GW01280669

PRAISE FOR *RELIGIOUS LIBERTY AND THE HERMENEUTIC OF CONTINUITY*

"How did the human right to religious liberty become an essential piece of modern Catholic teaching? R. Michael Dunnigan's contribution to the literature on Vatican II's *Dignitatis Humanae* brings to bear his keen theological and legal acumen not only to defend its compatibility with prior periods of Catholic teaching, but also to show its positive contribution in promoting human integrity in the modern world. Dunnigan explains how *Dignitatis Humanae* develops Church teaching on human dignity and the roles of civil authority and of law in both fostering and limiting the exercise of religion, and he lends his voice to recent arguments that regard the law of nations and the condition of reciprocity as grounding a development in justice that requires religious liberty among and within societies. Dunnigan's grasp of magisterial teaching, secular and ecclesiastical jurisprudence, and the post-conciliar literature is most impressive."

Barrett Turner
Mount St. Mary's University

"This is an extraordinarily competent and lucid investigation of the right to religious liberty promulgated by the Second Vatican Council. There might indeed be stronger rights or lesser rights to religious liberty, and perhaps different reasons for each, but Professor Dunnigan insists on getting to the precise right adopted by the Council. This is not easy work. He sifts through both the history of the conciliar debates and the plethora of post-conciliar opinions. I deem it fair not only to the Council but, perhaps just as importantly, to the scholarly debates thereafter."

Russell Hittinger
Catholic University of America

"One problem with *Dignitatis Humanae* is not what it said but what it didn't say. There was so much left to the imagination and future theological reflection. With this volume Dunnigan presents the principles of *Dignitatis Humanae* in the context of the broader theological tradition rather than leaving people to believe that the declaration was an endorsement of philosophies undergirding the French and/or American Revolutions. The work is essential reading for anyone interested in Catholic jurisprudence and political theory."

Tracey Rowland
University of Notre Dame (Australia)

"Dr. Michael Dunnigan has written a thorough and masterful study of *Dignitatis Humanae* that shows both its doctrinal continuity with previous Church teachings and its prophetic significance on the prudential plane. While refusing to shy away from the difficulties the text poses for interpreters concerned to reconcile the document with the teachings of nineteenth-century popes, Dunnigan convincingly demonstrates that *Dignitatis Humanae* roots religious liberty in the human desire to seek truth without coercion. He thus provides a subtle corrective to John Courtney Murray's highly influential view, according to which the text is founded on an acknowledgement on the part of the Church of the powerlessness of the state in the religious sphere. Dunnigan's book will be a standard reference in the field. Highly recommended."

Keith Lemna
Saint Meinrad Seminary

RENEWAL WITHIN TRADITION

SERIES EDITOR: MATTHEW LEVERING

Matthew Levering is the James N. and Mary D. Perry Jr. Chair of Theology at Mundelein Seminary. Levering is the author or editor of over thirty books. He serves as coeditor of the journals *Nova et Vetera* and the *International Journal of Systematic Theology*.

ABOUT THE SERIES

Catholic theology reflects upon the content of divine revelation as interpreted and handed down in the Church, but today Catholic theologians often find the scriptural and dogmatic past to be alien territory. The *Renewal within Tradition Series* undertakes to reform and reinvigorate contemporary theology from within the tradition, with St. Thomas Aquinas as a central exemplar. As part of its purpose, the Series reunites the streams of Catholic theology that, prior to the Council, separated into neo-scholastic and *nouvelle theologie* modes. The biblical, historical-critical, patristic, liturgical, and ecumenical emphases of the Ressourcement movement need the dogmatic, philosophical, scientific, and traditioned enquiries of Thomism, and vice versa. *Renewal within Tradition* challenges the regnant forms of theological liberalism that, by dissolving the cognitive content of the gospel, impede believers from knowing the love of Christ.

PUBLISHED OR FORTHCOMING

Reading the Sermons of Thomas Aquinas: A Beginner's Guide
Randall B. Smith

The Culture of the Incarnation: Essays in Catholic Theology
Tracey Rowland

Self-Gift: Humanae Vitae and the Thought of John Paul II
Janet E. Smith

On Love and Virtue: Theological Essays
Michael S. Sherwin, O.P.

Aquinas on Beatific Charity and the Problem of Love
Christopher J. Malloy

The One Church of Christ: Understanding Vatican II
Stephen A. Hipp

*O Lord, I Seek Your Countenance: Explorations
and Discoveries in Pope Benedict XVI's Theology*
Emery de Gaál

*One of the Trinity Has Suffered:
Balthasar's Theology of Divine Suffering in Dialogue*
Joshua R. Brotherton

The Bible and Catholic Ressourcement: *Essays on Scripture and Theology*
William M. Wright IV

*Conforming to Right Reason: On the Ends of the Moral Virtues
and the Roles of Prudence and Synderesis*
Ryan J. Brady

Vessel of Honor: The Virgin Birth and the Ecclesiology of Vatican II
Brian A. Graebe

*The Love of God Poured Out: Grace and the Gifts of
the Holy Spirit in St. Thomas Aquinas*
John M. Meinert

A Living Sacrifice: Liturgy and Eschatology in Joseph Ratzinger
Roland Millare

The Primacy of God: The Virtue of Religion in Catholic Theology
R. Jared Staudt

*The Trinitarian Wisdom of God: Louis Bouyer's
Theology of the God-World Relationship*
Keith Lemna

*The Order and Division of Divine Truth:
St. Thomas Aquinas as Scholastic Master of the Sacred Page*
John F. Boyle

A Bride Adorned: Mary–Church Perichoresis
in Modern Catholic Theology
John L. Nepil

Christ, the Logos of Creation: An Essay in Analogical Metaphysics
John R. Betz

*Saved as through Fire: A Thomistic Account of Purgatory,
Temporal Punishment, and Satisfaction*
Luke Wilgenbusch

Religious Liberty and the Hermeneutic of Continuity

Religious Liberty and the Hermeneutic of Continuity

Conservation and Development of
Doctrine at Vatican II

R. MICHAEL DUNNIGAN

EMMAUS
ACADEMIC

Steubenville, Ohio
www.emmausacademic.com

EMMAUS
ACADEMIC

Steubenville, Ohio
www.emmausacademic.com
A Division of The St. Paul Center for Biblical Theology
Editor-in-Chief: Scott Hahn
1468 Parkview Circle
Steubenville, Ohio 43952

© 2023 R. Michael Dunnigan
All rights reserved. Published 2023.
Printed in the United States of America.

Library of Congress Cataloging-in-Publication Data applied for
ISBNs 978-1-64585-332-9 hardcover | 978-1-64585-333-6 paperback | 978-1-64585-334-3 ebook

Unless otherwise noted, Scripture quotations are taken from The Revised Standard Version Second Catholic Edition (Ignatius Edition) Copyright © 2006 by the Division of Christian Education of the National Council of the Churches of Christ in the United States of America. Used by permission. All rights reserved.

Excerpts from the Catechism of the Catholic Church, Second Edition, Copyright © 1997, Libreria Editrice Vaticana—United States Conference of Catholic Bishops, Washington, D.C. Noted as "CCC" in the text.

Cover design and layout by Allison Merrick
Cover Image: *The Tribute Money* by Theodoor Boeyermans, 1674

For My Mother and Father

Table of Contents

Acknowledgements xv
Notes and Abbreviations xvii

Part 1—Introduction to the Debate

Chapter 1—An Impossible Reconciliation? 1
Chapter 2—The Stakes of the Debate over Religious Liberty 9
    2.1. Archbishop Lefebvre and the Declaration on Religious Liberty 10
    2.2. Father Charles Curran and the Teaching of Moral Theology 21
    2.3. Curran and Lefebvre 31
    2.4. Religious Liberty and the Church's Witness to Justice 31
    2.5. The Church's Diplomatic Activity and Her Relationship to Modernity ... 33
Chapter 3—Development, Method, and the Issues 35
    3.1. Development in Doctrine versus Corruption in Doctrine 35
    3.2. The Method and the Issues 47

Part 2—Church and State

Chapter 4—The Proper Relationship between Church and State 61
    4.1. Separation of Church and State 63
    4.2. The Need for Humility in Interpreting *Dignitatis Humanae* 65
    4.3. Gelasian Dualism 70
    4.4. The Drafting of *Dignitatis Humanae* 81
    4.5. Special Civil Recognition 86
    4.6. The Last-Minute Change to *Dignitatis Humanae* 92
    4.7. Does the Declaration Foreclose the Re-emergence of the
         Confessional State? 95
    4.8. Murray's Disappointment and Davies's Acknowledgement 99
    4.9. Murray, Paul VI, and the "Nothing but Freedom" Argument 101
    4.10. Further Significance 113
Chapter 5—The Appeal to "Changed Circumstances," Part 1:
    The Near-Disappearance of the Catholic State 115
    5.1. The Historical Inquiry 116

5.2. Limitations of the Historical Inquiry 119
5.3. Christopher Wolfe 121
5.4. A Word on the Islamic World 123

Part 3A—Analysis of the Right to Religious Liberty: The Scope and Object of the Right

Chapter 6—The Nineteenth-Century Magisterium 127
   6.1. Gregory XVI, *Mirari Vos* (1832) 128
   6.2. Bl. Pius IX, *Quanta Cura* (1864) 134
   6.3. Bl. Pius IX, *The Syllabus of Errors* (1864) 137
   6.4. Leo XIII, *Immortale Dei* (1885) and *Libertas* (1888) 143

Chapter 7—The Scope of the Right to Religious Liberty 147
   7.1. Some Preliminary Notes on Conscience 150
   7.2. The Nineteenth-Century Union of the Moral and Juridical Realms 155
   7.3. Consequences of the Blurring of the Moral and Juridical Realms 158
   7.4. The Vatican II Distinction between the Moral and Juridical Realms 174
   7.5. An Extension of the Nineteenth-Century Teaching 178
   7.6. The Relevance of the Scope of the Right to the Larger Question 186

Chapter 8—The Object of the Right to Religious Liberty 189
   8.1. The Central Dispute 190
   8.2. Positive Rights and Negative Rights 196
   8.3. The Right as *Ius Exigendi* 197
   8.4. The Davies Objection 198
   8.5. Related Observations 202
   8.6. Two Facets of Liberty 205

Part 3B—Analysis of the Right to Religious Liberty: The Crucial Question of the Foundation of the Right

Chapter 9—The Search for the Proper Foundation 209
   9.1. Allusions to the Right to Religious Liberty 210
   9.2. Early Attempts to Make Conscience the Foundation of the Right 211
   9.3. The "Juridical" Argument for the Incompetence of the State 216
   9.4. The Council's Choice of Human Dignity as the Foundation 229

9.5. The Remarkable Resiliency of the Incompetence Argument 235

9.6. Murray's "Sufficiency" Argument 253

Chapter 10—The Dog That Didn't Bark 261

10.1. Some Qualifications 262

10.2 A Note on the "Juridical Approach" and the "Incompetence Argument" 265

10.3. The Practical Problems with the "Incompetence Argument" 278

10.4. Doctrinal Difficulties 311

10.5. A Response to the Question: "Might It Have Been Otherwise?" 336

Chapter 11—Starting with the Person, Not the State 339

11.1. The Ontological Argument 339

11.2. The Social Argument (Part 1) 341

11.3. The Social Argument (Part 2: An Excursus on Thomas Pink) 342

11.4. The Argument about "Avoiding the Political" 357

11.5. Human Integrity 358

Part 4—Limitations on the Right to Religious Liberty

Chapter 12—The Challenge of *Quanta Cura* 369

12.1. The Need for Limitations on Religious Practice 369

12.2. *Quanta Cura* (1864) 371

12.3. A Matter of Translation 379

12.4. A Limitless Freedom? 381

12.5. The Public Order and the Common Good 387

12.6. Contemporary Applications 392

Chapter 13—Public Law and Policy 395

13.1. Teaching and Policy 396

13.2. The Vatican II Change in Policy or Public Law 398

13.3. Analysis of Harrison's Public Law Argument 401

13.4. Papal Administrative Practice 406

13.5. Doctrine and Policy 408

Chapter 14—The Burning of Heretics 409

14.1. Leo X's Bull against Luther 410

14.2. The Drafting of *Exsurge Domine* 414

Chapter 15—The Appeal to "Changed Circumstances," Part 2:
   Social Harm, Both Real and Perceived 417
   15.1. Noonan and O'Neil 418
   15.2. St. Augustine 422
   15.3. St. Thomas Aquinas 429
   15.4. Coercion of the Baptized 435
   15.5. Insights and Limitations of the O'Neil Approach 440

Conclusion

Chapter 16—The Appeal to "Changed Circumstances," Part 3:
   The Delay in Recognizing the Right to Religious Liberty 445
   16.1. Murray after the Council 445
   16.2. An Assumption 447
   16.3. Kasper's Contribution 448
   16.4. The Final Piece 452
   16.5. Conclusion 453

Bibliography 455
Index 479

Acknowledgements

I first became interested in the Vatican II religious liberty declaration almost twenty-five years ago, and I wish to begin by thanking the advisor on my first thesis on this subject, the late Dr. James B. Sauer of St. Mary's University in San Antonio. I am indebted to him for his tremendous insight, his infectious enthusiasm, and his constant encouragement.

I also wish to thank the advisor for my second thesis on this topic, Professor Vicente Prieto of the Pontifical University of the Holy Cross in Rome. His astute guidance and friendly advice were very valuable, especially in locating relevant English- and Italian-language sources when the subject still was relatively new to me.

Professor José Tomás Martín de Agar was the second reader for my licentiate thesis and the advisor for my doctoral dissertation, and I am extremely grateful for his encouragement, his careful reading of my text, his outstanding suggestions, and especially his remarkable patience in awaiting the long-delayed completion of my work.

I wish to thank Dr. Barrett Hamilton Turner of Mount St. Mary's University for sharing with me his own doctoral work on the religious liberty declaration. His clear and insightful dissertation became a valuable source for my own work. For helping in the completion of my dissertation, I first wish to thank my longtime friend and colleague Dr. David H. Delaney, for his review of many draft chapters and for his excellent comments and insights. I also thank my friends Mr. Ryan Chism and Dr. John Kieffer for their review of several passages and for their helpful observations and comments. For assistance in preparing for my defense, I thank Avv. Rosamaria Lojacono. For help in the publication of my dissertation, I would like to thank Mr. Edward Pentin, Avv. Andrea Zanni, and Mrs. Tammy Schuetter. I also would like to thank Messrs. Massimiliano Rosati and Domenico Sorgini of the Academic Secretariat of the Pontifical University of the Holy Cross for their helpfulness and kindness in a multitude of ways over a period of many years.

For his help in making this book possible, I wish to thank Dr. Matthew Levering of Mundelein Seminary for his lively interest in this subject, his excellent advice, and his help and support in a multitude of ways. I also wish to thank Mr. Christopher Erickson of Emmaus Academic for his valuable assistance and advice all throughout the editing and production process. For his help in preparing my manuscript for publication, I wish to thank Mr.

ACKNOWLEDGEMENTS

Robert Erickson of Emmaus. His diligence and attention to detail resulted in many improvements in the text. For additional valuable help in preparing the manuscript, I thank my research assistant at Saint Meinrad Seminary, Mr. Thomas Day, a seminarian of the Archdiocese of Indianapolis.

Finally, for his indispensable spiritual guidance and support, I wish to thank Father Cyril Guise, O.C.D., of Holy Hill Shrine in Hubertus, Wisconsin.

Notes and Abbreviations

Unless otherwise noted, all quotations from papal pronouncements are taken from the translations provided in the Vatican online document library, https://www.vatican.va/content/vatican/en.html.

    Citations to canons are abbreviated "can." in the singular and "cann." in the plural, and unless otherwise noted, are from the current Code, the *Codex Iuris Canonici* (1983).

AA	Second Vatican Council, Decree on the Apostolate of the Laity *Apostolicam Actuositatem* (Nov. 18, 1965) [AAS 58 (1966): 837–64].
AAS	*Acta Apostolicae Sedis* (1909–present).
Abbott	Walter M. Abbott, ed., *The Documents of Vatican II* (New York: Herder and Herder, 1966).
AS	*Acta Synodalia Sacrosancti Concilii Oecumenici Vaticani II* (Rome: Typis Polyglottis Vaticanis, 1976).
	N.B. Citations to the Acts of the Second Vatican Council or the *Acta Synodalia Sacrosancti Concilii Oecumenici Vaticani II* are by volume, part (of the volume), and page number. Thus, a citation to volume IV, part 5 (of volume IV), page 84, is rendered as follows: AS IV/5, 84.
ASS	*Acta Sanctae Sedis* (1865–1908).
CCC	Catechism of the Catholic Church, 2nd ed. (Vatican City: Libreria Editrice Vaticana, 1997).
CR	Pope Pius XII, Discourse to Italian Jurists *Ci Riesce* (Dec. 6, 1953) [AAS 45 (1953): 794–802].
C&RF	Kenneth L. Grasso and Robert P. Hunt, eds., *Catholicism and Religious Freedom. Contemporary Reflections on Vatican II's Declaration on Religious Liberty* (Lanham, MD: Rowman & Littlefield Publishers, Inc., 2006).
DDHC	*La Déclaration des droits de l'homme et du citoyen* (1789) (*The Declaration of the Rights of Man and the Citizen*).
DH	Second Vatican Council, Declaration on Religious Freedom *Dignitatis Humanae* (Dec. 7, 1965) [AAS 58 (1966): 929–41].
DV	Second Vatican Council, Dogmatic Constitution on Divine Revelation *Dei Verbum* (Nov. 18, 1965) [AAS 58 (1966): 817–36].

Notes and Abbreviations

Fesquet	Henri Fesquet, *The Drama of Vatican II* (New York: Random House, 1967).
Guminski/ Harrison	Arnold T. Guminski and Brian W. Harrison, *Religious Freedom: Did Vatican II Contradict Traditional Catholic Doctrine? A Debate* (South Bend, IN: St. Augustine Press, 2013).
GS	Second Vatican Council, Pastoral Constitution on the Church in the Modern World *Gaudium et Spes* (Dec. 7, 1965) [AAS 58 (1966): 1025–1115].
HG	Pius XII, Encyclical *Humani Generis* (Aug. 12, 1950) [AAS 42 (1950): 561–78].
ID	Leo XIII, Encyclical *Immortale Dei* (Nov. 1, 1885) [ASS 18 (1885–1886): 161–80] (English translation from EWTN website, https://www.ewtn.com/catholicism/library/on-the-christian-constitution-of-states-3479).
Küng/ Congar/ O'Hanlon	Hans Küng, Yves Congar, and Daniel O'Hanlon, eds., *Council Speeches of Vatican II* (Glen Rock, NJ: Paulist Press, 1964).
Leahy/ Massimini	William K. Leahy and Anthony T. Massimini, eds., *Third Session Council Speeches of Vatican II* (Glen Rock, NJ: Paulist Press, 1966).
LG	Second Vatican Council, Dogmatic Constitution on the Church *Lumen Gentium* (Nov. 21, 1964) [AAS 57 (1965): 5–75].
LP	Pope Leo XIII, Encyclical *Libertas* (June 20, 1888) [ASS 20 (1887–1888): 593–613].
LO	Pope Leo XIII, Encyclical *Longinqua Oceani* (Jan. 6, 1895) [ASS 27 (1894–1895): 387–99].
LRTC	Basile Valuet, *La liberté religieuse et la tradition catholique. Un cas de développement doctrinal homogène dans le magistère authentique*, 3rd rev. ed. (Barroux: Éditions Sainte-Madeleine, 2011).
LRTE	Basile Valuet, *Le droit à la liberté religieuse dans la Tradition de l'Eglise. Un cas de développement doctrinal homogène par le magistère authentique*, 2nd rev. ed. (Barroux: Éditions Sainte-Madeleine, 2011).
MV	Pope Gregory XVI, Encyclical *Mirari Vos* (Aug. 15, 1832) [ASS 4 (1868): 336–45] (English translation from EWTN website, https://www.ewtn.com/catholicism/library/on-liberalism—indifferentism-3371).

NPNF	Philip Schaff, ed., *A Select Library of the Nicene and Post-Nicene Fathers of the Christian Church*, First Series, 14 vols. (Edinburgh: T&T Clark, 1886–1900; reprint, Grand Rapids, MI: William B. Eerdmans Publishing Co., 1989).
PL	J. P. Migne, ed., Patrologia cursus completus, series latina (Paris: 1844 ff.).
PT	Pope John XXIII, Encyclical *Pacem in Terris* (Apr. 11, 1963) [AAS 55 (1963): 257–304].
QC	Pope Pius IX, Encyclical *Quanta Cura* (Dec. 8, 1864) [ASS 3 (1867): 160–67] (English translation from EWTN website, https://www.ewtn.com/catholicism/library/condemning-current-errors-3608).
QP	Pope Pius XI, Encyclical *Quas Primas* (Dec. 11, 1925) [AAS 17 (1925): 593–610].
RL&C	Brian W. Harrison, *Religious Liberty and Contraception: Did Vatican II Open the Way for a New Sexual Ethic?* (Melbourne: John XXIII Fellowship Co-op., 1988).
Schindler/Healy	David L. Schindler and Nicholas J. Healy Jr., eds., *Freedom, Truth, and Human Dignity: The Second Vatican Council's Declaration on Religious Freedom—A New Translation, Redaction History, and Interpretation of* Dignitatis Humanae (Grand Rapids, MI / Cambridge, UK: William B. Eerdmans Publishing Company, 2015).
ST	St. Thomas Aquinas, *Summa Theologica*, Christian Classics ed. (Benziger Brothers, 1947).
SVC&RL	Michael Davies, *The Second Vatican Council and Religious Liberty* (Long Prairie, MN: Neumann Press, 1992).
Syll.	Pope Pius IX, *Syllabus Errorum* (Dec. 8, 1864) [ASS 3 (1867): 170–76].
UR	Second Vatican Council, Decree on Ecumenism *Unitatis Redintegratio* (Nov. 21, 1964) [AAS 57 (1965): 90–112].
WHTT	John Courtney Murray, *We Hold These Truths: Catholic Reflections on the American Proposition* (Kansas City, MO: Sheed & Ward, 1960).
Yzermans	Vincent A. Yzermans, ed., *American Participation in the Second Vatican Council* (New York: Sheed & Ward, 1967).

PART 1

INTRODUCTION TO THE DEBATE

CHAPTER 1

An Impossible Reconciliation?

What have they done with history? It is impossible to reconcile this text with the magisterium of the nineteenth or even the twentieth century.

This was the exclamation of Bishop John Velasco of Amoy, China, during the Second Vatican Council's debate on religious liberty in September 1965. The bishop conceded that he might have misunderstood the draft Declaration on Religious Liberty, and then added, "But if that is the case, what about the faithful?"[1]

In the years since the close of the Council, the controversy surrounding the Declaration on Religious Liberty has not abated. The declaration today continues to raise questions concerning our understanding of the Church and her teaching office. Some have cited it as the justification for their establishment of a parallel hierarchy and for withholding obedience from the Holy See. Others have cited it in support of dramatic changes to the Church's moral teaching. The paradox of the declaration is that although it has been the occasion of much division within the Church, it also suggests answers to some of the most troubling questions facing the Church and indeed modern man.

The difficulty that the Declaration on Religious Liberty, *Dignitatis Humanae*, presents is whether it can be reconciled with the previous teaching of the Church. The nineteenth-century popes wrote a great deal about the relationship between the Church and secular governments, and several of their encyclicals describe the ideas of freedom of conscience and freedom of

---

[1] September 16, 1965, oral intervention of Velasco (AS IV/1, 253–54); partial English translation in Henri Fesquet, *The Drama of Vatican II* (New York: Random House, 1967), 599 (hereinafter cited as Fesquet).

worship as "insanity."[2] The nineteenth-century popes taught that although it sometimes is permissible for a Catholic state to *tolerate* the public rites of non-Catholic religions, there can be no *right* to non-Catholic public worship.[3] However, *Dignitatis Humanae* teaches that no person may be restrained from acting according to his religious convictions "whether privately or publicly."[4] All commentators appear to agree that the difference between toleration and a right is a difference not merely in *degree* but in *kind*.[5]

This is indeed a serious difficulty. Catholics traditionally have understood the Church as "indefectible."[6] The Lord promised the apostles, "When the Spirit of truth comes, he will guide you into all the truth" (John 16:13). From this promise and from the Lord's assurance that the gates of hell would not prevail against the Church (Matt 16:18), Catholics have understood that the Holy Spirit would preserve the Church from ever teaching error. However, if the Church's Vatican II teaching contradicts the teaching of her nineteenth-century popes, then it becomes difficult to escape the conclusion that the Church has indeed taught error.

I will attempt to answer the question, *What is the place of the Vatican II teaching on religious liberty in the tradition and life of the Catholic Church?* This question has two principal aspects, one that can be called the *doctrinal* inquiry and another that can be called the *prudential* inquiry. The first aspect concerns whether the teaching of Vatican II on religious liberty contradicts what the Church has taught in the past, especially the teachings of

---

[2] Pope Gregory XVI, Encyclical *Mirari Vos* (Aug. 15, 1832) [ASS 4 (1868): 341] (hereinafter cited as MV); Pope Pius IX, Encyclical *Quanta Cura* (Dec. 8, 1864), §3 [ASS 3 (1867): 162] (hereinafter cited as QC).

[3] Cf. Pope Leo XIII, Encyclical *Libertas* (June 20, 1888), §33 [ASS 20 (1887–1888): 609–10] (hereinafter cited as LP).

[4] Second Vatican Council, Declaration on Religious Liberty *Dignitatis Humanae* (Dec. 7, 1965), §2a [AAS 58 (1966): 929–41, at 930] (hereinafter cited as DH).

[5] "Religious freedom is different in kind from toleration." Franklin H. Littell, "A Response," in *The Documents of Vatican II*, ed. Walter M. Abbott (New York: Herder and Herder, 1966), 697 (hereinafter, the larger work is cited as Abbott). Cf. Patrick M. O'Neil, "A Response to John T. Noonan, Jr. Concerning the Development of Catholic Moral Doctrine," *Faith & Reason* (Spring/Summer 1996), EWTN, accessed Dec. 19, 2020, https://www.ewtn.com/catholicism/library/response-to-john-t-noonan-jr-concerning-the-development-of-catholic-moral-doctrine-10041; Fernando Ocáriz, "Sulla libertà religiosa. Continuità del Vaticano II con il Magistero precedente," *Annales theologici* 3 (1989): 71–97, at 89: "il principio di tolleranza non è equivalente al principio di libertà religiosa."

[6] Indefectibility is the immunity of the Church from falling away from the Faith. James T. O'Connor, *The Gift of Infallibility* (Boston: St. Paul Editions, 1986), 102.

the nineteenth-century popes. The second aspect concerns the relationship between conflict and doctrine. Even if the Vatican II and the nineteenth-century teachings could be harmonized, the prudential inquiry asks why the Church would pronounce a teaching that would result in so much conflict. Stated differently, the prudential inquiry examines whether there is a particular problem—or set of problems—to which *Dignitatis Humanae* provides the solution. Both questions run throughout this work.

This work is divided into four parts and a conclusion. The first part introduces the debate. This chapter provides a brief general overview. The next one (chapter 2) discusses the high stakes of the religious liberty debate, which has important implications both within the Catholic Church and outside of it. In short, it implicates the credibility of the Church as a teacher of truth, the legitimacy or illegitimacy of the Lefebvrist traditionalist movement, the authority of the Church to teach the faithful in matters of morality, and perhaps even the viability of the Church's diplomatic activity. Chapter 3 sets forth the key issues and a method for examining them. It identifies three key issues arising from the nineteenth-century context. The chief among them, however, is the question of whether non-Catholics living in a Catholic state have a right to public worship. It also provides a method for making the evaluation of whether there is indeed a contradiction of doctrine. Such an evaluation demands an appreciation of the need for doctrine to maintain *continuity* with the Church's past teachings, but also to allow for legitimate *development* of doctrine.[7]

The second part addresses the question of Church and state in two chapters. Chapter 4 clarifies the declaration's actual teaching and, in particular, it engages and offers a critique of John Courtney Murray's interpretation of the document on this question. Chapter 5 introduces the theme of "changed circumstances" and their impact on the attempt to harmonize the teachings of Vatican II and the nineteenth-century popes. In particular, chapter 5 addresses the question of whether the near disappearance of confessional states in our own day obviates the need to harmonize these teachings.

Parts 3A and 3B make up the heart of the work, as they contain my analysis of the actual right that Vatican II recognized. Part 3A begins with a review of the key nineteenth-century papal pronouncements (chapter 6), and it then proceeds to analyze the scope (chapter 7) and object (chapter 8) of the right to religious liberty recognized by Vatican II. Part 3B is devoted

---

[7] One important example of this understanding is Pope Leo XIII's description of the magisterium as both *living* and *permanent*. Pope Leo XIII, Encyclical *Satis Cognitum* (June 29, 1896), §9 [ASS 28 (1895–1896): 721].

to the key question of the foundation of the right. I attempt to show that the right to religious liberty as understood by the Council is different from the right or rights that the nineteenth-century popes rejected. In addition, part 3B (especially chapter 10) offers a lengthy review and critique of Murray's claim that state incompetence in religious matters furnishes the best foundation for the right to religious liberty.

Part 4 concerns the question of limitations on the right to religious liberty. It examines the standards for such restrictions, as contained in Pope Pius IX's famous encyclical *Quanta Cura* (1864) and in the Vatican II declaration (chapter 12). It also addresses changes to public ecclesiastical law effected by the Vatican II teaching (chapter 13), and it considers whether the religious liberty declaration contradicts Pope Leo X's sixteenth-century teaching on the burning of heretics (chapter 14). Finally, chapter 15 returns to a theme that first appeared in chapter 5, namely, the impact of changed circumstances. Whereas chapter 5 considers the changed circumstance of the near disappearance of the confessional state, chapter 15 discusses changing evaluations throughout history of the danger posed by heresy or by the religious practice of members of minority religions.

Finally, I include a conclusion in a single chapter, which again returns to the question of changed circumstances. In particular, it addresses the frequent charge that the Church is a latecomer to the cause of religious liberty, and it considers the reasons for this delay.

My own conclusion as to whether Vatican II contradicts the previous teaching is that, although it may be regrettable that the council fathers did not explain fully how the teachings are consistent, and although they included language in *Dignitatis Humanae* that rendered this task difficult, it ultimately is possible to reconcile the declaration with the previous teaching of the Church. Even the most ardent defenders of the orthodoxy of the declaration concede that it is a deceptively difficult text that must be interpreted with extreme care.[8] As already mentioned and as discussed more fully in chapter 2, the lack of clarity regarding the place of *Dignitatis Humanae* in the tradition has contributed to some of the worst internal Church crises since the close of the Council. However, despite these serious difficulties, I believe that a precise inquiry into the object, scope, and foundation of the right to religious liberty recognized by Vatican II reveals

---

[8] Cf. Ocáriz, "Sulla libertà religiosa," 96; Brian W. Harrison, "Roma Locuta Est—Causa Finita Est," *Living Tradition* 57 (March 1995), Roman Theological Forum, accessed Dec. 19, 2020, http://www.rtforum.org/lt/lt57.html.

that there is no doctrinal conflict between that teaching and the teaching of the nineteenth-century popes on religious tolerance.

In one sense, the prudential inquiry takes up where the doctrinal inquiry leaves off, though both run throughout the work, especially in parts two and three. Given the difficulty of reconciling the teachings, the prudential inquiry asks why the Church would pronounce a teaching that would result in so much conflict. Stated differently, one fairly can ask why the Vatican II fathers let the Church in for so much turmoil, not only at the Council itself but for decades afterward and up to the present.

This is because the Church took a great risk in issuing the declaration. The fathers of the Council must have known that critics would charge the Church with doing precisely what she says she cannot do, namely contradicting her own teaching.[9] One would hope that the fathers would not have taken such a risk and would not have exposed the Church to such criticism unless the declaration were expected to make some vital contribution to the Church and to humanity. The boldest way to summarize the prudential inquiry is to ask, *Was there some reason or circumstance that made it necessary for the Church to issue Dignitatis Humanae?*

There was no shortage of reasons put forward in support of the declaration at Vatican II. However, some of those reasons arguably are problematic. Some council fathers cited ecumenism and the necessity of responding to the Marxist world as justifications for the declaration. The very practical nature of these motivations cast something of a shadow over the declaration, because these motives lent themselves to the impression that the fathers—or at least some of them—may have been willing to ignore the previous teaching of the Church in pursuit of their own more immediate goals.

However, despite the controversy and despite the multitude of motivations for the declaration, *Dignitatis Humanae* makes an essential contribution to the Church and to the world. That is, it is a corrective to a mistaken notion of the human person that prevails throughout much of the world today, especially in the West. The prevailing modern ideas of rights and religious freedom flow in large part from those aspects of the Enlightenment that were genuinely insightful, namely the insistence on respect for individual rights and equal application of the law. However, the

---

[9] Shortly after the Council, journalist Henri Fesquet said, "Vatican II has shaken the conviction widely held by Catholics that doctrine is unchangeable" (Fesquet, 355). Paul Blanshard, a Protestant critic of the Catholic Church but a supporter of *Dignitatis Humanae*, said that John Courtney Murray's role at the Council "was to give the pedestrian bishops the right words with which to change some ancient doctrines without admitting that they were being changed." Paul Blanshard, *Paul Blanshard on Vatican II* (Boston: Beacon Press, 1966), 87.

Enlightenment also left many dark legacies, including a radical individualism that exalts the individual at the expense of the society.[10] In addition, the Enlightenment called into question the ability of the human person to know truth and, when these two principles—radical skepticism and radical individualism—are combined, they produce an image of modern man that looks distinctly unchristian: modern man often fixates on his own rights, feels little obligation to consider the good of the larger society in making his decisions, and tends ever increasingly to compartmentalize the private sphere of his life and to recognize few restrictions on his actions there.[11] Perhaps the unchristian character of this vision of man should not be surprising, given the well-known anticlericalism of the Enlightenment, but what should concern everyone is the sheer inhumanness of this vision, that is, the specter of the isolated, individualistic, compartmentalized, and socially-disconnected modern man.[12] This is a vision of man that alarmed not only the Vatican II fathers, but also the nineteenth-century popes. In fact, I believe that the most surprising and elusive virtue of *Dignitatis Humanae* is its conservation of—and its making more explicit—the teaching of the nineteenth-century popes on the human person. This becomes apparent if one takes Pope Benedict XVI's counsel to apply a *hermeneutic of reform in*

---

[10] Cf. Gertrude Himmelfarb, *On Looking into the Abyss: Untimely Thoughts on Culture and Society* (New York: Alfred A Knopf, 1994), 77–78: J. S. Mill's notion of liberty establishes "radical disjunction" between individual and society.

[11] Cf. Richard John Neuhaus, *The Naked Public Square: Religion and Democracy in America*, 2nd ed. (Grand Rapids, MI: William B. Eerdmans Publishing Co., 1986), 139, discussing the Enlightenment attempt to privatize religion; Stephen L. Carter, *The Culture of Disbelief: How American Law and Politics Trivialize Religious Devotion* (New York: Basic Books, 1993), 8: "[W]e often ask our citizens to split their public and private selves"; Robert H. Bork, *Slouching Towards Gomorrah: Modern Liberalism and American Decline* (New York: ReganBooks/HarperCollins, 1996), 58–64, discussing the Enlightenment's promotion of individualism and privatization of morality.

[12] Cf. Charles Murray, *Coming Apart: The State of White America, 1960–2010* (New York: Crown Forum, 2012), 247–52. Charles Murray focuses on white America because he believes that the country is "coming apart," not along racial or ethnic lines, but along class lines. Class distinction is not new, of course, but the degree of class separation that has occurred over the last half century, Murray argues, is unlike anything that the country ever has experienced, and unless it is reversed, it will result in the disappearance of any common kinship between the new elite class and the new working class, and it will result in the end of "the American project." (Murray is by no means unconcerned with the nonwhite community, but he believes that the usual comparison of statistics on whites with those on African-Americans and Latinos tends to obscure the deterioration within the baseline itself. That is, the much commented upon decline in African-American working-class family life and community life is, in fact, characteristic of the new working class as a whole, both white and nonwhite.)

continuity to the interpretation of Vatican II, that is, if one interprets it in the light of previous magisterial teaching.

What the Church has done in *Dignitatis Humanae* is to affirm the right to religious liberty but to avoid the most unfortunate aspects of the Enlightenment. She does so by basing this right not on the Enlightenment's understanding of man as isolated and skeptical but rather on an understanding of man as possessing inherent dignity because of his creation by God the Father and his redemption by Jesus Christ. By basing religious liberty on a distinctively Christian foundation, the Church is able to affirm modern insights concerning human rights but to avoid the Enlightenment's dangerous and dispiriting tendency toward radical individualism.[13] In addition, if one considers *Dignitatis Humanae* carefully, one will see that it not only avoids the serious problems of modern society that are traceable to the Enlightenment but that it actually provides a positive corrective to them. It does this by promoting an understanding of man as both an individual and a social being, thereby beginning the work of restoring the integrity of the human person.

---

[13] The opposite system, collectivism, which subsumes the individual within society or the collectivity, also is traceable to the Enlightenment. It is an equally serious threat, and the Vatican II fathers certainly were alive to it. In fact, *Dignitatis Humanae* really responds to both threats, and both are addressed below. However, while collectivism was a formidable threat in the mid twentieth century, in our own day, radical individualism is ascendant.

CHAPTER 2

The Stakes of the Debate over Religious Liberty

> *Remember that the Church went in specifically for dangerous ideas; she was a lion tamer. . . . [I]f some small mistake were made in doctrine, huge blunders might be made in human happiness.*
>
> — G. K. CHESTERTON[1]

In two of the greatest internal Church crises since Vatican II, the Declaration on Religious Liberty has played a key role. These two crises, the largescale rejection of the Church's moral teaching by progressive Catholics and the establishment of a separate hierarchy by traditionalist Catholics, have emerged from opposite ends of the theological spectrum. However, their proponents share one important idea in common, namely the belief that *Dignitatis Humanae* represents a fundamental change in Church teaching. The protagonists of these two crises, Archbishop Marcel Lefebvre and Father Charles Curran, may have disagreed on most every other important question that concerns the Church, but they shared the same understanding of *Dignitatis Humanae* and its relationship to the Church's traditional teaching. That is, both considered the declaration to be a reversal of previous Church teaching. As a result of the importance that both men placed on their reading of the declaration, the legitimacy or illegitimacy of the ideas and actions of Lefebvre and Curran turns in large part on whether or not their understanding of *Dignitatis Humanae* is correct.

---

[1] G. K. Chesterton, *Orthodoxy* (London: The Bodley Head, 1908), ch. 6.

2.1. Archbishop Lefebvre and the Declaration on Religious Liberty

The name of Archbishop Marcel Lefebvre has become synonymous with the traditional Latin Mass.[2] Lefebvre objected to the Vatican II-era reform of the rite for the celebration of the Mass, which culminated in Pope Paul VI's promulgation of the 1970 *Roman Missal*. Lefebvre declined to celebrate according to the 1970 *Missal* and continued instead to celebrate Mass according to the pre-conciliar 1962 *Roman Missal*. However, despite the identification of Lefebvre with the traditional Mass, the most serious doctrinal dispute between him and the Church hierarchy concerns not the Mass but the Vatican II Declaration on Religious Liberty.

Archbishop Lefebvre was born in France in 1905 and consecrated a bishop in 1947. He attracted attention when he raised objections to two of the documents of the Second Vatican Council (1962–1965), the Pastoral Constitution on the Church in the Modern World *Gaudium et Spes* and the Declaration on Religious Liberty *Dignitatis Humanae*. His objection to *Gaudium et Spes* was that he considered it simply uncatholic in its ethos, but his objection to *Dignitatis Humanae* was doctrinal.[3]

In 1970 Lefebvre established the Ecône seminary in Switzerland and founded the Society of Saint Pius X (SSPX). Ordained SSPX priests proceeded to establish traditionalist chapels in Europe and the United States. In 1974, Lefebvre denounced both Vatican II and the Mass according to the 1970 *Roman Missal* (also known as the *Novus Ordo* Mass). In his declaration of November 21, 1974, Archbishop Lefebvre said, "[W]e refuse and have always refused to follow the Rome of neo-Modernist and neo-Protestant tendencies such as were clearly manifested during the Second Vatican Council, and after the Council in all the resulting reforms."[4] Pope St. Paul VI ordered Lefebvre to close his seminary, but the archbishop refused. In 1976, the pope suspended Lefebvre's priestly faculties.[5]

In 1983, Archbishop Lefebvre threatened to consecrate a successor bishop for the SSPX. Under Pope John Paul II, the Holy See took a more conciliatory stance toward Lefebvre than Pope Paul VI had taken. In 1984, the Holy See provided for the licit celebration of the Mass according to the

---

[2] This Mass also is known as the *extraordinary form* of the Mass or the Tridentine Mass.
[3] Michael Davies, *Archbishop Lefebvre and Religious Liberty* (Rockford, IL: TAN Books and Publishers, 1980), 1.
[4] Michael W. Cuneo, *The Smoke of Satan: Conservative and Traditionalist Dissent in Contemporary American Catholicism* (New York: Oxford University Press, 1997), 91–92, quoting Lefebvre's Nov. 21, 1974, declaration.
[5] Cuneo, *The Smoke of Satan*, 91–92.

1962 *Roman Missal* under certain circumstances.[6] However, this concession was insufficient to resolve the matter. Four years later Lefebvre again threatened to consecrate a successor. However, he reached and signed an agreement with the Holy See on May 5, 1988, providing that the SSPX would receive recognition and that Lefebvre would profess loyalty to the pope and would acknowledge the validity of the *Novus Ordo* Mass. However, Archbishop Lefebvre backed out of the agreement the next day. On June 30, 1988, Lefebvre consecrated four bishops. He claimed that this step was necessary to maintain the independence of the SSPX.[7]

As a result of these episcopal consecrations, Pope John Paul II excommunicated Lefebvre, his four new bishops, and the bishop who joined Lefebvre in the consecrations.[8] Archbishop Lefebvre died in 1991, and since his death, the SSPX has continued to grow.[9]

Despite the identification of Lefebvre with the traditional Mass, attentive observers long have understood that the Vatican II teaching on religious liberty presents the most formidable obstacle to reconciliation between Lefebvre's followers and the Church hierarchy. Until his death in 2004, Michael Davies was Archbishop Lefebvre's most prolific and articulate defender. Davies succinctly noted the disparity between the challenges presented by the traditional Mass and religious liberty:

> The archbishop's insistence on the Society being allowed to use the Tridentine Mass and pre-conciliar sacramental rites is a disciplinary matter, and could be conceded by the Pope without great difficulty;

---

[6] Cf. Congregation for Divine Worship, Circular Letter *Quattuor Abhinc Annos* (Oct. 3, 1984) [AAS 76 (1984): 1088–89].

[7] Cf. Cuneo, *Smoke of Satan*, 92.

[8] Canon law provides that the consecration of a bishop without a pontifical mandate is an excommunicable offense (can. 1382). At the time of the excommunications, Pope John Paul II issued a motu proprio providing for a more generous application of the norms allowing celebration of the traditional Mass according to the 1962 *Roman Missal*. Pope John Paul II, Apostolic Letter Motu Proprio *Ecclesia Dei Adflicta* (July 2, 1988) [AAS 80 (1988): 1495–98].

[9] See generally Cuneo, *Smoke of Satan*, 91–93. The SSPX is by no means the only community to identify itself as Catholic but to exist irregularly and independently from the hierarchy of the Catholic Church. One such organization that split off from the SSPX is the Society of St. Pius V (SSPV), which unlike the SSPX, takes the position that the popes since Vatican II have been elected *invalidly*. (Persons holding this view are called *sedevacantists*, from their belief that the Holy See—the *Sancta Sede*—is vacant.) In addition, there are other such organizations that have split off from the SSPV, or that exist independently of either society. However, the SSPX is the largest and most prominent of all these groups.

but the question of religious liberty involves a serious disagreement on a matter of doctrine.[10]

The prescience of Davies's observations would become clear a year after his death, when his friend Joseph Cardinal Ratzinger was elected to succeed John Paul II as pope.

As prefect of the Congregation for the Doctrine of the Faith under John Paul, Ratzinger had been responsible for the 1988 negotiations with Lefebvre and for attempts to reconcile the SSPX.[11] As Pope Benedict XVI, he accelerated these efforts. In 2007 he issued a motu proprio entitled *Summorum Pontificum* declaring that all priests were free to celebrate the traditional Latin Mass. The SSPX and other proponents of the traditional Mass welcomed this development enthusiastically, because it provided both freedom for priests to celebrate the Mass and also greater access for the faithful devoted to it. Equally important, it rejected the "hermeneutic of rupture," through which many of the Church's pastors had interpreted Vatican II as a nearly complete break from the previous traditions and life of the Church. The hermeneutic of rupture had led these pastors to neglect providing pastoral care to the traditionalist faithful and to treat as shameful their desire for a rite that predated the Council. Three years before his election, the future pontiff had expressed his complete bewilderment at the prejudice against the traditional Mass that many bishops harbored. The faithful devoted to this Mass, he said, were being treated like *lepers*, and the unreasoning intolerance of these bishops was preventing necessary reconciliation within the Church.[12] This attitude, he said, is destructive of the Church herself. "A community is calling its very being into question when it suddenly declares that what until now was its holiest and highest possession is strictly forbidden and when it makes the longing for it seem downright indecent."[13]

In addition to freeing the traditional Mass, in 2009 Pope Benedict lifted the excommunications of the bishops that Lefebvre had consecrated. Throughout Benedict's pontificate, the Holy See attempted to facilitate the

---

[10] Michael Davies, *Apologia Pro Marcel Lefebvre*, vol. 2, *1977–1979* (Dickinson, TX: Angelus Press, 1983), xiv. Lefebvre's position, and Davies's expansion upon it, will be considered in greater detail below.

[11] Cf. Pope John Paul II, Apostolic Letter Motu Proprio *Ecclesia Dei Adflicta* (July 2, 1988), §3, recounting the excommunication of Archbishop Marcel Lefebvre [AAS 80 (1988): 1496].

[12] Cf. Joseph Ratzinger, *God and the World* (San Francisco: Ignatius Press, 2002), 416.

[13] Joseph Ratzinger, *Salt of the Earth* (San Francisco: Ignatius Press, 1997), 176.

return of the SSPX to full communion with the Church. Between 2009 and 2012, the Holy See and the SSPX engaged in discussions about doctrine and about possible juridic structures to accommodate the return of the SSPX. The doctrinal discussions were confidential, but it was reported that one of the key issues was the Vatican II teaching on religious liberty.[14]

In the spring of 2012 an agreement reconciling the SSPX with the Holy See seemed imminent.[15] A draft doctrinal agreement reportedly was based on the 1988 Protocol that Lefebvre had signed but had repudiated one day later.[16] The 1988 document had referred to passages in the Vatican II texts that are "reconcilable with Tradition only with difficulty." In April 2012 the SSPX submitted to the Congregation for the Doctrine of the Faith a revised text that spoke of such passages as "not reconcilable with the previous Magisterium of the Church."[17]

In June 2012, the Pontifical Commission *Ecclesia Dei* presented a doctrinal declaration to the SSPX for its agreement, together with a proposal for canonically regularizing the SSPX.[18] The declaration reportedly required the SSPX to accept the continuity of the Vatican II texts with the previous magisterium.[19] The SSPX requested and was granted additional time to study

---

[14] Cf. Gregor Kollmorgen, "Interview with *Ecclesia Dei* Secretary—Full Text," New Liturgical Movement, Dec. 3, 2010, accessed Dec. 19, 2020, http://www.newliturgicalmovement.org/2010/12/interview-with-ecclesia-dei-secretary_03.html#.Ub0Nwtgn_XQ. During the discussions, SSPX authorities continued to criticize Vatican II in communications to their benefactors and in press interviews. Bernard Fellay, Letter 77, "To Friends and Benefactors," reprinted in part on *Rorate Caeli*, Dec. 6, 2010, accessed Dec. 19, 2020, https://rorate-caeli.blogspot.com/2010/12/fellay-it-is-still-quite-difficult-to.html; "Naming the 'False Brethren,' the 'Mute Dogs' and the 'Untrustworthy Leaders,'" *The Pastor's Corner*, U.S. District of the SSPX (website), reprinted on *Rorate Caeli*, Feb. 14, 2011, accessed Dec. 19, 2020, https://rorate-caeli.blogspot.com/2011/02/naming-false-brethren-mute-dogs-and.html.

[15] See the sources cited in Côme de Prévigny, "Setting Things Straight about the SSPX-Vatican Talks: What Exactly Happened in April–June 2012?" *Rorate Caeli*, July 7, 2013, accessed Dec. 19, 2020, https://rorate-caeli.blogspot.com/search?updated-max=2013-07-19T23:30:00Z&max-results=40 [hereinafter, Côme de Prévigny].

[16] Côme de Prévigny.

[17] Côme de Prévigny.

[18] Cf. Dichiarazione della Pontificia Commissione "Ecclesia Dei," Oct. 27, 2012, accessed Dec. 19, 2020, https://web.archive.org/web/20121101161603/http://press.catholica.va/news_services/bulletin/news/29911.php?index=29911&lang=it#TESTO.

[19] Cf. Côme de Prévigny. The declaration also reportedly required the SSPX to accept the *liceity* of the 1970 *Missal* of Paul VI. The 1988 Protocol reportedly had required acceptance of the *validity* of the 1970 *Missal*. This reportedly proved to be objectionable to the SSPX. It appears that they were willing to acknowledge the bare validity of the 1970 *Missal*, but perhaps that they considered acknowledgment of its liceity to be an endorsement of the liturgical reform.

the declaration. In July 2012, the General Chapter of the SSPX apparently voted to reject these conditions.[20] However, the SSPX never has responded formally to the Pontifical Commission.

In January 2013, the Vice President of the Commission, Archbishop Augustine Di Noia, issued a letter to all the priests of the SSPX. In that letter, Di Noia observed that the disagreement between the Holy See and the SSPX remained the same as it had been since the 1970s:

> With magisterial authority, the Holy See has consistently maintained that the documents of the Council must be interpreted in the light of Tradition and the Magisterium and not vice versa, while the Fraternity has insisted that certain teachings of the Council are erroneous and are thus not susceptible to an interpretation in line with the Tradition and the Magisterium.[21]

Di Noia criticized SSPX leaders for using the press to reiterate their positions on Vatican II publicly, while those positions were supposed to be the subject of confidential discussions. This conduct, Di Noia said, "cause[d] concern about the realistic prospects for reconciliation." He indicated that the Holy See was willing to permit the SSPX to discuss the passages of Vatican II that are difficult to reconcile with previous teaching, but he said that this cannot take place in the mass media. Moreover, he said, these difficulties should not be the focus of the SSPX's preaching and formation. He called on both sides to conduct an examination of conscience, and he reiterated that the Holy See expects a response to the doctrinal declaration that it had presented to the SSPX in June 2012.

Shortly after Di Noia issued his letter, Bishop Bernard Fellay, the Superior General of the SSPX, gave a homily in which he said that the purpose of the SSPX is to defend the faith, and "in comparison with this sublime reality, talking about whether or not to reach an agreement with Rome is something trivial." He went on to criticize Vatican II vigorously:

---

[20] "The Priests of the Fraternity of St. Pius X Rally behind Bishop Fellay," *Rorate Caeli*, Feb. 18, 2013, accessed Dec. 19, 2020, https://rorate-caeli.blogspot.com/2013/02/the-priests-of-fraternity-of-st-pius-x.html (hereinafter, Priests Rally Behind Fellay).

[21] "Full Text of Advent Letter of Archbishop J. Augustine Di Noia Vice-President of the Ecclesia Dei Commission to the Fraternity of St. Pius X," *Il Sismografo*, Jan. 19, 2013, accessed Dec. 19, 2020, http://ilsismografo.blogspot.com/2013/01/vaticano-full-text-of-advent-letter.html.

2.1. Archbishop Lefebvre and the Declaration on Religious Liberty

> [W]ith the Council, through the Council, and in the Council, some poisons were introduced that are harmful to the faith; they lead souls into error and no longer defend them, no longer defend them in their faith. We denounce this fact, and this is why they condemn us. Even today, the condition that they want to impose on us in order to recognize us with the title "Catholic" is to accept those very same things that demolish the faith.[22]

On February 11, 2013, Pope Benedict astonished the world by announcing his decision to abdicate the papacy. He was eighty-five years old, and he said that he no longer had the strength of mind and body to discharge the duties of the Roman Pontiff. Press reports indicated that Benedict had two great disappointments at the end of his pontificate. One of these was the criminal disclosure of the Holy Father's private documents by his butler, Paolo Gabriele (the so-called VatiLeaks scandal). The other was the failure of the Holy See and the SSPX to achieve a reconciliation.[23]

In the closing days of Benedict's pontificate, the Holy See reportedly made a final outreach to the SSPX. Some accounts indicate that the prefect of the Congregation for the Doctrine of the Faith, Archbishop Gerhard Müller, asked the SSPX to sign the doctrinal declaration of June 2012.[24] Other reports said that the prefect only asked the SSPX to return to negotiations with the Holy See.[25] In any event, the accounts indicated that if the Society refused this final overture, then the Holy See would attempt reconciliation with individual SSPX priests. Reports differ as to what type of canonical structure the Holy See offered the SSPX. Some say that the prefect offered a prelature (which would make the Society dependent on the

---

[22] Bernard Fellay, "Fellay: 'To Defend the Faith, to Keep the Faith, to Die in the Faith, This is the Essential Thing!" Rorate Caeli, Feb. 2, 2013, accessed Dec. 19, 2020, https://rorate-caeli.blogspot.com/2013/02/fellay-to-defend-faith-to-keep-faith-to.html.

[23] Cf. Carlo Angerer and Ian Johnston, "Pope's Brother: Pontiff was Troubled by Butler's Revelations," Feb. 12, 2013, accessed June 15, 2013, https://www.nbcnews.com/news/world/popes-brother-pontiff-was-troubled-butlers-revelations-flna1c8340362.

[24] Cf. "Priests Rally Behind Fellay."

[25] Cf. "A Last Chance for the SSPX?" Rorate Caeli, Feb. 13, 2013, accessed Dec. 19, 2020, https://rorate-caeli.blogspot.com/2013/02/a-last-chance-for-sspx-plus-sspx-in.html.

Holy See, rather than on individual bishops),[26] but other reports indicated that the type of canonical structure was unclear.[27]

Bishop Fellay declined to reach an agreement before the election of Benedict's successor. He reiterated the Society's position on Vatican II, namely, that "it is necessary to clarify and correct a certain number of points that are either erroneous or lead to error."[28] Despite the threat that the Holy See would approach individual SSPX priests, the clergy of the Society appeared to be united behind Fellay. One SSPX priest said,

> We are always open to proposals from the Holy See, but do not force us to accept Vatican II! For forty years we've been saying that! The Council has promulgated a text contrary to the Catholic faith—that concerning religious liberty. We cannot in good conscience accept this text.[29]

As a result of Benedict's special concern and sympathy for the traditionalist faithful, many feared that his abdication would prove to have marked the closing of the window of opportunity for the SSPX's reconciliation. Indeed, in his final homily as pope, on Ash Wednesday 2013, Benedict appeared to be speaking to the SSPX when he recounted the prophet Joel's call to return and St. Paul's warning about the shortness of time to respond to the call:

> [T]he Church proposes the powerful appeal which the prophet Joel addresses to the people of Israel, "Thus says the Lord, return to me with all your heart, with fasting, with weeping, and with mourning" (2.12). . . .
>
> This "return to me with all your heart," then is a reminder that not only involves the individual but the entire community. . . . The community dimension is an essential element in faith and Christian life. . . .

---

[26] Cf. "Benedict XVI—SSPX: Quarter to Midnight," *Rorate Caeli*, Feb. 20, 2013, accessed May 8, 2021, https://rorate-caeli.blogspot.com/2013/02/benedict-xvi-sspx-quarter-to-midnight.html.

[27] Cf. "A Last Chance for the SSPX?"

[28] "Fellay: 'I Thought That, with His Resignation, He Would Perhaps Make a Final Gesture in Our Favor as Pope. (Updated)," *Rorate Caeli*, Feb. 15, 2013, accessed Dec. 19, 2020, https://rorate-caeli.blogspot.com/2013/02/fellay-i-thought-that-with-his.html.

[29] "Priests Rally Behind Fellay," quoting Father Jean-Yves Cottard Tours.

"Well, now is the favourable time, this is the day of salvation" (2 Cor 6:2). The words of the Apostle Paul to the Christians of Corinth resonate for us with an urgency that does not permit absences or inertia. The term "now," repeated several times, says that this moment cannot be let go, it is offered to us as a unique opportunity, that will not be repeated.[30]

In March 2013, Jorge Cardinal Bergoglio was elected to succeed Benedict, and he took Francis as his papal name. Two months into his pontificate, a group of Italian bishops from the region of Puglia made their *ad limina* visit and urged him to repeal *Summorum Pontificum* and to curtail the freedom that his predecessor had granted for the celebration of the traditional Mass. Francis, however, decisively rejected this request, urging the bishops to treasure tradition and to create the conditions necessary to enable tradition to live alongside innovation.[31] Thus, Francis seemed to signal that he embraces the *hermeneutic of reform in continuity* that Benedict had championed in interpreting Vatican II in the light of previous tradition.

Another event early in Francis's pontificate seemed to cast doubt on the likelihood of a close understanding between the pope and traditionalists. In June 2013, Francis received representatives from a Latin American association of leaders of religious communities, the Confederación Latinoamericana y Caribeña de Religiosos y Religiosas (CLAR). An account of that informal meeting appeared in the press, and it seemed to suggest a bewilderment on the pope's part toward the attitude and devotions of traditionalists. He is reported to have said that there is a "Pelagian current" running through "some restorationist groups." He reportedly suggested that such people desire to live several decades in the past, and he criticized a particular group that had approached him (before he was pope) with a spiritual bouquet of 3,525 rosaries. He appreciated the prayers but was taken aback by the practice of counting rosaries.[32]

---

[30] Benedict XVI, Homily for Ash Wednesday (Feb. 13, 2013) [AAS 105 (2013): 270–71]. Interestingly, Benedict also made several references to themes that touch on the Vatican II teaching on religious liberty. He referred to the importance of community several times, and he also made reference to the importance of witnessing to the faith and overcoming individualism.

[31] Cf. Sandro Magister, "Tra confidenze ed esorcismi, un Francesco tutto da decifrare," L'Espresso, May 25, 2013, accessed June 15, 2013, http://magister.blogautore.espresso.repubblica.it/2013/05/25/tra-confidenze-ed-esorcismi-un-papa-tutto-da-decifrare/.

[32] Cf. "Pope to Latin American Religious: Full Text," *Rorate Caeli*, June 11, 2013, accessed June 15, 2013, http://rorate-caeli.blogspot.com/2013/06/pope-to-latin-american-religious-full.html.

For its part, the SSPX became more adamant in its rejection of Vatican II in the opening months of Francis's pontificate. In June 2013, the Society marked twenty-five years since the episcopal consecrations by Lefebvre. The SSPX bishops issued a declaration to commemorate the occasion, and in that document, they rejected outright Pope Benedict's interpretation of Vatican II through a hermeneutic of continuity:

> Following Archbishop Lefebvre, we affirm that the cause of the grave errors which are in the process of demolishing the Church does not reside in a bad interpretation of the conciliar texts—a "hermeneutic of rupture" which would be opposed to a "hermeneutic of reform in continuity" but truly in the texts themselves, by virtue of the unheard of choice made by Vatican II.[33]

This "unheard of choice" the SSPX bishops complain of consists in a "new humanism" and an embrace of the "cult of man." The bishops proceed to critique specific teachings of Vatican II, most notably those on religious liberty and ecumenism. With regard to religious liberty, they say:

> Religious liberty, as exposed by Dignitatis humanae and its practical application these last fifty years, logically leads to demanding God-made-Man to renounce His reign over man-who-makes-himself-God, which is equivalent to dissolving Christ. In the place of a conduct which is inspired by a solid faith in the real power of Our Lord Jesus Christ, we see the Church being shamefully guided by human prudence and with such self-doubt that she asks nothing other from the State than that which the Masonic Lodges wish to concede to her: the common law in the midst of, and on the same level as, other religions which she no longer dares to call false.[34]

---

[33] "For the Record: Declaration of Bishops of Society of St. Pius X on the Occasion of the 25th Anniversary of the Episcopal Ordinations," §3, *Rorate Caeli*, June 27, 2013, accessed May 5, 2021, https://rorate-caeli.blogspot.com/2013/06/for-record-declaration-of-sspx-bishops.html. The declaration was issued by three of the four bishops consecrated by Lefebvre and by Bishop Antonio de Castro Mayer, who had joined Lefebvre in consecrating the four. Those three bishops were the then-superiors of the SSPX, Bernard Fellay, and also Bishops Bernard Tissier de Mallerais and Alfonso de Galarreta. (The fourth consecrated bishop had been Richard Williamson. Shortly after Benedict XVI had lifted the excommunications, accounts appeared in the press to the effect that Williamson had denied the Holocaust.)

[34] "Declaration of SSPX Bishops," §6.

The critique of ecumenism is similar, claiming that inter-religious dialogue has silenced the truth about the one true Church, has killed the missionary spirit, and has promoted false unity through a message of a purely earthly peace.[35] This declaration and other statements of the SSPX leadership in 2013 suggested that the window of possibility for reconciliation indeed may have closed, or at least narrowed.

In fact, however, dialogue has continued during the current pontificate, albeit with a lower profile. The Society's discussions with the Congregation for the Doctrine of the Faith that had broken off in 2012 resumed in 2014. In 2015, for the upcoming 2016 Jubilee Year of Mercy, Pope Francis granted to the Society's priests the faculty to hear confessions validly. At the end of the year, he extended that faculty indefinitely, and at the same time expressed his hopes "for the recovery of full communion."[36] On April 2, 2016, Pope Francis met with Bishop Fellay in a private audience. Little was made public other than the decision to continue discussions. During the same visit to Rome, Fellay also met with the secretary of the Pontifical Commission *Ecclesia Dei*. The following year, Francis allowed Catholic bishops to appoint priests to assist at marriages of members of the SSPX.[37] What was foreseen was that a diocesan priest would request and receive the spouses' consent, and that a priest of the SSPX then would celebrate the nuptial Mass. However, if diocesan priests were unavailable, then even SSPX priests could be appointed to request and receive consent.

Recent developments have included the SSPX's 2018 election of a new superior, the Rev. Davide Pagliarani, and Pope Francis's 2019 suppression of the Pontifical Commission *Ecclesia Dei* and the transfer of its responsibilities to the Congregation for the Doctrine of the Faith. The CDF already had assumed responsibility for dialogue with the SSPX, and the suppression of PCED represents the progress that has been made on liturgical issues and the reality that the remaining issues with the Society are doctrinal rather than liturgical.

In 2021, however, Pope Francis adopted a significantly stricter line toward the faithful attached to the traditional Latin Mass. In his apostolic letter *Traditionis Custodes*, he announced that pastors and individual priests

---

[35] Cf. "Declaration of SSPX Bishops," §7. The declaration also criticizes episcopal collegiality and the 1970 *Missal* of Paul VI. Cf. "Declaration of SSPX Bishops," §§8–9.
[36] Pope Francis, Apostolic Letter *Misericordia et Misera* (Nov. 20, 2016), 12 [AAS 108 (2016): 1319–20].
[37] Cf. Edward Pentin, "Pope Francis' Approval of SSPX Marriages Offers Hopeful Step to Unity," *National Catholic Register* (Apr. 7, 2017), accessed June 18, 2022, https://www.ncregister.com/news/pope-francis-approval-of-sspx-marriages-offers-hopeful-step-to-unity.

no longer may celebrate the traditional Mass freely, but rather now must obtain (or confirm) the permission of their diocesan bishops.[38] Moreover, with few exceptions, these celebrations no longer may take place in parish churches.[39] Finally, the pontiff forbade diocesan bishops from authorizing the establishment of any new groups devoted to the traditional Mass.[40]

In an explanatory letter accompanying *Traditionis Custodes*, Pope Francis asserts that the intentions of his predecessors, Pope St. John Paul II and Pope Benedict XVI, to recover unity have been disregarded and have been "exploited to widen the gaps, reinforce the divergences, and encourage disagreements that injure the Church, block her path, and expose her to the peril of division." In addition, he says that use of the 1962 Missal is "often characterized by a rejection not only of the liturgical reform, but of the Vatican Council itself, claiming, with unfounded and unsustainable assertions, that it betrayed the Tradition and the 'true Church.'"

He concludes: "A final reason for my decision is this: ever more plain in the words and attitudes of many is the close connection between the choice of celebrations according to the liturgical books prior to Vatican Council II and the rejection of the Church and her institutions in the name of what is called the 'true Church.'" Moreover, he says, the faithful attached to the traditional Mass "need to return in due time to the Roman Rite promulgated by Saints Paul VI and John Paul II."

Reactions came quickly. Several U.S. bishops issued letters the very day that *Traditionis Custodes* appeared, either confirming permission for existing celebrations of the traditional Mass or else limiting it.[41] Individuals and associations—either devoted to the traditional Mass or sympathetic to its adherents—issued statements of shock and disappointment. Some of these statements took issue with the charge of rejection of Vatican II and the promotion of division within the Church.[42] That is, the faithful attached

---

[38] Pope Francis, Apostolic Letter *Traditionis Custodes* (June 16, 2021), §§4–5.
[39] Francis, *Traditionis Custodes*, §2.
[40] Francis, *Traditionis Custodes*, §6.
[41] Cf. Christine Rousselle, "Traditionis Custodes: Arkansas Bishop Limits Traditional Latin Mass across State to Two Parishes Administered by FSSP," *National Catholic Register* (July 19, 2021), accessed June 18, 2022, https://www.ncregister.com/news/traditionis-custodes-arkansas-bishop-limits-traditional-latin-mass-across-state-to-two-parishes-administered-by-fssp; Joan Frawley Desmond, "Bishop Paprocki Discusses 'Traditionis Custodes': Liturgical Unity Doesn't Mean Liturgical Uniformity," *National Catholic Register* (Aug. 4, 2021), accessed June 18, 2022, https://www.ncregister.com/interview/bishop-paprocki-discusses-traditionis-custodes-liturgical-unity-doesn-t-mean-liturgical-uniformity.
[42] This summary of the apostolic letter and the reactions to it is based on my article,

to this form of the Mass include not only the members of the SSPX, but also Catholics in an entirely regular situation who attend Masses celebrated under the auspices of the local ecclesiastical authorities, and many spoke up to defend these Catholics as obedient and faithful.

The Holy See, however, has kept to the path indicated by *Traditionis Custodes*, and indeed has impressed it more firmly. Six months after the apostolic letter, the Congregation for Divine Worship and the Discipline of the Sacraments issued a list of eleven *responsa ad dubia* generated by the provisions of the letter.[43] The import of these *responsa* was to restrict celebration of the traditional Mass even further than indicated in *Traditionis Custodes*. In addition, in the spring of 2022, the Holy See suspended the ordinations of a French diocese that has a reputation for openness to the traditional Mass.[44]

Thus, despite the continuation of dialogue with the SSPX during Francis's pontificate and despite his concessions to SSPX priests concerning the sacraments of penance and marriage, *Traditionis Custodes* now raises a formidable obstacle to regularizing the situation of these faithful. In the context of attempts to reconcile the SSPX, this is a dramatic setback. However, such pronouncements primarily are matters of policy or discipline, and as a result, even in the light of these recent developments, the larger obstacles to reconciliation remain the doctrinal ones.

2.2. Father Charles Curran and the Teaching of Moral Theology

At the polar opposite end of the Church, theologically speaking, the Declaration on Religious Liberty has been the subject of an equally serious controversy. Since the close of the Second Vatican Council, few American priests have become better known than Father Charles Curran. Father Curran

---

"*Traditionis Custodes* and the Raw Data on the Latin Mass," *Catholic World Report* (July 19, 2021), accessed July 16, 2022, https://www.catholicworldreport.com/2021/07/19/traditionis-custodes-and-the-raw-data-of-the-latin-mass/. For an example of an essay by a self-described "*Novus Ordo* man" defending the faithful attached to the traditional Mass, see George Weigel, "Liberal Authoritarianism and the Traditional Latin Mass," *First Things* (July 21, 2021), accessed July 16, 2022, https://www.firstthings.com/web-exclusives/2021/07/liberal-authoritarianism-and-the-traditional-latin-mass.

[43] Congregation for Divine Worship and the Discipline of the Sacraments, *Responsa ad Dubia*, On Certain Provisions of the Apostolic Letter *Traditionis Custodes* (Dec. 4, 2021).

[44] Cf. Elise Ann Allen, "Suspension of Ordinations in France an Unprecedented Surprise," *Crux* (June 8, 2022), accessed July 16, 2022, https://cruxnow.com/church-in-europe/2022/06/suspension-of-ordinations-in-france-an-unprecedented-surprise/.

rose to prominence following Pope Paul VI's promulgation in 1968 of the encyclical *Humanae Vitae*, which reaffirmed the Church's teaching that artificial contraception is intrinsically disordered and that every marital act must remain open to the transmission of life.[45] Curran, then a professor of moral theology at the Catholic University of America, declared his personal nonacceptance of this teaching, and he proceeded to organize dissent against it.[46]

In the ensuing years, Curran declared his dissent from the Church's teaching in several areas of morality. He publicly dissented from the teachings of the magisterium on the indissolubility of marriage and on the morality of abortion, euthanasia, masturbation, premarital sexual intercourse, homosexual acts, direct sterilization, artificial insemination, and, as already noted, artificial contraception. In general, the difference between Curran and the magisterium was that for many of the acts that the Church declared as always prohibited, Father Curran taught that they sometimes were permissible. Curran's positions are well known, but the role that the Vatican II religious liberty document played in the formulation of his positions is far less known.

2.2.1. *The Inquiry of the Congregation for the Doctrine of the Faith*

The Congregation for the Doctrine of the Faith began investigating Curran in 1979 and engaged in a lengthy exchange of correspondence with him that lasted until 1986. Curran objected to the procedural posture of the investigation. He believed that the debate should begin with a statement from the Congregation declaring when dissent was permissible. In particular, Curran contended that his own actions were consistent with the norms for licit dissent that the American bishops had established in their 1968 pastoral letter, *Human Life in Our Day*.[47]

Just as then Cardinal Ratzinger (the future Pope Benedict XVI) was at

---

[45] Cf. Pope Paul VI, Encyclical *Humanae Vitae* (July 25, 1968), §§11, 14 [AAS 60 (1968): 488, 490].

[46] Both Curran himself and Joseph Cardinal Ratzinger, then Prefect of the Congregation for the Doctrine of the Faith, have referred to Curran's organization of dissent against *Humanae Vitae*. Charles Curran, "Public Dissent in the Church," reprinted in *Origins* 16, no. 9 (1986): 180; Congregation for the Doctrine of the Faith, "Observations on Father Charles Curran's Positions," *Origins* 15, no. 41 (1986): 170 (April 1983 observations). Curran published the entire exchange of correspondence between himself and Cardinal Ratzinger in his book *Faithful Dissent* (Kansas City, MO: Sheed & Ward, 1986).

[47] "The expression of theological dissent from the magisterium is in order only if the reasons are serious and well-founded, if the manner of the dissent does not question or impugn the

2.2. Father Charles Curran and the Teaching of Moral Theology

the center of the Holy See's attempts to reconcile the SSPX in the 1980s, so also was he—at virtually the same time—the key figure in the Holy See's effort to address the issues that Father Curran's dissent raised. In general, Ratzinger focused on the specific facts of Curran's case rather than the general subject of dissent in the Church. However, after the matter was resolved, Cardinal Ratzinger and the Congregation for the Doctrine of the Faith issued several documents that addressed the question of dissent in detail.[48] Despite the disagreement between Curran and Ratzinger over the procedural aspects of the case, Curran never contended that the Congregation had misrepresented his views. That is, he acknowledged that his opinions in these areas were contrary to the teachings of the magisterium.

Although he acknowledged the variations between his own teachings and those of the Church, Curran justified himself by asserting that he dissented only from teachings of the *ordinary* magisterium that had not been declared infallibly. He maintained that he did not dissent from any defined dogmas of the faith or pronouncements of the *extraordinary* magisterium.[49] Furthermore, he asserted that dissent from non-infallible teaching was permissible and that the Church had changed its teaching in the past:

> [S]ome historical examples give me hope. Theologians who have been condemned have at later times been vindicated and their

---

teaching authority of the Church, and is such as not to give scandal." *Human Life in Our Day: A Collective Pastoral Letter of the American Hierarchy* (Nov. 15, 1968).

[48] Cf. Congregation for the Doctrine of the Faith, Instruction on the Ecclesial Vocation of the Theologian *Donum Veritatis* (May 24, 1990) [AAS 82 (1990): 1550–70]; Congregation for the Doctrine of the Faith, Norms on Theological Dissent (June 29, 1997) [AAS 89 (1997): 830–35; cf. Archbishop Tarcisio Bertone, "Magisterial Documents and Public Dissent," *L'Osservatore Romano* (Jan. 29, 1997).

[49] The Catholic Church distinguishes between the *ordinary* and the *extraordinary* magisterium. The extraordinary magisterium may be exercised by the pope himself (which most theologians hold has occurred only twice), or by the pope together with the bishops of the world gathered in an ecumenical council (there have been twenty-one such councils in the history of the Church). The *extraordinary* magisterium pronounces on truths that belong to either the *primary object* or the *secondary object* of infallibility, that is, truths that either are revealed (primary object) or else that have a historical or logical connection with revealed truth (secondary object).

The *ordinary* magisterium is exercised by the pope and by the bishops dispersed throughout the world (that is, *not* gathered in council), but although its pronouncements may be infallible, they usually are *authoritative* rather than infallible. Note, however, that a teaching proposed as authoritative in one time, may be proposed as infallible at a later time. (This represents the Church becoming more certain about a particular teaching that already had been a part of Catholic doctrine.)

teachings have been accepted. The experience of the Second Vatican Council illustrates this fact.[50]

Curran took the position that the ordinary magisterium had made errors in the past and that dissent from Church teachings had resulted in the correction of those errors.[51] Curran's primary example of a purported change in Church teaching was the doctrine on religious liberty:

> Vatican Council II changed many earlier teachings such as those on religious freedom and the relationship of the Roman Catholic Church to other Christian churches and to the true church of Jesus Christ.[52]

His examples of changes in the teachings of the Church's ordinary magisterium would sometimes vary, but Father Curran almost always included a mention of the teaching on religious liberty:

> History reveals many cases where the Catholic Church officially changed its teaching on important issues such as the meaning and purpose of human sexuality and religious liberty. These changes ultimately came about and were prepared for by the work of theologians within the church.[53]

At one point, Father Curran seemed almost to goad the Congregation for the Doctrine of the Faith over the Vatican II teaching on religious liberty:

> Would the congregation say that the change in the teaching of the church on religious liberty at the Second Vatican Council was based on an abuse? ... When did the teaching on religious liberty become true? Only when a document was signed at the Second Vatican Council? The conciliar document itself recognized that the newer teaching was true before the official church teaching changed.[54]

---

[50] Cf. Charles Curran, "Response to Doctrinal Congregation's Decision," *Origins* 16, no. 11 (1986): 206: Statement at Aug. 20, 1986, News Conference.
[51] "Father Charles Curran Asked to Retract Positions," *Origins* 15, no. 41 (1986): 673: Curran's Aug. 10, 1983, Response to the Congregation for the Doctrine of the Faith.
[52] Curran, "Public Dissent," 180.
[53] "Curran Asked to Retract," 666: Curran's Mar. 11, 1986, Press Statement.
[54] "Curran Asked to Retract," 680: Curran's Aug. 24, 1984, Response to the Congregation for the Doctrine of the Faith.

Thus, it is clear that Curran's interpretation of the Vatican II Declaration on Religious Liberty provided one of the major justifications—if not the primary justification—for his argument in favor of the legitimacy of public dissent from the teachings of the Church's ordinary magisterium.

The Congregation for the Doctrine of the Faith asked Curran to retract his dissenting statements and positions. It responded to his assertion of a right to dissent by citing the Vatican II Dogmatic Constitution on the Church *Lumen Gentium*. That constitution requires Catholics to give "[r]eligious submission of the will and the intellect" to the "authentic teaching authority of the Roman pontiff, even when he does not speak *ex cathedra*."[55] Cardinal Ratzinger rebuked Father Curran for his doctrinal minimalism. "[T]he church does not build its life upon its infallible magisterium alone but on the teaching of its authentic, ordinary magisterium as well."[56] In addition, Ratzinger reminded Curran of the Vatican II teaching that the infallible magisterium is not confined only to matters of faith or solemn definitions.[57]

Father Curran refused to retract his positions. After multiple warnings, the Congregation advised the chancellor of the Catholic University of America on July 25, 1986, that Father Curran "will no longer be considered suitable nor eligible to exercise the function of a professor of Catholic theology." The chancellor, Archbishop James Hickey of Washington, DC, then initiated the process for the withdrawal of Curran's license to teach Catholic theology. Curran now teaches at Southern Methodist University in Dallas.

2.2.2. The Ramifications of Curran's Teachings

Father Curran's case illustrates the importance of *Dignitatis Humanae* for the entire field of moral theology. The Congregation for the Doctrine of the Faith was correct that Curran's teachings differed from those of the Church in a multitude of areas. Moreover, almost all of these differences occurred in

---

[55] Second Vatican Council, Dogmatic Constitution on the Church *Lumen Gentium* (Nov. 21, 1964), §25a [AAS 57 (1965): 29–30] (hereinafter, LG). Cardinal Ratzinger cited this passage in letters to Father Curran dated April 1983, April 13, 1984, and July 25, 1986.

[56] "Vatican Says Father Curran Can't Teach Theology," *Origins* 16, no. 11 (1986): 203: Cardinal Ratzinger's July 25, 1986, Letter to Father Curran.

[57] Cf. "Curran Can't Teach Theology," 203. Cardinal Ratzinger cites section 25 of *Lumen Gentium*, which provides that when the bishops in communion with the pope are in agreement that a particular position on a question of faith or morals is to be held definitively, then they are teaching infallibly. An example of the infallibility of the ordinary magisterium is the teaching that "the direct and voluntary killing of an innocent human being is always gravely immoral." Cf. Pope John Paul II, Encyclical *Evangelium Vitae* (Mar. 25, 1995), §57 [AAS 87 (1995): 465].

the area of sexual morality, the precise field in which the Church's teachings attract the most attention and in which the faithful find the most challenges in giving obedience. However, with some exceptions, Curran was correct in arguing that the Church's teachings in these areas had not been defined infallibly by the Church's extraordinary magisterium.[58]

As a result, it becomes important to determine whether Father Curran is correct that the Church has changed the teaching of its ordinary magisterium several times in the past—most notably in its doctrine on religious liberty. (In the next chapter, I discuss the difference between authentic developments of doctrine and illegitimate corruptions or changes. See section 3.1 below.) If Father Curran is correct in his interpretation of *Dignitatis Humanae*, then his position has far-reaching implications for virtually every area of moral theology. The reason is that moral theology by its nature is likely only rarely—if ever—to be the subject of ex cathedra definitions. The extraordinary magisterium concerns itself much more frequently with questions of systematic theology such as the nature of Christ, the Trinity, and the Virgin Mary. Even in these areas, however, the Church's pronouncements are infrequent.[59] If Father Curran is correct, then, for all practical purposes, the Church retains little authority to bind the faithful in matters of morality.

A cautionary note is necessary. One must remember that the magisterium does not propound all truths with the same degree of certainty. Thus, if, as some have proposed, the Church's teaching on artificial contraception is infallible, then a development or even a change in the teaching on religious liberty might not necessarily justify dissent on the question of contraception unless the teaching on religious liberty enjoyed at least the same level of authority. In the next chapter, I examine this circumstance more closely, and

---

[58] Cardinal Ratzinger pointed out that Curran's dissent regarding the indissolubility of marriage did conflict with a teaching of the extraordinary magisterium at the Council of Trent (cf. "Curran Can't Teach Theology," 203). Curran asserted in response that his position was the same as that of the Greek Orthodox Church, which applies the principle of "economy" (*oikonomia*) to permit divorce (Curran, "Response," 205). In addition, see the discussion below of whether the Church's pronouncements on artificial contraception constitute an infallible teaching of the *ordinary* magisterium.

[59] In the two millennia of the Church's life, there have been only twenty-one ecumenical councils. Only two popes have availed themselves of the only other expression of the extraordinary magisterium, a solemn *ex cathedra* definition on faith or morals. Pope Pius IX declared the Virgin Mary's Immaculate Conception in 1854 (Pope Pius IX, Apostolic Constitution *Ineffabilis Deus* [Dec. 8, 1854] [*Acta Pii IX*, pars 1, vol. 1]), and Pope Pius XII declared her Assumption into heaven in 1950 (Pope Pius XII, Apostolic Constitution *Munificentissimus Deus* [Nov. 1, 1950] [AAS 42 (1950): 753–73]).

2.2. Father Charles Curran and the Teaching of Moral Theology

I set forth my reason for believing that recourse to the levels of teaching is not the best way to address this question. See subsection 3.2.3 below.

The action of the Congregation for the Doctrine of the Faith against Curran did not end this matter. Many theologians from the progressive side of the Church have taken up Curran's position, both his premise concerning religious liberty and his conclusion concerning the liceity of public dissent from the Church's moral teachings. With regard to the teaching of Vatican II on religious liberty, theologians such as Hans Küng, Richard McBrien, and Leon Hooper echo Curran's argument that the Church has changed its teaching.[60] These ideas have spread to the wider culture and society by means of the writings of historians, journalists, and popular writers on religion.[61] The journalist Henri Fesquet covered the Council and, in his account of *Dignitatis Humanae*, he said that "Vatican II has shaken the conviction widely held by Catholics that doctrine is unchangeable."[62]

As stated above, from this premise that Vatican II changed the Church's teaching on religious liberty, Curran draws the conclusion that this purported change legitimizes dissent from other teachings that have not been defined infallibly. At least one moral theologian, Father Joseph Eagan, S.J., has adopted and applied this argument in such a way as to argue that a

---

[60] Cf. Richard P. McBrien, *Catholicism* (New York: Harper & Row, 1981), 273–81: "History of Catholic Teaching on Religious Toleration"; McBrien, 1020: "Church has Changed its Teaching on Religious Liberty and Usury"; J. Leon Hooper, introduction to *Religious Liberty: Catholic Struggles with Pluralism*, by John Courtney Murray (Louisville, KY: Westminster/John Knox Press, 1993), 12–13 (hereinafter, *Catholic Struggles with Pluralism*): *Dignitatis Humanae* "reversed long-standing Roman Catholic opposition to the separation of church and state and to the freedom of religion"; Interview with Hans Küng, *National Catholic Reporter*, Oct. 21, 1977: Küng: "Vatican II completely reversed Vatican I's position without explanation" (quoted and discussed in Michael Davies, *The Second Vatican Council and Religious Liberty* (Long Prairie, MN: Neumann Press, 1992), 203 (hereinafter, SVC&RL). With regard to the liceity of public dissent, Father Joseph Eagan's position is discussed below. Father Richard McBrien's view is similar in principle but, unlike Eagan, McBrien indicates that he believes that such dissent should be only occasional (McBrien, *Catholicism*, 72, 76). For additional similar views on the liceity of dissent, see Brennan R. Hill, Paul Knitter, and William Madges, *Faith, Religion, & Theology: A Contemporary Introduction*, rev. ed. (Mystic, CT: Twenty-third Publications, 1997), 306–10; Dennis M. Doyle, *The Church Emerging from Vatican II: A Popular Approach to Contemporary Catholicism* (Mystic, CT: Twenty-Third Publications, 1992), 101, 107.

[61] E.g., Doyle, *The Church Emerging*, 194: *Dignitatis Humanae* "illustrate[s] a dramatic reversal on an important issue: whether people should be free to worship in whatever religion they choose."

[62] Henri Fesquet, *The Drama of Vatican II* (New York: Random House, 1967), 355. The author went on to say, "[E]verything that is not strictly an article of faith is subject to changes according to the well-known adage, *Ecclesia semper reformanda*" (Fesquet, 355).

Catholic may take a position contrary to that of the magisterium on virtually any moral issue:

> Since moral teaching is part of the church's *ordinary* magisterium and is not in all cases infallible teaching, three consequences follow: the teaching can be *incomplete* and even considered erroneous in future centuries; it can be further developed and thus *changed*; and it therefore admits of responsible **dissent** by moral theologians and knowledgeable sincere Catholics.[63]

Instead of making the crucial distinction between *changes* and *developments* in doctrine, this quotation equates the two concepts. Later in the same work, *Restoration and Renewal*, Eagan makes it much clearer that in his mind, moral theologians are virtually free of constraints. He converts his position that moral teaching is "*not in all cases* infallible"[64] to a position that "the church has wisely *never* defined infallibly a moral question."[65] Reading these two quotations together enables one to complete Eagan's syllogism:

Major premise: One may dissent from any non-infallible teaching (Eagan, 286).
Minor premise: No moral teaching is defined infallibly (Eagan, 347).
Conclusion: Therefore, one may dissent from *any* Catholic moral teaching.

Thus, for nearly every action that the Church declares inconsistent with Christian living, Father Eagan's logic seemingly would justify that action in some circumstances. For Eagan, artificial insemination, premarital sex, homosexual acts, and artificial contraception all would be morally permissible in some situations.[66] In particular, they are permissible if a *proportionate reason* for them exists, that is, a reason sufficient to outweigh the harm of the action.[67] Father Curran's position is equivalent.[68] However, neither Eagan nor Curran place any limitations on the circumstances that a person may consider

---

[63] Joseph F. Eagan, *Restoration and Renewal: The Church in the Third Millennium* (Kansas City, MO: Sheed & Ward, 1995), 286 (emphasis in original).
[64] Eagan, *Restoration and Renewal*, 286 (emphasis added).
[65] Eagan, *Restoration and Renewal*, 347 (emphasis added).
[66] Cf. Eagan, *Restoration and Renewal*, 290.
[67] "[P]remoral evil becomes moral evil and sinful when it is done without a proportionate reason" (Eagan, *Restoration and Renewal*, 290). Cf. *Restoration and Renewal*, 289.
[68] Curran justifies his position on abortion by "a theory of proportionate reason" and his

as possible justifications for engaging in premarital sex, homosexual acts, or artificial insemination.[69] This fact gives rise to at least two problems. First, the practical effect of applying the proportionalist theory is that the person making the decision almost invariably will decide in favor of premarital sex, artificial insemination, or whatever the contemplated action is. Cardinal Ratzinger cited the human impulse toward self-justification as a major problem with this type of theory.[70] Kenneth Melchin is sympathetic to some of Curran's goals, but he reaches the same conclusion as Ratzinger: "After all, we can all marshal proportionate reasons to justify things we want."[71]

The second problem with proportionalist theories is that because an individual's judgment as to proportionate reason in a concrete situation is the sole determinant of the morality of an act, no role whatsoever remains for a public moral authority such as the Roman magisterium.[72] By the same token, proportionalism removes from the discipline of moral theology its most basic task of "mak[ing] clear how faith should shape Christian life."[73]

Proportionalist theories of morality render the Church's moral teaching

---

position on homosexual acts by "a theology of compromise" ("Curran Asked to Retract," 669 [Curran's March 11, 1986, press statement]).

[69] Cf. Kenneth R. Melchin, "Revisionists, Deontologists, and the Structure of Moral Understanding," *Theological Studies* 51, no. 3 (1990): 389–416, at 397.

[70] Cf. "Curran Asked to Retract," 671.

[71] Melchin, "Revisionists, Deontologists," 394. "The tendencies of human subjects towards rationalization, towards taking the easier road, towards egoism are well known" ("Revisionists, Deontologists," 408 [footnote omitted]). Melchin believes that the relevant context of moral decisions should be expanded to include additional data, but he argues that the *revisionist* moral theologians, who advance the proportionalist theories, have failed to provide adequate criteria to specify how far the circle of relevant data extends.

[72] Cf. Melchin, "Revisionists, Deontologists," 394. However, Melchin believes that this problem might be solved if adequate criteria were developed to define the limits of the context that is relevant to making a moral decision. Cf. "Revisionists, Deontologists," 412–15. It is not clear that Melchin's approach survives Pope John Paul II's 1993 rejection of proportionalism in *Veritatis Splendor*. However, Melchin's work can be harmonized with the encyclical if one interprets it not as providing a context to determine whether an act is objectively disordered, but rather as providing criteria for judging a person's subjective culpability. This reading of Melchin would be consistent with that of the Catechism, which reaffirms the objective disorder of acts such as masturbation and suicide, but also recognizes that subjective factors sometimes lessen culpability. Catechism of the Catholic Church, 2nd ed. (Vatican City: Libreria Editrice Vaticana, 1997), §§2282, 2352 (hereinafter, CCC).

[73] Germain Grisez, *The Way of the Lord Jesus*, vol. 1, *Christian Moral Principles* (Chicago: Franciscan Herald Press, 1983), 6. "Moral theology cannot do its full job if it remains at the level of general principles. It also must show the relationship between divine revelation and Catholic teaching on particular issues, such as the morality of choosing one's profession, of paying taxes, of sexual activity, and so on" (*Christian Moral Principles*, 7).

less and less important with the passage of time. One of Father Curran's arguments in support of his position is that these moral issues are very "complex."[74] (Given this complexity, Cardinal Ratzinger wondered how Father Curran could be so certain "that the magisterium is, in fact, wrong so completely and so often.")[75] In the three decades since the decision of the Congregation concerning Father Curran, moral issues have become even more complex. For example, in vitro fertilization, human cloning, and fetal experimentation are issues that have risen to prominence since the mid-1980s. If the magisterium's teaching on homosexual acts, based as it is on Scripture itself,[76] is open to question, then how much more open to question are the Church's teachings on subjects that were wholly unknown until the post-conciliar period? Pope John Paul II responded to the crisis in moral theology by issuing his 1993 encyclical *Veritatis Splendor*. However, although the encyclical rejected proportionalist theories of moral theology,[77] those theories have by no means disappeared from the field of Catholic moral theology. In fact, John Paul referred to the "crisis of obedience vis-à-vis the Church's Magisterium" as one of the "shadows" on the present age.[78]

Brian Harrison realized the import of Father Curran's arguments almost immediately. In response, he wrote a book entitled *Religious Liberty and Contraception*, the arguments of which are discussed at length below.[79] Harrison wrote his book to refute Father Curran's position on contraception. However, to do so, Harrison builds his case on a thorough analysis of *Dignitatis Humanae*. Thus, nine of his eleven chapters are devoted exclusively to *Dignitatis Humanae*. This degree of emphasis reveals the extent to which the future of the Church's moral teaching depends upon a proper understanding of the Vatican II Declaration on Religious Liberty.

---

[74] Cf. "Curran Asked to Retract," 678. Cf. Eagan, *Restoration and Renewal*, 290.
[75] "Curran Asked to Retract," 671 (April 1983 observations).
[76] CCC, §2357.
[77] Cf. Pope John Paul II, Encyclical *Veritatis Splendor* (Aug. 6, 1993), §§75–76, 79 [AAS 85 (1993): 1193–95, 1197]; cf. *Veritatis Splendor*, §§56, 65 [AAS 85 (1993): 1178–79, 1184–85].
[78] Pope John Paul II, Apostolic Letter *Tertio Millenio Adveniente* (Nov. 10, 1994), §36 [AAS 87 (1995): 28].
[79] Cf. Brian W. Harrison, *Religious Liberty and Contraception: Did Vatican II Open the Way for a New Sexual Ethic?* (Melbourne: John XXIII Fellowship Co-op, 1988) (hereinafter cited as RL&C).

2.3. Curran and Lefebvre

Some might be tempted to consider it nothing more than a coincidence that Archbishop Lefebvre and Father Curran, despite their radically different ideas, share the same understanding of *Dignitatis Humanae*, namely, that it represents a fundamental change in Catholic teaching. However, it is not the case that they simply *happen* to agree on this lone point. Rather, the fact is that for both of these clerics, the Vatican II Declaration on Religious Liberty lies at the very heart of their reasons for staking out positions opposed to the hierarchy of the Church. One of them interprets this purported change as justifying individual theologians in dissenting from the Church's teaching and in publicly advocating additional and far-reaching changes in Catholic morality. The other interpreted it as a betrayal of Catholic teaching, as proof of the illegitimacy of the Second Vatican Council, and as justification for establishing a parallel Church hierarchy.[80]

2.4. Religious Liberty and the Church's Witness to Justice

The importance of *Dignitatis Humanae* is not limited to the ecclesial controversies generated by Archbishop Lefebvre and Father Curran, but it naturally extends to the subject matter of the declaration itself, namely the vitally important question of religious liberty. One of the Council's motivations for issuing a Declaration on Religious Liberty was to enable the Church to respond to religious repression in the Marxist world. In some regions of the globe, notably Eastern Europe, the condition of Christians and other believers has improved in the time since *Dignitatis Humanae* was issued. Some council fathers intended the declaration to give the Church the moral authority to speak credibly on these issues, and it appears to have done so. It is no coincidence that Pope John Paul II, who made human

---

[80] Archbishop Lefebvre's views may seem extreme to the majority of Catholics but, within the context of Catholic traditionalism, one almost can describe his positions as moderate. For example, in 1983 a group of nine American SSPX priests challenged the validity of the elections of all of the popes following Pius XII. (Archbishop Lefebvre had accepted the Vatican II and post-Vatican II popes as validly elected.) The SSPX expelled these priests, and they formed a rival organization, the Society of Saint Pius V (SSPV). As with Archbishop Lefebvre and the SSPX, religious liberty figures prominently in the motivations of the SSPV and other *sedevacantists*. In asserting that the visible structure of the Church has broken with the Catholic faith, *sedevacantists* cite the teaching of *Dignitatis Humanae* as a key example. One *sedevacantist* layman asks, "Would a true pope . . . teach such obvious falsehoods as religious liberty and ecumenism?" (Cuneo, *Smoke of Satan*, 113).

rights a centerpiece of his papacy,[81] attended the Council as archbishop of Cracow and participated in the debates on the religious liberty declaration.[82] However, the problem of religious repression is far from solved. In the world's most populous nation, repression not only continues but is in fact on the rise. Moreover, neither the declaration nor any other attempt to secure religious rights holds any sway in the greater part of the Islamic world.[83]

Although the United States often is identified closely with this cause, religious liberty seems under threat even there. In particular, President Obama's universal healthcare legislation, the Affordable Care Act (and its implementing regulations), require employers to provide free access to artificial contraception, and this requirement applies even to organizations connected with a religion that teaches the immorality of such practices. In addition, attacks are increasing on "conscience protections" that allow healthcare workers to avoid assisting with measures such as abortion or sterilization if these interventions violate their beliefs. Also, a number of U.S. localities have excluded Catholic organizations from publicly-funded adoption programs because such organizations decline to place children with same-sex couples.

The Church no doubt will continue to proclaim human rights, including the right to religious liberty. However, the serious questions surrounding the declaration are bound to have an impact on the effectiveness of the Church's witness. If the Church's teaching on religious liberty is entirely cut off from its previous tradition, then observers and commentators might well question whether religious liberty is or ever can be an authentic part of the Christian message at all.

The Church recently has become not only a proponent of religious liberty but its chief defender. Commentators sometimes call *Dignitatis Humanae* the "American document" of Vatican II because of the prominence of American bishops—and the American *peritus* John Courtney Murray—in the drafting of the declaration. Also, in the post-World War II period, a number of Church leaders came to appreciate the American model of religious liberty because, although it did not allow the adoption

---

[81] See generally J. Bryan Hehir, "*Dignitatis Humanae* in the Pontificate of John Paul II," in John T. Ford, ed., *Religious Liberty: Paul VI and Dignitatis Humanae* (Brescia, Italy: Istituto Paulo VI, 1995), 169–83.

[82] Pope Benedict XVI also emphasized human rights during his pontificate, and he too had participated in the Council (as a *peritus*). Pope Francis did not attend the Council, but early in his pontificate, he too spoke about the importance of religious liberty.

[83] Cf. Pope John Paul II, Address to the Diplomatic Corps Accredited to the Holy See (Jan. 13, 1990), 16 [AAS 82 (1990): 869].

of a state religion, it did permit broad freedom. In this freedom, the Church in America flourished, and by the time of Vatican II, the U.S. had become a leader in Church attendance among Western nations.

As mentioned, though, in recent years, the future of religious liberty in America itself has become more doubtful. Thus, although religious liberty may have entered Church teaching by way of America, it seems to have taken a curious historical turn. That is, in the New Evangelization, it seems that it may have fallen to the Church to re-evangelize America, not only in the faith but even in its own heritage of cherishing and defending religious rights. If the Church is to take up this task, however, she must be certain that religious liberty has a legitimate place in her teaching.

2.5. The Church's Diplomatic Activity and Her Relationship to Modernity

The Holy See has a rich diplomatic history, and the Vatican II teaching on religious liberty is crucial to the current activity of the papacy in this realm. For the two centuries preceding the Second Vatican Council, one of the most important specialties in canon law was *Ius Publicum Ecclesiasticum* or the public law of the Church. This branch of the Church's law was concerned with the hierarchical structure of the Church, and with her relations with secular governments. Moreover, this field served an apologetic purpose by reasserting the Church's prerogatives in the face of hostile civil governments, particularly in Europe. As a result of the prominence of this branch of law over a sustained period, it is striking that there have been no major new texts in the field of public ecclesiastical law since Vatican II (or, for that matter, since World War II). In fact, the subject seems practically to have disappeared, except as a topic of historical interest.

Of course, the content of this subject has not entirely vanished, but the place that public ecclesiastical law formerly occupied in the Church now has been filled largely by the Vatican II religious liberty declaration *Dignitatis Humanae*. The Church's diplomatic activity is concerned primarily with the defense of human rights, the particular defense of religious liberty, and the freedom of the Church. In promoting these principles, the popes and the diplomatic corps rely in large measure on *Dignitatis Humanae*.[84] Although the religious liberty declaration is one of the shortest of all the

---

[84] See generally Giorgio Filibeck, *I diritti dell'uomo nell'insegnamento della Chiesa. Da Giovanni XXIII a Giovanni Paolo II* (Città del Vaticano: Libreria Editrice Vaticana, 2001).

pronouncements of Vatican II, it has become the true cornerstone of papal diplomacy today.

Given the importance of the declaration in this realm, the question once more arises as to whether this document truly has a legitimate place in the Church's life and tradition. If the Lefebvrists and others are correct in arguing the negative, then the Holy See's largely successful diplomatic activity of the last several decades would seem to have been built on an unsound foundation. That is, the question arises as to whether *Dignitatis Humanae* represents a "co-opting" of the Catholic Church. Vatican II sometimes is described as the Church's *coming to terms with modernity*. Some Catholics no doubt bristle at this suggestion, but as discussed above, it seems that this reconciliation—or at least partial reconciliation—already was beginning in the late nineteenth century under Pope Leo XIII. Thus, the key question is *in what sense* has the Church come to terms with modernity?

In the context of the religious liberty declaration, the more precise question is whether Vatican II amounts to the Church's wholesale embrace of Enlightenment theories of human and political rights. That is, does the Church's acceptance of universal human rights entail an acceptance of the Enlightenment rationalism and skepticism that led to the discovery—or, at any rate, the most influential articulation—of these rights?

On the other hand, however, perhaps this embrace was selective. In the end, the Church did indeed come to a conclusion similar to that of leading Enlightenment thinkers, namely, the recognition of a universal right to religious liberty. However, the reason for the Church's seemingly long delay in recognizing this right may have been her desire to withhold recognition until such time as she was able to separate the wheat from the chaff, thus embracing the right but not its historical underpinnings in rationalism and skepticism.[85] That is, the difficulty may not have been in recognizing the right itself but rather in locating a new and *distinctively Christian* foundation for it.[86]

---

[85] Needless to say, the difficulties were not only intellectual and theoretical. The French Enlightenment and the succeeding revolutions of 1789, 1830, and 1848 were so hostile to the Church, and elicited such a defensive response from the Church, that it is difficult to imagine the Church quickly embracing any ideas so closely associated with that movement.

[86] Cf. Walter Kasper, "The Theological Foundations of Human Rights," *The Jurist* 50 (1990): 148–66. See also chapter 16 below.

CHAPTER 3

Development, Method, and the Issues

How is it that mortal man can develop what he would not know unless God had revealed it?

— BERNARD LONERGAN[1]

The Vatican II teaching on religious liberty is controversial not only in itself, but also because it implicates the question of doctrinal development. The idea of doctrinal development is associated with St. John Henry Newman in particular, and an understanding of this idea is necessary for an examination of the right to religious liberty. This chapter briefly discusses doctrinal development, and then proceeds to outline both the *method* that will guide this study and the *questions* at the center of the controversy over *Dignitatis Humanae*.

3.1. DEVELOPMENT IN DOCTRINE VERSUS CORRUPTION IN DOCTRINE

It is crucial to understand what it means for doctrine to *develop*. The importance of the distinction between the phenomenon of doctrinal development and other phenomena eludes some authors. For example, Jesuit priest Joseph Eagan asserts that the teaching of the Church's ordinary magisterium "can be *incomplete* and even considered erroneous in future centuries; it can

---

[1] Bernard J. F. Lonergan, *Method in Theology* (London: Darton, Longman, & Todd Ltd., 1972; reprint, Toronto: University of Toronto Press, 1996), 302.

be further developed and thus *changed*."[2] Note that instead of making the crucial distinction between *changes* and *developments* in doctrine, Eagan equates the two concepts. However, a serious discussion of religious liberty requires a clear distinction between these two ideas.

The better course is to introduce greater precision in the use of terms. In particular, one should take a step back from both the terms *change* and *development* and recognize both as different *species* of the *genus* of *modification*. A doctrine may be modified in several different ways. If it is modified in such a way as to render it more precise, to describe it in more accessible language, or to extend it to analogous situations, then one can speak of the modification as a legitimate *development*. That is, the modification enhances some aspect of the doctrine in the same way that an adjective modifies a noun. However, modification also can mean a change in form or character, that is, a true change from what a thing is into a different thing. If this type of modification occurs, then the result is not a legitimate and continuous development but rather a radical *change* or *corruption* of doctrine.[3]

Thus, it is never sufficient to know simply that doctrine has been modified. One must ask whether the modification is, on the one hand, logically and substantively consistent with previous doctrine, or, on the other hand, a repudiation of previous doctrine. Following Newman, I will adopt the word *development* to describe the type of modification that is harmonious and consistent with previous doctrine, and the words *corruption* and *change* to denote modifications that result in a contradiction with earlier doctrine.[4]

The history of the Church's teaching on the nature of Christ provides a good example of a genuine *development* in doctrine. That is, the progress in the Church's teaching on the relationship between the divine in Christ and the human in Christ from the First Council of Nicaea (325) to the Council of Chalcedon (451) demonstrates how the Church's teaching can develop without contradicting itself. The First Councils of both Nicaea and

---

[2] Joseph F. Eagan, *Restoration and Renewal: The Church in the Third Millennium* (Kansas City, MO: Sheed & Ward, 1995), 286 (emphasis in original).

[3] NB, *The American Heritage Dictionary* (AHD), Second College ed. (Boston: Houghton Mifflin, 1982) gives a tertiary meaning for *modification*: "A small alteration, adjustment, or limitation." However, it gives as a primary meaning for *modify*: "To change in form or character; alter." NB, under "change," AHD has several synonyms: *change* implies fundamental difference or substitution; *vary* implies shifting circumstances that cause differences with some regularity; *modify* means to limit, restrict, qualify, or to make less extreme. *Modification* is useful as the *genus* in this discussion because it can mean either a minor alteration or a fundamental change.

[4] Cf. John Henry Newman, *An Essay on the Development of Christian Doctrine* (B. M. Pickering, 1878; reprint, Notre Dame, IN: University of Notre Dame Press, 1989), 38, 41.

3.1. Development in Doctrine versus Corruption in Doctrine

Constantinople (381) affirmed that there is an essential union of the human and the divine in Christ. However, these councils did not describe the nature of that union. The heresy of Nestorianism arose and asserted that there are two natures in Christ, but that the two natures are not ontologically united.[5] Stated differently, Christ's two natures exist side by side. The implication of Nestorianism would be that Christ really is two persons. The Council of Ephesus (431) condemned Nestorianism and taught that there is a *substantive* or *hypostatic* union between Christ's divine and human natures. Note that Ephesus did not repudiate the teachings of Nicaea and Constantinople but instead built upon them, or, one could say, *developed* them. The heresy of Eutychianism then arose and asserted that the nature of the union is a *mixture*. According to Eutyches, the human and divine aspects of Christ could not be distinguished; rather, the divine absorbs the human (as the ocean absorbs a drop of water), such that only the divine nature remains. The Council of Chalcedon (451) responded by condemning Eutychianism and by teaching that Christ is a single divine person, but that he has two natures, one human and one divine, that are distinct.

The Chalcedonian doctrine endures today. In reviewing the progress of this doctrine over the course of the 126 years between Nicaea and Chalcedon, one can see that each council represents "a permanent acquisition of knowledge,"[6] and that each succeeding council built upon the previous one to *develop* further the Church's understanding of Christ and to answer new questions in a way that was consistent with the previous teaching. Note that this is a real *development*. The fathers at Ephesus drew on the teachings of Nicaea but could not resolve the questions raised there simply by repeating the teaching of Nicaea.

By contrast, what Newman called a *corruption* in doctrine occurs when the new teaching cannot logically and substantively be reconciled with the previous teaching. That is, to affirm both the previous teaching and the later teaching would be a contradiction. The Mormon teaching on polygamy provides an example of what Newman would have considered a modification that amounts to an actual corruption. According to a revelation that Joseph Smith claimed to receive in the nineteenth century, polygamy was

---

[5] Nestorius did propose a type of union, a "prosopon of union," that united two separate *hypostases*. The reason was that his metaphysics required that each *physis* must have its own *hypostasis* to exist. However, this resulted in a union that was merely phenomenological or moral rather than ontological.

[6] Aidan Nichols, *From Newman to Congar: The Idea of Doctrinal Development from the Victorians to the Second Vatican Council* (Edinburgh: T&T Clark, 1990), 172, discussing Ambroise Gardeil's theory of doctrinal development.

necessary for salvation for those able to practice it.[7] However, pursuant to a later revelation to another president of the Mormon Church, the practice was discontinued and became grounds for excommunication.[8] The Mormon doctrine of continuing revelation allows for such doctrinal changes,[9] but it does not seem that any neutral principle of logic or historical development can reconcile the two teachings. Thus, one can harmonize these two teachings (or rather, simply render the contradiction acceptable) only if one accepts the Mormon religious doctrine of *continuing revelation*. Needless to say, this rationale is unavailable to Catholics seeking to reconcile doctrinal pronouncements because the Catholic Church teaches that public revelation closed with the death of the last apostle.[10] In addition, the Church teaches

---

[7] Joseph Smith specifically approved of polygamy in section 132 of the Mormon scripture *Doctrines and Covenants*. Cf. Isaiah Bennett, "Mormon Changes in Practice," *This Rock Magazine*, May 1999, 27; Peg McEntee, "Why Do People Practice Polygamy?; Utah & the United States; Nationally, Polygamists Cite Theological Roots," *Salt Lake Tribune*, Sept. 20, 1998, accessed Dec. 2, 1999, https://archive.sltrib.com/article.php?itype=story-ID&id=100F3CF37932951B. See also Associated Press, "Mormon President Denounces Polygamy," *Richmond Times-Dispatch*, Oct. 11, 1998.

[8] Bennett, "Mormon Changes," 27; cf. Frank S. Mead and Samuel S. Hill, *Handbook of Denominations in the United States* (Nashville, TN: Abingdon Press, 1995), 168. Wilford Woodruff, a later church president, promulgated the *Manifesto of 1890* discontinuing the practice of polygamy.

[9] Cf. Mead and Hill, *Denominations*, 167–68. Mormons believe that both Smith's scriptural injunction in favor of polygamy and the *Manifesto's* later prohibition of the practice are based on divine revelations. Cf. McEntee, "Polygamists Cite Theological Roots"; W. John Walsh, "Why Did the Church Abandon Polygamy?" Light Planet (Mormons website), accessed Feb. 28, 2023, https://www.lightplanet.com/mormons/response/qa/plural_revelation.htm; Paul H. Peterson, "The Manifesto of 1890," Light Planet (Mormons website), accessed Feb. 28, 2023, https://www.lightplanet.com/mormons/daily/history/plural_marriage/manifesto_eom.htm. Because Joseph Smith had declared polygamy to be necessary for salvation, one cannot consider this question akin to what Catholics refer to as a matter of Church discipline rather than doctrine. However, there are at least a few Mormons who attempt to make this argument. They argue that the *Manifesto of 1890* did not change church teaching, but that it merely suspended the *practice* of polygamy. W. John Walsh and Jeff Lindsay, "Have Your Doctrines Changed?" Light Planet (Mormons website), accessed Feb. 28, 2023, http://www.lightplanet.com/mormons/response/qa/doctrines_changed.htm; Walsh, "Polygamy"; Peterson, "Manifesto of 1890." However, this is clearly a minority position, because most Mormons resolve the issue simply with reference to the Mormon doctrine of continuing revelation.

[10] Cf. Holy Office, Decree *Lamentabili Sane* (July 3, 1907), §21 [ASS 40 (1907): 473]. See also First Vatican Council, Dogmatic Constitution on the Church of Christ *Pastor Aeternus* (July 18, 1870) [ASS 6 (1870–1871): 46].

that, in Christ, the fullness and definitiveness of divine revelation was accomplished and perfected. As a result, the content of revelation is fixed.[11]

The First Vatican Council taught that when the pope or a council defines a dogma, this action does not result in a new revelation but rather in the expounding of the revelation that already has been transmitted.[12] A century later, the Second Vatican Council reaffirmed the same understanding:

> This teaching office is not above the word of God, but serves it, teaching only what has been handed on, listening to it devoutly, guarding it scrupulously and explaining it faithfully in accord with a divine commission and with the help of the Holy Spirit, it draws from this one deposit of faith everything which it presents for belief as divinely revealed.[13]

The popes and councils continually have taught that the deposit of faith is permanent, and that the purpose and duty of the magisterium is to hand on what has been received. Indeed, this principle originates with the earliest Christian witness. St. Paul describes his own teaching as a transmission of the Lord's instruction, "For I received from the Lord what I also delivered to you" (1 Cor 11:23; cf. 1 Cor 15:3). By the same token, Paul instructs Timothy to pass on the same teaching without corruption, "[W]hat you have heard from me before many witnesses entrust to faithful men who will be able to teach others also" (2 Tim 2:2). Throughout its history, the Church has understood its teaching as essentially immutable, and the First Vatican Council solemnly affirmed this understanding of Catholic doctrine.[14] Pope St. Pius X, in particular, emphasized the permanence of revelation and the incorruptibility of dogma.[15]

However, this understanding of revelation and dogma gives rise to an

---

[11] Congregation for the Doctrine of the Faith, Declaration on the Unicity and Salvific Universality of Jesus Christ and the Church *Dominus Iesus* (Aug. 6, 2000), §§5–8 [AAS 92 (2000): 745–49].

[12] Cf. First Vatican Council, *Pastor Aeternus*, ch. 4n6: The Church's duty is to "religiously guard and faithfully expound" revelation [ASS 6 (1870–1871): 46].

[13] Second Vatican Council, Dogmatic Constitution on Divine Revelation *Dei Verbum* (Nov. 18, 1965), §10b (hereinafter cited as DV).

[14] "[T]hat understanding of its sacred dogmas must be perpetually retained, which Holy Mother Church has once declared." First Vatican Council, Dogmatic Constitution concerning the Catholic Faith *Dei Filius* (Apr. 24, 1870), 4 [ASS 5 (1869–1870): 490].

[15] Cf. Pius X, Encyclical *Pascendi Dominici Gregis* (Sept. 8, 1907), §§13, 26, 38 [ASS 40 (1907): 603, 617–18, 630–32]; Holy Office, *Lamentabili Sane*, §§21, 54, 58 [ASS 40 (1907): 473, 477].

important question: *If the task of the Church's teaching office is to hand on what it has received, and if revelation has been closed since the death of the last apostle, then why is there a need for additional doctrinal pronouncements after the apostolic age? Should not the revelation that already has occurred be sufficient? Indeed, why is there a need for a teaching office at all? Why should any further teaching be necessary if revelation already is complete?*

The reason is that although revelation indeed has been completed, the faithful lack a perfect knowledge of revelation. Pius XII explained that "each source of divinely revealed doctrine contains so many rich treasures of truth, that they can never really be exhausted."[16] Moreover, just as the state of the law becomes known through the arising of new disputes and through their resolution,[17] so do new heresies and crises prompt the magisterium to return to the sources of revelation and to "explain what is contained in the deposit of faith only obscurely and implicitly."[18] That is, the magisterium draws doctrine out from the deposit of faith (cf. DV, §10b). Again, this activity of the magisterium does not generate a new revelation but rather results in a deepening of knowledge of the revelation to the apostles that already has taken place.

St. Vincent of Lérins classically taught that "what all men have at all times and everywhere believed must be regarded as true."[19] However, Newman observed that this is a better rule for determining what *does* belong to the faith than for determining what *does not*.[20] Moreover, Vincent himself recognized that modification is permissible in the sense of providing a clearer explanation of the meaning of a doctrine.[21] The popes and councils have said the same thing. Pope Bl. Pius IX taught that the Church's teaching office must "investigate and explain" the ancient dogmas,[22] and the First Vatican Council taught that the popes "religiously guard and faithfully expound the revelation or deposit of faith transmitted by the apostles."[23] Note that even though revelation already has been complete for a number of centuries, the need still remains for the Church further to *investigate*, *explain*, and *expound*

---

[16] Pope Pius XII, Encyclical *Humani Generis* (Aug. 12, 1950), §21 [AAS 42 (1950): 568–69].
[17] Newman, *Essay on the Development*, 149–50.
[18] Pius XII, *Humani Generis*, §21 [AAS 42 (1950): 569].
[19] Vincent of Lérins, *Commonitorium Primum* 2 [PL 50:640].
[20] Cf. *The Catholic Encyclopedia* (New York: Encyclopedia Press, 1913), s.v. "St. Vincent of Lérins."
[21] Cf. Vincent of Lérins, *Commonitorium Primum* 23 [PL 50:668], cited in Avery Dulles, *Magisterium: Teacher and Guardian of the Faith* [Naples, FL: Sapientia Press, 2007], 25.
[22] Pope Pius IX, Apostolic Constitution *Ineffabilis Deus* (Dec. 8, 1854) [*Acta Pii IX*, pars 1, vol. 1].
[23] First Vatican Council, *Pastor Aeternus*, ch. 4 [ASS 6 (1870–1871): 46].

3.1. Development in Doctrine versus Corruption in Doctrine

it. Revelation does not explain itself but rather the Holy Spirit aids the Church's teaching office so that it might expound revelation.

Thus, despite the completeness of revelation and the permanence of dogma, the faithful still require a *living* teaching authority.[24] In the words of Pope Leo XIII, "Christ instituted in the Church a living, authoritative and permanent Magisterium."[25] The quality of being *both permanent and living* is the distinctive characteristic of the teaching office.

What is permanent is the transmission—in each generation—of the same faith that the apostles themselves received, that is, "the ancient and unchanging faith of the whole church";[26] what is living—in all times—is the pope and the members of the college of bishops to whom this duty is entrusted. In addition, the faithful who receive this teaching also, of course, are living. Finally, perhaps even the doctrines themselves may be understood as *living—not in the sense of being corruptible*[27] but in the sense meant by Pius IX and Vatican I in describing them as *growing within their own genus*.[28] In this way, one might say that the Christological teaching of Nicaea gave life to the teaching of Ephesus. At Ephesus, nothing of the Nicene doctrine was lost or corrupted, and yet the knowledge of the faithful after Ephesus was greater than it had been beforehand.

The Council of Ephesus did not generate "some new doctrine,"[29] but rather it further *developed* the doctrine on the human and the divine in Christ. Doctrinal development may occur in a number of ways. As discussed above, the magisterium can explain a doctrine more clearly or more precisely. Indeed, Pius XII taught that the terminology, not only of theologians but even that of the magisterium, "is capable of being perfected and polished."[30]

The same Pope pointed to another way in which doctrine may develop. The magisterium draws out the meaning of revelation over time.[31] This phenomenon can occur because the treasures of revelation are so rich as to be inexhaustible. Thus, it is the task of the magisterium "to elucidate and explain what is contained in the deposit of faith only obscurely and

---

[24] Cf. Pius XII, *Humani Generis*, §§8, 21 [AAS 42 (1950): 563, 568].
[25] Pope Leo XIII, Encyclical *Satis Cognitum* (June 29, 1896), §9 [28 ASS (1895–1896): 721].
[26] First Vatican Council, *Pastor Aeternus*, intro [ASS 6 (1870–1871): 41].
[27] Cf. Pius X, *Pascendi*, §§13, 38 [ASS 40 (1907): 603, 630–32].
[28] Cf. Pius IX, *Ineffabilis Deus*; cf. First Vatican Council, *Dei Filius*, §14 [ASS 5 (1869–1870): 490].
[29] Cf. First Vatican Council, *Pastor Aeternus*, ch. 4 [ASS 6 (1870–1871): 46].
[30] Pius XII, *Humani Generis*, §16 [AAS 42 (1950): 566].
[31] Cf. Pius XII, *Humani Generis*, §21 [AAS 42 (1950): 569]; DV, §8c.

implicitly."[32] Pope St. Paul VI expressed this idea in similar terms, "[T]hat which was assumed, is now explicit; that which was uncertain, is now clarified; that which was meditated upon, discussed and sometimes argued over, is now put together in one clear formulation."[33] By the same token, the Second Vatican Council said that "there is a growth in the understanding of the realities and the words which have been handed down" (DV, §8c).

In his landmark encyclical *Pascendi*, Pope St. Pius X taught that there are dangers in conceiving of doctrine as something that evolves. The reason for this caution was that he was combating a Modernist theory (or set of theories) that conceived of doctrine as erroneous, utterly changeable, subject to evolution, and in need of being adapted to the believer.[34] As discussed above, Pius X's understanding of the faith as unchanging is taught as well by the other popes and the councils. However, without allowing for actual change or corruption, other popes have affirmed what Newman called *development of doctrine*.

Pius IX had combined these two characteristics of doctrine—permanence and development—in his 1854 definition of the dogma of the Immaculate Conception. With regard to dogmas, he said, the Church "never changes anything, never diminishes anything, never adds anything to them."[35] However, she does "investigate and explain" the dogmas in an effort to make them always clearer. In this process, though, the dogmas are conserved, even as they grow. That is, they "will retain their full, integral, and proper nature, *and will grow only within their own genus*—that is, within the same dogma, in the same sense and the same meaning."[36] Pope St. John Paul II would say that tradition is not an "unchanging repetition of formulas" but rather is a living heritage. That is, tradition is "a living reality which grows and develops, and which the Spirit guarantees precisely because it has something to say to the people of every age."[37]

---

[32] Pius XII, *Humani Generis*, §21 [AAS 42 (1950): 569].

[33] Pope Paul VI, Homily on the Occasion of the Closing of the Third Session of the Second Vatican Council (Nov. 21, 1964) [AAS 56 (1964): 1009–10].

[34] Cf. Pius X, *Pascendi*, §§13, 26, 36, 38 [ASS 40 (1907): 603, 617–18, 629, 630–32]; Holy Office, *Lamentabili Sane*, §§21, 22, 54, 58 [ASS 40 (1907): 473, 477].

[35] Pius IX, *Ineffabilis Deus*.

[36] Pius IX, *Ineffabilis Deus*; cf. First Vatican Council, *Dei Filius*, 14 [ASS 5 (1869–1870): 490]. Note that the end of the Vatican I constitution closes in almost the same way that *Ineffabilis Deus* ends, namely, by calling for an increase in knowledge and wisdom but only "in its own proper kind, that is to say, in the same doctrine, the same sense, and the same understanding."

[37] Pope John Paul II, Apostolic Letter *Orientale Lumen* (May 2, 1995), 8 [AAS 87 (1995): 752]. See also Benedict XVI, Wednesday Catechesis, "St. Irenaeus of Lyons" (Mar. 28,

3.1. Development in Doctrine versus Corruption in Doctrine

Thus, the dogmas may grow, as the dogma on the divine and human natures of Christ grew from Nicaea to Chalcedon, but this growth must occur within the same *genus*. It must be a natural development rather than a radical change or corruption.

One final word is necessary on the subject of doctrinal development. In an attempt to emphasize the importance of precision in this discussion, I wish to return to Father Eagan's statement that the teaching of the Church's ordinary magisterium "can be *incomplete* and even considered erroneous in future centuries; it can be further developed and thus *changed*."[38] This assertion demonstrates the danger of equating *change* in doctrine with *development* of doctrine. The implication is that change in this context means radical change or complete transformation. Thus, Eagan declares as morally permissible several actions that the Church teaches are inconsistent with Christian living, including artificial insemination, premarital sex, homosexual acts, and artificial contraception.[39] It is seriously irresponsible to identify this type of change with a true development in doctrine.

The name of Newman has become virtually synonymous with development in doctrine,[40] and his works make clear that the type of complete transformation of doctrine that Father Eagan has in mind is not to be understood as a genuine development. The better course is to recognize that there are two relevant species of the *genus* of *modification*, and to go forward with precision as Newman does, specifying exactly the type of modification that one is ascribing to Catholic doctrine—whether, on the one hand, it is radical and transforming change (or corruption), or, on the other hand, logical and natural development.

Eagan has overstated drastically the extent to which the pronouncements of the magisterium may contain deficiencies. He is correct that in some cases, such pronouncements indeed may be deficient in a sense. The Congregation for the Doctrine of the Faith acknowledged as much in the 1990 instruction *Donum Veritatis*.

> When it comes to the question of interventions in the prudential order, it could happen that some Magisterial documents might not be free from all deficiencies. Bishops and their advisors have

---

2007): "Tradition is always enlivened from within by the Holy Spirit, who makes it live anew, causes it to be interpreted and understood in the vitality of the Church."

[38] Eagan, *Restoration and Renewal*, 286 (emphasis in original).
[39] Cf. Eagan, *Restoration and Renewal*, 290.
[40] Cf. Owen Chadwick, *From Bossuet to Newman: The Idea of Doctrinal Development* (Cambridge: Cambridge University Press, 1957), 48.

not always taken into immediate consideration every aspect or the entire complexity of a question.... This is not to be understood in the sense of a relativization of the tenets of the faith. The theologian knows that some judgments of the Magisterium could be justified at the time in which they were made, because while the pronouncements contained true assertions and others which were not sure, both types were inextricably connected. Only time has permitted discernment and, after deeper study, the attainment of true doctrinal progress.[41]

In parts 3 and 4, I will discuss the application of these principles to the subject of religious liberty. However, the context of the Congregation's statement makes clear that such instances are rare, and that the Congregation appears to limit its statement to "the prudential order," that is, the realm in which Church teachings intersect with the administration, governance, and pastoral judgments of the Church. In addition, although Eagan refers to the possibility of authentic teaching being "erroneous," the Congregation uses the word "deficiency" (*defectus*) rather than "error." Eagan, it appears, would leverage this limited principle into a justification for dissent from any Church teaching that has not been declared infallibly.[42] The text itself makes clear that such an application of this principle is misguided.

But it would be contrary to the truth, if, proceeding from some particular cases, one were to conclude that the Church's magisterium can be habitually mistaken in its prudential judgments, or that it does not enjoy divine assistance in the integral exercise of its mission.[43]

Thus, the Congregation's instruction serves as a reminder that acknowledging "doctrinal progress"[44] or development does not in any way imply that the Church's teaching office is habitually mistaken or that Catholic moral theologians are entitled to the type of license to dissent from moral doctrine that Eagan claims. On the contrary, a sound theory of doctrinal development helps one to distinguish genuine developments from illegitimate corruptions.

Newman proposes "seven notes" as criteria for making such distinctions. These notes are contained in his seminal 1845 work *An Essay on the Development of Christian Doctrine*. Although other commentators frequently

---

[41] Congregation, *Donum Veritatis*, §24 [AAS 82 (1990): 1560–61].
[42] See chapter 2 above.
[43] Congregation, *Donum Veritatis*, §24 [AAS 82 (1990): 1560].
[44] Congregation, *Donum Veritatis*, §24 [AAS 82 (1990): 1560].

propose images to explain doctrinal development, none of them propose a test as elaborate as Newman's for the judging of alleged developments. Newman's seven notes for judging such a doctrine are as follows:

> There is no corruption if [1] it retains one and the same type, [2] the same principles, [3] the same organization; [4] if its beginnings anticipate its subsequent phases, and [5] its later phenomena protect and subserve its earlier; [6] if it has a power of assimilation and revival, and [7] a vigorous action from first to last.[45]

A prominent Newman expert recently has argued that DH satisfies all seven of these "notes," thus indicating a legitimate development.[46] This judgment is sound, but it is important to remember that Newman's test, although useful, has some important limitations.

First, this famous system is better suited to explaining developments in doctrines of the *faith* than to explaining either doctrines of *morality* or *mixed questions* of faith and morals.[47] Religious liberty and toleration fall into this latter category as mixed questions, or, as the Congregation describes, ones sometimes bound together with prudential judgments. Thus, one should not expect to find a trajectory of development concerning religious liberty that is as neat as the development of the Christological dogmas. The reason is that the debate over religious liberty is driven in large measure by actual historical events and experience with actual political regimes. By contrast, the great dogmatic debates of the fourth and fifth centuries, although they may have been precipitated by actual events, did not revolve around those events in the substantive content of their discussions. The Christological debates sought to explain the truth of the unchanging Godhead, but debates over Church and state or over religious liberty are oriented as much to the here and now as to the eternal. That is, they are concerned not only with finding the truth but also with applying the truth to concrete circumstances. Thus, although one can see gradual and incremental development in the doctrinal trajectory leading to the Chalcedonian definition of the nature of Christ, one generally sees a different type of growth in moral doctrines and in mixed questions. That is, instead of gradual growth, one may be

---

[45] Newman, *Essay on the Development*, 171.
[46] Cf. Ian Ker, *Newman on Vatican II* (Oxford: Oxford University Press, 2014), 65–71.
[47] Cf. Patrick M. O'Neil, "A Response to John T. Noonan, Jr. Concerning the Development of Catholic Moral Doctrine," *Faith & Reason* (Spring/Summer 1996), EWTN, accessed Dec. 19, 2020, https://www.ewtn.com/catholicism/library/response-to-john-t-noonan-jr-concerning-the-development-of-catholic-moral-doctrine-10041.

faced with applications of doctrine that appear very different from previous applications in different contexts.[48] The task of the theologian is to come to a judgment as to whether there has in fact been a corruption in doctrine.

A second limitation of this system is that, quite surprisingly, Newman himself provides no example of how to apply his seven notes to a specific doctrinal problem. Although Newman sets forth these notes as a way to distinguish a doctrinal development from a corruption, he actually uses the notes in his *Essay* for a very different purpose. That is, he applies them not to judge the legitimacy of specific doctrines but rather to judge whether the Catholic Church of his day represents a genuine development of the ancient Church that Christ founded in the first century.[49]

A third limitation is connected with this circumstance of Newman not applying his seven notes to actual developments of doctrine. As a result of this fact, the seven notes present a less than perfect system for evaluating doctrine. Newman himself acknowledged as much.[50] Perhaps if he had applied the notes more systematically, he might have refined his system. For the purposes of this analysis, the principal drawbacks to the seven notes are that they are somewhat redundant, at times obscure, and, as already noted, not always well-suited toward analyzing moral doctrine or mixed questions.

---

[48] "[Some teachings of Vatican II] are innovations in the sense that they explain new aspects which have not previously been formulated by the Magisterium, but which do not doctrinally contradict previous Magisterial documents. This is so even though, in certain cases—for example, concerning religious freedom—these innovations imply very different consequences at the level of historical decisions concerning juridical and political applications of the teaching, especially given the changes in historical and social conditions." Fernando Ocáriz, "On Adhesion to the Second Vatican Council," *L'Osservatore Romano* (Dec. 2, 2011).

[49] Newman stated that applying the notes to all the Church's doctrines would be the work of a lifetime (cf. Newman, *Essay on Development*, 31). Given his own faith journey and the time in which he was writing, it understandably seemed to him that defending the apostolic quality of the Catholic Church was the most pressing matter (cf. Nichols, *Newman to Congar*, 54–55). It is important to recall that Newman published the original version of the *Essay* in 1845, years before the Church made its pronouncements on the Immaculate Conception and papal infallibility. He published a revised version in 1878 and, no doubt, must have had these doctrines in mind in making his revisions. However, he addressed those doctrines most directly in other works.

[50] Owen Chadwick is particularly critical of the seven notes on development. "Newman provided certain tests for distinguishing between developments, tests which convinced no one and which he himself once admitted to be incapable of performing their ostensible purpose" (Chadwick, *From Bossuet to Newman*, 143). Chadwick states that Newman put the seven notes forward "half-heartedly," and that the notes "are rather pegs on which to hang a *historical* thesis than solid supports for a doctrinal explanation" (*From Bossuet to Newman*, 155).

However, despite these limitations, Newman's *Essay* remains the classic work on doctrinal development and an important component of most discussions on the subject. Therefore, I will bring Newman's seven notes to bear on my discussion of the scope of the right to religious liberty in chapter 7 (see especially subsection 7.5.1), but I also will suggest that some of the notes have more relevance than others to this discussion.

3.2. The Method and the Issues

Although history is important to any inquiry into religious liberty, my method is not primarily historical. That is, it does not survey the teachings of all the popes and theologians who have addressed topics relevant to this one. Rather, I focus more or less discretely on the key disputed points that have arisen since the promulgation of the Vatican II Declaration on Religious Liberty, and I attempt to examine them in depth and with precision. Thus, my method begins by identifying these issues.

3.2.1. The Issues

One can identify the central issues by reviewing the most significant papal pronouncements and, in particular, the sources relied on by the key disputants in the debate over DH. This is not a particularly difficult task, as there is significant agreement on the main points at issue (and on the most relevant nineteenth-century papal pronouncements). My own review suggests that there are three key issues.

1. The first is the question of the relationship between Church and state.[51] This question concerns especially the fate of the Catholic confessional state (described in chapter 4). Does DH sound the death knell for this type of regime, as numerous commentators have suggested (most with approval, but some with disapproval)? Is DH reconcilable with previous teaching on the duty of the civil authority to the Creator? Is it possible to avoid a doctrinal conflict by pointing to the difference in political regimes of our day from those of a century or two

---

[51] I use the terms *Church* and *state* here because they are the familiar terms in contemporary discussions. However, the discussion in the next chapter (especially in section 4.3 on Gelasian dualism) will include historical antecedents, such as the Scriptural dichotomy of God and Caesar (cf. Matt 22:21), as well as the dichotomies between emperor and pope, and eventually between temporal order and religious order.

earlier (or those before the age of revolution)? The next part of this study—part 2—devotes two chapters to these and related questions. That part will focus especially on the question of whether DH announces a teaching on the Church-state relationship that contradicts the pronouncements of the nineteenth-century popes.

2. The second question is the very heart of this study, namely, the analysis of the right to religious liberty that the Council recognized. Did Vatican II embrace the same rights to freedom of conscience and religious liberty that the nineteenth-century popes—particularly Gregory XVI in *Mirari Vos* (1832) and Pope Bl. Pius IX in *Quanta Cura* (1864)—had rejected? Does Vatican II represent an embrace of Enlightenment theories of human rights and political liberties? The crucial issue at the center of the debate concerns the rights of non-Catholics. The nineteenth-century popes had spoken only of toleration of their (non-Catholics) public worship and religious expression, but Vatican II refers not to toleration but to an actual right to religious liberty that belongs to all persons. The key nineteenth-century documents (in addition to those already mentioned) are Pius IX's *Syllabus of Errors*[52] and two esteemed encyclicals of Pope Leo XIII, *Immortale Dei* (1885)[53] and *Libertas* (1888). Can these nineteenth-century teachings be reconciled with DH? The central part of this work, parts 3A and 3B, addresses these questions in six chapters.

3. The third issue is related to the second. However, its focus is not the rights of non-Catholics but the authority of civil governments. The question is *when may the civil authority restrict religious expression or activity*. All agree that it must have some prerogative to do so, or else a person would be justified in doing any action whatsoever as long as he could claim a religious motivation for it. The disputed issue is the *standard* for such governmental intervention. Critics charge Vatican II with

---

[52] Cf. Pope Pius IX, *Syllabus Errorum* (Dec. 8, 1864) [ASS 3 (1867): 170–76] (hereinafter cited as Syll.).

[53] Cf. Pope Leo XIII, Encyclical *Immortale Dei* (Nov. 1, 1885) [ASS 18 (1885–1886): 161–80] (hereinafter cited as ID).

embracing a minimal standard that permits the government to intervene only for the sake of public safety or preventing violence, thus allegedly contradicting the broader scope for such intervention envisioned by Pius IX in *Quanta Cura*. Part 4 of this study addresses these questions in four chapters.

3.2.2. A Jurisprudential Hermeneutic

I analyze these issues with a method that I describe as a *jurisprudential hermeneutic*. That is, I believe that some of the tools of legal analysis and scholarship may be useful in this inquiry. My hope is that they will provide the rigor and precision necessary to enable one to arrive at clear judgments. This is vitally important in the enterprise of investigating modifications of doctrine to determine whether they are legitimate developments or illicit corruptions.

For this reason, two of the Church's greatest interpreters of doctrine in the nineteenth century expressly analogized theology to law when it comes to the interpretation of doctrines. Both St. John Henry Newman and Bishop Félix Dupanloup of Orléans, France, used the legal analogy to explain how one might come to understand Pope Pius IX's *Syllabus of Errors*. Newman said that just as legal courts employ traditional rules of interpretation, so must one follow accepted theological rules of construction to understand the *Syllabus*.[54] Bishop Dupanloup, in his famous pamphlet expounding the *Syllabus*, anticipates the argument that such rules of construction might be interpreted as legalistic hair-splitting. "Yes, theology, like philosophy and jurisprudence, has great niceties of distinction, because, evidently, in questions of doctrine, as in questions of law, nice distinctions must be drawn, to avoid dangerous misapprehensions."[55]

Dupanloup's observation points to the key danger that one must avoid

---

[54] Cf. John Henry Newman, Letter to the Duke of Norfolk (December 27, 1874), reprinted in *Newman and Gladstone: The Vatican Decrees*, with an introduction by Alvan S. Ryan (Notre Dame, IN: University of Notre Dame Press, 1962), 164.

[55] Félix Dupanloup, *Remarks on the Encyclical of the 8th of December 1864*, trans. W. J. M. Hutchinson (London: George Cheek, 1865), 21. Bishop Dupanloup's pamphlet explaining how to interpret the *Syllabus* in the proper context set at ease the minds of so many of his brother bishops that he received letters of thanks from over six hundred of them throughout the world. Cf. E. E. Y. Hales, *Pio Nono: A Study in European Politics and Religion in the Nineteenth Century* (London: Eyre & Spottiswoode, 1954), 261. It appears that the full text of Dupanloup's pamphlet never was translated into English. The Hutchinson translation comprises only that section of the pamphlet concerning the *Syllabus*, omitting the other section that addresses the contemporary political situation. For the full text in the original

in employing a jurisprudential hermeneutic, namely, falling into legalism. Legalism in the context of theology is an attempt to confine spiritual realities within a narrow set of rules. The erroneous tendency of legalism is to make the rule an end in itself. One rightly rejects such legalism even in the field of law, and all the more so in the area of theology and doctrine.[56] However, a true jurisprudential hermeneutic avoids this pitfall. It recognizes the importance of terminology, but it attends not only to terms and words but to the *meaning* behind the words. It brings precision to bear on the questions at issue, and it attempts to make a fair evaluation of opposing arguments. Thus, it makes possible a thorough and accurate examination of the question.

In referring to a jurisprudential hermeneutic, I have the Anglo-American common law tradition in mind. The distinctive feature of that system is that judicial decisions themselves acquire the force of law. Newman noted the parallel between the common law tradition and the development of Christian doctrine. That is, the state of both the law and Catholic doctrine becomes better known through the arising and resolution of disputes.[57] (This is not the only way, of course, but it is the most frequent and the most important one.)

French, see Félix Dupanloup, *La convention du 15 septembre et l'encyclique du 8 décembre* (Paris, 1865).

[56] A bad name follows legalism across virtually every theological discipline. In the field of moral theology, both Pope St. John Paul II and Germain Grisez attempted to shift the focus away from legalism. As Grisez says, the key deficiency in classical moral theology was that it "focused on the detailed specification of duties, while ceasing to clarify the meaning of good and bad in terms of the total Christian vocation." Germain Grisez, *The Way of the Lord Jesus*, vol. 1, *Christian Moral Principles* (Chicago: Franciscan Herald Press, 1983), 13. This emphasis fostered a conception of moral theology characterized by voluntarism, legalism, and minimalism. The specification of duties was seen as originating exclusively or primarily in God's will rather than in his goodness or wisdom. A tendency arose to view moral precepts as arbitrary and to consider the Church's pronouncements, like civil laws, as subject to change. As a result, the faithful most often viewed morality as prescribing the minimum standards of conduct for the avoidance of mortal sin. In his landmark encyclical on moral theology, John Paul uses the biblical passage about the rich young man to show that moral theology is concerned with much more than legal requirements. "For the young man, the *question* is not so much about rules to be followed, but *about the full meaning of life*." Pope John Paul II, Encyclical *Veritatis Splendor* (Aug. 6, 1993), §7 [AAS 85 (1993): 1138]. "Jesus shows that the commandments must not be understood as a minimum limit not to be gone beyond, but rather as a path involving a moral and spiritual journey toward perfection, at the heart of which is love" (*Veritatis Splendor*, §15 [AAS 85 (1993): 1145]). By the same token, the desire to escape legalism is a prominent theme in other branches of theology, such as the study of the sacraments. E.g., Joseph Martos, *Doors to the Sacred* (Liguori, MO: Triumph Books, 1991), 109–10, 287, 304–7.

[57] Cf. Newman, *Essay on the Development*, 149–50.

By the same token, in both law and doctrine, the relationship that current decisions or pronouncements have with the past is crucial. Thus, when the magisterium revisits an issue, its later pronouncement either must reaffirm its earlier ones or else must be explainable as a legitimate development of previous teaching (or alternately, as implied by the Congregation for the Doctrine of the Faith in *Donum Veritatis*, the magisterium may need to separate out earlier assumptions that were rooted in the prudential order). Similarly, in the common law tradition, the principle of *stare decisis* requires a court to follow the precedent of its own previous decisions (and the decisions of other courts of superior rank). When a court's own past decision lends itself to several interpretations, the court may need to decide which interpretation will be the authoritative one. In this way, the court may be able to *harmonize* the past decision with a new decision embodying a development in the law. Along similar lines, Newman concedes that in the field of the Church's doctrine, "[T]here are in fact certain apparent variations in its teaching, which have to be explained."[58]

This function of harmonization is consistent with Pope Benedict XVI's admonition that in interpreting the Vatican II documents, one should apply a *hermeneutic of reform in continuity* rather than a *hermeneutic of discontinuity and rupture*.[59] That is, one should read the Vatican II documents in the light of tradition and thus attempt to find the continuity running throughout all of tradition, including Vatican II. This is in contrast to the approach often employed in the decades immediately following the Council, by which commentators frequently depicted Vatican II as inaugurating an entirely new era, thereby representing a *rupture* from the Church's previous tradition. Needless to say, both law and doctrine, although embodying strong preferences for continuity and harmonization, need to reckon with the possibility of contradiction. This is less stressful in the law because it is clear that, where necessary, a court may overrule a precedent that was wrongly decided. In doctrine, however, a contradiction or reversal is more likely to provoke a crisis.

3.2.3. Levels of Authority

For doctrines described as *authentic*—that is, those belonging to neither the primary nor the secondary object of infallibility—the possibility of some deficiency (*defectus*) is not entirely excluded. "When it comes to the

---

[58] Newman, *Essay on the Development*, 7.
[59] Cf. Benedict XVI, Address to the Roman Curia (Dec. 22, 2005) [AAS 98 (2006): 46].

question of interventions in the prudential order, it could happen that some Magisterial documents might not be free from all deficiencies [*non fuerint a defectibus immunia*]."[60] As a result, it seems that analysis and comparison of the levels of teaching might be one way to resolve the apparent conflict between DH and the pronouncements of the nineteenth-century magisterium.[61] However, several good reasons suggest that this option should be a last resort.

First, it simply is preferable, if possible, to grapple with the actual *substance* of these documents rather than to resolve the dispute by comparing their authority. As with the common law, harmonization is preferable to overruling. Indeed, if it is possible to harmonize the documents, then the faithful's understanding of all the relevant documents likely will be deepened.

Second, even if authentic doctrine admits the remote possibility of some deficiency, still the faithful are obliged to assent to it with religious submission of the will and intellect (cf. LG, §25a). Having recourse to a comparison of the authority of magisterial pronouncements usually would entail the assumption that there is indeed a contradiction. A Catholic should not embrace this premise lightly but rather only if it is unavoidable.[62]

Third, as the advocacy of Fathers Curran and Eagan shows, all too many commentators are overeager to interpret this slight possibility of deficiency in authentic teaching as a license to dissent from the full range of teachings that fall outside of the primary and secondary objects of infallibility. To embrace the premise of contradiction prematurely is to contribute (intentionally or not) to the Curran project of weakening the authentic magisterium. Indeed, it no longer is uncommon to encounter members of the faithful who regard authentic non-infallible teachings as merely optional.

---

[60] Congregation, *Donum Veritatis*, §24 [AAS 82 (1990): 1560]; but cf. *Donum Veritatis*, §24: "But it would be contrary to the truth, if, proceeding from some particular cases, one were to conclude that the Church's Magisterium can be habitually mistaken in its prudential judgments, or that it does not enjoy divine assistance in the integral exercise of its mission."

[61] For an example of this approach, see Martin Rhonheimer, "Benedict XVI's 'Hermeneutic of Reform' and Religious Freedom," *Nova et Vetera* (English ed.) 9, no. 4 (2011): 1038–47. For my own part, I believe that the more fruitful course is to examine the content of the right that the nineteenth-century popes rejected and the content of the right that Vatican II recognized, so as to determine whether they are indeed the same right. This is my own approach throughout this study, especially in its central portion, parts 3A and 3B, chapters 7–11.

[62] Only the magisterium of the Church herself enjoys the certain guidance of the Holy Spirit, and as a result, an individual theologian would do well to assume in the first instance that it is more likely that his own judgment is mistaken than that such a deficiency truly is present in a magisterial pronouncement.

3.2. The Method and the Issues

As then Cardinal Ratzinger reminded Curran, however, the Church simply cannot build her life on her infallible magisterium alone.[63]

Fourth, such recourse to levels of Church teaching might prove to be a merely temporary resolution. Traditionalist critics of DH have enthusiasm for this route, because although few if any commentators consider DH infallible, two nineteenth-century encyclicals often set in opposition to the declaration, namely, *Mirari Vos* (1832) and *Quanta Cura* (1864), often are interpreted as containing infallible teaching. This approach, however, does not take account of the half century of history since the Council. In that time, the popes frequently have cited and reaffirmed DH, and indeed, in many ways, they have made this declaration the very cornerstone of their diplomatic activity.[64]

What is the import of the post-conciliar popes' frequent repetition and reaffirmation of the teaching of DH? At the outset, it is necessary to say that it seems doubtful that a pope could enhance the authority of a conciliar document itself. After all, once the Council is concluded, that particular exercise of the magisterium by the college of bishops has come to a close. Thus, it does not seem possible for a pope to deem DH to have been an exercise of the charism of infallibility unless this is clear from the action of the college at the time of the Council. Moreover, it seems that few, if any, commentators—whether arguing for or against DH's continuity with tradition—believe that the Church has proposed DH as infallible.

However, it is possible to distinguish DH itself from the teaching that it contains. The individual popes following the Council have made this teaching their own. They not only have repeated it frequently and emphasized its significance, but they also have based their diplomatic activity in large measure on this teaching. This does not increase the authority of DH as a conciliar declaration, but it does mean that the teaching contained in DH has become part of the papal magisterium as well, and as such, the authority of this teaching indeed may be enhanced by frequent repetition (cf. LG,

---

[63] Cf. "Vatican Says Father Curran Can't Teach Theology," *Origins* 16, no. 11 (1986): 203 (Cardinal Ratzinger's July 25, 1986, Letter to Father Curran): "[T]he church does not build its life upon its infallible magisterium alone but on the teaching of its authentic, ordinary magisterium as well."

[64] See generally Giorgio Filibeck, *Human Rights in the Teaching of the Church: From John XXIII to John Paul II* (Vatican City: Libreria Editrice Vaticana, 1994), ch. 23 (compilation of papal statements between 1961 and 1991 on the right to freedom of religion); Basile Valuet, *La liberté religieuse et la tradition catholique. Un cas de développement doctrinal homogène dans le magistère authentique*, 3rd rev. ed. (Barroux: Éditions Sainte-Madeleine, 2011), vol. IIA, 1291–1416 (compilation of pronouncements of post-conciliar popes relevant to DH), hereinafter cited as LRTC.

§25a). Thus, it would seem that the argument from levels of Church teaching is becoming more challenging with time, as the authority of the teaching contained in DH increases with these papal reaffirmations.[65]

3.2.4. Applying the Method to the Issues

In what else does the jurisprudential hermeneutic consist? As set forth above, most fundamentally, it begins with an attempt to isolate all of the key areas of conflict—or potential conflict—between DH and previous teaching. My goal is not to summarize the entire history of the Church's relationship with the secular power or of the treatment of non-Catholics. Rather, my objective is to focus with precision on those areas where an actual doctrinal contradiction appears to exist or at least to be possible.

Identifying the areas of possible conflict is relatively easy because the scholarship on DH is so extensive. Thus, the three issues described above stand out as the crucial questions in the debate over DH. In addition, the documents of the nineteenth-century magisterium discussed above (in the enumeration of key issues) are the ones around which every extensive treatment of this subject revolves. Other papal pronouncements also are

---

[65] As a result of the fact that DH proclaims a natural right to religious liberty, it is possible that this teaching one day could be included within the secondary object of infallibility. Indeed, the declaration's teaching on the freedom of the act of faith (that is, the teaching against coercing religious acts) conceivably could be included within the *primary* object of infallibility, given that this part of DH's teaching finds abundant support in Scripture and in long-standing tradition. "It is one of the major tenets of Catholic doctrine that man's response to God in faith must be free: no one therefore is to be forced to embrace the Christian faith against his own will. This doctrine is contained in the word of God and it was constantly proclaimed by the Fathers of the Church." Second Vatican Council, Declaration on Religious Liberty *Dignitatis Humanae* (December 7, 1965), §10 [AAS 58 (1966): 936]. This first part of the right recognized by DH is not identical with the ancient teaching on the necessary freedom of the act of faith, but it can be understood as flowing from it. See section 9.6 below, quoting John Courtney Murray, "The Declaration on Religious Liberty: A Moment in Its Legislative History," in *Religious Liberty: An End and a Beginning* (New York: MacMillan, 1966), 30. With regard to the second (and more controversial) part of the right—namely, the right to noninterference with religious acts, provided that they do not violate the just public order—this support is less apparent. Cf. Kevin Flannery, "*Dignitatis Humanae* and the Development of Doctrine," *Catholic Dossier* 6, no. 2 (March–April 2000): 31: DH may be part of the "secondary object of infallibility," but it is based primarily on reason alone, rather than Revelation. Indeed, chapter 16 of this study will consider the reasons for the delay in the recognition of the right to religious liberty.

significant and will be discussed, but the encyclicals of Gregory XVI, Pius IX, and Leo XIII mentioned above truly are at the center of the controversy.

The primary inquiry for each issue is simply whether a contradiction exists between the nineteenth-century teaching and Vatican II. Stated differently, *is it logically possible to affirm both teachings?* One necessary step is to examine these areas of possible conflict and to determine whether any of them might be explained by something other than a doctrinal corruption. For example, as discussed in part 4 (chapter 12), at least some of the confusion over DH's possible contradiction of *Quanta Cura* on the question of religious repression arose because of a mistranslation of a key term in the nineteenth-century encyclical.

By the same token, part 2 on the Church-state relationship concerns especially the question of whether the Catholic confessional state survives DH, at least in theory. The influential Council *peritus* John Courtney Murray argued forcefully that it does not, and he based his position in large measure on Paul VI's speech to world leaders at the close of the Council, *Aux gouvernants*. However, after careful examination of that speech and several similar ones by the same Pope, my own conclusion is that this speech largely has been misread. As a result, I believe that Murray's interpretation of this speech (already weakened by the analysis of scholars such as Brian Harrison, Basile Valuet, and Russell Hittinger) now has become untenable.

As mentioned above, a significant aspect of the jurisprudential hermeneutic is its requirement for precision. This is particularly important in using terms like the *confessional state* (addressed primarily in part 2)[66] and the *incompetence of the state in religious matters* (discussed in part 3B).

It also is vitally necessary to consider not only terms and formulas but also the meaning behind those terms. There is no doubt that both the nineteenth-century pronouncements and Vatican II contain the term *religious liberty* (or similar terms), the former in condemnatory language and the latter in approving terms. However, one must inquire whether the Council and the nineteenth-century popes were discussing the same thing. That is, *Is the right that Vatican II embraced the same one that Pius IX and other nineteenth-century popes condemned?* Answering this question is the most important task of this study, and it also is one to which the jurisprudential hermeneutic is well-adapted. I will seek to address this question through a

---

[66] The declaration does not use the term *confessional state*, but as discussed below in section 4.5, it acknowledges the possibility of one religion receiving *special civil recognition* (DH, §6c). It refers to such recognition generally, so that the same passage of the declaration addresses official recognition of Catholicism as well as the possibility of a civil government recognizing a different religion.

careful analysis that examines the foundation, object, and scope of the right to religious liberty that DH recognizes.

The focus on these three aspects is not original to me. Since shortly after the close of the Council, a number of commentators have realized the utility of analyzing the right in terms of its foundation, object, and scope.[67] The chief innovations in this study are four. As described above, one of them is what I believe to be a new reading of Pope St. Paul VI's important 1965 *Aux gouvernants* speech, which I will discuss in part 2. The next two innovations are contained in parts 3A and 3B, which make up the heart of this study. In chapter 7 (in part 3A) on the *scope* of the right to religious liberty, I suggest not only that the nineteenth-century teachings and Vatican II are noncontradictory but that there is in fact a profound harmony and continuity between them. The principle of continuity is their common focus on the integrity of the human person. It is nascent and sometimes merely implied in the pronouncements of the nineteenth-century popes, but Vatican II will extend it and develop it more fully. In part 3B, chapters 9 and 10 concern the foundation of the right to religious liberty, and they give special attention to the possibility of identifying the *incompetence of the state* as an alternate foundation for the right to religious liberty. This was the favorite argument of Murray, and although the Council did not embrace it, many commentators continue to assert that it would have been an equally valid foundation (or indeed, a better one). I disagree, and I believe that this argument is significantly more problematic than it appears at first blush. I hope to subject this argument to a searching analysis and to show that it entails a number of significant difficulties. The fourth innovation (perhaps less significant than the other three) is contained in part 4, and it concerns the sixteenth-century papal bull *Exsurge Domine*. The relevant passage in that bull concerns the burning of heretics, and the question arises as to whether *Exsurge Domine* poses a difficulty for reconciling DH with tradition. Like Harrison and Valuet, I believe that it does not. For my own part, I believe that I have treated this document at greater length than other commentators and that I am putting forth some additional significant reasons for concluding that it may be reconciled with DH.

As mentioned above, in both doctrine and the common law, the relationship between current pronouncements and the past is crucial. I do not mean only past pronouncements but the past itself. Sometimes the facts or historical circumstances of two cases are so dissimilar that the same rule

---

[67] E.g., Pietro Pavan, "Le droit à la liberté religieuse en ses éléments essentiels," *Unam Sanctam* 60 (Paris: Éditions du Cerf, 1967): 149–64.

cannot be applied to both. Similarly, a court may find an earlier decision to be of limited use because of a change in facts or circumstances, but rather than overrule it, the court may "limit it to its facts" while announcing a new rule for most other cases. The same considerations affect the understanding and development of doctrine. For example, these considerations come into play when considering Church teaching on usury. That is, a significant change in economic circumstances led to a new situation in which lending money for interest could no longer be considered per se exploitative. The Church's teaching against economic exploitation remained constant, but the application shifted with this change in circumstances. This change included the discoveries that money has a time-value, and that the risk of loss on a loan and the foregoing of other economic opportunities are detriments to the lender that justly could be compensated.[68]

To what extent do "changed circumstances" impact the debate over religious liberty? This is an important but difficult question. It goes without saying that significant historical and political changes occurred between the time of the nineteenth-century popes and the Vatican II teaching on religious liberty. Moreover, the import of *Donum Veritatis* is that these changes should be taken into account in some way when examining doctrine. At the same time, however, the danger in resorting too quickly or too frequently to a "changed circumstances" argument is readily apparent. That is, the awareness of the need to maintain doctrinal consistency could be lost altogether. Theologians like Father Eagan already seem close to this point. Thus, at three different stages in this study, I include chapters on the relevance of "changed circumstances" to this debate. One (chapter 5) considers the historical shift away from the confessional state and toward constitutional government in the West. Another (chapter 15) concerns changing evaluations of the social harm caused by non-Catholic religious worship and expression. Finally, the last one (chapter 16) forms my conclusion, and it examines those factors and circumstances that account for the delay in the Church's recognition of the right to religious liberty.

---

[68] Cf. O'Neil, "Response to Noonan."

PART 2

CHURCH AND STATE

CHAPTER 4

The Proper Relationship between Church and State

Murray ... a devout American.

— BRIAN HARRISON[1]

Several hazards are likely to obstruct a person who is attempting to understand the Catholic Church's doctrine on religious liberty. The question itself leads almost inevitably to a multitude of additional questions concerning the relationship between Church and state. This subject is acutely sensitive and highly complex. Although these Church-state questions can provide important context for the discussion of religious liberty, they often loom so large as to cause one to lose sight of the actual doctrinal controversy. As a result, it is important to emphasize that this work is not concerned with examining all aspects of the Church-state relationship but rather with evaluating the charge that the Church has reversed its teaching on religious liberty. Thus, it is necessary to examine the various controversies that have arisen from the Vatican II teaching and to determine which of them presents a live doctrinal dispute.

The Church's teaching on religious liberty has generated controversy both for doctrinal reasons and for other reasons, such as the pastoral prudence of issuing such a declaration. As a result, it is necessary to identify the areas of potential conflict and to set to one side those issues that have arisen in the context of discussing *Dignitatis Humanae* that do not concern

---

[1] Brian W. Harrison, *Religious Liberty and Contraception: Did Vatican II Open the Way for a New Sexual Ethic?* (Melbourne: John XXIII Fellowship Co-op., Ltd., 1988), 157.

doctrine. This is not meant to denigrate those issues but only to show that they do not pertain to doctrine (or that, if they do, the doctrinal question already has been resolved). As noted above (in section 3.2.1), the extensive scholarly literature on the declaration reveals that there are three issues of potential doctrinal conflict: (a) the proper Church-state relationship, (b) legitimate restriction on religious expression, and (c) the question of whether non-Catholics have a right *publicly* to worship and to practice their religion. I will address these issues in turn, and I will explain why I believe that the final question is the only one that presents a live doctrinal dispute. Part 2 of this study will address the Church-state relationship, and each of the following two parts will discuss one of the remaining issues.

Before proceeding, I note that I refer initially to the relationship between *Church and state* because this framing is familiar and is current in our own time. As discussed below in section 4.3, however, it is necessary to recall that this dichotomy has historical antecedents in the dichotomies between empire and papacy, and between civil society and ecclesiastical society. Moreover, in our own day, the dichotomy between Church and state remains relevant, but the compound term *Church and state* can be ambiguous. That is, it continues to be used in the strict sense to refer to the civil power's relationship with the Catholic Church herself, but it more often is used generically to refer to relations between the state and any religious community. (The latter usage is particularly widespread in the United States. However, I often will use it in the first sense because one of questions concerning the declaration is whether it is consistent with the existence of Catholic confessional states.) There is a certain commonality underlying all of these distinctions and dichotomies, but there also are important and substantive differences among these terms. As a result, one should be careful to avoid simply equating these dichotomies with each other. (See generally section 4.3 below.)

* * *

At first blush, *Dignitatis Humanae* appears to differ from previous Church teaching on the matter of whether a state should adopt Catholicism as its official religion.[2] As a result of the fact that *Dignitatis Humanae* emphasizes

---

[2] At the outset, I refer to state *establishment* of religion and I discuss the *confessional state*. I use these terms because they are familiar and because they arise frequently in connection with discussions on *Dignitatis Humanae*. However, I hope that it will become clear, as this chapter proceeds, that rather than speaking of papal teaching on the confessional state, it is more accurate to speak of papal teaching on the duty of the state (or the governing authority) toward religion. In addition, to the extent that one does speak of the confessional

the right of all persons to religious liberty, it often is assumed that state neutrality toward religion must go hand-in-hand with true religious liberty. Indeed, Jesuit priest John Courtney Murray, a *peritus* at the Council and one of the persons most responsible for the eventual issuance of a document on religious liberty, took precisely this position. During the Council, Murray wrote an article in which he described the legal establishment of religion and religious intolerance as "twin institutions,"[3] and just after the Council, he argued that *Dignitatis Humanae* embraced more or less his own position, thus rejecting the confessional state and adopting a position of Church-state separation or disestablishment. "The Church," Murray says, "does not make, as a matter of right or of divine law, the claim that she should be established as the 'religion of the state.' Her claim is freedom, nothing more."[4]

4.1. Separation of Church and State

If Murray accurately has described the Council's Declaration on Religious Liberty, then indeed there does seem to be a doctrinal problem. The reason is that previous papal statements repeatedly condemned the separation of Church and state. Thesis 55 of Pope Pius IX's *Syllabus of Errors* rejected the statement that the Church "ought to be separated from the State." Pope Leo XIII taught that the state must have care for religion and that it must not be

---

state, the discussion in section 4.3 below identifies several possible forms that such regimes might take.

[3] John Courtney Murray, "The Problem of Religious Freedom," *Theological Studies* 25, no. 4 (1964): 566. See also John Courtney Murray, "Religious Freedom," in *Freedom and Man* (New York: P. J. Kenedy & Sons, 1965) (speech at Georgetown University in summer 1964), 134: "Given the institution of establishment, it follows by logical and juridical consequence that no other religion, *per se* and in principle, can be allowed public existence or action within the state"; John Courtney Murray, "The Issue of Church and State at Vatican Council II," *Theological Studies* 27, no. 4 (December 1966): 594: If Catholicism is established as the religion of the state, then with regard to members of other religions, "certain civil disabilities logically follow."

[4] John Courtney Murray, "Religious Freedom," in *The Documents of Vatican II*, ed. Walter M. Abbott (New York: Herder and Herder, 1966), 693n52. A more subtle interpretation than Murray's might be that the declaration simply acknowledges that confessional states now have disappeared, or almost disappeared. In chapter 5, I address the question of whether the decline or disappearance of the Catholic confessional state might render it unnecessary to attempt to reconcile DH with previous papal teaching.

godless.[5] Pope Pius X stated directly that separation between Church and state "is a thesis absolutely false, a most pernicious error."[6]

Murray argued that the *type* of Church-state separation that the popes had uppermost in mind was the militantly anti-Catholic state of nineteenth-century Continental Liberalism rather than the system established by the United States Constitution.[7] The difficulty with Murray's argument is that one of these popes—Leo XIII—wrote directly about the American system, and although he did appreciate the freedom that it allowed to the Church, he also said that the American system was not the best.

> [T]hanks are due to the equity of the laws which obtain in America and to the customs of the well-ordered Republic. For the Church amongst you, unopposed by the Constitution and government of your nation, fettered by no hostile legislation, protected against violence by the common laws and the impartiality of the tribunals, is free to live and act without hindrance. Yet, though all this is true, it would be very erroneous to draw the conclusion that in America is to be sought the type of the most desirable status of the Church, or that it would be universally lawful or expedient for State and Church to be, as in America, dissevered and divorced. The fact that Catholicity with you is in good condition, nay, is even enjoying a prosperous growth, is by all means to be attributed to the fecundity with which God has endowed His Church, in virtue of which unless men or circumstances interfere, she spontaneously expands and propagates herself; but she would bring forth more abundant fruits if, in addition to liberty, she enjoyed the favor of the laws and the patronage of the public authority. (LO, §6)

Murray, however, was a proponent of Church-state separation, both generally and in his interpretation of the declaration. He deals with the pronouncements of previous popes—particularly Leo XIII—by attempting

---

[5] Pope Leo XIII, Encyclical *Immortale Dei* (Nov. 1, 1885), §6 [ASS 18 (1885–1886): 161–80]; Encyclical *Libertas* (June 20, 1888), §21 [ASS 20 (1887–1888): 593–613]. See also Pope Leo XIII, Encyclical *Longinqua Oceani* (Jan. 6, 1895), §6, praising freedom of the Church under U.S. Constitution but asserting that Church would be more fruitful if it enjoyed not only liberty, but also the favor of the laws [ASS 27 (1894–1895): 390] (hereinafter cited as LO).

[6] Pope Pius X, Encyclical *Vehementer Nos* (Feb. 11, 1906), §3 [ASS 39 (1906): 5].

[7] Cf. John Courtney Murray, "Leo XIII: Separation of Church and State," *Theological Studies* 14, no. 2 (1953): 169, 185–86.

to limit them to a specific historical and geographical context, namely, the nineteenth-century European anti-clerical secular state.[8] Murray is correct that the nineteenth-century popes, in rejecting Church-state separation, had uppermost in mind the anti-clerical trends in Europe that followed in the wake of the French Revolution rather than the American constitutional system of more or less benevolent governmental neutrality toward the Catholic Church and all other religious organizations. However, is he also correct in limiting their pronouncements to the nineteenth-century context? More to the point of this discussion, Is he correct that *Dignitatis Humanae* essentially embraces the American model of Church-state separation, or something like it?[9] I will return to this question below after some general observations on interpreting the declaration.

4.2. The Need for Humility in Interpreting *Dignitatis Humanae*

Interpretation of the Vatican II Declaration on Religious Liberty calls for humility. For the task of squaring this document with the teachings of the nineteenth-century popes—or, as Pope Emeritus Benedict XVI would say, reading it in the light of Tradition—the document's *silences* are at least as important as its words.[10] One of the keys to understanding *Dignitatis Humanae* is the circumstance that the Council did not intend to provide a complete description of relations between Church and state.[11] Where many readers demand that the declaration speak, the document itself is reticent.

---

[8] Cf. Murray, "Leo XIII: Separation of Church and State," 185–86.

[9] In his pre-conciliar writings, Murray argues that the U.S. system represents an outgrowth of the Church's own natural law tradition. Cf. John Courtney Murray, *We Hold These Truths: Catholic Reflections on the American Proposition* (Kansas City, MO: Sheed & Ward, 1960), 10, and in his conciliar and post-conciliar writings, he sometimes claims that *Dignitatis Humanae* represents the Council's adoption of this theory. Cf. John Courtney Murray, "Commentary," in Vincent A. Yzermans, ed., *American Participation in the Second Vatican Council* (New York: Sheed & Ward, 1967), 671: "Caught in the more disastrous aberrations derivative from the French Revolution, the Church long failed to recognize the validity of the American development of what was, in fact, her own tradition. The Declaration accords the belated recognition" (hereinafter, larger work cited as Yzermans).

[10] Russell Hittinger, in particular, emphasizes the need "to respect the silences of *DH*." "Religion, Human Law, and the Virtue of Religion: The Case of *Dignitatis Humanae*," *Nova et Vetera* (English ed.) 14, no. 1 (2016): 176. Cf. Hittinger, 155.

[11] Fernando Ocáriz, "Sulla libertà religiosa. Continuità del Vaticano II con il Magistero precedente," *Annales theologici* 3 (1989): 73: "DH non è una dichiarazione circa l'intera dottrina cattolica sui rapporti tra libertà umana e religione, né sui rapporti tra Chiesa e Stato."

The declaration makes limited references to previous teaching and to civil recognition of religion, but for the most part it is silent about the confessional state. In a February 1963 meeting in advance of the second session of the Council, the Secretariat for Promoting Christian Unity (which ultimately would assume responsibility for the drafting of the declaration) decided to set to one side the question of the relationship between Church and state.[12] In addition, the official relator of the document, Bishop Émile De Smedt of Bruges, Belgium, noted in one of his official reports (*relationes*) that the declaration does not address the Church-state question directly.[13] As a result, one must resist the temptation to look to it for the answers to questions that it does not intend to address.[14] Thus, in introducing the first draft of what eventually would become the Declaration on Religious Liberty, De Smedt cautioned the council fathers, "I beseech you, Venerable Fathers, not to force the text to speak outside of its historical and doctrinal context, not, in other words, to make the fish swim out of water."[15]

What in fact does the declaration say about Church-state separation or Church-state union?

---

[12] Cf. Mathijs Lamberigts, "Msgr. Emiel-Jozef De Smedt, Bishop of Bruges, and the Second Vatican Council," in *Experience, Organisations and Bodies at Vatican II: Proceedings of the Bologna Conference, December 1996*, ed. M. T. Fattori and A. Melloni (Leuven, Belgium: Bibliotheek van de Faculteit Godgeleerdheid, 1999), 447n83.

[13] "In our present declaration, we do not directly treat of the juridical relations between church and state, the theological problem of the right and mission of the Church to proclaim the Gospel, the moral doctrine that must be adopted with regard to non-Christians, or the arguments that make tolerance morally obligatory." Émile De Smedt, Oral *Relatio* on the *Textus Emendatus* (Nov. 19, 1964) [AS III/8, 452]; English translation in Henri Fesquet, *The Drama of Vatican II* (New York: Random House, 1967), 541. Note that, in section 9.5.1 below (in connection with my discussion of Thomas Pink), I caution against some uses of the *relationes*. In particular, I criticize Pink's attempt to interpret the declaration through comments in the November 1964 *relatio* on passages of the *Textus Emendatus* that did not survive the redaction process. However, I believe that the present citation to the November 1964 *relatio* is sound. That is, the principle cited here—the avoidance of a detailed discussion of Church and state—remained a feature not only of the *Textus Emendatus*, but of the final document as well. See also Murray, "Commentary," in Yzermans, 673: The Council "wisely" avoided being "carried . . . into the problem of 'Church and State.'"

[14] Cf. Russell Hittinger, "How to Read *Dignitatis Humanae* on Establishment of Religion," *Catholic Dossier* 6, no. 2 (March–April 2000): 15; Brian W. Harrison, "Vatican II and Religious Liberty: Contradiction or Continuity?," *Catholic Dossier* 6, no. 2 (March–April 2000): 23.

[15] Émile De Smedt, Oral *Relatio* on Chapter V of *De Oecumenismo* (Nov. 19, 1963) [AS II/5, 491–92]; English translation in Michael Davies, *The Second Vatican Council and Religious Liberty* (Long Prairie, MN: Neumann Press, 1992), 294.

Very little really.

Dignitatis Humanae neither reaffirms nor repudiates the teaching of Pius IX, Leo XIII, and Pius X against Church-state separation. Rather, it simply is silent—or almost silent—on the subject. (As we shall see, the document's sole statement touching on this question reinforces its determination to remain almost entirely silent.) The declaration never expressly recapitulates the teaching of the nineteenth-century popes, but neither does it contradict them. The reason appears to be that the council fathers chose to address the political situation actually prevailing in the world today, that is, modern constitutional government. "[T]he council intends to develop the doctrine of recent popes on the inviolable rights of the human person and the constitutional order of society."[16]

Archbishop Roland Minnerath asserts that the Vatican II religious liberty declaration pronounced the end of the era of the confessional state. "With its declaration on religious freedom *Dignitatis Humanae*, the council took note that the time of confessional states was definitely over."[17] This is true—if at all—only in a certain sense, however. By addressing itself to the modern constitutional state, perhaps the declaration acknowledges—albeit implicitly—that the previous era is over in the sense that confessional states are less prevalent in the world today.[18] However, the declaration does not say that confessional states cannot or should not re-emerge at some point

---

[16] See also section 4.6 below on the significance of another passage, providing that the Council "leaves untouched traditional Catholic doctrine on the moral duty of men and societies toward the true religion and toward the one Church of Christ." Cf. Second Vatican Council, Declaration on Religious Liberty *Dignitatis Humanae* (December 7, 1965), §1c.

[17] Roland Minnerath, "How Should State and Church Interact?," *The Jurist* 70, no. 2 (2010): 476.

[18] Brian Harrison, however, identifies the Wallis and Futuna Islands as perhaps "the last totally Catholic society on earth" (RL&C, 85n3). Moreover, Minnerath himself notes that some small European states—Monaco, Malta, and Lichtenstein—remain officially Catholic (Minnerath, "State and Church," 482). Still others, though not adopting a state religion, recognize the importance of Catholicism in the life of the people and the history of the nation (cf. RL&C, 79–82, emphasizing Colombia and the Philippines). As discussed below in section 4.5, the Council will refer not to confessional states but to states in which a particular religion enjoys *special civil recognition* (cf. DH, §6c). That is, it refers to this possibility in general rather than exclusively in connection with official recognition of Catholicism. In this connection, one should recall—as Minnerath himself notes—that there also remain countries in which non-Catholic Churches or communities are established. Thus, Lutheranism is established in Norway and Denmark, and the Church of England in the United Kingdom. Similarly, Orthodoxy enjoys special privileges in Greece and in some other Eastern countries (cf. Minnerath, "State and Church," 481–84). See also Pew Research Center, "Many Countries Favor Specific Religions, Officially or Unofficially," Pew Research

in the future. By the same token, neither does the declaration say that they *should* re-emerge. The document simply is silent on the question.[19] (Section 4.5 below on "special civil recognition" of religion briefly discusses some possible reasons for the declaration's silence on this question.)

Before proceeding, we should pause to ask what exactly a *confessional state* is or was. The popes actually do not use the phrase *confessional state*, but rather they refer to the *Catholic state*. Even so, they nearly always take the notion for granted rather than defining or describing it. In fact, Basile Valuet identifies only a single papal document that defines the Catholic state. Moreover, even this definition is brief. That document, a 1929 chirograph by Pius XI, describes the Catholic state as one that accords with Catholic doctrine and practice, not only in the order of practical action but in the order of ideas and doctrines as well.[20] For his part, Pope Bl. Pius IX in the nineteenth century had emphasized the duty of the civil power to protect the Church (cf. QC, §§3, 8), while his successor Leo XIII did the same and also called attention to the state's duty to worship God (cf. ID, §21).

The confessional state or the Catholic state is an idea that has been more lived out than defined with precision.[21] Valuet, however, makes some useful distinctions among types of confessional states. The first is between, on the one hand, *formal* or *legal* confessionality, and, on the other hand, confessionality that is *substantial* or *tacit*. A state that is *formally* confessional explicitly declares itself to be such in a text. That is, it adopts a state religion. By contrast, a *substantially* confessional state lacks this explicit

---

Center, Oct. 3, 2017, accessed Apr. 5, 2021, https://www.pewforum.org/2017/10/03/many-countries-favor-specific-religions-officially-or-unofficially/ (hereinafter, Pew Study).

[19] This discussion is concerned primarily with *Christian* confessional states, particularly *Catholic* ones. However, even if the Christian confessional state is less common today, the continuing relevance of these matters is readily apparent in the fact that confessional states are abundant in the Islamic world (see Pew Study).

[20] Cf. Basile Valuet, *Le droit à la liberté religieuse dans la Tradition de l'Eglise. Un cas de développement doctrinal homogène par le magistère authentique*, 2nd rev. ed. (Barroux: Éditions Sainte-Madeleine, 2011), 298 (hereinafter, LRTE), quoting Pope Pius XI, *Ci si è domandato* (May 30, 1929) [AAS 21 [1929]: 303].

[21] In discussing Maurice Blondel's theology of doctrinal development, Aidan Nichols refers to institutions that arise in the life of the Church and acquire doctrinal significance, even though their precise definition remains elusive or receives surprisingly little attention. Cf. Aidan Nichols, *From Newman to Congar: The Idea of Doctrinal Development from the Victorians to the Second Vatican Council* (Edinburgh: T&T Clark, 1990), 151. The cited passage discusses Blondel's understanding of doctrine as both *conserving* and *conquering*. "This conserving power is at the same time conquering, which discovers and formulates truths that the past has lived out without having been able to enunciate them or define them explicitly" (*Newman to Congar*, 151).

declaration, but the juridic functioning of society depends de facto on the confessionality of the society.²²

Further, among *formally* confessional states, there is an additional distinction. The state's formal confessionality is *doctrinal* if the relevant text declares the state religion to be true. However, if the declaration makes no judgment of truth but rather recognizes the importance of the religion in the nation's past or as the majority religion of the people, then the state's confessionality is *historico-sociological*.

As discussed below, the text of *Dignitatis Humanae* makes clear that a state at least may recognize a particular religion in the historico-sociological sense. This is apparent from the declaration's famous reference to a state's *special civil recognition* of a particular religion in article 6:

> If, in view of peculiar circumstances obtaining among peoples, special civil recognition (*specialis civilis agnitio*) is given to one religious community in the constitutional order of society, it is at the same time imperative that the right of all citizens and religious communities to religious freedom should be recognized and made effective in practice. (DH, §6c)

However, although it is clear that this passage permits the type of historico-sociological confessionality discussed by Valuet, commentators disagree over the question of *doctrinal* confessionality, that is, whether according to *Dignitatis Humanae*, a state legitimately may recognize a religion *as true*. This question is addressed below.

Before proceeding, however, a brief word is in order concerning the relationship between the terms *special civil recognition* and the *confessional state*. Murray and like-minded commentators sharply distinguish the terms and insist that special civil recognition is not the confession of a religion by the state but merely a historical or demographic recognition of the state's majority religion.²³ Others, such as Harrison, Valuet, and Ocáriz interpret special

---

²² Cf. Valuet, LRTE, 383–84.
²³ Cf. Murray, "Church and State at Vatican II," 595: "It is therefore clearly the mind of the Council that the establishment of Catholicism as the religion of the state is no more than a matter of historical circumstances, and not a matter—or even a consequence—of doctrine"; Richard Regan, "John Courtney Murray, the American Bishops, and the *Declaration on Religious Liberty*," in John T. Ford, ed., *Religious Liberty: Paul VI and Dignitatis Humanae* (Brescia, Italy: Istituto Paolo VI, 1995), 61, asserting that under *Dignitatis Humanae*, state religions are a product of historical circumstance, not theological doctrine; Pietro A. D'Avack, "La Chiesa e lo Stato nella nuova impostazione conciliare," in *Il Diritto*

civil recognition as including the confessional state.[24] According to this view, although article 6 mentions only certain "circumstances" as supporting civil recognition of a religion, it does not exclude doctrinal confession of religion. I will return to—and will attempt to resolve—this question below in section 4.5 of this chapter. For present purposes, it is sufficient to note that all the commentators appear to agree that the crucial question is whether a state may recognize a particular religion *as true*. Thus, unless otherwise noted, from this point forward, I will refer to confessionality in this more specific sense, namely, what Valuet calls formal confessionality of the doctrinal type.

4.3. Gelasian Dualism

Another pronouncement of the Council actually comes closer than *Dignitatis Humanae* to addressing the questions of the confessional State and Church-state separation (or union). The Pastoral Constitution on the Church in the Modern World *Gaudium et Spes* speaks of something like Church-state separation, but it takes an approach somewhat different from the one that Murray advocated. The council fathers say, "The Church and the political community in their own fields are autonomous and independent from each other."[25] Although this might appear to be an embrace of separation between Church and state, it actually is a reaffirmation of an ancient Catholic principle, the Gelasian dyarchy or Christian dualism.[26]

---

ecclesiastico e rassegna di diritto matrimoniale (Milano, Italy: Giuffrè, 1971), 33, asserting that confessionality of a Catholic state cannot have the character of an act of faith but rather "constitutes a mere pragmatic-juridical disposition founded on the faith of the citizens."

[24] Cf. Harrison, RL&C, 77: A last-minute amendment to article 1 of DH—the addition of the phrase *and societies*—"explicitly reaffirmed this traditional doctrine" on the civic community's duty to God and the Church; Valuet, LRTE, 394; Ocáriz, "Sulla libertà religiosa," 93: Nothing in *Dignitatis Humanae* prevents the state from recognizing the true religion.

[25] Second Vatican Council, Pastoral Constitution on the Church in the Modern World *Gaudium et Spes* (December 7, 1965), §76c [AAS 58 (1966): 1025–1115, at 1099] (hereinafter, GS).

[26] Neither Council text discussed here—GS §76 nor LG §36—mentions the principle of Gelasian dualism or cites Pope St. Gelasius I himself. However, LG §36d cites two encyclicals of Leo XIII, whom Murray credits with reviving Gelasian dualism (see the main text of this section). Moreover, the two passages cited—ID §13 and *Sapientiae Christianae* §30 [ASS 22 (1889–1890): 397]—are strong affirmations of this principle. Both carefully delineate the religious and the temporal spheres, and what is central to the point discussed in this section, the latter makes clear that this distinction between the two powers does not equate to a separation or severance between them. "The Church alike and the State, doubtless, both possess individual sovereignty. . . . It does not hence follow, however, that Church and State are in any manner severed, and still less antagonistic" (*Sapientiae*

4.3. Gelasian Dualism

Late in the fifth century, Pope St. Gelasius I recalled the Lord's command "Render unto Caesar the things that are Caesar's" (Matt 22:21) and taught that there are two distinct realms or powers, the temporal and the spiritual. In a justly famous letter to Emperor Anastasius, Gelasius writes:

> There are two, august Emperor, by which this world is governed, the sacred authority [*auctoritas*] of priests and the royal power [*potestas*]. . . . Hence, you realize that, in the religious sphere, in matters concerning the reception and correct administration of the sacraments, you must submit rather than rule, because in these matters you must follow their judgment and not try to bend them to your will.
>
> If, indeed, the bishops themselves, recognizing that your office has been conferred on you by the will of God, obey your laws as far as public order is concerned lest they seem to oppose your decisions in temporal matters, what, I ask, should be your attitude to those charged with the administration of the sacred mysteries?[27]

As a result of the the fact that Gelasian dualism distinguishes between two realms or two powers, one might be tempted to assume that there is a substantial identity between this concept and the modern idea of *separation of Church and state*. However, although there are commonalities, there also

---

Christianae §30 [*Acta Leonis XIII* 10, 29 = ASS 22 (1889–1890): 397]). On the location of GS §76 in the tradition of Gelasian dualism, see José Tomás Martín de Agar, "Derecho y relaciones iglesia—sociedad civil," *Ius Ecclesiae* 32, no. 1 (2020): 48: Vatican II reaffirms Christian dualism; key text is GS, §76 (Martín de Agar, 50).

[27] Gelasius, "Letter Twelve to Emperor Anastasius" (494). English translation in Hugo Rahner, *Church and State in Early Christianity*, trans. Leo Donald Davis (San Francisco: Ignatius Press, 1992), 173–76, at 174. Curiously, Gelasius's discussion of "Render to Caesar" comes not in his famous letter to Emperor Anastasius (494) but rather in a tract that he wrote shortly before his death in 496. "For Christ, mindful of human frailty, regulated with an excellent disposition what pertained to the salvation of his people. Thus he distinguished between the offices of both powers according to their own proper activities and separate dignities, wanting his people to be saved by healthful humility and not carried away again by human pride, so that Christian emperors would need priests for attaining eternal life, and priests would avail themselves of imperial regulations in the conduct of temporal affairs. . . . Thus the humility of each order would be preserved, neither being exalted by the subservience of the other, and each profession would be especially fitted for its appropriate functions" (Gelasius, "Fourth Tract on the Bond of Anathema," ch. 11, in Hugo Rahner, *Church and* State, 177–78, citing B. Tierney, *The Crisis of Church and State* [Toronto, 1988], 14–15). Although he does not quote the verse, it is clear from the context that "Render to Caesar" is the one that Gelasius is expounding.

are differences. Gelasian dualism has a long and complex history, and it has given rise to several dichotomies of terms. Rather than attempting simply to equate these terms with each other, one instead should attend to the various stages in the progress of Gelasian dualism.[28]

José Tomás Martín de Agar notes that, although the foundational text—"Render to Caesar" (Matt 22:21)—does not necessarily imply the demarcation of distinct temporal and religious realms, Church leaders early on began invoking the passage in support of the Church's freedom and that of individual believers.[29] With Theodosius's establishment of Christianity as the official religion of the Roman Empire in the late fourth century, the focus shifted from individual freedom to the relations between the *two powers*, the emperor and the pope.[30] This emphasis on the two powers has been a historical constant, but later one also will come to speak of *two orders* (religious and temporal) and *two societies* (ecclesiastical and civil). In the *respublica christianorum* of the Middle Ages, civil society and ecclesiastical society become amalgamated. As a result, this period is characterized by the presence of the two powers within the one Christian society.[31] Secular currents arise in time and lead to the predominance of the temporal power and to limitations on ecclesiastical jurisdiction.[32] The Church eventually will reassert her spiritual authority, and the theory will arise of the Church and the state as *two perfect societies*.[33]

Vatican II does not mention Gelasian dualism expressly, but it both reaffirms and adapts the basic doctrine. Classically the focus had been on the two powers, the two orders, or the two perfect societies. Vatican II emphasizes the reciprocal autonomy between the Church and the political community, as well as the supremacy of each within its own ambit.[34]

Gelasian dualism has something in common with Church-state

---

[28] Cf. Martín de Agar, "Derecho y relaciones iglesia—sociedad civil," 33: the author cautions against the neglect of taking into account the various understandings of Christian dualism throughout time.

[29] Martín de Agar, "Derecho y relaciones iglesia—sociedad civil," 29.

[30] Martín de Agar, "Derecho y relaciones iglesia—sociedad civil," 31.

[31] Cf. Martín de Agar, "Derecho y relaciones iglesia—sociedad civil," 33–34.

[32] Cf. Martín de Agar, "Derecho y relaciones iglesia—sociedad civil," 36.

[33] Cf. Martín de Agar, "Derecho y relaciones iglesia—sociedad civil," 37, 41.

[34] Cf. Martín de Agar, "Derecho y relaciones iglesia—sociedad civil," 48, 50. Although GS §76 speaks of the relations between the Church and the political community, DH and other conciliar documents (as well as the pronouncements of the post-conciliar popes) make clear that the Church also is attentive to such relations between governmental authorities and non-Catholic religious bodies. Moreover, article 76 opens with an acknowledgment of the prevalent contemporary context of the pluralistic society. This passage does not use

separation, namely, the insistence on a clear distinction between the two realms and their spheres of authority. In other important ways, however, the Gelasian principle is very different from the type of strict separationism or disestablishment that Murray promoted.[35]

Although Murray himself praises Gelasian dualism and credits Leo XIII with reviving the tradition,[36] he and other strict separationists seem not fully to appreciate the differences between separationism and Gelasian dualism. Thus, Murray famously identified the American constitutional system as a development of the Church's own tradition.[37] As Murray's biographer Donald Pelotte observes, Murray does not simply recall the Gelasian theory but rather he reformulates it around the American experience.[38] Thus, where the popes habitually emphasize the need for the spiritual and temporal realms to cooperate and to collaborate,[39] Murray's separationism is nearly absolute.[40]

---

the classical terms the two *powers* or the two *societies*, but it does retain some of the classical terminology in referring to the temporal *order*.

[35] Cf. International Theological Commission, *Religious Freedom for the Good of All* (Apr. 16, 2019), 61n64, citing Gelasius and Leo XIII, and noting that in Leo's *Immortale Dei* "one finds an appropriate distinction between the political and religious orders without a radical separation."

[36] Cf. Murray, "Problem of Religious Freedom," 540.

[37] Cf. Murray, "Commentary," in Yzermans, 671: "Caught in the more disastrous aberrations derivative from the French Revolution, the Church long failed to recognize the validity of the American development of what was, in fact, her own tradition. The Declaration accords the belated recognition." See also Murray, *We Hold These Truths*, 10.

[38] Cf. Donald E. Pelotte, *John Courtney Murray: Theologian in Conflict* (New York: Paulist Press, 1975), 145–46. See also John Courtney Murray, "Contemporary Orientations of Catholic Thought on Church and State in the Light of History," *Theological Studies* 10 (1949): 188–89, asserting that First Amendment of U.S. Constitution stands for the state's "non-competence in the field of religion" and locating its premise in the "Christian dualist concept of man."

[39] E.g., LP, §18: "[A]lthough the civil authority has not the same proximate end as the spiritual, nor proceeds on the same lines, nevertheless in the exercise of their separate powers they must occasionally meet. For their subjects are the same, and not infrequently they deal with the same objects, though in different ways."

[40] Cf. Pelotte, *Theologian in Conflict*, 124–25. Murray's separationism manifests itself, among other ways, in assertions that state establishment of religion necessarily entails intolerance. Cf. Murray, "Religious Freedom" (Georgetown speech), 134: "Given the institution of establishment, it follows by logical and juridical consequence that no other religion, *per se* and in principle, can be allowed public existence or action within the state." Indeed, in his famous 1964 *Theological Studies* article, Murray calls establishment and intolerance "twin institutions" (cf. "Problem of Religious Freedom," 566). As a result, Murray asserts the incompetence of the state in religious matters as the basis both for religious liberty and separationism (or rejection of state establishment of religion). Thus, the drafts of DH for which Murray had primary responsibility (discussed below in section 4.4) contain forceful

Most significantly, Gelasian dualism is an effort to *distinguish* the two realms rather than to *separate* them absolutely or to isolate them from each other entirely.[41] Like the popes, the Council speaks of collaboration between the two realms[42] and of the dangers of isolating the two spheres from each other.[43]

By contrast, the American type of separationism (or at least one influential formulation of it) tends in the other direction, that is, to a strict and stark separation that leaves little room for cooperation between the two realms. Thomas Jefferson famously characterized the First Amendment as erecting "a wall of separation between church and state,"[44] and that opinion and image increasingly have gained currency, both culturally and jurisprudentially. Indeed, the U.S. Supreme Court adopted Jefferson's view in its landmark 1947 *Everson* decision,[45] and although the Jeffersonian interpretation of the First Amendment does not enjoy universal support, it

---

assertions of state incompetence that later were removed and therefore did not appear in the final version of the declaration. Cf. *Textus Emendatus*, §4e: Competence of the civil power "is restricted to the earthly and temporal order" (AS III/8, 432); English translation by Patrick T. Brannan and Michael Camacho, in David L. Schindler and Nicholas J. Healy Jr., *Freedom, Truth, and Human Dignity: The Second Vatican Council's Declaration on Religious Freedom—A New Translation, Redaction History, and Interpretation of* Dignitatis Humanae (Grand Rapids, MI / Cambridge, UK: William B. Eerdmans Publishing Co., 2015), 293 (hereinafter, cited as Schindler/Healy); *Textus Reemendatus*, §3: "The competence of the civil power . . . is restricted in its purpose to the earthly and temporal order. . . . The civil power must therefore be said to exceed its limits if it involves itself in those matters that concern the very ordination of man to God" (AS IV/1, 150; English translation by Brannan and Camacho in Schindler/Healy, 323).

[41] "Al ser universal y distinguir—sin confundir ni separar, al menos en teoría—lo religioso de lo temporal, el cristianismo introduce, como se ha dicho, un nuevo modo de entender las relaciones entre religion y política" (Martín de Agar, "Derecho y relaciones iglesia—sociedad civil," 28). See also ITC, "Religious Freedom for All," 60n64; *Lorenzo Spinelli, Lo Stato e la Chiesa. Venti secoli di relazioni* (Turin, Italy: UTET, 1988), 71–72: Vatican II, especially GS §42, embraces a distinction between the two realms, rather than a separation.

[42] Cf. GS, §76c. See also Vicente Prieto, *Diritto dei rapporti tra Chiesa e società civile* (Rome: Edizioni Università della Santa Croce, 2003), ch. 2: "[O]ccore, per il bene della persona, che ci sia un'armonico rapporto fra queste due società e poteri."

[43] Cf. Second Vatican Council, Dogmatic Constitution on the Church *Lumen Gentium* (Nov. 21, 1964), §36d, acknowledging that the temporal sphere is governed by its own principles, but warning against the "ominous doctrine" that attempts to build society without regard for religion (citing ID [ASS 18 (1885): 166 ss.]); Leo XIII, *Sapientiae Christianae* (Jan. 10, 1890) [ASS 22 (1889–1890): 397 ss.]; Pius XII, Discorso *Ai marchigiani residenti in Roma* (Mar. 23, 1958): "la legittima sana laicità dello Stato" [AAS 50 (1958): 220].

[44] Thomas Jefferson, Letter to the Danbury Baptist Association (Jan. 1, 1802), in *The Portable Thomas Jefferson*, ed. Merrill D. Peterson (New York: Penguin Books, 1977), 303.

[45] Everson v. Board of Education, 330 U.S. 1, 16 (1947) (Black, J.): "In the words of Jefferson, the clause against the establishment of religion by law was erected to set up a 'wall of

remains influential. Murray, to his credit, opposed the *Everson* decision.[46] It seems, however, that as Murray's thought developed, it became increasingly separationist.[47] As a result, his own stark separation of the two realms in his later thought regrettably seems to tend in a direction similar to that of the *Everson* decision.

It is important to avoid caricaturing Murray's views. Writing after the Council, he is aware of the call for cooperation between the two realms in *Gaudium et Spes*.[48] Nevertheless, his reading of the Vatican II documents' treatment of Church and state remains strongly separationist, though more subtly so than in his famous 1964 article (discussed above in this section and in section 4.4 below).[49] As discussed below, these references also suggest that Murray sees nearly all questions as falling on one side or the other of the temporal-spiritual divide without taking much account of *mixed questions* that cross between them. By contrast, Leo's teaching makes clear that the more flexible principle of Gelasian dualism makes provision for such questions.

> [I]nasmuch as each of these powers has authority over the same subjects, . . . it might come to pass that one and the same thing—related differently, but still remaining one and the same thing—might belong to the jurisdiction and determination of both. (ID, §13)

Murray's theory attempts to preserve a social role for religion by distinguishing—again, quite sharply—between society and the state, and this distinction is a welcome reminder that the state must not occupy the

---

separation between church and state'"; *Everson*, 330 U.S. at 18: "The First Amendment has erected a wall between church and state. That wall must be kept high and impregnable."

[46] Cf. John Courtney Murray, "A Common Enemy, A Common Cause," *First Things*, no. 26 (October 1992): 29–37 (a previously unpublished address by Murray on the *Everson* decision, delivered May 3, 1948, in Wilmington, Delaware).

[47] Cf. Brian W. Harrison, "John Courtney Murray: A Reliable Interpreter of *Dignitatis Humanae*?" in *We Hold These Truths and More*, ed. Donald J. D'Elia and Stephen M. Krason (Steubenville, OH: Franciscan University Press, 1993), 137–38, discussing Murray's 1964 article "Problem of Religious Freedom," which is cited below in section 4.4.

[48] Cf. Murray, "Church and State at Vatican II," 603, quoting GS, §76.

[49] Cf. Murray, "Church and State at Vatican II," 591: Government may not make judgments of truth; government's care of religion "is primarily negative" (597); the Church's mission in the temporal sphere is "entirely of the spiritual order" (601); the Church's entrance into politics is "purely spiritual" (604); "[E]ven in the temporal order" the Church's mission is "purely spiritual" (605); GS leads the Church "to impose self-denying ordinances on the whole range of her action within the temporal order" (605); privilege of governments to nominate bishops "was always per se an abuse" (606).

entirety of the social sphere. However, in a time of increasing government encroachment and regulation of more and more aspects of the citizens' lives, the opportunities to infuse the temporal order with the spirit of the Gospel are contracted as the government comes to occupy an increasing share of the social realm. (As mentioned above, in several parts of the United States, Catholic institutions have been excluded from participating in government-funded adoption programs because they refuse to place children with same-sex couples.)[50] The growth of the regulatory state and the interpenetration of the spheres of society and state have caused at least one commentator to propose a possible rethinking of Murray's state-society distinction.[51]

Murray and other separationists frequently seem to assume that all public questions belong to only one of the two realms, temporal or spiritual.[52]

---

[50] Cf. U.S. Conference of Catholic Bishops Office of Religious Liberty, "Discrimination Against Catholic Adoption Services," USCCB, 2018, accessed Sept. 3, 2018, http://usccb.org/issues-and-action/religious-liberty/discrimination-against-catholic-adoption-services.cfm.

[51] Cf. David Hollenbach et al., "Theology and Philosophy in Public: A Symposium on John Courtney Murray's Unfinished Agenda," *Theological Studies* 40, no. 4 (1979): 708–9, observation of Robin W. Lovin calling for a rethinking of Murray's distinction between society and the state because, in contemporary life, these two realms interpenetrate each other and because state policy has an "unavoidable impact . . . on the moral possibilities open to persons in society." See also Francis Canavan, "Religious Freedom: John Courtney Murray, S.J., and Vatican II," *Faith & Reason* 13 (Summer 1987): 323–38, reprinted in *John Courtney Murray and the Amereican Civil Conversation*, ed. Robert P. Hunt and Kenneth L. Grasso (Grand Rapids, MI: William B. Eerdmans Publishing Co., 1992), 168: "Society overall is organized as the state, but only for certain purposes and for the performance of certain functions relative to those purposes."

[52] Murray's biographer Donald Pelotte summarizes Murray's position and views. Cf. Pelotte, *Theologian in Conflict*, 83–84: The government's only interest in religion is to protect religious liberty; the character of the spiritual power is "absolutely spiritual" (124); and spiritual power "extends to nothing that is not necessarily related to Christ's redemptive work" (125). Note that Pelotte situates Murray's thought in relation to John Ireland and others of the so-called "Americanist" bishops of the nineteenth century, and in this connection consider as well the words of Ireland: "The limitations of jurisdiction in both Church and State are well defined, and, each one confining itself to its own sphere, no conflict can arise between them" (Pelotte, *Theologian in Conflict*, 143, quoted in John Ireland, "The Catholic Church and Civil Society," in *The Church and Modern Society*, 2nd ed. [New York: D. H. McBride & Co., 1897], 34–35). Thus, for Ireland, the two realms are so far separated from each other that conflict between them is impossible! Note also that Pietro Pavan, like Murray, sometimes reads DH as embracing the broader incompetence argument that appeared in the third schema of the declaration, which the two of them largely were responsible for drafting, even though this argument was reduced drastically in the final text. Cf. Pietro Pavan, "Introduction and Commentary on the Declaration on Religious

Murray does not expressly adopt Jefferson's "wall of separation" image, but, functionally, he comes close to doing so.[53] This theory lends itself to a type of *political Nestorianism*. Thus, as discussed above, Murray separates the two realms further than Gelasius and his successors have done. In particular, "Murray's thought clearly indicates the presence of two distinct orders of reality in contrast with the earlier theory of two functions within one society."[54] This identification of two "orders" is not unique to Murray, as the development of Gelasian dualism has resulted in several shifts in focus throughout history, including a movement from concentration on the two "powers" (the emperor and the pope) to one emphasizing two "orders" (the temporal and the religious). What is distinctive of Murray, though, is the sharpness and seemingly absolute character of his distinction between the two orders. With the fracturing of Christendom and the rise of the nation state, the "one society" paradigm has been lost (or at least is in a very extended eclipse). However, the popes preserve the Gelasian insight by insisting on unity between the realms, even while distinguishing them clearly.[55] Thus, where Murray insists on the modern state's absolute incompetence in religious matters,[56] the papal concept generally is less doctrinaire and more fluid.

Freedom," in *Commentary on the Documents of Vatican II*, vol. 4, ed. Herbert Vorgrimler (New York/London: Herder and Herder/Burns & Oates Limited, 1969), 69: "[B]y their very nature the religious acts transcend the order of terrestrial and temporal affairs, while the competence of governments is restricted to this sphere" (commentary on DH §3); Pavan, 80: Civil authority "must be respected and obeyed, when it is exercised legitimately within its own sphere, that is, in the sphere of earthly and temporal ends" (commentary on DH §11); larger work cited hereinafter as Vorgrimler. By contrast, a relation based on Christian dualism is characterized by "a fruitful functional relationship." Joseph Ratzinger, *Church, Ecumenism and Politics: New Essays in Ecclesiology* (New York: Crossroad, 1988), 162–63.

[53] This is particularly the case in his insistence of an absolute or nearly absolute state incompetence in religious matters.

[54] Pelotte, *Theologian in Conflict*, 125.

[55] Cf. ID, §§13–14; Pius XII, Discorso *Ai marchigiani residenti in Roma*. Pius says that a part of Church tradition is the continual effort to maintain the two powers as distinct, but united ("il continuo sforzo per tenere distinti, ma pure, sempre secondo I retti principi, uniti I due poteri") [AAS 50 (1958): 220].

[56] Cf. Murray, "Problem of Religious Freedom," 558: "Is it in any sense the function of government to authorize the public existence of any religion, true or false? The answer is no! . . . [T]he public power is not competent to confer such empowerments." See also the third draft of DH, on which Murray served as "first scribe"; *Textus Emendatus*, §4e: Competence of the civil power "is restricted to the earthly and temporal order" [AS III/8, 432; English translation by Brannan and Camacho in Schindler/Healy, 293].

(In the context of this debate over DH, David L. Schindler calls attention to the fascinating dispute that arose concerning the "Augustinian" and "Thomist" views of the Council,[57] So-called "transcendental Thomists," like Murray, insisted on a sharp distinction between the temporal and spiritual realms [and, in other contexts, between nature and grace]. The Augustinians [led by Henri de Lubac] countered that if the temporal world has its own proper end, then faith would appear to be merely optional, rather than central, to "real" life. On the other hand, the difficulty for Augustinians is that the temporal world might seem to lack solidity for them. In addition, their hopes for the temporal world's full embrace of the faith seems sure to be disappointed. From the discussion that follows, note that although Vatican II does not resolve this dispute, it, like the nineteenth-century and twentieth-century popes, avoids the pitfalls of both schools. That is, although taking a distinct temporal realm for granted, the Council always insists on a vibrant principle of unity between it and the spiritual realm. Note that it is not the case that the statements of the different popes merely "balance" each other out over time, but rather that the individual popes themselves [particularly Leo XIII, Pius XII, and John XXIII] embrace both principles. That is, they acknowledge the autonomy of the two spheres, but they also insist on unity between them.)

The two realms are indeed distinct, and each is autonomous and independent. However, the boundary between the two—although it is a true boundary—is not Jefferson's "high and impregnable"[58] wall but rather is more like *a semi-porous membrane*. Thus, although the state's finality is temporal, it nevertheless may not ignore man's ultimate supernatural end.

> [A]lthough its proximate end is to lead men to the prosperity found in this life, yet, in so doing, it ought not to diminish, but rather to increase, man's capability of attaining to the supreme good in which his everlasting happiness consists: which never can be attained if religion be disregarded. (LP, §21)[59]

---

[57] Cf. David L. Schindler, "Religious Freedom, Truth, and American Liberalism: Another Look at John Courtney Murray" *Communio* 21 (Winter 1994): 700n5. Schindler lists de Lubac, Ratzinger, and Balthasar as representatives of the Augustinian school, and Rahner, Congar, Murray, and others as representatives of the transcendental Thomists. He identifies the more conservative fathers as neo-Scholastics.

[58] *Everson*, 330 U.S. at 18 (Black, J.): "The First Amendment has erected a wall between church and state. That wall must be kept high and impregnable."

[59] See also Pope John XXIII, Encyclical *Pacem in Terris* (Apr. 11, 1963), §57: Civil authorities "should promote simultaneously both the material and the spiritual welfare of the

4.3. Gelasian Dualism

By the same token, although the religious power has a supernatural end, it is by no means unconcerned with the problems of this world.

> [T]he Church, whilst directly and immediately aiming at the salvation of souls and the beatitude which is to be attained in heaven, is yet, even in the order of temporal things, the fountain of blessings so numerous and great that they could not have been greater or more numerous had the original purpose of her institution been the pursuit of happiness during the life which is spent on earth. (LO, §4)

Indeed, the Council teaches that "a hope related to the end of time does not diminish the importance of intervening duties but rather undergirds the acquittal of them with fresh incentives."[60]

The superiority of the Gelasian approach is particularly important for mixed questions—such as marriage and education—that legitimately concern both realms. As a result of the fluidity of the Gelasian system, it is more able than the separationist theory to address these issues in a realistic and just way that takes account of the prerogatives of both powers.[61] It is only in light of this expectation of mutual cooperation between the realms that Pope Pius XII could both denounce the separation of civil authority from dependence on God,[62] and also acknowledge "a legitimate and healthy secularity of the State" (*la legittima sana laicità dello Stato*).[63]

It is not unusual for a commentator on *Dignitatis Humanae* to argue

---

citizens;" *Pacem in Terris*, §59: "[T]he common good is to be procured by such ways and means which not only are not detrimental to man's eternal salvation but which positively contribute to it" [AAS 55 (1963): 273] (hereinafter, PT).

[60] GS, §21c. See also GS, §39b: "[T]he expectation of a new earth must not weaken but rather stimulate our concern for cultivating this one. For here grows the body of a new human family, a body which even now is able to give some kind of foreshadowing of the new age."

[61] Cf. Richard J. Regan, *The American Constitution and Religion* (Washington, DC: Catholic University of America Press, 2013), 77–83: A critique of the U.S. Supreme Court's jurisprudence on the First Amendment's Establishment Clause and its application of a test for Establishment Clause cases derived from the Court's decision in *Lemon v. Kurtzman*, 403 U.S. 602 (1971).

[62] Pope Pius XII, Encyclical *Summi Pontificatus* (Oct. 20, 1939) [AAS 31 (1939): 550; English trans.]. Valuet notes that the document is incomplete in the AAS, that is, it is missing two pages. Cf. *La liberté religieuse et la tradition catholique. Un cas de développement doctrinal homogène dans le magistère authentique*, 3rd rev. ed. (Barroux: Éditions Sainte-Madeleine, 2011), vol. IIA, 1185n5312.

[63] Pope Pius XII, Discorso *Ai marchigiani residenti in Roma* [AAS 50 (1958): 220].

or assume that the declaration embraced Murray's strict separationism and rejected state establishment of religion.[64] As discussed above, however, one searches in vain for support of this interpretation within the four corners of the declaration itself. Indeed, the document's relator himself disclaimed an intention directly to engage the question of the juridical relationship between Church and state.[65]

Moreover, the mind of the Council becomes clearer when one reads DH in light of the Council's constitutions on the Church, both the dogmatic and the pastoral. The pastoral constitution, *Gaudium et Spes*, like *Dignitatis Humanae*, is a Vatican II document that traditionalists often criticize. However, it makes an important point in this context that should reassure traditionalists. That is, although the council fathers may have judged that we are living in a time where the Church's witness is enhanced by foregoing governmental privileges, the Council makes clear that these privileges themselves are legitimate.

> The Church ... does not place her trust in the privileges offered by civil authority. She will even give up the exercise of certain rights which have been legitimately acquired, if it becomes clear that their use will cast doubt on the sincerity of her witness or that new ways of life demand new methods. (GS, §76e)[66]

---

[64] Cf. David L. Schindler, "Freedom, Truth, and Human Dignity: An Interpretation of *Dignitatis Humanae* on the Right to Religious Freedom," in Schindler/Healy, 106: Murray put in place "[t]he current dominant juridical reading of the Declaration"; Schindler/Healy, 173n46: "Murray's juridical interpretation has largely been taken for granted as the proper hermeneutic for reading the Declaration." See also Gerard V. Bradley, preface to *Religious Freedom: Did Vatican II Contradict Traditional Catholic Doctrine? A Debate*, by Arnold T. Guminski and Brian W. Harrison (South Bend, IN: St. Augustine Press, 2013), 2: "[S]cholarly treatments of *DH* have read way too much of John Courtney Murray into that document" (larger work cited hereinafter as Guminski/Harrison). See also the discussion of Roland Minnerath in section 4.2 above. In a recent dissertation, Barrett Turner notes that the interpretation of DH as "hostile to any establishment of religion ... is thanks, in large part, to the post-conciliar commentary of Murray." Barrett Hamilton Turner, "*Dignitatis Humanae* and the Development of Moral Doctrine: Assessing Change in Catholic Social Teaching on Religious Liberty" (PhD diss., Catholic University of America, 2015), 304.

[65] Cf. De Smedt, Oral *Relatio* on the *Textus Emendatus* [AS III/8, 452]: "In our present declaration, we do not directly treat of the juridical relations between church and state" (English translation in Fesquet, 541).

[66] Hittinger makes this point in connection with state recognition of a particular religion: "Privileges are not required, but they are not absolutely forbidden by the Council." "Political Pluralism and Religious Liberty: The Teaching of *Dignitatis Humanae*," in *Universal Rights in a World of Diversity: The Case of Religious Freedom*, Proceedings of

Moreover, far from embracing an isolating separationism, *Gaudium et Spes* insists—every bit as much as Leo XIII did—on mutual cooperation between the spiritual and temporal realms.

> The Church and the political community in their own fields are autonomous and independent from each other. Yet both, under different titles, are devoted to the personal and social vocation of the same men. The more that both foster sounder cooperation between themselves . . . the more effective will their service be exercised for the good of all. For man's horizons are not limited only to the temporal order; while living in the context of human history, he preserves intact his eternal vocation. The Church, for her part, founded on the love of the Redeemer, contributes toward the reign of justice and charity within the borders of a nation and between nations. (GS, §76c)

In addition, taken together with the teaching of the dogmatic constitution *Lumen Gentium*, this teaching becomes even clearer and more forceful. That is, any attempt to isolate the Church from public life only can be regarded as an "ominous doctrine" (LG, §36d). Thus, it becomes clear that the Council rejects the stark isolation of the Church from public life as something harmful both to states and to persons.

4.4. The Drafting of *Dignitatis Humanae*

Let us return to the discussion of Murray's separationist views and the question of whether the Council adopted them. Although Murray read the declaration as embracing a theory very much like his own, the actual drafting history of the document tells a more complicated tale.

What that history shows is that although the Murray position in favor of strict Church-state separation and against the confessional state was one that the Council *initially* appeared ready to embrace, it later rejected that position. (This is not to say that Vatican II promoted the confessional state—it did not—but only that it did not repudiate it.) The religious liberty declaration went through more drafts than any other Council document,

---

the 17th Plenary Session, Pontifical Academy of Social Sciences, Acta 17, ed. Mary Ann Glendon and Hans F. Zacher (Vatican City: Pontifical Academy of Social Sciences, 2012), 52. Thus, state recognition of a particular religion is not necessarily incompatible with religious liberty, provided that the religious rights of all citizens and communities are respected (cf. "Political Pluralism and Religious Liberty, 52).

and a review of its drafting history helps to separate the influential views of Murray from the principles that the Council actually embraced.[67]

The second draft[68] of the Declaration on Religious Liberty—the *Declaratio Prior*, dated April 27, 1964—contained a passage denying the competence of the state in spiritual matters,[69] and the *relatio* or oral report of Bishop De Smedt described its meaning as follows: "For it is manifest ... that the State, precisely because of the juridical quality of its authority is not qualified to make judgments of truth in religious matters."[70]

(This argument from the second draft pertains not only to the issue of the confessional state but also to the crucial question of what the *foundation* of the right to religious liberty is. Throughout his writings on religious liberty, Murray had put forward several different rationales for the right of religious liberty, but his favorite one appears quite clearly to have been this one based on the state's *incompetence* in religious matters.[71] The specific

---

[67] The necessity of making this distinction is the subject of an important article by Harrison. Cf. Harrison, "Reliable Interpreter" (cited above in the previous section).

[68] The Declaration on Religious Liberty began as a part of the document on ecumenism. Thus, the first draft (Nov. 18, 1963) was chapter V ("De libertate religiosa") of the document *De Oecumenismo* (cf. AS II/5, 433–41). The first draft is not directly relevant to the question at issue here. The second draft is the first one in which religious liberty is contemplated as the subject of a distinct document.

[69] "Civil powers have no direct capacity or competence to determine or regulate the relationship between citizens and their Creator and Savior, and therefore cannot subordinate religious communities to the temporal ends of the state. The more that civil society provides favorable conditions for fostering religious life, however, the more it will enjoy those goods that come forth everywhere from men's fidelity to their divine vocation." *Declaratio Prior* (Apr. 27, 1964), §30 [AS III/2, p. 321; English translation by Patrick T. Brannan and Michael Camacho, in Schindler/Healy, 271].

[70] Émile De Smedt, Oral *Relatio* on the *Declaratio Prior* (Sept. 23, 1964) [AS III/2, 352–53; English translation by Harrison in RL&C, 65]. This *relatio* is cited in Valuet, LRTE, 390, and in Silvia Scatena, *La fatica della libertà. L'elaborazione della dichiarazione* Dignitatis humanae *sulla libertà religiosa del Vaticano II*, Istituto per le scienze religiose—Bologna, Testi e ricerche di scienze religiose, nuova serie, 31 (Bologna, Italy: Il Mulino, 2003), 173. Note, however, that both Harrison and Russell Hittinger identify—or appear to identify—this passage as having been contained in the *Declaratio Prior* itself, rather than in De Smedt's oral report on it (cf. Harrison, RL&C, 65; Hittinger, "*Dignitatis Humanae* on Establishment," 16).

[71] This is evident from Murray's famous *Theological Studies* article published during the Council. Part of that article argues for religious freedom on the basis of man's social nature (cf. Murray, "Problem of Religious Freedom," 525–27). However, he cites the incompetence of the state as an alternate argument and devotes most of his attention to it. Cf. Murray, 527–28: "The political-legal argument reaches and enforces the same conclusion"; Murray, 558: "Is it in any sense the function of government to authorize the public existence of any

question of the foundation for the right of religious liberty—including whether the incompetence of the state could furnish such a foundation—will be discussed at length below in chapter 9. For the time being, however, note the importance of the incompetence argument to Murray. As his biographer says, "It mattered little to Murray whether one spoke of the relation between Church and State or of religious liberty or of cooperation. All three represented various ways of speaking about the same issue."[72] For Murray, the state's incompetence in religious matters was both the basis of religious liberty and the basis of Church-state separation. The state has no authority in religious matters for Murray and, therefore, it may neither adopt a state religion nor compel or inhibit individual religious acts.)

Murray served as "first scribe" of the next draft, the third schema or the *Textus Emendatus* (dated November 17, 1964),[73] and, accordingly, it and the fourth schema (the *Textus Reemendatus*, dated May 28, 1965) contained strong assertions of state incompetence in religious matters. The third draft described the state's competence as "restricted to the earthly and temporal order," and it said that the public power acts beyond its authority if it assumes any role in the care of souls.[74] The fourth draft contained similar language, describing the civil power as "restricted in its purpose to the earthly and temporal order" and asserting that it exceeds its authority "if it involves itself in those matters that concern the very ordination of man to God."[75] In the final months of the Council, however, Pope St. Paul

---

religion, true or false? The answer is no! . . . [T]he public power is not competent to confer such empowerments." Similarly, he suggests in a related vein that tolerance or liberty cannot coexist with state establishment of religion. Cf. Murray, 566, describing establishment and intolerance as "twin institutions." See also Murray, 508, 564, 572.

[72] Pelotte, *Theologian in Conflict*, 16.

[73] Nicholas J. Healy, "The Drafting of *Dignitatis Humanae*," in Schindler/Healy, 220.

[74] "In performing these [religious] acts, therefore, man is not subject to the civil power, whose competence, on account of its end, is restricted to the earthly and temporal order. . . . The public power completely exceeds its limits if it involves itself in any way in the governing of minds or the care of souls" (*Textus Emendatus*, §4e [AS III/8, 432; English translation by Brannan and Camacho in Schindler/Healy, 293]). Note that the language "restricted to the earthly and temporal order" is absolute or nearly absolute for Murray, although it (or similar terminology) is not for the popes, particularly Leo XIII. On this point, see the quotations from Leo XIII, Pius XII, and St. John XXIII above in section 4.3.

[75] "[R]eligious acts, in which men and women privately and publicly order themselves toward God out of a sense of inner conviction, by their nature transcend the earthly and temporal order of things. The competence of the civil power, however, on account of its proper end—which today is more accurately perceived and described in terms of the demands of the dignity of the person and his rights—is restricted in its purpose to the earthly and temporal order. . . . The civil power must therefore be said to exceed its limits if it involves itself in

VI took a number of steps to address the concerns of the fathers who did not believe that these passages adequately acknowledged the earlier papal teaching on the state's duties in the religious field. His concern no doubt was motivated by the substance of these fathers' comments, but in addition, he was concerned with the high number of "no" votes (*non placet*) that the declaration was likely to receive. Most other Council documents had received—or would receive—only a handful of negative votes (as opposed to two thousand or more positive or *placet* votes), but an estimate for the final vote on the religious liberty declaration predicted as many as three hundred *non placet* votes.[76]

Accordingly, the fifth and sixth drafts (the *Textus Recognitus*, dated October 25, 1965, and the *Textus Denuo Recognitus*, dated November 19, 1965, respectively) significantly modified and limited the discussion of the state's incompetence in religious matters. The fifth draft *deleted* the sentence restricting the state's competence "to the earthly and temporal order."[77] In addition, the statement in the fourth draft excluding the civil authority's competence "in those matters that concern the very ordination of man to God" was revised and limited to read, "The civil power must therefore be said to exceed its limits if it either impedes or directs those matters that by their nature transcend the earthly and temporal order of things."[78] However, the revision process was not yet complete.

There were two different complaints about the remaining language in the fifth draft asserting state incompetence in religious matters. As is well known, the conservative International Group of Fathers (which included Archbishop Marcel Lefebvre) continued to object to the passage as insufficiently consistent with the teachings of previous popes on the duties of the state to religion. In addition, however, the Polish bishops objected for a different reason. They feared that some regimes, especially Communist

---

those matters that concern the very ordination of man to God" (*Textus Reemendatus*, §3 [AS IV/1, 150; English translation by Brannan and Camacho in Schindler/Healy, 323]).

[76] Cf. Scatena, *La fatica della libertà*, 553–54: Even after concessions to the minority, an estimate predicted that the declaration could receive between 150 and 300 *non placet* votes. Nine of the Council's sixteen documents would receive fewer than 10 *non placet* votes, while receiving over 2,100 *placet* votes. The document to receive the most *non placet* votes was *Inter Mirifica*, the Decree on the Means of Social Communications, which was approved by a vote of 1,960 to 164.

[77] Healy, "The Drafting of *Dignitatis Hum*anae," in Schindler/Healy, 229.

[78] Healy, "The Drafting of *Dignitatis Hum*anae," in Schindler/Healy, 230, citing *Textus Recognitus*, §3 [AS IV/5, 81; English translation by Brannan and Camacho in Schindler/Healy, 353].

4.4. The Drafting of *Dignitatis Humanae*

ones, would use this separationist language to exclude the Church from public life.[79]

After the third schema in November 1964—the draft of the declaration most influenced by Murray—the argument from the incompetence of the state diminished increasingly.[80] However, it did not disappear entirely. A faint remnant of the incompetence argument remains in article 3 of DH. That passage asserts that religious acts transcend temporal affairs. It does not demand Church-state separation or reject the confessional state, however, but rejects only state action that *commands* or *inhibits* religious acts.[81] Stated differently, the limiting principle contained in the final version of the declaration is not grounded in political theory but rather in the dignity of the person. *Dignitatis Humanae* does not say that state establishment of a religion is unjust. What it says is unjust is the state's coercion of religious belief, or its prohibition of religious practice without a sufficient reason. Said yet another way, the declaration retains a remnant of Murray's "incompetence" argument, but the object of the state's incompetence is not the establishment of a state religion but only the commanding or inhibiting of religious acts.[82]

A note about the incompetence argument is in order. The Council's reduction of the argument here is significant, but the key fact is the *context* of the rejection or reduction of this argument. Murray wished to found the right to religious liberty on the state's incompetence in religious matters, but the Council rejected this idea. It founded the right instead on the dignity of the human person (DH, §2a). To the extent that the incompetence argument survives at all in the declaration, it is merely as a "further consideration" (DH, §3e) and not as the foundation (or even an alternative foundation) for the right to religious liberty. The incompetence argument is legitimate in other contexts, and some authors describe Gelasian dualism in terms

---

[79] Cf. Scatena, *La fatica della libertà*, 547: Complaints regarding fifth draft or *Textus Recognitus*. See also Scatena, 539–40: Similar complaints regarding fourth draft or *Textus Reemendatus*.

[80] Regan, "American Bishops," 58, discussing various drafts of *Dignitatis Humanae*. For detailed discussions of the progression of the various drafts, see Valuet, LRTE, 389–95; Healy, "The Drafting of *Dignitatis Humanae*," in Schindler/Healy, 211–42.

[81] These and other crucially important revisions throughout the drafting of the declaration show that Kenneth Whitehead is most seriously mistaken when he asserts that "despite the fact that the schema went through so many different drafts[,] very little of substance was changed in the document in the course of the extensive discussions, speech-making, and parliamentary maneuvers which accompanied all these successive revisions." Kenneth D. Whitehead, "Summarizing the Controversy," *Catholic Dossier* 6, no. 2 (March–April 2000): 8–9.

[82] Cf. Valuet, LRTE, 393.

of mutual incompetence between the two spheres or two authorities.[83] (As described above in section 4.3, though, it is problematic to separate the spheres too completely or to fail to take account of mixed questions that legitimately concern both.)[84] However, serious problems arise when one attempts to base religious liberty on state incompetence in religious matters. Part 3B will discuss these difficulties. Thus, although this chapter and chapters 9 through 11 (in part 3B) offer a critique of the incompetence argument, the reader should keep the context uppermost in mind. That is, this critique is not a rejection of every attempt to delineate the competencies of the two spheres (or of the two powers historically, or of Church and state in our day), but rather it is an argument against a *specific application* of the incompetence idea, namely, the attempt to identify it as the foundation for religious liberty.

4.5. Special Civil Recognition

Let us resume the discussion begun in section 4.2 above on the relationship between confessionality and what the declaration calls "special civil recognition" of religion. The fifth draft of the declaration (the *Textus Recognitus*, dated October 25, 1965) introduced the possibility of a state granting civil recognition to a particular religion. This too was part of the set of changes aimed at conciliating the conservative fathers and reducing the number of *non placet* votes. Thus, article 6 of the final version of the declaration provides as follows:

---

[83] Cf. Martín de Agar, "Derecho y relaciones iglesia—sociedad civil," 52: While classical formulations of Christian dualism focused on the competencies of the powers, the contemporary formulation concerns incompetencies ("la Iglesia no es competente en asuntos políticos y el Estado no lo es en asuntos religiosos en cuanto tales [sí para reglamentar las manifestaciones de la religion en al ámbito civil: la libertad religiosa"]).

[84] These, too, are shortcomings of Murray's conception of state incompetence. His notion is a stark and seemingly absolute one. That is, his understanding is more Jeffersonian than truly Gelasian. Murray entirely separates the religious and temporal spheres from one another, and he takes little or no notice of the *mixed matters* that necessarily are the concern of both realms. (Note how the two drafts of the declaration over which he had charge restricted the civil power—seemingly absolutely—to the temporal order.) By contrast, the quotations from the popes in the preceding section (4.3) suggest a sound and realistic framework that recognizes a real distinction between the realms, but that avoids the pitfall of a hard and fast separation between them. (The Council too, in the final version of the declaration, would identify the temporal common good as the civil power's proper concern, but it would omit the characteristic Murray language restricting it absolutely to the earthly order [cf. DH, §3e].)

> If, in view of peculiar circumstances obtaining among peoples, special civil recognition is given to one religious community in the constitutional order of society, it is at the same time imperative that the right of all citizens and religious communities to religious freedom should be recognized and made effective in practice. (DH, §6c)

The question arises as to whether this passage amounts to a reaffirmation—admittedly muted—of the confessional state.

Murray distinguishes sharply between state and society, and he believes that religion is the proper concern of society but not of the state. That is, society may recognize a duty to the Church, but the state must not do so.[85] Does the Council embrace this understanding? Some commentators argue that DH definitively closes the book on the confessional state,[86] while others argue that it still permits states to acknowledge the Catholic religion as true.[87]

Those who assert that a state may *not* recognize the truth of Catholicism point to the phrase "peculiar circumstances," and argue that it refers only to the history and demographic makeup of a people. That is, this type of recognition approved by the Council amounts simply to the state taking notice of the religion of a great majority of its people. Murray himself makes this argument forcefully:

> It is therefore clearly the mind of the Council that the establishment of Catholicism as the religion of the state is no more than a matter of historical circumstances, and not a matter—or even a consequence—of doctrine. It is not thesis but hypothesis.[88]

Further, because the declaration mentions no scenario other than a people's "peculiar circumstances," they argue that this rationale is the exclusive

---

[85] Cf. Murray, "Problem of Religious Freedom," 520–21. See also Pelotte, *Theologian in Conflict*, 134, 138n22.

[86] Cf. Minnerath, "State and Church," 476; Murray, "Church and State at Vatican II," 587, 591; D'Avack, "La Chiesa e lo Stato nella nuova impostazione conciliare," 32: The state acts *ultra vires* if it presumes to judge which is the true religion.

[87] Ocáriz, "Sulla libertà religiosa," 93: Nothing in *Dignitatis Humanae* prevents the state from recognizing the true religion; Harrison, "Reliable Interpreter," 160. Gerard Bradley takes a similar position. Cf. Gerard V. Bradley, "Pope John Paul II and Religious Liberty," *Ave Maria Law Review* 6, no. 1 (2007): 41: The authorHe holds that *Dignitatis Humanae* is silent on whether state legitimately may acknowledge Catholicism as true.

[88] Murray, "Church and State at Vatican II," 595. See also Regan, "American Bishops," 61: DH §6 "made clear that state religions are the product of historical circumstance, not a matter of theological doctrine."

one permitting state recognition. As a result, the confessional state—in the sense of a state that formally recognizes Catholicism as true—is excluded.[89]

As mentioned above, others argue that nothing in the text of the declaration prohibits a state from recognizing a particular religion as true. That is, they object to Murray's relegation of state establishment of religion to the past by implying that only "historical" circumstances justify a state's recognition of a particular religion. Indeed, although an earlier draft of this passage (in the fifth schema or *Textus Recognitus*) had limited this type of recognition to the "historical circumstances" of the people, this phrase was replaced with the broader term "peculiar circumstances" in the final version of the declaration.[90] These commentators argue either that this broader term is sufficient to include recognition of a religion on the basis of its truth, or that the "peculiar circumstances" mentioned in article 6 do not exhaust all of the legitimate reasons that would justify a state's recognition of a religion. The reason that the document is silent about such other reasons is simply that it is addressing itself primarily to the situation most prevalent today, and in most current regimes, the constitution does not empower the governing authority to make such judgments of truth.

The drafting history of this provision in particular is highly complex, and it points to several different motivations behind this passage. Barrett Turner sheds light on the background of this provision.[91] The final text is very much a compromise among several positions. Some fathers considered it inopportune to treat the matter of state establishment of religion at all. Others wanted a clear statement that the civil power may recognize the true religion. Still others focused on contexts in which Catholicism was a minority religion. They noted that although Christian confessional states might recognize the rights of minorities, non-Christian confessional states often do not. As a result, these fathers were wary of an endorsement of religious establishment, not necessarily because they were opposed to the

---

[89] Cf. D'Avack, "La Chiesa e lo Stato nella nuova impostazione conciliare," 33, asserting that confessionality of a Catholic state cannot have the character of an act of faith but rather "constitutes a mere pragmatic-juridical disposition founded on the faith of the citizens."

[90] Harrison, "Reliable Interpreter," 157. Note that here, as elsewhere, Murray expounds the declaration as if this amendment never had occurred. See also Harrison, 157, in Murray's commentary on the declaration, contained in the version of the Vatican II documents edited by Walter Abbot (discussing articles 1 and 13 in particular): "[V]ital amendments ... are passed over in complete silence by Fr. Murray." See also subsections 9.3.4 and 10.4.1.1 below on Murray's post-conciliar commentary on DH §6. For the draft mentioning "historical circumstances" (that is, the fifth schema), see *Textus Recognitus*, §6 [AS IV/5, 84; English translation by Brannan and Camacho in Schindler/Healy, 357].

[91] Cf. Turner, "*Dignitatis Humanae* and the Development of Moral Doctrine," 303–7.

establishment of Catholicism but rather because they did not wish to see the Council grant a blanket approval of confessional states and thus seem to justify non-Christian confessional states in denying the religious liberty of Catholics and other minorities.[92] The commission found it impossible to avoid addressing the question because state recognition or establishment of religion remained prevalent in many places throughout the world. In a famous and influential intervention early in the fourth session of the Council, Bernard Cardinal Alfrink (of Utrecht) proposed framing the possibility of official recognition in the conditional mode.[93] The commission included the Alfrink proposal in the fifth draft (the *Textus Recognitus* of October 25, 1965), and it remained in the final text as well.[94] As already noted, the text includes not only the situation in which Catholicism is the religion that receives official recognition but also situations in which other religions receive that status.

Participants on both sides of the debate note that article 6 is not the only provision relevant to the question of the declaration's attitude toward the confessional state. The other key passage is article 1, which provides as follows: "Religious freedom . . . leaves untouched traditional Catholic doctrine on the moral duty of men and societies toward the true religion and toward the one Church of Christ" (DH, §1c). Again, commentators have different interpretations of this passage. Those who generally align with Murray's views emphasize the drafters' choice of the word "societies" rather than "the state" or "the public power." This appears to amount to an embrace of Murray's state-society distinction. That is, the duty toward the Church seems to run not necessarily from the governing power itself but rather from the society generally.

However, others point out that even if the text does not mention the state or the governing authority in this context, it does not exclude them either. If the debate were to cease there, it might seem that the Murray camp has the better of the argument and the more plausible reading of the declaration. However, Brian Harrison's study of the redaction history of article 1 places the question in another light entirely.

---

[92] Cf. Turner, "*Dignitatis Humanae* and the Development of Moral Doctrine," 305–6.

[93] Cf. Sept. 15, 1965, intervention of Bernard Cardinal Alfrink (AS IV/1, 218); partial English translation and summary in Fesquet, 593.

[94] Cf. Jérôme Hamer, "Histoire du texte de la Déclaration," *Unam Sanctam* 60 (1967): 97; Richard J. Regan, *Conflict and Consensus: Religious Freedom and the Second Vatican Council* (New York/London: Macmillan/Collier-Macmillan Ltd., 1967), 134–35, 160; Scatena, *La fatica della libertà*, 458n51.

THE PROPER RELATIONSHIP BETWEEN CHURCH AND STATE

* * *

Before proceeding to Harrison's study, however, a word is necessary about two distinctions that Harrison draws.[95] Up to this point, I have referred to Harrison's interpretation as finding religious liberty to be compatible with confessionality. This is indeed the case. The type of confessionality that I primarily have been discussing is what Valuet calls doctrinal confessionality, and it is characterized by the state's recognition of the religion in question as true. It is clear from Harrison's scholarship that he believes that the declaration raises no bar to this recognition.[96] Harrison, however, uses the phrase *confessional state* relatively infrequently, and his reason for this usage is instructive.

That is, he shows that the recognition of Catholicism as the religion of the state in a legal or constitutional text is something that neither Vatican II nor the nineteenth-century popes ever required.[97] Harrison is clear that the community does indeed have a duty to God and to the Church, but "written constitutions and law-codes are only one historically-conditioned form of recognition."[98] Thus, although it is not inaccurate to discuss Harrison and Valuet together in connection with the argument that the declaration is compatible with the confessional state, it is useful to keep in mind that although Valuet's frame of reference is a legal or constitutional text establishing a state religion, Harrison's frame is wider and includes a number of ways in which the community could fulfill its duty to God and to the Church.

Harrison's second distinction is even more significant. He believes that much of the disagreement and confusion at the Council resulted from the failure to address the ambiguity in the term *state*.[99] The Latin word usually translated into English as *state* is *civitas*, literally "the city." The word *state*, however, has multiple connotations, and it is not always clear which one is intended. In particular, Harrison identifies three main meanings: (1) a sovereign nation, such as Portugal; (2) a semi-autonomous region within a nation, such as Texas; or (3) the governing authority within a nation, together with its agencies. As a result of this ambiguity, Harrison usually avoids the term *state* and instead translates *civitas* as "civic community." Thus, rather than

---

[95] See generally Harrison, RL&C, 69–82. The distinctions discussed in this paragraph and the following paragraphs can be found in Harrison's articles as well, but are expounded most completely in RL&C.
[96] Cf. Harrison, RL&C, 69.
[97] Cf. Harrison, RL&C, 70.
[98] Harrison, RL&C, 70.
[99] See generally Harrison, RL&C, 76–79.

speaking of the confessional state, Harrison generally refers to Church teaching on *the civic community's duty to God and to the Church*.[100]

To an extent, then, Harrison accepts the argument of Murray and others that the *state* (understood as the governing authority) may be incompetent to establish a religion. That is, the sovereign in a constitutional republic is not the governing authority but rather the whole body of citizens, and it would be illegitimate for the governing authority to reserve such decisions to itself. In practice, however, the religiously pluralistic composition of the citizenry often may render it impossible or undesirable to establish a religion.[101]

Even if adoption of a state religion is not obligatory, however, Harrison makes clear that the community still has a duty to God and to the Church. Harrison keeps uppermost in mind the teachings of the nineteenth-century and twentieth-century popes on the social duties of the civic community to religion, and he frequently recalls Pope Pius XI's injunction on the obligation of the rulers of a people to honor God publicly.[102] He also points out a few modern examples of civic communities such as Colombia and the Philippines acting in fulfillment of this duty, notwithstanding the absence of any declaration establishing Catholicism as the religion of the state.[103]

In light of these distinctions, Harrison does not focus primarily on the legal establishment of religion but rather on the nineteenth-century popes' teachings on the duty of the civic community to God and the Church. In

---

[100] Valuet agrees with Harrison and accordingly translates *civitas* as *city*, *civil society*, or *state-society*. Cf. LRTC, vol. IA, 345n1467, noting disagreement with Davies, who translates *civitas* as *state*; LRTE, 243n1269 (same).

[101] Cf. Harrison, RL&C, 78. Another relevant shift from the early modern period to the present day concerns the identity of the sovereign and of the public power. The *sovereign* in most cases no longer is a monarch who rules personally in the fullest sense, but as Harrison says, it is the whole body of the people. By the same token, the *public power* generally no longer is a monarch but rather is a body (or a number of structured bodies) of office-holders who rule according to law. Thus, although some contemporary nations do indeed have official or established religions, the literal notion of a confessional state—in the sense of one where the public power actually "confesses" a particular religion on behalf of the people—is rather distant from the contemporary context of the juridical state or constitutional government. Cf. Martín de Agar, "Derecho y relaciones iglesia—sociedad civil," 41, 51. See also José T. Martín de Agar, "Ecclesia y Polis," *Ius Canonicum* (2008): 403, 405.

[102] Cf. Harrison, "Reliable Interpreter," 141, quoting Pope Pius XI, Encyclical *Quas Primas* (December 11, 1925), §32: "[N]ot only private individuals but also rulers and princes are bound to give public honour and obedience to Christ . . . for His kingly dignity demands that the State should take account of the commandments of God and of Christian principles."

[103] Cf. Harrison, RL&C, 79–82.

addition, he is, of course, vitally concerned with the question of whether this teaching survives Vatican II.

I now proceed to consider the redaction history of article 1 in the declaration.

4.6. The Last-Minute Change to *Dignitatis Humanae*

Most important to the issue of the confessional state is a crucial amendment to article 1 of the declaration. At virtually the last minute before the final vote on the document, the first article of *Dignitatis Humanae* was amended in a significant way. This change concerns a passage relating to the state's religious duties.

The fifth schema, the *Textus Recognitus* (October 25, 1965), had recognized the "moral duty individuals have toward the Church."[104] The oral *relatio* of Bishop De Smedt acknowledged having received the mission on September 21, 1965, to "show in a more explicit fashion that RL [religious liberty] does not absolve (*exonère*) men and societies from the moral duty that binds them to the Catholic religion."[105] De Smedt met with Paul VI a few days later, and that meeting was in the same vein:

> Bishop Émile De Smedt provides an important note from an audience with Paul VI a few days later, on September 30, 1965, summarizing the pope's instructions to the committee charged with revising schema 4: "to emphasize the obligation of seeking the truth; to present the traditional teaching of the ecclesiastical magisterium; to avoid basing religious freedom solely on freedom of conscience; *to state the doctrine in such a way that the lay state would not think itself dispensed from its obligations to the Church*;

---

[104] *Textus Recognitus*, §1: "[R]eligious freedom . . . leaves intact the Catholic teaching on the one true religion, the one Church of Christ, and the moral duty individuals have toward the Church" (AS IV/5, 78; English translation by Brannan and Camacho in Schindler/Healy, 351).

[105] Valuet, LRTE, 393. The English translation is mine. De Smedt's account is found in AS IV/5, 77. Valuet reproduces it in LRTC, vol. IIB, 1529. This reference to the moral duties of *societies* did not appear in the fifth draft (*Textus Recognitus*) itself or in De Smedt's written report on that draft, but rather it appeared for the first time in De Smedt's fifth oral report, that is, his *relatio* on the fifth draft or *Textus Recognitus* (cf. LRTE, 393). This duty then was included in the sixth and final draft of the declaration, the *Textus Denuo Recognitus*.

to specify the authority of the declaration (doctrinal, dogmatic, juridical, or practical?)."[106]

Although this fifth draft recognized the duty of *individuals* to the Church, Paul VI requested further accommodations to the minority.[107] As a result, the sixth (and final) schema, the *Textus Denuo Recognitus* (November 19, 1965), was strengthened from the standpoint of the minority. That is, it specified that it was affirming "traditional" Catholic doctrine and that the moral duty to the Church falls not only to individuals but also to "societies." In consequence of these last-minute revisions, the final text (with changes indicated in italics) states that the right to religious liberty "leaves intact the *traditional* Catholic teaching on the moral duties individuals *and societies* have toward the true religion and the one Church of Christ."[108]

As mentioned in the previous section, however, this language still arguably lends itself to the interpretation that it embraced Murray's state-society distinction, that is, the idea that society has a duty to the Church, but that the state does not—indeed that the state *must* not—recognize the truth of Catholicism.

Despite the ambiguity of this passage, however, Harrison notes that an official interpretation of the passage makes clear that the Council does not adopt this stark dichotomy between state and society. On the contrary, in his final *relatio* on the declaration, De Smedt says that the Council's reference to the duty of "societies" to the Church does not exclude the public power but rather includes it. He says outright that the purpose of this final change to DH §1 is to recall this duty on the part of the public power (*potestas publica*):

> The text that is presented to you today recalls more clearly (see nos. 1 and 3) the duties of the public authority towards the true religion (*officia potestatis publicae erga veram religionem*); from which it is manifest that this part of the doctrine has not been overlooked (*ex quo patet hanc doctrinae partem non praetermitti*).[109]

---

[106] Schindler, "Freedom, Truth, and Human Dignity," in Schindler/Healy, 168n34, citing Alberigo, vol. 5, 111n239 (emphasis added).

[107] Cf. Scatena, *La fatica della libertà*, 552.

[108] This new English translation of DH §1 is by Brannan and Camacho in Schindler/Healy, 385. The English translation on the Vatican website reads: "Therefore it leaves untouched traditional Catholic doctrine on the moral duty of men and societies toward the true religion and toward the one Church of Christ." DH, §1, The Holy See, Dec. 7, 1965, https://www.vatican.va/archive/hist_councils/ii_vatican_council/documents/vat-ii_decl_19651207_dignitatis-humanae_en.html.

[109] Émile De Smedt, Oral *Relatio* on the *Textus Denuo Recognitus* (Nov. 19, 1965) [AS IV/6,

Again, however, what is the relation between the final version of DH §1 and the Catholic state? De Smedt's *relatio* makes clear that the Council "leaves untouched" the traditional teaching on the moral duty of societies (including the public power) to the Church. However, why is this acknowledgment so muted?

De Smedt provides the answer. The reason is that while leaving the previous teaching on society's duty to the Church untouched, "the special object of our Declaration is to clarify the second part of the doctrine of recent Supreme Pontiffs—that dealing with the rights and duties which emerge from a consideration of the dignity of the human person."[110]

Harrison's scholarship on De Smedt's final *relatio* became possible only after the Acts of the Council (*Acta Synodalia*) became available in the 1970s. Even earlier, however, an influential commentator on the declaration had put forward a similar reading of the phrase "and societies" (*ac societatem*). Jérôme Hamer was the only person who worked actively on the document throughout all of its various stages,[111] and in his well-regarded 1967 article on the elaboration of the text, he comments on the language of article 1 on the moral duty to the Church. This duty, he says, concerns not only individuals but all social groups as well, from small and spontaneous associations all the way up to nations and states.[112]

Thus, once more, it is vitally important to attend to what *Dignitatis Humanae* does *not* say. Indeed, when it comes to the question of the confessional state, there is a great deal that the declaration does not say. It neither

---

719; English translation by Harrison, RL&C, 75]. See also Harrison, "Reliable Interpreter," 155–58. Harrison was the first to note the significance of De Smedt's final *relatio* in this context. He also noted that the position quoted above represented a reversal of De Smedt's previous position (cf. Harrison, RL&C, 75). In addition, he has drawn attention to the fact that De Smedt's final *relatio* is the *sole official interpretation* of article 1 (cf. Harrison, "Reliable Interpreter," 157). Valuet acknowledges—as all commentators on DH should—the significance of Harrison's use of the final *relatio* to interpret DH §1 (cf. Valuet, LRTE, 394n2149).

[110] De Smedt, Oral *Relatio* on the *Textus Denuo Recognitus* (AS IV/6, 719; English translation by Harrison, RL&C, 75).

[111] Cf. Valuet, LRTC, vol. IIIA, 2016n8980.

[112] "En outre, la déclaration souligne que ce 'devoir' (*officium*) n'affecte pas seulement les individus mais les collectivitiés, c'est-à-dire les hommes agissant en commun. Il s'agit ici de tous les groupes sociaux depuis les plus modestes et les plus spontanés jusqu'aux nations et aux États, en passant par tous les intermédiaires: syndicats, associations culturelles, universités.... L'idée du schéma est simplement d'éliminer une sort d'interprétation purement individualiste de ce devoir primordial" (Hamer, "Histoire du texte de la Déclaration," 99–100). See also Jérôme Hamer, *La libertà religiosa nel Vaticano II*, 2nd ed. (Torino, Italy: Elle Di Ci, 1967), 145 (similar).

forecloses the confessional state nor calls for its return. Its relationship with previous papal teaching on the duty of states and societies to the Church is simply to leave that doctrine "untouched."

The text contains neither the rejection of the confessional state sought by the progressive Catholic nor the point-by-point recapitulation of the nineteenth-century teaching desired by the traditionalist Catholic. If many readers find the declaration unsettling because it did not treat this issue comprehensively, this is understandable. However, the argument that *Dignitatis Humanae* reversed previous Church teaching on this question is untenable. That is, although the prudential question remains open, the doctrinal question has been resolved.[113]

4.7. Does the Declaration Foreclose the Re-emergence of the Confessional State?

If a confessional state should arise in the future, what would be its status under *Dignitatis Humanae*?

Again, I refer to *confessionality* in the broad sense in which Valuet uses the term, without usually distinguishing between it and *establishment* or *civil recognition* of religion. I adopt this usage for two reasons, first, because Valuet helpfully identifies various types and subtypes of confessionality and he does so without distinguishing this concept from establishment,[114] and second, because this chapter is in large measure a response to an important question raised by Murray, who generally seems to treat the terms as rough equivalents.[115]

---

[113] For further observations on the late amendments to articles 1 and 6, see subsections 9.3.4 and 10.4.1–2 below.

[114] See section 4.2 above (citing Valuet, LRTE, 383–84). Note, however, that a 2002 Doctrinal Note included several negative references to "confessionalism" and seemed to identify the idea with intolerance. Cf. Congregation for the Doctrine of the Faith, "Note on Some Questions Concerning the Participation of Catholics in Political Life" (Nov. 24, 2002), §§5–6 (emphasis added) [AAS 96 (2004): 365–67]. Valuet interprets these references as applying only to a certain type of confessionalism that confuses the religious and the temporal orders or that would attempt to compel adherence to a particular faith (LRTE, 403).

[115] Murray does seem to be aware, however, of the question that Martín de Agar will raise, namely, whether the impersonal governing structures of contemporary constitutional states are capable of confessing a religion in the sense that Christian monarchs once did on behalf of their subjects (see section 4.5 above, citing commentaries by Martín de Agar). Cf. John Courtney Murray, "Vers une intelligence du développement de la doctrine de l'Église sur la liberté religieuse," *Unam Sanctam* 60 (1967): 128: Leo was influenced by the historic notion of personal political power exercised in a paternalistic fashion. The likely reason

Murray is correct that confessional states sometimes violated the religious rights of their citizens or subjects, but is he correct in assuming a necessary connection between confessionality and the violation of religious rights? (See introduction of this chapter, preceding section 4.1.) The history is more varied and complicated than Murray acknowledges. That is, it discloses as many periods of toleration as persecution.[116] In any event, the declaration never makes the same inexorable connection between establishment and persecution that Murray insists upon so ardently. *Dignitatis Humanae* hardly addresses the question of the confessional state, and it contains no repudiation of such regimes. Indeed, the drafting commission as a whole did not consider establishment to be irreconcilable with religious liberty.[117]

However, this is not to say that *Dignitatis Humanae* has nothing to say to the hypothetical confessional state that might arise in the future. On the contrary, its clear implication is that where such states still exist, or if they should arise again in the future, there would be some important limitations on the concrete ways that the state could manifest its official religion.[118] Thus,

---

for Murray not focusing on a distinction between confessionality and establishment is the near-absolute nature of his separationism. That is, his first preference quite clearly is to reject any confessionality or establishment (regardless of any possible difference between them), although he will reconcile himself to civil recognition based on exclusively historical factors (see [sub]sections 4.5 above and 9.6, 9.3.4, and 10.4.1.1 below).

[116] Cf. A. Vermeersch, *Tolerance*, trans. W. Humphrey Page (New York: Benziger Brothers, 1912), 104–5: "In regard to its practice, tolerance of opinions and creeds may be combined with the recognition of a state religion, with favors reserved to the true religion, or to religion in general"; Vermeersch, 105: "The most liberal tolerance does not require official indifference in religious matters." See also Vermeersch, 212; Gerard V. Bradley, "John Courtney Murray and the Privatization of American Religion," in Donald J. D'Elia and Stephen M. Krason, eds., *We Hold These Truths and More* (Steubenville, OH: Franciscan University Press, 1993), 127: Establishment of a state religion or government aid to one religious body does not necessarily coerce members of other bodies.

[117] "The *relationes* indicate that the drafting commission as a whole and over the entire drafting process saw establishment or endorsement as compatible with religious liberty, provided that all citizens and communities enjoy true religious liberty" (Turner, "*Dignitatis Humanae* and the Development of Moral Doctrine," 305). See also Turner, 307: "As for the theoretical question of whether religious liberty is compatible with establishment or endorsement, the drafting commission was unequivocal." Note that section 4.4 above quoted De Smedt's second oral *relatio* to the effect that the state may not make judgments of truth in religion. However, what this passage from the *relatio* rejected—at this juncture in the drafting process (long before the last-minute additions to article 1)—was what Valuet calls *formal* confessionality of the *doctrinal* type. It did not necessarily reject other varieties, such as *substantial* confessionality or *formal* confessionality of the *historico-sociological* type. (See section 4.2 above, discussing Valuet's typology of confessional states.)

[118] Cf. Vermeersch, *Tolerance*, 256.

the declaration raises no barrier to the return of the confessional state,[119] but it does lay down a key condition: a confessional state, like all others, would be obliged to recognize the religious rights of all citizens and religious communities (DH, §6c). In addition, the government would need to ensure the equality of all citizens (DH, §6d) and to prevent discrimination among citizens on the basis of religion (DH, §6e).

That is, the state's recognition of an official religion would need to stop short of coercing non-majority religionists to practice the official religion (or prohibiting them from practicing their own religion, except in limited circumstances discussed in chapters 10 and 11 below). In the nineteenth century and earlier, confessional states (including the Papal States) sometimes made Church attendance compulsory. *Dignitatis Humanae* would seem to allow a state to manifest its official religion in a number of ways, but not in such a way as would coerce belief or practice or that would deny religious liberty to other citizens and religious communities.

Martin Rhonheimer seems to agree with Murray that confessional states are incompatible with the declaration.

> It seems clear to me that a confessional state, in the traditional sense of the term, would be essentially incompatible with the doctrine of Vatican II and in general with the civil right to freedom of religion, since, necessarily, civil discrimination would be inevitable in a confessional state, especially in the public sphere.[120]

---

[119] Interestingly, *Gaudium et Spes* arguably is slightly warmer toward the confessional state than *Dignitatis Humanae* is. See section 4.3 above. Although the council fathers teach that the Church "does not place her trust in the privileges offered by civil authority," they give no indication that such privileges are beyond the state's competence. In fact, the same passage even says that the Church's rights "have been legitimately acquired" (cf. GS, §76e). Note that Vatican II does not absolutely renounce these privileges but rather says that the Church will give them up *if* they cast doubt on her sincerity or if new circumstances call for renouncing them. Still, both *Gaudium et Spes* and *Dignitatis Humanae* are relatively cool toward—or disinterested in—the confessional state, and the reasons seems to be that the council fathers prefer instead to focus on the regimes actually existing in the world today.

[120] Martin Rhonheimer, "Benedict XVI's 'Hermeneutic of Reform' and Religious Freedom," *Nova et Vetera* (English ed.) 9, no. 4 (2011): 1047–48n11. Rhonheimer also contends that Pope Benedict XVI's 2005 Christmas message to the Roman Curia takes a position against religious establishment (cf. Rhonheimer, 1031). The passage from Benedict that Rhonheimer cites perhaps is open to this interpretation. "The ancient Church naturally prayed for the emperors and political leaders out of duty (cf. 1 Tm 2:2); but while she prayed for the emperors, she refused to worship them and thereby clearly rejected the religion of the State." However, David L. Schindler offers a more plausible reading of the passage, namely, that what the Church rejected was not all state religion but the *Roman* religion

Evaluation of this claim depends, however, on what Rhonheimer means by "the traditional sense of the term." The declaration is by no means incompatible with discrimination in the sense of a distinction among religions. The very idea of "special civil recognition" (even as understood by Murray) necessarily entails a recognition of one particular religion and non-recognition of all others. In this sense, Vatican II does not exclude the confessional state "in the traditional sense." That is, it does not raise a barrier, for example, to the granting of a special role to the official religion at state ceremonies. However, the declaration is indeed incompatible with discrimination in the sense of coercing religious acts by non-majority religionists or interfering with their public religious activity (unless it threatens the just public order). It also is incompatible with discrimination among citizens on the basis of religion. If one understands "the traditional sense" of the confessional state to include compulsory religious attendance or the prohibition of public worship by members of non-majority religions, then the declaration is indeed incompatible with this understanding.[121]

The Council says that it intends to address the modern constitutional state. Another term for *constitutional government* is *government limited in its powers*. In a sense, the declaration is saying that *all governments* are limited in their powers. That is, the legitimate action of all governments is limited.[122] However, the principle of limitation is not the type of strict separationism that Murray championed. Rather, the principle of limitation is the human person and his or her natural rights.[123] Thus, although the Council may be agnostic on the confessional state, it is by no means agnostic on the rights

---

in particular. The reason is that it refused to recognize the transcendence of the God that the Christians worshipped and that by identifying the state with Roman religion in this way, it refused to recognize the freedom of others to fulfill their duty to the transcendent God (Schindler, "Freedom, Truth, and Human Dignity," in Schindler/Healy, 110).

[121] On the compatibility of religious liberty and confessionality, see section 9.4 below, particularly on the interventions of Heenan and Wright in the Council debates.

[122] Indeed, one can read both Gelasius's fifth-century teaching on the two powers and Pius XI's twentieth-century teaching on subsidiarity from the same perspective, namely, as limitations on governmental action. Cf. Pope Pius XI, Encyclical *Quadragesimo Anno* (May 15, 1931), §§79–80: "Just as it is gravely wrong to take from individuals what they can accomplish by their own initiative and industry and give it to the community, so also it is an injustice and at the same time a grave evil and disturbance of right order to assign to a greater and higher association what lesser and subordinate organizations can do.... The supreme authority of the State ought, therefore, to let subordinate groups handle matters and concerns of lesser importance, which would otherwise dissipate its efforts greatly. Thereby the State will more freely, powerfully, and effectively do all those things that belong to it alone because it alone can do them" (AAS 23 [1931]: 203).

[123] "Comme l'homme est antérieur à l'État,' les compétences de l'État sont limitées par certains

of the person. If a confessional state should arise, it would be difficult to cite any provision of *Dignitatis Humanae* as either a clear endorsement or a clear rejection. What is clear, though, is that the declaration would require that confessional state to refrain from coercing the religious practice of any citizen and to refrain from discriminating among citizens on the basis of religion.[124]

4.8. Murray's Disappointment and Davies's Acknowledgement

Ardent "progressives" are no more likely than ardent "traditionalists" to be completely satisfied with the declaration. The main thrust of the document may appear to be progressive in the sense that it recognizes the religious liberty of all persons. However, the final amendments to article 1 were an important concession to the conservative fathers' critique that the earlier drafts were insufficiently continuous with older papal teachings. Consequently, although few Catholics are entirely content with *Dignitatis Humanae*, it is at least clear that the document did not overturn traditional papal teaching on the relationship between Church and state. The declaration may not have reaffirmed each point of previous papal teaching on this issue, but it certainly did not contradict that teaching. Indeed, it said outright that it was leaving this doctrine intact. Traditionalists should attend to the reaction of two men in particular to *Dignitatis Humanae*, one a fellow traditionalist and the other a theological opponent.

Until his death in 2004, Michael Davies was perhaps the leading lay promoter of the traditional Latin Mass. Indeed, he served for twelve years as President of the International Federation "Una Voce," the largest organization dedicated to promoting this cause. Davies wrote a book criticizing *Dignitatis Humanae*, and he engaged in a debate with Brian Harrison over the orthodoxy of the document. Davies always remained critical of the declaration, but he eventually seemed to come to acknowledge that Harrison's argument in favor of its orthodoxy was correct. Davies believed that the amendments to article 1 were contrary to the predominant spirit of the

---

droits naturels de l'individu et de la famille, non seulement à la propriété, mais à la libertté" (Valuet, LRTE, 283, quoting Pope Leo XIII, Encyclical *Rerum Novarum* (May 15, 1891).

[124] This is a significant modification of the nineteenth-century theory of the confessional state, but as far as the life of the citizens is concerned, the change is less dramatic. The reason is that the nineteenth-century popes recognized that a Catholic state legitimately could allow public non-Catholic worship in appropriate circumstances, and in fact, many did so.

declaration, but, at the end of the day, he essentially conceded that Harrison was correct about their doctrinal significance and that they do indeed safeguard the orthodoxy of *Dignitatis Humanae* on this point.[125]

The reaction of John Courtney Murray to the final text is even more significant. As an apparent result of the decision of the council fathers not to reject the confessional state, Murray judged that "the final text of the Declaration is inadequate in its treatment of the limitations imposed on government by sound political doctrine."[126]

By the same token, Murray supporters and like-minded commentators complained bitterly about the late additions to the final text of the declaration that Paul VI ordered in response to objections from the conservative fathers. Murray's biographer Donald Pelotte criticizes the revisions in the final month as "a number of altogether unnecessary phrases" that "weakened the Declaration and left it somewhat ambiguous."[127] This remark would seem to refer to the modifier "traditional" to describe the previous teaching that the declaration leaves "untouched," as well as to the clarification that the moral duty toward the Church falls not only to individuals but also to "societies." Similarly, Silvia Scatena, a representative of the progressive Bologna School, laments the "compromises" in the final redaction of the declaration.[128]

Murray's disappointment with the document is as significant as Davies's grudging acceptance of its orthodoxy. Just as traditionalists should be

---

[125] "Harrison is correct . . . that the finalized Article 1 is of considerable doctrinal significance" (Davies, SVC&RL, 173). At the same time, Davies maintains with Henri Fesquet that reading this phrase strictly "would be artificial since the spirit of the schema as a whole is far different" (Davies, SVC&RL, 173, quoting Fesquet). Davies interprets this phrase as contrary to the predominant spirit of the document as a whole (which he does not approve), but he appears to acknowledge that it does at least safeguard the declaration's orthodoxy. "I pointed out on several occasions in *Pope John's Council* how the insertion of some evidently orthodox terminology into conciliar documents with a definite Liberal bias, usually upon the insistence of Pope Paul VI himself, had a double-edged effect in that while, to a greater or lesser extent, this helped to safeguard orthodoxy, it also served to neutralize conservative opposition to basically Liberal documents" (Davies, SVC&RL, 174).

[126] Murray, "Church and State at Vatican II," 587. This seems to be in tension with his annotations to the declaration, which were published the same year (cf. Abbott, 693n52, introduction and annotations to *Dignitatis Humanae* by Murray.

[127] Pelotte, *Theologian in Conflict*, 99. See also Mathijs Lamberigts, "Msgr. Emiel-Jozef De Smedt, Bishop of Bruges, and the Second Vatican Council," in *Experience, Organisations and Bodies at Vatican II: Proceedings of the Bologna Conference, December 1996*, ed. M. T. Fattori & A. Melloni (Leuven, Belgium: Bibliotheek van de Faculteit Godgeleerdheid, 1999), 465 (adopting Pelotte's position).

[128] Scatena, *La fatica della libertà*, 581.

comforted by Davies's acceptance, so also should they be encouraged that the leading proponent of the strictly separationist reading of the declaration was dissatisfied with the finished document. That is, the withholding of a repudiation of the confessional state should be as much of a relief to traditionalists as it was a frustration to Murray.[129]

4.9. Murray, Paul VI, and the "Nothing but Freedom" Argument

In arguing that *Dignitatis Humanae* supports his separationist preference, Murray strongly emphasizes a passage of the declaration that, taken in isolation, appears to provide some support to his position that the document requires nothing but freedom for the Church. It is article 13 of *Dignitatis Humanae*, which states, "The freedom of the Church is the fundamental principle in what concerns the relations between the Church and governments and the whole civil order." The freedom of the Church (*libertas Ecclesiae*) is an important principle. Pope Leo XIII championed it, and Vatican II placed it at the center of its teaching on religious liberty. Murray, however, would make it not only the *center* of the Church's teaching on her relation to the state but, in some of his writings at least, practically the *totality* of that teaching. Indeed, Murray even read Leo XIII this way.[130]

The above examination of the text of *Dignitatis Humanae* reveals that Murray's equating of the Council's teaching with his own position is more a matter of wishful thinking as to what the declaration *might* have said (or nostalgia for the third and fourth drafts that had reflected more of his own thought) rather than an accurate description of what the final version of the document actually *did* say. The same may be true of Murray's "nothing but freedom" argument as well, but this point presents an additional difficulty. The reason is that it was not only Murray who characterized the declaration in this way but—at least apparently—Pope Paul VI as well.

At the close of Vatican II, Paul VI issued an address to political leaders

---

[129] Needless to say, others besides traditionalists and progressives are interested in the question of the continuity of DH with earlier teaching. However, the concerns of traditionalists have great practical importance because DH presents the major obstacle to their regularization within the Church.

[130] Cf. Murray, "Problem of Religious Freedom," 541: "His central notion was 'the freedom of the Church'"; cf. Murray, 541–43, 568: Leo XIII "began . . . to restore the traditional centrality of the Church's ancient claim to freedom in the face of the public power"; John Courtney Murray, "The Declaration on Religious Freedom," *Concilium* 5, no. 2 (May 1966): 6: Leo's "essential claim" was the freedom of the Church.

(*Aux gouvernants*) that Achille Cardinal Liénart delivered.[131] The address says, "What does the Church ask of you today? She tells you in one of the major documents of this council. She asks of you only liberty."[132] Murray emphasized this speech in support of his interpretation of article 13, though the translation he used was slightly different: "[S]he asks of you nothing but freedom."[133]

In fact, Paul made similar statements on at least three other occasions. Interestingly, one of those occasions was almost two years *before* the declaration was promulgated. It was Paul's famous 1964 speech in Bethlehem, which occurred at a time when the drafting of the declaration was in its early stages. That speech contained the following precursor to his "nothing but freedom" position in *Aux gouvernants*:

> Our only concern is to proclaim our faith. *We ask nothing more than freedom* to profess and propose, to whomever wishes, in complete freedom, to embrace this religion, this bond instituted between human beings and God through Jesus Christ, our Lord.[134]

Paul's Bethlehem speech no doubt is emblematic of his policy, but it cannot be an interpretation of *Dignitatis Humanae*. Paul made this speech only a few months after the first draft of the declaration had appeared, and that draft (unlike the final version of nearly two years later) did not refer to the *libertas Ecclesiae*, the precise point to which Murray seeks to link it. This fact itself provides a first indication that Murray's attempt to connect the "nothing but freedom" notion to the *libertas Ecclesiae* deserves scrutiny.

The speech cited by Murray (*Aux gouvernants*) is from the close of the Council in December 1965, and Paul will reprise his "nothing but freedom" theme only weeks later in his Christmas radio message. "The Church comes to you without pride, without expecting any privileges for itself.... It has no ambitions of domination or wealth, *if anything it asks you for freedom*

---

[131] Cf. Hittinger, "*Dignitatis Humanae* on Establishment," 18–19.

[132] Pope Paul VI, Address to Rulers at the Close of the Second Vatican Council *Aux Gouvernants* (Dec. 8, 1965) [AAS 58 (1966): 10].

[133] Cf. Abbott, 693n52 (annotations to DH by Murray).

[134] Pope Paul VI, Address from Bethlehem (Jan. 6, 1964) [AAS 56 (1964): 176–77; English translation by Luigi Mistò, "Paul VI and *Dignitatis Humanae*: Theory and Practice," in John T. Ford, ed., *Religious Liberty: Paul VI and Dignitatis Humanae* (Brescia, Italy: Istituto Paulo VI, 1995), 32 (emphasis added). The passage in the original French is as follows: "Nous n'avons pas d'autre intérêt que celui d'annoncer notre foi. Nous ne demandons rien, sinon la liberté de professer et de proposer à qui veut bien, en toute liberté, l'accueillir, cette religion, ce lien nouveau instauré entre les hommes et Dieu par Jésus-Christ, notre Seigneur."

for its inner faith and freedom for its outer proclamation."[135] This speech is discussed more fully below.

Russell Hittinger argues that it is vitally important to place the "nothing but freedom" statement in *Aux gouvernants* in the entire context of that speech to world leaders at the Council's end. That is, although Paul may have made a hasty (and perhaps unfortunate) characterization of the declaration (and, one could add, may himself have been influenced by Murray's thought), the Pope also issued the following exhortation to world leaders in the same speech: "Allow Christ to exercise his purifying action on society. Do not crucify Him anew." This quotation shows that it is necessary for the Church not simply to be left alone by secular governments but also to permeate society. Thus, Hittinger argues, it is an incomplete reading of Paul's speech to interpret it merely as a plea for external freedom.[136]

Moreover, a number of other provisions of *Dignitatis Humanae* and other Council documents cut against the "nothing but freedom" interpretation of article 13. For example, the passage cited above by Hittinger finds echo in another conciliar pronouncement, namely the Decree on the Apostolate of the Laity *Apostolicam Actuositatem*. That document speaks of the lay apostolate infusing the Christian spirit not only into the mentality and behavior of society but even into its laws and structures.[137] As with Paul's closing speech, this conciliar provision likewise claims (at least implicitly) something more than freedom, namely, the need for civil society to open itself to permeation by the spirit of the Gospel.

By the same token, *Gaudium et Spes*, in its passage on the relationship between the Church and civil society, not only claims freedom for the Church but also asserts—or at least implies—that the Church should be acknowledged as a moral judge (cf. GS, §76b). Moreover, *Dignitatis Humanae* itself claims more for the Church than bare freedom. It declares that the state must take account of the religious life of its citizens and even

---

[135] Pope Paul VI, Christmas Radio Message (Dec. 23, 1965) [AAS 58 (1966): 95; English translation by Mistò, "Paul VI and *Dignitatis Humanae*," 30n26 (emphasis added)]. The passage in the original Italian is as follows: "[L]a Chiesa del Concilio ... viene a voi senza orgoglio alcuno, senza pretendere per sé privilegio alcuno. Ella ... non ha alcuna ambizione né di dominio, né di ricchezza; se una cosa chiede è la libertà per la sua fede interiore e la libertà di darne l'annuncio esteriore."

[136] Cf. Hittinger, "*Dignitatis Humanae* on Establishment," 19–20.

[137] "The apostolate in the social milieu, that is, the effort to infuse the Christian spirit into the mentality, customs, laws, and structures of the community in which one lives, is so much the duty of the laity that it can never be performed properly by others." Second Vatican Council, Decree on the Apostolate of the Laity *Apostolicam Actuositatem* (Nov. 18, 1965), §13 [AAS 58 (1966): 849].

must favor it (DH, §3e). This is more than a request for bare state neutrality, and it too seems to be a departure from a position of strict separation.

What then is one to make of Paul's repeated assertions that the Church asks the state for nothing but freedom?

Hittinger points primarily to different passages of Paul's closing speech in support of his reading. Indeed, he argues persuasively that an exclusive focus on "nothing but freedom" is incomplete and that other parts of the same speech make this clear. In light of these difficulties, Hittinger argues against a "doctrinal" reading of Paul's references to "nothing but freedom," which he says *Dignitatis Humanae* does not support.[138]

The fact that all of Paul's pronouncements in this vein appear in speeches, rather than in more formal teaching documents, provides some support for this position. One could add other reasons as well. For example, the pope who makes the most frequent reference to the declaration, John Paul II, rarely takes up this theme. He appears to make perhaps a single reference to the "nothing but freedom" argument and, for the most part, is much more interested in urging collaboration between the temporal and spiritual realms.[139]

Brian Harrison takes a position similar to Hittinger's, asserting that the text of *Aux gouvernants* itself undercuts a doctrinal reading of this phrase. "Indeed, the first two interrogatory sentences, emphasizing the constantly changing nature of the Church's *de facto* relationships with civil rulers throughout history, support a merely prudential and pastoral interpretation of this message, in keeping with the Council's overall goals."[140] The entire passage from Paul's speech is as follows:

> In your earthly and temporal city, God constructs mysteriously His spiritual and eternal city, His Church. And what does this Church ask of you after close to 2,000 years of experiences of all kinds in her relations with you, the powers of the earth? What does the Church ask of you today? She tells you in one of the major documents of this council. She asks of you only liberty, the liberty to believe and to preach her faith, the freedom to love her God and serve Him, the freedom to live and to bring to men her message of life. She is made after the image of her Master, whose mysterious action does

---

[138] Cf. Hittinger, "*Dignitatis Humanae* on Establishment," 19.

[139] Cf. Message to Congress on Secularism and Religious Liberty (Dec. 7, 1995), in *L'Osservatore Romano*, English ed. (Dec. 10–27, 1995), quoted in Valuet, LRTC, vol. IIA, 1396: "The Church ... asks only to be allowed to address man in freedom."

[140] Harrison, "Reliable Interpreter," 153.

not interfere with your prerogatives but heals everything human of its fatal weakness, transfigures it and fills it with hope, truth and beauty.

Allow Christ to exercise His purifying action on society. Do not crucify Him anew.[141]

In addition to calling attention to Paul's reference to the constantly changing arrangements of the Church-state relationship, Harrison emphasizes Paul's use of the word "today." That is, *today* it is appropriate to ask only for freedom because—Harrison says—so few nations are united in the profession of Catholicism. "Civil rulers whose task is the *representative* government of largely or predominantly non-Catholic populations cannot reasonably be expected to enact laws recognizing Catholicism as the true religion *under those existing conditions*."[142] However, this does not mean that mere freedom exhausts the Church's rights as a matter of doctrine, even if she is not insisting on them at this present time. "[O]ne does not *renounce* one's rights simply by not insisting on them in a determined situation."[143]

Harrison's interpretation may seem to prove too much. Indeed, one commentator believes that Harrison reads too much of the confessional state into *Dignitatis Humanae*.[144] After all, could not Paul VI have enunciated his policy without citing the declaration? The pope not only announces an apparent policy, but he seemingly alludes to the declaration in support of it. Harrison's exegesis of article 1 may provide a possible explanation. As discussed above, he shows that the reason for adding "and societies" to the passage on duties to religion was to make clear that the traditional teaching on that point remains "untouched," even while the Council chooses to focus on the second aspect of the papal doctrine, namely, the rights of the person. Reading Paul's *Aux gouvernants* speech in light of the late amendments to

---

[141] *Aux Gouvernants* [AAS 58 (1966): 10–11].
[142] Harrison, "Reliable Interpreter," 154.
[143] Harrison, "Reliable Interpreter," 154. Lamberigts notes that the declaration concerns religious liberty in general, rather than a résumé of all of the Church's rights. Cf. Lamberigts, "Msgr. Emiel-Jozef De Smedt," 463, citing Émile De Smedt, Oral *Relatio* on the *Textus Recognitus* (Oct. 25, 1965) [AS IV/5, 99–104]. See also Turner, "*Dignitatis Humanae* and the Development of Moral Doctrine," 307, discussing the same point and citing the same *relatio* at AS IV/5, 102.
[144] Cf. David Rooney, "Murray: Beacon of Light?," review of *We Hold These Truths and More*, ed. Donald J. D'Elia and Stephen M. Kraso, *Lay Witness Newsletter*, May 1994, 7–10, arguing that Harrison reads too much of the confessional state into *Dignitatis Humanae* but agreeing with him on the necessity of distinguishing the teaching of the declaration from the thought of Murray.

article 1 shows how the pope could announce a mere policy and also claim the declaration's support for it. As Harrison suggests, the decision is not necessarily to renounce the Church's rights but rather to emphasize instead the right of the person to religious liberty and the right of the Church to freedom. Note that, at least in practical terms, such an approach is not far removed from that of Leo XIII. Thus, Leo praised the U.S. constitutional system for allowing freedom to the Church and attributed the Church's flourishing in America "to the fecundity with which God has endowed his Church, in virtue of which unless men or circumstances interfere, she spontaneously expands and propagates herself" (LO, §6).[145] Leo issues this favorable judgment, even as he makes clear that the American system is not the perfect arrangement of relations between Church and state. Other commentators too, prescinding from the question of the Church's rights, have made similar observations on the ability of the Church to flourish if she at least enjoys freedom.[146]

Thus, Harrison's reading of Paul's speech as belonging to the prudential order seems quite sound. Interestingly, however, Paul's own diplomatic administration sometimes tended away from this stated policy and toward a more traditional direction.

That is, "nothing but freedom" does not seem to be a completely accurate statement even of Paul's own policy as pope. Valuet calls attention to a concordat that the Holy See negotiated with Lower Saxony during Paul's pontificate. Far from providing for "nothing but freedom," that agreement recognizes Sunday observance (and observance of solemnities), requires respect for Catholic religious sentiments in the media, and provides for the teaching of the Catholic religion in public schools.[147] As a result, although Paul's closing speech initially may appear to support Murray's strict

---

[145] Recall also the late-eighteenth-century and nineteenth-century context, in which the United States was one of few governments to allow the Church freedom. Cf. Philip Hughes, *A Popular History of the Catholic Church* (Macmillan, 1947; Image Books Edition, 1954), 219: "Certainly by 1790, outside the States of the Church and the new United States of America, there was not a single country in the world where the Catholic religion was free to live fully its own life, and not a single Catholic country where there seemed any prospect but of further enslavement and gradual emasculation."

[146] E.g., Vermeersch, *Tolerance*, 51: "From those who do not know her the Church asks one thing only—freedom to speak and to convince." Although freedom may be sufficient for the Church, Vermeersch asserts at the same time that unity between Church and state, if based on the truth, benefits the state (cf. *Tolerance*, 192–93). See also *Tolerance*, 212.

[147] Cf. Valuet, LRTE, 550, citing the concordat with Lower Saxony (Feb. 26, 1965), arts. 1, 7, 10, and 14 [AAS 57 (1965): 835, 839, 842, and 844–45]. The concordat predated Paul's speech by several months. However, if it had proven to be difficult to reconcile with

4.9. Murray, Paul VI, and the "Nothing but Freedom" Argument

separationism, a close reading suggests that it is a statement of policy rather than doctrine, and even as policy, by no means an exceptionless one.

Note that the concordat is dated nine months *before* the promulgation of *Dignitatis Humanae*. Could this be the reason for the disconnect with Paul's apparent policy that the Church should demand "nothing but freedom"? This is unlikely. Recall that Paul had embraced the "nothing but freedom" policy as early as his trip to the Holy Land in January 1964. Just as Hittinger counsels against a "doctrinal" reading of the "nothing but freedom" language, so might one say that even on the policy plane, this language might be more a matter of rhetoric and aspiration rather than an iron-clad principle of either policy or diplomacy.

Hittinger and Harrison provide good reasons for limiting Paul's closing speech to its context and for rejecting Murray's invitation to read it as a definitive interpretation of article 13 and, more broadly, of the declaration's position on the confessional state. In addition, however, there may be another even more basic reason to reject the Murray interpretation. That is, although commentators on Paul's speech seem to take it for granted that the pope—in calling for "nothing but freedom"—is drawing on *Dignitatis Humanae*, it is possible that he is not referring to this document at all!

It seems at first blush that Paul's closing speech *Aux gouvernants* (and his Christmas radio message—both from December 1965) refer to *Dignitatis Humanae* but, in fact, this is not necessarily the case. Neither speech mentions the declaration outright, and the famous closing message refers only to "one of the major documents of this council." Murray (and apparently all other commentators up to now) have assumed that Paul is referring to *Dignitatis Humanae*. However, it is possible that he is referring instead to *Gaudium et Spes*.

One reason for this possibility is that both conciliar documents treat the freedom of the Church. As discussed above, *Dignitatis Humanae* does so in article 13, but *Gaudium et Spes* treats this subject too. "[T]he Church should have true freedom to preach the faith, to teach her social doctrine, to exercise her role freely among men" (GS, §76e). In this same passage of *Gaudium et Spes* claiming freedom—article 76—the Council also announces an intention to forgo state privileges, and it is this entire passage toward the end of the article (concerning both the freedom of the Church and the foregoing of privileges) that I believe Paul may be interpreting as the Church's

---

Dignitatis Humanae, the Holy Father likely would have insisted upon revisions to it, as he did in the case of the 1953 concordat with Spain.

demand for "nothing but freedom." A reading of the whole passage from GS §76 discloses the plausibility of this interpretation:

> The Church herself makes use of temporal things insofar as her own mission requires it. She, for her part, does not place her trust in the privileges offered by civil authority. She will even give up the exercise of certain rights which have been legitimately acquired, if it becomes clear that their use will cast doubt on the sincerity of her witness or that new ways of life demand new methods. It is only right, however, that at all times and in all places, the Church should have true freedom to preach the faith, to teach her social doctrine, to exercise her role freely among men, and also to pass moral judgment in those matters which regard public order when the fundamental rights of a person or the salvation of souls require it. (GS, §76e)

Thus, when Paul says in *Aux gouvernants* that the Church seeks only freedom and when he cites a "major" Council document to this effect, he could be referring not to *Dignitatis Humanae* but rather to this passage of *Gaudium et Spes* announcing a willingness to forgo secular privileges but insisting upon the Church's freedom. Indeed, because this document is one of the Council's four constitutions, Paul's reference to a "major" document seems more appropriate as a reference to *Gaudium et Spes* than to *Dignitatis Humanae*, which is only a declaration.[148]

If these observations raise some doubt as to whether the quotation from *Aux gouvernants* refers to *Dignitatis Humanae*, still other circumstances suggest that it seems, in fact, *more likely* that Paul is referring to *Gaudium et Spes*. As mentioned above, two weeks after he closed the Council with *Aux gouvernants*, Paul delivered his Christmas radio message, and his theme was "encounter." He described the recently concluded Council as an encounter with the Church itself, with the people of today, and with the world. In that connection, he said:

> The Church comes to you without pride, without expecting any privileges for itself.... It has no ambitions of domination or wealth, *if anything it asks you for freedom for its inner faith and freedom for*

---

[148] Standing alone, however, this point is not dispositive. As discussed below, in another discourse, Paul refers to *Dignitatis Humanae* as "one of the greatest documents" of Vatican II (cf. Mistò, "Paul VI and *Dignitatis Humanae*," 13).

its outer proclamation; but it does not impose on anyone, rather it wants supreme responsibility and decisive choice of conscience, even in the face of religious truth, to be respected and safeguarded.[149]

Immediately after his call for "if anything... freedom," Paul mentions a particular conciliar document on his theme. "The encounter of the Church with today's world was described in the wonderful pages of the final constitution of the Council."[150] Needless to say, the document that Paul means here cannot be *Dignitatis Humanae* (which is a declaration rather than a constitution). Instead, it must be *Gaudium et Spes*, given that Paul refers to the "final Constitution," and *Gaudium et Spes*, the Pastoral Constitution on the Church in the Modern World, was indeed the last of the Council's four constitutions to be promulgated.[151]

Note also how this passage from the Christmas message touches on a point that appears in *Gaudium et Spes* but not in *Dignitatis Humanae*. That point is the foregoing of state privileges. This theme is contained both in *Gaudium et Spes* ("The Church... does not place her trust in the privileges offered by civil authority") and in Paul's Christmas 1965 radio message ("The Church comes to you... without expecting any privileges"). However, this theme is absent from *Dignitatis Humanae*. In his radio message, then, it is clear that Paul is drawing on *Gaudium et Spes* in calling for "if anything... freedom." Accordingly, I am suggesting that one should read the ambiguous conciliar reference in *Aux gouvernants* in light of the very similar but unambiguous reference that Paul makes to *Gaudium et Spes* only two weeks later, in his 1965 Christmas radio message. Thus, I believe that both of these speeches are in dialogue, not with the religious liberty declaration but with the pastoral constitution.

---

[149] Paul VI, Christmas Message (1965) [AAS 58 (1966): 95]; English translation by Mistò, "Paul VI and *Dignitatis Humanae*," 30n26 (emphasis added). The passage in the original Italian is as follows: "[L]a Chiesa del Concilio... viene a voi senza orgoglio alcuno, senza pretendere per sé privilegio alcuno. Ella... non ha alcuna ambizione né di dominio, né di ricchezza; se una cosa chiede è la libertà per la sua fede interiore e la libertà di darne l'annuncio esteriore; ma ella non si impone ad alcuno, anzi vuole che la responsabilità suprema e la scelta decisiva delle coscienze, anche di fronte alla verità religiosa, siano rispettate e tutelate."

[150] Paul VI, Christmas Message (1965) [AAS 58 (1966): 95].

[151] In order of their promulgation, the Council's four constitutions are (1) the Constitution on the Sacred Liturgy *Sacrosanctum Concilium* (Dec. 4, 1963), (2) the Dogmatic Constitution on the Church *Lumen Gentium* (Nov. 21, 1964), (3) the Dogmatic Constitution on Divine Revelation *Dei Verbum* (Nov. 18, 1965), and (4) the Pastoral Constitution on the Church in the Modern World *Gaudium et Spes* (Dec. 7, 1965).

There is yet another relevant speech to consider. It too is a discourse of Paul VI from December 1965, and it too contains a phrase similar to the "nothing but freedom" passage that Murray emphasizes. This discourse is a message to the envoys in attendance at the close of the Council, and it was delivered on December 7, 1965, one day before *Aux gouvernants*. In this speech, Paul says, "[T]he Church demands today, for herself, nothing besides the liberty to announce the Gospel."[152]

Unlike Paul's other speeches calling for "nothing but freedom" (or the equivalent), this one does indeed make a clear reference to *Dignitatis Humanae*. However, although this discourse does cite the declaration, it does *not* cite it in support of "nothing but freedom" but on another point entirely. The following is the passage citing *Dignitatis Humanae*:

> [I]n a declaration which will undoubtedly remain one of the greatest documents of this Council, the Church echoes the aspiration to civil and social freedom in religious matters, universally felt today; i.e., that no one should be forced to believe; that no longer should anyone be prevented from believing or professing his or her faith, since it is a fundamental right of the human person.[153]

That is, Paul cites *Dignitatis Humanae* on its signal contribution, namely, the pronouncement that all persons possess a right to religious freedom. He does not cite it in support of the "nothing but freedom" position that is absent from the declaration, which Murray seeks to read into it. Moreover, unlike his other speeches, there can be no doubt that Paul is citing DH here. First he refers to a declaration, which is the precise genre of DH. Second, he refers to "social and civil liberty," which is a phrase from DH's own subtitle. And third, his description of the document accurately summarizes the key provision of the declaration, namely, article 2.[154]

By contrast, when Paul comes to the "nothing but freedom" passage in

---

[152] Paul VI, *Discours aux membres des missions extraordinaires* (Dec. 7, 1965), in AAS 58 (1966): 74. The English translation is mine. The original French reads: "l'Église ne demande aujourd'hui, pour elle, rien d'autre que la liberté d'annoncer l'Évangile."

[153] Paul VI, *Aux membres des missions extraordinaires* (English translation in Mistò, "Paul VI and *Dignitatis Humanae*," 13). The original is as follows: "[D]ans une Déclaration qui restera sans doute, elle aussi, comme un des grands documents de ce Concile, l'aspiration si universellement ressentie aujourd'hui à la liberté civile et sociale en matière religieuse. Que nul ne soit forcé à croire; mais que nul non plus ne soit empêché de croire et de professer sa foi, droit fondamental de lat personne humaine."

[154] The only other Vatican II declarations are *Gravissimum Educationis* on Christian education and *Nostra Aetate* on the relation of the Church to non-Christian religions, neither

4.9. MURRAY, PAUL VI, AND THE "NOTHING BUT FREEDOM" ARGUMENT

the same discourse, far from citing *Dignitatis Humanae*, he cites a different Council document entirely. Paul proceeds to discuss the Church's demand of civil governments that she be left free in the choice and nomination of her pastors, and he refers to the passage of *Christus Dominus* (the Decree concerning the Pastoral Office of Bishops in the Church) discussing this matter. Paul says that this policy should be advantageous to both the Church and the civil power. Then he says, "The Church demands nothing for herself today besides the liberty to announce the Gospel."

Although Paul does not cite *Gaudium et Spes* here, I believe that it remains in the immediate background of this statement. In his Christmas 1965 radio message, Paul's "if anything . . . freedom" statement comes in connection with a clear reference to the Pastoral Constitution. Moreover, because Paul uses his radio message to disclaim any desire on the Church's part for domination or riches, I believe the passage of *Gaudium et Spes* that he has in mind is article 76, where the Church announces an intent to forgo state privileges.

This statement of December 7, 1965, (only two weeks earlier) represents the other side of the same coin. That is, the Church will forgo state privileges, as stated in *Gaudium et Spes*, but the necessary reciprocal condition—as specified in *Christus Dominus*—is that civil governments must forgo privileges concerning the nomination of bishops.[155]

As a result, when one examines all four of Paul's speeches declaring that the Church seeks "nothing but freedom" (or the equivalent), it becomes clear that Paul does not derive this idea from *Dignitatis Humanae*. Indeed, one of the relevant speeches took place nearly two years before the issuance of that declaration. Moreover, the key speech cited by Murray, *Aux gouvernants*, contains only an ambiguous reference to an unnamed Council document, and the other two documents provide context suggesting that the "nothing but freedom" idea (as Paul developed it from January 1964 to December 1965) relies on article 76 of *Gaudium et Spes* (on the Church foregoing civil privileges) and the reciprocal passage found in article 20 of *Christus Dominus* (on governments foregoing the nomination of bishops).

Even if my interpretation is correct, however, *does anything turn on it?* That is, if this analysis defeats Murray's strictly separationist reading of

---

of which, for the reasons stated in the main text, can be mistaken for *Dignitatis Humanae* here.

[155] Cf. Second Vatican Council, Decree concerning the Pastoral Office of Bishops in the Church *Christus Dominus* (Oct. 28, 1965), §20 [AAS 58 (1966): 683].

article 13 of *Dignitatis Humanae*, does it not simply shift the problem to another Vatican II document, or worse yet, to two other Council documents?

Not necessarily.

Disengaging the "nothing but freedom" language from *Dignitatis Humanae* renders it much clearer that this language indeed is a matter of policy (or of addressing the pastoral needs of contemporary society) rather than doctrine. Hittinger and Harrison are correct that *Aux gouvernants* contains several indications that "nothing but freedom" should be read as a policy statement. However, Murray's attempt to tie the speech to article 13 of *Dignitatis Humanae* amounts to an attempt to insist on a doctrinal reading, that is, a reading that excludes the confessional state. The reason is that article 13 is not a passage discussing policy or the vicissitudes of history but rather is one discussing permanent things—"things therefore that are always and everywhere to be kept secure and defended against all injury"—especially the *libertas Ecclesiae*. As a result, although Hittinger and Harrison offer careful and plausible readings of *Aux gouvernants*, the difficulty remains that as long as one assumes a connection between this speech and *Dignitatis Humanae*, the Murray position still remains plausible, albeit somewhat weakened by Hittinger and Harrison. In addition, if *Aux gouvernants* truly is an interpretation of *Dignitatis Humanae*, then it would seem somewhat difficult for Hittinger and Harrison to escape the uncomfortable implication that Paul VI himself, who was very much involved in the final redaction of the declaration, has misunderstood the document to a significant degree. That is, while Murray seems to insist on a doctrinal reading of Paul's *Aux gouvernants*, Hittinger asserts that *Dignitatis Humanae* will not support such a reading.

However, if I am correct that *Aux gouvernants* draws not on *Dignitatis Humanae* but on *Gaudium et Spes* (together with *Christus Dominus*), then it becomes nearly undeniable that it is a statement of policy (or pastoral prudence) rather than doctrine. Recall that article 13 of *Dignitatis Humanae* concerns itself with permanent things, especially one particular permanent thing, namely, the *libertas Ecclesiae* or the freedom of the Church. Note that article 76 of *Gaudium et Spes* also treats of the same permanent thing: "[A]t all times and in all places, the Church should have true freedom." However, unlike DH §13, GS §76 does not *confine* itself to permanent things.

On the contrary, GS §76, like *Aux gouvernants*, treats of the vicissitudes of history and the shifting arrangements between Church and state throughout time. Article 76 begins with the premise that "a pluralistic society" predominates today, and it notes the need for clarity in the notion of the relationship between the two realms. GS §76 proceeds to make clear that the Church is not identified with any particular political system. Then follows a discussion of the competencies of the two realms that amounts to a reprise of Gelasian dualism. Toward the end of the article comes the key passage. As quoted above, the Council says that the Church does not place her hope in privileges offered by civil authority. It adds that the Church will forgo certain rights, although she has acquired them legitimately, if their use compromises the Church's witness or if "new ways of life demand new methods" (GS, §76e).

Harrison's analysis of *Aux gouvernants* (discussed above) shows that the context of that speech is the shifting arrangements between Church and state throughout history. This review of the final part of GS §76 immediately above shows that the same is true of this article of the pastoral constitution. The Church always will insist on her freedom. She could perhaps insist on more, but, given the social and religious pluralism that predominates today, the Church of our day is willing to forgo even legitimate rights and privileges to promote an encounter with the people of today.[156] That is, the Church's request for "nothing but freedom" does not originate in a doctrine providing that this is all that the Church ever could claim legitimately. Rather, it is a matter of policy and prudence tailored to the present moment in history.

4.10. Further Significance

The question of the relationship between Church and state reappears throughout this work. In particular, it resurfaces in connection with the inquiry into what the *foundation* is for the right to religious liberty that Vatican II recognized. There are three main candidates for the foundation of this right, and one of them—the assertion that the state is *incompetent* in religious matters—is similar to Murray's argument in favor of Church-state separation, which I have addressed in this chapter and section. Here I have argued that Vatican II *did not in fact* adopt the strict separationist argument that Murray promoted. In chapters 9 and 10, I examine Murray's closely connected argument that the state's incompetence in religious matters is the foundation of the right to religious liberty, and I argue that Vatican II *did not* adopt this argument, and that it *could not have done so* without the risk of raising difficulties much more serious than those contained in the final text of the declaration.

---

[156] Cf. Lamberigts, "Msgr. Emiel-Jozef De Smedt," 463: DH does not present a résumé of all of the Church's rights (citing De Smedt's Oral *Relatio* on the *Textus Recognitus*).

CHAPTER 5

The Appeal to "Changed Circumstances"

Part 1: The Near-Disappearance of the Catholic State

> *I fear that our question has been discussed thus far with excessive pragmatism.*
> —BISHOP JOHN WRIGHT, DURING THE
> VATICAN II DEBATE ON RELIGIOUS LIBERTY[1]

A comparison of Leo XIII's teachings (discussed above in sections 3.2.1, 4.1, and 4.2, and below in chapter 6) with those of DH gives rise to a crucial threshold question: *Nearly a century elapsed between Leo's pronouncements and those of Vatican II, and in that time, the world situation—and even the forms of government—changed significantly. Given these changes, is it really necessary to harmonize Leo with the council fathers?*

Stated differently, Can we resolve the doctrinal dispute simply by asserting that Leo's teaching (that only the true religion could be the object of a right, while others could be the object only of toleration) was suitable to the regimes that he encountered in his day, while DH similarly is addressed to the very different regimes of the mid twentieth century and beyond? That is, perhaps the teachings of Leo and Vatican II need not be harmonized at all because they are addressed to such different factual and historical contexts. In particular, the key "changed circumstance" is the near disappearance of

---

[1] AS III/2, 573; English translation in William K. Leahy and Anthony T. Massimini, eds., *Third Session Council Speeches of Vatican II* (Glen Rock, NJ: Paulist Press, 1966), 57 (hereinafter, Leahy/Massimini).

the Catholic state. The teaching of Leo that seems to be most at odds with DH concerns the posture of the Catholic state toward non-Catholic public worship. *Now that Catholic states are much less prevalent than they once were, perhaps the Leonine teaching simply is inapplicable to our time.*

This is an important question, and it is one of several significant questions premised on a change in circumstances. Accordingly, at several points in this work, I will have occasion to address such arguments predicated on changed historical or factual circumstances. All of these arguments shed light on the key doctrinal issue, but their sufficiency to resolve the doctrinal question (or to remove the need to resolve it) frequently is less adequate than appears at first blush.

Here, I will address the arguments such as those premised on the "changed circumstance" of the near disappearance of the Catholic state. As the discussion below will show, these arguments are appealing because they possess an air of straight-forwardness and common sense. At the end of the day, however, the arguments tend to "prove too much." That is, although it is true that the world situation changed a great deal between the mid nineteenth century and the mid twentieth century, it still remains necessary to compare—and, if possible, to harmonize—the two teachings, because the nineteenth-century teaching addressed the optimal state situation and the Vatican II teaching declared a universal right.[2] As a result, although each teaching arises in a specific historical context, neither one can be confined neatly within its context. While both Leo and the Vatican II fathers took careful notice of their contemporary contexts, both also spoke beyond those contexts.

5.1. The Historical Inquiry

The following is a summary and analysis of the positions of the council fathers who placed decisive emphasis on these changes in historical circumstances, and also of the influential *peritus* John Courtney Murray who also took this position both during and after the Council.

Richard Cardinal Cushing of Boston was one of the fathers to put this argument forward. During one of the conciliar debates on religious liberty, he made the statement that, "[T]he doctrine of the Church on religious liberty in *modern civil society* has not yet been declared clearly and

---

[2] Cf. Christopher Wolfe, "The Church's Teaching on Religious Liberty," *Faith & Reason* 9, no. 3 (Fall 1983): 190.

unambiguously."[3] Other council fathers made similar arguments. Archbishop Gabriel-Marie Garrone of Toulouse, France, said, "Now contradictions exist concerning the same matter under the same aspect. But in the case at hand the discussion in no way concerns the same thing or the same aspect."[4]

The heart of this argument is that fundamental changes took place in the political situation from the nineteenth century to the twentieth century. This was a favorite argument of John Courtney Murray, who asserted that the encyclicals of Leo XIII do not apply with full force to the twentieth-century situation because they were addressed chiefly to the situation of nineteenth-century Continental Liberalism and its militantly anti-Catholic states.[5] Indeed, dramatic and rapid changes did take place in the political situation. Most significantly, by the time of the Council, the Catholic Church no longer was under the attacks that it had faced during the French Revolution, the German *Kulturkampf*, and the period of the formation of the Italian nationalist state. By the time of Vatican II, this type of state-sponsored persecution of the Church in Western Europe had ceased. One of the milestones in this development was the solution to the vexing "Roman Question." Following Italy's annexation of the Papal States in 1860 and Rome in 1870, the problem arose as to how to secure the Church's independence from civil governments. This problem was solved finally by the ingenious device of creating Vatican City as an independent nation in the Lateran Agreements of the 1929 Concordat between the Holy See and Italy. However, if the challenges of the twentieth century were markedly different from those of the nineteenth century, they were by no means less threatening.

The great and ominous political development of the twentieth century was the advent of modern totalitarianism. The distinctive feature of totalitarianism is the claim by the government to the right to control every aspect of the lives of its subjects. Concern over totalitarianism was a recurring theme of Vatican II, which took place during the height of the Cold War. Bishop Émile De Smedt, the relator of *Dignitatis Humanae*, alluded implicitly to Marxist-Leninist regimes when he said that the Church cannot remain silent when half the world is denied religious freedom by atheistic

---

[3] Sept. 23, 1964, intervention of Richard Cardinal Cushing of Boston (AS III/2, 361–62); English translation in Leahy/Massimini, 41 (emphasis added).
[4] Sept. 25, 1964, oral intervention of Archbishop Gabriel-Marie Garrone of Toulouse (AS III/2, 533); English translation in Leahy/Massimini, 51.
[5] Cf. John Courtney Murray, "Leo XIII: Separation of Church and State," *Theological Studies* 14, no. 2 (1953): 169–73; "Current Theology on Religious Freedom," *Theological Studies* 10, no. 3 (1949): 422.

materialism.[6] By the same token, Franz Cardinal König of Vienna would later say that *Dignitatis Humanae* was primarily a defense of human rights against Marxist-Leninist regimes.[7] The rise of totalitarian regimes engendered a profound appreciation for constitutional governments, which were distinguished by placing limits on the prerogatives of governmental authority. Thus, the declaration specifically states that its intent is to develop teaching "on the constitutional order of society" (DH, §1c).

An appreciation of constitutional government was bound to focus attention on the United States and the "American experience." Thus, although Leo XIII had expressed some caution regarding the American system,[8] that system gained a great deal of respect in the wake of the rise of totalitarianism. Moreover, American prestige was at its zenith in the mid twentieth century not only because of the example that its form of government set but also because, as a result of its entry into World War II, the United States had become the foremost opponent of totalitarianism in the world. In addition, it also had become apparent by the time of Vatican II that the situation of government neutrality toward religion in the United States had enabled members of the various religions to live together in peace, and that it had allowed the Catholic Church in particular to flourish.[9] In fact, the American people had elected a Catholic president in the most recent election preceding the Second Vatican Council. Albert Cardinal Meyer of Chicago spoke to the Council about these matters on September 23, 1964.

> Men of our day long for the Church to promote rather than to fear religious freedom. This longing arises from a certain common experience by which, on the one hand, they have noted religious persecutions wherever the unlimited power of the State prevailed, and, on the other, they have observed religion flourishing in regions where peaceful coexistence of various religious groups is allowed.[10]

---

[6] Émile De Smedt, Oral *Relatio* on Chapter V of *De Oecumenismo* (Nov. 19, 1963) [AS III/8, 491]; English translation in Hans Küng, Yves Congar, O.P., and Daniel O'Hanlon, S.J., eds., *Council Speeches of Vatican II* (Glen Rock, NJ: Paulist Press, 1964), 237 (larger work hereinafter cited as Küng/Congar/O'Hanlon).

[7] Franz König, "The Right to Religious Freedom: The Significance of *Dignitatis Humanae*," in *Vatican II Revisited By Those Who Were There*, ed. Alberic Stacpoole (Minneapolis, MN: Winston Press, 1986), 284.

[8] Cf. Pope Leo XIII, Encyclical *Longinqua Oceani* (Jan. 6, 1895), §6, rejecting the proposition "that in America is to be sought the hope of the most desirable status of the church."

[9] See section 4.9 above, citing and quoting Philip Hughes, *A Popular History of the Catholic Church* (Macmillan, 1947; Image Books Edition, 1954), 219.

[10] Sept. 23, 1964, oral intervention of Albert Cardinal Meyer of Chicago (AS III/2, 368);

Several American bishops adverted to the "American experience" specifically as supporting adoption of the declaration.[11] As a result of all of these circumstances, *Dignitatis Humanae* sometimes is referred to as Vatican II's "American document."[12]

An appreciation of the historical setting of the Council is helpful to an understanding of the Declaration on Religious Liberty. Most importantly, these circumstances explain why the council fathers saw the need to address this question and why they considered it necessary to consider the actual situation prevailing in the contemporary world rather than previous historical paradigms of the relation between Church and state. In this sense, the historical situation justifies the Council's decision to leave to one side the question of the perfect relationship between Church and state and to concentrate instead on the situation of modern constitutional government.

5.2. Limitations of the Historical Inquiry

However, there also is a danger in an exclusive focus on historical circumstances as an explanation for a doctrinal development. That is, although this focus sheds a great deal of light on the council fathers' motivations and on the reasons for their strong desire to promulgate a Declaration on Religious Liberty, it does little to resolve the doctrinal question. The reason is that putting forward "changed historical circumstances" as the sole or primary rationale for a doctrinal development simply proves too much. That is, this argument renders it *too easy* to explain a doctrinal development. The claim that the current period is different from past periods always will be true, or at least there always will be a great number of persons willing to believe that it is true to supply the premise for the argument that the Church should revise a particular teaching.[13] Moreover, once one applies this argument to the case of religious liberty, it can be applied perhaps to any moral question. Such a method has the potential to transform virtually all of Catholic moral

---

English translation in Vincent A. Yzermans, ed., *American Participation in the Second Vatican Council* (New York: Sheed & Ward, 1967), 645.

[11] Cf. Yzermans, 636–37.

[12] Cf. Yzermans, 617, 623. See also John Tracy Ellis, "Religious Freedom: An American Reaction," in Stacpoole, *Vatican II Revisited*, 294: Impact of American hierarchy "decisive" in bringing about *Dignitatis Humanae*.

[13] Cf. Kenneth R. Melchin, "Revisionists, Deontologists, and the Structure of Moral Understanding," *Theological Studies* 51, no. 3 (1990): 389–416, at 408: "The tendencies of human subjects towards rationalization, towards taking the easier road, towards egoism are well known."

teaching. As discussed in chapter 2, this potential transformation of Catholic moral teaching is one of the problems that launched the instant discussion. Thus, instead of serving as an *explanation* of a doctrinal *development*, the argument from changed circumstances has the potential to become a mere *excuse* for doctrinal *contradiction*.

This is not to say that reliance on the argument from changed circumstances is illegitimate in seeking to understand doctrinal developments. In fact, in the area of moral teachings or mixed questions of faith and morals, it almost always will be necessary to take some account of changed circumstances because these teachings invariably address the concrete human situation.[14] However, one cannot allow the argument from changed circumstances to take the place of a serious theological and doctrinal inquiry. Some of the speeches of the council fathers are unsettling because they seem to reveal a willingness to approve a declaration without making this inquiry.

Some of the American council fathers and *periti* in particular placed such an emphasis on the practical benefits of a declaration that they were willing to ignore the doctrinal issues almost entirely. Thus, even Murray, whose ideas provided the theological rationale for some drafts of the declaration, said simply that the Council left the explanation of the doctrinal development embodied in *Dignitatis Humanae* to be explained by future theologians.[15] Lawrence Cardinal Shehan of Baltimore attempted to avoid direct confrontation with Leo XIII's teachings by reducing and restricting them to a single oversimplified idea: "[T]he heart of Leo's teaching was the freedom of the Church."[16] This idea appears to have been taken almost verbatim from Murray's writings.[17] The difficulty with this interpretation is

---

[14] Cf. Congregation for the Doctrine of the Faith, Instruction on the Ecclesial Vocation of the Theologian *Donum Veritatis* (May 24, 1990), §24 [AAS 82 (1990): 1560–61]; Pope Leo XIII, Apostolic Letter *Au Milieu des Sollicitudes* (Feb. 16, 1892), §15 [ASS 24 (1891–1892): 523].

[15] John Courtney Murray, "Religious Freedom," in *The Documents of Vatican II*, ed. Walter M. Abbott (New York: Herder and Herder, 1966), 673.

[16] Sept. 20, 1965, intervention of Lawrence Cardinal Shehan (AS IV/1, 397); English translation in Yzermans, 663. Valuet suggests that Murray may have ghost-written this intervention. Cf. Basile Valuet, *La liberté religieuse et la tradition catholique. Un cas de développement doctrinal homogène dans le magistère authentique*, 3rd rev. ed. (Barroux: Éditions Sainte-Madeleine, 2011), vol. IIB, 1733n7620: "On sent le main de Murray derrière cette intervention, au demeurant intéressante."

[17] "The phrase, 'the freedom of the Church,' states the dominant theme of Leo XIII's whole pontificate." John Courtney Murray, "Leo XIII: Two Concepts of Government," *Theological Studies* 14, no. 4 (1953): 561. "In the context of this question—the value of law in society—there recurs Leo XIII's endless, insistent theme, the necessity of religion in society,

that it attempts to sidestep Leo's clear teaching on toleration of non-Catholic worship (and also perhaps on the duty of the state to the true religion). One American cardinal's disregard for doctrinal consistency was positively alarming. In September 1964, Joseph Cardinal Ritter of St. Louis told his colleagues, "Venerable Fathers, this Declaration on Religious Liberty is valid and certain, even if the reasons are weak or even invalid."[18] The posture of the debate caused Bishop John Wright of Pittsburgh to declare in 1964 that the discussion of religious liberty was being conducted "with excessive pragmatism."[19]

These council fathers' reflections on changed political circumstances are interesting and important for historical reasons, but they do little to solve the doctrinal problem. In fact, these arguments are a cause for concern because they sometimes seem to present a temptation to ignore the issue of doctrine.

5.3. Christopher Wolfe

Christopher Wolfe explains why a historical inquiry—standing alone—is insufficient to reconcile the teachings of Leo XIII and Vatican II on the issue of non-Catholic worship in a Catholic state. The reason is that the nineteenth-century teachings address the optimal situation, and the Vatican II teaching declares a universal right.[20]

That is, although some of the nineteenth-century pronouncements might be limited to their context, the more significant ones—such as Leo's encyclicals—cannot be. Some of the allocutions cited in the *Syllabus of Errors* indeed are addressed to specific contemporary situations and locations. For example, thesis 78 of the *Syllabus*[21] is supported by a citation to Pius IX's allocution *Acerbissimum* (September 27, 1852), and this statement did indeed address the situation in a particular place, namely, New Granada

---

and to this end, the freedom of the Church" ("Two Concepts of Government," 556). Cf. Murray, "Leo XIII: Separation of Church and State," 203, 205; John Courtney Murray, "Leo XIII on Church and State: The General Structure of the Controversy," *Theological Studies* 14, no. 1 (1953): 27.

[18] Sept. 23, 1964, oral intervention of Joseph Cardinal Ritter (AS III/2, 368–69); English translation in Yzermans, 647.

[19] Sept. 28, 1964, oral intervention of Bishop John Wright (AS III/2, 573); English translation in Leahy/Massimini, 57.

[20] Wolfe, "Teaching on Religious Liberty," 190.

[21] Thesis 78, one of key propositions in the *Syllabus*, provides, "Hence it has been wisely decided by law, in some Catholic countries, that persons coming to reside therein shall enjoy the public exercise of their own peculiar worship."

(now Colombia).[22] However, the same cannot be said about major statements like Leo's encyclicals.

That is, Leo and the other popes did not limit themselves to addressing contemporary crises only, but rather they also went on to teach about the optimal relationship between Church and state. The optimal situation, Wolfe notes, is one that necessarily would need to take account of a universal right.[23] Thus, the nineteenth-century and twentieth-century teachings do indeed engage each other directly. Vatican II did not declare a mere civil right in DH but rather a natural right, that is, a universal right to religious liberty. Thus, at least implicitly, the Vatican II teaching—like that of the nineteenth-century popes—also addresses the optimal situation, even if the Council's primary concern is to address constitutional government and contemporary regimes as they actually exist today.[24]

That is, Vatican II declares a universal right, and as a result, the recognition of this right would be obligatory in all situations, including the optimal. Thus, both the nineteenth-century and twentieth-century teachings address the optimal situation, albeit indirectly in the case of the twentieth-century teaching. Vatican II does not address the optimal situation directly, but rather it specifies minimum standards that apply to all states, including Catholic ones (if they should arise again)[25] and including states whose relationship to the Church is optimal.[26]

However, the nineteenth-century pronouncements appear to deny the very universal right that Vatican II recognizes. That is, in the optimal situation of the Catholic state, the nineteenth-century teaching apparently would deny the natural right that, according to Vatican II, all regimes are obliged to recognize. As a result, resolution of the doctrinal question will require more than an illustration of the varying historical contexts in which

---

[22] See section 6.3 below.
[23] Wolfe, "Teaching on Religious Liberty," 191.
[24] Cf. Second Vatican Council, Declaration on Religious Liberty *Dignitatis Humanae* (December 7, 1965), §1c: The Council "intends to develop the doctrine of recent popes on the inviolable rights of the human person and the constitutional order of society."
[25] It is a disputed point whether the re-emergence of Catholic states would be consistent with DH, and there are distinguished authors on both sides of the question. See the discussion above in sections 4.2 and 4.7, arguing that DH neither encourages nor forecloses this possibility.
[26] DH does not specify any particular arrangement of the Church-state relationship as optimal, but rather, as discussed in the main text, it specifies minimum standards that all states are obliged to follow. From the text of DH, however, one may conclude that the two most significant components of the optimal situation are the guarantee of both religious liberty and the liberty of the Church (cf. DH §§2a, 13a).

the two sets of teaching arose. As discussed below, it will require an inquiry into the precise foundation, scope, and object of the right to religious liberty that Vatican II recognized.

Following the Council, theologians continued to put forward arguments based on changed historical circumstances. However, these arguments generally took greater care than some of the council fathers initially did to avoid relying exclusively on changed circumstances. As a result, these arguments also take account of theological and doctrinal questions.

Although the appeal to "changed historical circumstances" sometimes tends to "prove too much," it nonetheless helps to shed light on the doctrinal inquiry. The significance of "changed circumstances" is a theme in this inquiry, and it will appear again at various points in this work.

5.4. A Word on the Islamic World

Finally, on a different but relevant matter, one might pause to consider that although Catholic states are relatively rare today, there is a realm in which confessional states remain common, namely, the Islamic world. This circumstance does not touch on the instant doctrinal issue, which concerns Catholic states' treatment of non-Catholic religious expression, but it nonetheless might have some practical significance. If the Catholic teachings of the nineteenth and twentieth centuries can be harmonized, then the hypothetical existence or re-emergence of Catholic states remains relevant. That is, in dialogue and engagement with the Islamic world, this possibility might serve to help to achieve parity or reciprocity between the Christian (or formerly Christian) West and the Islamic world. In this type of engagement, acknowledging the possibility (however remote) of the return of the Catholic state serves to illustrate that all states are obliged to recognize religious liberty, Islamic and Catholic states included. If this possibility is discounted entirely, then Muslims might well charge Catholics with hypocrisy, just as Protestants did before the Council. Protestants charged Catholics with advocating liberty when they were in the minority but with denying it to non-Catholics when they were in the majority.[27] By the same token, if Catholic states are marginalized entirely or if their possible return is considered an impossibility, Muslims might well see a certain cynicism in the Church's having waited until the near disappearance of its own confessional states before embracing religious liberty, and thus regard with

---

[27] Cf. A. F. Carrillo de Albornoz, "Roman Catholicism and Religious Liberty," *Ecumenical Review* 11, no. 4 (July 1959): 417–20.

skepticism any urging that their Islamic regimes should adhere to the same principle. To some degree, such a reaction may be inevitable, but perhaps it could be softened if the Catholic interlocutors could recall the few states that remain officially Catholic and the handful of others where the laws and constitutions are animated by a Catholic ethos.[28] In this way, Catholics might lead by example, showing that they are not asking more of Muslims than they are willing to do themselves, and providing a model to demonstrate that religious liberty is compatible with a state religion.

---

[28] See section 4.2 above (citing Harrison and Minnerath on the remaining Catholic states).

PART 3A

ANALYSIS OF THE RIGHT TO RELIGIOUS LIBERTY: THE SCOPE AND OBJECT OF THE RIGHT

CHAPTER 6

The Nineteenth-Century Magisterium

Explaining the origins of the prudential judgments in favor of toleration, however, will never be enough in this case, for Vatican II raised toleration from something morally permissible to something morally obligatory.

— PATRICK M. O'NEIL[1]

This chapter reviews the key papal pronouncements of the nineteenth-century popes that are relevant to the question of whether *Dignitatis Humanae* contradicts the earlier magisterium. The popes whose teachings most often are put forward as having been contradicted by Vatican II are Gregory XVI (1831–1846), Bl. Pius IX (1846–1878), and Leo XIII (1878–1903). Before the nineteenth century, a few popes made pronouncements relevant to the questions addressed here. In the wake of the French Revolution, Popes Pius VI and Pius VII issued relevant documents that will be discussed briefly in this chapter.[2] In addition, at the beginning of the Protestant Reformation, Pope Leo X issued his bull condemning the teachings of Martin Luther, *Exsurge Domine* (1520). This document will be the subject of chapter 13.

---

[1] Patrick M. O'Neil, "A Response to John T. Noonan, Jr. Concerning the Development of Catholic Moral Doctrine," *Faith & Reason* (Spring/Summer 1996), EWTN, accessed Dec. 19, 2020, https://www.ewtn.com/catholicism/library/response-to-john-t-noonan-jr-concerning-the-development-of-catholic-moral-doctrine-10041.

[2] On the relevant pronouncements of both Pius VI and Pius VII, see generally Basile Valuet, *La liberté religieuse et la tradition catholique. Un cas de développement doctrinal homogène dans le magistère authentique*, 3rd rev. ed. (Barroux: Éditions Sainte-Madeleine, 2011), vol. IA, 290–301 [= Basile Valuet, *Le droit à la liberté religieuse dans la Tradition de l'Eglise. Un cas de développement doctrinal homogène par le magistère authentique*, 2nd rev. ed. (Barroux: Éditions Sainte-Madeleine, 2011), 195–205].

The following is a brief review of the most important pronouncements of the nineteenth-century popes. For the most part, these documents only are introduced here. They will be addressed at more length in the following chapters. However, special considerations apply to Pope Bl. Pius IX's *Syllabus of Errors*, and as a result, I will discuss it in somewhat greater depth here.

6.1. Gregory XVI, *Mirari Vos* (1832)

The pronouncements of the nineteenth-century papal magisterium concerning religious liberty, toleration, and related subjects begin in earnest with Pope Gregory XVI's encyclical *Mirari Vos* in 1832. The encyclical famously denounces indifferentism:

> Now We consider another abundant source of the evils with which the Church is afflicted at present: indifferentism. This perverse opinion is spread on all sides by the fraud of the wicked who claim that it is possible to obtain the eternal salvation of the soul by the profession of any kind of religion, as long as morality is maintained. (MV, §13)

In the very next paragraph, the document describes "liberty of conscience" as an error that finds its origin in indifferentism:

> This shameful font of indifferentism gives rise to that absurd and erroneous proposition [*deliramentum*] which claims that liberty of conscience must be maintained for everyone. It spreads ruin in sacred and civil affairs, though some repeat over and over again with the greatest impudence that some advantage accrues to religion from it. (MV, §14)

Note that what Gregory rejects is not religious liberty but liberty of conscience. Is *Mirari Vos* nonetheless relevant to this inquiry concerning the religious liberty declaration of Vatican II?

One challenge in answering this question is the circumstance that Gregory does not define the idea that he is condemning. However, he does say that liberty of conscience *originates* in indifferentism, which he does define, and which does concern religion. Brian Harrison, noting that the encyclical is directed at the French priest Félicité de Lamennais, argues persuasively that *liberty of conscience* refers to an idea representative of Lamennais's thought, namely, the advocacy of a nearly absolute civil liberty in religious matters.[3] Basile Valuet reaches a similar conclusion, thus identifying liberty of conscience with one of the rights proclaimed by the central document of the French Revolution, the *Declaration of the Rights of Man and the Citizen* of 1789 (the DDHC or *la Déclaration des droits de l'homme et du citoyen*).[4] The relevant provision of the DDHC is paragraph 10: "No one shall be disquieted on account of his opinions, including his religious views, provided their manifestation does not disturb the public order established by law."[5]

There is no doubt that Gregory XVI directed *Mirari Vos* at Lamennais. This is clear from the fact that the pope's secretary of state, Bartolomeo Cardinal Pacca, wrote a letter to Lamennais informing him that the pontiff had his writings chiefly in mind when issuing the encyclical.[6] Moreover, in that letter, Pacca referred especially to the advocacy of liberty of worship (*liberté des cultes*) as problematic.[7] This right usually is called *liberty of conscience and of cults*. It is not absolutely certain that this is what Gregory meant by liberty of conscience, but it seems clear that the idea either is the same or else is quite closely related.[8] In any event, Valuet notes that the difference is insignificant, given that Lamennais used the terms interchangeably.[9]

Before proceeding further to discuss *Mirari Vos*, it is necessary to take note of some earlier papal pronouncements that confronted the ideas coming out of the French Revolution, and, in particular, those appearing in the DDHC. The first major application of the DDHC was the Civil Constitution of the Clergy of 1790 (the CCC or *la Constitution civile du clergé*). The CCC entirely reorganized the French Church, reduced the number of dioceses, provided for the election of bishops and pastors, excluded the Holy See from governance, and provided for governance by

---

[3] Cf. Brian W. Harrison, *Religious Liberty and Contraception: Did Vatican II Open the Way for a New Sexual Ethic?* (Melbourne: John XXIII Fellowship Co-op., Ltd., 1988), 38–40.

[4] Cf. Valuet, LRTE, 212, 216. Valuet asserts that Pope Bl. Pius IX's 1856 allocution *Nunquam fore* supports his reading of *Mirari Vos*, that is, his interpretation of *liberty of conscience* as referring to DDHC, art. 10, and *liberty of opinions* as referring to DDHC, art. 11 (cf. LRTE, 221).

[5] English translation at website of Yale University's Avalon Project, "Declaration of the Rights of Man—1789," accessed Jan. 6, 2021, https://avalon.law.yale.edu/18th_century/rightsof.asp.

[6] Cf. Alec R. Vidler, *Prophecy and Papacy: A Study of Lamennais, the Church, and the Revolution* (London: SCM Press Ltd., 1954), 212–13 (includes an English translation of a long excerpt of the letter).

[7] Cf. Vidler, *Prophecy and Papacy*, 213. See also Valuet, LRTE, 209.

[8] Cf. Valuet, LRTE, 211.

[9] Cf. Valuet, LRTE, 209n1106.

secular authorities. Most French bishops and pastors protested, but the National Assembly retaliated by requiring French priests to take an oath of allegiance to the CCC.[10]

Pope Pius VI (1775–1799) responded by condemning the CCC in his 1791 letter *Quod Aliquantum*. The pope addressed the document to the bishop members of the National Assembly, and in it he also warned of the absolute and immoderate freedom proclaimed by articles 10 and 11 of the DDHC.[11] As discussed above, article 10 pertains to religious opinions. Article 11 concerns the right of speech and publication:

> The free communication of ideas and opinions is one of the most precious of the rights of man. Every citizen may, accordingly, speak, write, and print with freedom, but shall be responsible for such abuses of this freedom as shall be defined by law.[12]

Pius VI warns against both of these provisions of the DDHC in the following language:

> It is according to such a view that this absolute liberty is proposed as a human right in society: a liberty which not only assures to each one the right not to be disturbed on account of his religious opinions, but which also grants the licence of thinking, saying, writing, and even printing with impunity anything which might occur to the wildest imagination in regard to religion. This monstrous right, however, is seen by the Assembly as pertaining to that equality and liberty which are natural to all men. But what could be more irrational than to establish among men this unbridled equality and liberty, which seems to extinguish reason—nature's most precious gift to man, and the only one that distinguishes him from the animals?[13]

---

[10] Cf. James MacCaffrey, *History of the Catholic Church in the Nineteenth Century (1789–1908)*, 2nd rev. ed., vol. 1 (Dublin/St. Louis: M.H. Gill and Son, Ltd./B. Herder, 1910), 15–17. Only four bishops (including Talleyrand) and about a third of the clergy took the oath (cf. MacCaffrey, 17).

[11] Cf. Valuet, LRTE, 195–97. Pius VI does not refer expressly to articles 10 and 11, but as Valuet shows, a comparison of the substance of these provisions with the substance of the condemnations leaves little or no doubt.

[12] English translation at website of Yale University's Avalon Project, "Declaration of the Rights of Man—1789," accessed Jan. 6, 2021, https://avalon.law.yale.edu/18th_century/rightsof.asp.

[13] Pope Pius VI, Encyclical *Quod Aliquantum* (Mar. 10, 1791); English translation in Harrison, RL&C, 39. It appears that the first full English translation of this document

6.1. Gregory XVI, *Mirari Vos* (1832)

The key feature of the liberty that Pius VI is rejecting is its absolute or near-absolute character. Gregory XVI will use similar language in *Mirari Vos*, referring not only to liberty of conscience but, in the same paragraph, to another idea that flows from it, namely, the "immoderate freedom of opinion, license of free speech, and desire for novelty" (MV, §14). By the same token, Gregory says, the proponents of these ideas claim the "freedom to publish any writings whatever and disseminate them to the people" (MV, §15). Both popes are concerned with the sheer breadth of the claimed right and the dangers that such an unbridled right of expression and publication will pose. In addition, they are concerned that the only limitations on such expression that articles 10 and 11 of the DDHC recognize are those of the positive civil law. (The concern of Pius VI is the DDHC itself, while Gregory XVI's chief concern is the largescale embrace of these principles by Catholics under the sway of Lamennais.) Part 4 of this study will address the specific question of legitimate limitations on religious activity.

Note also how Pius VI draws out that the asserted liberties are claimed to be natural rights. As Valuet notes, articles 10 and 11 are applications of the first and foundational paragraph of the DDHC: "Men are born and remain free and equal in rights."[14] Pius VI treats articles 10 (on freedom of conscience and religion) and 11 (on freedom of opinion and publication) as a single right, and he connects them to the foundational article 1: "This monstrous right, however, is seen by the Assembly as pertaining to that equality and liberty which are natural to all men." *Quod Aliquantum*, as Valuet says, is the key to understanding the statements of all the nineteenth-century popes in this area.[15]

Given the significance of *Quod Aliquantum*, why is it not more central to this study? The reason is that it is not a universal teaching. At that time, the ideas that Pius VI was addressing concerned only France. Indeed, the pope does not direct his letter even to the whole of the French episcopacy but only to the bishop members of the assembly. Similarly, although the next pope, Pius VII (1800–1823), also would engage these issues, he too limited his interventions to the French context and even to difficulties with particular governmental enactments.

Thus, Pius VII expressed his concerns about the oath of anointing Napoleon (1804), by which the emperor promised to respect and ensure the

---

appeared only in 2016. Cf. Jeffrey Langan, *The French Revolution Confronts Pius VI* (South Bend, IN: St. Augustine's Press, 2016), 41–83; see especially Langan, 46.

[14] Cf. Valuet, LRTC, vol. IA, 292 [= LRTE, 197]. English translation at website of Yale University's Avalon Project, accessed Jan. 6, 2021, avalon.law.yale.edu.

[15] Cf. Valuet, LRTC, vol. IA, 290 [= LRTE, 195].

liberty of worship (*liberté des cultes*). However, the Church was able to clarify that this promise referred to civil tolerance rather than to a positive approval of all forms of worship.[16] Nevertheless, the Pope found the 1814 senatorial constitution and the *Charte octroyée* (the constitution granted by King Louis XVIII following the Congress of Vienna) more problematic. The senatorial constitution promised support and patronage to the liberty of conscience and of cult, while article 5 of the *Charte* said, "Each professes his religion with an equal liberty and obtains the same protection for his worship [*son culte*]." The king's ambassador partially allayed the Pope's concerns about the *Charte* by assuring him that this provision was a matter only of civil liberty and not of dogma (and also by declaring Catholicism to be the religion of the state). Note that Pius VII was not opposed to toleration or what he called the favoring of individuals but rather to the positive promotion of all forms of worship without distinction.[17]

Returning now to *Mirari Vos*, the development that had prompted Gregory XVI to issue the encyclical was the advent of Catholic Liberalism. Lamennais, the leader of the movement, was an ultramontane, but because he hated Gallicanism and the Bourbon monarchy, he advocated a temporary embrace of the liberal principles deriving from the French Revolution. He formulated his famous maxim: "On tremble devant le libéralisme: eh bien, catholicisez-le, et la Société renaître" (People tremble before liberalism: well then, let us Catholicize it, and society will be reborn).[18]

As discussed below in section 7.3.1.3, Lamennais did this by means of his theory of certitude, which he set forth in the second volume of his *Essai sur l'indifférence en matière de religion* in 1820. Critical of the Enlightenment deification of reason, Lamennais asserted that *individual* reason cannot lead to certitude. Only *general* reason (the universal consent of mankind) can give certitude. Catholicism, he said, is the highest expression of mankind's universal consent, which is evidenced by the large number of its adherents. Because the people collectively are the repository of truth, they need to be free. As a result, he said, they must be allowed all manner of liberty, including liberty of conscience, worship, and the press.[19]

As a result of his support for popular revolutionary movements and

---

[16] Cf. Félix Dupanloup, *Remarks on the Encyclical of the 8th of December 1864*, trans. W. J. M. Hutchinson (London: George Cheek, 1865), 30.

[17] Cf. Valuet, LRTC, vol. IA, 299–300 [= LRTE, 204].

[18] Vidler, *Prophecy and Papacy*, 160, citing Letter from Lamennais, in *Correspondance de F. de Lamennais*, ed. E. D. Forgues, 2 vols. (1855–1858), 2:106.

[19] Cf. Charles Poulet and Sidney A. Raemers, *A History of the Catholic Church*, vol. 2 (St. Louis, MO: B. Herder Book Co., 1934), 585–86.

6.1. Gregory XVI, *Mirari Vos* (1832)

his continued criticism of the French clergy's Gallicanism, Lamennais's orthodoxy was called into question. He traveled to Rome in 1831 to plead his case, and he expected to be vindicated because a previous pope, Leo XII, had commended him for his defense of the papacy.[20] However, Gregory XVI issued his decision several months later by way of publishing *Mirari Vos*, warning against a number of theories and ideas, including indifferentism and liberty of conscience. Although he did not refer to Lamennais by name, the letter of Cardinal Pacca made known to him that it was his doctrines that the pope especially had in mind. (See section 7.3.1.3 below for a more complete account of this episode.)

Gregory issued another encyclical concerning Lamennais two years later. That document, *Commissum Divinitus*, sheds light on the authority of *Mirari Vos*. In it, Gregory recounts the content of the earlier encyclical (*Mirari Vos*), and he uses the word *define* to refer to his previous condemnation of liberty of conscience:

> Against the oath solemnly given in his declaration, he [Lamennais] cloaked Catholic teaching in enticing verbal artifice, in order ultimately to oppose it and overthrow it. We expressed this in Our letter mentioned above [*Mirari Vos*] concerning both the dutiful submission towards authorities and the prevention of the fatal contamination of the people by indifferentism. It also concerned measures to use against the spreading license of ideas and speeches. Finally, it concerned that freedom of conscience which should be thoroughly condemned and the repulsive conspiracy of societies enkindling destruction of sacred and state affairs, even from the followers of false religions, as We have made clear [*definivimus*] by the authority handed down to Us.[21]

As a result of Gregory's use of the word *definivimus*,[22] some commentators consider the condemnation of liberty of conscience to be definitive.[23] Arnold

---

[20] Cf. Vidler, *Prophecy and Papacy*, 95–97, 194–96; Thomas Bokenkotter, *Church and Revolution: Catholics in the Struggle for Democracy and Social Justice* (New York: Image Books, 1998), 44.

[21] Pope Gregory XVI, Encyclical *Singulari Nos* (June 25, 1834), §3 [*Acta Gregorii XVI*, vol. 1 (Rome 1901): 433–34]. Gregory also recalls the unlimited or nearly unlimited nature of the rights claimed by Lamennais, noting that "he thrusts forth every kind of opinion, speech, and freedom of conscience" (*Singulari Nos*, §4 [*Acta Gregorii XVI*, vol. 1, 434]).

[22] The quoted English translation reads "as We have made clear," but a more accurate translation would be "as We have defined."

[23] Cf. Valuet, LRTE, 218; Marcel de Corte et al., *Lettre à Quelques Évêques* (Paris: Société

Guminski disagrees, arguing that "it is highly unlikely that the mere use of 'definire' in one encyclical can be properly taken as persuasive evidence of an intent to make an *ex cathedra* definition in an earlier papal document especially since *Mirari Vos* was issued well before the definition of papal infallibility by Vatican I in 1870."[24] Guminski also asserts that the popes (presumably those before 1870) often used the word *define* in a broad sense to refer to any authentic teaching.[25] Regardless of whether the teaching of *Mirari Vos* fully qualifies as definitive in the strict sense (that is, as part of the secondary object of infallibility), it is at least clear that *Commissum Divinitus* enhances the previous document's authority by repetition and strong reaffirmation. Moreover, as described below, Gregory's successor Pius IX will repeat and reaffirm the teaching of *Mirari Vos* as well.[26]

6.2. Bl. Pius IX, *Quanta Cura* (1864)

Pope Bl. Pius IX's encyclical *Quanta Cura* addresses the question of religious liberty—or at least of freedom of worship—expressly. It also cites and reaffirms *Mirari Vos*, and it seems to give an interpretation of the earlier encyclical.

> [T]hey [proponents of naturalism] do not fear to foster that erroneous opinion, . . . called by Our Predecessor, Gregory XVI, an "insanity" [citing *Mirari Vos*], viz., that "liberty of conscience and worship is each man's personal right, which ought to be legally proclaimed and asserted in *every* rightly constituted society; and that a right resides in the citizens to an *absolute* liberty, which should be restrained by *no* authority whether ecclesiastical or civil, whereby they may be able openly and publicly to manifest and declare *any* of their ideas whatever, whether by word of mouth, by the press, or in *any* other way." (QC, §3)

Saint-Thomas-d'Aquin, 1983), 93.

[24] Arnold T. Guminski and Brian W. Harrison, *Religious Freedom: Did Vatican II Contradict Traditional Catholic Doctrine? A Debate* (South Bend, IN: St. Augustine Press, 2013), 105n27 (opinion of Guminski). Guminski is a lawyer who engaged in a book-length debate with Brian Harrison over the question of whether DH contradicts previous papal teaching. Guminski argues that it does, and Harrison argues that it does not.

[25] Cf. Guminski/Harrison, 105n27.

[26] Cf. Second Vatican Council, Dogmatic Constitution on the Church *Lumen Gentium* (Nov. 21, 1964), §25a: The intention of a pope is known by repetition, his manner of speaking, and the character of the pronouncement.

Note that despite the fact that Gregory XVI had mentioned only "liberty of conscience" in *Mirari Vos*, Pius IX summarizes his predecessor's encyclical as pertaining to "liberty of conscience *and worship*."

How should one understand this difference? Has Pius simply made a mistake in recounting the content of *Mirari Vos*, or is he intentionally resolving the difficulty raised by Gregory's not having specified what he meant by liberty of conscience? Stated differently, is Pius declaring that Gregory's terminology should be interpreted to mean both liberty of conscience *and of worship* (*libertatem conscientiae et cultuum*)? Given that there already were weighty reasons to conclude that Gregory's term included liberty of worship, it seems safe to assume that Pius intended this clarification.

Another feature of Pius's discussion of his predecessor's encyclical is more puzzling. Note that the cited passage contains two quotations, and that Pius seems to attribute both of them to Gregory in *Mirari Vos*. The first is a single word—*insanity* (*deliramentum*)—and it does indeed appear in the earlier encyclical.[27] The second quotation is much longer, and it specifies the content of the condemned idea of liberty of conscience and of worship. However, this latter quotation appears nowhere in *Mirari Vos*. In addition, *Quanta Cura* cites no other source, so it is impossible to tell the origin of the quotation. Perhaps the source citation simply was omitted by mistake. It also is possible that there is no source. The language placed in quotation marks may be a characterization of the extreme nature of the purported right that Gregory had condemned. This is the most likely explanation, but the quotation marks leave some doubt. They also are open to the interpretation that the quoted language originates with Lamennais or another of the proponents of the right.[28]

Whatever the source of this quotation, Pius's use of it shows that he is particularly alarmed at the seemingly absolute nature of the claimed right. Indeed, virtually the entire passage consists of repeated emphasis of the quality of these asserted rights as having no limits. The same concern was prominent in Pius VI's *Quod Aliquantum* and Gregory XVI's *Mirari Vos* and *Commissum Divinitus*.

Part 4 of this study is dedicated to the question of when it is legitimate to restrict religious worship or practice, and it is there that my most extensive treatment of *Quanta Cura* will be found. That discussion will consider

---

[27] The English translation of *Mirari Vos* quoted above reads "that absurd and erroneous proposition," but the instant English translation of *Quanta Cura* quoted here is more accurate in translating *deliramentum* as "insanity."

[28] This is the assumption of Valuet, namely, that the quotation is from a condemned document rather than from a previous magisterial document (cf. LRTE, 229).

whether religious liberty—as recognized by Vatican II—is a limited right or a limitless right. The quoted passage from *Quanta Cura* raises this question and renders it necessary to address it. In addition, immediately before this passage, Pius IX had raised the question of the proper *standard* for determining when repression of religious practice by the civil authorities is legitimate. In particular, Pius rejects the idea that protection of the *public peace* is the only justification for such intervention.[29] The key question on this topic is whether Vatican II embraced the standard that Pius IX had rejected in *Quanta Cura*, and this question is the subject of chapter 12 below.

Note also the *nature* of the right or rights that the pontiff is condemning. As discussed in chapter 1, the right to religious liberty that Vatican II recognizes is an *immunity*. That is, it is a right to noninterference in religious matters (within limits, as discussed below in chapter 7). However, Pius IX is discussing a right that not only is an immunity, but that also is a *positive authorization*. That is, it is a right not only to non-coercion and noninterference in religious acts but also a right attaching to the *content* of the various religions. The crucial difference between these concepts will be addressed in chapter 8 on the object of the right to religious liberty.

Finally, it is necessary to take note of the authority of *Quanta Cura*. After describing the offending ideas covered in the encyclical, the pontiff then proceeds to condemn them in forceful terms:

> Therefore, by our Apostolic authority, we reprobate, proscribe, and condemn all the singular and evil opinions and doctrines severally mentioned in this letter, and will command that they be thoroughly held by all children of the Catholic Church as reprobated, proscribed and condemned. (QC, §6)

Some traditionalist critics of DH assert that Pius IX's invocation of his apostolic authority indicates an intention to make an infallible declaration.[30] Brian Harrison agrees, specifying that the document belongs to the

---

[29] "And, against the doctrine of Scripture, of the Church, and of the Holy Fathers, they do not hesitate to assert that 'that is the best condition of civil society, in which no duty is recognized, as attached to the civil power, of restraining by enacted penalties, offenders against the Catholic religion, except so far as the public peace may require.'" Pope Pius IX, Encyclical *Quanta Cura* (Dec. 8, 1864), §3. Note that here, too, Pius includes an extended passage in quotation marks without providing a source. This further suggests that these quotations are not taken from actual documents but are exemplary of proponents of the theories in question.

[30] Cf. Marcel Lefebvre, *Religious Liberty Questioned*, trans. Jaime Pazat de Lys (Kansas City,

secondary object of infallibility, while his interlocutor Arnold Guminski disagrees.[31] Valuet's opinion is that the document has exceptional authority and may amount to a confirmation of an infallible teaching of the ordinary magisterium.[32] In any event, this invocation of the pope's apostolic authority renders the question of the compatibility of *Dignitatis Humanae* and *Quanta Cura* particularly important.

For my own part, I take no position on whether *Mirari Vos* and *Quanta Cura* belong to the secondary object of infallibility and therefore qualify as definitive teachings of the ordinary magisterium. As set forth in chapter 3, I believe that a comparison of the levels of authority of *Dignitatis Humanae* and previous pronouncements is legitimate but should be a last resort. I do not believe that such a comparison is necessary in this case. In addition, although I acknowledge the significant weight of both documents, I believe that the textual issues identified in this chapter and below in chapter 12 leave some doubt as to the precise contours of the ideas that Gregory XVI and Pius IX condemn.[33]

6.3. Bl. Pius IX, *The Syllabus of Errors* (1864)

The next possible source for comparison to Vatican II is the famous appendix to *Quanta Cura*, Pius IX's *Syllabus of Errors*. The *Syllabus* (like *Quanta Cura*) was prompted by the spread of the revolution to Italy and the Papal States. By 1860, the Italian nation-state largely had been unified under the House of Savoy. The Piedmontese nationalists had captured the Papal States, and the sole temporal possession left to the pontiff was the city of Rome. Pius depended largely on the French forces of Emperor Napoleon III to prevent the loss of Rome. Although the Pope had planned for years to release a compendium of errors,[34] his secretary of state, Giacomo Cardinal Antonelli, did

---

MO: Angelus Press, 2002). The original title, *Mes doutes sur la liberté religieuse* (Clovis, 2000), 29–30, argues in favor of infallibility. Cf. Michael Davies, *The Second Vatican Council and Religious Liberty* (Long Prairie, MN: Neumann Press, 1992), 270: "*Quanta Cura* certainly fulfils all the requirements for an infallible pronouncement."

[31] Cf. Guminski/Harrison, 97–99 (Guminski), 155 (Harrison). Harrison's opinion as to the document's infallibility also appears in his review of Michael Davies's book on the declaration. Cf. Brian W. Harrison, "The Center is Holding," review of *The Second Vatican Council and Religious Liberty*, by Michael Davies, *Living Tradition* 44 (1993), Roman Theological Forum, accessed Oct. 29, 2000, http://www.rtforum.org/lt/lt44.html (hereinafter, "Review of SVC&RL").

[32] Cf. Valuet, LRTE, 234n1231.

[33] Cf. can. 749, §3: No teaching is understood to be infallible unless manifestly demonstrated.

[34] Sources disagree as to the length of time that a document like the *Syllabus* had been

not wish to offend Napoleon, who embraced many of the propositions eventually listed in the *Syllabus* and whose government was organized around a number of the liberal principles that the *Syllabus* rejected. In September 1864, the French emperor negotiated a convention with the Italian nationalists, providing for the withdrawal of French forces from Rome in exchange for a guarantee not to attack Rome. Pius was infuriated by the convention (and by its negotiation without his consent or consultation), and despite his continued reliance on the French forces, he issued the encyclical and the *Syllabus*.[35]

Other factors also played a role in the composition and timing of the *Syllabus*. As with his predecessor's encyclical, *Mirari Vos*, Pius IX aimed his own encyclical and the *Syllabus* at the ideas of Lamennais and other Liberal Catholics. In 1863 two Catholic congresses had been held (one in Malines and the other in Munich), and they had received a great deal of attention for their promotion of liberal ideas. Although Lamennais by now was dead, his one-time ally Charles Montalembert continued to promote Liberalism. In addition, he began to *absolutize* those ideas. That is, instead of claiming simply that liberal reforms such as toleration, free speech, and disestablishment are appropriate in *some* contexts, he now asserted that in the modern world, they should be the rule *everywhere*.[36] The Holy See rebuked Montalembert and issued a brief on the Munich Congress. "The way for the publication of the Syllabus was thus paved."[37]

The *Syllabus of Errors* is a perplexing document. It presents problems of both authority and interpretation. The problem of *authority* is that the *Syllabus* was published as an appendix to the encyclical *Quanta Cura* but was not signed by the Pope. As a result, it is not at all clear that the *Syllabus* has the same authority as the encyclical.[38] Cardinal Antonelli described it

---

contemplated. Cf. Frank J. Coppa, *Pope Pius IX: Crusader in a Secular Age* (Boston: Twayne Publishers, 1979), 146 (since February 1862, that is, two to three years); E. E. Y. Hales, *Pio Nono: A Study in European Politics and Religion in the Nineteenth Century* (London: Eyre & Spottiswoode, 1954), 257 (at least four years); Peter Doyle, "Pope Pius IX and Religious Freedom," in *Persecution and Toleration: Papers Read at the Twenty-second Summer Meeting and the Twenty-third Winter Meeting of the Ecclesiastical History Society*, ed. W. J. Sheils (Padstow, UK: Ecclesiastical History Society, 1984), 331 (13 years); MacCaffrey, *History of the Catholic Church*, 1:439–40: Since close to the beginning of his pontificate in 1846.

[35] See generally Hales, *Pio Nono*, 255–57.
[36] Cf. Hales, *Pio Nono*, 265–66.
[37] Hales, *Pio Nono*, 271. On the developments described in this paragraph, see generally Hales, 266–71. See also MacCaffrey, *History of the Catholic Church*, 1:439–41.
[38] This is an important question, given that, as discussed above, Pius IX invoked his apostolic authority in issuing the encyclical (cf. QC, §6).

merely as a memorandum of references to earlier condemnations.[39] In his famous letter to the Duke of Norfolk, St. John Henry Newman took the position that the *Syllabus* "has no dogmatic force."[40] However, other authorities regard it as authentic teaching but not (or probably not) infallible.[41] In addition, succeeding popes have relied on it and have cited it in their own encyclicals.[42] As a result, it seems that Newman discounted the document's value too much in his attempt to ease the concerns of those alarmed by the *Syllabus*. The document does have doctrinal weight, and it almost certainly amounts to an authentic teaching.

The problem of *interpretation* arises because the format of the *Syllabus* is simply a list of eighty erroneous statements grouped into several categories. As Newman says, "There is not a word in it of the Pope's own writing; there is nothing in it at all but the Erroneous Propositions themselves."[43] As a result, there is little guidance within the document as to the mind of the Pope. The *Syllabus* gives no explication of the erroneous statements that it lists, although each statement is followed by a citation to an encyclical or allocution that discusses the particular error. The distinctive *genre* of the *Syllabus* provides a crucial principle of interpretation: "[I]n accordance with the peculiar character of the Syllabus, the meaning of the thesis is determined by the meaning of *the document it is drawn from*."[44]

Indeed, Pope Pius IX himself had set down this principle of interpretation. The British diplomat Odo Russell recounts a conversation that he had with the Pope on the proper interpretation of the *Syllabus*. Pius told him that one must have recourse to the documents cited in the *Syllabus* itself. He

---

[39] Cf. Coppa, *Pope Pius IX*, 146.

[40] John Henry Newman, Letter to the Duke of Norfolk (Dec. 27, 1874), reprinted in *Newman and Gladstone: The Vatican Decrees*, with an introduction by Alvan S. Ryan (Notre Dame, IN: University of Notre Dame Press, 1962), 153.

[41] E.g., Valuet, LRTE, 234.

[42] Cf. Pope Leo XIII, Encyclical *Immortale Dei* (Nov. 1, 1885), §34n22, citing Pope Pius IX, *Syllabus Errorum* (Dec. 8, 1864), §§19, 29, 55, and 79; Pius X, Encyclical *Pascendi Dominici Gregis* (Sept. 8, 1907), §28n12, citing Syll., §5; *Pascendi*, §42n18, citing Syll., §13 [ASS 40 (1907): 620–21, 636–37].

[43] Newman, Letter to the Duke of Norfolk, 150–51.

[44] *The Catholic Encyclopedia* (New York: Encyclopedia Press, 1913), s.v. "Syllabus" (emphasis added). This article from the *Catholic Encyclopedia* is significant because it was published long before there was any need to harmonize the *Syllabus of Errors* with Vatican II. The corresponding article from the *New Catholic Encyclopedia* contains the same principle of interpretation. *The New Catholic Encyclopedia* (New York: McGraw-Hill Book Co., 1967), s.v. "Syllabus of Errors." The latter article notes that in interpreting the *Syllabus*, one must pay attention to the "exact wording" of the theses.

reiterated, "The true meaning of my words I have *'in petto,'*—to understand them you must read the original Documents."[45]

In fact, this method is similar to the one that Bishop Félix Dupanloup of Orléans, France, used in his celebrated exposition of the *Syllabus*.[46] Some commentators charge Dupanloup with *explaining away* the Syllabus rather than simply explaining it.[47] However, the pope himself expressed appreciation for Dupanloup's work.[48] In any event, even if some of Dupanloup's interpretations might neutralize the *Syllabus* excessively, he undeniably is on firm ground where he reads it in light of the original documents cited in the *Syllabus* itself.

The *Syllabus* was controversial from the start. It caused turmoil in diplomatic circles, and it confused many Catholics and caused resentment among Protestants. The Pope himself was distressed at the shock that the *Syllabus* had caused.[49] One reason for the hostile reaction to the *Syllabus* was that the condemned propositions seemed to be framed in the most provocative way possible.[50] However, when one looks to the original documents supporting the rejected theses, it becomes clear that many of the condemnations are less sweeping than they appear to be at first glance.

This principle of having recourse to the original documents is particularly important with regard to thesis 15 because it has long been recognized that this thesis, though described as an error, admits of a correct interpretation.[51] Thesis 15 implicates liberty of worship by rejecting the proposition that "[e]very man is free to embrace and profess that religion which, guided by the light of reason, he shall consider true."[52]

---

[45] Damian McElrath, *The Syllabus of Pius IX: Some Reactions in England* (Louvain, Belgium: Publications Universitaires de Louvain, 1964), 30–31.

[46] Cf. Félix Dupanloup, *La convention du 15 septembre et l'encyclique du 8 décembre* (Paris, 1865), 21, 26.

[47] Cf. McElrath, *Reactions in England*, 57; Doyle, "Pius IX and Religious Freedom," 330.

[48] The Pope's letter to Dupanloup is published at the beginning of the pamphlet (cf. Dupanloup, *Remarks on the Encyclical*, 1–4).

[49] Cf. Hales, *Pio Nono*, 273.

[50] The historian E. E. Y. Hales, however, suggests that the format and genre of the document also are significant in this regard. "Read straight through, as though it were an independent document in its own right, it is as irritating and as indigestible as any summarised index of condemnations read consecutively must necessarily be" (Hales, *Pio Nono*, 256).

[51] *Catholic Encyclopedia*, s.v. "Syllabus"; *New Catholic Encyclopedia*, s.v. "Syllabus of Errors."

[52] Syll., §15. Along similar lines, Pope Leo XII had issued an 1824 encyclical criticizing the philosophical idea that "God has given every individual a wide freedom to embrace and adopt without danger to his salvation whatever sect or opinion appeals to him on the basis of his private judgment." Pope Leo XII, Encyclical *Ubi Primum* (May 5, 1824), §13 [Bull. Rom. IV (Continuatio) (Prato), VIII (1854), 53–57].

6.3. Bl. Pius IX, *The Syllabus of Errors* (1864)

The *Syllabus* here does not condemn *every* principle of freedom of conscience or freedom of religion but only the one that is contained in the citations that follow thesis 15. Those citations refer to two previous pronouncements of Pius IX, one from 1851 and the other from 1862. When one turns to these documents, one discovers that the type of freedom of conscience or religion that is condemned is freedom in the sense that it is expounded by a Peruvian priest, Francisco de Paula Vigil, in his work *Defensa*.[53] Vigil held that one must follow one's human reason *to the exclusion of divine reason*. That is, Vigil taught that one must refuse to consider or follow supernatural revelation in one's acceptance of religious truth.[54]

Thus, the statement condemned in thesis 15 does not mean what it, at first blush, might appear to mean to contemporary readers—that one has no freedom in religion and that human reason must be entirely excluded from consideration of such matters. Rather, its meaning is simply that one may not exclude revelation in seeking religious truth. Indeed, Dupanloup, in his pamphlet on the *Syllabus*, recalls the multiple times that Pius IX has praised reason. "He is doing what the Church has always done. He is vindicating the cause both of reason and of faith! He defends reason against the sophists, and faith against the impious."[55]

Thesis 55 concerns separation of Church and state. The proposition that it rejects is the following: "The Church ought to be separated from the State, and the State from the Church." The intention here seems *not* to be to condemn all disestablishment but rather to reject the absolutizing claims of some Liberal Catholics asserting that separation should be the rule everywhere.[56] Along similar lines, thesis 77 rejects the following proposition: "In the present day it is no longer expedient that the Catholic religion should be held as the only religion of the State, to the exclusion of all other forms of worship." The document cited in support of thesis 77 is the allocution *Nemo Vestrum* (1855).[57] This allocution concerned Spain's unilateral breach of its Concordat with the Holy See, providing that Catholicism would be

---

[53] Pope Pius IX, Allocution *Maxima Quidem* (June 9, 1862) [*Acta Pii IX* 3:451–61]; Pope Pius IX, Damnatio *Multiplices Inter* (June 10, 1851) [*Acta Pii IX* 1:280–84]. The full title of the work in which Vigil puts forth his theories is his *Defensa de la autoridad de los Gobiernos y de los Obispos contra las pretenciones de la Curia Romana* (1848). *Multiplices Inter* is addressed to Vigil's *Defensa* specifically, and *Maxima Quidem*, one of the most frequently cited documents in the *Syllabus*, discusses a number of different issues.

[54] Cf. *Catholic Encyclopedia*, s.v. "Syllabus"; *New Catholic Encyclopedia*, s.v. "Syllabus of Errors."

[55] Dupanloup, *Remarks on the Encyclical*, 24. See also Dupanloup, 23–24.

[56] Cf. Hales, *Pio Nono*, 265–66.

[57] Pope Pius IX, Allocution *Nemo Vestrum* (July 26, 1855) [*Acta Pii IX* 2:441].

the sole religion of the state. Thus, as Harrison points out, the meaning of thesis 77 is simply that in overwhelmingly Catholic Spain, it remains expedient for Catholicism to be the sole religion of the state. It does not call for establishment everywhere but simply rejects the Liberal Catholic demand for disestablishment everywhere.[58] These issues of separation between Church and state are addressed at length above in chapter 4 of this study.

Perhaps the most significant provision for the purposes of this inquiry is thesis 78. It rejects the proposition that "it has been wisely decided by law, in some Catholic countries, that persons coming to reside therein shall enjoy the public exercise of their own peculiar worship." This statement indeed comes close to taking a position directly opposite to that of *Dignitatis Humanae*. In the discussion below of Leo XIII, we will see that this question of the rights of non-Catholics in a Catholic state is indeed one of the most crucial and most difficult issues. With regard to the *Syllabus*, though, the method of considering the cited supporting document again shows the thesis to be less broad than it initially appears.

The original document from which thesis 78 is taken was addressed to the situation of immigrants to New Granada (now Colombia).[59] That is, the original document was addressed not to the universal Church but to a specific situation in a single country. One can see this by the fact that thesis 78 addresses only the situation of *immigrants*. If a general rule of applicability had been intended, one would not have expected the pope to single out immigrants. After all, it is difficult to find any principled reason to distinguish public worship by non-Catholic *immigrants* from public worship by non-Catholic *natives* of a Catholic state.[60] This circumstance recalls the discussion above of Popes Pius VI and Pius VII, whose pronouncements are indeed significant but are limited to addressing the situation in France. However, although thesis 78 presents little difficulty for reconciliation with Vatican II, it raises the matter of the rights of non-Catholics in Catholic states. This will be a key theme of Leo XIII, and it will be one of the crucial questions in the attempt to harmonize *Dignitatis Humanae* with the teachings of the nineteenth-century popes.

One final observation on the *Syllabus* is in order. Even if the principle of recourse to the original documents significantly softens several of the

---

[58] Cf. Harrison, RL&C, 57. Harrison treats thesis 77 at length. See generally RL&C, 55–60.

[59] Cf. Pope Pius IX, Allocution *Acerbissimum* (Sept. 27, 1852) [*Acta Pii IX* 1:383–95].

[60] One reason that the nonuniversal character of this document is significant is that pronouncements of the teaching office can be infallible only if they apply to the universal Church. Cf. First Vatican Council, Dogmatic Constitution on the Church of Christ *Pastor Aeternus* (July 18, 1870), ch. 4 [ASS 6 (1870–1871): 47]; LG, §25c.

theses listed there, still the question that remains is why Bl. Pius IX would allow the *Syllabus* so often to give the impression of condemning a wider range of ideas than the underlying documents really do condemn. This question is especially important because Pius seems to have intended to be provocative in issuing the *Syllabus*. He reportedly referred to the Syllabus as "raw meat, needing to be cooked and seasoned."[61] Disputes over the *Syllabus* did not arise only with Vatican II, but rather the *Syllabus* sparked controversy as soon as it was published. An answer to the question of the Pope's motivations is beyond the scope of the present inquiry. However, part of the answer no doubt lies in the sheer number and magnitude of the threats that the Church faced from both the civil governments and the world of intellectual ideas during Pius's reign. His successor, Leo XIII, was blessed with a much less tumultuous reign and generally was more receptive to modern ideas than Pius was, but Leo too saw the need to protect the faithful from dangerous intellectual trends.[62] Keeping the number and gravity of the mid-nineteenth-century threats in mind, one might imagine Pius making his own the explanation that twentieth-century fiction writer Flannery O'Connor would offer for the frequently stark and disturbing content of her own work: "To the hard of hearing you shout, and for the almost blind you draw large and startling figures."[63]

6.4. Leo XIII, *Immortale Dei* (1885) and *Libertas* (1888)

Michael Davies (1936–2004), a traditionalist critic and prominent apologist for Archbishop Lefebvre, was precise in his framing of the key doctrinal issue concerning Vatican II and religious liberty.[64] He cited the key passage of *Dignitatis Humanae*, article 2, and its proclamation that all men have a right to religious liberty (that is, to non-coercion of religious acts and to noninterference with one's own religious acts, within due limits), and he contrasted it with the teachings of the nineteenth-century popes, who had taught that

---

[61] Hales, *Pio Nono*, 273.
[62] Cf. Pope Leo XIII, Encyclical *Providentissimus Deus* (Nov. 18, 1893), concerning biblical studies.
[63] Flannery O'Connor, "The Fiction Writer and His Country," in *Mystery and Manners: Occasional Prose*, ed. Sally Fitzgerald and Robert Fitzgerald (New York: Farrar, Straus & Giroux, 1969), 34.
[64] Michael Davies, *Archbishop Lefebvre and Religious Liberty* (Rockford, IL: TAN Books and Publishers, 1980), 9–11. Cf. Michael Davies, "Pope Leo XIII on True Liberty," *Latin Mass* (Summer 1998): 62–66.

a Catholic state could *tolerate* the public worship of non-Catholics but that such worship was not the object of a *right*. Davies saw the Vatican II teaching as a seeming contradiction of the Church's previous teaching.[65]

The encyclicals of Pius IX's successor, Pope Leo XIII (1878–1903), present the clearest examples of statements with which Vatican II is in apparent conflict on the issue of non-Catholic worship in a Catholic state. For example, Leo's encyclical *Immortale Dei* (1885) rejects the idea that all religions should be treated as equal.

> [I]t is not lawful for the State . . . to hold in equal favor different kinds of religion; the unrestrained freedom of thinking and of openly making known one's thoughts is not inherent in the rights of citizens, and is by no means to be reckoned worthy of favor and support. (ID, §35)

Three years later, in his encyclical *Libertas* (1888), Leo made the same point even more forcefully.

> Justice therefore forbids, and reason itself forbids, the State to . . . treat the various religions (as they call them) alike, and to bestow upon them promiscuously equal rights and privileges. Since, then, the profession of one religion is necessary in the State, that religion must be professed which alone is true, and which can be recognized without difficulty, especially in Catholic States, because the marks of truth are, as it were, engraven upon it. (LP, §21)

These two quotations raise the question of the proper relationship between Church and state. As discussed above in chapter 4, *Dignitatis Humanae* shifted the focus of the Church-state discussion in a new direction, but it did not overturn the papal teaching of the nineteenth century on the duty of the civic authority to religion. These quotations also raise the issue of *indifferentism*, the idea that one may attain salvation by the profession of any religion at all. As suggested in the discussion of *Mirari Vos* above, this concern loomed large in the thought of the nineteenth-century popes, and it is the prism through which the Vatican II fathers most often interpreted those earlier papal teachings. This perspective will be discussed

---

[65] Davies was careful not to argue that Vatican II necessarily contradicts previous teaching but rather that he personally is unable to see how the teachings are consistent (cf. SVC&RL, 2–3).

below in sections 7.2 and 7.3.1.2–4. However, the most significant teaching of *Libertas* concerned neither the Church-state relationship nor the question of indifferentism. Rather, it concerned the posture of a Catholic state toward public non-Catholic worship. On this matter, Leo taught that the state might tolerate non-Catholic worship as a necessary evil but that it could never endorse it as a positive good.

> [W]hile not conceding any right to anything save what is true and honest, she [the Church] does not forbid public authority to *tolerate* what is at variance with truth and justice, for the sake of avoiding some greater evil, or of obtaining or preserving some greater good. God Himself in His providence, though infinitely good and powerful, permits evil to exist in the world, partly that greater good may not be impeded, and partly that greater evil may not ensue. In the government of States it is not forbidden to imitate the Ruler of the world. . . . But if, in such circumstances, for the sake of the common good (and this is the only legitimate reason), human law may or even should tolerate evil, *it may not and should not approve or desire evil for its own sake*; for evil of itself, being a privation of good, is opposed to the common welfare which every legislator is bound to desire and defend to the best of his ability.[66]

Leo went on to say that "the more a State is driven to tolerate evil, the further it is from perfection" (LP, §34). In addition, he made clear that the extent of toleration must be strictly circumscribed by the benefit to public welfare that justifies the policy of toleration (LP, §34).

Thus, the key conflict is established: Leo taught that although it sometimes is permissible for a Catholic state to *tolerate* public worship by non-Catholics, non-Catholics do not have a *right* to public worship. However, the Vatican II Declaration on Religious Liberty *Dignitatis Humanae* seems to contemplate just such a *right* by providing that no person may be restrained from acting according to his religious convictions "whether privately or publicly" (DH, §2a). Nearly all commentators appear to agree that this difference between toleration and a right is a difference not merely in *degree* but in *kind*. This is the essence of Patrick O'Neil's position reflected in the quotation at the head of this chapter. Fernando Ocáriz and José Martín de Agar take similar positions.[67]

---

[66] Pope Leo XIII, Encyclical *Libertas* (June 20, 1888), §33 (emphasis added); cf. ID, §36.
[67] Cf. Fernando Ocáriz, "Sulla libertà religiosa. Continuità del Vaticano II con il Magistero

Other popes would reaffirm these principles, most significantly Pope Pius XI in his encyclical *Quas Primas* instituting the liturgical Feast of Christ the King.[68] However, the content of this teaching remained essentially the same and no pope expounded it more fully than Leo XIII. For this reason, the most serious discussions about Vatican II and nineteenth-century teaching on toleration return repeatedly to Leo's encyclicals.[69] Therefore, with regard to the rights of non-Catholics to religious liberty, Leo's two encyclicals *Immortale Dei* and *Libertas* will serve as a key baseline of nineteenth-century papal thought that must be reconciled with *Dignitatis Humanae*, or vice versa, to avoid a doctrinal contradiction.

---

precedente," *Annales theologici* 3 (1989): 89: "il principio di tolleranza non è equivalente al principio di libertà religiosa." Cf. José T. Martín de Agar, "Ecclesia y Polis," *Ius Canonicum* (2008): 411: "*lo que se tolera nunca es un derecho.*"

[68] Pope Pius XI, Encyclical *Quas Primas* (Dec. 11, 1925) [AAS 17 (1925): 593–610] (hereinafter cited as QP).

[69] See, e.g., the following articles by Murray: "Leo XIII on Church and State: The General Structure of the Controversy," *Theological Studies* 14, no. 1 (1953); "Leo XIII: Separation of Church and State," *Theological Studies* 14, no. 2 (1953); "Leo XIII: Two Concepts of Government." *Theological Studies* 14, no. 4 (1953); "Leo XIII: Two Concepts of Government (II): Government and the Order of Culture," *Theological Studies* 15, no. 1 (1954): 1–33.

CHAPTER 7

The Scope of the Right to Religious Liberty

A double minded man is inconstant in all his ways.

— JAMES 1:8[1]

A thing as old as the Catholic Church has an accumulated armoury and treasury to choose from; it can pick and choose among the centuries and brings one age to the rescue of another. It can call in the old world to redress the balance of the new.

— G. K. CHESTERTON[2]

This chapter constitutes the beginning of my analysis of the Vatican II right to religious liberty proper. This analysis concerns the scope, object, and foundation of the right to religious liberty recognized in *Dignitatis Humanae*, and it runs through this chapter and the following four.

This chapter examines the *scope* of the right. That is, it will consider the *realms* within which this right exists: private and public, moral and juridical, etcetera. It also will begin to consider what sort of limitations constrain

---

[1] The Holy Bible: Douay-Rheims Version, rev. Bishop Richard Challoner, 1749–1752 (Rockford, IL: TAN Books and Publishers, Inc., 1989). The RSVCE (verses 6-8) says, "[H]e who doubts is like a wave of the sea that is driven and tossed by the wind. For that person must not suppose that a double-minded man, unstable in all his ways, will receive anything from the Lord."

[2] G. K. Chesterton, *The Catholic Church and Conversion* (New York: MacMillan Company, 1926), ch. 5.

this right and its exercise, though this question will be dealt with at greater length in part 4, especially in chapter 12.

The next chapter will consider the *object* of the right, and then all three chapters of part 3B will investigate its *foundation*. The groundwork for this analysis has been laid especially in the previous chapter, which has identified the key papal statements with which DH must be reconciled. The key question in the analysis running throughout these five chapters is whether the right to religious liberty that Vatican II recognizes is the same one that the nineteenth-century popes rejected. I hope to demonstrate that the answer to this question is *no*.

As discussed in chapter 3, the analysis of the right to religious liberty requires the drawing of some distinctions. This is particularly important in this chapter and the four that follow. In studying the scope of the right to religious liberty here, it is necessary to come to an understanding of the *ambit* within which the Council recognizes this right to religious liberty. That is, it is necessary to distinguish the individual *moral* realm from the *social* or *juridical* realm.

Throughout this chapter, I distinguish frequently between the private and public spheres and between the moral and juridical realms. For the purposes of discussing DH and the nineteenth-century papal teaching, there is a *rough* correspondence between these two dichotomies. That is, the *private* corresponds approximately to the individual *moral* realm (or, perhaps more precisely, the individual moral realm corresponds to a *part* of the private sphere), and the *public* roughly corresponds to the *juridical*. This correspondence applies here for the special purpose of comparing these teachings at the outset, but it is by no means a perfect correspondence. (Indeed, later in this chapter, I will need to distinguish the private from the moral.) When I say below that the right recognized by DH is not a moral right, I have in mind the context of the individual or private moral decision. That is, DH does not imply that every individual or private religious choice is morally justified. I believe that this rough correspondence is clear, but by identifying the private sphere with the (individual) moral realm for part of the discussion in this chapter, I do not wish to suggest that morality is confined to the private sphere. Similarly, there is a rough correspondence between the public sphere and the juridic realm. This is because the law is concerned especially with acts that impact the common good, that is, acts with some public or social significance.[3] Again, this rough correspondence

---

[3] Cf. St. Thomas Aquinas, *Summa Theologica*, Christian Classics ed. (Benziger Brothers, 1947), I/II, q. 96 (hereinafter, ST).

should be clear, but so should its limitations. That is, despite the law's predominant concern with the social or public sphere, it is obvious that acts done in private also can have juridic significance.[4]

In short, the nineteenth-century popes often united the two realms (moral and juridic), and when they rejected *the liberty of conscience and of cults*, they generally were rejecting a right that they understood to straddle both realms. In the private sphere, this claimed right concerned the individual moral realm. It was an alleged right to believe whatever one chose to believe. The popes rejected this right for several reasons but above all as an embrace of *indifferentism*, namely, the idea that one might obtain salvation by the profession and practice of any religion whatsoever. At the same time, they usually concerned themselves equally with the *social* ramifications of this asserted right and especially with the claimed right to propagate any ideas whatsoever and any form of worship.

This attentiveness to both the private and public spheres (or the moral and the juridical realms) is a particular strength of the approach of the nineteenth-century popes. Indeed, I believe that it represents the beginning (or at least the modern beginning) of an implicit teaching on the human person—concerning his social dimension—that will come to fruition and that will become explicit at Vatican II. I will refer to this development in the remainder of this chapter and in chapters 9 through 11.

Throughout this part of my study, I am attempting to show that the right that DH recognizes is *not* the same right that the nineteenth-century popes rejected. This chapter offers a component of this argument by demonstrating that these rights differ in their *scope*, that is, in the realms in which they are operative. As mentioned above and as discussed more fully below, the *liberty of conscience and of cults* that the nineteenth-century popes rejected was a right that its proponents asserted in both the moral and the juridical realms. By contrast, the scope of the Vatican II right to religious liberty is narrower. Although it applies both in private and in public, it does not apply in the realm of individual morality but rather in the juridical realm. Moreover, within the juridical realm, the Vatican II right is not the unlimited or nearly unlimited right that the nineteenth-century popes

---

[4] The same is true of acts that affect relations between persons. That is, the law is concerned with such actions, even in the absence of an apparent impact on society or the common good. Thus, Hervada makes clear that law concerns not only the individual's duties to the community and the community's duties to the individual but also the duties of one person to another. Cf. Javier Hervada, *Critical Introduction to Natural Law*, trans. Mindy Emmons (Montreal: Wilson & Lafleur, 2006), 39–40.

condemned but rather a right that applies only "within due limits." Chapter 8 and the whole of part 4 discuss additional differences as well.[5]

7.1. Some Preliminary Notes on Conscience

This inquiry into the scope of the right to religious liberty will focus especially on liberty of conscience. As discussed above, Pope Gregory XVI began by addressing *liberty of conscience* in *Mirari Vos* (1832), and although he does not define this term, it at least seems closely related to the *liberty of conscience and of cults* (or the *liberty of conscience and worship*) originating with the French Revolution. Thus, in reaffirming *Mirari Vos*, Gregory's successor Pius IX describes it as rejecting *liberty of conscience and worship* (QC, §3). Pius and his own successor Leo XIII will speak more often of liberty of worship, but in this section, the focus is on the pronouncements of the early and mid nineteenth century, which refer more frequently to liberty of conscience.

It is necessary to keep in mind the relationship between these three terms: *liberty of conscience, liberty of worship*, and *liberty of conscience and of cults* (or *worship*). The terms are bound very closely together. In fact, the first two are components of the third. However, it seems that when the popes use one of the first two terms—*liberty of conscience* or *liberty of worship*—they nearly always are referring to the more comprehensive idea that unites both components. I say that this *seems* to be the case, because, owing to the sometime absence of definitions of terms, it is difficult to speak with

---

[5] Although the Council limited the right to religious liberty to the juridical realm, it did not neglect the moral realm. On the contrary, it reaffirmed the duty of the person to seek the truth in religious matters. Cf. Second Vatican Council, Declaration on Religious Liberty *Dignitatis Humanae* (December 7, 1965), §1b. It simply limited the right to religious liberty to the juridical realm. Stated differently, Vatican II does not speak of a right before God or a right objectively to believe anything that one wishes to believe. Religious liberty is not a moral right in this sense. Cf. Jérôme Hamer, "Histoire du texte de la Déclaration," *Unam Sanctam* 60 (1967): 96 (the fifth draft makes clear that DH does not concern the relationship between man and God); Fernando Ocáriz, "Sulla libertà religiosa. Continuità del Vaticano II con il Magistero precedente," *Annales theologici* 3 (1989): 74 (DH does not treat the relationship between man and God, but the relationships between persons in human and civil society). Rather, it is a juridic right. It is an immunity that protects religious belief and practice in civil society. However, its purpose is to make possible the exercise of the moral right to seek the truth and to embrace it. Cf. Basile Valuet, *Le droit à la liberté religieuse dans la Tradition de l'Eglise. Un cas de développement doctrinal homogène par le magistère authentique*, 2nd rev. ed. (Barroux: Éditions Sainte-Madeleine, 2011), 420–21: Adherence to the truth is the finality of the right to religious liberty but is not its foundation. See also LRTE, 428, 432.

certainty about all instances of the popes' use of these terms. Nevertheless, as discussed immediately above, it is clear that Pius IX (in *Quanta Cura*) reads his predecessor's encyclical (*Mirari Vos*) in exactly this way. Thus, a reader must be aware that the nineteenth-century popes sometimes use these terms interchangeably. This is the case even though the reference to *conscience* may seem to imply a concern with the private or moral realm, while the reference to worship seems to indicate a greater concern with the public or juridical realm.[6]

In addition, despite the many papal rejections of liberty of conscience, it is necessary to recall that this phrase admits of an orthodox—as well as an unorthodox—interpretation. In this way, it is like thesis 15 of the *Syllabus of Errors*—concerning the following of one's reason in religious matters—discussed above in section 6.3. Some traditionalist critics reject the type of analysis proposed in this (and succeeding) chapters. In at least some of their arguments, they seem to assert that it is sufficient to demonstrate a contradiction simply by recalling that the nineteenth-century popes rejected liberty of worship and that Vatican II embraced a concept with the same (or a similar) name.[7] In fact, however, the popes themselves acknowledge that certain phrases can be understood either in accordance with Catholic doctrine or in opposition to it.[8] Thus, in accordance with the method employed here, one must look behind the words to their meaning.

John Henry Cardinal Newman took up the issue of liberty of conscience in his famous 1874 letter to the Duke of Norfolk. That letter was a public reply to William Gladstone's criticisms of Pope Pius IX's *Quanta Cura*,

---

[6] As discussed above in the introduction to this chapter and below in section 7.2, I do not mean to suggest an exact correlation between the public realm and the juridic realm, or between the private and the moral. Rather, these distinctions mark approximate delineations only.

[7] Cf. Marcel de Corte et al., *Lettre à Quelques Évêques* (Paris: Société Saint-Thomas-d'Aquin, 1983), 117, arguing that a difference in foundations between the right that Pius IX rejected and the one that Vatican II recognized is irrelevant. See also de Corte, 76, arguing that the philosophical and historical context of the nineteenth-century condemnations is irrelevant. In other parts of the *Lettre*, however, de Corte and his co-authors do inquire into the meaning of terms and the context of the nineteenth-century pronouncements. Cf. de Corte, 83, concerning the meaning of liberty of conscience; de Corte 88–95, concerning the context of *Mirari Vos*; and de Corte, 102–4, concerning the meaning of conscience and liberty of conscience. However, their study largely treats the terms as clear on their face and as having been called into question only after Vatican II and only as a result of the need to reconcile DH with previous teaching (cf. de Corte, 81, 84, 95).

[8] See the discussion shortly below in this section of Leo XIII's teaching on *liberty of conscience* in his 1888 encyclical *Libertas*.

his *Syllabus of Errors*, and the First Vatican Council's definition of papal infallibility. Although Gladstone aims his criticism at Pius IX, Newman understands that in the area of liberty of conscience, the key teaching is that of Pope Gregory XVI in *Mirari Vos* (discussed above in section 6.1).

Newman begins his defense of the papal teachings by distinguishing between two different notions of conscience. The traditional Catholic idea of conscience is that it is a person's apprehension in his mind of the natural law. Newman's description calls to mind the biblical image of a law inscribed by God on the human heart (Jer 31:33; Rom 2:14–16).[9] According to traditional Catholic teaching, a person is obliged to follow his conscience, even if it is mistaken. In this sense, the conscience is indeed free and, if Gregory XVI or Pius IX had spoken against conscience under this meaning, they would have been wrong.

However, it is a different sense of conscience that the popes speak against in rejecting liberty of conscience. That is, by the nineteenth century, philosophers had put forward a flawed notion of conscience. Under this second meaning, conscience was considered not the divine law written on the human heart but rather simply a creation of man himself. Newman describes both the correct understanding of conscience and its distortion:

> Conscience is a stern monitor, but in this century it has been superseded by a counterfeit, which the eighteen centuries prior to it never heard of, and could not have mistaken for it, if they had. It is the right of self-will.[10]

According to Newman, it is this second notion of free conscience that the popes reject. Nevertheless, the erroneous notion of conscience endures even into our own day. Germain Grisez provides a late-twentieth-century description of what Newman seems to have had in mind when he referred to *self-will*:

---

[9] The Catechism of the Catholic Church defines *conscience* as "a judgment of reason whereby the human person recognizes the moral quality of a concrete act." Catechism of the Catholic Church, 2nd ed. (Vatican City: Libreria Editrice Vaticana, 1997), (CCC, §1778). Citing Newman's letter to the Duke of Norfolk, the Catechism says that it is by the judgment of conscience that one "perceives and recognizes the prescriptions of the divine law" (CCC, §1778).

[10] John Henry Newman, Letter to the Duke of Norfolk (Dec. 27, 1874), reprinted in *Newman and Gladstone: The Vatican Decrees*, with an introduction by Alvan S. Ryan (Notre Dame, IN: University of Notre Dame Press, 1962), 130.

7.1. Some Preliminary Notes on Conscience

> [C]onscience today is often confused with arbitrariness. This is expressed by such statements as, 'My conscience tells me it's all right to do this, so it is all right for me.' Such moral subjectivism rests on two confusions. First, the fact that conscience is one's own grasp of moral truth is taken to mean that moral truth itself is whatever one makes it. Second, moral principles, which are the source of conscience's authority, are mistaken for legal impositions, which it is the task of the conscience to judge.[11]

As Newman's discussion shows, it is not sufficient simply to focus on the word *conscience* or the phrase *liberty of conscience*. A narrow and exclusive focus on the words themselves, rather than the meaning behind them, renders a serious inquiry into the doctrinal question difficult or impossible. A *contradiction* exists when two statements cannot both be true at the same time and *in the same respect*. One can determine what the relevant *respect* is only by looking behind the words to the meaning that they signify.[12] Newman makes this clear by distinguishing sharply between the traditional and modern ideas of conscience.

A decade later Pope Leo XIII would make a distinction very much along Newman's lines, and he would leave no doubt that liberty of conscience, though often rejected by his predecessors, admits of a sound and orthodox interpretation as well.

> Another liberty is widely advocated, namely, liberty of conscience. If by this is meant that everyone may, as he chooses, worship God or not, it is sufficiently refuted by the arguments already adduced. But it may also be taken to mean that every man in the State may follow the will of God and, from a consciousness of duty and free from every obstacle, obey His commands. This, indeed, is true liberty, a liberty worthy of the sons of God, which nobly maintains the dignity of man and is stronger than all violence or wrong—a liberty which the Church has always desired and held most dear. (LP, §30)

These principles should be familiar to Catholics who have received a sound formation, but they nevertheless bear reaffirmation and new emphasis.

---

[11] Germain Grisez, *The Way of the Lord Jesus*, vol. 1, *Christian Moral Principles* (Chicago: Franciscan Herald Press, 1983), 88–89.

[12] Cf. Bernard J. F. Lonergan, *Method in Theology* (London: Darton, Longman, & Todd Ltd., 1972; reprint, Toronto: University of Toronto Press, 1996), 323: "[T]he permanence [of doctrine] attaches to the meaning and not to the formula."

The reason is that the nineteenth-century popes' condemnation of liberty of conscience left many people, especially Protestants, with the impression that the Church rejected *every* principle of conscience. Indeed, it may have created the suspicion in some quarters that the Church sought to control the very thoughts of her faithful. Newman's correspondent, Gladstone, is a key example. Gladstone recently had been Prime Minister of the United Kingdom (and eventually would serve three more times in this post), and he had been instrumental in the disestablishment of the Church of Ireland, which meant that Irish Catholics no longer would be compelled to support the official Protestant Church. Thus, Gladstone, a sincere Protestant, was not lacking in sympathy for—or in a desire to do justice to—Catholics. However, Gladstone feared that the papal pronouncements and the teaching on infallibility would divide the loyalty of British Catholics between two sovereigns. Thus, Newman's—and later, Leo's—engagement on this issue were crucial.

Half a century later, Pope Pius XI would make the same point as Leo XIII, but in a different way. In his encyclical *Non Abbiamo Bisogno* (1931), Pius recognized that misunderstandings over conscience or liberty of conscience could be resolved through a shift in terminology. Thus, he distinguished between an inadmissible principle of freedom of *conscience* (singular) and the legitimate principle of freedom of *consciences* (plural).[13] This may seem like hair-splitting or like drawing an excessively fine distinction, but it is not. Rather, it is an acknowledgement of the fact that *liberty of conscience* is a *term of art* and that in the context of the papal responses to it, it signifies a particular theory originating in the late eighteenth century and spread widely in the nineteenth century. It grows out of the French Revolution and is embodied especially in articles 10 and 11 of the DDHC. It is this particular notion of *liberty of conscience* that the popes condemn, and not necessarily all other possible meanings of the term.

---

[13] "È in considerazione di questo duplice diritto delle anime, che Ci dicevamo testè lieti e fieri di combattere la buona battaglia per la libertà delle coscienze, non già (come qualcuno forse inavvertitamente Ci ha fatto dire) per la libertà di coscienza, maniera di dire equivoca e troppo spesso abusata a significare la assoluta indipendenza della coscienza, cosa assurda in anima da Dio creata e redenta." Pope Pius XI, Encyclical *Non Abbiamo Bisogno* (June 29, 1931), §41 [AAS 23 (1931): 301–2]. In a speech to the Council, Bishop De Smedt called attention to this distinction. Cf. Émile De Smedt, Oral *Relatio* on Chapter V of *De Oecumenismo* (Nov. 19, 1963) [AS II/5, 485–95]; English translation in in Hans Küng, Yves Congar, O.P., and Daniel O'Hanlon, S.J., eds., *Council Speeches of Vatican II* (Glen Rock, NJ: Paulist Press, 1964), 249–50.

7.2. The Nineteenth-Century Union of the Moral and Juridical Realms

The distinction between the moral and juridical realms is one of the Second Vatican Council's most important insights, and it denotes an approach that differs somewhat from that of the nineteenth-century popes. That is, although Vatican II discusses the moral realm, it makes clear that the right to religious liberty that it is recognizing belongs not to that sphere but rather to the juridical realm.[14] Thus, the subtitle of the declaration is crucial: "On the Right of the Person and of Communities to Social and Civil Freedom in Matters Religious."[15]

However, when the nineteenth-century popes taught against liberty of conscience (or liberty of conscience and worship), they often were making reference to the moral and social (or juridical) realms *at the same time*. Thus, they rejected the assertion that in the individual moral realm a person has a right to believe whatever he wishes, and they also rejected the social or juridical consequences of this claim to liberty, namely the assertion that a person has a right openly to propagate and publish any opinions whatsoever in society.[16]

This characteristic of unity between the two realms (public and private,

---

[14] As discussed in chapter 8, the right that DH proclaims is a right in civil society, that is, a right in the juridical realm. As discussed in chapter 9, however, the foundation of this right is the dignity of the human person and, in particular, his duty to seek the truth, especially the truth about God. Thus, DH proclaims a right in the juridical realm, but its finality is located in the moral realm. See section 7.1 above, citing Valuet, LRTE, 420–21, 428, 432.

[15] Fernando Ocáriz in particular calls attention to the subtitle in making clear the scope and ambit of the Vatican II right to religious liberty (cf. "Sulla libertà religiosa," 73).

[16] Again, I do not mean to suggest an exact correspondence between the private/public distinction and the moral/juridical distinction. After all, public morality is as much a reality as private morality, and indeed the Council envisions the spirit of the Gospel permeating even the juridical realm. Cf. Second Vatican Council, Decree on the Apostolate of the Laity *Apostolicam Actuositatem* (Nov. 18, 1965), §13: "[T]he effort to infuse the Christian spirit into the mentality, customs, laws, and structures of the community" is the duty of the laity [AAS 58 (1966): 849]. In addition, I will discuss the *social* realm as corresponding to both the *public* sphere and the *juridical* realm.

I do, however, mean to suggest a *rough* or *approximate* correspondence between these two dichotomies. The main reason is that the thought of Lamennais tends toward the consignment of morality to the private realm. It does not necessarily banish morality from the public realm, but at least as a practical matter, it tends strongly in this direction by severing the link between private and public morality.

By the same token, the juridical realm may not be coextensive with the public realm. Much human activity takes place in public that does not have juridical significance, at least not in the usual understanding. In addition, activity in the private realm can indeed have juridical import in some cases. However, to the extent that it is common to consider the juridical realm as concerning matters that impact the common good and not only an

or juridical and moral) appears most clearly in the pronouncements of Pope Pius VI (1775–1799) and Pope Bl. Pius IX (1846–1878). Recall Valuet's admonition that Pius VI's *Quod Aliquantum* is the key to understanding all of the nineteenth-century papal statements in this area.[17] Pius VI, writing at the very beginning of the Revolutionary period, condemns the Civil Constitution of the Clergy (1790) and warns against the immoderate freedom proclaimed by articles 10 and 11 of the *Declaration of the Rights of Man and the Citizen*. Article 10 concerns freedom of conscience and religion, while article 11 proclaims freedom of opinion and publication. However, Pius VI very significantly treats them as components of *a single right*, which, largely because of its unlimited or nearly unlimited nature, he calls "this monstrous right."[18]

In *Mirari Vos*, Gregory XVI (1831–1846) separates the realms slightly but still treats them as closely linked. Thus, he begins in the private or moral realm by condemning indifferentism, but he quickly moves to the social or juridical realm by rejecting an error that he says finds its origin in indifferentism, namely, liberty of conscience. This claimed right, he says, spreads ruin in both sacred and civil affairs. In this, he includes the asserted right to publish any writings whatsoever (MV, §§14–15).

Pope Pius IX will repeat Gregory's teaching, but he will tie the moral and juridical realms more closely together. Like Pius VI, he refers to *a single right*, which he calls "liberty of conscience and worship," but he discusses it in terms of both the individual moral realm and its social implications. Thus, beginning with the moral realm, he refers to the claim that "a right resides in the citizens to an absolute liberty." He immediately proceeds to the social manifestations of this right by specifying that the claimed right is "restrained by no authority whether ecclesiastical or civil," and that it includes the right of the people "openly and publicly to manifest and declare any of their ideas whatever, either by word of mouth, by the press, or in any other way" (QC, §3).[19]

---

individual's good, this rough correspondence between the juridical and the public realms should be clear.

[17] Cf. Basile Valuet, *La liberté religieuse et la tradition catholique. Un cas de développement doctrinal homogène dans le magistère authentique*, 3rd rev. ed. (Barroux: Éditions Sainte-Madeleine, 2011), vol. IA, 290 [= LRTE, 195].

[18] Pope Pius VI, Encyclical *Quod Aliquantum* (Mar. 10, 1791); English translation in Brian W. Harrison, *Religious Liberty and Contraception: Did Vatican II Open the Way for a New Sexual Ethic?* (Melbourne: John XXIII Fellowship Co-op., Ltd., 1988), 39.

[19] Thus, I disagree with Martin Rhonheimer's claim that Pius IX was condemning only a *civil right* to religious liberty. Cf. Rhonheimer, "Benedict XVI's 'Hermeneutic of Reform' and Religious Freedom," *Nova et Vetera* (English ed.) 9, no. 4 (2011): 1042: "[T]he freedom of

7.2. The Nineteenth-Century Union of the Moral and Juridical Realms

Leo XIII (1878–1903) frequently distinguishes the two realms clearly, but in discussing liberty of conscience, he too sometimes will treat the moral right and the juridical right as a single right. Thus, in *Immortale Dei* (1885), he begins by discussing private judgment in religion, and he easily transitions to the problem of the unlimited freedom to publish:

> [I]t is a part of this theory that all questions that concern religion are to be referred to private judgment; that everyone is to be free to follow whatever religion he prefers, or none at all if he disapprove of all. From this the following consequences logically flow: that the judgment of each one's conscience is independent of all law; that the most unrestrained opinions may be openly expressed as to the practice or omission of divine worship; and that everyone has unbounded license to think whatever he chooses and to publish abroad whatever he thinks. (ID, §26)

Later in the same encyclical, however, Leo distinguishes the two realms quite clearly. He equates indifferentism with atheism, and he discusses the two concepts in the context of private judgment.[20] Then, in the very next passage, he discusses liberty of thought and of publication, and he does so in in the context of the social or juridical realm.[21] In the encyclical *Libertas* three years later, Leo again clearly distinguishes the two realms but never forgets the close connection between them. Moreover, he makes clear that the errors he is discussing extend to both realms. "What naturalists or

---

religion that he [Pius IX] was condemning was nothing other than the civil right to freedom of worship." As the discussion in the main text makes clear, Pius IX was condemning a single right that bridged the moral and juridical realms.

[20] "To hold, therefore, that there is no difference in matters of religion between forms that are unlike each other, and even contrary to each other, most clearly leads in the end to the rejection of all religion in both theory and practice. And this is the same thing as atheism, however it may differ from it in name. Men who really believe in the existence of God must, in order to be consistent with themselves and to avoid absurd conclusions, understand that differing modes of divine worship involving dissimilarity and conflict even on most important points cannot all be equally probable, equally good, and equally acceptable to God." Pope Leo XIII, Encyclical *Immortale Dei* (Nov. 1, 1885), §31. Note that the individual moral realm is at issue here. That is, Leo is discussing the consequences for man himself rather than the social ramifications.

[21] "So, too, the liberty of thinking, and of publishing, whatsoever one likes, without any hindrance, is not in itself an advantage over which society can wisely rejoice" (ID, §32). Here Leo is focusing on the application in the juridical realm and on the resulting harm to society.

rationalists aim at in philosophy, that the supporters of liberalism . . . are attempting in the domain of morality and politics" (LP, §15). He begins by addressing the moral realm.

> [T]hese followers of liberalism deny the existence of any divine authority to which obedience is due, and proclaim that every man is the law to himself; from which arises that ethical system which they style independent morality, and which, under the guise of liberty, exonerates man from any obedience to the commands of God, and substitutes a boundless license. (LP, §15)

Leo then proceeds to discuss the social consequences. This moral system harms both individuals and the state. It destroys the principle of unity in society and the distinction between good and evil. It undermines authority and paves the way for tyranny (LP, §16).

What conclusions do these observations yield? The nineteenth-century popes do not all treat liberty of conscience (and of cults) in precisely the same way, but all see a very close connection between the private and public realms (or between the moral and the juridical). Some, like Pius VI and Pius IX (and sometimes Leo XIII), see only a single right at issue, albeit one with harmful implications in both spheres, the moral and the juridical. Others, such as Gregory XVI (and sometimes Leo XIII), distinguish the realms more sharply but nonetheless recognize the close bond between them. Thus, Gregory speaks of indifferentism in the moral realm but connects it closely to liberty of conscience in the juridical realm and the associated right to promote and publish any ideas whatsoever. As discussed in the next section, this uniting of the two realms in the minds of the nineteenth-century popes is both revealing and challenging. It is revealing in that it seems to offer an implicit teaching on the two aspects of the human person—the individual and the social—and on the necessity of maintaining consistency or integrity among them. However, it also is challenging because this straddling of the moral and juridical realms sometimes has led to misunderstandings of the nineteenth-century popes' teachings and their key concerns.

7.3. Consequences of the Blurring of the Moral and Juridical Realms

This blurring of the realms in some of the nineteenth-century papal pronouncements, as suggested immediately above, presents both an insight and a challenge. I begin with the challenge.

7.3. Consequences of the Blurring of the Moral and Juridical Realms

7.3.1. The Challenge

The challenge presented by this uniting of the moral and juridical realms becomes especially clear in considering the position of St. John Henry Newman in the nineteenth century and the critique of it by Father Brian Harrison in the twentieth century.

7.3.1.1. The Newman Position

Newman's engagement and debate with William Gladstone concerning the mid-nineteenth-century papal pronouncements yielded a much-needed reaffirmation and clarification of the correct understanding of conscience. (See section 7.1 above.) In addition, however, it also yielded a seeming difficulty in interpreting the nineteenth-century popes.

As discussed above, Newman recalls Gregory XVI's teaching in *Mirari Vos*, and he proceeds to offer an important clarification of what conscience is. He then proceeds to consider *Mirari Vos*, *Quanta Cura*, and the *Syllabus of Errors*, and he concludes that they are condemning only an extreme and unprecedented notion of freedom of conscience. "What if a man's conscience embraces the duty of regicide? Or infanticide? Or free love?"[22] That is, according to Newman, the popes are condemning only the radical idea that a person may embrace *any idea whatsoever*. This is a plausible reading, given these popes' frequent references to unlimited or unbridled freedoms. Gregory refers to a type of liberty in which "all restraints are removed" (MV, §14) and Pius IX refers to "an absolute liberty" that is "restrained by no authority" and that claims the right to propagate "any . . . ideas whatever" (QC, §3).

However, there is a difficulty with Newman's interpretation. Anticipating his opponent's objection, Newman says, "Perhaps he [Gladstone] will say, 'Why should the Pope take the trouble to condemn what is so wild?'"[23] Gladstone did indeed raise this objection, seriously questioning why Pius IX would bother to condemn a situation that does not exist and has never existed. That is, there has never been a nation that imposed no restrictions whatsoever on the publication and propagation of ideas. In a postscript to the letter, Newman answers by asserting that Pius issued his condemnation on account of the theories of certain writers that if taken to their *logical conclusion*, would result in this type of unbridled license of liberty.[24]

Newman's position is not entirely convincing. As Father Brian Harrison

---

[22] Newman, Letter to the Duke of Norfolk, 148.
[23] Newman, Letter to the Duke of Norfolk, 149.
[24] Newman cites the example of John Stuart Mill (cf. Letter to the Duke of Norfolk, 216).

says, Newman offers a reasonable explanation of *Mirari Vos* and *Quanta Cura*, but the price of this explanation is the necessity of admitting that the popes were "jousting only with a man of straw."[25] That is, they were writing encyclicals about problems that did not really exist and about theories that were so extreme that they hardly required condemnation.

7.3.1.2. The Harrison Critique

Harrison disagrees with Newman's analysis, arguing that the evils addressed by Gregory XVI and Pius IX were indeed real and were not at all theoretical as Newman seems to concede. This disagreement highlights the tension in the nineteenth-century encyclicals discussed above in section 7.2. This tension arises because it is not always clear whether the popes, in rejecting liberty of conscience, are referring to the individual moral realm or the realm of civil society. The erroneous modern notion of conscience—conscience as personal self-will—gives rise to two applications. First, it gives rise to the claim that a person has the *moral right* to embrace any idea that pleases him. Second, it gives rise to the claim to a *legal or civil right* to propagate any idea that one chooses, without interference from civil authorities.

As stated above, sometimes the popes seem to be concerned primarily with the individual moral realm. In an earlier nineteenth-century encyclical not yet discussed here, Pope Leo XII (1823–1829) expresses this concern when he criticizes the idea that "God has given every individual a wide freedom to embrace and adopt without danger to his salvation whatever sect or opinion appeals to him on the basis of his private judgment."[26] Note that Leo XII is speaking not of a person's rights in civil society but of his rights before God. Thesis 15 of the *Syllabus of Errors* expresses the same concern in rejecting the proposition that "[e]very man is free to embrace and profess that religion which, guided by the light of reason, he shall consider true." However, the nineteenth-century conception of freedom of conscience quickly gives rise to a claim for freedom of worship or freedom of religion (so much so that, as discussed above, the two often are joined under the single formulation *liberty of conscience and of worship*). As a result, Pius IX connects these two ideas in *Quanta Cura*. If a person's conscience is free of all constraints, then this freedom extends to the choice of religious ideas as well. The popes were concerned about the connection between these theories and *indifferentism*, the theory "that it is possible to obtain the eternal salvation

---

[25] Harrison, RL&C, 34.
[26] Pope Leo XII, Encyclical *Ubi Primum* (May 5, 1824), §13 [Bull. Rom. IV (Continuatio) (Prato), VIII (1854), 53–57].

7.3. Consequences of the Blurring of the Moral and Juridical Realms

of the soul by the profession of any kind of religion, as long as morality is maintained" (MV, §13). Liberty of conscience in the moral realm often is identified very closely with indifferentism, and when the popes discuss liberty of conscience in the juridical realm, they see its origin in indifferentism. Again, some will refer to a single right having ramifications in both realms, while others will speak of indifferentism in the individual moral realm and liberty of conscience in the social (or juridical) realm. These differences in treatment are relatively minor, given that all of these popes express alarm at both personal indifferentism and the unbridled freedom to propagate and publish ideas in society.

However, as an apparent result of the fact that both the moral and the juridical realms are at issue in the nineteenth-century papal statements, these pronouncements often are considered to be primarily a caution against, and a rejection of, indifferentism. That is, it is often said that the reason for the encyclicals *Mirari Vos* and *Quanta Cura* was to caution the faithful against the idea that all religions are equal or that all lead to salvation. As Harrison says, Newman is concerned primarily with this personal moral aspect of freedom of conscience. However, Harrison believes that the proper focus is not on the individual moral realm but on the realm of civil society (or the public sphere, or the juridical realm).

Just as the nineteenth-century popes sometimes seem to address the moral realm in their encyclicals discussing freedom of conscience, at other times they seem more concerned with the impact of freedom of conscience on civil society. Both *Mirari Vos* and *Quanta Cura* are concerned with the assertion of a right not only to hold various opinions as an intellectual and volitional matter but also to propagate them publicly (cf. MV, §15; QC, §3). Gregory says that an unrestrained liberty results in "the ruin of Church and State" (MV, §14). After rejecting freedom of conscience, Gregory speaks of the right to publish in similar words. "Here We must include that harmful and never sufficiently denounced freedom to publish any writings whatever and disseminate them to the people, which some dare to demand and promote with so great a clamor" (MV, §15). Pius IX too seems to be referring to the civil or juridical realm when he speaks of a liberty "restrained by no authority" (QC, §3).

For Harrison, it is crucial that the popes were concerned not only with personal moral freedom but with the civil order as well. Newman's mistake is to interpret the papal statements as directed only or primarily to the personal moral realm.[27] This mistake has persisted down to the Vatican II era. The

---

[27] Martin Rhonheimer takes the opposite position, namely, that the right that Pius IX was

nineteenth-century papal statements often are assumed to have applied only to a moral duty before God. That is, they sometimes are taken to reject only the claim that one has no duty in conscience to seek God or to follow his law. Indeed, some Vatican II fathers sought to reconcile *Dignitatis Humanae* with the nineteenth-century statements in this way.[28] They attempted to reconcile these teachings by asserting that the earlier papal statements apply only to personal moral freedom, but that the Vatican II Declaration on Religious Liberty applies to liberty in civil society and therefore considers the issue from a completely different perspective.

Harrison argues that this reasoning is flawed. It is not correct, he says, that Gregory XVI and Pius IX were concerned exclusively, or even primarily, with theories concerning personal moral freedom. Rather, like Vatican II, these popes were concerned with the rights of persons in civil society.

Harrison's critique is an important corrective. In some places, he seems to suggest that the real concern of the nineteenth-century popes was with the social realm rather than the moral realm. However, it is necessary to keep the nineteenth-century popes' own approach in mind, and that approach reveals that they were quite concerned with both realms. I doubt that Harrison would disagree with this, and I do not believe that it takes anything away from his critique and analysis. Indeed, he may well be correct that the popes' primary concern was with civil society. However, my own sense is that they were nearly as concerned—and possibly equally concerned—with the personal moral realm.

The question arises: Why did a luminary like Newman and a number of council fathers at Vatican II misinterpret the nineteenth-century popes

---

rejecting was only a civil right. Cf. Rhonheimer, "Benedict XVI's 'Hermeneutic of Reform' and Religious Freedom," 1042: "The contradiction arises only at the level of the assertion of the civil right." Rhonheimer makes the same connection between indifferentism and the right in the public realm discussed here. Cf. Rhonheimer, 1039: the nineteenth-century popes' conviction "was that a civil right to freedom of religion" implied indifferentism. However, as Pius VI made clear and as Valuet emphasizes, the claimed right that the popes condemned in both the private and the public realms is not merely a civil right, but rather it is akin to a natural right. See section 6.1 above, discussing *Quod Aliquantum*.

[28] Cf. De Smedt, Oral *Relatio* on Chapter V of *De Oecumenismo*, advancing an argument similar to that of Newman, stating that freedom of worship was condemned in the nineteenth century because it was based on indifferentism [AS II/5, 485–95; English translation in Küng/Congar/O'Hanlon, 247]; Sept. 25, 1964, oral intervention of Archbishop Gabriel-Marie Garrone of Toulouse [AS III/2, 534–35] (English translation in Leahy/Massimini, 53): "Here we are looking from another viewpoint; we are dealing not with principles such as liberalism and indifferentism, which were previously condemned and remain condemned, but with a course of action toward persons insofar as their religious life is concerned."

as being concerned almost exclusively with the personal moral realm? One reason seems to be that the nineteenth-century popes were indeed alarmed about indifferentism, and they mentioned it often in the statements under consideration here. As a result, perhaps the condemnation of indifferentism was so vivid and memorable as to obscure the popes' equal or greater concern with civil society. A second reason may be that the notion of an idea or an asserted right having significant applications in both the moral and juridical realms may have been difficult to grasp, especially since the popes—though all united in their concerns—varied somewhat in their terminology and in their conceptualization of liberty of conscience. Third, one of the signal consequences of the Enlightenment has been the fragmentation of the human person and of human life. For twentieth-century and twenty-first-century readers at least, it may be a challenge to determine when the nineteenth-century popes are addressing each distinct realm—moral or juridical—precisely because those popes were writing in a time before fragmentation and compartmentalization had become so pervasive, whereas, in our own day, Enlightenment thought has made such destructive inroads on the culture that the separation—or even isolation—of the public from the private (and the juridical from the moral) has come to seem normal and even natural to us.

Two consequences follow from Harrison's critique of Newman. First, it is more difficult to reconcile *Dignitatis Humanae* with *Mirari Vos* and *Quanta Cura* than some of the Vatican II fathers may have assumed. That is, although it is true that DH is not indifferentist,[29] it is incorrect to suggest that indifferentism was the sole concern of the nineteenth-century popes in their pronouncements on liberty of conscience and worship. Second, there is some lack of clarity as to the ideas that the nineteenth-century popes, especially Gregory XVI, really were rejecting. When one comes to understand these ideas, one realizes that they were not at all hypothetical ideas, as Gladstone charges and as Newman comes close to conceding. Rather, the encyclicals *Mirari Vos* and *Quanta Cura* were addressed to real situations. Harrison argues convincingly that the papal condemnations of freedom of conscience are aimed primarily at a single author, the French priest, Félicité de Lamennais. Father Harrison's argument merits serious attention, and although the previous chapter already has discussed these encyclicals as a response to Lamennais (see sections 6.1 to 6.3 above), a full appreciation of the Harrison critique requires a more thorough consideration of the thought of Lamennais.

---

[29] See chapter 8, especially sections 8.4 and 8.5 below.

7.3.1.3. The Importance of Lamennais

One might describe Félicité de Lamennais as a modern-day Tertullian. Like the great Patristic era theologian, Lamennais enlisted his considerable intellectual gifts in the service of an embattled Church. Both Tertullian and Lamennais made valuable contributions to the Church's intellectual life and assisted greatly in her defense against hostile forces. However, the similarities extend all too far. Like Tertullian, Lamennais followed a path that led him into conflict with the Church that he once had served so well. For all of their gifts, both thinkers were flawed by obstinacy. These defects caused both Tertullian and Lamennais to prefer their own ideas to communion with the Church, and to die without the Church's consolations.

Lamennais's formative years were a time of great turmoil for France. He grew up during the period of the French Revolution and came to manhood during the Napoleonic Wars. The chief combatants during this period were the partisans of the Revolution and the monarchs of the Bourbon dynasty. Lamennais eventually would develop strong animosities toward both.

With the close of the Napoleonic Wars, an era of conservatism emerged in France and throughout Europe. The quarter-century of bloodshed inaugurated by the Revolution had called into question the Enlightenment ideas that progress was inevitable, and that man was inherently good.[30] In 1815 the Congress of Vienna restored the Bourbon monarchy to the French throne. A period of relative peace followed, and a Catholic revival took place in France. Led by thinkers such as Chateaubriand and de Maistre (and by the spiritual example of the Curé d'Ars), the French came to a renewed appreciation of the Catholic Church and the papacy.

No thinker was more important to this revival than Lamennais. Under the influence of his older brother, the priest Jean-Marie Robert de La Mennais, Félicité had begun writing in defense of the Church.[31] He was the first French cleric of his day openly to denounce Gallicanism.[32] His writings on Gallicanism earned Lamennais the enmity of most of the French bishops and the Bourbons. Together with de Maistre, Lamennais championed the cause of Ultramontanism, the position that Catholics should look "across the mountains"—to Rome—for leadership.

---

[30] Cf. Thomas Bokenkotter, *A Concise History of the Catholic Church* (Garden City, NY: Image Books, 1979), 302.

[31] The surnames of the two brothers generally are written differently. The original family name of both Jean-Marie and Félicité was *La Mennais*, but, after he became enamored of democratic ideas, Félicité began writing his name *Lamennais* to eliminate any aristocratic connotation.

[32] Cf. *The Catholic Encyclopedia* (New York: Encyclopedia Press, 1913), s.v. "Lamennais."

7.3. Consequences of the Blurring of the Moral and Juridical Realms

In addition to Gallicanism, the other major intellectual trend that Lamennais denounced was religious indifference. In 1817 he published the first volume of his *Essai sur l'indifférence en matière de religion*. Lamennais's *Essai* denounced ideas of indifference, such as the view of religion as merely a political institution, and also initiatives to dilute religion by removing revelation or by reducing it to a small number of fundamental articles. The *Essai* brought notoriety and acclaim to Lamennais.

Then, however, Lamennais's thought took a fateful turn. In a sense, he was caught between the Church, the Bourbon monarchy, and the ideas of Liberalism.[33] The Liberals—who generally were associated with the spirit of the French Revolution—advocated freedom of conscience, worship, and the press. In the popular mind, the Church was linked with the Bourbon monarchy. However, Lamennais's staunch defense of the Church put him at odds with the Bourbons because of his opposition to their Gallicanism. He could not adopt the ideas of Liberalism without reserve because that movement embodied the personal religious indifference that he deplored. Lamennais sought to solve this dilemma with a type of compromise, namely, his famous injunction concerning Liberalism: "Let us Catholicize it."[34]

Lamennais did this by means of his theory of certitude, which he set forth in the second volume of his *Essai* in 1820. Rejecting the Enlightenment valorization of reason, Lamennais said that *individual* reason cannot lead to certitude. Only *general* reason or the universal consent of mankind truly can give certitude. He believed that Catholicism was the highest expression of mankind's universal consent, and he supported his position by calling attention to the large number of its adherents. Lamennais devoted the third and fourth volumes of his *Essai* (1823) to attempting to demonstrate that the dogmas of Christianity are professed throughout most of the world. As a result of the role of the people as the repository of truth, Lamennais believed that they must be free. Therefore, they must be allowed all manner of liberty, including liberty of conscience, of worship, and of the press.[35]

---

[33] As a political idea, one can describe Modern Liberalism as the resurgence and expansion of Enlightenment ideas after the Congress of Vienna (1815). The predominant characteristic of Liberalism is the call for greater individual freedom and civil liberty. As an intellectual or moral idea, one can describe the more radical brand of Liberalism as the claim to be free from any authority that does not originate within oneself. Cf. *Catholic Encyclopedia*, s.v. "Liberalism"; *The New Catholic Encyclopedia* (New York: McGraw-Hill Book Co., 1967), s.v. "Liberalism."

[34] Alec R. Vidler, *Prophecy and Papacy: A Study of Lamennais, the Church, and the Revolution* (London: SCM Press Ltd., 1954), 160, citing Letter from Lamennais, in *Correspondance de F. de Lamennais*, ed. E. D. Forgues, 2 vols. (1855–1858), 2:106.

[35] Cf. Charles Poulet and Sidney A. Raemers, *A History of the Catholic Church*, vol. 2

Lamennais already was hostile to the Bourbons, and these developments in his thought only increased the hostility. However, Lamennais believed that the Church did not need the monarchy. In fact, he believed that the Church's true freedom required its total separation from the state. The state, Lamennais believed, was an obstacle to religious truth.[36] Lamennais's ultimate goal was to ensure a strong papacy in both the spiritual and the temporal realms, but his means for achieving it was to advocate radical short-term liberty in the temporal realm.[37] He believed that if persons were left entirely free in the social realm, then they and their nations eventually would submit to the authority of the Church. Thus, Lamennais became a pioneer in two movements that usually are considered incompatible, namely Ultramontanism and Liberalism. As Harrison observes, "Lamennais's brand of liberalism was very utopian, and paradoxical almost to the point of being schizoid."[38]

As a result of his support for various popular revolts and his continued opposition to the Gallicanism of the clergy, Lamennais's orthodoxy was called into question. As mentioned briefly above (section 6.1), he suspended the publication of his journal *L'Avenir* and traveled to Rome to plead his case. He expected to be vindicated because a previous pope, Leo XII, had commended Lamennais eight years earlier for his defense of the papacy.[39] However, Pope Gregory XVI issued his decision several months later in the encyclical *Mirari Vos*, warning against a number of intellectual trends, including indifferentism and liberty of conscience. Although he did not mention Lamennais specifically, Gregory made known to him that it was his doctrines that he had in mind.[40]

It may seem strange that an encyclical directed at Lamennais would focus so sharply on indifferentism. Moreover, indifferentism is not merely one among many concerns for Gregory, but it is the very source that the pontiff identifies for the error of liberty of conscience. Gregory does not even reach the question of liberty of conscience until he has first considered indifferentism. He connects these liberties with indifferentism—not to

---

(St. Louis, MO: B. Herder Book Co., 1934), 585–86.

[36] Cf. Poulet and Raemers, 2:398–99; *New Catholic Encyclopedia*, s.v. "Lamennais, Hugues Félicité Robert de."

[37] Cf. Harrison, RL&C, 35.

[38] Harrison, RL&C, 34.

[39] Thomas Bokenkotter, *Church and Revolution: Catholics in the Struggle for Democracy and Social Justice* (New York: Image Books, 1998), 44.

[40] Cf. Harrison, RL&C, 38; *Catholic Encyclopedia*, s.v. "Lamennais"; *New Catholic Encyclopedia*, s.v. "Lamennais, Hugues Félicité Robert de."

exonerate Lamennais, who was not personally an indifferentist, but rather to make clear that regardless of Lamennais's personal opinions, the true origin of the ideas and the liberties that he advocates lies in indifferentism.

At first, Lamennais submitted to the pope's judgment. However, he became embittered and soon abandoned all priestly functions. In 1834 he published *Paroles d'un croyant*, a denunciation of what he called the conspiracy of priests and princes against the people. Gregory responded with an encyclical, *Commissum Divinitus*, censuring the book by name. About *Paroles d'un croyant*, Gregory said, "Though small in size, it is enormous in wickedness."[41] Lamennais continued to advocate revolutionary causes and died in 1854 unreconciled to the Church.

7.3.1.4. Evaluation of the Harrison Critique

Father Harrison's contribution to the discussion of this issue is a corrective for much mistaken consideration of liberty of conscience. He shows convincingly that it is not the case, as Newman believed, that Popes Gregory XVI and Pius IX addressed their encyclicals only to hypothetical evils or to evils that would result only if certain dangerous ideas were taken to their logical extreme. Rather, they were addressing actual ideas that were promoted at the time by a popular author. Lamennais really did advocate the kind of unrestrained or virtually unrestrained liberty that the popes rejected.

Another of Harrison's contributions is to show that contrary to widespread opinion, it is not the case that the nineteenth-century popes addressed their encyclicals exclusively to the problem of personal indifferentism. As Harrison reminds us, Lamennais was no indifferentist. Despite advocating unbridled freedom in the civil sphere, Lamennais rejected the claim that all religions are equal or that man has no duty to God in his intellectual activity. Harrison's interpretation is that *Mirari Vos* and its reaffirmation in *Quanta Cura* are addressed to Lamennais's call for widespread liberty in the realm of civil society.

Many circumstances bolster the argument that the principal statements of the nineteenth-century popes were targeted primarily at Lamennais. With regard to *Mirari Vos*, there can be no doubt. Gregory XVI assigned his secretary of state, Bartolomeo Cardinal Pacca, to inform Lamennais that the pontiff had his writings chiefly in mind when issuing the encyclical.[42] Pacca

---

[41] Pope Gregory XVI, Encyclical *Singulari Nos* (June 25, 1834), 2 [*Acta Gregorii XVI* 1:433–34].

[42] Cf. Vidler, *Prophecy and Papacy*, 212–13 (includes an English translation of a long excerpt of the letter).

mentioned the advocacy of liberty of worship, in particular, as problematic. In addition, Gregory's description of the rejected theories sounds very much like the ideas of Lamennais. Thus, he and later popes refer to a liberty that spreads ruin in both sacred and civil affairs.[43] This seems to be a reference to Lamennais's call for complete liberty in civil society. As stated above, Gregory also connects the error of freedom of conscience closely to the idea of freedom to publish. His successor will make the same point.

> [T]hey [proponents of naturalism] do not fear to foster that erroneous opinion, . . . called by Our Predecessor, Gregory XVI, an "insanity" [citing *Mirari Vos*], viz., that "liberty of conscience and worship is each man's personal right, which ought to be legally proclaimed and asserted in *every* rightly constituted society; and that a right resides in the citizens to an *absolute* liberty, which should be restrained by *no* authority whether ecclesiastical or civil, whereby they may be able openly and publicly to manifest and declare *any* of their ideas whatever, whether by word of mouth, by the press, or in *any* other way." (QC, §3)

Gregory makes it a special point to reject the argument that the Church itself will benefit from a widespread freedom of conscience or freedom to publish.[44] These statements, too, make it clear that Gregory is speaking of Lamennais. The argument that the Church herself will profit from recognition of such liberties is one of the hallmarks of Lamennais's thought and of Catholic Liberalism. That is, Lamennais claimed that an unlimited civil liberty to propagate and publish ideas would result in the submission of all nations to the authority of the pope.

All of these features of *Mirari Vos* show that, as Harrison argues, Gregory is concerned with more than the personal moral realm. If personal indifferentism were Gregory's sole concern, then it is unlikely that he would have spoken so forcefully about the societal ramifications of liberty of conscience.

---

[43] Cf. Pope Gregory XVI, Encyclical *Mirari Vos* (Aug. 15, 1832), §14. See also Pope Pius IX, Encyclical *Quanta Cura* (Dec. 8, 1864), §3, rejecting "an absolute liberty . . . restrained by no authority whether ecclesiastical or civil"; Pope Leo XIII, Encyclical *Libertas* (June 20, 1888), §§15–16.

[44] Gregory rejects liberty of conscience despite the fact that "some repeat over and over again with the greatest impudence that some advantage accrues to religion from it" (MV, §14). With regard to freedom to publish, he says, "Some are so carried away that they contentiously assert that the flock of errors arising from them is sufficiently compensated by the publication of some book which defends religion and truth" (MV, §15).

7.3. Consequences of the Blurring of the Moral and Juridical Realms

Rather, one would have expected him to concentrate on the personal spiritual danger of indifferentism and perhaps only to take some note of the indirect societal repercussions. Instead, however, Gregory speaks about direct and grievous harm to both the Church and civil society from liberty of conscience. Moreover, later events make clear that his successors shared the same concerns.

Pius IX reaffirms *Mirari Vos* expressly in his own encyclical *Quanta Cura*, and Leo XIII will focus on another characteristically Lamennaisian feature, namely, the stark split between the private and public spheres. "[I]t is unlawful to follow one line of conduct in private life and another in public, respecting privately the authority of the Church, but publicly rejecting it" (ID, §47).

Thus, Harrison succeeds in showing that it is an oversimplification to reduce the nineteenth-century encyclicals to an exclusive concern with indifferentism and with the private moral realm. If one truly wishes to reconcile Vatican II with the papal teachings, one cannot simply relegate the nineteenth-century teachings to the private realm (or the moral realm), in the hope of leaving the social realm a blank slate at the complete disposal of the Vatican II fathers.

7.3.2. The Insight

The identification of Lamennais as the key figure in the freedom of conscience debate has far-reaching implications. As Father Harrison shows, when one considers Lamennais's ideas, one realizes that Popes Gregory XVI and Pius IX were not addressing merely hypothetical ideas in their encyclicals on freedom of conscience, but rather they were addressing actual theories that Lamennais was putting forward and that were taking hold in Europe. An appreciation for Lamennais's importance also shows that the debate over freedom of conscience raises an important question regarding the integrity of the human person.

Father Harrison describes Lamennais's utopian brand of Liberalism as almost "schizoid." This is forceful language, but it is nonetheless accurate. As discussed above, Lamennais was a leader in two movements that would have seemed incompatible to most thinkers, namely, Ultramontanism and Liberalism. However, the schizoid character of Lamennais's thought appears most clearly when one contrasts his opinions on indifferentism with his opinions on civil liberty.

As Harrison points out, Lamennais was no indifferentist. In fact he first achieved his fame by writing against religious indifferentism. Lamennais recognized the moral duty that all persons have to God and, as an ultramontanist, he certainly equated this duty to God with a duty to the Catholic Church. Thus, Lamennais's ultimate goal was for all persons and nations to submit to papal authority. However, Lamennais's strategy for achieving this goal was to secure radical freedom in the area of civil liberties, such as freedom of speech, the press, and publication. He believed that unbounded freedom would lead the people to truth and ultimately to submission to the Catholic Church.

The consequence of Lamennais's theories and strategies is strange indeed. On the one hand, he insists that the individual person has a duty to God and to the Church, but, on the other hand, he recognizes virtually no obligations of the person in society. It is a bedrock principle of Western and Christian thought that the human person has both an individual and a social aspect.[45] However, in Lamennais's thought, there is "a radical disjunction"[46] or fragmentation between these two aspects of the person. For Lamennais, a person in society has no obligations and has virtually unlimited freedom but, in private life, the same person is strictly bound by moral duties.

Father Harrison does not raise the issue of the integrity of the human person in the context of the religious liberty debate or the debate over liberty of conscience,[47] but this idea is a useful hermeneutic for interpreting this

---

[45] "The human good is at once individual and social" (Lonergan, *Method in Theology*, 47). Appreciation of the correlation between the individual and the social aspects of the person is in fact a keystone of Western thought. Cf. Plato, *Republic*, trans. Allan Bloom (New York: Basic Books, Inc, 1968), II, 369a; Aristotle, *Nichomachean Ethics*, Loeb Classical Library, I, ii, 8; Aristotle, *Politics*, ed. and trans. Ernest Barker (London/Oxford/New York: Oxford University Press, 1958) I, ii, 9. However, since the mid nineteenth century, the appropriation of Enlightenment principles by Western societies has resulted in the virtual separation of the two. Cf. John Stuart Mill, *On Liberty* (Cambridge: Cambridge University Press, 1989); Jeremy Bentham, "An Introduction to the Principles of Morals and Legislation," in *A Bentham Reader*, ed. Mary Peter Mack (New York: Pegasus, 1969), I, 4: "The community is a fictitious *body*, composed of the individual persons who are considered as constituting as it were its *members*. The interest of the community then is, what?—the sum of the interests of the several members who compose it."

[46] Cf. Gertrude Himmelfarb, *On Looking into the Abyss: Untimely Thoughts on Culture and Society* (New York: Alfred A Knopf, 1994), 77–78. Himmelfarb's essay concerns John Stuart Mill rather than Lamennais, but her critique applies equally to both.

[47] I am unaware of any other commentator emphasizing human integrity to the extent that this work does. However, David L. Schindler does mention this principle. "The text [of DH]...bears a unity of meaning, one that, I have argued, consists in its affirmation of an intrinsic relation between freedom and truth, and of this positive relation as the internal context for the negative meaning of the right to religious freedom. My contention is that it is such an affirmation that alone can bring together the two overarching concerns voiced

area of magisterial teaching. The reason is that it ties together the specific concerns of the popes, and it provides an explanation of the papal teaching as something more than a reactionary movement against modern liberties. This hermeneutic of human integrity applies to the nineteenth-century papal teaching in the following ways.

First, the popes express a constant concern for the welfare not only of individuals but also of society. The modern liberties that are at issue in the papal pronouncements are generally personal rights to believe or to act, but the popes continually call attention to the impact on society that recognition of such rights is likely to have or is already having. For example, Pope Gregory XVI says that unrestrained liberties result in "the ruin of Church and State" (MV, §14). Similarly, Pius IX emphasizes the social ills that he says will result from the recognition of modern liberties (QC, §§1–2, 4). Leo XIII says that Liberalism's ethical system known as "independent morality" is a doctrine that is "most hurtful both to individuals and to the State" (LP, §§15–16). Moreover, Leo seems to refer to Lamennais's thought when he rejects the ideas of those thinkers "who affirm that the morality of individuals is to be guided by the divine law, but not the morality of the State" (LP, §18).

Second, several of the papal pronouncements on toleration and religious liberty are based expressly on the intimate connection between the individual and society. This is especially clear in the teachings of Leo XIII. Leo criticizes theories of liberty that proceed "just as if there were no God; or as if He cared nothing for human society; or as if men, whether in their individual capacity or bound together in social relations owed nothing to God" (ID, §25). The divine law is a gift from God, and those who contend

---

during the course of the redactions of the Declaration: to affirm *both* the intrinsic good of the right to religious freedom *and* the integrity of the human person in his natural ordering toward the truth, in relation to God." David L. Schindler, "Freedom, Truth, and Human Dignity: An Interpretation of *Dignitatis Humanae* on the Right to Religious Freedom," in David L. Schindler and Nicholas J. Healy Jr., *Freedom, Truth, and Human Dignity: The Second Vatican Council's Declaration on Religious Freedom—A New Translation, Redaction History, and Interpretation of* Dignitatis Humanae (Grand Rapids, MI / Cambridge, UK: William B. Eerdmans Publishing Co., 2015), 93. In addition, Schindler's signature theme of the ontological unity between freedom and truth arguably implies a concern with integrity, even where Schindler does not mention it expressly. See generally Schindler/Healy, 93. Among historians of the declaration, Silvia Scatena appears to be unique in demonstrating a particular interest in the issue of human integrity. Cf. Silvia Scatena, *La fatica della libertà. L'elaborazione della dichiarazione* Dignitatis humanae *sulla libertà religiosa del Vaticano II*, Istituto per le scienze religiose—Bologna, Testi e ricerche di scienze religiose, nuova serie, 31 (Bologna, Italy: Il Mulino, 2003), 208, 215, 217, 257, 261, 298, and 375–76.

that God is concerned only with our private lives underestimate him and impose limitations on him. They fail to understand that God concerns himself with the good of the whole person, both his individual identity and his social nature.[48] Leo bases his teaching on religious toleration and liberty on the parallel between the individual and the community. "[I]t is not lawful for the State, any more than for the individual, either to disregard all religious duties or to hold in equal favor different kinds of religion" (ID, §35). Leo says specifically that man is naturally inclined toward society (ID, §3) and that "what applies to individual men applies equally to society—domestic alike and civil."[49] Indeed, Leo refers directly to the need to maintain integrity across the private and public realms.

> [I]t is unlawful to follow one line of conduct in private life and another in public, respecting privately the authority of the Church, but publicly rejecting it; for this would amount to joining together good and evil, and to putting man in conflict with himself; whereas he ought always to be consistent, and never in the least point nor in any condition of life to swerve from Christian virtue. (ID, §47)[50]

In his encyclical on liberty, Leo says, "[T]he eternal law of God is the sole standard and rule of human liberty, not only in each individual man, but also in the community and civil society, which men constitute when united" (LP, §10; cf. LP, §11). Pope St. Pius X makes the same point forcefully in discussing the Lord's teachings and the way of the Cross: "These are teachings that it would be wrong to apply only to one's personal life in

---

[48] Cf. Second Vatican Council, Dogmatic Constitution on the Church *Lumen Gentium* (Nov. 21, 1964), §9a: "God, however, does not make men holy and save them merely as individuals, without bond or link between one another. Rather has it pleased Him to bring men together as one people, a people which acknowledges Him in truth and serves him in holiness."

[49] Pope Leo XIII, Encyclical *Sapientiae Christianae* (Jan. 10, 1890), §2 [ASS 22 (1889–1890): 385].

[50] Pope St. John XXIII will express a concern very similar to that of Pope Leo XIII. Reflecting that although Christians have contributed to founding secular institutions exhibiting scientific and technical excellence, these institutions bear few marks of Christian inspiration, John asks: "How does one explain this? It is Our opinion that the explanation is to be found in an inconsistency in their minds between religious belief and their action in the temporal sphere. It is necessary, therefore, that their interior unity be re-established, and that in their temporal activity Faith should be present as a beacon to give light, and Charity as a force to give life." Pope John XXIII, Encyclical *Pacem in Terris* (Apr. 11, 1963), §152.

7.3. Consequences of the Blurring of the Moral and Juridical Realms

order to win eternal salvation; these are eminently social teachings."[51] The most striking teaching in this area is that contained in the 1925 encyclical of Pope Pius XI establishing the Feast of Christ the King in the liturgy of the Church. The entire basis for this encyclical is that a person has a duty to Christ both in his individual life and in his social life. Although the specific jurisdiction of the Catholic Church is limited to its actual members, Christ's reign extends to all mankind:

> Thus the empire of our Redeemer embraces all men.... Nor is there any difference in this matter between the individual or family and the State; for all men, whether collectively or individually, are under the dominion of Christ. In him is the salvation of the individual, in him is the salvation of society.[52]

From these statements, it is clear that the popes are insisting on coherence of belief and action both in a person's private life and in his public life. Accordingly, I suggest that there is a true nineteenth-century papal teaching—at least an implicit one, or at least the beginning of one—on the integrity of the human person. That is, the human person is both an individual and a being destined for society. He has both an individual or personal identity and a social nature, and coherence and integrity between the person's private moral beliefs and his public actions is essential. Moreover, in some ways, this implicit teaching seems to be at the heart of papal teaching on religious liberty and toleration.

That is, the nineteenth-century papal teaching on religious liberty can be understood as an affirmation of this vision of the integrity of the human person. One reason that the popes so often criticized modern liberties was that they were concerned about threats to this integrity.

The nineteenth-century popes opposed the public worship of non-Catholics in a Catholic state as a matter of right because it seemed to them that this would be a denial of the social duty to Christ. For this reason, Leo XIII equates indifferentism with godlessness. That is, because the *individual* Catholics in a Catholic state have a duty to Christ and his Church,

---

[51] Pope Pius X, Letter to the French Archbishops and Bishops *Our Apostolic Mandate* (Aug. 25, 1910) [AAS 2 (1910): 630].

[52] Pope Pius XI, Encyclical *Quas Primas* (Dec. 11, 1925), §18. Like Pius XI, Vatican II also teaches that there is a connection between Christ and all persons. "For, by his incarnation, he, the son of God, has in a certain way united himself with each man." Second Vatican Council, Pastoral Constitution on the Church in the Modern World *Gaudium et Spes* (December 7, 1965), §22b.

so must the *community* also have a corresponding duty.[53] To deny this duty would be to embrace the Lamennaisian principle of a radical disjunction between individual life and social life.

Third, these considerations finally provide an explanation for the somewhat confusing way in which Gregory XVI and the other popes discuss liberty of conscience. As noted at the beginning of this discussion, when the popes speak of freedom of conscience, they sometimes seem to refer to a private right to believe, but other times they seem to mean an external civil right to speak or to publish one's ideas openly. My contention is that this ambiguity may be intentional, and that, in any event, it is meaningful. Indeed, it provides a richer understanding of the papal teachings. Wisdom lies hidden in this sometimes-obscure way of speaking. By treating both private belief and public action under the title "freedom of conscience," Gregory and the other popes provide an implicit defense of the integrity of the human person. That is, Gregory denies the legitimacy of a theory like Lamennais's that radically separates the person's individual identity from his social nature. Thus, one cannot truly separate a Christian's right to believe from his right to act or to proclaim his beliefs. The same obligations that the person has in private must also find some corresponding public analog.

7.4. The Vatican II Distinction between the Moral and Juridical Realms

7.4.1. Vatican II and the Moral Realm

Like the nineteenth-century popes, the Vatican II fathers address both the moral and the juridical realms, but the council fathers draw a much sharper distinction between them. That is, *Dignitatis Humanae* briefly addresses the moral realm, but it makes clear that the right to religious liberty that it recognizes pertains—not to the moral realm or to the realm of conscience—but rather to the juridical realm.[54] With regard to the realm of morality and conscience, the Council says,

---

[53] As discussed below in section 7.5, the nineteenth-century popes' concern was for the moral integrity and coherence of their Catholic subjects in particular.

[54] Bishop De Smedt, the relator for the declaration, made this clear in his oral *relatio* on the fifth draft of the document. Cf. Émile De Smedt, Oral *Relatio* on the *Textus Recognitus* (Oct. 20, 1965): The declaration does not concern relations between man and the truth, or between man and God, but rather relations among men, between men and social groups, and between men and the civil power [AS IV/5, 102].

> [A]ll men should be at once impelled by nature and also bound by a moral obligation to seek the truth, especially religious truth. They are also bound to adhere to the truth, once it is known, and to order their whole lives in accord with the demands of truth. (DH, §2b)

As a result, the Council makes clear that man has no right before God to embrace any opinions whatsoever.[55] It also conveys Newman's insight that contrary to widespread opinion, conscience is not individual self-will. Thus, the right to religious liberty that the Council recognizes is not a right to embrace any religious opinion that pleases one. (See, especially, section 4.6 above.) Vatican II is in full agreement with the nineteenth-century popes on this point.

7.4.2. The Social-Juridical Realm

The right that the Council recognizes is a right in the social or juridical realm. "Religious freedom . . . has to do with immunity from coercion in civil society" (DH, §1c). Fernando Ocáriz rightly emphasizes the importance of the declaration's subtitle in locating the ambit within which the right to religious liberty is recognized.[56] That subtitle summarizes the content of *Dignitatis Humanae* in the following language: "On the Right of the Person and of Communities to Social and Civil Freedom in Matters Religious." Thus, what is at issue in the declaration is not a right before God to believe whatever one likes but rather a right before human powers to be immune from coercion in religious matters. As Ocáriz says, the declaration—in embracing a right to religious liberty—does not treat the relationship between man and the truth or the relationship between man and God; rather, it treats the relationships between persons in human and civil society.[57]

---

[55] See section 7.1 above (citing Valuet, LRTE, 420–21, 428, 432); see also section 7.2.

[56] Cf. Ocáriz, "Sulla libertà religiosa," 73.

[57] Cf. Ocáriz, "Sulla libertà religiosa," 74. The declaration does discuss the relationship between man and God, but as Valuet makes clear, this is the *finality* of the right to religious freedom, not its *foundation*. See section 7.1 above (citing LRTE, 420–21). Ocáriz is correct that in describing what the right to religious liberty is, the declaration makes clear that religious liberty is a right in human and civil society rather than a right before God.

David L. Schindler criticizes Murray's primarily "negative" framing of the right to religious liberty, and he argues that the right should be understood primarily as "positive," that is, as emphasizing man's openness to the truth and also the intrinsic connection between freedom and truth. Cf. "Religious Freedom, Truth, and American Liberalism: Another Look at John Courtney Murray," *Communio* (Winter 1994): 716, 721. This is problematic

Because this right pertains to the social and juridical realm, some authors view religious liberty as a *civil right*.[58] Cardinal Pavan notes that many council fathers shared this belief as well.[59] In fact, however, this right is not merely a civil right. Pavan argues that the purpose of the declaration's subtitle is to make this point clear. If the right were merely a civil right, then it would be a right only against one's own government, and the existence of this right would depend on the state's recognition or conferral of it.

7.4.3. A Natural Right

The right that Vatican II recognizes is not only a civil right, but it also is a *natural* right to religious liberty.[60] Brian Harrison cites an important

---

as an interpretation of DH, however. As discussed below in chapter 8, strictly speaking the right is indeed a negative right. That is, the nature or object of the right is an immunity rather than the content of any particular religion or belief (cf. AS IV/6, 725). That said, it also is true that the right has a positive finality, namely, the search for (and embrace of) the truth (see section 7.1, citing LRTE, 420–21). Valuet unites these ideas nicely by describing the right as *formally negative* (in its essence), but *ultimately positive* (in its finality): "La 'liberté religieuse' de DH est *formellement*, c'est-à-dire dans son essence, une liberté négative (*libertas a*), et *ultimement*, c'est-à-dire dans sa raison d'être, dans sa finalité, une liberté positive (*libertas ad*)" (Valuet, LRTC, vol. IB, 644 [= LRTE, 428]).

[58] E.g., Thomas Pink. See the following articles and essays by Pink: "Conscience and Coercion: Vatican II's Teaching on Religious Freedom Changed Policy, Not Doctrine," *First Things* 225 (August 2012): 46: "The declaration is not a statement about religious liberty in general but about a specifically civil liberty"; Pink, "What is the Catholic Doctrine of Religious Liberty?" (expanded version, June 15, 2012), Academia, §6, p. 33, referring to religious liberty in DH as "a specifically civil liberty of religion"; Pink, §7, at 43: "[T]he declaration proposes to address a specifically political or civil liberty" (accessed July 16, 2022, https://www.academia.edu/es/639061/What_is_the_Catholic_doctrine_of_religious_liberty); Pink, "Jacques Maritain and the Problem of Church and State," *The Thomist* 79 (2015): 17: "We have a distinctively political right to religious liberty, just as *Dignitatis Humanae* teaches." Pink recognizes the right to religious liberty merely as a right to immunity from coercion *by the state*. Indeed, he invariably describes DH as a teaching on state coercion, despite the declaration's express language rejecting coercion much more broadly, that is, "on the part of individuals, social groups and of any human power" (DH, §2a). See section 11.3. In addition, Pink claims that the declaration is not primarily a matter of doctrine but rather of mutable ecclesiastical policy (see Pink, "Problem of Church and State," 17). This supposed vulnerability of the right to shifts in Church policy is difficult or impossible to square with the Council's apparent reference to the right as "inviolable" (cf. DH, §1c). See also section 11.3.

[59] Cf. Pietro Pavan, *La dichiarazione conciliare* Dignitatis humanae *a 20 anni dalla pubblicazione* (Casale Monferrato, Italy: Edizioni Piemme di Pietro Marietti, 1986), 37. See also Harrison, RL&C, 116–17.

[60] Cf. Ocáriz, "Sulla libertà religiosa," 72; Pavan, *La dichiarazione conciliare*, 38.

exchange during the Council debates between a group of conservative fathers and the official relator of the declaration, Bishop Émile De Smedt of Bruges, Belgium. This group of council fathers sought to harmonize the Vatican II teaching with Pope Leo's teaching on toleration by amending the declaration to describe religious liberty as only a civil right. Bishop De Smedt rejected these proposed amendments because, he said, religious liberty is a right that pertains to the human person. That is, it is (in this sense) a moral right.[61] However, this right pertains to the immunity of the person from coercion, not necessarily to the *content* of his beliefs and religious practices.[62] (Chapter 8, on the *object* of the right to religious liberty, addresses this point in some depth.) As Harrison summarizes the conclusion of the exchange, the right that Vatican II recognized was not merely "a *civil* right to liberty" but rather "a *right* to civil liberty."[63]

Although the declaration does not refer to religious liberty expressly as a natural right, it nevertheless is clear that this is how the Council understands it. The text itself makes this plain by referring to the right as "inviolable,"[64] by asserting that all men possess this right (cf. DH, §2a) and by locating the foundation of the right in the "very nature" of the human person (cf. DH, §2c).[65] The drafting commission itself conceived of religious liberty as a natural right,[66] and the Catechism of the Catholic Church later would confirm this understanding.[67]

---

[61] It is a moral right in the sense that denying it to someone would be a violation of something due to the human person himself, regardless of whether the civil law recognizes the right. The first draft of DH recognized religious liberty as a natural right (cf. Draft of Chapter V of *De Oecumenismo* [Nov. 19, 1963] [AS II/5, 434–36]), but the language of natural rights regrettably was omitted in later drafts. Cf. Hamer, "Histoire du texte de la Déclaration," 64.

[62] Cf. Harrison, RL&C, 115–17, citing AS IV/6, 725.

[63] Harrison, RL&C, 117 (emphasis added), citing AS IV/6, 726. Cf. Jérôme Hamer and Clemente Riva, *La libertà religiosa nel Vaticano II* (Torino, Italy: Elle di Ci, 1966), 151: The reference in the declaration's subtitle to social and civil liberty clarifies that the right to religious liberty is not founded on positive civil law (hereinafter cited as Hamer/Riva).

[64] "[T]he council intends to develop the doctrine of recent popes on the inviolable rights of the human person and the constitutional order of society" (DH, §1c).

[65] For his part, Thomas Pink sometimes refers to natural law, but he does so primarily with reference to the inherent powers of the state rather than to the rights due to the human person as such. See section 11.3.

[66] Cf. Hamer "Histoire du texte de la Déclaration," 64: Although the language of natural rights was not retained after the first draft of Nov. 19, 1963, the drafting commission understood religious liberty as a natural right.

[67] Cf. CCC, §2108.

7.5. An Extension of the Nineteenth-Century Teaching

If one interprets the nineteenth-century papal teachings as an implicit defense of the integrity of the human person (as suggested above in section 7.3.2), then the continuity between those teachings and Vatican II becomes clearer. Although I contend that nineteenth-century papal teaching defends this integrity of the human person, it would be more accurate to say that it defends the integrity of the *Catholic* person. It equates the duty that a person owes to the truth and to God with a duty to the Catholic Church. Leo XIII says that if one takes care to consider the marks of the true Church of Christ, it cannot be difficult to discern the identity of that Church.[68] Consequently, the social duty also corresponds to this individual duty to the Church.

However, the fact of religious pluralism presents a difficulty. The Church may not perhaps embrace pluralism as the best possible condition, but it does accept it as a fact in our day. In this regard, the traditional pronouncements on non-Catholic worship in a Catholic state present a serious challenge. Consider the following: If a Catholic state tells its non-Catholic citizens that they may worship in private but not in public, what is the state really saying? It seems to be saying that one effectively must deny one's religious identity in public. One is not forced to renounce his beliefs, but one is prohibited from expressing his religious identity in public. What is the result of this policy? It tends toward fragmenting the integrity of these non-Catholic persons. That is, the effect of the policy is to declare to non-Catholics that they may live as Lutherans or Jews in their private lives in a Catholic state, but they may not do so in their social or public lives. In a sense, then, adopting such a policy threatens, as a practical matter, to force these non-Catholics into embracing the Lamennaisian error of radically separating their individual identity from their social nature.[69]

---

[68] Cf. ID, §7; LP, §21.

[69] The idea that religious persecution can destroy a person's integrity can be found in the writings of Sébastien Castellio and Roger Williams. One of Castellio's arguments against religious persecution was that persons who are forced to recant their religious opinions sometimes suffer a complete disintegration in their moral lives. Similarly, Roger Williams observed that persons who are mistaken but sincere in their religious beliefs (he had Catholics in mind) often live more upright lives than persons of correct beliefs. Roland H. Bainton, *The Travail of Religious Liberty: Nine Biographical Sketches* (Philadelphia: Westminster Press, 1951), 120, 221, 223. Cf. Bainton, 14, 256, and 259–60, Bainton's own reflections on the tendency of religious persecution, whether by believing Christians or atheistic governments, to destroy the integrity of the persecuted. By the same token, Franco Biffi argues that the problem with the revocation of the Edict of Nantes was that it forced one million people to renounce their own identities. Cf. Biffi, "Chiesa, società

7.5. An Extension of the Nineteenth-Century Teaching

In this regard, it is helpful briefly to revisit Leo XIII's policy of toleration. That policy was based almost verbatim on Thomas Aquinas's teaching. However, Thomas spoke only of tolerating non-Christians such as Jews and Muslims. For Christians who departed from Catholic doctrinal orthodoxy and professed heresy, Thomas sanctioned capital punishment.[70] However, by the nineteenth century, Leo found it just to extend this teaching on tolerance in a way that Thomas could not have foreseen, namely, to grant toleration to non-Catholic Christians in a Catholic state.

By the same token, it is altogether appropriate to do what Vatican II did, namely, to extend the principle that can be discerned in the nineteenth-century teaching on the integrity of the human person. That is, the Church is rightly concerned with defending the integrity of all persons of good will, whether or not they are Catholic or even Christian. One can read Vatican II as accomplishing precisely this in its recognition that all persons have a right to religious liberty, both in private and in public.

Here, it is necessary to distinguish the private realm from the moral, although up until now, I have been using them as rough equivalents. It was necessary for Vatican II to recognize the right to religious liberty in both the private and public realms because of the importance of the principle that the person is to maintain integrity across these realms, as opposed to confining religion and morality artificially to the private sphere. However, the Council makes clear that this right is a juridical one and not a moral one. That is, it is not a positive authorization to believe anything that one wishes. Rather, as discussed in the next chapter, it is an immunity from coercion in the realm of religious activity. The person still has the moral duty to seek the truth about God, and, once he has found it, to embrace it (DH, §1b).

However, is it really the case that the Church does—or should—take an interest in the integrity of non-Catholic persons? Yes. The reason is that totalitarianism and radical individualism are attacks on the human person from opposite directions. Moreover, both result in cultures and societies that not only lack (or marginalize) the Christian ethos but that indeed grow notably less human. It is indeed the Church's business to oppose these trends—not only to defend her own children and others of good will but

---

civile e persona di fronte al problema della libertà religiosa. Dalla revoca dell'Editto di Nantes al Concilio Vaticano II," in *Teologia e diritto canonico* (Vatican City: Libreria Editrice Vaticana, 1987), 148. See also section 11.4 below, recounting the intervention of Josef Cardinal Beran during the Council debate on religious liberty: "[G]rave temptations . . . easily corrupt people who lack true freedom of conscience."

[70] Cf. ST II-II, q. 10, a. 8, reply obj. 1; ST II-II, q. 11, a. 3–4.

also to ensure that Catholics in public life do not visit these errors on those for whom they have responsibility.

If one interprets the teachings of Vatican II and the nineteenth-century popes in this way, one can see Vatican II not as a "rollback" of nineteenth-century papal teaching but rather as an advance and extension of the principle that animates the previous papal teaching. Confronted with the theories of Lamennais and his followers, the popes reacted by defending the integrity of the human person. It is easy to understand why these popes would associate this integrity with fulfillment of the social duty to Christ and the Church. First, the threats to the Catholic Church in the nineteenth century, from both political and intellectual trends, naturally caused the popes to focus primarily on their own flock in their teaching documents. Second, in considering non-Catholic, Christian denominations, the focus of the time was on points of division rather than on points of unity. Third, the ideas in dispute emanated from a nation that not only had a great Catholic past but that long had been recognized as the Church's "eldest daughter."

However, Vatican II extends this principle of human integrity. Although the Council "leaves intact the traditional Catholic teaching on the moral duty of individuals and societies toward the true religion and the one Church of Christ" (DH, §1c), it also recognizes that the principle of human integrity that underlies that teaching applies as well to non-Catholics and non-Christians. The Church does not renounce its truth claims by this action, but it acknowledges that it is harmful to pit any person's individual identity against his social nature, especially where matters of religion are concerned. Given the circumstance of a pluralistic state in particular, it is better that non-Catholics consider their own religious and moral principles to apply both in private and in public (as long as the public manifestation of these principles comports with the just public order [see chapter 12]). The alternative is to impose upon non-Catholics a system that separates the public from the private, thereby confining religion and morality to the private realm. This relegation of religion to the realm of private morality is an Enlightenment principle rather than a Catholic one.[71]

By contrast, the emphasis on the social nature of the human person appears in both the text of *Dignitatis Humanae* and in the Council debates. Some of the council fathers refer to a new awareness of the social nature of

---

[71] Cf. Richard John Neuhaus, *The Naked Public Square: Religion and Democracy in America*, 2nd ed. (Grand Rapids, MI: William B. Eerdmans Publishing Co., 1986), 139, discussing the Enlightenment's attempt to privatize religion.

man as a justification for a Declaration on Religious Liberty.[72] Bishop Ernest Primeau of Manchester, New Hampshire, argued that it is improper to accept a dichotomy between the individual and social aspects of the human person.[73] The declaration itself incorporates this idea in certain respects: "The social nature of man, however, itself requires that he should give external expression to his internal acts of religion" (DH, §3c). Moreover, "Religious communities are a requirement of the very nature of man and of religion itself" (DH, §4a). The idea that the human person is both individual and social is not new. However, the declaration and the Council debates incorporate a new emphasis on this social aspect and draw new implications from it. The reason may be a desire to respond to new threats against the integrity of the human person. Just as the nineteenth-century popes did combat against Enlightenment and Liberal ideas that emphasized the individual and his rights at the expense of society, so did the Church in the twentieth century oppose the equal and opposite error of totalitarianism, which subsumes the individual entirely within the state. *Dignitatis Humanae*, then, is an attempt to recover the integrity of the human person and to restore balance by emphasizing both his individual identity and his social nature.

7.5.1. The Virtues of This Hermeneutic

Several circumstances commend the integrity of the human person as a valuable hermeneutic for interpreting both the nineteenth-century teaching and Vatican II.[74] *First*, although, this interpretation may not be *commanded* by the texts, it is certainly *consistent* with them. Indeed, it seems to be the

---

[72] Cf. written intervention of Bishop Robert Tracy of Baton Rouge (AS IV/2, 273–74); English translation in Vincent A. Yzermans, ed., *American Participation in the Second Vatican Council* (New York: Sheed & Ward, 1967), 641: "[M]en are naturally social, and religion of its nature is social"; Sept. 25, 1964, oral intervention of Archbishop Gabriel-Marie Garrone of Toulouse [AS III/2, 534–35] (English translation in Leahy/Massimini, 53): "Actually, the question is completely changed because of an evolution of social matters and because of reflection on the person in society."

[73] Cf. Sept. 24, 1964, oral intervention of Bishop Ernest Primeau of Manchester, New Hampshire (AS III/2, 495–97); English translation in Leahy/Massimini, 49. By the same token, Primeau argues against separating the personal order from the juridico-social order (cf. AS III/2, 495–97; English translation in Leahy/Massimini, 48; another translation is found in Yzermans, 629).

[74] By integrity, I mean especially the continuity or consistency between a person's private life and his public life. See subsection 7.3.2 above, quoting *Immortale Dei*: "[I]t is unlawful to follow one line of conduct in private life and another in public, ... for this would amount to ... putting man in conflict with himself."

most likely interpretation. The popes spoke often of the unity between the individual and society, and Vatican II refers directly to the social nature of the person and its relevance to religious liberty. This explains why the immunity from coercion that the declaration recognizes applies both in private and in public. As mentioned in the previous subsection, the council fathers' references to man's social nature show that this hermeneutic is by no means alien to their intentions.

Second, the principle of human integrity is connected closely to the principle of human dignity that the Council acknowledges as the source of the declaration. An understanding of the human person as possessing a nature that is both individual and social necessarily inspires increased appreciation for the complexity and dignity of the person.

Third, this hermeneutic is consistent with the contemporary concerns that the council fathers expressed. As discussed above, many fathers considered it crucial to respond to totalitarianism in general and to Marxist-Leninist totalitarianism in particular. The hermeneutic of human integrity ties the declaration to this issue by emphasizing the threat that totalitarianism poses in its attempt to subsume the individual within the state. Moreover, by referring to public religious worship as a requirement of man's nature, *Dignitatis Humanae* exposes the injustice of the religious restrictions that such regimes invariably impose.[75] This specific virtue of the hermeneutic also shows the Vatican II teaching as corresponding to two of Newman's seven notes of authentic doctrinal development, namely, the sixth and seventh, power of assimilation and vigorous action. That is, the concern of the nineteenth-century popes for human integrity—particularly in the sense of the person as both an individual and a social being—easily takes its place in the powerful critique of totalitarianism of the twentieth-century popes and many bishops at Vatican II.

Fourth, this hermeneutic is useful because it addresses the specific doctrinal problem that arises from Vatican II. That is, it helps to explain why non-Catholics may worship publicly in a Catholic state. The immunity from coercion extends not only to the private realm but also to the public realm because of the requirements of man's social nature. Moreover, this hermeneutic shows this question in a new light. As critics of DH argue, viewed from the usual perspective, it certainly does represent an apparent conflict between Vatican II and the nineteenth-century popes. However, viewed from the perspective of this hermeneutic of human integrity, DH

---

[75] Of course, restrictions on religious practice are not always unjust, and part 4 below treats the situations in which such restrictions are legitimate.

appears as an extension of the nineteenth-century popes' principle of the crucial importance of integrity (that is, harmony and consistency across the individual and social realms) and as a fulfillment of their nascent teaching on this point.

Fifth, this hermeneutic avoids the dangers that some other interpretations encounter. As discussed in subsection 7.3.1.1, a temptation exists to reduce the nineteenth-century teachings to a single thematic affirmation to avoid confronting the specific magisterial statements that are the most controversial. Although this hermeneutic also seeks to distill a core message from those teachings, it does not do so in an attempt to explain away the doctrinal conflict.

Sixth, and most importantly, this hermeneutic ties the Vatican II teaching to the nineteenth-century teaching without denigrating or minimizing either one. The nineteenth-century teaching often is described *negatively* as a teaching against religious freedom, but it is truer to describe it *positively* as a teaching (albeit often an implicit one) that the human person possesses an innate integrity such that the religious obligations that he has as an individual apply with the same force to his life in society. As foreign as some of the popes' expressions may sound to us today, their teachings are a cause for neither scandal nor embarrassment. Rather, they are the source of a keen insight regarding the human person. The nineteenth-century teaching strongly implies the importance of man's social nature and the need for integrity in private and public morality, and Vatican II makes this implicit teaching explicit.[76] True to its word, "This Vatican Council... searches into the sacred tradition and doctrine of the Church—the treasury out of which the Church continually brings forth new things that are in harmony with the things that are old" (DH, §1a). Thus, Vatican II seizes upon the insight of the nineteenth-century popes concerning human integrity and extends its application from the Catholic faithful to all persons.[77]

This quality of preserving the nineteenth-century teaching without minimizing it also suggests the satisfaction of three of Newman's notes of authentic development. As already discussed, the sixth note is the power of assimilation. If one views both the nineteenth-century pronouncements and Vatican II as teachings on the human person, and especially on the necessity of human integrity, it becomes clear that the declaration does not

---

[76] Cf. Pope Paul VI, Homily on the Occasion of the Closing of the Third Session of the Second Vatican Council (Nov. 21, 1964) [AAS 56 (1964): 1009–10]. See also Second Vatican Council, Dogmatic Constitution on Divine Revelation *Dei Verbum* (Nov. 18, 1965), §8c–d.

[77] Paul VI, Homily on the Closing of the Third Session [AAS 56 (1964): 1009–10].

simply avoid contradicting the previous popes but that it in fact bolsters, emphasizes, and revivifies the nineteenth-century papal teachings.[78] By the same token, one sees the declaration satisfying the fifth note, that is, the quality of the later teaching as protecting the earlier one. Related to the fifth note is the fourth, namely, the quality of the beginning anticipating subsequent phases of the teaching. Needless to say, not everyone will agree that the nineteenth-century teaching anticipates DH. Viewed from the standpoint of human integrity though, one can see the pronouncements of the nineteenth-century popes come to fruition in DH. That is, one sees their sometimes-implicit concern for human integrity become explicit at Vatican II.

Newman's first three notes are that the later development retains the same type, has the same principles, and has the same organization as the earlier teaching. Again, it is understandable if some readers have difficulty in discerning the thread running through Gregory, Pius, Leo, and Vatican II. If one attends to the concern for human integrity running throughout all of these teachings though, then it becomes clear that DH satisfies even these first three of Newman's notes. As I acknowledge at the beginning of this subsection, human integrity is not the only lens through which one might view the nineteenth-century and Vatican-II teachings. However, this interpretation is by no means forced. The popes' and the Council's concern for the unity between a person's private life and his public life is readily apparent. In addition, this hermeneutic avoids a simple reduction of any of the teachings (for example, as being concerned exclusively with indifferentism) and it accounts for the presence of everything in them (the concern for private life, for public activity, for dangerous currents of thought, and for the limitations on governmental action). Moreover, this hermeneutic reveals not only the bare non-contradiction of the teachings but the profound underlying unity between them.

---

[78] The fecundity of this hermeneutic appears from its relevance to different but related contexts. Thus, in discussing the Council's teaching on the freedom of the faithful in temporal affairs, Martín de Agar notes that this freedom is an application of the Council's formulation of Gelasian dualism, but he cautions against interpreting the distinction between the religious and temporal realms as a complete separation. Indeed, he says, there must be a "harmony of coherence" centered in the person himself. "[E]sta novedosa proyección del dualismo en el ámbito jurídico personal no consiste en la mera distinción de órdenes, lo importante es la armonía de la coherencia: que en su conducta personal 'recuerden que, en cualquier asunto temporal, deben guiarse por la conciencia cristiana, ya que ninguna actividad humana, ni siquiera en el orden temporal, puede sustraerse al imperio de Dios' (LG 36)." José Tomás Martín de Agar, "Derecho y relaciones iglesia—sociedad civil," *Ius Ecclesiae* 32, no. 1 (2020): 62.

7.5.2. One Age Rescues Another

In a book that he wrote to explain his conversion to Catholicism, G. K. Chesterton praises the Church for her uncanny ability to navigate new currents of thought and to emerge always with the correct position and a sound judgment on whatever movements and trends arise.[79] Thus, in another work, he extols the Church for defending faith in the nineteenth century when the Enlightenment trend was to believe only in reason, and much more remarkably, Chesterton notes that the Church emerges in the twentieth century as almost the sole remaining defender of reason, once men had come to lose belief even in this.[80] "We do not really want a religion that is right where we are right. What we want is a religion that is right where we are wrong."[81]

What enables the Church to exercise such an impeccable judgment? Needless to say, the chief cause is the assistance she receives from the Holy Spirit to preserve the faith intact (cf. DV, §10b). Chesterton, however, focuses his own attention on the Church's long history and the perspective that it gives her teachers and pastors in judging new ideas and movements. Indeed, Chesterton's insight sheds light on the fruitful cooperation of the pastors' human wisdom in the mission of the Holy Spirit. In this light, his observations on the Church's life and history are instructive.

> There is a sort of rotation of crops in religious history; and old fields can lie fallow for a while and then be worked again. But when the new religion or any such notion has sown its one crop of wild oats, which the wind generally blows away, it is barren. A thing as old as the Catholic Church has an accumulated armoury and treasury to choose from; it can pick and choose among the centuries and brings one age to the rescue of another. It can call in the old world to redress the balance of the new.[82]

Chesterton's notion of one age of the Church rescuing another is an outstanding insight, and one can perceive it working in this very development of the teaching on religious liberty. In this case, however, which age is the rescuer, and which is the beneficiary of the rescue? Does the age of the nineteenth-century teaching rescue the era of Vatican II? Or is it the

---

[79] Cf. Chesterton, *The Catholic Church and Conversion*, ch. 5.
[80] Cf. G. K. Chesterton, "Why I am a Catholic," in *Twelve Modern Apostles and Their Creeds* (New York: Duffield & Co., 1926): "Catholicism is not mere mysticism; it is even now defending human reason against the mere mysticism of the Pragmatists."
[81] Chesterton, *Catholic Church and Conversion*, ch. 5.
[82] Chesterton, *Catholic Church and Conversion*, ch. 5.

time of the Council that rescues the timeTable of Chesterton's implication seems to be that it is the earlier age that rescues the later. However, what the hermeneutic of human integrity most clearly reveals is the Vatican II "rescue" of the nineteenth-century teaching. As discussed above, this hermeneutic reveals the nineteenth-century teaching not only *negatively*, as a teaching against religious liberty, but also *positively*, as an insistence on coherence across the individual and social realms (or the moral and the juridical). The nineteenth-century popes' teaching on human integrity usually is implicit, but Vatican II "rescues" it by making it explicit. That is, DH extends the nineteenth-century teaching on this point and gives it new life.[83]

At the same time, however, it is possible to glimpse how the age of the nineteenth-century popes also might be said to "rescue" the time of Vatican II. One sees this especially in the elaboration of the religious liberty teaching throughout the Council. There was a widespread desire to promulgate a document on religious liberty, but some of the supporting theories were incomplete or problematic. The following two chapters—on the object and foundation of the right to religious liberty—will discuss some of the pitfalls and problematic bases asserted for this teaching. That the final document avoided these pitfalls is largely thanks to the efforts of those fathers who insisted on a declaration that would be consistent with previous teaching. Most of these fathers actually hoped to avoid the promulgation of a document on religious liberty, and although they failed in this initiative, they had an outsized impact on the final form of the document. Indeed, their efforts resulted in a final version that reaffirmed traditional teaching on the duty of the public power to the Church (see section 4.6 above). In addition, as discussed below in chapter 9, their efforts also seem to have foreclosed efforts to found the right on bases that would have given rise to several practical and doctrinal difficulties.

7.6. The Relevance of the Scope of the Right to the Larger Question

The full analysis of the right to religious liberty requires examination of its scope, object, and foundation. This chapter has considered its scope and has

---

[83] Other parts of the nineteenth-century teaching remain vibrant as well, such as the rejection of indifferentism and the defense of the *Libertas Ecclesiae*. However, the point in the main text is that the principle of integrity animating the very teaching at issue in the debate over DH comes to fruition at Vatican II.

attempted to contribute toward distinguishing the Vatican II right from the one (or ones) that the nineteenth-century popes rejected.

First, while the nineteenth-century popes rejected a broad right of conscience that applies in both the moral realm and the juridical realm, the Vatican II right applies only in the juridical realm. In the moral realm, Vatican II reaffirms the traditional teaching on the duty of all persons to seek the truth. Indeed, it reaffirms the duty of individuals toward "the true religion and the one Church of Christ" (DH, §1c). (See section 4.6 above.) Thus, the Vatican II right is different because it is by no means a right before God to profess whatever one wishes, but rather it is a right in civil society.

Second, in the realm of civil society too, the Vatican II right differs in several respects from the one rejected by the nineteenth-century popes. Those popes were particularly concerned about a right to worship or publish that they described as absolute, unbounded, and limitless. By contrast, the Vatican II right exists only "within due limits" and it must be exercised in accordance with the "just demands of public order" (DH, §§2a, 4b). Thus, the Council does not approve of the radical and virtually unlimited right in the civil realm that the French Revolution inaugurated and that Lamennais championed. (See chapter 12 below, which is devoted entirely to the question of the limits of this right.) In addition, Vatican II avoids indifferentism in the social realm by reaffirming the duty of societies (including their public authorities) toward the Catholic Church (cf. DH, §1c). (See section 4.6 above.)

Finally, the content of the right is entirely different. The nineteenth-century right was a positive authorization for any type of worship, but the Vatican II right is merely an immunity from coercion. This aspect of the right is the subject of the next chapter.

CHAPTER 8

The Object of the Right to Religious Liberty

Could it be that in certain circumstances He would not give men any mandate, would not impose any duty, and would not even communicate the right to impede or to repress what is erroneous and false?

— POPE PIUS XII[1]

The preceding chapter established that the *realm* in which the Vatican II right to religious liberty exists is the juridical (as opposed to the moral) sphere, and this chapter concerns the *nature* or *object* of that right. Within the juridical realm, *Dignitatis Humanae* declares that every person has a right to religious liberty. What precisely does this mean? What is *the exact thing* that is the right of each person?

The key to understanding the nature or object of the right to religious liberty is that this right is an *immunity*. That is, the object of the right to religious liberty is not the *content* of any particular religion, but it is instead the *immunity* from coercion in religious matters.[2] It is this peculiar nature of the right *as an immunity*—above all else—that preserves the declaration from contradicting previous papal teaching.[3]

---

[1] Pope Pius XII, Discourse to Italian Jurists *Ci Riesce*, §V (Dec. 6, 1953) [AAS 45 (1953): 798–99] (hereinafter cited as CR).

[2] Cf. Fernando Ocáriz, "Sulla libertà religiosa. Continuità del Vaticano II con il Magistero precedente," *Annales theologici* 3 (1989): 75; Pietro Pavan, *La dichiarazione conciliare Dignitatis humanae a 20 anni dalla pubblicazione* (Casale Monferrato, Italy: Edizioni Piemme di Pietro Marietti, 1986), 28–29.

[3] As an immunity, the nature of the right to religious liberty is negative. However, the right

8.1. The Central Dispute

The central doctrinal dispute in the religious liberty debate concerns the status of public non-Catholic worship in a Catholic state (see sections 3.2.1 and 6.4 above). Chapter 5 provided an investigation into the change in circumstances from the time of the nineteenth-century papal pronouncements to the Vatican II teachings to consider the question of whether those historical changes themselves might resolve the debate and render a theological inquiry unnecessary. Although the historical inquiry illuminated the context of the religious liberty debate, it was insufficient to resolve it. As a result, further theological and juridical inquiry remains necessary. Chapter 6 set forth the key pronouncements of the nineteenth-century magisterium, and chapter 7 began the analysis proper by investigating the *scope* of the right to religious liberty that Vatican II recognizes. In this chapter I now continue that analysis by turning to the *object* of the Vatican II right to religious liberty. (The following three chapters will treat the *foundation* of the right.)

The teaching of the nineteenth-century popes (especially Leo XIII) was that although non-Catholics have no *right* to worship publicly, a Catholic state legitimately might decide to *tolerate* such worship. However, *Dignitatis Humanae* declares that every person (which necessarily includes a non-Catholic in a Catholic state) has the right to religious liberty, that is, the right not to be coerced into performing a religious act and the right to freedom from interference in his conduct of his own religious acts.[4] *Is this not the affirmation of precisely what the popes have taught could not be the object of a right?*

Traditionalist critic Michael Davies identified this as the key dispute over *Dignitatis Humanae* and the possibility of reconciling it with previous papal teaching.[5] An answer to this question requires one to come to an understanding of the terms *toleration* and *right*.

---

has a positive purpose or finality, namely, man's orientation toward seeking and embracing the truth. See section 7.1, citing Basile Valuet, *Le droit à la liberté religieuse dans la Tradition de l'Eglise. Un cas de développement doctrinal homogène par le magistère authentique*, 2nd rev. ed. (Barroux: Éditions Sainte-Madeleine, 2011), 420–21, and subsection 7.4.2 (citing LRTE, 428).

[4] This right must be exercised "within due limits," and the legitimate limitations on this right are the subject of part 4 of this study.

[5] Cf. Michael Davies, *Archbishop Lefebvre and Religious Liberty* (Rockford, IL: TAN Books and Publishers, 1980), 9–11. See also Davies, "Pope Leo XIII on True Liberty," *Latin Mass* (Summer 1998): 62–66.

8.1.1. The Notion of a Right

A *right* may be defined as "that which justly accrues or falls to anyone; what one may properly claim; one's due."[6] As stated below, however, in the debate over *Dignitatis Humanae*, it is crucial to distinguish different types of rights and to come to an understanding of the precise nature of the right that Vatican II recognized. Several attempts to describe the nature of this right are discussed below (see section 8.2).

The difficulty is that one can have an affirmative right to embrace and to propagate only what is true.[7] Needless to say, every non-Catholic religion denies some truths of the Catholic faith. *How then can the embracing and the spreading of these other beliefs be the object of a right?*

In his encyclical *Immortale Dei* (1885), Pope Leo XIII rejected the idea that a Catholic state should treat all religions as equal.

> [I]t is not lawful for the State . . . to hold in equal favor different kinds of religion; the unrestrained freedom of thinking and of openly making known one's thoughts is not inherent in the rights of citizens, and is by no means to be reckoned worthy of favor and support. (ID, §35)[8]

Three years later, in his encyclical *Libertas* (1888), Leo made the same point even more forcefully.

---

[6] *The Shorter Oxford English Dictionary on Historical Principles* (Oxford: Clarendon Press, 1968), s.v. "Right." On the notion of "right" as "one's own" or as "what is owed to one," see Javier Hervada, *Critical Introduction to Natural Law*, trans. Mindy Emmons (Montreal: Wilson & Lafleur, 2006), 1–2, 6, 50, 67–68. Hervada is clear, however, that the person is a holder not only of *rights* but also of *obligations* (cf. Hervada, 104, 107). On the notion of "subjective right" as including a faculty to require or to claim something, see Álvaro del Portillo, *Laici e fedeli nella Chiesa* (Milano, Italy: Giuffrè, 1999), 42–46.

[7] Cf. Pope Leo XIII, Encyclical *Libertas* (June 20, 1888), §33: The Church does "not conced[e] any right to anything save what is true and honest"; CR, §V: "[T]hat which does not correspond to the truth and to the moral norm has objectively no right either of existence or of self-propagation or of action." See the discussion in section 8.1.2 below.

[8] Note that Leo refers to the state generally rather than to the Catholic state in particular. However, the context suggests that he has the Catholic state in mind, and in any event, he suggests elsewhere that this teaching is tailored to Catholic states in particular. Cf. LP, §21: "[T]hat religion must be professed which alone is true, and which can be recognized without difficulty, especially in Catholic states, because the marks of truth are, as it were, engraven upon it." In addition, note Leo's concern with indifferentism. The charge that DH promotes indifferentism was addressed above (see section 4.6 above).

Justice therefore forbids, and reason itself forbids, the State to ... treat the various religions (as they call them) alike, and to bestow upon them promiscuously equal rights and privileges. Since, then, the profession of one religion is necessary in the State, that religion must be professed which alone is true, and which can be recognized without difficulty, especially in Catholic States, because the marks of truth are, as it were, engraven upon it. (LP, §21)

8.1.2. Leo XIII on Toleration

Toleration is a different matter from a right. Peter Garnsey provides a useful definition. He describes *toleration* as a position that implies disapproval coupled with an unwillingness to take action against those who are viewed with disfavor. Garnsey describes toleration as an *active* concept, unlike indifference or apathy, both of which are *passive*.[9] Similarly, Judge John T. Noonan describes toleration as "permission of what is frankly described as an evil, but a lesser evil."[10] The distinction between rights and toleration is important because Leo XIII described public religious worship by non-Catholics in a Catholic state as a matter of toleration rather than right. Leo taught that the state might tolerate non-Catholic worship as a necessary evil, but that it could never endorse it as a positive good (see section 6.4).

> [W]hile not conceding any right to anything save what is true and honest, she [the Church] does not forbid public authority to *tolerate* what is at variance with truth and justice, for the sake of avoiding some greater evil, or of obtaining or preserving some greater good. God Himself in His providence, though infinitely good and powerful, permits evil to exist in the world, partly that greater good may not be impeded, and partly that greater evil may not ensue. In the government of States it is not forbidden to imitate the Ruler of the world. . . . But if, in such circumstances, for the sake of the common good (and this is the only legitimate reason), human law may or even should tolerate evil, *it may not and should not approve or desire evil for its own sake*; for evil of itself, being a

---

[9] Peter Garnsey, "Religious Toleration in Classical Antiquity," in *Persecution and Toleration*, ed. W. J. Sheils (Oxford: Basil Blackwell, 1984), 1.

[10] John T. Noonan Jr., "Development in Moral Doctrine," *Theological Studies* 54, no. 4 (1993): 668.

privation of good, is opposed to the common welfare which every legislator is bound to desire and defend to the best of his ability.[11]

Leo went on to say that "the more a State is driven to tolerate evil, the further it is from perfection" (LP, §34). In addition, he made clear that the extent of toleration must be strictly circumscribed by the benefit to public welfare that justifies the policy of toleration (cf. LP, §34). As stated above, there is a near-consensus in the scholarly literature that the difference between toleration and a right is a difference not merely in degree but also in kind. (Harrison, for his part, will describe the right to religious liberty as a *right to be tolerated*,[12] and section 8.4 below will examine this concept.)

The Church's pronouncements on the toleration of non-Catholic worship are rooted in the teachings of St. Thomas Aquinas. Thomas wrote on several subjects that bear closely on the questions of religious liberty and toleration. For example, he taught that the rites of Jews and Muslims may be tolerated to achieve some good or to avoid some evil. He reasoned that human government should imitate divine government, which permits evils that it might otherwise prevent, so that unbelievers gradually might be won to the faith.[13] Leo adapted the teaching of St. Thomas Aquinas to nineteenth-century circumstances. That is, whereas Thomas taught that the rites of *Jews and Muslims* might be tolerated, Leo applied the same principle to the public worship of *non-Catholic Christians*. The principle of toleration left intact the idea that the state, like the individual, has a duty to God and the Church.[14] However, it also took account of the emerging reality that forbidding worship by non-Catholics often resulted in more harm than good.[15] Leo's successors in turn extended the policy of toleration and applied

---

[11] LP, §33 (emphasis added). Cf. Pope Leo XIII, Encyclical *Immortale Dei* (Nov. 1, 1885), §36.

[12] Brian W. Harrison, *Religious Liberty and Contraception: Did Vatican II Open the Way for a New Sexual Ethic?* (Melbourne: John XXIII Fellowship Co-op., Ltd., 1988), 117.

[13] St. Thomas Aquinas, *Summa Theologica*, Christian Classics ed. (Benziger Brothers, 1947), II-II, q. 10, a. 11.

[14] Cf. ID, §6: "[T]he state ... is clearly bound to act up to the manifold duties linking it to God." The principle of the state's or the community's duty to God is set forth most fully in Pope Pius XI's encyclical instituting the Feast of Christ the King. Cf. Pope Pius XI, Encyclical *Quas Primas* (Dec. 11, 1925), §18.

[15] Toleration grew out of the "thesis-hypothesis" theory. In that theory, the thesis was an abstract and ideal rule (such as, *the state should permit public worship of only the Catholic religion*), and the hypothesis was a rule of conduct that took actual circumstances into account (*in this situation, it is best to tolerate public worship of non-Catholic religions*). Cf. Henri Fesquet, *The Drama of Vatican II* (New York: Random House, 1967), 353.

it with increasing generosity and with increasing recognition of the actual social, political, and religious circumstances present in the world (cf. CR).

Leo XIII made it clear in both *Immortale Dei* and *Libertas* that it is not permissible for all religions to be treated in the same way. Leo's concern was with the error of *indifferentism*, the idea that one can attain salvation by the profession of any religion. In addition, however, it is clear that Leo also based his teaching on the proposition that Catholicism is uniquely true. That is, Leo's "toleration only" teaching was rooted in the Catholic Church's claim that it is unique in containing the fullness of the means necessary for salvation (cf. LP, §21; see also ID, §7).

8.1.3. The Challenge of Vatican II

The Second Vatican Council introduced a momentous shift of emphasis from Leo's description of non-Catholic churches and communities as "evil" (LP, §33) to the conciliar description of Orthodox and Protestant Christians as "our separated brethren."[16] This striking shift in emphasis ushered in a new period of ecumenism, but it did not result in the Church's renunciation of her truth claims.[17] Vatican II would retain this principle but would shift the emphasis away from the points that divide the various Christian denominations and toward an appreciation of the many points that are held in common (cf. LG, §8b; UR, §3c). (Although there is a great difference of emphasis between Leo's teachings discussed here and those of the Second Vatican Council, one should not forget that, at least in his later pronouncements, Leo himself was willing to acknowledge the sincerity of the beliefs of non-Catholic Christians.[18] In addition, it is noteworthy that his encyclical on the political situation in France, although addressed to French Catholics, included an appeal to non-Catholics as well.)[19]

---

[16] Second Vatican Council, Decree on Ecumenism *Unitatis Redintegratio* (Nov. 21, 1964), §3e [AAS 57 (1965): 93] (hereinafter cited as UR).

[17] Cf. UR, §3a; Congregation for the Doctrine of the Faith, Declaration on the Unicity and Salvific Universality of Jesus Christ and the Church *Dominus Iesus* (Aug. 6, 2000), §16, 16n56 [AAS 92 (2000): 757–58].

[18] Cf. Pope Leo XIII, Encyclical *Longinqua Oceani* (Jan. 6, 1895), §20; Pope Leo XIII, Encyclical *Testem Benevolentiae Nostrae* (Jan. 22, 1899) [ASS (1898–1899): 478–79].

[19] Pope Leo XIII, Apostolic Letter *Au Milieu des Sollicitudes* (Feb. 16, 1892), §§4, 6–7, 26, 30 [ASS 24 (1891–1892): 519–21, 527–29]. Moreover, although use of the phrase *separated brethren* to refer to non-Catholic Christians may seem to be a distinctive innovation of Vatican II, it appears that in fact this phrase may originate with Leo himself! Murray in particular credits Leo with coining the phrase *separated brethren* in this context. John Courtney Murray, "Leo XIII on Church and State: The General Structure of the

8.1. The Central Dispute

This creates a difficulty for reconciling Vatican II with Leo's teaching. That is, the reason that Leo taught that non-Catholic worship was the object only of toleration and not of a right was that non-Catholic religions and denominations could not make the same truth claims as the Catholic Church. To the extent that the teachings and sacramental life of these bodies differed from Catholicism, to that extent, they were not in full concord with the truth. Thus, for Leo, there could be no objective right for non-Catholic religious bodies to propagate their teaching. Pope Pius XII repeated the same teaching less than a decade before the opening of the Council.[20]

The difficulty that *Dignitatis Humanae* presents is that the language that it uses in recognizing religious liberty may seem to suggest that the Council did indeed recognize an objective right on the part of non-Catholics to propagate non-Catholic religion.

> This Vatican Council declares that the human person has a right to religious freedom. Such freedom consists in this, that all men and women should be immune from coercion on the part of individuals, social groups or any human power, so that no one is to be forced to act against his conscience in religious matters, or prevented from acting according to his conscience, in private or in public, whether alone or in association with others, within due limits.[21]

Indeed, this language often is described as affirming a *positive right* to profess and to propagate any religion.[22]

Controversy," *Theological Studies* 14, no. 1 (1953): 2–3: "Leo XIII was the first Pope, as far as I know, to use the expression, 'fratelli nostri separati da noi.'"

[20] Cf. CR, §V: "[T]hat which does not correspond to the truth and to the moral norm has objectively no right either of existence or of self-propagation or of action."

[21] Second Vatican Council, Declaration on Religious Liberty Dignitatis Humanae (December 7, 1965), §2a; English translation from David L. Schindler and Nicholas J. Healy Jr., Freedom, Truth, and Human Dignity: The Second Vatican Council's Declaration on Religious Freedom—A New Translation, Redaction History, and Interpretation of *Dignitatis Humanae* (Grand Rapids, MI / Cambridge, UK: William B. Eerdmans Publishing Co., 2015), 387. Note that a problem is present in some prominent English translations of DH §2, including the one on the Vatican website (site accessed Apr. 14, 2019). The problem is that they translate DH §2 as providing a right to freedom from coercion, but do not include the right to be prevented from acting in accordance with one's conscience. See also *Declaration on Religious Freedom:* Dignitatis Humanae, NCWC translation (Boston: St. Paul Books & Media) (same problem).

[22] Cf. Valuet, LRTE, 37–38n102 [= Basile Valuet, *La liberté religieuse et la tradition catholique. Un cas de développement doctrinal homogène dans le magistère authentique*, 3rd rev. ed. (Barroux: Éditions Sainte-Madeleine, 2011), vol. IA, 63].

However, a close look at the precise language of the declaration reveals something important. What Vatican II asserts is *not* a right to profess and to propagate any religion that one chooses. Rather, the Council asserts a right to freedom from coercion of religious acts and freedom from interference in religious acts. Thus, the *object* of this right is not the *content* of any particular religious faith but rather it is *immunity* for religious acts.

Recall that Pope Leo XIII had taught that although a Catholic state could *tolerate* public non-Catholic religious worship, the state could not *approve* or desire such worship for its own sake (LP, §33). The character of the Vatican II right as an immunity makes possible the affirmation of a right to religious liberty on the part of all persons *without* any necessary approval of the content of their beliefs. (Although this concept initially may be difficult to grasp, it is analogous to a familiar principle of American jurisprudence concerning the First Amendment, namely, that the constitution's recognition of a right to freedom of speech on the part of each citizen does not equate to positive governmental or constitutional approval of any given individual's particular use of his right.) Because the *object* of the right is *immunity from coercion* rather than the *content* of any particular religion, the right to religious liberty is not strictly speaking an *affirmative right* to practice non-Catholic religious worship. This is a challenging concept, and some authors frankly acknowledge that it is difficult to grasp how *Dignitatis Humanae* does not "effectively recognize a 'right to error.'"[23] Recognition of a positive right to propagate false teaching would be "incompatible with the traditional doctrine of the Church."[24] However, several scholars have advanced various theories to show that the right to religious liberty that the Council recognizes is not in fact a right to error.

8.2. Positive Rights and Negative Rights

Some scholars, including Pietro Pavan, distinguish between *positive* rights and *negative* rights.[25] Under this formulation, the right to religious liberty is not a positive right to act but is instead a negative right. That is, religious liberty is not a positive or affirmative right to practice a certain religion, but it is rather a negative right to immunity from coercion in religious matters.

A similar formulation distinguishes *active* rights from *passive* rights. An

---

[23] Kevin Flannery, "*Dignitatis Humanae* and the Development of Doctrine," *Catholic Dossier* 6, no. 2 (March–April 2000): 33.
[24] Harrison, RL&C, 114–15. See also CR, §V.
[25] Cf. Pavan, *La dichiarazione conciliare*, 30–31; Valuet, LRTE, 30–31.

active right is understood as the right to do something, and a passive right is understood as the right to receive something.[26]

8.3. The Right as *Ius Exigendi*

However, Brian Harrison provides a more thorough discussion of the various categories of rights that are relevant to the question of religious liberty. In particular, Harrison distinguishes among (1) the right to do something (*ius agendi*), (2), the right to have something (*ius habendi*), and (3) the right to require someone else or some institution to do something or to refrain from doing something (*ius exigendi*).[27] In common parlance, religious liberty generally is spoken of as an active right or in terms of *ius agendi*, that is, the affirmative right to worship in public or in private. However, Harrison notes that the language of Vatican II pertains more to the nature of a *ius exigendi*. That is, Vatican II speaks of religious liberty as an *immunity* rather than as a *ius agendi* or a right to do something.[28]

Thus, Harrison argues, the right to religious liberty is not a positive right to propagate non-Catholic religion or to worship publicly in non-Catholic rites,[29] but rather it is an immunity from interference in these activities.[30] The immunity that is at issue is immunity from coercion in civil society.[31] Stated differently—and paradoxically—Harrison describes the right to religious liberty as "a right to be tolerated."[32] (The next section will include a consideration of whether this is a coherent concept.) Religious liberty is a *ius exigendi* and its content is the right to require civil authorities not to

---

[26] Cf. Brian Tierney, *The Idea of Natural Rights: Studies on Natural Rights, Natural Law, and Church Law (1150–1625)* (Atlanta, GA: Emory University, 1997), 3.

[27] Cf. Harrison, RL&C, 117–18; cf. Brian W. Harrison, "Religious Liberty: 'Rights' versus 'Tolerance,'" *Living Tradition* 16 (March 1988), Roman Theological Forum, accessed Apr. 23, 2003, http://www.rtforum.org/lt/lt16.html#II (NB, this article is substantially the same as chapter 8 of RL&C).

[28] Harrison, RL&C, 117–18. Tierney describes the right to worship as an active right (Tierney, *Idea of Natural Rights*, 3). However, Harrison's argument shows how this right can be reformulated as a right to immunity from government interference rather than a positive right to act. Valuet's position is much the same as Harrison's (cf. Valuet, LRTE, 37–38n102, 39).

[29] This is especially clear, Harrison notes, from the late addition to DH §1 affirming the duty of all men and societies to Christ and His Church (cf. Harrison, RL&C, 115).

[30] Brian W. Harrison, "Vatican II and Religious Liberty: Contradiction or Continuity?," *Catholic Dossier* 6, no. 2 (March–April 2000): 28.

[31] Harrison, RL&C, 114.

[32] Harrison, RL&C, 117.

interfere with a person's practice of his religion, provided that he acts in accordance with the requirements of public order.

Harrison observes that the Council employs the concept of *ius exigendi* "in a novel and unexpected way."[33] This concept traditionally had been used to describe the right of superiors to require their subjects to do (or not to do) something. The Council, however, inverts this usage by attributing the *ius exigendi* to "subjects" against their "superiors" at the head of civil governments. Thus, the individual citizen may demand that others, especially governmental actors, refrain from compelling religious belief or practice, and also refrain from interfering with religious worship or activity (unless harm to the public order occurs).[34]

8.4. THE DAVIES OBJECTION

Michael Davies argued that Harrison's attempt to reconcile *Dignitatis Humanae* with Catholic tradition by positing a right to be tolerated was merely "a semantic quibble."[35] That is, Davies did not accept the distinction between (1) a right to *propagate* non-Catholic religion in public, and (2) a right to *immunity from coercion in propagating* non-Catholic religion in public. Indeed, such a distinction is quite fine.[36]

However, despite the fineness of the distinction, Harrison's analysis does stand up to scrutiny. With regard to whether there is a real distinction between a right to propagate and a right to immunity, Michael Davies himself cites an example that validates this distinction. He argues that the only instance of a legitimate distinction along these lines pertains to private life.

---

[33] Harrison, RL&C, 118.

[34] The right to religious liberty is concerned especially with immunity from governmental coercion, but it is important to remember that it also protects against coercion from private individuals. Cf. Paul VI, Consistory and Wishes to the Sacred College and the Roman Prelature, Dec. 20, 1976: DH concerns right with regard to human authorities, especially the state; Giorgio Feliciani, "La libertà religiosa nel magistero di Giovanni Paolo II," in *Escritos en honor de Javier Hervada*, Ius Canonicum, volumen especial (Pamplona, Spain: Instituto Martín de Azpilcueta, 1999), 928.

[35] Michael Davies, *The Second Vatican Council and Religious Liberty* (Long Prairie, MN: Neumann Press, 1992), 230. However, after years of debating the issue privately with Harrison, Davies appears to have revised his position to accept this distinction. Cf. "Letters," *The Latin Mass Magazine* (Winter 2000): 8–9 (letter from Harrison).

[36] Ocáriz agrees with Davies and refers to a "right to toleration" as a contradiction in terms (Ocáriz, "Sulla libertà religiosa," 89). However, Ocáriz resolves this difficulty by making reference to the limits on the power of the state in confronting the human person (Ocáriz, 89–90).

8.4. The Davies Objection

That is, St. Thomas taught that it was improper to baptize Jewish children against the wishes of their parents.[37] Davies recognizes the right of parents in the same terms that Harrison discusses religious liberty—not as the right to teach any religion to one's children but as the right to immunity from coercion in making such decisions within the home.[38] Although Davies strenuously argues that this principle does not extend to the public realm, he concedes Harrison's most important point, namely, that a right to immunity can exist even when no objective right to do the underlying act exists.[39] This is precisely the situation that St. Thomas addresses. In addition, one can see this most clearly in the case of atheism. The Church teaches that every person has the duty to seek God (DH, §1b; can. 748, §1). However, even though a person has no objective moral right to refuse to fulfill this duty (that is, no right according to nature and no right before God), he does have a right not to be compelled to fulfill it (cf. DH, §2a; can. 748, §2).[40] Moreover, as discussed above, this is not merely a civil right but is rather a requirement of the inherent dignity of each person.[41] In addition to the

---

[37] ST II-II, q. 10, a. 12. Cf. ST III, q. 68, a. 10.

[38] Davies, SVC&RL, 216–17.

[39] In speaking of rights, one must always remain aware of the relevant context. That is, in discussing religious liberty, one might be referring to the rights that a person has in the *objective moral order*, or one might be referring to the rights that one has in *civil society* (cf. Davies, SVC&RL, 18). In discussing religious liberty it is sometimes difficult to separate these two contexts. On the one hand, *Dignitatis Humanae* is addressed primarily to rights in civil society, that is, the rights that persons have in relation to their governments and other human powers. (The context of civil society is vitally important for *Dignitatis Humanae*, but, as discussed below, religious liberty cannot be reduced to a mere civil right.)

[40] Thus, one of the most frequently uttered sentiments during the debates on religious liberty was that error may not have rights but persons in error do. Cf. Sept. 18, 1965, oral intervention of John Cardinal Heenan of Westminster [AS IV/1, 295–96] (English translation in Fesquet, 606); Sept. 20, 1965, oral intervention of Lawrence Cardinal Shehan of Baltimore [AS IV/1, 396–99] (English translation Vincent A. Yzermans, ed., *American Participation in the Second Vatican Council* [New York: Sheed & Ward, 1967], 663); Sept. 21, 1965, oral intervention of Charles Cardinal Journet, Professor at Fribourg [AS IV/1, 424–25] (English translation in Fesquet, 615).

[41] This observation raises the issue of the *origin* of rights. In short, the two predominant theories are of rights as *natural* and rights as *positive*. The theory that rights are natural posits certain rights as inherent in the human person. The theory of rights as positive makes rights dependent on the actual laws enacted by one's own government. That is, no right exists unless the government recognizes it. The tradition of the Catholic Church is that there are certain rights that are natural. The modern popes, starting with Leo XIII, have given a great deal of attention to natural rights and have located the source of these rights in the dignity of the human person. "No man may with impunity outrage that dignity which God Himself treats with great reverence." Pope Leo XIII, Encyclical *Rerum Novarum* (May

chief example discussed here—the right of Jewish parents to educate their children—Valuet notes other situations in which Thomas recognizes that tolerance is obligatory, even where the underlying act is not the object of a positive right. In particular, he points to Thomas's teachings on the illegitimacy of coercing the act of faith and on the obligatoriness of permitting Jewish worship.[42]

The teaching of Pope Pius XII provides support for Harrison's argument that a right to immunity can exist even in the absence of what the Church would recognize as an objective right to perform the underlying action. In a 1953 address to Italian jurists, *Ci Riesce*, Pius considered the commands of God in this area:

> Could it be that *in certain circumstances* He would not give men any mandate, would not impose any duty, and would not even communicate the right to impede or to repress what is erroneous and false? A look at things as they are gives an affirmative answer. . . . Hence the affirmation: religious and moral error must always be impeded, when it is possible, because toleration of them is in itself immoral, is not valid *absolutely and unconditionally*. (CR, §V)

This teaching is particularly important in light of the Council's announced intention "to develop the doctrine of recent popes" (DH, §1c). The distinction that both Pius XII and Harrison make, at least implicitly, between a positive right and an immunity is echoed in the Council's invocation of the parable of the wheat and the tares as support for its teaching on religious liberty (DH, §11a). As Henri Fesquet notes, one person described the teaching of the declaration as "the divine right of tares."[43]

Thus, Harrison succeeds in showing that a right to immunity can exist even when there is no right to do the underlying act. In addition, the support that Thomas's teaching and Pius XII's discourse lend to the Harrison argument validate his claim that the idea of a right as an immunity "was already

---

15, 1891), §40. "[P]recisely because he is a person, [every human being] has rights and obligations flowing directly and simultaneously from his very nature." Pope John XXIII, Encyclical *Pacem in Terris* (Apr. 11, 1963), §9. Cf. Thomas J. Paprocki, *Vindication and Defense of the Rights of the Christian Faithful Through Administrative Recourse in the Local Church* (Ann Arbor, MI: UMI, 1995), 158–72, summarizing modern papal teaching on human rights. By contrast, it is quite common today for citizens of modern nation-states to regard their rights as the creation of their governments.

[42] Cf. Valuet, LRTE, 156. See also LRTE, 153, citing ST II-II, q. 10, a. 8, 11.
[43] Fesquet, 609, quoting Jean Vogel.

implicit in Catholic tradition,"[44] even if it remains difficult to understand how this can be the case as a logical matter.

* * *

Is Harrison also correct that one can speak of religious liberty as a *right to be tolerated*? Commentators on both sides of the question bring convincing arguments to bear. On the one hand, under Leo XIII's framing of the issue, tolerance and liberty seem to be mutually exclusive.[45] One has a *right* to practice the true religion, but the practice of other religions can be the object only of *toleration*. Basile Valuet, however, draws an interesting distinction in light of *Ci Riesce*.[46] One can speak of toleration in two senses, he says. First, there is the usual sense of toleration as *not impeding that which one has a right to impede*. Second, however, there is another sense of the term, that is, toleration as *not impeding that which one has no right to impede*. To deny the possibility of a *right to be tolerated*, Valuet notes, is to deny that between the two alternatives of the *presence of a right to act* and the *absence of a right to act*, there exists a third possibility—that of *Ci Riesce*—namely, the *absence of a right to act coupled with the absence of a right to hinder by another authority*. As Valuet frames it in this fashion, it does seem logically possible to speak of a right to be tolerated.

At the same time, however, one must acknowledge that this second sense in which he uses the word *tolerate* is quite unusual. Moreover, the specific use of the word tolerance in this context does not seem to be essential to either his or Harrison's argument. Neither Harrison nor Valuet denies the dichotomy between liberty and toleration in the first sense (the sense in which Leo uses it). That is, neither one believes that the repeated granting of toleration (in the first sense) can transform the object of toleration into the object of a right. As a result, this question seems to be one more of terminology than of substance.

One way to clarify matters would be to speak of toleration in the first sense as *toleration proper* and to refer to Valuet's second concept as *toleration in the paradoxical sense*. Perhaps a more manageable usage would be to adopt a distinction between *active* and *passive* toleration. Yet another possibility would be to reserve toleration to its usual or proper sense (the first sense) and to adopt another term to correspond to the *Ci Riesce* situation (the

---

[44] Harrison, "Contradiction or Continuity," 28.

[45] Cf. Ocáriz, "Sulla libertà religiosa," 89: A right to toleration is a contradiction in terms; José T. Martín de Agar, "Ecclesia y Polis," *Ius Canonicum* (2008): 411: "*lo que se tolera nunca es un derecho.*"

[46] Cf. Valuet, LRTE, 334 [= LRTC, vol. IA, 442–44].

second sense). Thus, within the *genus* of *noninterference*, one could identify two *species* of noninterference, namely, *toleration* and *immunity-recognition*.

8.5. Related Observations

A brief consideration of two additional scholars sheds light on this problem.

Valuet's discussion of rights is lengthier and more technical than Harrison's, but his conclusion and his interpretation of its significance are much the same. In addition, he discusses positive and negative rights at greater length, and thus in a sense combines the Harrison approach with the Pavan approach described above. Thus, Valuet describes a positive authorization to act as a permission (or right-as-permission, that is, *droit affirmatif-permission*). For example, the Church herself has from Christ such an authorization to preach the Gospel throughout the world (cf. Matt 28:19, Mark 16:15, Luke 24:47). However, the right to religious liberty that Vatican II recognizes is not a permission, but a negative right (*droit négatif-exigence*).[47] Where Harrison uses the word *immunity*, Valuet generally uses the word *noninterference*.[48] Thus, the Vatican II right is a right to noninterference, that is, freedom from being compelled to perform a religious act and freedom from interference in one's own religious worship and practices (provided that they do not harm the public order).

The difference between these two rights—the permission and the immunity—is that, for the Church, the right (that is, the right-as-permission) concerns preaching and teaching in themselves. It is a *positive authorization* to undertake these activities. However, what DH recognizes as religious liberty is a negative right. That is, the right consists not in a positive provision of assistance but rather in an abstention from interfering in an action.[49] It is not a positive authorization to choose any religion or no religion, nor is it a

---

[47] Just as the nineteenth-century popes sometimes blurred the distinction between the moral and juridical realms (see chapter 7 on the "Scope of the Right"), it also seems to be the case that neither they nor the nineteenth-century liberals distinguished well between the concepts of *droit affirmatif-permission* and *droit négatif-exigence*. Cf. Valuet, LRTC, vol. I, 59n113; see also LRTE, 34n91.

[48] That is, he uses the word *non-empêchement* (e.g., Valuet, LRTE, 31). I translate this word as *noninterference*, but in some contexts, it alternatively may be translated as *non-hindrance* or *non-impediment*.

[49] Valuet, LRTE, 38. A *ius exigendi* can be either positive or negative. It is positive if what one has the right to demand is an action (for example, from the government), and it is negative if what one may demand is an abstention from acting. Religious liberty is a negative *ius exigendi* because the right is in demanding abstention from interference in one's religious acts (LRTE, 34–35); cf. LRTE, 36.

8.5. RELATED OBSERVATIONS

permission to engage in any type of religious worship. Rather, it is a negative right to noninterference, that is, a right not to be compelled to make any religious profession, nor (within broad limits) to be impeded from engaging in one's chosen form of worship and religious activity.[50]

Although some commentators refer to religious liberty as a right to act freely,[51] Valuet argues convincingly that this formulation is insufficiently precise and that it blurs the distinction between a permission (*ius agendi*) and a *ius exigendi*.[52] The correct formulation is that of a right not to be constrained to act and not to be hindered from acting.[53]

Thus, Vatican II does not recognize an objective moral right to believe whatever one wishes or to worship in any way imaginable, but rather it recognizes religion as a sphere within which all persons have a right not to be hindered or impeded, regardless of their religious beliefs (unless they cause harm to the public order).

William Marshner pursues this question by distinguishing between a thing that is the object of a right per se and a thing that is the object of a right *accidentally*. He argues that error cannot be the object of a right per se, but that it can be the object of a right accidentally. Thus, to use Thomas's example, parents have no right per se to raise their children in a non-Catholic religion; however, parents do have a natural right to educate their own children and, as a result of this right, they have a right accidentally to decide upon the religious upbringing of their children, even if this choice involves error.[54] Similarly, Marshner argues, no one has a right per se

---

[50] Kevin Flannery also contrasts these two rights, arguing that the right to religious liberty recognized by Vatican II is a limited right, whereas the Church's right is a right to as much liberty as the care of souls requires (cf. Flannery, "*Dignitatis Humanae* and the Development of Doctrine," 34); cf. Flannery, 32, citing and discussing Leo XIII, Encyclical *Officio Sanctissimo* [ASS 20 (1888): 269]. Flannery is correct that the right recognized by DH to freedom of religious worship and practice is limited by the requirements of public order, but the right not to be coerced is, on the other hand, regarded by many commentators as absolute. Cf. John T. Ford, ed., *Religious Liberty: Paul VI and Dignitatis Humanae* (Brescia, Italy: Istituto Paolo VI, 1995), 43 (comment of Luigi Mistò). But see Richard J. Regan, *Conflict and Consensus: Religious Freedom and the Second Vatican Council* (New York/London: Macmillan/Collier-Macmillan Ltd., 1967), 123: "[T]here are a number of cases where governments apparently force citizens with good cause to do things that their consciences forbid." See also section 12.4 below, citing Regan and the case of *Application of the President and Directors of Georgetown College*, 331 F., 2nd 1000 (DC Cir. 1964), *cert. denied*, 84 S. Ct. 1883 (1964).

[51] Tierney, *Idea of Natural Rights*, 3.

[52] Valuet, LRTE, 37–38n102; cf. LRTE, 39.

[53] Valuet, LRTE, 39.

[54] Cf. William H. Marshner, "*Dignitatis Humanae* and Traditional Teaching on Church and

to embrace erroneous religious opinions; however, by reason of the state's disability to punish religious error, citizens have an accidental right to profess error.[55] Marshner's result and reasoning are similar to Harrison's and Valuet's, but he uses Thomistic philosophical terminology, rather than legal terms of art, to arrive there.

All of the frameworks discussed here present ways to understand how the Vatican II right to religious liberty is not a right to error. However, among these explanations, the most significant is Harrison's, because it provides the clearest explanation of how the Council could affirm a right to religious liberty without affirming a positive right to propagate error. Valuet adds further precision to the Harrison approach and, in particular, uses this framework to draw a sharp distinction between, on the one hand, the limited and negative right that the Council affirmed and, on the other hand, the absolute and positive right of the DDHC that the nineteenth-century popes rejected. For those who prefer philosophical to legal terminology, Marshner provides an alternate path to the same destination. An important intervention by one of the council fathers provides another less technical explanation of the same distinctions. Bishop Ernest Primeau of Manchester, New Hampshire, was the U.S. bishop most involved in the actual drafting of the declaration, and his intervention provides a fitting summary of this discussion:

> By "right" we mean a type of moral faculty. This moral faculty can be duplex. It is a faculty for action and a faculty for demanding that our action be not impeded by others. One affirms immunity in action; the other affirms a positive command to act. In our subject, confusing the two senses involved in the notion of right would give rise to endless confusion. In its contemporary technical sense, well understood by experts, religious liberty is a true right in the sense that it is a true juridic immunity from any legal or social force in religious matters. In this modern sense the Declaration proclaims the right of all and of all Churches to religious liberty in society. By this proclamation we do not by any means say that all men and all Churches have from the all-good God the positive mandate to spread their doctrine and worship. This would involve accepting religious indifferentism.

State," *Faith & Reason* 9, no. 3 (1983): 236.

[55] Marshner, "*Dignitatis Humanae* and Traditional Teaching on Church and State," 236.

> Anyone reading this Declaration on Religious Liberty in such a way as to see in it a touch of indifferentism confesses that he has completely misunderstood the matter under discussion.[56]

8.6. Two Facets of Liberty

The task of harmonizing the Vatican II declaration with the teachings of the nineteenth-century popes is indeed formidable. An inquiry like this one into the object of the right to religious liberty places one of the reasons in sharp focus. That is, the nineteenth-century popes and the Vatican II fathers begin with different perspectives on liberty. The nineteenth-century popes understand liberty primarily as an affirmative right, a right to do something (what Harrison calls a *ius agendi*), and such a right necessarily can be a right only to do something *good* or to embrace something *true*.

This perspective renders it difficult indeed to conceive of how all persons can enjoy a right to religious liberty. At first blush, such a right seems to imply a positive authorization to embrace any religion or belief whatsoever, without regard to its truth. Indeed, as Valuet notes, many readers of the declaration mistakenly continue to describe it in precisely these terms, that is, as an affirmative right to act or to practice a religion (*ius agendi*).

The Vatican II perspective, however, is at once both novel and traditional. It is novel because it speaks of the right to religious liberty, not as a *ius agendi* but rather as a *ius exigendi*. The idea is not a positive authorization but a negative immunity from coercion. Moreover, as Harrison shows, the Council employs this idea, not in the usual way, to vindicate the rights of "superiors" (such as government actors), but rather to assert the rights of "subjects" or, more properly, of citizens. Yet, one finds the source of these innovations not in the *Declaration of the Rights of Man and the Citizen* but rather in the Church's own tradition, most notably in the writings of St. Thomas.

If one conceives of liberty as a gem, there is no doubt that the gaze of the Vatican II fathers and that of the nineteenth-century popes fall on different facets of it. However, both facets truly exist, and both enjoy recognition in the Church's tradition, the affirmative right to act and the negative right to immunity from coercion or interference. Moreover, the shift in the gaze of the Vatican II fathers by no means repudiates the perspective or teachings of

---

[56] Sept. 24, 1964, oral intervention of Bishop Ernest Primeau (AS III/2, 495–97); English translation in Yzermans, 629.

the nineteenth-century popes. On the contrary, the real value of the Vatican II insight is precisely that it provides a way of recognizing a universal right to religious liberty *without* indifferently affirming every use of the right and without affirming a positive right to embrace and to promote any idea or belief whatsoever.

Thus, the Vatican II approach actually *conserves* the insights of the nineteenth-century popes.[57] Those popes taught that there can be no positive right to embrace false teaching, and Pope Pius XII—one of the two popes whose teaching Vatican II especially develops—reiterated this teaching not long before the Council.[58] Moreover, two key architects of the declaration made clear that they shared the same understanding. The relator, Bishop De Smedt, assured the council fathers that the declaration did not—and could not—affirm a right to propagate error,[59] and John Courtney Murray was similarly emphatic. Indeed, Murray succinctly captured both the innovativeness of the Council's formulation and its conservation of the earlier teaching: "Neither error nor evil can be the object of a right, only what is true and good. It is, however, true and good that a man should enjoy freedom from coercion in matters religious."[60]

---

[57] In his book on doctrinal development, Aidan Nichols discusses Maurice Blondel's understanding of doctrine as both *conserving* and *conquering*. Cf. Aidan Nichols, *From Newman to Congar: The Idea of Doctrinal Development from the Victorians to the Second Vatican Council* (Edinburgh: T&T Clark, 1990), 151.

[58] Cf. CR, §V: "[T]hat which does not correspond to the truth and to the moral norm has objectively no right either of existence or of self-propagation or of action." On the Council's intention particularly to develop the teaching of Pius XII, Barrett Turner notes that of the twenty-five references to modern papal teaching in DH, Pius XII and John XXIII are cited most often, that is, eight times and nine times, respectively. Leo XIII is cited four times, and Pius XI and Paul VI each twice. Cf. Barrett Hamilton Turner, "*Dignitatis Humanae* and the Development of Moral Doctrine: Assessing Change in Catholic Social Teaching on Religious Liberty" (PhD diss., Catholic University of America, 2015), 179.

[59] Cf. Émile De Smedt, responses to *modi* on the *Textus Denuo Recognitus* (Nov. 19, 1965), AS IV/6, 725: "Nowhere is it affirmed—nor could it be truly affirmed, as is evident—that there is any right to propagate error" (English translation in Harrison, "Vatican II and Religious Liberty," 28).

[60] John Courtney Murray, "Religious Freedom," in *The Documents of Vatican II*, ed. Walter M. Abbott (New York: Herder and Herder, 1966), 678n5.

PART 3B

ANALYSIS OF THE RIGHT TO RELIGIOUS LIBERTY: THE CRUCIAL QUESTION OF THE FOUNDATION OF THE RIGHT

CHAPTER 9

The Search for the Proper Foundation

Every one then who hears these words of mine and does them will be like a wise man who built his house upon the rock; and the rain fell, and the floods came, and the winds blew and beat upon that house but it did not fall, because it had been founded on the rock. And every one who hears these words of mine and does not do them will be like a foolish man who built his house upon the sand; and the rain fell, and the floods came, and the winds blew and beat against that house, and it fell; and great was the fall of it.

— MATT 7:24–27

One cannot understand *Dignitatis Humanae* unless one understands that the right to religious liberty that the declaration recognizes is founded on the nature and dignity of the human person. This may not appear to be a controversial statement, but the question of the foundation of the right to religious liberty was one of the most difficult issues that the Second Vatican Council addressed. In addition, even though the Council resolved this issue by basing the right to religious liberty on the dignity of the person, confusion and controversy over the foundation of this right still persists.

This question (the foundation of the right) may appear, at first blush, to amount to a mere technicality or a matter of less significance than the fact of the Church's recognition of the right. As I hope the following discussion will show, however, it is crucial. As a practical matter, the foundation will determine who is protected by the right to religious liberty. As a matter of theology and doctrine, the question of whether it is possible to reconcile *Dignitatis Humanae* with the teachings of the nineteenth-century popes will depend in large measure on the foundation that the Church chooses for the right that she recognizes. Indeed, the question of continuity or rupture between Vatican II and the nineteenth-century popes comes down, in large measure, to a question of the right's foundation.

9.1. Allusions to the Right to Religious Liberty

Discussions of the right of religious liberty often begin with Pope St. John XXIII. However, it is possible to go back further to find some examples of earlier foreshadowing of the Church's recognition of this right.

Pope Pius XI alludes to it as early as the 1930s in his famous encyclical against Nazism, *Mit Brennender Sorge*. "The believer has an absolute right to profess his Faith and live according to its dictates. Laws which impede this profession and practice of Faith are against natural law."[1] Marcel Lefebvre, however, interprets *Mit Brennender Sorge* to be referring only to the rights of Catholics.[2] More surprisingly, Richard Regan, a protégé of John Courtney Murray, reads Pius XI (and Pius XII) the same way. "[T]he citations of Pius XI were directed only toward vindicating the rights of Catholics ... Pius XII's affirmation of 'the right to private and public worship of God' similarly referred in context only to the right of Catholics."[3] Basile Valuet, however, argues that Pius XI is asserting a natural right on the part of each person to practice his religion.[4] Valuet's analysis is convincing, and it is bolstered by Pius XI's earlier call for the Soviet Union to respect the conscience, worship, and property of Orthodox Christians.[5]

Pius XI, however, does not address the crucial question at issue in this chapter. That is, although he recognizes—or at least alludes to—the right of religious liberty, he does not specify what the foundation of the right is.

---

[1] Pope Pius XI, Encyclical *Mit Brennender Sorge* (Mar. 14, 1937), §31 [AAS 29 (1937): 160].

[2] Cf. Marcel Lefebvre, Letter to Cardinal Seper (Feb. 26, 1978), in Michael Davies, *Apologia Pro Marcel Lefebvre*, vol. 2, *1977–1979* (Dickinson, TX: Angelus Press, 1983), 153.

[3] Richard J. Regan, *Conflict and Consensus: Religious Freedom and the Second Vatican Council* (New York/London: Macmillan/Collier-Macmillan Ltd., 1967), 46, citing Pius XII, *Nuntius Radiophonicus* (Dec. 24, 1942) [AAS 35 (1943): 19]. On Regan as protégé, see the dedication of *Conflict and Consensus* to Murray, whom the author refers to as "my friend and mentor."

[4] Cf. Basile Valuet, *La liberté religieuse et la tradition catholique. Un cas de développement doctrinal homogène dans le magistère authentique*, 3rd rev. ed. (Barroux: Éditions Sainte-Madeleine, 2011), vol. IA, 415: "un droit de tout croyant à pratiquer *sa* foi"; Basile Valuet, *Le droit à la liberté religieuse dans la Tradition de l'Eglise. Un cas de développement doctrinal homogène par le magistère authentique*, 2nd rev. ed. (Barroux: Éditions Sainte-Madeleine, 2011), 306–7.

[5] Cf. Pius XI, Chirograph *Ci Commuovono* (Feb. 2, 1930) [AAS 22 (1930): 89]. For Valuet's discussion, see LRTC, vol. IA, 413–14 [= LRTE, 304–5].

(Pius XII's key discourse relating to religious liberty, *Ci Riesce*, is addressed in the previous chapter in section 8.4.)

9.2. Early Attempts to Make Conscience the Foundation of the Right

Pope St. John XXIII's initial articulation of the right to religious liberty had a foundation very different from the one on which Vatican II based the right. His landmark encyclical *Pacem in Terris* is one of the first pronouncements recognizing this right. However, John located the origin of the right to religious worship in the right of conscience. "Also among man's rights is that of being able to worship God in accordance with the right dictates of his own conscience, and to profess his religion both in private and in public" (PT, §14). Indeed, the first two drafts of the declaration also based the right to religious liberty on conscience.[6]

Richard Regan notes that some difficulties arise from basing the right to religious liberty on the duty and right to obey one's conscience.[7] The primary difficulty is that the right to follow one's conscience is sufficient to defend a right to liberty on the part of only *some* persons, namely those who sincerely follow their consciences. If a person were in the position of being both (1) aware that he had a duty to God but (2) nonetheless unwilling to fulfill that duty, he would seem to have no right to religious liberty. That is, a right based on conscience would not afford him any protection (because he evidently is not following his conscience) and it would seem that such a formulation would allow religious coercion of such a person (at least in theory).[8] Another possible difficulty with basing the right to

---

[6] Cf. Draft of Chapter V of *De Oecumenismo* (Nov. 19, 1963), 3 [AS II/5, 434]; *Declaratio Prior* (Apr. 27, 1964), §26 [AS III/2, 317]. See also Richard Regan, "John Courtney Murray, the American Bishops, and the *Declaration on Religious Liberty*," in John T. Ford, ed., *Religious Liberty: Paul VI and Dignitatis Humanae* (Brescia, Italy: Istituto Paolo VI, 1995), 53, discussing drafts of *Dignitatis Humanae*.

[7] Cf. Regan, "American Bishops," 53.

[8] This might apply (again, at least theoretically) to a person who was lax in his religious observance—that is, aware of his duty but disinclined to fulfill it. Such a person arguably would have no right to object to being compelled to fulfill that duty (if conscience were the foundation for the right to religious liberty). Such compulsion might be unpleasant to him (and almost certainly would be an unwise governmental policy), but in the case of a lax practitioner, it arguably would not be a violation of his conscience.

By contrast, Bishop Alfred Ancel's "theological" or "ontological" foundation for religious liberty (discussed below in section 9.4) emphasizes both man's orientation to the truth and his response to it in freedom. Thus, under the Ancel approach, although compulsion

religious liberty on conscience is that such a grounding of the right could be interpreted to justify governments in making intrusive inquiries to determine the sincerity of the beliefs of their citizens. John Courtney Murray in particular argued against conscience as a basis for the right of religious liberty, on the ground that "it is neither within the power nor within the competence of government to judge whether conscience be erroneous or not, in good faith or in bad faith."[9] Finally, although this type of formulation of the right to religious liberty seems to defend liberty for a broad range of religious traditions, it is not clear that it would defend a person's decision not to practice any religion.[10]

This being said, one should be careful not to overestimate the difficulties with liberty of conscience as a basis for religious liberty. There is no doubt a connection between the two areas. It is no accident that liberty of conscience and religious liberty are connected in history and often are linked in secular constitutions and human rights conventions. The reason is that both ideas concern the most intimate dimension of the human person, namely, "his self-determination as a rational and free being with regard to the most profound and vital questions."[11] In fact, some authors even after the Council continue to locate the foundation of the right to religious liberty in the right and duty to follow one's conscience.[12]

However, the difficulties with basing the right to religious liberty solely on the right and duty to follow one's conscience are indeed serious, and, in the final analysis, the right of conscience is not a sufficient basis by

---

of the lax practitioner theoretically might avoid violating his conscience, it undoubtedly would violate his freedom.

[9] John Courtney Murray, "Religious Freedom," in *Freedom and Man* (New York: P. J. Kenedy & Sons, 1965) (speech at Georgetown University in summer 1964), 137. As discussed below in subsection 10.3.4.1, government sometimes inquires into the sincerity of religious beliefs to verify eligibility for benefits like tax exemptions. These legitimate inquiries could give rise to abuses. This can be a cause for concern, but it is not nearly as fundamental a threat as the one that Murray identifies, namely, an inquiry into conscience as a precondition for exercising religious liberty in any measure.

[10] Cf. Regan, "American Bishops," 56. For a recent article examining the problems with basing religious liberty on conscience, see Barrett Turner, "Is Conscience the Ultimate Ground of Religious Liberty?" *Political Theology* (June 10, 2016), Political Theology Network, accessed May 15, 2021, https://politicaltheology.com/is-conscience-the-ultimate-ground-of-religious-liberty-barrett-turner/.

[11] José T. Martín de Agar, "Problemas jurídicos de la objeción de conciencia," *Scripta Theologica* 27, no. 2 (1995): 519–43.

[12] Cf. E. William Sockey III, "Religious Freedom and Human Rights," *Faith & Reason* 9, no. 3 (1983): 214–15, 217–18; William H. Marshner, "*Dignitatis Humanae* and Traditional Teaching on Church and State," *Faith & Reason* 9, no. 3 (1983): 242.

itself for the right to religious liberty that the Council recognized. In fact, both John Courtney Murray and his conservative opponents at the Council agreed on this point. However, although they agreed that conscience was an insufficient foundation for a universal right to religious liberty, Murray, unlike his opponents, believed that it was possible to find other adequate foundations for this right.[13]

As an aside, one should keep in mind that the various drafts of what eventually would become the Declaration on Religious Liberty usually asserted more than one basis for the right to religious liberty. Nicholas Healy characterizes the first draft as having been based on freedom of conscience and on the free character of the act of faith.[14] Needless to say, these two bases are closely related. The first draft mentions human dignity but does not establish it as the foundation of the right (as the final text of DH would do).[15] By the same token, the second draft contains the first mention of the argument that the state is incompetent in religious matters—an argument that would achieve prominence in the third and fourth drafts prepared under Murray's direction—but again, this basis was not yet advanced in the second draft as the foundation of the right.[16] The challenge with identifying a foundation for the right to religious freedom is in locating one or more principles sufficient to support *both* parts of the right that the Council would recognize: (1) immunity from coercion in religious acts (that is, freedom from being compelled to perform an act of religion), and (2) immunity from interference with one's own religious acts (or freedom from being hindered in the exercise of one's acts of religion). The history of the drafting of DH shows that locating a foundation for the second part of the right presented a much greater challenge than locating one for the first part. As discussed below (in section 9.5), Kenneth Grasso explains that one should distinguish between the two aspects of the right that Vatican II recognized. The first right is a freedom from coercion, that is, the right not to be coerced into acting against one's own beliefs. If the declaration had limited itself to this right, then conscience would have been a sufficient foundation for it. However, the Council went further and proclaimed that not only is one

---

[13] Cf. Regan, "American Bishops," 56–57.
[14] Cf. Nicholas J. Healy, "The Drafting of *Dignitatis Humanae*," in *Freedom, Truth, and Human Dignity: The Second Vatican Council's Declaration on Religious Freedom—A New Translation, Redaction History, and Interpretation of* Dignitatis Humanae, ed. David L. Schindler and Nicholas J. Healy (Grand Rapids, MI / Cambridge, UK: William B. Eerdmans Publishing Company, 2015), 216.
[15] Cf. Draft of Chapter V of *De Oecumenismo* (Nov. 19, 1963) [AS II/5, 433].
[16] Cf. *Declaratio Prior* (Apr. 27, 1964), §31 [AS III/2, 321–22].

not to be coerced into acting but neither is one to be restrained from acting according to one's religious beliefs (except where there is a breach of the "just public order"). It is this second right, the freedom from constraint, that presents the difficulty and that requires another foundation.[17]

John Courtney Murray had not been present for the first session of the Council in 1962. Indeed, he and some other theologians apparently were excluded or disinvited from participating.[18] However, Murray was present for the second and third sessions in 1963 and 1964, and he had a strong influence on the work of the Secretariat for Promoting Christian Unity (SCU), the body responsible for the draft texts on religious liberty.

Murray acted as "first scribe" on the third draft (*Textus Emendatus*) of the declaration,[19] and he deserves the lion's share of the credit for recognizing the inadequacy of conscience as a basis for the right to religious liberty. Indeed, he argued tirelessly both during and after the Council that conscience did not—and could not—serve as the basis for the right.[20] Although the final version of the declaration veered away from Murray's theories in

---

[17] Cf. Kenneth L. Grasso, "John Courtney Murray, 'The Juridical State,' and the Catholic Theory of Religious Freedom," *The Political Science Reviewer* 33 (2004): 15. See also Regan, *Conflict and Consensus*, 61–62 (making the same point).

[18] Cf. Xavier Rynne, *Vatican II: An Authoritative One-Volume Version of the Four Historic Books* (New York: Farrar, Straus, and Giroux, 1968), 33–34.

[19] Cf. David L. Schindler, "Freedom, Truth, and Human Dignity: An Interpretation of *Dignitatis Humanae* on the Right to Religious Freedom," in Schindler/Healy, 162n6.

[20] Cf. John Courtney Murray, "The Problem of Religious Freedom," *Theological Studies* 25, no. 4 (1964): 526: Religious freedom is not a "deduction" from freedom of conscience; Murray, "Religious Freedom" (Georgetown speech), 136–37: Basing religious liberty on conscience moves from the subjective order to the objective order, and it also implies that government may inquire into the good faith or bad faith of a citizen's conscience; Murray, "Religious Freedom," in *The Documents of Vatican II*, ed. Walter M. Abbott (New York: Herder and Herder, 1966), 679n5: "[T]he Declaration does not base the right to the free exercise of religion on 'freedom of conscience.' ... This is a perilous theory. Its particular peril is subjectivism—the notion that, in the end, it is my conscience, and not the objective truth, which determines what is right or wrong, true or false"; John Courtney Murray, "Arguments for the Human Right to Religious Freedom," in *Religious Liberty: Catholic Struggles with Pluralism*, ed. J. Leon Hooper (Louisville, KY: Westminster/John Knox Press, 1993), 233: "[T]he Council's third schema—entitled 'corrected text'—abandoned this line of argument that would ground the right to religious freedom in the dictates of conscience." See also Silvia Scatena, *La fatica della libertà. L'elaborazione della dichiarazione* Dignitatis humanae *sulla libertà religiosa del Vaticano II*, Istituto per le scienze religiose—Bologna, Testi e ricerche di scienze religiose, nuova serie, 31 (Bologna, Italy: Il Mulino, 2003), 573: Murray's imposition of the juridic-political dimension marks the abandonment of the conscience perspective of the "ecumenical" version of the Declaration; Regan "American Bishops," 53: The difficulty with basing religious liberty on conscience is that the right

9.2. Early Attempts to Make Conscience the Foundation of the Right

important respects, one must recognize that he made at least four enduring and essential contributions to the document. *First*, the fact that the Council issued a Declaration on Religious Liberty *at all* is in large measure due to Murray's scholarship beginning in the 1940s and to the esteem in which the American bishops held him. It is possible that if it had not been for Murray, there would have been no such declaration. *Second*, although his may not have been the lone voice raised against founding the right on conscience,[21] it does seem to have been the clearest, the most vigorous, and the most influential. *Third*, Murray also was influential in the framing of the right in negative terms as an immunity rather than in positive terms that would have implied approval of the content of all religious beliefs (see generally chapter 8). This idea appeared for the first time in the third schema, for which Murray had primary responsibility. In addition, this negative conception of the right is a hallmark of his own "juridical" approach to the right to religious liberty. *Fourth*, in searching for a standard to evaluate when restriction on religious activity is legitimate, Murray was largely responsible for moving the discussion from the use of the "common good" as the standard to adopting "public order" as a more precise standard. This concept would require further refinement to tie "public order" to objective standards of justice and morality,[22] but its first inclusion in Murray's third draft undoubtedly was a key step (see generally chapter 12).[23]

---

would protect only those who sincerely follow their consciences; one cannot deduce external social freedom from internal personal freedom (57).

[21] Valuet credits both Murray and Guy de Broglie with moving the Council away from basing the right to religious liberty on conscience (cf. LRTE, 418n2294).

[22] Cf. Schindler, "Freedom, Truth, and Human Dignity," in Schindler/Healy, 120: "[T]he Declaration's references to public order in schema 3 were qualified in later drafts by terms such as *iustus, verus, legitimus*, and the like, all of which qualify public order in terms of a substantive order of justice or moral truth."

[23] I believe that Murray made a *fifth* enduring contribution as well. In both his scholarship and his work at the Council, he put forward multiple bases for the right of religious liberty. One of these was the nature of the human person. Unfortunately, Murray himself was more enamored with the argument from state incompetence (and also the argument from historical consciousness), and as a result, his argument from the nature of the person received relatively little attention from him (at least in connection with identifying a basis for religious liberty). Nevertheless, Murray's reflections on the person contain some unique and valuable insights (discussed below in chapter 11).

9.3. The "Juridical" Argument for the Incompetence of the State

In his scholarship and his work at the Council, John Courtney Murray advanced several arguments in favor of religious liberty, but his favorite one was the assertion that the state is incompetent in religious matters.[24] According to Murray, the state has no right to adopt an official religion or to act coercively in matters of religion, because the religious realm is a sphere of activity in which it lacks competence. Murray believed that confessional states inevitably were intolerant.[25] Thus, he put forward the argument of the state's incompetence both to justify recognition of a right to religious liberty and also to reject state establishment of religion.[26] (For this reason—Murray's attempt to base *both* religious liberty *and* Church-state separation on the incompetence of the state—some repetition regrettably is necessary of the previous discussion in chapter 4 of the relationship between Church and state.)

* * *

Much of this chapter and the next one will be taken up with examining the incompetence argument as a possible foundation for religious liberty. I expect this chapter to show that the Council rejected state incompetence as a foundation, and I expect chapter 10 to show that it (the Council) almost certainly had to do so. That is, state incompetence could not have served even as an alternate foundation for the right. Recall, however, (as noted in section 4.4 above) that the critique found in this chapter is directed to a *specific context*, namely, the attempt to found the right to religious liberty on state incompetence. This critique is *not* a rejection of every assertion of state incompetence in religious matters. On the contrary, a certain notion of

---

[24] This seems clear from Murray's famous "Problem of Religious Freedom" article that he wrote during the Council. That article identifies several possible arguments for religious freedom, such as historical and political consciousness, the incompetence of the state, and human integrity. See generally Murray, "Problem of Religious Freedom." Murray's preference for the incompetence argument appears quite clearly in that article. Cf. Murray, 528: "[T]he State, under today's conditions of growth in the personal and political consciousness, is competent to do only one thing in respect of religion, that is, to recognize, guarantee, protect, and promote the religious freedom of the people." Moreover, this preference appears even more clearly in his activity at the Council and in his later writings. See also section 4.4 above.

[25] Murray, "Problem of Religious Freedom," 507, 564, 572. Cf. Murray, "Religious Freedom" (Georgetown speech), 134: "Given the institution of establishment, it follows by logical and juridical consequence that no other religion, *per se* and in principle, can be allowed public existence or action within the state."

[26] Cf. Murray, "Problem of Religious Freedom," 558.

state incompetence is relevant to the analysis of the right to religious liberty. That is, as a result of the foundation of religious liberty in the very nature of the person—or, stated differently, as a result of the recognition of religious liberty as a natural right—it necessarily follows as a *consequence* that the state is incompetent to violate that right (cf. DH, §3e). See section 10.1 below.[27]

This chapter and the next one will examine the incompetence argument at length, not because every invocation of state incompetence requires such an examination but because the attempt to establish incompetence *as the foundation for religious liberty* requires it. This is particularly true of John Courtney Murray's framing of the argument. He begins with the state's competence and argues that as a result of its lack of competence in religion, a space is left for religious freedom.[28] That is, the state's competencies do not include religion and, therefore, the state generally is incompetent to compel or restrict religious practice. This framing necessarily requires a *precise* delineation of state competence and incompetence—to verify that such a space really does remain—and it also seems to require a *broad* formulation of state incompetence to ensure that the remaining space is indeed sufficiently ample to give rise to the right. Thus, the examination in this chapter and the next asks whether the need for such a precise and such a broad formulation of state incompetence raises any difficulties with basing the right on this foundation.

9.3.1. The Third Draft

As discussed above, Murray moved the Secretariat for Promoting Christian Unity (SCU) away from the argument that *conscience* is the foundation for the right to religious liberty. In its place, he substituted this argument based on *the state's incompetence*. It usually is called the "juridical" or

---

[27] For another example of the placement of this notion in a proper context, see subsection 10.3.2, discussing the incompetence of the state in *ecclesiastical* matters, a concept that would appear to be widely accepted.

[28] This idea of a *sphere*, *space*, or *zone* of liberty is by no means incorrect, but it is open to misinterpretation. That is, one might take it to suggest the image of an impenetrable enclave of freedom from all governmental interference. See subsection 10.3.5.1 below. As a result, it is important to recall that the right to religious liberty is not unlimited (see generally part 4 of this study, which is devoted to limitations on the right). In addition, although the civil power may not deny the right, it may regulate the manner of its exercise in some respects. Cf. José Tomás Martín de Agar, "Derecho y relaciones iglesia—sociedad civil," *Ius Ecclesiae* 32, no. 1 (2020): 52: "la Iglesia no es competente en asuntos politicos y el Estado no lo es en asuntos religiosos en cuanto tales [sí para reglamentar las manifestaciones de la religión en el ámbito civil: la libertad religiosa]."

"constitutional" argument, and it is associated generally with the American and Italian bishops. (The most influential Italian proponent of this argument was Murray's close collaborator, Pietro Pavan.) Accordingly, this argument was featured prominently in the draft for which Murray had primary responsibility, namely, the third schema or the *Textus Emendatus* (dated November 17, 1964).

The third schema actually contained several arguments in support of a right to religious freedom, but Murray's juridical argument had pride of place. The schema began with an assertion that religious freedom often is understood as having its foundation in the dignity of the person.[29] Murray then provided five specific foundations for the right, namely, arguments from the integrity of the person, the person's duty to seek the truth, the nature of religion itself, human conscience, and the incompetence of the state.[30] Despite this multitude of arguments or possible foundations, it was clear that the juridical argument—asserting the incompetence of the state in religious matters—was the central one.[31] There does not seem to be any dispute over this point, and it seems clear from the fact that the third schema approved the current juridical practice of those governments that recognize religious liberty.[32] That is, although this draft put forward several different foundations for the right to religious liberty, its distinct focus was the political realm.[33]

Murray's third draft of the declaration describes the civil power's

---

[29] Cf. *Textus Emendatus* (Nov. 17, 1964), §2 [AS III/8, 426].

[30] Cf. *Textus Emendatus*, §4 [AS III/8, 430–32].

[31] Cf. Regan, *Conflict and Consensus*, 159: "[F]ive different arguments were enumerated, although the dignity of man and the correlative constitutional principle held the primacy."

[32] Although the "incompetence" argument achieved a new prominence in the third draft, it first had appeared in the second draft, albeit in a position subordinate to the "conscience" argument. Cf. Regan, *Conflict and Consensus*, 69: The first mention of state incompetence appears in the second draft. In the September 1964 Council debate on the second draft, this argument was one of the most significant of the several criticisms of the text. "The paragraph denying the 'direct capacity and competence' of the state in religious matters was the most controversial of the additions to the second conciliar text on religious freedom" (Regan, 90).

[33] Murray himself alluded to the critique that the third draft was excessively political. Cf. John Courtney Murray, "Commentary," in Vincent A. Yzermans, ed., *American Participation in the Second Vatican Council* (New York: Sheed & Ward, 1967), 673: The Council avoided political arguments because "a serious effort to make the political argument for religious freedom would have carried the Council into the problem of 'Church and State,' so called, a much broader and more complicated problem which the Council wisely wished to avoid." See also Regan, *Conflict and Consensus*, 172: "[M]any liberals thought the argument [of the third and fourth drafts] too political and legal."

9.3. The "Juridical" Argument for the Incompetence of the State

competence as "restricted to the earthly and temporal order," and it proclaims that "the public power completely exceeds its limits if it involves itself in any way in the governing of minds or the care of souls."[34] Although a vote on the third draft had been expected during the Council's third session in 1964, no such vote took place. The reason was that the extensive additions to that draft rendered it, in effect, a new document, rather than simply a revision of the previous draft.[35] However, the relator, Émile De Smedt, solicited comments in the interval between the third and fourth sessions.

9.3.2. The Fourth Draft

In light of those comments, the fourth draft (*Textus Reemendatus*, dated May 28, 1965) would be restructured, but it would maintain the same line of argument as the third draft.[36] It continued to show Murray's influence, and its description of the civil power's incompetence was broadened to say that it exceeds its limits "if it involves itself in those matters that concern the very ordination of man to God."[37]

Although Murray's juridical argument was prominent in the third and fourth drafts, the Council soon would depart from it. (See section 4.4 above and subsection 9.3.3 below.) Indeed, the "incompetence" argument, which was at the heart of Murray's juridical approach, was reduced in the fifth draft and was eliminated almost entirely from the final text of *Dignitatis Humanae*.[38] Murray nevertheless would continue to believe that the juridical

---

[34] *Textus Emendatus*, §4e [AS III/8, 432]; English translation at Schindler/Healy, 293.

[35] Cf. Ralph M. Wiltgen, *The Rhine Flows into the Tiber: A History of Vatican II* (Rockford, IL: TAN Books, 1985), 235–38. See also Rynne, *Vatican II*, 415–22. The fathers and *periti* most concerned with the issuance of a religious liberty document severely criticized the decision not to hold a vote, and this decision resulted in a great deal of tumult on the floor of the Council. Indeed, it resulted in an appeal to the Holy Father on behalf of hundreds of bishops. (The pope rejected it.) This episode would contribute toward the Dutch bishops calling the final week of the Council's third session "Black Week" (cf. Wiltgen, 235). Wiltgen agrees that the Rules of Procedure themselves compelled the delay, while Rynne disagrees, asserting that the rules were in fact "vaguely worded and not conclusive" (cf. Rynne, 421; and Wiltgen, 238). In any event, Murray himself ultimately recognized the wisdom of the decision to postpone the vote. Cf. Murray, "Religious Freedom" (Georgetown speech), 133: "[T]he decision not to call a vote was technically correct.... Moreover, in retrospect (although not at the moment), it was generally recognized that the decision to postpone a vote was wise."

[36] Cf. Regan, *Conflict and Consensus*, 172.

[37] *Textus Reemendatus*, §3 [AS IV/1, 150]; English translation in Schindler/Healy, 323.

[38] Cf. Regan, "American Bishops," 58, discussing various drafts of *Dignitatis Humanae*; see also Russell Hittinger, "How to Read *Dignitatis Humanae* on Establishment of Religion,"

argument is the only one sufficient to provide a foundation for the right to religious liberty (this view is discussed in section 9.5 and chapter 11 below).[39]

9.3.3. The Fifth and Sixth (Final) Drafts

The fifth draft (*Textus Recognitus*, dated October 25, 1965) would shift the declaration away from Murray's "incompetence" (or "juridical") argument, and the final version (*Textus Denuo Recognitus*, dated November 19, 1965) would preserve only a remnant of it.[40] The reasons for this shift are discussed below in section 9.4 and chapter 10. Thus, where Murray had advocated a broad understanding of incompetence, "restrict[ing]" the civil power to the temporal order and barring its involvement in matters concerning "the very ordination of man to God," the Council preserves only a much narrower version of this argument, declaring the civil power to transgress its limits only "were it to presume to command or inhibit acts that are religious" (DH, §3e). That is, the Council considers the state incompetent not broadly, as Murray had hoped in the entire realm of religious matters, but only narrowly, if it should presume to compel or hinder religious acts.[41]

Murray's protégé Richard Regan asserts that a late change to the declaration partially vindicated Murray's "juridical" argument. That change took place between the fifth draft (October 22, 1965) and the sixth or final version (November 19, 1965). Murray's *third* draft had opened by recognizing modern man's demand for freedom and for juridical limits to the public power.[42] The *fourth* draft (for which Murray also chiefly was

---

Catholic Dossier 6, no. 2 (March–April 2000): 16, discussing second schema of the declaration, the *Declaratio Prior*, and later amendments. See also quotations from the third and fourth drafts cited and discussed in this section.

[39] Cf. Murray, "Arguments for the Human Right," 241 (an article based on a September 19, 1966, speech).

[40] Below, in section 10.2, I distinguish Murray's juridical approach in general from that part of it based on the incompetence of the state. Although the final version of the declaration eliminated Murray's incompetence argument almost entirely, it still retained a number of key elements of his juridical approach, broadly considered.

[41] Perhaps it is an obvious point, but this repudiation of the Murray position may suggest that some limited or indirect involvement of the civil power in the "care of souls," or at least in orienting man to God, is permissible. This seems to be how the popes view things: though civil government corresponds roughly to the temporal sphere, it should not ignore man's final destiny. See section 4.3 (on Gelasian dualism) above, citing Pope Leo XIII, Encyclical *Libertas* (June 20, 1888), §21; Pope Leo XIII, Encyclical *Longinqua Oceani* (Jan. 6, 1895), §4; Second Vatican Council, Pastoral Constitution on the Church in the Modern World *Gaudium et Spes* (December 7, 1965), §21.

[42] Cf. *Textus Emendatus* (Nov. 17, 1964), §1 [AS III/8, 426].

responsible) continued to open with a reference to modern man's demand for freedom, but it no longer referred to his demand for juridical limits.[43] It did, however, speak directly of the limitations on the state—not only as an aspiration of modern man but rather in terms of religious acts, by their nature, transcending the temporal order.[44] Indeed, this was the highpoint of the "incompetence" argument. The *fifth* draft retained the language of modern man's demand for freedom, but it limited the "juridical" argument and gave pride of place to the "theological" or "ontological" argument concerning man's duty to seek the truth.[45] This dramatic shift was based in large measure on the interventions of Alfred Ancel, Auxiliary Bishop of Lyons, and Carlo Colombo, Auxiliary Bishop of Milan. The *sixth* draft (which the Council would approve) limited the "juridical" argument still further. Whereas the fifth had declared it improper for the civil authority to impede or direct those matters that transcend the temporal order, the sixth narrowed and specified this requirement further by stating only that the civil power exceeds its authority if it presumes to command or inhibit religious acts.[46] However, the demand of modern man for constitutional limits on governments—which had originated in the *third* draft, had taken a different form in the *fourth*, and had disappeared from the *fifth*—reappeared in the opening paragraph of the *sixth* draft.[47] Regan referred to this late addition as a partial vindication of Murray's argument. "By reinstating this sentence of the *textus emendatus*, the final text partially rescued the constitutional principle from the limbo to which it had been consigned in the *textus recognitus*."[48]

It is true that the final version of the declaration includes this brief passage that had originated in Murray's third draft, but Regan overestimates the significance of this amendment. One reason is that the assertion in question—that modern man demands constitutional limitations on government—is unremarkable in itself. It certainly recounts an important development, but coming in the wake of World War II and at the height of the Cold War (that is, during and after the reigns of the twentieth-century totalitarian regimes), it strikes one largely as a simple truism. Indeed, it

---

[43] Cf. *Textus Reemendatus* (May 28, 1965), §1 [AS IV/1, 146].
[44] Cf. *Textus Reemendatus*, §3 [AS IV/1, 150].
[45] Cf. *Textus Recognitus* (Oct. 22, 1965), §§1–2 [AS IV/5, 77–79].
[46] Compare *Textus Recognitus*, §3 [AS IV/5, 81], with Second Vatican Council, Declaration on Religious Liberty *Dignitatis Humanae* (December 7, 1965), §3e.
[47] "The demand is likewise made that constitutional limits should be set to the powers of government, in order that there may be no encroachment on the rightful freedom of the person and of associations" (DH, §1a).
[48] Regan, *Conflict and Consensus*, 164.

contains no *direct* reference to the signature Murray theme of the state's incompetence in religious matters.[49] In addition, this amendment did not come close to restoring the Murray argument to its former prominence. In the third and fourth drafts, the incompetence argument was the very foundation of the right to religious liberty (or at least the primary one). In the final version, the principal remnant of the Murray argument—the prohibition on the state commanding or inhibiting religious acts—is reduced to "a further consideration" (DH, §3e). The change cited by Regan is to the opening paragraph of the declaration. It is understandable why the proponents of the constitutional argument would take a measure of solace in this amendment. If their argument no longer was prominent in the argumentation, a shadow of it at least was prominent in its final placement. Regan is not necessarily incorrect to refer to this change as a partial rescue of the Murray argument, but it might have been more accurate to refer to it not as "partial" but as "fractional."

9.3.4. Other Provisions of the Declaration

In addition to the revisions to the passages on the foundation of the right, late amendments to other provisions of the declaration served further to undercut Murray's incompetence argument. As described above in chapter 4, to Murray's apparent displeasure, a last-minute change to article 1 of the declaration reaffirmed the traditional teaching of the Church on the moral duty of both men and societies to the one Church of Christ, and indeed the declaration's relator explained that the reference to "societies" having a duty to the Church includes *the public power itself*:

> The text that is presented to you today recalls more clearly (see nos. 1 and 3) the duties of the public authority towards the true religion (*officia potestatis publicae erga veram religionem*); from which it is

---

[49] Below in section 10.2, I distinguish Murray's "juridical approach" from his "incompetence argument." The incompetence argument often is identified closely or even entirely with the juridical approach, but this is a mistake. It is indeed the key feature of Murray's juridical approach, but it is by no means the sole feature. On the contrary, other important elements of that approach are the description of the right as an immunity, the adoption of the "public order" standard for judging restrictions on religious practice, and the equality of all persons. See generally section 9.2 above, on Murray's contributions to the declaration. Thus, Regan plausibly can claim that the elements discussed here also belong to Murray's juridical approach, but because the central feature of that approach was limited so profoundly, I believe that Regan overstates the "rescue" of Murray's juridical approach.

manifest that this part of the doctrine has not been overlooked (*ex quo patet hanc doctrinae partem non praetermitti*).[50]

Thus, Murray would judge that "the final text of the Declaration is inadequate in its treatment of the limitations imposed on government by sound political doctrine."[51] As discussed below in subsection 10.4.2, the full implications of this late addition to article 1 are not clear, at least not from the text of the declaration and the relator's *relationes*. One key question is the significance of the Council's description of the duty to the true religion as a *moral* duty. Is this to be understood in distinction from a *juridical* duty? The declaration does not say. What seems clear, however, is that, although the Council's recognition of this duty might not be incompatible with all notions of state incompetence in religious matters, it is incompatible with Murray's notion. The reason is that Murray has bound his notion of state incompetence to a very strict—nearly absolute—notion of separation of Church and state. (See chapter 4 introduction and section 4.3 above.) Article 1's recognition of the moral duty of the public powers to the true religion (as officially interpreted by De Smedt) seems wholly incompatible with Murray's separationism and his notion of state incompetence. This seems clearly to be the reason (or one of the reasons) for Murray's criticism of the late amendments to the declaration, and for the similar positions of commentators who largely share his views. (See section 4.8 above, discussing Murray, Pelotte, and Scatena.)

The Council's affirmation of the public power's duty to religion was not the only blow to Murray's argument regarding state incompetence in religious matters. The final text also acknowledges in article 6 the possibility of a state according "special civil recognition" to a particular religious community. (As discussed above in subsection 3.2.4 and section 4.5, this

---

[50] De Smedt, Oral *Relatio* on the *Textus Denuo Recognitus* (Nov. 19, 1965) [AS IV/6, 719]; English translation in Brian W. Harrison, *Religious Liberty and Contraception: Did Vatican II Open the Way for a New Sexual Ethic?* (Melbourne: John XXIII Fellowship Co-op., Ltd., 1988), 75. Hamer supports this position as well. "En outre, la déclaration souligne que ce 'devoir' (*officium*) n'affecte pas seulement les individus mais les collectivités, c'est-à-dire les hommes agissant en commun. Il s'agit ici de tous les groupes sociaux depuis les plus modestes et les plus spontanés jusqu'aux nations et aux États, en passant par tous les intermédiaires: syndicats, associations culturelles, universités. . . . L'idée du schéma est simplement d'éliminer une sort d'interprétation purement individualiste de ce devoir primordial." Jérôme Hamer, "Histoire du texte de la Déclaration," *Unam Sanctam* 60 (1967): 99–100).

[51] John Courtney Murray, "The Issue of Church and State at Vatican Council II," *Theological Studies* 27, no. 4 (December 1966): 587.

reference is generic in that it treats official recognition of any religion and not only of Catholicism [cf. DH, §6c].) Murray repeatedly claims that only "historical" circumstances—as distinguished from truth claims—justify such recognition. (See section 4.5 above.) However, this is not what the Council said. Although the fifth draft or schema (*Textus Recognitus*, dated October 25, 1965) had indeed specified "historical circumstances" as the predicate for this type of recognition, this phrase was amended to read "peculiar circumstances" in the final version of the declaration. Nevertheless, after the Council, Murray would continue to assert that the deleted standard—"historical circumstances"—provides the sole justification for state recognition of religion.[52]

Indeed, Murray seemed to wish to conceal this part of the text of article 6. In a December 1966 *Theological Studies* article, he recounts the development of this passage, quoting the third, fourth, and fifth drafts at length.[53] The fifth contains the "historical circumstances" phrase. Next he acknowledges that there were additional changes before the document was finalized, but he does not quote them. He discusses a rejected suggestion to change the conditional language back to the declarative mood. "The rest proposed merely verbal alterations."[54] He conceals the fact that the "historical circumstances" language that he favored was replaced. Indeed, he entirely misrepresents the final version: "It is therefore clearly the mind of the Council that the establishment of Catholicism as the religion of the state is no more than a matter of *historical circumstances*."[55]

Murray certainly was aware of what article 6 actually said. In a popular article that he published in April of the same year, Murray correctly stated the applicable article 6 standard as "peculiar circumstances."[56] Even here, however, Murray attempted to equate the authentic term with the discarded standard. "[T]he notion is dismissed into history, beyond recall."[57]

Harrison speculates that the reason for the change from "historical" to "peculiar" was to avoid the implication that "special civil recognition" is a

---

[52] Cf. Murray, "Church and State at Vatican II," 595, asserting that it is "clearly the mind of the Council" that establishment "is no more than a matter of historical circumstances"; Murray, "Religious Freedom," in Abbott, 685n17 (comment on DH, §6): "[E]stablishment ... is a matter of historical circumstance."
[53] Cf. Murray, "Church and State at Vatican II," 594–95.
[54] Murray, "Church and State at Vatican II," 595.
[55] Murray, "Church and State at Vatican II," 595 (emphasis added).
[56] John Courtney Murray, "The Declaration on Religious Freedom: Its Deeper Significance," *America* 114 (Apr. 23, 1966): 593, quoting DH, §6. NB, this is the only source that I have come across in which Murray correctly states the DH §6 standard.
[57] Murray, "Declaration on Religious Freedom," 593.

9.3. The "Juridical" Argument for the Incompetence of the State

mere relic of the past. Valuet notes that Harrison adduces no proof for this assertion, but he nonetheless seems to embrace a similar reading, namely, that history is not the sole justification for such recognition.[58] The precise intention of the council fathers is unclear, but this change at least seems to suggest a choice for some additional breadth or flexibility in the legitimate grant of "special civil recognition," beyond that corresponding to historical reasons alone.[59]

This example brings to light a key characteristic of Murray's post-conciliar writings. Owing to his stature and his important role at the Council, Murray's word often was considered authoritative. "So influential was Murray as an architect of *Dignitatis Humanae* that there has often been a tendency almost to identify his own theses . . . with the teaching of the Council itself."[60] In addition, although he died less than two years after the close of the Council, Murray wrote and spoke prolifically during his final years. Thus, his opinions became quite widespread, and many commentators have adopted his positions.[61] However, as this and other episodes show, Murray used his access to the bully pulpit not simply to explain DH but also to shape its interpretation and even to relitigate disputes that he had lost at the Council. (See also section 4.9 above.) Thus, despite the replacement of

---

[58] Cf. Valuet, LRTE, 493, 493n2830.

[59] Although the original Latin phrase *circumstantiis peculiaribus* usually is translated as *peculiar circumstances*, it also could be translated as *specific circumstances*. A new translation published by Schindler and Healy translates it as *particular circumstances* (Schindler/Healy, 397).

[60] Brian W. Harrison, "John Courtney Murray: A Reliable Interpreter of *Dignitatis Humanae*?" in *We Hold These Truths and More*, ed. Donald J. D'Elia and Stephen M. Krason (Steubenville, OH: Franciscan University Press, 1993), 134. Harrison was speaking in particular of Murray's views on Church and state, but his point is equally applicable to other topics.

[61] On this question of the predicate for "special civil recognition," a number of authors follow Murray in interpreting DH, §6—not according to the standard that it adopts, namely, "peculiar" circumstances but rather according to the standard contained in the penultimate draft, "historical" circumstances. Cf. Regan, *Conflict and Consensus*, 175: "[T]he text . . . make[s] clear that the institution of establishment is the product of historical circumstance"; Francis Canavan, "The Catholic Concept of Religious Freedom as a Human Right," in *Religious Liberty: An End and a Beginning*, ed. John Courtney Murray (New York: MacMillan, 1966), 77: "The declaration . . . grants it [establishment] only a rather reluctant recognition as an historical fact." Regan is particularly interesting in this regard. He not only took this position shortly after the Council, as he did in his 1967 book *Conflict and Consensus*, but he maintained this position even decades later. Cf. Regan, "American Bishops" (1995), 61: DH §6 "made clear that state religions are the product of historical circumstance, not a matter of theological doctrine."

Murray's preferred standard, "historical circumstances" (in the fifth draft), with the seemingly broader term "peculiar circumstances" (in the sixth and final text), Murray persisted in interpreting the Council's meaning by way of the discarded phrase rather than the language of DH itself. As a result, there is a growing awareness that Murray's commentary is not always reliable in every respect and that reading too much of his thought into DH can lead to misunderstandings of the Council's teaching.[62] Indeed, Barrett Turner notes that the widespread belief that the declaration embraced a separationist position is largely due to Murray's post-conciliar writings.[63] Brian Harrison was one of the first to note this trend in Murray's scholarship. He is particularly critical of Murray's annotations to DH in the Walter Abbott compilation of the Vatican II documents (one of the earliest compilations), and he charges Murray with simply "pass[ing] over in complete silence" a number of "vital amendments" introduced late in the redaction process.[64]

There can be little doubt that the final version of article 6 is incompatible with Murray's theory of state incompetence. His repeated misrepresentation of the final text alone seems to make this clear. Moreover, the only part of Murray's juridical approach that is threatened by official establishment of religion is his notion of state incompetence. A question that seems not to have been asked is why Murray believed that civil recognition of religion *on the basis of historical factors* (the position of the penultimate schema) *was consistent* with his incompetence theory. Needless to say, the practical realities of competing positions and differing views at and after the Council likely played some role. However, given the strictness of his separationism, it is not a foregone conclusion that he would accept any type of establishment or confessionality, even the type that Valuet calls *historico-sociological* (see section 4.2 above). Recall Murray's assertion that establishment and intolerance are "twin institutions" (see section 4.4). It seems that Murray is able to accept this position—but not the declaration's final position—by way

---

[62] Cf. Gerard V. Bradley, preface to *Religious Freedom: Did Vatican II Contradict Traditional Catholic Doctrine? A Debate*, by Arnold T. Guminski and Brian W. Harrison (South Bend, IN: St. Augustine Press, 2013), 2, noting agreement between Guminski and Harrison "that way too many scholarly treatments of DH have read way too much of John Courtney Murray into that document."

[63] Cf. Barrett Hamilton Turner, "*Dignitatis Humanae* and the Development of Moral Doctrine: Assessing Change in Catholic Social Teaching on Religious Liberty" (PhD diss., Catholic University of America, 2015), 304: The interpretation of DH as "hostile to any establishment of religion . . . is thanks, in large part, to the post-conciliar commentary of Murray."

[64] Harrison, "Reliable Interpreter," 157; cf. "Reliable Interpreter," 155.

of creating an exception to his notions of incompetence and separationism. (See subsections 10.3.5.2 and 10.4.1.1 below.)

9.3.5. *Other Documents of the Council*

As discussed in chapter 4, if Murray's argument as to the state's incompetence did not survive as the basis for the right of religious liberty, other conciliar pronouncements contain passages on a similar theme. (See generally section 4.3.) In particular, the Pastoral Constitution on the Church in the Modern World *Gaudium et Spes* draws a clear distinction between the spiritual realm and the temporal realm. "The Church and the political community in their own fields are autonomous and independent from each other" (GS, §76c). Although this principle recalls the tradition of Gelasian dualism (see section 4.3 above), it is crucial to observe that the Council's expression of the distinction between the temporal and spiritual realms is less absolute than the separation that Murray advocated. Thus, although the Council says that the Church "does not place her trust in the privileges offered by civil authority," it gives no indication that extending such privileges is outside the state's competence. Indeed, the same passage says nearly the opposite, namely, by referring to rights that "have been legitimately acquired" (GS, §76e).[65] Similarly, the Dogmatic Constitution on the Church *Lumen Gentium* teaches that "the temporal sphere is governed by its own principles" but, nonetheless, strongly warns against attempts to construct society without regard to religion (LG, §36d). Thus, the *distinction* between the temporal and spiritual realms must not be interpreted as a strict *separation* between them.[66] In particular, there are "mixed questions," such as marriage

---

[65] This seems at least to tend in the direction of supporting Ocáriz's assertion that nothing in DH bars the state from recognizing the true religion, or at least an absence of intention in DH to reject previous Church-state arrangements. Cf. Fernando Ocáriz, "Sulla libertà religiosa. Continuità del Vaticano II con il Magistero precedente," *Annales theologici* 3 (1989): 93. Recall also that the Church once offered privileges to the state, such as the prerogative to veto a papal election. Needless to say, such a practice is difficult to reconcile with a position of absolute state incompetence in religious matters. Indeed, Murray makes clear that he considers such arrangements always to have been an abuse (cf. Murray, "Church and State at Vatican II," 606).

[66] Cf. Ocáriz, "Sulla libertà religiosa," 92–93; Franco Biffi, "Chiesa, società civile e persona di fronte al problema della libertà religiosa. Dalla revoca dell'Editto di Nantes al Concilio Vaticano II," in *Teologia e diritto canonico* (Vatican City: Libreria Editrice Vaticana, 1987), 136–37: Church and state are distinct, but they must cooperate with each other.

and education, which are legitimate concerns of both the spiritual and the temporal realms.[67] (See section 4.3 above.)

The tradition of Christian dualism (or the "dyarchy," as Murray called it)[68] is crucial to an understanding of the Church's relationship to the temporal realm. This tradition is associated closely with the late fifth-century pope St. Gelasius I and the eleventh-century pope St. Gregory VII, and Murray credits Pope Leo XIII with reviving the tradition in the nineteenth century.[69] Vatican II both reaffirmed and adapted the principle of Christian dualism.[70] Despite the importance of this principle (see section 4.3 above), the history of the various drafts of the Declaration on Religious Liberty shows that this is not the foundation (or at least not the primary foundation) of the right to religious liberty that the Second Vatican Council recognized (see section 4.4 above).

Despite the Council's rejection of the "incompetence" argument as a foundation, that position has proven to be strikingly durable in the post-conciliar commentary and scholarship on *Dignitatis Humanae*. (See section 9.5 below.) Some commentators claim outright—against all evidence—that the declaration based religious liberty on "the incompetence of the state." Others assert more modestly—but still, I would say, against the evidence—that the Council did not settle the question of the foundation of the right to religious liberty, and that, therefore, they are free to argue for state incompetence as the basis for the right. Murray himself used various strategies in attempting (quite successfully) in the years immediately following the Council to revive his argument from state incompetence that the Council had rejected or severely limited. The following section (9.4) discusses the actual basis for religious liberty that the Council enunciated, namely, human dignity, and after that (in sections 9.5 and 9.6), I will return to the "juridical" argument to ask why it has endured so tenaciously in the scholarship, and (in chapter 10) whether it could have served as the foundation for the right that *Dignitatis Humanae* recognizes. Chapter 11 will engage Murray's assertion that the incompetence argument is the only one sufficient to provide a foundation for the right to religious liberty.

---

[67] Cf. Biffi, "Chiesa, società civile e persona," 137.
[68] Murray, "Problem of Religious Freedom," 540–41.
[69] Murray, "Problem of Religious Freedom," 540–41.
[70] Cf. Martín de Agar, "Derecho y relaciones iglesia—sociedad civil," 48, 50.

9.4. The Council's Choice of Human Dignity as the Foundation

The Council states in the clearest language that "the right to religious freedom has its foundation in the very dignity of the human person" (DH, §2a). The difference between founding the right on the dignity of the human person rather than on conscience is the difference between founding it on man's very nature versus founding it on his subjective disposition.[71] Fernando Ocáriz notes that locating the foundation of the right to religious liberty in the inherent dignity of the person may seem to contradict the teaching of Leo XIII, which asserted that man's dignity is to adhere to true ideas, and that man loses his dignity when he embraces false ideas.[72] In fact, however, Ocáriz proceeds to show that there is no contradiction. The declaration does not deny that man's dignity is to embrace the truth. Even though the declaration speaks of an aspect of human dignity that is rooted in human nature itself, it does not identify this aspect with the *whole* of human dignity. That is, it does not state that man's dignity is identified *solely* with his human nature. Thus, *Dignitatis Humanae* does not deny Leo's teaching that it is man's dignity to embrace the truth, but it simply adds that man also has a basic dignity that does not disappear even when he does not embrace the truth and even when he neglects his religious duties.[73] Pietro Pavan formulates the issue in a similar way. Although religious liberty is founded on the dignity of the human person, he says, it is not founded on dignity in the *moral* sense, which derives from having a right conscience. Rather, it is founded on dignity in the *existential* sense, which derives from man's very nature as a being equipped with reason and free will.[74] Recall man's creation in the "image" and "likeness" of God. One might say that God's image, reflected in man's nature as a rational creature, is ineradicable. One's "likeness" to God—that is, his goodness—however, may be lost through serious sin.[75] The gravamen of the Ocáriz and Pavan interpretations is that religious liberty

---

[71] Cf. Ocáriz, "Sulla libertà religiosa," 81.

[72] Cf. Ocáriz, "Sulla libertà religiosa," 81–82, discussing Pope Leo XIII, Encyclical *Immortale Dei* (Nov. 1, 1885), §32. "If the mind assents to false opinions, and the will chooses and follows after what is wrong, neither can attain its native fullness, but both must fall from their native dignity into an abyss of corruption" (ID, §32).

[73] Cf. Ocáriz, "Sulla libertà religiosa," 82.

[74] Pietro Pavan, *La dichiarazione conciliare* Dignitatis humanae *a 20 anni dalla pubblicazione* (Casale Monferrato, Italy: Edizioni Piemme di Pietro Marietti, 1986), 31.

[75] Cf. Peter Lombard, *Sent.* Ii, D, xvi, in *The Sentences*, book 2, *On Creation*, trans. Giulio Silano (Toronto: Pontifical Institute of Mediaeval Studies, 2008), 70: "[I]n his image according to memory, intelligence, and love; in his likeness according to innocence and justice"; Lombard, xvi: "[The] image is considered in the knowledge of truth, his likeness

is based on human dignity in this first sense, namely, human dignity in the existential or ontological sense rather than in the moral sense.[76]

As a result of its foundation in the very nature of the human person, the right to religious liberty applies to all persons, even atheists and skeptics.[77] The reason is that even when a person neglects or refuses to fulfill his religious duties, there nonetheless remains in him a basic dignity that is inherent in his nature. For this reason, human dignity understood in the existential or ontological sense provides the foundation for a broader right to religious liberty than does the right and duty to follow one's conscience.

In addition, the criterion of human dignity is relevant to the council fathers' intention "to develop the doctrine of recent popes on the inviolable rights of the human person and the constitutional order of society" (DH, §1c). John Courtney Murray and Fernando Ocáriz are correct in interpreting this reference to "constitutional" society or government to mean *limited government*.[78] That is, the council fathers' reflections on religious liberty signify an appreciation for constitutional government or government limited in its powers.[79] This reflection no doubt was inspired in large measure by the counter-examples of totalitarian regimes in the twentieth century. Human dignity is important because it provides the crucial limiting principle for

---

in the love of virtue." See also St. Thomas Aquinas, *Summa Theologica*, Christian Classics ed. (Benziger Brothers, 1947), I, q. 93, a. 9, citing Lombard.

[76] The Congregation for the Doctrine of the Faith has confirmed that DH based religious liberty on man's dignity in the ontological sense. Cf. Congregation for the Doctrine of the Faith, "Note on Some Questions Regarding the Participation of Catholics in Political Life" (Nov. 24, 2002), §8: Freedom of conscience and religion are "based on the ontological dignity of the human person."

[77] Cf. Jérôme Hamer and Clemente Riva, *La libertà religiosa nel Vaticano II* (Torino, Italy: Elle di Ci, 1966), 178. See also Murray, "Commentary," in Yzermans, 670: Although DH does not refer explicitly to the atheist, "nevertheless, its definition and doctrine of religious freedom clearly extends to him"; Giorgio Feliciani, "La libertà religiosa nel magistero di Giovanni Paolo II," in *Escritos en honor de Javier Hervada*, Ius Canonicum, volumen especial (Pamplona, Spain: Instituto Martín de Azpilcueta, 1999), 925.

[78] Cf. Ocáriz, "Sulla libertà religiosa," 90; Murray, "Problem of Religious Freedom," 519.

[79] The principle of *limited government* itself could be considered merely relative because the term itself seems to leave the nature and extent of governmental limitations unspecified. However, I use the term here (and in subsection 10.4.4.2 below) in an almost abstract sense to stand for the idea that the state is not all-powerful and that it may not occupy the whole of the citizens' lives. That is, constitutional government is (or at least should be) anti-totalitarian in several senses, including in the maintenance of internal checks on the exercise of governmental authority, and in the positive recognition of human rights.

Catholic social teaching might frame this idea in more positive terms, such as the obligation of government to serve the common good and to recognize the rights of persons and of the Church.

constitutional government (as well as the end and source of governmental power, properly understood). That is, the most important limitation on the exercise of governmental authority is that it must acknowledge that certain rights belong to the person simply by virtue of his human nature, and government, therefore, must respect these rights (cf. DH, §6a). Thus, religious liberty and other human rights exist not because states *confer* them, but rather states recognize these rights because they *already exist* in their citizens and in others simply by virtue of human nature and the inherent dignity of the human person.[80]

However, there are challenges involved with basing the right to religious freedom on the dignity of the human person. First, a reference to human dignity standing alone is quite open-ended. It is necessary to specify either *what is meant* by human dignity, or else *which specific aspect* of this dignity supports the right to religious freedom. Second, it is necessary to establish a connection between this notion of human dignity and the right itself. That is, it must be made clear why this idea supports—or even commands—religious liberty.

In one way or another, each of the drafts leading up to the Vatican II Declaration on Religious Liberty refers to the dignity of the person.[81] As stated above, not all of the drafts recognized human dignity as the foundation

---

[80] Cf. Pavan, *La dichiarazione conciliare*, 49; Feliciani, "La libertà religiosa nel magistero di Giovanni Paolo II," 924.

[81] Cf. Draft of chapter V of *De Oecumenismo* (Nov. 19, 1963), introductory section: "The Catholic Church earnestly urges each man and all men ... to direct all their energy ... to defending the honor of God and the dignity of the human person created and redeemed by him" [AS II/5, 433; English translation in Schindler/Healy, 245]; *Declaratio Prior* (Apr. 27, 1964), §29: "For the divine vocation ... in truth constitutes the highest dignity of the human person" [AS III/2, 319; English translation in Schindler/Healy, 267]; *Textus Emendatus* (Nov. 17, 1964), §1: "Religious freedom is commonly understood today to be a true right, having its foundation in human dignity" [AS III/8, 426; English translation in Schindler/Healy, 285]; *Textus Reemendatus* (May 28, 1965), §§1–2: "1. Men and women of our time are becoming more conscious every day of the dignity of the human person.... 2. This Vatican Council declares that the right to religious freedom has its foundation in the very dignity of the human person" [AS IV/1, 146–47; English translation in Schindler/Healy, 319]; *Textus Recognitus* (Oct. 22, 1965), §1: "Men and women of our time are becoming more conscious every day of the dignity of the human person" [AS IV/5, 77; English translation in Schindler/Healy, 349]; *Textus Recognitus*, §2: "[T]his Council declares that the right to religious freedom has its foundation in the very dignity of the human person" [AS IV/5, 79; English translation in Schindler/Healy, 351]; DH, §§1a, 2a: "1. A sense of the dignity of the human person has been impressing itself more deeply on the consciousness of contemporary man.... 2. [T]he right to religious freedom has its foundation in the very dignity of the human person."

of the right, but it is significant—and even reassuring—that this is a theme running throughout all of the various drafts. Indeed, although Murray's third draft is known for its basis in the "juridical" approach, his protégé Richard Regan would describe that schema as basing religious liberty "on the dignity of the human person and the corresponding constitutional principle of the state's competence in matters of religion."[82] Regan's characterization illustrates both the significance and endurance of the theme of human dignity and its potentially problematic generality, breadth, and open-endedness.

One of the key interventions of the Council—indeed the very final oral intervention in the final debate on religious liberty—sought to address these challenges. Bishop Alfred Ancel, Auxiliary Bishop of Lyons, France, spoke on behalf of over one hundred French bishops.[83] He said that the argument simply asserting human dignity as the foundation of religious liberty was insufficient. Rather, as others had noted before, it is necessary to provide the *theological* or *ontological* basis for the right. Ancel proposed that the human person's obligation to seek the truth (and, once found, to embrace it) provides just such a basis. That is, man's obligation to search out the truth is intimately connected to religious freedom. Man can fulfill this obligation—in the way in which the Lord wishes him to fulfill it—only if he enjoys both psychological freedom and immunity from coercion.[84]

Bishop Carlo Colombo, Auxiliary Bishop of Milan and former private theologian to Pope Paul VI, had made a similar proposal,[85] and both he and Ancel are credited with providing the primary argument for the fifth draft, which would carry over into the final version of DH.[86] In addition, though, several other fathers—including Archbishop Karol Wojtyła—had made interventions along similar lines calling for demonstration of a closer connection between freedom and truth.[87]

---

[82] Regan, *Conflict and Consensus*, 172.

[83] Cf. Sept. 22, 1965, oral intervention of Ancel (AS IV/2, 16–18).

[84] A recent book by David L. Schindler and Nicholas J. Healy Jr. emphasizes the importance of Ancel's influence on the final text of DH. Cf. David L. Schindler and Nicholas J. Healy Jr., *Freedom, Truth, and Human Dignity: The Second Vatican Council's Declaration on Religious Freedom—A New Translation, Redaction History, and Interpretation of* Dignitatis Humanae (Grand Rapids, MI / Cambridge, UK: William B. Eerdmans Publishing Company, 2015), 52, 227–28, 229, 234. Schindler and Healy provide the Latin original and an English translation (by Michael Camacho) of the intervention of Ancel discussed above. Cf. Schindler/Healy, appendix II, 460–63.

[85] Cf. Sept. 25, 1964, oral intervention of Colombo (AS III/2, 554–57).

[86] Ancel had made the same point in the third-session debate on the second draft or *Declaratio Prior*. Cf. written intervention of Bishop Alfred Ancel on the second draft (AS III/2, 616–17).

[87] Cf. Sept. 25, 1964, oral intervention of Archbishop Karol Wojtyła of Cracow, Poland (AS

9.4. The Council's Choice of Human Dignity as the Foundation

Ancel's intervention was one of the most influential in the conciliar debates over religious liberty. It responded to a desire on the part of a number of council fathers (especially among the French bishops) for a more theological basis for religious liberty than Murray and his collaborators had included in the third and fourth drafts.[88] Basing the right on the obligation to seek the truth was not an entirely new idea, but rather was one that Ancel, Colombo, and others previously had raised during the Council.[89]

In addition, several council fathers were troubled by the implications of the juridical argument. Although this argument was featured prominently in the third text under Murray's leadership, it first appeared in the second draft. The council fathers had debated the second draft (the *Declaratio Prior*) during the second session, in September 1964, and the relevant passage of that draft had stated:

> Civil powers have no direct capacity or competence to determine or regulate the relationship between citizens and their Creator and Savior, and therefore cannot subordinate religious communities to the temporal ends of the state. The more that civil society provides favorable conditions for fostering religious life, however, the more it will enjoy those goods that come forth everywhere from men's fidelity to their divine vocation.[90]

This was the first appearance of the "incompetence" argument in any draft document on religious freedom, and it also was one of the most highly criticized passages of the second draft.[91] Several fathers were concerned that the passage implied the illegitimacy of state establishment of religion. As a

---

III/2, 530–32); Sept. 15, 1965, oral intervention of Giovanni Cardinal Urbani of Venice (AS IV/1, 211–15); Sept. 16, 1965, oral intervention of Bishop Stanislaus Lokuang of Taiwan (AS IV/1, 250–51); Sept. 17, 1965, oral intervention of Archbishop Antoni Baraniak of Poznan, Poland (AS IV/1, 306–8).

[88] Cf. Regan, *Conflict and Consensus*, 118 (French critique of third draft).

[89] See footnotes in this section containing citations to the *Acta Synodalia*.

[90] *Declaratio Prior* (Apr. 27, 1964), §30 [AS III/2, 321; English translation in Schindler/Healy, 271]. See also *Declaratio Prior*, §31: "[T]here is a growing consciousness by all ... that the state, on account of the juridical structure of its government, is considered unfit to pass judgment on truths that concern religious matters" [AS III/2, 321–22; English translation in Schindler/Healy, 271].

[91] Cf. Regan, *Conflict and Consensus*, 69: first mention of state incompetence argument; Regan, 90: "The paragraph denying the 'direct capacity and competence' of the state in religious matters was the most controversial of the additions to the second conciliar text on religious freedom."

result, some of the fathers intervened to assure their colleagues that religious liberty is not incompatible with establishment. Archbishop John Heenan of Westminster pointed out that despite the establishment of the Church of England in his country, all persons enjoy religious freedom.[92] Similarly, Bishop John Wright of Pittsburgh assured the bishops that religious freedom was compatible with state recognition of a particular religion.[93]

The council fathers never debated Murray's third draft (the *Textus Emendatus*), but at the beginning of the fourth (and final) session, they did debate the fourth draft (the *Textus Reemendatus*), which still bore Murray's strong influence. As with the debate on the second draft, some fathers continued to express concern about the compatibility of the declaration with state establishment of religion.[94] Several fathers also feared that the text implied religious indifferentism. William Cardinal Conway of Armagh, Ireland, was concerned that the fourth draft's strong assertion of state incompetence in religious matters would lead to an entirely secularized temporal order.[95]

As a result of persistent dissatisfaction with the incompetence argument and also as a result of the desire among many council fathers for a more positive and theological foundation for the right of religious liberty, the Ancel argument would become—and would remain—the predominant one. Indeed, such was the admiration for the argument from man's obligation to seek the truth that both Ancel and Colombo were invited to join the subcommission of the SCU charged with revising the fourth draft.

After the Council, Murray would describe the turning point in the drafting of DH as the transition between the second and the third drafts. That is, the key moment for him was the abandonment of the conscience argument and the adoption of the constitutional or juridical argument (as well as the formulation of the right itself as an immunity). He would minimize the remaining drafts by describing them essentially as adjustments to the third draft.[96] In fact, however, there are *two* key moments in the drafting history.

---

[92] AS III/2, 570. See also Regan, *Conflict and Consensus*, 86, discussing this intervention.
[93] AS III/2, 575. See also Regan, *Conflict and Consensus*, 87, discussing this intervention.
[94] Cf. intervention of Ernesto Cardinal Ruffini, Archbishop of Palermo (AS IV/1, 205); intervention of Bishop Gregorio Modrego y Casáus (AS IV/1, 257). However, Lorenz Cardinal Jäger, Archbishop of Paderborn, Germany (speaking for all 150 bishops of the episcopal conference of Germany), assured the fathers that the schema did not exclude the possibility of a state granting a privileged position to one religion (cf. AS IV/1, 239).
[95] Cf. AS IV/1, 298.
[96] Cf. John Courtney Murray, "The Declaration on Religious Liberty: A Moment in Its Legislative History," in *Religious Liberty: An End and a Beginning*, ed. John Courtney Murray (New York: MacMillan, 1966), 16, arguing that a new doctrinal line was taken

The first is the one that Murray indicates. However, the second is even more significant. It is the transition between the fourth and the fifth drafts. That is, it is the SCU's move largely away from Murray's argument and toward the ontological argument of Ancel and Colombo.[97] It is the transition from Murray's constitutional argument to the argument from human dignity, with increased precision as to the meaning of human dignity in grounding the right to religious liberty.

9.5. The Remarkable Resiliency of the Incompetence Argument

The text of DH leaves no doubt as to the foundation of the right to religious liberty: "This Vatican Council ... declares that the right to religious freedom has its foundation in the very dignity of the human person as this dignity is known through the revealed word of God and by reason itself" (DH, §2a). Moreover, as discussed above (in sections 4.4 and 9.4), the difficult drafting history of the declaration reveals the Council's initial attempts to base the right on conscience (in the first and second drafts) and on the incompetence of the state (in the third and fourth drafts) before settling on human dignity (and man's obligation to seek the truth) as the primary foundation for the right (in the fifth and sixth drafts).

Nevertheless, Murray's argument from the incompetence of the state has proven to be surprisingly resilient. Despite the clarity of the Council's language and its chosen foundation for religious liberty, Murray continued to assert in the years following the Council that the incompetence of the state is (or should be) the foundation of the right to religious liberty. Moreover, several other commentators made the same or similar arguments.

9.5.1. The First Two Forms of the Argument

This argument takes a number of forms. The first one simply asserts outright that state incompetence is the true basis for the right to religious liberty that

---

in the third schema, and that it "remained substantially the same through the subsequent three revisions."

[97] The importance of this second key moment is the focus of the recent book by David L. Schindler and Nicholas J. Healy Jr. mentioned above. Cf. Schindler, "Freedom, Truth, and Human Dignity," in Schindler/Healy, 40: "[T]he prevalent readings of DH today, while rightly recognizing the Council's shift of emphasis away from the notion of truth formally considered to the notion of the person, fail for the most part to take note of the profound ways in which the issue of truth emerges once more, *precisely from within this new context centered in the person*."

DH recognized. Pietro D'Avack is perhaps the boldest proponent of this position. He claims that the Council "does not hesitate to proclaim in the most drastic terms the absolute incompetence of the State."[98] It is true that the Council (in DH, §3) teaches that the civil authority exceeds its power if it presumes to compel or prohibit religious acts. However, D'Avack's notion of state incompetence extends much further. He asserts that any confessionality on the part of the state must stop short of affirming the value of the religion in question, and he argues that several consequences flow from this, including the right to religious liberty.[99] That is, his claim is that the

---

[98] Pietro A. D'Avack, "La Chiesa e lo Stato nella nuova impostazione conciliare," in *Il Diritto ecclesiastico e rassegna di diritto matrimoniale* (Milano, Italy: Giuffrè, 1971), 32. The English translation is my own. The original passage is as follows: "Contrariamente alla dottrina tradizionale passata . . . la dottrina conciliare attuale non esita invece a proclamare nei termini più drastici l'assoluta incompetenza dello Stato per le opzioni religiose e per le professioni e atti fideistici, contestando al medesimo ogni diritto a una sua possibile qualifica di Stato confessionista in senso proprio e all'elevazione di una qualunque fede religiosa a vera religione di Stato."

In the first instance, D'Avack correctly asserts that this incompetence applies to the government's purporting to make religious choices (*opzioni religiose*) for the citizens. However, as the discussion in the main text and in this longer quotation shows, he extends this notion of incompetence to the state's recognition of a religion as true, and he later asserts that it is the basis or foundation for the right of religious liberty (or at least that it is one of three or four foundations for the right).

[99] Cf. D'Avack, "La Chiesa e lo Stato nella nuova impostazione conciliare," 33–34. D'Avack is concerned more with disestablishment than with religious liberty, and as a result, he does not usually speak directly in terms of state incompetence as the foundation of the right to religious liberty. However, his works make clear that, like Murray, he has a broad understanding of state incompetence, and he does indeed conceive of it as the foundation for both disestablishment and religious liberty. Like Murray, he acknowledges a limited form of confessionality, but he entirely excludes the state from judgments of truth about religion. However, he predicates this limited confessionality on sociological conditions, whereas Murray predicated in on historical circumstances. Cf. Pietro Agostino D'Avack, "La libertà religiosa (diritto canonico)," in *Enciclopedia del Diritto*, vol. 24 (Varese: Giuffrè Editore, 1974), 612. In his encyclopedia article on religious liberty, D'Avack lists three fundamental principles undergirding the Council's "new official doctrine" (*nuova dottrina ufficiale*), and one of these is the incompetence of the state in religious choices (*l'incompetenza dello Stato in tema di opzioni religiose*). D'Avack, 610: The other two are the freedom of the act of faith and respect for the human person. See also D'Avack, "La Chiesa e lo Stato nella nuova impostazione conciliare," 32–34, especially 34, seemingly suggesting that religious liberty flows from state incompetence. D'Avack's phrasing of state incompetence—that is, in regard to "religious choices" (*opzioni religiose*)—differs somewhat from that of most other commentators. However, his writings make clear that his understanding of incompetence is quite broad and is at least comparable with that of the commentators who refer to state incompetence "in religious matters." That is, like Murray, he sharply separates the religious

state's incompetence is the foundation of the right to religious liberty. (On the question of whether the civil authority may recognize a religion as true, see sections 4.5 and 4.6, comparing D'Avack and Ocáriz.)[100]

Silvia Scatena is the author of a detailed history of the origin, drafting, and redaction of the declaration, and she takes a similar position. Like many commentators who share Murray's outlook (or significant parts of it), she regrets the late changes to the document that Pope St. Paul VI insisted upon in his attempts to conciliate the minority of council fathers opposed to the draft declaration.[101] Scatena complains that these revisions introduced timidity and incoherence into the text, and that they largely failed truly to conciliate the minority in any event. Notwithstanding these amendments, Scatena argues that religious liberty still "is founded at bottom on the principle of the incompetence of the State in religious matters" (*trova la sua base teorica nel principio dell'incompetenca dello Stato in materia religiosa*).[102]

A more recent proponent of this first form of the argument—simply asserting that state incompetence is the foundation for the right of religious liberty—is Thomas Pink. He has a novel reading of the declaration, interpreting it not primarily as a teaching document but rather as a shift in ecclesiastical *policy*. (See subsection 7.4.2.) For Pink, the document marks the Church's withdrawal of her authorization for the state to engage in religious coercion on her behalf. This argument rests on three premises: *first*, that when Catholic princes repressed or restricted non-Catholic religious activity in the past, they were doing so largely for *religious* ends rather than for *secular* ends; *second*, that the civil power possesses no authority *of its own* to coerce religiously; and *third*, that when Catholic princes restricted non-Catholic worship, they did so on the basis of authority that the Church

---

and the temporal realms. Cf. Pietro Agostino D'Avack, "La libertad religiosa en el magisterio actual de la Iglesia Católica," *Ius Canonicum* 5, no. 2 (1965): 379–80. Also, like Murray, he excludes the state from recognizing which is the true religion, and he acknowledges only a limited form of confessionality (cf. "La Chiesa e lo Stato nella nuova impostazione conciliare," 32).

[100] Franco Biffi appears to take a position similar to D'Avack's. He asserts that the Edict of Nantes was based on the state's incompetence, and he claims that Vatican II "definitively clarified" this position. Biffi, "Chiesa, società civile e persona," 143.

[101] Barrett Turner makes the important point that contrary to a frequently asserted characterization, the late changes to the declaration were not solely for the purpose of conciliating the minority. Rather, the comments of strong supporters like Ancel and Wojtyła prompted a number of the changes. Cf. Turner, "*Dignitatis Humanae* and the Development of Moral Doctrine," 287–88.

[102] Scatena, *La fatica della libertà*, 569. The English translation is mine.

had *delegated* to them.[103] Pink, like Murray, starkly separates the religious realm from the secular realm, and he claims that this separation—and, in particular, the state's incompetence in religious matters—is the basis of the right to religious liberty that the Council recognized.

> The state is forbidden to coerce in matters of religion, not because such coercion is illicit for any authority whatsoever, but because such coercion lies beyond the state's particular competence.[104]
>
> *Dignitatis Humanae* bases the right to religious liberty on a claim that religion transcends the authority of the state.[105]

In asserting that the declaration bases religious liberty on the distinct competencies of Church and state, Pink relies heavily on some of the *relationes* or reports of the official relator of the declaration at Vatican II, Bishop Émile De Smedt of Bruges, Belgium. Pink relies in particular on De Smedt's *relationes* of November 19, 1964, and September 15, 1965, and at first glance, they do indeed seem to provide some support for his (Pink's) stark dichotomy between the two realms. The November 1964 *relatio*, in treating of legitimate state restriction on religious practice, says:

---

[103] See generally Thomas Pink, "Dignitatis Humanae: Continuity after Leo XIII," in *Dignitatis Humanae Colloquium*, Dialogos Institute Proceedings, vol. I (Dialogos Institute, 2017), 105–6: The popes demanded state action for religious ends; Pink, 110 (similar); Pink, 113, civil power's authority to coerce came from the Church; Pink, 127 (similar); Pink, 114: The state has no coercive authority of its own in religious matters; Pink, 145 (similar). See also section 11.3. Pink's theory has met with many critical responses. See generally Martin Rhonheimer, "*Dignitatis Humanae*—Not a Mere Question of Church Policy: A Response to Thomas Pink," *Nova et Vetera* (English ed.) 12, no. 2 (2014): 445–70; John Finnis, "Reflections and Responses [26: Response to Thomas Pink]," in *Reason, Morality, and Law: The Philosophy of John Finnis*, ed. John Keown and Robert P. George (Oxford: Oxford University Press, 2013), 566–77. For arguments specifically challenging Pink's three premises described here, see Roger W. Nutt and Michael R. De Salvo, "The Debate over Dignitatis Humanae at Vatican II: The Contribution of Charles Cardinal Journet," *The Thomist* 85 (2021): 200–203, 206–7; Arnold T. Guminski, "Further Reflections about Thomas Pink's Theory of the Meaning of *Dignitatis Humanae*" (Apr. 2, 2020), §§6–17, Academia, accessed July 16, 2022, https://www.academia.edu/42924123/Further_Reflections_About_Thomas_Pinks_Theory_of_the_Meaning_of_Dignitatis_Humanae.

[104] Thomas Pink, "Conscience and Coercion: Vatican II's Teaching on Religious Freedom Changed Policy, Not Doctrine," *First Things* 225 (August 2012): 46.

[105] Pink, "Continuity after Leo XIII," 131.

9.5. The Remarkable Resiliency of the Incompetence Argument

> [I]t is not permissible for the public power to restrict the public exercise of any religion by law or governmental action on the basis that this or that religion is judged to be false or that its exercise proceeds from an erroneous conscience or that it harms the goods of the Church. *For then the public power's coercive action would intrude into the order of religion as such, which is unlawful (nefas).*[106]

By the same token, the September 1965 *relatio* says that "the nature of religious liberty rests on this distinction of orders [the civil and the religious]."[107] However, although Pink's reliance on these *relationes* is essential to his argument, that reliance also is misplaced. The reason that these two *relationes* are crucial to Pink is that he contends that the Council adopted his own sharply separationist understanding of the religious and temporal realms. Pink refers to his theory as "Leonine" because he bases it on his reading of two passages from Leo XIII's 1885 encyclical *Immortale Dei*.[108] The evidence that Pink adduces to show the Council's adoption of a so-called "Leonine" reading (like his own) comes chiefly from the November 1964 and September 1965 *relationes*.[109]

The reason that Pink's reliance on these documents is misplaced is that they are *relationes*, not on the final version of the declaration but on the third and fourth drafts, the *Textus Emendatus* and *Textus Reemendatus*, respectively. These are the two drafts for which John Courtney Murray had chief responsibility, and accordingly they are the ones that sought to base religious liberty on the incompetence of the state in religious matters. Thus, these two *relationes* do not correspond to the final version of the declaration

---

[106] AS III/8, 462–63, quoted in Pink, "Continuity after Leo XIII," 107 (emphasis supplied).

[107] AS IV/1, 193, quoted in Pink, "Continuity after Leo XIII," 122.

[108] Cf. Pink, "Continuity after Leo XIII," 121, asserting that the *relationes* show that DH "is to be read and understood in Leonine terms."

[109] What follows here is a critique of Pink's use of these two *relationes*. In addition, however, I believe that Pink's reading of Leo XIII is incorrect or at least seriously incomplete. Arnold Guminski convincingly shows, *first*, that the two passages from *Immortale Dei* that Pink relies on are not necessarily inconsistent with some inherent authority of the civil power in religious matters, and *second*, that other passages in the same encyclical (and in Leo's 1888 encyclical *Libertas*) undercut Pink's strictly separationist reading of it. Cf. Arnold T. Guminski, "Reflections about Thomas Pink's Theory," §§6–10, 12–15, 17. Note, however, that although I believe that Guminski's two essays examining the Pink thesis offer one of the most thorough and insightful critiques of that theory, I believe that both Guminski and Pink rely incorrectly on the November 19, 1964, *relatio* (as Pink also does on the September 15, 1965, *relatio*). See the discussion immediately below. (For Guminski's other essay offering a critique of the Pink theory, see the Bibliography.)

but rather to the earlier Murrayite drafts.[110] Indeed, the relator consulted Murray in the drafting of the September 1965 *relatio*.[111]

Harrison notes that, at the time of the November 1964 *relatio*, De Smedt still was in agreement with Murray's incompetence argument. (The same seems to be true of the September 1965 *relatio*.) However, late in the drafting process, De Smedt departed sharply from Murray's view, and as discussed at length above in sections 4.4 and 9.4, the fifth and sixth (final) drafts reduced Murray's incompetence argument almost to the vanishing point.[112] Moreover, the final version entirely omitted any mention of state incompetence as a foundation of the right to religious liberty, referring to it instead only as a "further consideration" (DH, §3e).

Thus, Pink is interpreting the final version of the declaration by means of passages from two *relationes* that were explaining provisions of Murray's drafts that eventually would be *omitted* from the fifth draft and from the final version. That is, the passages from the November 1964 and September 1965 *relationes* that Pink quotes are points in support *not of any provisions that appear in the final version of the declaration itself* but of ones that appear in the *earlier Murrayite drafts* but that did not survive into the final text. Note the starkly separationist tone characteristic of the earlier Murrayite drafts themselves (and note in particular that the following language does not merely *distinguish* between the temporal and religious realms, but rather seeks to *separate the realms entirely and seemingly absolutely*):

> In performing these [religious] acts, therefore, man is not subject to the civil power, whose competence, on account of its end, is restricted to the earthly and temporal order. . . . The public power completely exceeds its limits if it involves itself in any way in the governing of minds or the care of souls. (*Textus Emendatus*, §4e)[113]

---

[110] Cf. Guminski/Harrison, 210–12: Harrison's critique of Guminski's reliance on De Smedt's Nov. 19, 1964, *relatio*. My observations in this section on Pink's use of some of the *relationes* are indebted to Harrison's critique of Guminski.

[111] Cf. Scatena, *La fatica della libertà*, 446.

[112] Cf. Guminski/Harrison, 210–11. Note that Harrison refers to the Murrayite drafts of the declaration as the second and third texts, while I refer to them as the third and fourth. Despite these variations in the counting of the schemata, it is clear that the ones concerned were those for which Murray had chief responsibility, the *Textus Emendatus* (Nov. 17, 1964) and the *Textus Reemendatus* (May 28, 1965).

[113] *Textus Emendatus*, §4e [AS III/8, 432; English translation by Brannon and Camacho in Schindler/Healy, 293].

9.5. The Remarkable Resiliency of the Incompetence Argument

The competence of the civil power, however, on account of its proper end . . . is restricted in its purpose to the earthly and temporal order. The civil power must therefore be said to exceed its limits if it involves itself in those matters that concern the very ordination of man to God. Nor can it be said to be deprived in any way of its inherent worth, provided it performs its duty toward the community, restricting itself to secular matters." (*Textus Reemendatus*, §3)[114]

The key difference between, on the one hand, the position of Pink and Murray and, on the other hand, the final text of the declaration is that while Pink and Murray exclude the state completely from acting in the realm of religion,[115] the final version of the declaration does not. As Harrison notes, the final version does acknowledge that the government's distinctive or proper end is the temporal common good,[116] but it no longer says (as Murray would have it) that this is its only purpose.[117] In addition, where Murray and Pink would ground religious liberty on the incompetence of the state in religious matters, the final version of the declaration refers to the distinction of the two realms not as the basis for religious liberty but only as a "further consideration." See section 4.4.[118]

---

[114] *Textus Reemendatus*, §3 [AS IV/1, 150; English translation by Brannon and Camacho in Schindler/Healy, 323].

[115] More precisely, Pink argues that the state has no inherent authority to act in religious matters, except to safeguard the just public order. Nonetheless, he asserts, the state may indeed act in religious matters or in the order of religion if the Church authorizes or delegates it to do so. See subsection 9.5.1.

[116] Cf. Guminski/Harrison, 211–12.

[117] Pink curiously will distance himself from arguments based on state incompetence. "The Catholic debate about religious liberty needs to move on from what is, where religion is concerned, the secondary issue of the authority and competence of the state" (Pink, "Conscience and Coercion," 50). This is surprising, given that Pink's own thesis is a version of the incompetence argument. Cf. Pink, 46: "[C]oercion lies beyond the state's particular competence." Nonetheless, what is needed, he says, is a theology of the Church that explains the Church's power to coerce (cf. Pink, 50–51). Again, it is strange that in an article on the religious liberty declaration, Pink would issue such a call. The reason is that, as Pink himself indicates, DH is not (or at least not primarily) about the Church's power to coerce. Cf. Thomas Pink, "The Interpretation of *Dignitatis Humanae*: A Reply to Martin Rhonheimer," *Nova et Vetera* (English ed.) 11, no. 1 (2013): 108–9, 111. (But see subsection 11.3.1 on whether the Church is a "human power" within the meaning of DH, §2.) Why does Pink seek to shift the debate in this direction? It seems that Pink's chief interest is the coercive power of the Church and that his interest in the declaration is primarily an attempt to enlist it in support of his vision of the Church's coercive power.

[118] Pink also relies on De Smedt's October 25, 1965, *relatio* on the fifth draft or *Textus Recognitus* (cf. Pink, "Continuity after Leo XIII," 123–24), but his use of this *relatio* is not

The attempt to maintain the incompetence argument takes a second, subtler form as well. Commentators taking this second approach usually acknowledge that the Council shifted its focus away from Murray's juridical approach and toward Ancel's "ontological" argument.[119] Nevertheless, they assert that the Council's teaching on state incompetence remains implicit. Murray himself often adopted this strategy. As discussed above (in section 9.3), he quite *successfully* but—along with Schindler and Healy, I would say—*incorrectly* asserted that the lone key moment in the drafting of DH was the transition from the second to the third drafts. The key feature of this transition was the abandonment of conscience as the primary foundation for religious liberty in favor of Murray's assertion of the state's incompetence. Thus, Murray refers to the first three schemata as *drafts* or *texts* but to the subsequent three, including the crucial fifth one, merely as *revisions* to his own third schema.[120] He makes these points in his article, "A Moment in Its [DH's] Legislative History," and he also says there, "Inherent, therefore, in the notion of religious freedom is the notion of governmental incompetence in matters religious."[121] This article is one of the clearer examples of Murray not simply serving as a disinterested authority after the Council, but rather of his attempting to shape the interpretation of DH, and even of his continuing to litigate issues on which his preferred position had not prevailed at the

---

open to precisely the same criticism that I propose here. First, the October 1965 *relatio* was on a draft that was much more similar to the final version of the declaration than either of Murray's drafts (the third and fourth). Second, the passage of the October 1965 *relatio* that Pink uses pertains to a provision that remained in the final version, namely, the subtitle of the document. The quoted passage says that religious liberty, as addressed in the declaration, is a right to social and civil liberty rather than a right before God or a right of the faithful before Church authorities. In general, there is little or no difficulty in using the October 1965 *relatio*. However, Pink attempts to use it to bolster his use of the November 1964 and September 1965 *relationes*. This particular usage fails because, for the reasons stated here, the quoted passages from those earlier *relationes* are of no value in interpreting the final text of the declaration.

[119] The juridical or constitutional argument often is identified with the American and Italian bishops, largely because of the prominence of Murray and Pavan in the drafting of the third and fourth schemata. By the same token, Ancel's ontological (or theological) argument often is identified with the French bishops.

[120] Cf. Murray, "A Moment in Its Legislative History," 15–16, referring to each of the first three schemata as a "draft," "text," "schema," and/or "draft-text," but referring to the final three schemata as "revisions." Pietro Pavan, Murray's close collaborator on the third and fourth drafts, takes a very similar position. "Mais au troisième schéma, on posait le problème en des termes nouveaux, qui demeurent en substance ceux du présent document" Pavan, "Le droit à la liberté religieuse en ses éléments essentiels," *Unam Sanctam* 60 (1967): 164.

[121] Murray, "A Moment in Its Legislative History," 36–37.

9.5. The Remarkable Resiliency of the Incompetence Argument

Council. (See also section 9.3.4 above, concerning Murray's interpretation of "special civil recognition," not in terms of the standard contained in the final text of the declaration itself but rather in terms of a standard that had appeared in the penultimate schema.)

Another key figure in the drafting of the declaration, Jérôme Hamer, adopts a version of the incompetence notion that is similar to Murray's in some respects, but that diverges from Murray in others. Hamer and Clemente Riva argue that the recognition of a right to religious liberty on the part of all persons implies state incompetence in judgments of value or truth in religious matters.[122] This is similar to Murray's statement above that the very idea of religious freedom implies state incompetence. However, although Hamer and Riva describe the public power as incompetent in religious matters, they say that it should not be entirely neglectful of religion.[123] In addition, they do not conceive of state incompetence as the foundation of the right to religious liberty,[124] but rather they apparently see it as a consequence of the right.[125]

As discussed in subsection 9.3.3, Murray's protégé Richard Regan acknowledges that the Secretariat for Promoting Christian Unity significantly reduced the prominence of the incompetence argument in later drafts, but he argues that a late addition to DH §1 partially restored that argument. That "restoration," however, merely amounted to a recognition that contemporary man demands limits on the powers of government. This addition may have provided some consolation to the Murray camp, but it did nothing to restore state incompetence as the foundation of the right.

Murray himself had made an argument similar to Regan's shortly after the Council. That is, he too acknowledged that the SCU had shifted its focus away from the incompetence argument as the foundation for religious liberty. However, he claimed nonetheless that "the elements of the political

---

[122] Cf. Hamer/Riva, 179. On this question, see sections 4.5 and 4.6 above.

[123] Cf. Hamer/Riva, 187.

[124] They note that the human person is the foundation of the right, and also that the declaration later speaks of the foundation as residing in eternal law and man's duty to God. Cf. Hamer/Riva, 173–74.

[125] That is, they seem to see the idea of state incompetence as flowing from religious liberty rather than vice versa. This is similar to the basic position that I am suggesting in this chapter. However, in my opinion, what follows from this natural right to religious liberty is only the limited notion of incompetence remaining in DH §3, namely, state incompetence to command or inhibit religious acts (unless they violate the just public order). Hamer and Riva, however, describe a broader notion of state incompetence flowing from the right, that is, one that apparently would exclude all judgments of truth concerning religion.

argument are stated in later articles (6 and 7)."[126] This is only partially true and, even then, only in the most general sense. DH §6 emphasizes a point dear to Murray, namely, that the protection of rights, especially the right to religious liberty, is an essential duty of government. At the same time, though, this passage recognizes positive duties of government that are difficult to harmonize with Murray's strict notion of state incompetence in religious matters. In particular, DH §6 states that government is to create favorable conditions to promote religious life. Even admirers of Murray note that his concept of state incompetence seems to leave little room for this affirmative governmental action in favor of religion.[127]

The other passage that Murray cites as purportedly containing some of the "elements" of the juridical argument, DH §7, concerns the standard for restriction on religious practice. This provision establishes *public order*, rather than the *common good*, as the applicable standard. Murray contributed significantly toward this provision. That is, his third schema originated the adoption of *public order* as the correct standard. This is one of Murray's achievements and he deserves credit for it (see section 9.2 above). Like DH §6, it concerns the government's duty to protect the religious liberty of all, but it does not touch on the crucial question of the foundation of the right to religious liberty, at least not directly. As a result, it is difficult to understand why Murray believed that either of these passages contained any of the key "elements" of his juridical argument (at least if state incompetence is understood to lie at the heart of that argument).

9.5.2. The Third Form of the Argument

Murray did not limit himself to the argument that state incompetence is implicit in the declaration (the second form of the argument), but rather he introduced a third form of it as well. In the months and years following the close of the Council, he argued repeatedly that its binding authority falls only on its assertion of the right to religious liberty, and not on the reasons that it gave in support of the declaration. "It was not the intention of the Council to affirm that the argument, as made in the text, is final and decisive."[128] As a result, Murray claimed, "We can legitimately debate how better to construct the argument. For the Council's teaching authority falls upon

---

[126] Murray, "Religious Freedom," in Abbott, 680n7.
[127] Cf. Kenneth L. Grasso, "John Courtney Murray, 'The Juridical State,' and the Catholic Theory of Religious Freedom," *The Political Science Reviewer* 33 (2004): 32–33.
[128] Murray, "Religious Freedom," in Abbott, 680n7. See also John Courtney Murray, *Religious Liberty: An End and a Beginning* (New York: Macmillan, 1966), 168n7 (same).

what is affirmed, not upon the reasons it adduced for its affirmation."[129] Stated differently, Murray says, "One is free to construct the argument in the form which may seem more convincing."[130]

In *what way* does Murray wish to "better . . . construct" the Council's arguments? It is especially in this very matter of the *foundation* of the right that he wishes to do so. Above all else, Murray seeks to reintroduce his own idea of state incompetence as the foundation (or at least as one foundation) for the right. That is, he acknowledges that between the fourth and fifth drafts of the declaration, the focus shifted from state incompetence to man's duty to seek the truth.[131] An interesting aspect of Murray's position is that he does not seek to supplant the ontological argument entirely. On the contrary, he recognizes it as valid. However, he does not believe that it is *sufficient* to provide the foundation for the right to religious liberty.[132] As discussed previously (see section 9.2), it is the second part of the right—that is, the immunity from restriction in religious practice—that presents the key difficulty. Murray believed that only the juridical argument was sufficient to provide the necessary foundation here. Chapter 10 will discuss whether the incompetence argument could have furnished a foundation for the right, and chapter 11 will assess Murray's claim that only this argument is sufficient to provide a foundation for it. The subsection immediately following (subsection 9.5.3) will evaluate the three forms of the argument, seeking to keep alive state incompetence as the foundation for religious liberty, especially this third form of the argument, which asserts that the Council intended to leave the question open.

Before proceeding to that evaluation, however, it is worthwhile to pause for a moment to consider again the resilience of this argument. This subsection and the previous one already have discussed several authors who embrace one form or another of this attempt to revive the incompetence argument. This final form of the argument has been especially successful. That is, many authors either have reached the same conclusion as Murray or else have adopted this position in reliance on him. Least surprisingly, Pietro

---

[129] Murray, "Arguments for the Human Right," 230 (article based on a Sept. 19, 1966, speech).
[130] Murray, "Religious Freedom," in Abbott, 680n7.
[131] Murray, "Religious Freedom," in Abbott, 680n7: "American theorists are generally disposed to relate religious freedom to a general theory of constitutional government, limited by the rights of man, and to the concept of civic equality. The Declaration, however, lays less stress on this political argument than it does on the ethical foundations of the right itself."
[132] Murray, "Arguments for the Human Right," 235–36. Indeed, Murray acknowledges human dignity as a foundation of the right as well. Cf. Murray, "Religious Freedom," in Abbott, 678n5: "The reason why every man may claim immunity from coercion in matters religious is precisely his inalienable dignity as a human person." As stated in the main text, though, Murray believed that state incompetence was a necessary foundation as well.

Pavan, Murray's partner in drafting the third and fourth schemata, adopted a similar position.[133] By the same token, theologian Joseph Komonchak asserts that there is no agreement on the theology underlying DH.[134]

Kenneth Grasso is an admirer of Murray's but, at the same time, he is willing to subject Murray's thought to careful scrutiny and criticism. On this question, though, he and his coauthor Robert Hunt agree with Murray.[135] "The Declaration, in short, did not attempt to resolve definitively the complicated question of the intellectual foundations of the right it proclaims."[136] At least one scholar, John Crosby, seems to adopt this position solely in reliance on Murray.[137]

9.5.3. Evaluation of These Arguments

The text of DH itself refutes the first form of the argument discussed above, that is, the one that simply asserts that state incompetence is the true

---

[133] Cf. Pietro Pavan, "Introduction and Commentary on the Declaration on Religious Freedom," in *Commentary on the Documents of Vatican II*, vol. 4, ed. Herbert Vorgrimler (New York/London: Herder and Herder/Burns & Oates Limited, 1969), 80 (commentary on DH, §11): "[T]he civil authority is not competent in the religious sphere; not a few theologians believe that this incompetence is one of the deepest roots of the right of the person to religious freedom." Pavan makes this point not in commenting on DH §2, which concerns the foundation of the right, but rather in DH §11, which quotes the Lord's famous injunction to "Render to Caesar the things that are Caesar's and to God the things that are God's" (Matt 22:21).

[134] Cf. Joseph Komonchak and Riccardo Burigana, "Discussion Summary: First Day," in *Religious Liberty: Paul VI and Dignitatis Humanae*, ed. John T. Ford (Brescia, Italy: Istituto Paulo VI, 1995), 45–46 (comment by Komonchak).

[135] Kenneth L. Grasso and Robert P. Hunt, introduction to *Catholicism and Religious Freedom: Contemporary Reflections on Vatican II's Declaration on Religious Liberty* (Lanham, Maryland: Rowman & Littlefield Publishers, Inc., 2006), xxi: "Indeed, even today when the existence of a right to religious liberty is almost universally acknowledged, an intense argument continues to rage about the foundation, nature, and scope of this right" (larger work cited hereinafter as C&RF).

[136] Grasso and Hunt, "Introduction," xxv. Grasso takes the same position elsewhere. Grasso, "Murray, 'the Juridical State,' and Religious Freedom," 4: The Council "left to the future the task of systematically elaborating the intellectual foundations of the right affirmed by *DH*."

[137] In an article on DH and personalism, Crosby opens with Murray's position that although the declaration's teaching on the right to religious liberty "is 'clear, distinct, and technically exact,' the philosophical and theological foundations of this right are not equally clear and distinct." John F. Crosby, "On Proposing the Truth and Not Imposing It: John Paul's Personalism and the Teaching of *Dignitatis Humanae*," in C&RF, 135. As a result of this apparent vacuum, Crosby suggests that "the Christian personalism of John Paul II might assist us in securing the foundations of the right to religious freedom" (Crosby, 135).

foundation of the right to religious liberty. The text says outright that the foundation of the right is the dignity of the human person. The Council explains itself with reference to the Ancel/Colombo/Wojtyła argument that the right is based on man's duty to seek the truth and, once found, to embrace it. Man can fulfill this duty in a way consistent with his own nature only if he enjoys immunity from coercion (DH, §2b).

Analysis of the second form of the argument—the one contending that state incompetence is implicit in the declaration—is largely a matter of emphasis. As discussed above (in section 4.4), it is indeed true that a remnant of Murray's incompetence argument remains in the final text. That is, the Council declares, the state exceeds its own proper limitations if it presumes to command or inhibit religious acts (DH, §3e). Thus, the second form of the argument is correct as far as it goes, but it does not go nearly as far as Murray would have liked. State incompetence is implicit in the declaration, but that incompetence encompasses only attempts by the temporal authority to command or prohibit religious acts. It does not extend—as Murray would have had it—to all "religious matters."[138] Note also that the declaration entirely avoids the Murray terminology. That is, even in the remnant of this argument (as well as throughout the rest of the declaration), the Council never uses the language of *incompetence* or *competence*. Finally, even to the extent that a remnant of the incompetence argument does survive, it is not as a foundation of the right but only as a "further consideration" (DH, §3e).

The third form of the argument—the assertion that the Council never intended to settle the question of the foundation of the right—is the most interesting and important variety of this argument. Although Murray asserts outright that the Council never intended its reasons in favor of DH to be binding, he never supports this assertion with citations to DH, to other Council documents, or to rulings of the Theological Commission.

It seems clear that Murray has uppermost in mind the foundation of the right to religious liberty, for that is the subject to which he repeatedly returns in seeking to "better . . . construct" the Council's argument. However, from the outset, Murray's position is implausible. The fathers vigorously debated the question of the foundation of the right to religious liberty. Why would they have expended so much time and energy on a matter that they did not intend to resolve?

Indeed, as a result of the difficulty of these very discussions, Joseph Cardinal Ritter of St. Louis proposed during the third session that the Council affirm the right to religious liberty, but that it do so without providing reasons:

---

[138] Cf. Murray, "Problem of Religious Freedom," 558.

> The arguments of this Declaration have neither simplicity, clarity nor certitude. A Declaration restricted to a simple affirmation and advocation of religious liberty by omitting all argumentation would be much better. . . . Venerable Fathers, this Declaration on Religious Liberty is valid and certain, even if the reasons are weak or even invalid.[139]

If the Council had adopted the Ritter proposal, then Murray indeed might have the space that he seeks to provide his own foundation for the right. However, the Council never adopted this proposal. Moreover, as the relator for the declaration made clear after the Council, it was necessary that the fathers avoid embracing such a proposal: "The Council did not limit itself to affirming that persons and associations possess a true right to social and civil liberty in the religious domain; it was bound to explain with precision the foundation of this right."[140]

Murray himself acknowledges that it would have been inappropriate for the Council to affirm the right entirely without any reasons. Had it done so, the declaration would have appeared as a mere practical measure or an opportunistic concession to contemporary sensibilities. (Hamer makes the same point.)[141] However, Murray then proceeds to empty the Council's reasoning of nearly all meaning and significance:

> It was necessary for the Council to present an argument for the principle of religious freedom, lest anyone should mistakenly think that the Church was accepting religious freedom merely on pragmatic grounds or as a concession to contemporary circumstances. However, it was not the intention of the Council to affirm that the argument, as made in the text, is final and decisive. Complete and systematic study of the arguments for religious freedom is a task left to the scholars of the Church, working in ecumenical spirit

---

[139] Sept. 23, 1964, oral intervention of Joseph Cardinal Ritter of St. Louis (AS III/2, 368–69); English translation from Yzermans, 647.

[140] Émile-Joseph De Smedt, "Les conséquences pastorales de la Déclaration," *Unam Sanctam* 60 (1967): 215. The English translation is mine. The original French is as follows: "Il ne s'est pas borné à affirmer que les personnes et les associations possèdent un droit véritable à la liberté sociale et civile dans le domaine religieux; il a tenu à exposer avec précision, autant que faire se pouvait, le fondement de ce droit."

[141] Hamer says that it was necessary for the Council to include reasons for its teaching on religious liberty, so as to avoid the impression that the Church simply finds the idea acceptable in the present day. Cf. Hamer, "Histoire du texte de la Déclaration," 77.

with scholars of other religious Communities, and in humanist spirit with scholars of no religious convictions who are concerned with the exigencies of human dignity. The Council merely presents certain lines or elements of argument.[142]

Note Murray's reference to the Council's "argument." As David L. Schindler notes, this characterization is "highly ambiguous."[143] When Murray says that the Council's "argument" is not decisive, there is some truth to this. That is, some of the Council's observations about the desires of contemporary man are matters about which people may disagree. In addition, one might ask why the fathers chose the examples and citations that they did. For example, Jean Willebrands, the Secretary for the SCU, regretted that the fathers, although citing St. Paul on Christian freedom (Rom 8:21), did not base the right to religious liberty more directly on this principle.[144]

However, Murray seeks not simply to take issue with some of the observations or argumentation contained in the declaration but rather to provide an entirely different *foundation* for the right. This question of the right's foundation was perhaps the most crucial question in the entire religious liberty debate,[145] and it is the key to determining whether it is possible to reconcile DH with the teachings of the nineteenth-century popes. Proponents of early formulations of the right to religious freedom in the fifteenth and sixteenth centuries often based it on the impossibility of knowing the truth.[146] If this were the only possible foundation for the right, then the

---

[142] Murray, *An End and a Beginning*, 168n7.

[143] Schindler, "Freedom, Truth, and Human Dignity," in Schindler/Healy, 89. Schindler goes on to say that "Murray's apparent openness to different arguments ... is rigged in advance" (Schindler/Healy, 89). His concern is Murray's advocacy of a "negative" right, not only in the sense of an immunity but also in the sense of a "freedom from" rather than a "freedom for." That is, Schindler asserts, Murray's openness is an openness only to supporting the juridical notion of "freedom from" rather than Ancel's ontological notion of "freedom for."

[144] Cf. Jean Willebrands, "La liberté religieuse et l'œcuménisme," *Unam Sanctam* 60 (1967): 248.

[145] Indeed, one of Murray's signal contributions was to move the SCU away from basing the right on conscience. See section 9.2 above.

[146] The first major thinker to put forward ideas of toleration as a solution to religious strife in the modern period was the Dutch theologian and humanist Desiderius Erasmus (1466?–1536). Erasmus advocated shifting the focus of religion from dogma to morality. He was skeptical about the possibility of arriving at definite answers to dogmatic questions, and he seems to have hoped that focusing on morality rather than dogma would put an end to religious strife, which resulted most often from dogmatic disputes. Cf. Paul Johnson, *A History of Christianity* (New York: Atheneum, 1985), 275.

Erasmus's ideas did not prevail during his own life, but, by the late sixteenth century,

Church never could approve it, because the basis or premise of the right would be an untruth.

Thus, the foundation of the right to religious liberty is not simply one of several possible arguments or reasons adduced in favor of the declaration. On the contrary, the Council's locating the foundation for the right is as important as the affirmation of the right itself. Thus, several theologians note that the most authoritative provisions of DH are articles 1 and 2, namely, the passages that describe the right *and its foundation*.[147] As a result, while De Smedt (like Murray) expresses an openness to further examination of some of the argumentation contained in the declaration,[148] he (unlike Murray) does not extend this openness to the question of the foundation for the right.[149]

As discussed above, Murray provides little or no support for his argument that the Council did not intend its arguments (including its choice of a foundation for the right) to be decisive. Note, however, that Murray claims that the task and prerogative to "better . . . construct" the Council's work is left to "scholars." By the same token, his protégé Regan contends that the Council's praxis "left to professional theologians, philosophers, and political scientists the task of critically evaluating specific arguments."[150] Echoing Murray, Regan says, "It was the affirmation of the principle of religious freedom which the Council proclaimed unreservedly to the faithful

---

several states had begun to enact toleration laws that reflected his thought. These laws expressed above all the desire to end or to avoid religious warfare. Poland had not suffered in the religious wars, but the Polish nobility formed the Warsaw Confederation in 1573 as a measure to avoid the strife that had wracked Poland's neighbors. The Confederation reflected both Erasmus's overarching desire for peace and his doubt concerning the ability to find agreement on theological matters: "As there is wide disagreement in our state on matters related to the Christian religion, and in order to prevent any fatal outburst such as ha[s] been witnessed in other kingdoms, we, who differ on religion, bind ourselves for our own sake and that of our posterity in perpetuity . . . to keep the peace among ourselves on the subject of differences of religion" (Johnson, *History of Christianity*, 293).

[147] Yves M.-J. Congar, "Que faut-il entendre par 'Déclaration'?" *Unam Sanctam* 60 (1967): 51; Pavan, "Introduction and Commentary," in Vorgrimler, 64–65. Cf. Turner, "*Dignitatis Humanae* and the Development of Moral Doctrine," 252–53: Congar, Pavan, and Valuet all assert that DH §1 and §2 are the most authoritative sections of the declaration.

[148] Cf. De Smedt, "Les conséquences pastorales," 215: "La pertinence des considérations émises par le Concile fera peut-être l'objet de discussions."

[149] "The Council did not limit itself to affirming that persons and associations possess a true right to social and civil liberty in the religious domain; *it was bound to explain with precision the foundation of this right*" (De Smedt, "Les conséquences pastorales," 215 [emphasis added]).

[150] Regan, *Conflict and Consensus*, 159.

9.5. The Remarkable Resiliency of the Incompetence Argument

and the world."[151] These references to theologians and scholars raise the possibility that Murray and Regan may have believed that their position enjoyed sanction from the relator, Bishop De Smedt. In his final *relatio*, De Smedt did indeed refer to theologians and other experts:

> Some Fathers affirm that the Declaration does not sufficiently show how our doctrine is not opposed to ecclesiastical documents up till the time of the Supreme Pontiff Leo XIII. As we said in the last *relatio*, this is a matter for future theological and historical studies to bring to light more fully.[152]

This passage might appear at first glance to support the Murray position, but it does not. As discussed above, De Smedt by no means wishes to foreclose theological comment on the declaration. At the same time, however, he makes clear that the Council was bound to resolve the matter of the foundation of the right to religious liberty, and that it did so. This passage from De Smedt's last *relatio* again welcomes theologians and historians to examine the declaration, but the relator gives no indication that this welcome extends to providing a new foundation for the right.[153]

9.5.4. Related Positions

Before leaving this subject, a word about some other scholars is appropriate. The positions described above have in common the attempt to revive the incompetence argument in some way. That is, they assert (1) that state incompetence is the true foundation of the right, (2) that this argument remains implicit despite the Council's shift to the "ontological" approach, or (3) that the Council intended to leave scholars free to continue to argue in favor of state incompetence as the foundation of the right. For the reasons discussed above, I believe that the first and third positions are problematic and the second is ineffective.

In addition to the positions described above, there are scholars who

---

[151] Regan, *Conflict and Consensus*, 159.

[152] AS IV/6, 719; English translation in Harrison, RL&C, 75. See also Scatena, *La fatica della libertà*, 551, recounting similar statement by Augustin Cardinal Bea.

[153] Schindler gives another reason for taking a skeptical attitude toward Murray's attempt to keep the foundation question open, namely, that the specific reason for the changes to the fifth and sixth drafts was to correct Murray's earlier drafts. Schindler, "Freedom, Truth, and Human Dignity," in Schindler/Healy, 89: "[T]he changes made in the final drafts of the Declaration were for the express purpose of *correcting* Murray's juridical view."

avoid these specific pitfalls but nonetheless remain interested in state incompetence as a foundation for the right.

For example, Francesco Finocchiaro acknowledges that the council fathers did indeed base the right to religious liberty on human dignity, but he argues that the right equally could have been founded on the principle of civil incompetence in matters of religious choice.[154] As a *logical* matter, this probably is true. That is, the assertion that the state is incompetent in religious matters certainly does lead to the conclusion that people are immune from religious coercion. However, chapter 10 below will consider whether basing the right on state incompetence might entail other unacceptable consequences.

Similarly, Basile Valuet is clear that the Council based the right to religious liberty on the dignity of the person,[155] and that it progressively diminished the significance of the incompetence argument,[156] but he nonetheless maintains a lively interest in the latter. In particular, he discusses the subject at length in his treatment of DH §3 (where the remnant of the incompetence argument is preserved) and DH §13 (on the Church's claim for freedom in the face of the civil powers). He emphasizes a 1971 audience in which Pope Paul VI asserted the state's incompetence in religious matters, and he concludes that both Paul and the Council located the *internal* foundation of the right to religious liberty in the dignity of the human person and located the *external* foundation in the incompetence of the state in religious matters.[157]

Thus, both Finocchiaro and Valuet acknowledge that the Council identifies the dignity of the person as the foundation of religious liberty, but both also seem to identify the incompetence of the state as what a lawyer would call "an argument in the alternative." Finocchiaro takes the position that the Council equally could have based the right on state incompetence. Valuet does not explain precisely what he means in contrasting the "internal" and "external" foundations of the right, but he seems to see the two as

---

[154] "Inoltre, proprio perché il fine del potere civile è quello di realizzare 'il bene comune temporale,' tale potere evade dalla sua competenza 'se presume di dirigere o di impedire gli atti religiosi' (cfr. D.H., n. 3). Così, nel diritto delle società civili, la libertà religiosa, oltre che sui principi della libertà della fede e della dignità della persona umana, dovrebbe essere fondata anche sul principio dell'incompetenza civile in materia delle scelte religiose dei cittadini." *Enciclopedia giuridica* (Roma: Istituto della Enciclopedia Italiana, 1990), s.v. "Libertà, VI) Libertà Religiosa—Diritto Canonico," 3.2.

[155] Cf. Valuet, LRTE, 416, 419.

[156] Cf. Valuet, LRTE, 389–95, review of evolution of the schemata.

[157] Cf. Valuet, LRTE, 554 [= LRTC, vol. IB, 837].

complementary. Although he is very aware of the Council's reduction of the importance of the incompetence argument, Valuet nonetheless seems to believe that this argument remains quite important.[158]

The next section (9.6) will consider what Murray believed to be at stake with the incompetence argument. That is, it will consider his "sufficiency" argument in which he asserts that only the incompetence argument is fully sufficient to ground the right to religious liberty. The next chapter discusses whether the Council could have maintained the incompetence argument as the foundation for religious liberty, or whether this argument entails insurmountable difficulties. Then chapter 11 will return to Murray's "sufficiency" argument and will attempt to respond to his claim that only the incompetence argument is sufficient to ground the right to religious liberty.

9.6. Murray's "Sufficiency" Argument

The preceding section (9.5) and other passages of this work have taken issue with a number of John Courtney Murray's positions. They have discussed some problematic aspects of his scholarship, especially in the years following the Council. It is difficult to escape the sense that Murray's claim that the Council did not intend its argumentation to be decisive seems to have been a strategy to enable him to rebuild the declaration around his own position—namely, the incompetence argument—that the council fathers themselves had rejected (or severely limited). Moreover, with regard to the question of a government's special civil recognition of a given religion, Murray seems to have misrepresented the relevant passage (DH, §6) by repeatedly interpreting it not in light of the standard that the final text adopts, "peculiar circumstances," but rather in light of the discarded standard from the penultimate schema, "historical circumstances." (See section 9.3.4 above.)

Although Murray outlived the Council by only two years, he wrote and spoke extensively during that time. Given the high regard in which the U.S. bishops held him and given his service as a *peritus* during the second and third sessions of the Council, Murray's word long was accepted as authoritative in interpreting DH. In recent years, however, increasing numbers of scholars have taken note of the shortcomings in Murray's commentary and have come to realize that his post-conciliar statements sometimes obscure the meaning of the final text of the declaration.[159] (See section 9.3.4 above.)

---

[158] This issue is discussed at greater length below in subsection 10.3.5.1.
[159] Cf. Gerard V. Bradley, preface to Guminski/Harrison, 2, noting agreement between Guminski and Harrison that "that way too many scholarly treatments of DH have read way

That said, it would be a mistake to interpret these unfortunate features in Murray's scholarship as mere vanity or pride of authorship. On this crucial question of the foundation of the right to religious liberty, Murray sought to revive his own incompetence argument—not only to relitigate a battle that he had lost at the Council but to provide the right to religious liberty with a foundation that he believed it needed.

Murray believed that the only foundation sufficient to support the right was his own notion of the state's incompetence in religious matters. Moreover, he believed that this argument alone was sufficient. He did not object to the inclusion of Ancel's ontological argument, but he did not believe it necessary. That is, he thought that the incompetence argument by itself was sufficient to ground the right to religious liberty.[160]

Following the Council, Murray set out to strengthen the incompetence argument that he had put forward there.[161] He did so primarily in two works, an article and a speech.[162] The key to Murray's argument is that, in a sense, DH recognized not one right, but two, or rather "a twofold immunity."[163]

The first is the right *not to be forced* to act contrary to one's own beliefs, and the second is the right *not to be restrained from acting* according to one's conscience, especially in religious matters (DH, §§2a, 3c). Although these rights may seem to be two sides of the same coin, they present different problems when it comes to identifying their foundation. Kenneth Grasso provides an excellent summary and analysis of Murray's argument, and accordingly, following Murray, he points out that the great problem is with identifying a foundation for the *second* right.[164]

The first right—the immunity from being coerced to perform religious acts—is similar to one that, as the declaration makes clear, the Church always has recognized.

---

too much of John Courtney Murray into that document"; Schindler, "Freedom, Truth, and Human Dignity," in Schindler/Healy, 173n46: Murray's juridical interpretation has been taken for granted as the proper reading of DH, although Murray himself acknowledged that the final document gives pride of place not to his argument, but to the "religious" or "ontological" argument.

[160] Cf. Murray, "Arguments for the Human Right," 241 (this work is based on a Sept. 19, 1966, speech by Murray).

[161] Cf. Murray, *Catholic Struggles with Pluralism*, 229 (Hooper's annotation to a 1966 Murray speech).

[162] Cf. Murray, "A Moment in Its Legislative History," 15–42; Murray, "Arguments for the Human Right," 229–44 (based on a 1966 Murray speech).

[163] Murray, "A Moment in Its Legislative History," 30.

[164] Grasso, "Murray, 'the Juridical State,' and Religious Freedom," 15.

> It is one of the major tenets of Catholic doctrine that man's response to God in faith must be free: no one therefore is to be forced to embrace the Christian faith against his own will. This doctrine is contained in the word of God and it was constantly proclaimed by the Fathers of the Church. (DH, §10)

The first right that the declaration recognizes is a broader version of the freedom of the act of faith. That is, just as coercion of the Christian faith is prohibited, so also is coercion of a person to act against his conscience (within due limits). There are several possible foundations for this right. One is the duty to obey one's conscience, and, in principle, another is the necessary freedom of the act of faith. Murray echoes the latter idea:

> From the necessary freedom of the act of Christian faith—or of any other kind of final religious commitment, even one of atheist tenor—it does indeed follow that no man may be constrained either to believe against his will or to act in a manner contrary to his own beliefs.[165]

In addition, although Murray was successful in arguing that the rights of conscience were an insufficient foundation for the second right (the right not to be hindered), he acknowledged that this notion did provide an adequate grounding for the first right, or the first part of the twofold immunity.[166] Indeed, as set forth by the Council, the first right incorporates the notion of conscience: "[N]o one is to be forced to act in a manner contrary to his own beliefs (*contra suam conscientiam*) [DH, §2a].... [H]e is not to be forced to act in a manner contrary to his conscience (*contra suam conscientiam*) [DH, §3c]."

The second right presented a more difficult challenge. To begin, in the second right (or the second aspect of the twofold immunity), the right that is protected is not simply the right not to be coerced, but the right to *immunity from being hindered in one's religious acts* (provided that one exercises his rights within the boundaries of the just public order [see generally part 4]). As a result, the second right is much more consequential for society at large because it concerns not only one's refusal to adhere to a religion

---

[165] Murray, "A Moment in Its Legislative History," 30. This is not to say that the first right that the declaration mentions is identical with the freedom of the act of faith, but rather that it can and should be understood as following from it.
[166] Cf. Murray, "A Moment in Its Legislative History," 30.

(as the first right does) but also one's positive, outward religious actions in both private and public. Thus, the second aspect of the immunity protects the dissemination of even false religious information, provided that one's action is peaceful and in accord with the limits of the just public order.[167]

If one's conscience is both sincere and correct, then the rights of conscience support even this second immunity.[168]

> There is no difficulty, of course, in the case of the man of both right and true conscience. What his conscience dictates him to do is in accord with the objective order of truth. He has the duty to do it; he has the right to do it; the others have the duty to recognize the rightfulness of his claim to act; and they have no grounds on which to deny it, precisely because the action in question is in accord with objective truth.[169]

However, the Council wished to vindicate a right on the part of all persons, not only those with a correct conscience (and not only those who are sincere).[170] The rights of conscience are insufficient to provide a foundation for liberty in the case of those with an erroneous conscience. As Murray succinctly puts it, "If the conscience in question is right but erroneous, it cannot give rise to a juridical relationship between persons. From one human being's erroneous conscience no duty follows for others to act or perform or omit anything."[171]

This measuring of the conscience argument against the second part of the twofold immunity accounts for Murray's success in moving the SCU away from the conscience argument. One grasps the insufficiency of the conscience argument only if one first recognizes the difference between the two parts of the twofold immunity—*non-coercion* and *non-hindrance*—and if one then realizes the greater difficulty involved in locating a foundation for the second part.

---

[167] Murray, "Arguments for the Human Right," 232.

[168] Murray, "Arguments for the Human Right," 233: "No difficulty arises if the conscience in question is right and true."

[169] Murray, "A Moment in Its Legislative History," 24.

[170] Needless to say, the Council did not wish to approve the abuse of the right to religious liberty, but such abuses may be addressed by the public authority only when they amount to juridical abuses, that is, violations of the *just public order*, and not when they are confined to the moral realm (cf. DH, §7c).

[171] Murray, "Arguments for the Human Right," 233. Murray acknowledges that one with a sincere but erroneous conscience has a moral obligation to act according to his conscience, but not necessarily a moral-juridical right to do so. Cf. "A Moment in Its Legislative History," 24–25.

9.6. Murray's "Sufficiency" Argument

The first two drafts of the declaration had identified conscience as the foundation for the right to religious liberty, until Murray's third draft supplanted the conscience argument with his own distinctive argument from state incompetence (the key component of his juridical approach). Although Murray's incompetence argument did not survive as the foundation for the right, his movement of the SCU away from the conscience argument did indeed endure.[172]

However, in his post-conciliar writings and speeches (especially the two discussed here), Murray bolsters his incompetence argument. It is not surprising that he would continue to argue the insufficiency of the conscience argument and the significance of the Council's move away from it, and this indeed is one of the major themes in his post-conciliar writing. However, Murray proceeds to argue that even the foundations identified in the final version of the declaration are insufficient to support the right to religious liberty that the Council recognizes.

The foundations that have pride of place in the final declaration are the Ancel/Colombo "ontological" argument concerning man's duty to seek the truth, and the need for man to do so in a manner consonant with his human dignity and with the social nature of the human person. As already discussed, the conscience argument was displaced as a foundation, but contrary to the implication that one might draw from Murray's writing, conscience remained a theme in the document.[173] By the same token, as already noted, the Council eliminated Murray's incompetence argument as a foundation of the right, and preserved it only in small measure, that is, as a "further consideration" and as a prohibition on state action that would "presume to command or inhibit" religious acts (DH, §3e).

Murray treats the declaration's foundation as two distinct arguments: the duty to seek the truth, and the social nature of man. He begins with the duty to seek the truth. Far from disagreeing with the argument, he

---

[172] This is not to say that conscience is irrelevant to religious liberty, of course. The "theological" or "ontological" argument of Ancel presupposes a subject who follows his conscience, or who at least must be left free to do so. In addition, as already noted, conscience is indeed sufficient to ground the first part of the declaration's two-fold right, namely, the right not to be compelled to act against one's conscience. However, it is the second part of the two-fold right—the right to non-hindrance in one's religious acts—that requires an additional foundation.

[173] "In fact, the language of the 'rights of conscience' argument was not limited to the first two drafts. There remains some residual 'rights of conscience' terminology in the Declaration, a fact used by some who want to argue that the Council did not advance beyond the 'conscience' argument" (Murray, *Catholic Struggles with Pluralism*, 243n5; Hooper's annotation to Murray's "Arguments for the Human Right of Religious Freedom" speech).

describes it as "valid and on target."[174] However, he does not believe that it is sufficient to provide a foundation for the second immunity. In his speech on "Arguments for the Human Right to Religious Freedom," Murray constructs an imaginary response from governmental authorities claiming the right to repress a person's religious error, notwithstanding the ontological argument from man's duty to seek the truth:

> We acknowledge and deeply respect the impulse to seek truth implanted in human nature. We acknowledge, too, your moral obligation to conform your life to truth's demands. But, sorry to say, we judge you to be in error. For in the sphere of religion we possess objective truth. More than that, in this society we represent the common good as well as religious truth—in fact religious truth is an integral part of the common good. In your private and in your family life, therefore, you may lawfully act according to your errors. However, we acknowledge no duty on our part to refrain from coercion in your regard when in the public life of society, which is our concern, you set about introducing your false forms of worship or spreading your errors. Continue, then, your search for truth, until you find it—we possess it—so that you may be able to act in public in keeping with it.[175]

Thus, Murray finds the ontological argument insufficient to ground the twofold immunity, because suppression of religious error is not necessarily inconsistent with man's duty to seek the truth. Indeed, one might add, the public powers may well consider these measures suppressing religious error as providing assistance to man in promoting and channeling his search for the truth.[176] (Chapter 11 responds to this argument.)

Murray next considers the argument from man's social nature. He recapitulates the argument as claiming that there is a necessary connection between one's internal religious acts and the social or external manifestations of those acts in a public way. As a result, just as no human power may forbid the internal religious acts, none may forbid the external ones. Murray responds that this argument begs the question. That is, it assumes the matter to be proven, namely, that the public power may not hinder external religious actions.[177]

---

[174] Murray, "Arguments for the Human Right," 234.
[175] Murray, "Arguments for the Human Right," 235.
[176] Murray, "Arguments for the Human Right," 235–36.
[177] Murray, "Arguments for the Human Right," 236–37.

Grasso's summary and synthesis of Murray's "sufficiency" argument reveals at least one reason why Murray was so attached to his own argument from the state's incompetence. In a sense, this argument is indispensable in Murray's view (and in Grasso's). The arguments from the duty to seek the truth and from man's social nature were legitimate as far as they went, but they simply did not go far enough. No argument could be sufficient unless it were joined to the incompetence argument. The reason is that, for Murray (and for Grasso), religious liberty inevitably is a political question.[178] As a result, one simply cannot avoid the question of the powers of the government.

> When all is said and done, a theory of religious freedom cannot avoid "the crucial issue" of "the competence of the powers with regard to passing judgment on forms of religious expression in society." A persuasive argument to ground the right affirmed by DH simply cannot be constructed without engaging the question of why "the public power" possesses neither "the duty" nor "right to repress opinions, practices, religious rites" that "are erroneous to the common good."[179]

Indeed, Grasso asserts that DH requires—but does not itself provide—"a full-fledged theory of the state."[180]

Thus does Murray raise the stakes of the incompetence argument. He seeks to revive his argument as the foundation for the right, and he claims not only that incompetence is the best possible foundation but that it is the sole foundation that fully can support this right to religious liberty. The next chapter considers whether, on the one hand, the Council could have located the right's foundation in the state's religious incompetence, or, on the other hand, whether the Murray argument entailed insurmountable practical and doctrinal difficulties. The following chapter returns to the question of "sufficiency" and will seek to address Murray's claim that state incompetence provides the only sufficient foundation for the right.

---

[178] "[T]his political argument is of primary importance. Without it any other argument would not sufficiently settle the questions. For the very question concerns the limits of public power in religious matters." Murray, "Arguments for the Human Right," 237.

[179] Grasso, "Murray, 'the Juridical State,' and Religious Freedom," 20 (citations omitted). The phrases in quotation marks are from Murray's speech, "Arguments for the Human Right of Religious Freedom," and from his 1964 *Theological Studies* article, "The Problem of Religious Freedom."

[180] Grasso, "Murray, 'the Juridical State,' and Religious Freedom," 21.

CHAPTER 10

The Dog That Didn't Bark

"Is there any other point to which you would wish to draw my attention?"
"To the curious incident of the dog in the nighttime."
"The dog did nothing in the nighttime."
"That was the curious incident," remarked Sherlock Holmes.

— ARTHUR CONAN DOYLE[1]

It is clear that the Council based the right to religious liberty on the dignity of the human person. (See section 9.3 above.) The question next arises as to whether this was a *necessary* choice. *Might it have been otherwise?* That is, could the council fathers have based this right on a different foundation, such as one of the others discussed above in chapter 9? Most significantly, could the Council have adopted as the foundation for religious liberty *the state's incompetence in religious matters*?

At least as a purely *logical* matter, the answer initially seems to be a qualified *yes*. That is, the assertion that the state is incompetent in religious matters certainly does lead to the conclusion that people are immune from religious coercion. Indeed, this is the great appeal of the incompetence argument. Once the state is defined as incompetent in religious matters, religious liberty becomes a right *by default*, that is, by the state's disqualification from acting in the religious sphere.[2]

However, founding the right to religious liberty on the incompetence

---

[1] Arthur Conan Doyle, "Silver Blaze," in *The Memoirs of Sherlock Holmes* (Pleasantville, NY: The Reader's Digest Association, Inc., 1988), 28.

[2] Cf. Kenneth L. Grasso, "John Courtney Murray, 'The Juridical State,' and the Catholic Theory of Religious Freedom," *The Political Science Reviewer* 33 (2004): 20. See also section 9.6 on Murray's "sufficiency" argument.

of the state would have entailed other unacceptable consequences. Some of these difficulties are practical, but others seem to be doctrinal. The following section will set some parameters for this discussion, and the succeeding ones will attempt to demonstrate the practical and doctrinal difficulties with founding the right to religious liberty on the state's incompetence in religious matters.

10.1. Some Qualifications

This discussion is not limited to John Courtney Murray's version of the incompetence argument, but it will keep his formulation of the argument uppermost in mind. His articulation of the argument is the most significant one for the reason that he succeeded in basing two schemata of the declaration on it. In addition, he is the foremost proponent and defender of this argument, and indeed, as discussed above in section 9.5, he has been quite successful in promoting it. (This is not to shortchange Murray's close collaborator Pietro Pavan, whose notion of incompetence also will receive attention.)

However, I do not believe that any version of the incompetence argument is able to ground the right to religious liberty in an acceptable way. Even if a particular version of the argument is not vulnerable to all of the same criticisms as the Murray formulation, I believe that each one entails practical problems, doctrinal difficulties, or both.

The remainder of this chapter will show why state incompetence is not a proper foundation for the right to religious liberty. That said, I do not deny that, at some level of abstraction, one must recognize that the incompetence argument does contain truth. (See section 10.3 below on the contours of the argument and the various ways in which its proponents frame it.)

Along these lines, although I will show that the dignity of the person is the sole proper foundation of the right, I also will show that this foundation does indeed yield conclusions that one can describe as limiting the state's competence. To state the matter simply, the dignity of the person is the basis for the human right (and natural right) to religious liberty that every man and woman possesses. As a result of this natural right (and as a result of man's natural orientation toward seeking and embracing the truth), civil authorities (and others) must respect the religious liberty of all persons. Thus, it is indeed true to say that the state is incompetent to violate the religious liberty of citizens and other residents. In fact, this is as far as the Council was willing to go in preserving a remnant of Murray's incompetence argument. "[I]t would clearly transgress the limits set to its [the government's] power, were it to presume to command or inhibit acts that are religious" (DH, §3e). However, state incompetence is a *consequence* of the foundation of the right in human dignity, or it is a consequence of the right itself. It is not the *foundation* of the right. The interplay between human dignity and state incompetence moves in only one direction. The existence of a human right or a natural right necessarily implies a limitation on state competence. However, the consequence does not flow in the opposite direction. That is, the fact of state incompetence over a given matter does not necessarily imply the presence of a human right.[3]

To take a simple example, the Third Amendment to the U.S. Constitution prohibits the quartering of soldiers in private houses during peace time. Thus, the U.S. government is incompetent to quarter troops in private homes during time of peace.[4] However, the right of the homeowner implied by this limitation on governmental power is not necessarily a human right or a natural right, but it appears to be only a positive right (albeit one touching on the rights of privacy and property). By the same token, with regard to natural rights, such as speech, assembly, and religion (all recognized in the First Amendment), the direction of the movement—from the natural right to the incompetence of the state—is clear. The person's social nature and his rational faculty are the reasons for the rights of free speech and peaceable assembly, and as a result, the state is incompetent to infringe these rights. The consequence does not flow in the other direction, however. That is, the government's incompetence to prevent peaceable assembly is not what gives rise to the natural right to assembly. In fact, the natural right exists regardless of whether the government recognizes it.[5]

---

[3] As discussed below, neither Murray nor the other proponents of the incompetence argument make clear precisely what it means for the state to be *incompetent*. See subsection 10.3.1, discussing the ambiguity over whether *incompetence* means, on the one hand, a *lack of ability* to judge a certain matter, or, on the other hand, a *lack of authority* to do so. The third and fourth drafts of the declaration (for which Murray had primary authority) arguably included both meanings, but it seems clear that the emphasis was on the latter, namely, *lack of authority*. See in particular (in subsection 10.3.1) the discussion of Martín de Agar's distinction between *doctrinal* incompetence and *juridical* incompetence.

[4] This is not exactly the same type of incompetence that Murray seems to mean in discussing religious liberty. That is, in this example, an inability or incompetence to judge the subject matter is not necessarily implied. However, this example is similar to Murray's assumptions in implying the lack of authority to act or the lack of authority to act licitly.

[5] Joseph Story, a Justice of the U.S. Supreme Court in the nineteenth century, wrote that the right to assembly is so basic that it need not have been specified in the First Amendment to the United States Constitution: "This would seem unnecessary to be expressly provided

This feature of the incompetence argument was the subject of a rare divergence between the views of Murray and Pavan. Murray acknowledges this reality at least implicitly. That is, he concedes that his chosen foundation, state incompetence, is not true at all times but only under present conditions.[6] As a result, unlike many other defenders of religious liberty, he is not particularly concerned to defend it as a natural right.[7] His emphasis on historical consciousness assumes that the recognition of state incompetence is an achievement and a welcome development. It seems likely that he personally anticipated the right to religious liberty as permanent, but this would have been more of a personal assumption on his part than a consequence of his incompetence theory. In a rare divergence with Murray, Pavan rejected this position, saying that the right is indeed permanent. That is, he recognized it expressly as a natural right. Thus, whereas Murray described historical (or political) consciousness as giving rise to state incompetence (and consequently to religious liberty), Pavan confined the role of historical circumstances to giving rise to the *awareness* of the right.[8]

---

for in a republican government, since it results from the very nature of its structures and institutions. It is impossible that it could be practically denied, until the spirit of liberty had wholly disappeared, and the people had become so servile and debased, as to be unfit to exercise any of the privileges of freemen." Joseph Story, *A Familiar Exposition of the Constitution of the United States* (1840; repr., Lake Bluff, IL: Regnery Gateway, 1986), §449.

[6] "It is not exact to say flatly that the state is incompetent in religious matters, as if this were some sort of transtemporal principle, derivative from some eternal law. The exact formula is that the State, under today's conditions of growth in the personal and political consciousness, is competent to do only one thing in respect of religion, that is, to recognize, guarantee, protect, and promote the religious freedom of the people. This is the full extent of the competence of the contemporary constitutional state." John Courtney Murray, "The Problem of Religious Freedom," *Theological Studies* 25, no. 4 (1964): 528.

[7] "From 1964 on, Murray attempts to ground religious freedom less on perduring factors of human nature—though the emphasis on such factors remains in the background—and more on what he calls the 'exigences' of the human person at the present stage of human history." Todd David Whitmore, "Immunity or Empowerment? John Courtney Murray and the Question of Religious Liberty," in *John Courtney Murray and the Growth of Tradition*, ed. J. Leon Hooper and Todd David Whitmore (Kansas City, MO: Sheed & Ward, 1996), 150. As the quotation in the preceding note suggests, Whitmore may be overemphasizing the degree to which Murray's attention to the enduring aspects of human nature survives the shift in his focus to developments in historical and political consciousness.

[8] Cf. Pietro Pavan, *La dichiarazione conciliare* Dignitatis humanae *a 20 anni dalla pubblicazione* (Casale Monferrato, Italy: Edizioni Piemme di Pietro Marietti, 1986), 31.

10.2. A Note on the "Juridical Approach" and the "Incompetence Argument"

Barrett Turner argues that both the juridical and the ontological arguments are necessary to the declaration. That is, although the Murray transition from the second to the third schema *supplanted* the conscience argument with the juridical argument, the "Ancel" transition from the fourth to the fifth schema *supplemented* the juridical approach with the ontological.[9]

Note that Murray's "juridical" approach or position includes the "incompetence" argument. That is, one of its features is the attempt to found the right to religious liberty on the incompetence of the state in religious matters. In this aspect, I believe that Murray is mistaken. However, his juridical approach includes other elements as well, such as the framing of the right in negative terms as an immunity, the equality of all persons, the move away from the attempt to base the right on conscience, and the adoption of the "public order" standard for limitations on religious practice.[10] With regard to these and other aspects of Murray's juridical argument or approach, I agree with Turner that they are indeed necessary or at least useful.[11] However, the incompetence argument is at the heart of Murray's juridical approach, and, as I have said above, I do not believe that it is a proper foundation for the right. Turner emphasizes the importance of the twentieth-century popes'

---

[9] Cf. Barrett Hamilton Turner, "*Dignitatis Humanae* and the Development of Moral Doctrine: Assessing Change in Catholic Social Teaching on Religious Liberty" (PhD diss., Catholic University of America, 2015), 256: The juridical argument repudiates the first two drafts of DH, but the ontological argument "completes" the juridical. See also Turner, 264–65: "[B]oth the juridical moment and the ontological moment were necessary to achieve DH without destroying the principles that animated previous teachings"; Barrett H. Turner, review of *Freedom, Truth, and Human Dignity: The Second Vatican Council's Declaration on Religious Freedom—A New Translation, Redaction History, and Interpretation of* Dignitatis Humanae, by David L. Schindler and Nicholas J. Healy Jr., *The Thomist* 80, no. 2 (Apr. 2016): 311–12: Ontological argument placed juridical elements of DH on a better foundation.

[10] See section 9.2 above, on Murray's authentic contributions to the elaboration of DH. Note, however, that these contributions do not pertain to the *foundation* of the right. Murray's signal contribution in this particular area is his critique of conscience as the proposed foundation for the right to religious liberty. See also section 9.6 above, qualifying the Council's move away from conscience as the foundation and noting the continuing relevance of conscience as a presupposition of the "ontological" argument.

[11] The adoption of the "public order" standard is useful but may not be necessary, strictly speaking. However, in light of the recognition of religious liberty as a natural right, it does seem necessary to adopt a narrower standard than the "common good." See chapter 13, which addresses this question. With regard to the other three features of the juridical approach mentioned in the main text, I believe that they are indeed necessary.

insights on political regimes (especially totalitarian ones). I do not disagree, but I believe that these teachings too, in the first place, are teachings about the requirements of human dignity and the natural rights of the person, even before they are teachings on the state and its limitations.[12] See subsections 10.2.1, 10.2.2, and 10.2.3 immediately below on the teachings of Pius XI, Pius XII, and St. John XXIII.

Thus, I must add a note of clarification. In the commentary on DH, one finds frequent identification of Murray's "juridical argument" with his attempt to found the right to religious liberty on the incompetence of the state. The incompetence aspect is indeed at the heart of the juridical argument or approach, but it is not the whole of it. Thus, I refer to Murray's "juridical argument" or "juridical approach" in the broad sense, that is, as including the incompetence argument but encompassing other aspects as well, such as the ones just mentioned above. Consequently, I will refer to Murray's "incompetence argument" in the narrower sense of that specific part of Murray's juridical approach that attempts to found the right on the state's incompetence in religious matters.

In this sense, I would agree with Turner that both the ontological argument and the juridical approach (understood broadly to include the concept of the right as an immunity, etc.) were necessary in the final formulation of the declaration. However, if the juridical approach is understood narrowly as more or less identical with the incompetence argument, then I would not agree that it is necessary.[13] On the contrary, while preserving several features of the juridical approach (in the broad sense), the Council drastically restricted the reach of the incompetence argument and eliminated it as a foundation for the right (cf. DH, §3e).

10.2.1. Pope Pius XI (1922–1939)

The pronouncements of Popes Pius XI and Pius XII against totalitarianism are indeed crucial. However, the key reason for the condemnation of these regimes is not that they act in fields in which they are incompetent, although

---

[12] Pope Pius XI, Encyclical *Non Abbiamo Bisogno* (June 29, 1931) is a good example. There, Pope Pius XI discusses the violation of the rights of education and association (see §§10–11, 39–41) before he turns to the question of the Italian fascist political regime itself (see §44) and the competence of the state generally (see §§45, 49, 72). See the discussion in subsection 10.2.1 below.

[13] Professor Turner was kind enough to exchange messages with me on this subject, and our correspondence (email messages dated Feb. 4 and 7, 2021, and April 22 and 28, 2023) suggests to me that our understandings on this point are similar.

10.2. A Note on the "Juridical Approach" and the "Incompetence Argument"

they do indeed do this, and although this is in fact unjust. The popes do sometimes speak of the proper competence of the state, but their emphasis is on these regimes' violations of natural rights and the rights of the Church.

Pius XI wrote three great encyclicals against totalitarianism in the 1930s: *Non Abbiamo Bisogno* (1931) against measures taken by the Italian fascist government, *Mit Brennender Sorge* (1937) against German National Socialism, and *Divini Redemptoris* (1937) against Soviet communism. In all of these documents, the Pope's criticism of the regime centers around the violation of natural rights and the rights of the Church. *Non Abbiamo Bisogno* concerns the Italian fascist government's suppression of the association known as Catholic Action. This measure, the Pope says, violates the natural right of association and the natural rights of the family. *Mit Brennender Sorge* concerns the German Reich's violation of its Concordat with the Holy See, especially in connection with confessional schools and Catholic education. It also condemns the Reich's idolatry of race and its encroachments on religious freedom. *Divini Redemptoris* exposes Soviet communism's wholesale denial of individual rights and its subordination of the individual entirely to the collective.

Although he emphasizes the violation of natural rights, Pius XI also speaks of the relative competencies of the Church and the civil authority. In the face of the Reich's idolatry of race and "the seduction of a national German Church," Pius says, only the universal Church is "qualified and competent" for a universal evangelical mission.[14] *Non Abbiamo Bisogno* addresses state competence most directly. Although condemning the Italian government's violations of the rights of education and association, it acknowledges that the state has rights and duties in the field of education.

> Such rights and duties are unchallengeable as long as they remain within the limits of the State's proper competency, a competence which in its turn is clearly indicated and determined by the role of the State, a role which, though certainly not only bodily and material, is by its very nature limited to the natural, the terrestrial and the temporal.[15]

The drafts of DH for which Murray was responsible (the third and fourth ones) cited this very passage in support of the principle of governmental incompetence in religious matters. However, just as the incompetence

---

[14] Pius XI, Encyclical *Mit Brennender Sorge* (Mar. 14, 1937), §22 [AAS 29 (1937): 156].
[15] Pius XI, Encyclical *Non Abbiamo Bisogno* (June 29, 1931), §45 [AAS 23 (1931): 303].

argument declined almost to the vanishing point in the successive drafts, so did the citation to this passage fall away. In the absence of a prominent argument from state incompetence, such a citation was unnecessary.

In addition, however, it is possible that a citation to this passage could have given a false impression. Although it is indeed true that the Church insists on a distinction between the two realms, the boundary between them is more "porous" than Murray and the incompetence argument suggest. (See section 4.3 above on Gelasian dualism.) One could view Murray's citation to this passage as a kind of "proof-texting" that neglects the fuller view of the matter. The fuller view is that expressed by Pope Leo XIII in *Immortale Dei*, namely, that although these two realms are distinct, there is some overlap between them.[16] The Church herself confers many temporal benefits. In addition, although the realm of the state is the temporal one, its citizen is a transcendent being, so even his temporal good is more than purely temporal.[17]

Pius XI addresses both the violation of natural rights and the government's overstepping of its competence. However, the reason for the encyclical is the violation of rights. This is the subject of nearly the entire document, and the violation of the right to association is mentioned repeatedly.[18] Pius also refers to violations of the natural rights of the family,[19] as well as to the rights of "souls," and the rights of the Church.[20]

His discussion of state competence is indeed important, but it is connected to the overarching theme of the violation of natural rights. That is, if a government violates the natural rights of citizens or residents, then it follows *ipso facto* that that regime has exceeded its competence.

Is this the only way that a government can exceed its proper competence? No. However, it is the most important one. Note the emphasis on natural rights in all three of Pius's great encyclicals against totalitarianism. Recall also the teaching of Leo XIII. His encyclical *Diuturnum Illud*

---

[16] See the discussion in the next subsection, 10.2.2, of Pius XII's teaching on unity between the two realms.

[17] See also Leo XIII, Encyclical *Diuturnum Illud* (June 29, 1881), §26: Things of a civil nature are under the power of the ruler, but where the decision belongs to both the sacred and the secular powers, there should be harmony between the two [ASS 14 (1881): 13]; Pope Gregory XVI, Encyclical *Singulari Nos* (June 25, 1834), §3 [*Acta Gregorii XVI*, vol. 1 (Rome 1901): 433–34]; Pius XI, *Divini Illius Magistri* (Dec. 32, 1929), §51: Regarding the two powers, "each has its own fixed boundaries" and yet "it may happen that the same matter, though from a different point of view, may come under the competence and jurisdiction of each of them" [AAS 22 (1930): 65].

[18] See especially *Non Abbiamo Bisogno*, §§5, 10–11, 22 [AAS 23 (1931): 287, 288–89, 294].

[19] Cf. *Non Abbiamo Bisogno*, §§44, 52 [AAS 23 (1931): 302, 305].

[20] Cf. *Non Abbiamo Bisogno*, §§39–41, 44 [AAS 301–2].

10.2. A Note on the "Juridical Approach" and the "Incompetence Argument"

addresses the civil power, and he does indeed place natural rights in the first place. A citizen is justified in disobeying civil authority, he says, only when that authority requires something that is "openly repugnant to the natural or the divine law."[21] The reason is clear: "[I]f the will of rulers is opposed to the will and the laws of God, they themselves exceed the bounds of their own power and pervert justice; nor can their authority then be valid, which, when there is no justice, is null."[22]

When else might the civil government exceed its competence? One example is when the government enacts legislation in a realm in which it has no authority under positive law. For example, the U.S. Constitution empowers Congress to regulate "interstate commerce," that is, commerce occurring within the U.S. but crossing borders between any of the fifty individual U.S. states. This authority does not extend to "*intra*state" commerce, namely, commerce taking place wholly within one of the several states.

However, suppose that the federal government limits the amount of wheat that a farmer may grow, even for his own use, on the grounds that it *impacts* commerce in other states. This scenario was the subject of a U.S. Supreme Court case concerning President Franklin Roosevelt's New Deal legislation.[23] Is such a measure a legitimate attempt by Congress to solve a national emergency, or is it rather a usurpation of the power of the several states on the pretext of regulating interstate commerce? Principles of Catholic teaching, such as subsidiarity and the government's proper competence, are relevant to this problem. However, the issue falls within an area in which the magisterium would not involve itself beyond the level of offering guiding principles. One reason is that resolution of the issue will require expertise in civil law, constitutional law, and perhaps political science, and even agriculture. In addition, the question might be one over which people of good faith legitimately could disagree. Indeed, even the experts in law and political science may disagree among themselves.

Note the wisdom in the popes' approach. They teach on what the proper

---

[21] *Diuturnum Illud*, §15 [ASS 14 (1881): 8].

[22] *Diuturnum Illud*, §15 [ASS 14 (1881): 8].

[23] This example is from the U.S. Supreme Court case, *Wickard v. Filburn*, 317 U.S. 111 (1942). An Ohio farmer grew more wheat than government quotas in President Franklin Roosevelt's New Deal administration allowed. When the farmer was penalized, he objected because the excess wheat was for his own use. As a result of the fact that it was unrelated to commerce, the farmer argued that the federal government had no right to regulate it. The U.S. Supreme Court disagreed. In a widely-criticized decision, it upheld the legislation on the ground that the farmer's activity had a *substantial effect* on commerce in other states (that is, it had an impact on interstate commerce, because by growing his own wheat, the farmer was said to reduce demand for wheat from neighboring states).

competence of the state is, but their own practice is to limit their pronouncements to the most serious and certain overreaches, namely, those involving violations of natural rights or the rights of the Church. This points to a key difficulty with Murray's approach. With good reason, his incompetence argument is included in an approach that is called "juridical" or "constitutional." As discussed below, however, Murray largely detaches his approach from natural law, preferring to tie it instead to developments in historical and political consciousness. (See section 11.2 below.)

The problem is that Murray places political science in the first position. His notion of state incompetence is based on what he believes are sound principles of political science. Thus, his theory seems to require a full-fledged outline of the competencies of the sacred and temporal realms. (See subsection 10.3.4.2 below, which considers whether Murray in fact provides this outline.) Even with such an outline, however, he still would be in the problematic position of making political science the driver of the Church's teaching on religious liberty.

By contrast, placing natural rights in the first position solves or ameliorates these problems. State competence or incompetence remains relevant, but its significance is secondary. It is not political science's inquiry into state competence or incompetence that founds the right. Rather, the state's incompetence to violate the right flows as a consequence from the basis of the right in human dignity, that is, from the status of the right as a natural right. When the action under consideration is the violation of a natural right, the state necessarily is incompetent to act.

This is not the full extent of the state's incompetence, but it is the clearest and most crucial aspect. It is the one that popes have emphasized, and it is the only one that is necessary to a discussion of the foundation of the Vatican II teaching on religious liberty.

10.2.2. Pope Pius XII (1939–1958)

Pope Pius XII's pronouncements on totalitarianism are complementary to those of Pius XI. This is unsurprising, given that he served as Pius XI's Secretary of State. Like his predecessor, Pius XII speaks repeatedly of the need for limitations on governmental power and of the obligation of all political regimes to adhere to the natural law.

Speaking toward the end of World War II, Pius XII examines specific governmental structures in more detail than his predecessor had. In his famous 1944 Christmas message, he discusses democracy, referring specifically to the three branches of government,[24] and he identifies the Legislative Assembly as the regime's center of gravity.[25] He even notes that some consider the democratic form of government to be "a postulate of nature imposed by reason itself."[26]

His warmth of disposition toward democracy is connected closely with the characteristic of modern democracy as placing limitations on state power. He warns repeatedly against the danger of "absolutism," and he is fully aware that even democracy is not necessarily immune to it. Moreover, avoiding absolutism depends on adhering to the natural law:

> A sound democracy, based on the immutable principles of the natural law and revealed truth, will resolutely turn its back on such corruption as gives to the state legislature an unchecked and unlimited power, and moreover, makes of the democratic regime, notwithstanding an outward show to the contrary, purely and simply a form of absolutism.[27]

The 1944 Christmas address provides one of Pius XII's most extensive treatments of principles of democratic government. However, the need for civil governments to adhere to the natural law is one of the constant themes throughout his pontificate especially in discussing the post-War rebuilding: "[M]an has certain liberties independent of the State."[28] The positive law, he says, must stay within its "natural competence," that is, it must conform to, or at least not oppose, "the absolute order set up by the Creator and placed in a new light by the revelation of the Gospel."[29] Indeed, the state has no authority to depart from the natural law. "The precise, bedrock, rules that govern society cannot be prejudiced by the intervention of human agency. They can be denied, overlooked, despised, transgressed, but they can never be overthrown with legal validity."[30] Indeed, the first duty of the state is to

---

[24] Cf. Pius XII, Christmas Radio Message (Dec. 24, 1944), §41 [AAS 37 (1945): 15].
[25] Pius XII, Christmas Message (1944), §43 [AAS 37 (1945): 16].
[26] Pius XII, Christmas Message (1944), §19 [AAS 37 (1945): 13].
[27] Pius XII, Christmas Message (1944), §47 [AAS 37 (1945): 17].
[28] Pius XII, Discourse, "Rome, Which Welcomes You," to a U.S. Parliamentary Commission (Dec. 4, 1949), not in AAS but in *L'Osservatore Romano* (Dec. 5–6, 1949).
[29] Pius XII, Christmas Message (1944), §49 [AAS 37 (1945): 17].
[30] Pius XII, Christmas Radio Message (Dec. 24, 1942) [AAS 35 (1943): 13]. See also Pius XII, Encyclical *Summi Pontificatus* [for the feast of Christ the King] (Oct. 20, 1939): Man and the family should not be considered in terms of national power; they are by nature anterior to the state and are given rights by the Creator [AAS 31 (1939): 552].

safeguard these rights.[31] "From the juridic order, as willed by God, flows man's inalienable right to juridical security, and by this very fact to a definite sphere of rights, immune from all arbitrary attack."[32]

Pius XII sometimes speaks of the competencies of the two realms, but his sense in doing so is quite different from Murray's hard and fast separationism. Pius affirms the distinction between the realms.[33] However, he calls for close collaboration between them. Indeed, he says, such collaboration is normal in principle, and in a Catholic country, the Church considers the ideal to be unanimity of action between her and the state.[34] In short, the best relationship between the two realms is their being "distinct" but "united."[35] In addition, he says that the distinction between the two realms by no means excludes the Church from public life.[36]

---

[31] Cf. Pius XII, Radio Message to the Whole World "La Solennità della Pentecoste" (June 1, 1941), safeguarding the intangible domain of the rights of the human person must be the essential role of every public power [AAS 33 (1941): 200]. See also Pius XII, Allocution "This Audience" to American Journalists (Jan. 23, 1950): "Then the individual man is recognized by all in his true stature as image of God gifted with inherent rights which no merely human power may violate; when the State is recognized in its true nature as divinely instituted to protect and defend the citizens, not to enslave them" (not in AAS, but in *L'Osservatore Romano* [Jan. 23-24, 1950]).

[32] Pius XII, Christmas Message (1942) [AAS 35 (1943): 21]. This quotation may give the impression that rights arise from state incompetence in religious matters (the Murray thesis). That is, Pius XII begins with the juridic order and then seems to derive a sphere of rights from it. However, in fact, Pius's approach is much different than Murray's. When Murray speaks of the political order, he means the order resulting from modern developments in human consciousness and political theory. Pius, however, discusses the juridic order only in reference to natural law, that is, the juridic order "as willed by God." In fact, for Pius, both ends of the *equation* depend on natural law: the role of the temporal power and the rights of individuals that government is bound to protect. By contrast, for Murray, neither side is especially concerned with natural law. He does not refer to natural law at all in discussing the obligations of the state, and, in discussing the right to religious liberty, he refers to it only occasionally, and even then, only in his own somewhat impoverished sense that is quite far removed from the traditional understanding. (On Murray's treatment of natural law, see section 11.2 below.)

[33] Cf. Pope Pius XII, Discourse *Vous avez voulu* to the Tenth International Conference of Historical Sciences (Rome, Sept. 7, 1955) [AAS 47 (1955): 677].

[34] Cf. Pius XII, *Vous avez voulu* [AAS 47 (1955): 679].

[35] Pope Pius XII, Discorso *Ai marchigiani residenti in Roma* (Mar. 23, 1958): "[la] tradizione della Chiesa [è] il continuo sforzo per tenere distinti, ma pure, sempre secondo I retti principi, uniti I due poteri" [AAS 50 (1958): 220]. See also Pius XII, Discourse "With the Special Affection" to Irish Prime Minister Eamon de Valera (Oct. 4, 1957) (praising Irish constitution for embodying "mutual trust between the authorities of Church and State, independent each in its own sphere, but as it were allied for the common welfare in accordance with the principles of Catholic faith and doctrine") [AAS 49 (1957): 953].

[36] Cf. Pius XII, Radio Message "La Famiglia" (Mar. 23, 1952): "The popes have not failed

10.2. A Note on the "Juridical Approach" and the "Incompetence Argument"

A notable feature of Pius XII's pronouncements at and after the end of the war is his assertion that the Church's struggles for her own freedom "were at the same time struggles for man's true liberty."[37] Similarly, in a 1947 message to U.S. President Harry Truman, the Pope recalls that the Church "has championed the individual against despotic rule, the labouring-man against oppression, Religion against persecution."[38]

These claims are indeed justified, and they show why the "Render to Caesar" doctrine has important ramifications for human freedom, despite the problematic attempt by some commentators[39] to draw a straight line from this passage, first, to state incompetence in religious matters and, second, to religious liberty.[40] Stated differently, although "Render to Caesar" is indeed

---

to insist on the principle that the order willed by God embraces all of life, not excluding public life in all its manifestations, persuaded that in this there is no restriction of true human liberty, nor any interference in the competence of the State, but an assurance against errors and abuses, against which Christian morals, if rightly applied, may protect" [AAS 44 (1952): 277]. The translation is mine.

[37] Pius XII, Christmas Message (1944), §83 [AAS 37 (1945): 22].

[38] Pius XII, Chirograph "We Have Just," in response to President Harry Truman (Aug. 26, 1947) [AAS 39 (1947): 380–82].

[39] Although he does not discuss the matter at length, Pierre Benoit believes that "Render to Caesar" should have been the basis for resolution of the religious liberty question. Cf. Pierre Benoit, "La droit à la liberté religieuse à la lumière de la Révélation," *Unam Sanctam* 60 (1967): 210, asserting that "Render to Caesar" contains the principle of solution for the whole problem of religious liberty. Valuet argues that the "Render to Caesar" principle establishes the distinction between the two powers until the end of time, and thus the distinction of their juridic competence. "Mt 22,21 fonde jusqu'à la fin du monde la doctrine de la *distinction* des deux pouvoirs, et donc de la différence de leur *compétence juridique*. Cette incompétence juridique de l'État lui interdit d'user de son pouvoir coercitif en matière religieuse." Basile Valuet, *La liberté religieuse et la tradition catholique. Un cas de développement doctrinal homogène dans le magistère authentique*, 3rd rev. ed. (Barroux: Éditions Sainte-Madeleine, 2011), vol. IB, 814n3665 [= Basile Valuet, *Le droit à la liberté religieuse dans la Tradition de l'Eglise. Un cas de développement doctrinal homogène par le magistère authentique*, 2nd rev. ed. (Barroux: Éditions Sainte-Madeleine, 2011), 534n3042], citing René Coste, *Théologie de la liberté religieuse. Liberté de conscience, liberté de religion* (Gembloux: Duculot, 1969), 75–76.

[40] David L. Schindler has identified the problem of equating the Church-state distinction with the sacred-secular distinction, and also with overemphasizing the autonomy of the two orders. Cf. "Religious Freedom, Truth, and American Liberalism," 730–31, responding to Leon Hooper's summary of Murray's conciliar argument as being based largely on Gelasian dualism. "What seems to be critical in Hooper's formulation here, is (a) his equating of the state-church distinction with the secular-sacred distinction, simultaneous with (b) his sense of the autonomy of these two orders relative to each other. . . . The easy manner in which these assertions are made seems to me extraordinary in light of the great debates within twentieth-century Catholicism. In what sense is the end of creation different from

relevant to the competence of the civil authority, it is problematic to identify the passage chiefly with this principle.

Reading this famous passage primarily or exclusively as a delimitation of competencies is problematic because so much of Church life and history seems characterized by heedlessness of this delineation of competencies. One thinks of Constantine's convoking of the Council of Nicaea and of the papal veto held by civil rulers even into the beginning of the twentieth century. Also, as Church historian Joseph Lecler says, even where Early Church leaders did insist on this delineation, this insistence often was opportunistic. (See subsection 10.3.5.2 below.) That is, they objected to secular interference in the religious realm that harmed Catholic interests, but they often ignored such intervention when it seemed to serve those interests.

This "line-drawing" also is problematic because, although the Church has had the "Render to Caesar" doctrine from the very beginning, it took her nearly two millennia to affirm a right to religious liberty. As a result, viewed from this optic, critics often charge the Church with arriving quite belatedly to the cause.[41] Moreover, even once this right is on the horizon, the attempt to base it on state incompetence remains problematic. See subsections 10.3.4.2 and 10.3.5.1 below, on the relative competencies of the two realms and on areas that continue to give rise to actual or potential conflicts between the two powers.

However, although this line-drawing presents difficulties, it is not entirely false. For core functions belonging exclusively to either the temporal realm or the religious realm, one indeed can distinguish the realms and recognize a sphere of authority protected from state interference. However, as discussed below, this corresponds most clearly to the civil authority's incompetence in *ecclesiastical* matters, rather than the broader realm of all *religious* matters. State incompetence in ecclesiastical matters, though, does not necessarily lead to recognition of the right to religious liberty (see section 10.3.1).

Then, in what sense is Pius XII correct in asserting that the Church's historical struggle for her own rights was, at the same time, a struggle for man's rights? The reason is that, notwithstanding the difficulties in identifying

---

the end of redemption: are there (simply) two ends?" Schindler, 730–31. On the question of equating these distinctions, see also José Tomás Martín de Agar, "Derecho y relaciones iglesia—sociedad civil," *Ius Ecclesiae* 32, no. 1 (2020): 29: "Asimismo una es la distinción entre Dios y César . . . y otro entre Iglesia y Estado: ni siempre ni todo lo que es de Dios, es de la Iglesia; en el tiempo han variado la relevancia y el modo de enfocar estas dualidades."

[41] Cf. Henri Fesquet, *The Drama of Vatican II* (New York: Random House, 1967), 335: "Considerably later than the secular forces for liberty, Vatican II has come to the defense of the cause of man, irrespective of belief, in the wake of a unique encyclical, *Pacem in Terris*."

10.2. A Note on the "Juridical Approach" and the "Incompetence Argument"

the specific competencies of both realms, what "Render to Caesar" does immediately establish in history is the presence on earth of another authority alongside the civil authority. Stated differently, what it establishes is the first limitation on state power.

This limitation always has been present in the Christian era, even in times when, to modern eyes, one realm has involved itself excessively in objects proper to the other. This is not to say that all of the Church's pastors have judged wisely in their relations with the civil authorities. However, it at least has meant that ever since "Render to Caesar," a power has been present in the world to deny that the state possesses absolute authority. This basic limitation is the beginning of political freedom.[42]

10.2.3. Pope St. John XXIII (1958–1963)

Pope St. John XXIII maintains the same interest that his two immediate predecessors show in the forms of government, but he makes it even clearer than they did that the question of the person is prior to the question of political structures. Recall that Murray places the political question first:

---

[42] Cf. Joseph Ratzinger, *Church, Ecumenism and Politics: New Essays in Ecclesiology* (New York: Crossroad, 1988), 147–58; see also Ratzinger, 161: Separation of the sacred from the secular is the origin of the idea of freedom in the West. As pope, Ratzinger said in his 2005 Christmas message to the Roman Curia that in DH, Vatican II adopted "an essential principle of the modern State" and also "recovered the deepest patrimony of the Church." Citing the "Render to Caesar" passage, Matthew 22:21, he said that the Council's action was "in full harmony with the teaching of Jesus himself." Commentators disagree, however, on what the "essential principle" is that the Council adopted. As a result of the fact that Pope Benedict goes on to discuss the Church's rejection of the Roman state religion, Martin Rhonheimer concludes that the principle is the rejection of state establishment of religion. Cf. Rhonheimer, "Benedict XVI's 'Hermeneutic of Reform' and Religious Freedom," *Nova et Vetera* (English ed.) 9, no. 4 (2011): 1031. David L. Schindler, however, challenges this reading (see section 4.7 above) and argues that "the essential element of modernity embraced by the Church consists in modernity's growing awareness of the subjectivity or interiority of the human person, coincident with the growing awareness in the realm of modern politics with respect to the right of religious freedom." Schindler, "Freedom, Truth, and Human Dignity," in *Freedom, Truth, and Human Dignity: The Second Vatican Council's Declaration on Religious Freedom—A New Translation, Redaction History, and Interpretation of Dignitatis Humanae*, ed. David L. Schindler and Nicholas J. Healy (Grand Rapids, MI / Cambridge, UK: William B. Eerdmans Publishing Company, 2015), 112. For my own part, I would suggest another possibility. The "essential principle" could be simply the concept of limited government. This is consistent with everything that Benedict says. A bedrock principle of modern constitutional theory is the limitation of government power, and "Render to Caesar" stands for the entirely compatible idea of the presence in the world of another authority in addition to the secular power.

as a result of the state's incompetence in religious matters, man has a right to religious freedom. (See subsection 10.2.1 above.) That is, the right arises more or less *by default*. Murray does not refer to the intrinsic value of religion as having any juridical relevance but simply to man's freedom in the realm that the state is excluded from entering. (See subsection 10.4.3 below.) By contrast, even at the high points of their interest in political regimes, the popes put the person first. The human person is the starting point, and once one understands his nature and his rights, only then can one proceed to the question of the state's obligations and its proper structure.

The great anti-totalitarian encyclicals of Pius XI make this clear. *Non Abbiamo Bisogno* perhaps is the clearest example. (See subsection 10.2.1 above.) This principle is present in Pius XII's pronouncements as well. It may not be quite as clear as it is in the encyclicals of Pius XI, but it is apparent from his strong emphasis on natural law. St. John XXIII, however, states the principle outright. That is, this principle (the priority of the human person) that we find in his predecessors by looking primarily to the emphasis and ordering of their pronouncements (that is, by implication, albeit *strong* implication) is one that John voices *directly* in his landmark encyclical *Pacem in Terris*.

> Any human society, if it is to be well-ordered and productive, must lay down as a foundation this principle, namely, that every human being is a person, that is, his nature is endowed with intelligence and free will. Indeed, precisely because he is a person he has rights and obligations flowing directly and simultaneously from his very nature. And as these rights and obligations are universal and inviolable so they cannot in any way be surrendered.[43]

John does not discuss totalitarianism directly, but he undoubtedly is building on his predecessors' pronouncements on this subject. *Pacem in Terris* cites relatively few sources, but it includes five citations to Pius XI's *Mit Brennender Sorge* and *Divini Redemptoris*, and fourteen citations to Pius XII's 1942 and 1944 Christmas messages.

Just as Pius XII is somewhat more specific about political structures than Pius XI, so John is more specific than Pius XII. With reference to constitutional democracy, Pius XII notes that some consider this form of government "a postulate of nature imposed by reason itself." (See subsection

---

[43] Pope John XXIII, Encyclical *Pacem in Terris* (Apr. 11, 1963), §9 [AAS 55 (1963): 259]. Translation from the NCWC, published by the Daughters of St. Paul.

10.2. A Note on the "Juridical Approach" and the "Incompetence Argument"

10.2.2 above.) Like Pius, John refers expressly to the three branches of government. Indeed, he goes further by suggesting that this division of powers "is in keeping with the innate demands of human nature" (PT, §68).

Another feature of constitutional democracy that John endorses is the enumeration of rights in a charter and its incorporation in the nation's constitution (cf. PT, §75). He calls for this measure after he first has provided an extensive discussion of the fundamental rights of the person (cf. PT, §§11–27). Moreover, he describes the safeguarding of the inviolable rights of the person as the chief duty of government (PT, §60).

Despite this adoption of some of the principles of constitutional democracy, John stops short of embracing this form as a universal model. "It is impossible," he says, "to determine, in all cases, what is the most suitable form of government, or how civil authorities can most effectively fulfill their respective functions" (PT, §67). Like Pius XII, John takes a lively interest in governmental structures, but these always are secondary to the question of the human person. Indeed, one may describe John's foundational principle simply as the *centrality of the person*.[44]

Note that with this sharper focus on the person and his natural rights, the need to discuss the competency of the state practically disappears, at least from the standpoint of rights theory. John does discuss the state's competency, but he never does so in the context of basing religious liberty—or any other natural right—on it. Murray was a great admirer of *Pacem in Terris*, but he seems to have overlooked this feature of the encyclical. Where John mentions competency outright, his references are unremarkable. He says simply that constitutions should describe the competence of public officials and that in relations with the government, individuals should follow the directives of civil authorities acting within their competence.[45] In his entire discussion enumerating the rights of the human person, John never refers to the competence of the state (cf. PT, §§11–27). This is inconvenient for Murray's theory, but the reason for it is clear. As discussed both above (in sections 10.1 and subsection 10.3.5.1) and below (in sections 10.5 and 11.4), a theory basing religious liberty in the nature of the human person largely obviates the need for a discussion of state competency. The competence of the state remains relevant, but only as a *consequence* of the right's foundation

---

[44] José T. Martín de Agar, "Ecclesia y Polis," *Ius Canonicum* (2008): 412: "[la] perspectiva que nace con la *Pacem in terris* y se desarrolla a partir del Concilio . . . se puede definir como *centralidad de la persona*"; Martín de Agar, "Derecho y relaciones iglesia—sociedad civil," 45–46 (similar).

[45] Cf. PT, §53 (on civil authorities acting within their competence); PT, §76 (on specifying the competence of public officials in the constitution).

in human nature. The existence of a natural right *necessarily* implies the incompetence of the state to violate it. "[I]f any government does not acknowledge the rights of man or violates them, it not only fails in its duty, but its orders completely lack juridical force" (PT, §61).

Elsewhere, *Pacem in Terris* contains brief references that are relevant to the state's competence, but that do not mention competency outright. These passages are more interesting than the ones that mention competency by name. What they suggest is that while John affirms the principle of Gelasian dualism that distinguishes clearly between the temporal and the religious realms, his idea is far from the strictly and starkly separationist view exemplified by Jefferson and adopted by Murray.[46] Thus, in promoting the common good, civil authorities are to do so "by ways and means that are proper to them." However, John says, "The common good touches the whole man," and as a result, civil authorities should respect the hierarchy of values and "should promote simultaneously both the material and the spiritual welfare of the citizens" (PT, §57).[47]

10.3. The Practical Problems with the "Incompetence Argument"

As mentioned above (at the beginning of this chapter), the incompetence argument has enormous appeal. Once one accepts the government's incompetence in religious matters, it becomes clear why religious liberty follows as a consequence. That is, *by default* the person is left free in the religious realm, as a function of the government's disqualification from acting in it.

Given this appeal of the incompetence argument, why did the Council not maintain it? Could the fathers not have preserved state incompetence as an alternate (and perhaps subordinate) foundation for the right?

It is clear that they did not do so. They state the right's foundation in human dignity, and to the extent that they preserve even a narrow slice of the incompetence argument, they do so not as the foundation (or even an

---

[46] On the strictly separationist conception of the relation between the two realms (primarily as conceived by Murray, but also by others), see sections 4.3 and 4.4 and subsection 9.5.1 above, and subsections 10.3.5.1 and 10.3.4.2 below.

[47] John does call for civil authorities to have a clear idea of the nature and scope of their duties, but at the same time, he acknowledges that relations with citizens and among them "cannot be regulated by inflexible legal provisions" (cf. PT, §72). As far as I am aware, the only remaining passage of the encyclical that is relevant to state competence is one concerning the establishment of an international authority. There, the pontiff simply says that such a step does not limit the action of the state (cf. PT, §141).

alternate or subordinate foundation) but merely as a "further consideration" (DH, §3e).

The reason seems to be that despite the argument's obvious appeal and high-profile support, it is inescapably problematic. It presents both practical and doctrinal difficulties. This section (10.3) addresses the practical problems, and the following one (10.4) discusses the doctrinal ones, though there is some overlap between the two categories.

10.3.1. Ambiguity about Incompetence

In the scholarship on the declaration, it is common to encounter references to the incompetence of the state. However, even the proponents of this argument acknowledge that there is surprisingly little agreement about precisely what this term means.[48] As a threshold matter, the meaning of the word *incompetence* itself is *ambiguous*.[49]

One possible meaning of incompetence is that the state might be ill-suited or ill-equipped to judge a certain issue. That is, the state may lack the necessary knowledge or expertise to judge a certain matter or type of matter (or at least to do so adequately or reliably). In this sense, incompetence equates to a *lack of ability* on the part of the state to pronounce on a specific question or class of questions.

However, incompetence also may mean that the state lacks the authority—or at least the *legitimate* authority—to act in a certain realm or with regard to a particular subject. Murray's writings emphasize the modern democracies' withdrawal of authority from the state to act in the religious realm. He usually describes this development as a result of increased historical or political consciousness. Incompetence in this sense equates to a *lack of authority*.

Needless to say, these two possible meanings—*lack of ability* and *lack of authority*—are not mutually exclusive.[50] In fact, a conviction that civil authorities have judged poorly in an area in the past might give rise to a

---

[48] Cf. A. F. Carrillo de Albornoz, *The Basis of Religious Liberty* (Guildford and London: World Council of Churches, 1963), 76 (difficulty of identifying exact boundaries on limitations of state incompetence).

[49] See section 10.1.

[50] By contrast with Murray and others discussed here, an author who *does* distinguish these two possible meanings of incompetence is Martín de Agar. He refers to the first type—inability or lack of expertise—as *doctrinal* incompetence, and he refers to the second—lack of authority—as *juridical* incompetence (Martín de Agar, "Derecho y relaciones iglesia—sociedad civil," 52).

decision in the present to withhold power from the public authority over a certain matter or realm.[51] The notion of state incompetence contained in the third and fourth drafts of the declaration (for which Murray had primary responsibility) arguably included both of these meanings, but it seems clear that it emphasized the second, namely, lack of authority.[52]

10.3.2. A Variety of Terms

In addition, there is great variety even in the *naming* of the argument based on *state incompetence*! The most common formulation speaks of incompetence in *religious matters*.[53] However, some scholars refer to incompetence in *spiritual matters*[54] or *ecclesiastical matters*.[55] Other formulations are incompe-

---

[51] James Madison in particular hoped that the U.S. Constitution's prohibition on Congress establishing a national religion would spare America the bloodshed of the sixteenth- and seventeenth-century wars of religion in Europe. "Torrents of blood have been spilt in the old world, by vain attempts of the secular arm to extinguish Religious discord, by proscribing all differences in Religious opinions." James Madison, *Memorial and Remonstrance Against Religious Assessments* (1785), 11, reprinted in *The Mind of the Founder: Sources of the Political Thought of James Madison*, rev. ed., ed. Marvin Meyers (Hanover: University Press of New England, 1981), 11. Madison's famous *Memorial and Remonstrance* quoted here was directed against a proposed law in the state of Virginia that would have supported religious denominations in a non-discriminatory way. Thus, although the U.S. Constitution constrained only the *national* government with regard to religious establishment, Madison opposed religious assessments by the governments of the several *states* as well.

[52] Some commentators cite the Scriptural principle "Render to Caesar" as the basis for state incompetence. As discussed in subsection 10.2., however, although this principle is relevant to the question of state competence or incompetence, it is problematic to identify it chiefly with this question.

[53] Cf. Murray, "Problem of Religious Freedom," 527, 558; A. F. Carrillo de Albornoz, "Roman Catholicism and Religious Liberty," *Ecumenical Review* 11, no. 4 (July 1959): 420: "[T]he state is by no means competent to interfere in religious matters"; Richard J. Regan, *Conflict and Consensus: Religious Freedom and the Second Vatican Council* (New York/London: Macmillan/Collier-Macmillan Ltd., 1967), 182–83: The declaration "states clearly the incompetence of the state in matters of religion"; Jérôme Hamer and Clemente Riva, *La libertà religiosa nel Vaticano II* (Torino, Italy: Elle di Ci, 1966), 187: Public powers are incompetent in religious matters. See also Valuet, LRTC, 837, asserting that Paul VI, like the Council, locates the internal foundation of religious liberty in the dignity of man in his orientation toward God, and its external foundation in the religious incompetence of the state ("*l'incompétence religieuse de l'État*").

[54] Cf. Carrillo de Albornoz, "Roman Catholicism and Religious Liberty," 33: "[I]ncompetence to interfere in spiritual matters."

[55] Valuet, LRTE, 104: Early church fathers were nearly unanimous "in proclaiming the juridic incompetence of the state in ecclesiastical matters" (*à proclaimer l'incompétence de l'État en matière ecclésiastique*).

10.3. The Practical Problems with the "Incompetence Argument"

tence in the *supernatural domain*[56] or in *religious options*.[57] Also, as discussed elsewhere (section 9.5.1), some speak of the state's incompetence to make *judgments of truth in religious matters*.[58]

Needless to say, these variations are by no means equivalent. The principle that the public power is incompetent in *spiritual* matters might not necessarily mean that it is incompetent in all *religious* matters. For example, the impact of zoning laws on churches could be considered *religious* matters, but it is less obvious that they also would qualify as *spiritual* matters.[59] The broadest formulation of the idea seems to be the assertion of incompetence in *religious matters*, while the assertion of incompetence in *ecclesiastical matters* is considerably narrower.

As the category grows broader, the difficulties increase. The most manageable version of the incompetence argument is the one pertaining to *ecclesiastical matters*. The popes and Curial offices sometimes have made assertions of governmental incompetence in this area, and they have provided lists indicating a clear idea of the boundary between legitimate and illegitimate governmental action. Pope Gregory XVI issued such a list in a nineteenth-century encyclical addressed to the clergy of Switzerland, in the wake of proposals to encroach on the Church's own distinctive functions:

---

[56] Valuet, LRTE, 406: State "incompetent in the supernatural domain" (*incompetent dans le domaine surnaturel*).

[57] Pietro A. D'Avack, "La Chiesa e lo Stato nella nuova impostazione conciliare," in *Il Diritto ecclesiastico e rassegna di diritto matrimoniale* (Milano, Italy: Giuffrè, 1971), 32: "[A]bsolute incompetence of the State in religious options and professions and acts of faith" (*l'assoluta incompetenza dello Stato per le opzioni religiose e per le professioni e atti fideistici*).

[58] Hamer/Riva, 179: Application of the right to all "implicitly insinuates also the incompetence of the public powers in judgments of value, of truth or not in religious matters" (*insinuando implicitamente anche qui l'incompetenza dei poteri pubblici nei giudizi di valore, di verità o meno in materia religiosa*); Hamer/ Riva, 208–9 (similar); D'Avack, "La Chiesa e lo Stato nella nuova impostazione conciliare," 33: State acts *ultra vires* if it presumes to judge which is the true religion ("*Lo Stato perciò agirebbe* ultra vires, *e cioè al di fuori della sua sfera di competenza e al di là dei compiti propri, se dovesse preoccuparsi di giudicare quale sia la religione vera e quale quella falsa*").

[59] Cf. Franco Biffi, "Le droit à la liberté religieuse et le rôle des pouvoirs politics selon le Concilie Vatican II," in *I diritti fondamentali della persona umana e la libertà religiosa: Atti del V Colloquio Giuridico, 8–10 marzo 1984* (Vatican City: Libreria Editrice Vaticana, 1985), 742–43: "Les pouvoirs civils dépasseraient leur compétence s'ils prétendaient déterminer le contenu de la croyance ou les modalités du culte: cela ne signifie pas qu'ils puissent se désintéresser des moyens (ex. Le terrain pour bâtir une église doit être prévu dans un plan d'aménagement du territoire)."

[I]f any secular power dominates the Church, controls its doctrine, or interferes so that it cannot promulgate laws concerning the holy ministry, divine worship, and the spiritual welfare of the faithful, it does so to the injury of the faith and the overturning of the divine ordinance of the Church and the nature of government.[60]

A more recent example is the 2002 "Note on some Questions Concerning the Participation of Catholics in Political Life," by the Congregation for the Doctrine of the Faith. It too contains a list delineating areas of state incompetence:

All the faithful are well aware that *specifically religious activities* (such as the profession of faith, worship, administration of sacraments, theological doctrines, interchange between religious authorities and the members of religions) are outside the state's responsibility.[61]

I said above (in section 10.1) that the incompetence argument contains elements of truth.[62] This is another example. If the scope of the incompetence argument is narrowed from "religious matters" to "ecclesiastical matters" (or "specifically religious activities," to take the term adopted in the 2002 "Note"), the truth of the assertion is readily apparent, and the applicable standard is manageable.

That is, the tasks and prerogatives listed in both Gregory's encyclical and the 2002 "Note" are functions at the center of religious practice. Gregory focuses on doctrine, the sacraments, the priesthood, and the spiritual care of the faithful. The 2002 document includes all of these and adds communication between religious leaders and the faithful.[63] The delimitation of these

---

[60] Cf. Gregory XVI, Encyclical *Commissum Divinitus* on Church and State; Addressed to the Clergy of Switzerland (May 17, 1835), §5; English translation from EWTN online library, https://www.ewtn.com/catholicism/library/on-church-and-state-3368.

[61] Congregation for the Doctrine of the Faith, "Note on Some Questions Concerning the Participation of Catholics in Political Life" (Nov. 24, 2002), §6 (emphasis added) [AAS 96 (2004): 366].

[62] That section argues that although state incompetence is not the foundation for religious liberty, nonetheless, some notion of state incompetence does indeed follow as a consequence of the right's foundation in the dignity of the human person. This section emphasizes another true aspect of the incompetence argument, namely, that in its narrow formulation as incompetence in *ecclesiastical* matters, it embodies an important principle that all or nearly all commentators on DH would embrace.

[63] The *Syllabus of Errors* includes a similar listing. It too rejects civil encroachment in the

matters as falling outside of the state's competence is hardly controversial. Scholars and commentators who are concerned with the protection of religious rights likely could achieve something close to a consensus on these points. Note, however, that the range of the state's incompetence is described here in precise and relatively narrow terms.

The problem for proponents of the incompetence argument in the context of DH, however, is that "incompetence of the state" in this narrower sense does not necessarily imply the right of religious liberty specified in DH. Rather, the exclusion of the state from these *ecclesiastical matters* goes more to the question of the *libertas Ecclesiae* or the freedom of the Church. This, too, is the subject of DH but not its central focus. The reason that the state's incompetence in ecclesiastical matters does not necessarily imply religious liberty is that a state could respect the Church's liberty without recognizing the right of all citizens not to be hindered in their religious practice. Indeed, this very thing seems to have been the expectation of the nineteenth-century popes.

10.3.3. Sorting Out the Terms (Incompetence to Do What?)

Is this variety of terms an insurmountable problem? Not necessarily. However, it may provide an initial warning that despite the pervasiveness of the idea of the *incompetence of the state*, some authors may be using this term rather reflexively and without giving sufficient attention to its actual content and limitations. It might also indicate that few authors appreciate the difficulty of defining this concept. Indeed, they may not have considered the possibility that this notion may evade definition altogether. Thus, this variety may foreshadow a particular difficulty for the incompetence argument, namely, that although the idea is quite familiar and resonates especially well with those in the Western democracies, the contours of the argument may be insufficiently defined and indeed may even elude definition.

---

administration of the sacraments and spiritual governance. However, it also refers more generally to interference in religion and morality. As a result, it appears to be open either to a narrow reading, along the lines of *ecclesiastical matters*, or a somewhat broader reading. Cf. Pope Pius IX, *Syllabus Errorum* (Dec. 8, 1864), §44 (listing the following thesis as an error): "The civil authority may interfere in matters relating to religion, morality and spiritual government: hence, it can pass judgment on the instructions issued for the guidance of consciences, conformably with their mission, by the pastors of the Church. Further, it has the right to make enactments regarding the administration of the divine sacraments, and the dispositions necessary for receiving them" (English translation from EWTN, https://www.ewtn.com/catholicism/library/syllabus-of-errors-9048).

As discussed above, the incompetence of the state in *ecclesiastical matters* is an important term. However, it is more relevant to the *libertas Ecclesiae* than to a universal right to religious liberty. As a result, we can set it aside for the time being. That is, although the term is important in its own context, it is too narrow of a concept to provide the foundation for the right to religious liberty.

By the same token, the term *incompetence of the state to make judgments of truth in religious matters* also is an important term, but it too seems to refer primarily to another question. It is the question addressed above in sections 4.5 and 4.6 on the confessional state and on whether or not DH raises an obstacle to a state recognizing a religion as true. As a result, this term is unlikely to provide the primary point of reference for this discussion, but we nonetheless should remain attentive to it. It is important to recall that proponents of the broad formulation—incompetence in religious matters—almost invariably embrace this position as well. That is, for most of these commentators, their concept of incompetence in religious matters encompasses the state's incompetence to make judgments of truth in religious matters.

Pietro D'Avack refers to state incompetence in *religious options* and in *professions of faith*.[64] What he seems to mean by these specific terms is that the state may not impose religious choices or creeds on its citizens or residents. On the face of it, this presents no difficulty, because as Murray says, it is a notion of non-coercion that should be understood simply as flowing in principle from the ancient Christian teaching on the necessity for freedom in the act of faith. (See section 9.6 above.) These notions are uncontroversial, but they are sufficient to support only the first part of the right to religious liberty (freedom from coercion); they do not necessarily support the second part of the right (freedom from being hindered in one's chosen religious practice). See section 9.6 on Murray's sufficiency argument. Thus, D'Avack's terminology here presents little difficulty, but one must recall that his notion of incompetence extends beyond the specific term used here, *religious options*. That is, he also will refer later to incompetence in making judgments of truth, and the context of his position suggests a broad understanding of state incompetence. Indeed, he will assert that the state's only role with regard to religion is to safeguard the public peace and other temporal ends.[65]

---

[64] Cf. D'Avack, "La Chiesa e lo Stato nella nuova impostazione conciliare," 32.

[65] D'Avack, "La Chiesa e lo Stato nella nuova impostazione conciliare," 33. See also Pietro Agostino D'Avack, "La libertad religiosa en el magisterio actual de la Iglesia Católica," *Ius Canonicum* 5, no. 2 (1965): 380.

10.3. The Practical Problems with the "Incompetence Argument"

Basile Valuet uses several of the terms listed above, thus referring in various places to state incompetence in *ecclesiastical matters*, in the *supernatural domain*, and in *religious matters*. Only the second of these terms, the *supernatural domain*, is unique to Valuet, and it is a term that he uses only rarely. Thus, it does not appear that he intends to give *incompetence in the supernatural domain* a different meaning than *incompetence in religious matters*.

However, although Valuet argues for state incompetence in religious matters, he is not a proponent of this argument in the usual sense. That is, he is critical of those who embrace an absolute notion of state incompetence, and he emphasizes rather than minimizes the late amendments to the declaration on society's (including the public power's) duty to God and on the possibility of a state extending special civil recognition to a given religion.[66]

Another difference in Valuet's formulation is that he is less concerned (though by no means unconcerned) about establishing state incompetence as a possible foundation for religious liberty. In his own unique approach, Valuet asserts that the dignity of the person is the "internal" foundation of the right to religious liberty, while state incompetence in religious matters is the "external" foundation.[67] Perhaps one could apply the phrase *incompetence in the supernatural domain* to this distinctive position of Valuet. Although this would be useful, it does not seem to be his own intention in using that term.

In any event, this term—incompetence in the supernatural domain—presents few difficulties here because it seems to be a synonym for incompetence in religious matters, or at least to be included within that term. Valuet's approach in general represents a sound distinction between the religious and the temporal realms. However, as discussed below, I believe that his notion of state incompetence as the external foundation of the right remains problematic. See subsection 10.3.5.1 below.

With regard to the remaining terms—incompetence in *religious matters* and in *spiritual matters*—it is difficult to analyze and compare them. As mentioned above, the ordinary use of the terms would suggest that the former is broader than the latter. However, when Carrillo uses the term *incompetence in spiritual matters*, his usage suggests that he intends it as a term equivalent to *religious matters*. The reason is that he uses *incompetence in spiritual matters* much like Murray uses *incompetence in religious matters*,

---

[66] Cf. Valuet, LRTE, 387–89.
[67] Cf. Valuet, LRTC, 837 [= LRTE, 554].

namely, as providing the basis for both religious liberty and separation between Church and state.[68]

The remainder of this discussion will focus primarily on the term *incompetence of the state in religious matters*. This is how the leading proponents of the argument—Murray, Pavan, and others—usually describe it, and it is the most common formulation. It also appears to be the broadest formulation of the idea of state incompetence. In addition, as discussed above, some of the other formulations either are synonyms for *incompetence in religious matters* or at least often are used as near-synonyms for it. The formulation that undeniably represents a different idea is *incompetence in ecclesiastical matters*. This is an important idea because it demonstrates a truth concerning the state's incompetence, namely, that it may not interfere with the distinctive functions at the core of religious practice. However, as discussed above, this concept is too narrow to furnish the foundation for the right to religious liberty.

10.3.4. An Amorphous Concept?

Despite the familiarity of the idea of state incompetence in religious matters, an influential promotor of the concept, A. F. Carrillo de Albornoz, acknowledges that it is difficult to define its content and limits.[69] By the same token, Jérôme Hamer and Clemente Riva also describe the state as incompetent in religious matters, but they too concede that the distinction between the temporal realm and the religious realm is not always clear.[70] This is indeed the case. Not all proponents of the idea specify what they mean by incompetence in religious matters, and, among those who do, there is significant variation in the precise boundaries of the state's competence or incompetence.

Archbishop Roland Minnerath's formulation is to describe this idea as state incompetence in "religious issues," and the lone example that he gives is "dictating internal rules to Church organizations."[71] This description creates

---

[68] Cf. Carrillo de Albornoz, "Roman Catholicism and Religious Liberty," 33–34.

[69] Carrillo de Albornoz, *The Basis of Religious Liberty*, 76 (difficulty of identifying exact boundaries on limitations of state incompetence).

[70] Hamer/Riva, 191. Note that although they argue in favor of state incompetence, they do not claim that it is the foundation of the right to religious liberty. Cf. Hamer/Riva, 179, 187, 200–201.

[71] "The State no longer claims to control all aspects of social life. In particular, it declares itself incompetent in religious issues, and has no interest in dictating internal rules to Church organizations. So, according to Vatican II, as long as the fundamental right to

10.3. The Practical Problems with the "Incompetence Argument"

the impression that his focus may be the narrower category of *ecclesiastical matters* rather than *religious matters* (or *religious issues*, as he says). However, he also refers more broadly to "religious issues," and he describes this idea of incompetence as creating "a sphere of activity in which the State will not interfere." This indicates that he has the broader idea of incompetence in religious matters in mind, but he does not specify precisely what the state is incompetent to do (besides establishing internal Church rules). Moreover, he concludes his description by once again emphasizing not religious liberty but the autonomy of Church organizations.[72]

Minnerath's conception almost seems to alternate between a broad conception of state incompetence and a narrow one. That is, he focuses especially on internal church rules, but he also refers more expansively to incompetence in "religious issues" and to a "sphere of activity" protected from state interference. As a result, his ultimate concept seems to be a broad one, though his references to the specific question of internal church

---

religious freedom is correctly guaranteed, there will be a sphere of activity in which the State will not interfere. The autonomy of churches is guaranteed within the self-proclaimed incompetence of the State in religious matters." Roland Minnerath, "How Should State and Church Interact?," *The Jurist* 70, no. 2 (2010): 477.

[72] Cf. Minnerath, "State and Church," 477. Minnerath has a broad conception of state incompetence, but he does not identify it as the foundation of the right to religious liberty. Rather, he correctly states that human dignity is the foundation, but he also says that the deeper foundation is man's moral duty to seek the truth. Cf. Roland Minnerath, "La concezione della chiesa sulla libertà religiosa," in *La libertad religiosa: Memoria del IX Congreso Internacional de Derecho Canónico* (Universidad Nacional Autónoma de México, 1996), 55: "Il Concilio fonda questo diritto alla libertà religiosa sulla dignità inerente ad ogni uomo"; Minnerath, 56: "l'obbligo morale di ogni uomo di ricercare la verità su Dio . . . è il vero fondamento della libertà religiosa." It is clear, though, that Minnerath's primary concern is not religious liberty but rather the independence of religious organizations. However, his idea of state incompetence probably is broad enough to provide at least an alternate foundation for religious liberty. Cf. Minnerath, "State and Church," 477: "The State no longer claims to control all aspects of social life. In particular, it declares itself incompetent in religious issues, and has no interest in dictating internal rules to Church organizations. So, according to Vatican II, as long as the fundamental right to religious freedom is correctly guaranteed, there will be a sphere of activity in which the State will not interfere. The autonomy of churches is guaranteed within the self-proclaimed incompetence of the State in religious matters." Although this suggestion (that Minnerath might accept state incompetence as an alternate basis for religious liberty) is speculative, his high opinion of Murray and his following of Murray's lead in interpreting DH provide additional reason for entertaining this possibility. Cf. "State and Church," 476, crediting Murray—excessively, it seems—for "the whole architecture of *Dignitatis Humanae*"; "La concezione della chiesa," 56, following Murray in strictly limiting role of the state and in claiming that DH embraced the idea of state incompetence.

rules suggests that this particular matter is one of special concern to him. However, how is this "sphere of activity" to be protected? That is, how can this sphere or zone be secured from state interference without a precise delimitation of the specific matters (or at least the categories of matters) in which the state is incompetent?

Franco Biffi describes state incompetence in more spiritual terms. Among the essential traits of the modern (lay) state, especially in the West, Biffi includes incompetence to give judgments in spiritual matters. He takes his idea from Pietro Pavan, who gives the following examples of such spiritual matters that are considered beyond the state's competence: the authenticity of works of art, the certitude of scientific theories and philosophical conceptions, the validity of public opinions, the consistency of moral convictions, and the truth of religious beliefs.[73] (Pavan's own concept of state incompetence is interesting and important, and it is discussed at greater length below.)

The position of Hamer and Riva also rejects the possibility of the state making judgments of value or truth in religious matters.[74] This is a consequence of the secular nature of the state. Thus, the state recognizes the rights of all "without claiming to put forward competence on the merits in judgments of truth and of conscience over individual doctrines and religious communities."[75]

Pietro D'Avack does not use the term *incompetence in religious matters*, but it seems quite clear that he has this idea in mind, given that he embraces a broad idea of state incompetence. He refers to the state's "absolute incompetence," and he describes that incompetence as encompassing the following:[76]

- religious options (the choice of religion or religious decisions for the citizens),
- professions of faith,

---

[73] Franco Biffi, "Chiesa, società civile e persona di fronte al problema della libertà religiosa. Dalla revoca dell'Editto di Nantes al Concilio Vaticano II," in *Teologia e diritto canonico* (Vatican City: Libreria Editrice Vaticana, 1987), 137, quoting Pavan, *Dignità della persona* (Napoli, 1980), 130ff. Biffi does not describe state incompetence outright as the foundation for religious liberty, but it is clear that his conception of state incompetence in religious matters is broad (cf. Biffi, 143). However, his primary concern is not with the foundation of the right but with the damage caused by governmental adoption of religion (particularly in the case of the revocation of the Edict of Nantes).

[74] Hamer/Riva, 179: The fact that the right applies to all "implicitly insinuates also the incompetence of the public powers in judgments of value, of truth or not in religious matters."

[75] Hamer/Riva, 208–9.

[76] D'Avack, "La Chiesa e lo Stato nella nuova impostazione conciliare," 32–33.

10.3. The Practical Problems with the "Incompetence Argument"

- acts of faith,
- judgment concerning which is the true religion, and
- judgment concerning the speculative value of a particular religion.

Thus, whereas Minnerath's focus is the autonomy of religious organizations and Biffi's is spiritual values, D'Avack's concern is with personal freedom and with denying that the state may recognize a specific religion as true (or even as having value). Thus, although these authors appear to embrace the same general concept of state incompetence in religious matters, their descriptions of the actual matters protected from governmental interference display a significant amount of variation.[77]

The most serious attempt to specify the state's incompetence in religious matters is that of Pietro Pavan in his well-regarded 1967 *Unam Sanctam* article and other works. He asserts that an increasing consciousness of human dignity has led to the creation of the constitutional state, and that this development has resulted in the recognition of religion as a "reserved zone" protected from the civil authorities.[78] Pavan begins by suggesting that nearly everyone will agree that the public powers "are not competent in what concerns the intrinsic content of a religion."[79] Thus, these powers are incompetent in judging the following questions:

- whether a person must have a religious faith,
- whether he is bound to one religion or another,
- whether he is obliged to worship,
- how to worship,
- whether he has a duty to witness or to spread his faith, and
- whether he must engage himself in penetrating temporal institutions with religious motivations.

---

[77] Robert T. Kennedy offers a description of state incompetence that shares some similarities with D'Avack's notion. However, the context of Kennedy's remarks is a review of the American system rather than a discussion of the foundation of the right contained in DH. "It has long been recognized in the United States that civil government has neither the competence nor the power to command or prohibit internal or external religious acts, impose the profession or repudiation of any religion, or hinder anyone from joining or leaving a religious body." Robert T. Kennedy, "Contributions of *Dignitatis Humanae* to Church-State Relations in the United States," in *Religious Liberty: Paul VI and* Dignitatis Humanae, ed. John T. Ford (Brescia, Italy: Istituto Paulo VI, 1995), 99. Unlike D'Avack, however, Kennedy does not address the question of state establishment of religion.

[78] Pietro Pavan, "Le droit à la liberté religieuse en ses éléments essentiels," *Unam Sanctam* 60 (1967): 166.

[79] Pavan, "Le droit à la liberté religieuse en ses éléments essentiels," 167.

Pavan then makes a move that is distinctly his own. He provides a list of six principles that he says require the protection of a "reserved zone" of religion from governmental interference. They are subsidiarity, interiority, transcendence, personal responsibility, divine positive law, and human positive law.[80] He includes a discussion of the relevance of these principles for state incompetence. Thus, in a sense, he reasons to the specifics of state incompetence *from two directions*. That is, *like the other authors*, he begins with the idea of state incompetence and makes some observations on impermissible state action, but then, *unlike the other authors*, he reasons from another direction as well, namely, from his list of principles that he says require a protected zone for religion. This discussion of incompetence represents a significant portion of Pavan's article, and it suggests that his efforts to specify the bounds of state incompetence are more thorough and more serious than those of other proponents of the incompetence argument. As he discusses each of these six principles, other areas become clear in which he believes the state is incompetent. The specific areas that appear from his discussion of the six principles are the following:

- incompetence to emit judgments of value on the content of a religious belief;[81]
- incompetence to evaluate (*apprecier*) interior human acts or to have authority over them;[82]
- incompetence to influence directly the intrinsic content of religious acts;[83] and
- incompetence to substitute for persons in deciding how the relationship between them and God must be arranged (*aménagé*) and lived.[84]

Pavan's approach is more interesting and (in a sense) conscientious than those of the other proponents of state incompetence. Perhaps his recourse to the six principles reveals his own doubts about the incompetence argument as a foundation for religious liberty, or at least some doubt about the

---

[80] Pavan, "Le droit à la liberté religieuse en ses éléments essentiels," 168.
[81] Pavan, "Le droit à la liberté religieuse en ses éléments essentiels," 172 (from the author's discussion of the subsidiarity principle).
[82] Pavan, "Le droit à la liberté religieuse en ses éléments essentiels," 173 (from the author's discussion of the principle of interiority).
[83] Pavan, "Le droit à la liberté religieuse en ses éléments essentiels," 174 (from the author's discussion of the transcendence of religious acts).
[84] Pavan, "Le droit à la liberté religieuse en ses éléments essentiels," 175.

10.3. The Practical Problems with the "Incompetence Argument"

complete sufficiency of that argument to ground the right. Pavan's inclusion of the principles of interiority, transcendence, and personal responsibility is somewhat reminiscent of the declaration's own approach. Pavan's observations on these principles might have bolstered the declaration's grounding of religious liberty in human dignity, given that some of his six principles are similar to the reasons contained in the declaration's grounding of the right or else are expansions upon themes contained elsewhere in the declaration. However, Pavan uses these principles not to ground the right directly but to argue for a "reserved zone" for religion. That is, he bolsters the incompetence argument *from a second direction*.

I believe that Pavan would have done better to focus on a set of principles that would ground the right to religious liberty directly, or that would bolster the declaration's grounding of it in human dignity. Such an approach, for the reasons discussed above, would have eliminated the need to justify state incompetence as the foundation of the right. (That is, if the right is established securely as a natural right, state incompetence to violate it naturally follows as a consequence of the existence of the natural right.)

For the purposes of the instant discussion on whether the principle of state incompetence is a manageable or definable concept, the significance of Pavan is that although he makes the most serious attempt to delineate the state's incompetence, the idea remains strikingly incomplete. Despite his broader frame of reference, Pavan's concerns, like those of the other authors, center on just a couple of areas, namely, preventing the state from interfering in acts of religion, from influencing the content of a religion, and from making judgments on spiritual values.

The variation in all of these authors' ideas of incompetence does not necessarily prove that state incompetence is an undefinable concept, but it does suggest that the idea may well be unworkable. Justifying state incompetence as the foundation for religious liberty depends on establishing a rather broad—or at least well-defined—zone of impermissible state action.[85] However, there is no real agreement among these proponents as to what precisely the state is incompetent to do, and there is little or no attempt among them to establish a comprehensive delineation of the areas of state incompetence.

---

[85] Note that although all of the authors discussed here are proponents of state incompetence, not all are concerned to establish it as the foundation for religious liberty. Some, such as Hamer and Riva, argue for state incompetence to exclude the state from adopting a religion, or at least from judging it as true. Most proponents, however, embrace it for both reasons.

10.3.4.1. Summary of the Attempts to Describe State Incompetence

Note the variety of understandings of state incompetence, even among those who are in agreement in embracing a rather broad formulation of the idea. There is some overlap, but there seems to be more variation. Each has a distinct concern, and his list of excluded areas of state interference reflects this concern. Hamer and Riva exclude the state from making judgments of truth in religious matters. Biffi and Pavan extend this incompetence to all spiritual matters, broadly considered, thus including art, science, and philosophy. Minnerath focuses on the autonomy of religious organizations and, in particular, on their prerogative to formulate their own internal rules. D'Avack is concerned especially to exclude the state from making religious judgments, either for individual citizens or for the state itself. Finally, Pavan is especially concerned to protect interior religious decisions and the content of religious belief.

All of these authors have a broad notion of state incompetence, but, in their lists of measures protected from state action, they make little attempt at comprehensiveness (with the possible exception of Pavan). Rather than specifying the full range of state incompetence, they seem to content themselves with emphasizing an area or two in which they have a particular interest. Moreover, when one considers the greatest proponent of state incompetence, these difficulties only increase. See subsection 10.3.4.2, immediately below.

10.3.4.2. The Dog That Didn't Bark

What of John Courtney Murray? When one considers the chief proponent of state incompetence in religious matters, what does one learn about the content of his notion of this idea? *Surprisingly little.*

Murray scholar Kenneth Grasso has written extensively on Murray's conception of the constitutional state. Grasso has great admiration for Murray, but he is by no means uncritical, and he faults Murray in particular on this question. That is, despite Murray's frequent references to state incompetence—and despite him raising this argument above all others as a justification for religious freedom—Murray gives almost no indication of what he actually means by state incompetence!

Other commentators, like the ones discussed above, give some indication of the areas in which they understand the state to be incompetent. In fact, they often give lists of the areas or categories of action in which they believe state interference is excluded (or at least of the areas where they consider exclusion of state action to be most important). Whether these lists are intended as exhaustive or exemplary is not entirely clear, but they at least give an indication of the author's key concerns.

Murray, however, appears to have provided no such listing. Grasso is an admirer of Murray and a student of his work. Moreover, he agrees with Murray's assertion that the incompetence argument—and it alone—is sufficient to provide the foundation for the right that DH recognizes (both the immunity from coercion and the immunity from interference with religious practice).[86] Nevertheless, Grasso to his credit identifies four important weaknesses in Murray's incompetence argument. One of these is that Murray never really specifies what he means by state incompetence in religious matters.[87]

This is, indeed, an unexpected circumstance. Murray is the leading proponent of the argument that the state is incompetent in religious matters, and yet, despite many articles and speeches on the subject of religious liberty, he seems never to have specified with detail and clarity what he means by state incompetence.

His biographer discusses a letter that Murray wrote to Francis Cardinal Spellman during the second session of the Council. In this letter, unlike in most of his published writings, he provides at least some indication of his notion of state incompetence. In fact, here he provides his own short list, like the ones described above. In putting forward the American system as the model for the Council, Murray says the following:

> The functions of government and law are limited to the temporal and terrestrial affairs of men. In particular, the First Amendment declared government to be incompetent in the field of religion; government is not a judge of religious truth; it has no right to repress error; it has no share in the *cura animarum*; its sole function in the field of religion is the protection and promotion of *freedom* of the Church and of the churches and of all citizens.[88]

---

[86] See section 9.6 (on the "sufficiency" argument).

[87] Grasso, "Murray, 'the Juridical State,' and Religious Freedom," 35: "Murray never really explores the meaning or implications of the religious 'incompetence' of the state in anything approaching a systematic fashion." The other three weaknesses that Grasso identifies are that Murray's idea is insufficient to ground the full range of principles that constitute the juridical state, that his concept of "public order" is too minimal, and that he does not sufficiently explain why he denies that the state has a mandate to promote the common good (cf. Grasso, 31–35).

[88] Letter from John Courtney Murray to Francis Cardinal Spellman (Nov. 18, 1963), quoted in Donald E. Pelotte, *John Courtney Murray: Theologian in Conflict* (New York: Paulist Press, 1975), 83. Note that, as discussed in chapter 4, not all commentators embrace

Despite the existence of this letter providing some illumination of Murray's concept of state incompetence, Grasso's point stands. This explanation of the Murray position appeared in a private letter rather than in one of his published articles. In addition, even here, Murray says little about what it means for the state to be "incompetent in the field of religion." One of his few other indications came in a 1964 speech at Georgetown University, where he said that "it is neither within the power nor within the competence of government to judge whether conscience be erroneous or not, in good faith or in bad faith."[89]

Grasso culls Murray's writings for indications of what the content of his notion of state incompetence might be. His conclusion is substantially the same as the points contained in the Spellman letter and the Georgetown speech. Quoting from Murray's "scattered discussions of the subject," Grasso summarizes Murray's idea of incompetence as including

> his insistence that the right to religious liberty proclaimed by *DH* involves the rejection of the idea that government is "*defensor fidei*," the rejection of the idea that government's "duty and right ... extend to what has long been called *cura religionis*, a direct care of religion itself." It involves, this is to say, the rejection of the ideas that the "function of government" encompasses a responsibility for "the protection and promotion ... of religious truth," that "government is to be the judge of religious truth, the defender of the true faith, or the guardian of religious unity, and that the state's duties encompass a "share in the *cura animarum* or in the *regimen*

Murray's strictly separationist reading of the First Amendment. Rather, a strong contrary opinion holds that although the federal government may not favor one or more particular religions, it may promote religion generally. Murray's protégé Richard Regan takes note of this position, even while embracing a somewhat separationist position himself (though perhaps less separationist than Murray's). Cf. Richard J. Regan, *The American Constitution and Religion* (Washington, DC: Catholic University of America Press, 2013), 38–41, 73–74. In addition, Murray distorts the American tradition by ignoring the circumstance that the First Amendment, as originally enacted, limited the authority only of the *federal* government, not the *state* governments. (The U.S. system, of course, is one of shared sovereignty [cf. Regan, 18].) Ten of the original thirteen colonies had an established religion, and even after adoption of the First Amendment, three states continued to maintain a state religion for decades. The Congregational Church remained the established religion of Connecticut until 1818, of New Hampshire until 1819, and of Massachusetts until 1833. In addition, some states allowed only Protestants to hold office (cf. Regan, 30).

[89] John Courtney Murray, "Religious Freedom," in *Freedom and Man* (New York: P. J. Kenedy & Sons, 1965) (speech at Georgetown University in summer 1964), 137.

animorum." One also thinks here of his contention that this right implies the recognition that "the function of government is secular," that "its powers are limited to the affairs of the temporal and terrestrial order of man's existence," and thus that the state is neither "the judge or the representative of transcendent truth with regard to man's eternal destiny" nor "man's guide to heaven."[90]

Note that the few areas of state incompetence that Grasso is able to identify in Murray's writings are repetitive and abstract. Most of them—government is not *defensor fidei*, government has no role in the *cura animarum*, etcetera—stand for a single principle, namely, that, for Murray, the state is absolutely secular. Moreover, none of these delimitations is helpful in addressing either "mixed questions" or the concrete areas in which even modern states inevitably continue to come into contact with religion (discussed below in subsection 10.3.4 and especially in subsection 10.3.4.1).

Why is the leading thinker on state incompetence so reticent about explaining what incompetence actually means? This is the import of the quotation from Arthur Conan Doyle at the head of this chapter. It comes from "The Adventure of Silver Blaze," an 1892 story in which Sherlock Holmes solves the crime of a stolen horse by asking why the owner's dog did not bark, even though it was nearby at the time of the theft. Thus, the image of *the dog that didn't bark* stands for the conspicuous absence of something that one would expect to find in the normal course of things.

So, why didn't the dog bark in this case? Why does the most prominent proponent of state incompetence in religious matters provide virtually no explanation of precisely what the state is incompetent to do?

One reason may be the difficulties pointed out in sections 10.1, 10.2, and 10.3. That is, although the idea of state incompetence sounds familiar and even may seem to have the ring of truth about it, there are some difficulties simply in naming the realm of state incompetence, and there are yet more challenges in trying to specify exactly what the state lacks competence to do.

However, there is another reason for Murray's reticence as well. His theory seems to demand an extreme notion of state incompetence. The way that his concept of incompetence leads to religious liberty is *by default*. That is, religious liberty follows from the modern state's incompetence to take any action in the religious field. In Murray's theory, historical and political consciousness is responsible in large measure for the development of the

---

[90] Grasso, "Murray, 'the Juridical State,' and Religious Freedom," 35–36 (ellipses in original; citations omitted).

modern state that is incompetent in religion. Religious freedom depends on the religious realm existing as a protected sphere or a zone of immunity in which the government may not interfere. As a result, this theory requires the maximum possible exclusion of the state from the religious realm.[91] As a result, this theory requires a well-defined zone of protection and an absolute or near-absolute exclusion of the state from it. In addition, it seems to tend toward a rather expansive zone or sphere of state noninterference rather than a narrow one.

Murray gives some indication of this in his Spellman letter. The state's exclusion from the religious realm is so complete that it remains competent to do only a single thing in this realm. "[I]ts sole function in the field of religion is the protection and promotion of *freedom* of the Church and of the churches and of all citizens."[92]

Recall some of the features of Murray's thought on the relationship between Church and state (see chapter 4 above). One of the key circumstances was that while an authentic notion of Gelasian dualism asserts a

---

[91] Murray proposed a number of arguments in favor of religious liberty. An article in which he asserts multiple foundations for religious liberty is his famous 1964 *Theological Studies* article written during the Council (cf. "Problem of Religious Freedom"). As the same article makes clear (and as his work on the third and fourth drafts of the declaration confirm), his favorite of his own arguments was the incompetence of the state in religious matters. Murray's affinity for this argument only increased with time. Thus, following the Council, he argued not only that the incompetence argument is necessary to provide an adequate foundation for religious liberty, but that it—standing alone—is sufficient to do so (even without the help of other arguments, though he was not opposed to the presence of other arguments). Cf. Murray, "Arguments for the Human Right," 237: "[T]his political argument is of primary importance. Without it any other argument would not sufficiently settle the questions."

In addition, note that Murray's argument seems to be purely political (or purely constitutional). The zone of immunity that religion enjoys does not result from the inherent value of religion but from the state's incompetence in the religious field. Grasso asserts that Murray seeks to ground DH's conception of the state on man's dignity. Cf. Grasso, "Murray, 'the Juridical State,' and Religious Freedom," 27, asserting that Murray grounds his conception of the state in man's dignity. It is true that Murray does discuss human dignity, but he does not invariably include it in his incompetence argument. My own sense is that it is more of an alternative argument for Murray rather than an essential component of his incompetence argument.

[92] Letter to Spellman, in Pelotte, *Theologian in Conflict*, 83. See also Murray, "Problem of Religious Freedom," 522: "[P]ublic care of religion is limited to public care of religious freedom"; Murray, 528: "[T]he state, under today's conditions . . . , is competent to do only one thing in respect of religion, that is, to recognize, guarantee, protect, and promote the religious freedom of the people"; Murray, 558: The state is not competent to adopt a religion.

somewhat fluid distinction between the two realms,[93] Murray by contrast embraces a strict—perhaps even absolute[94]—separation of Church and state. By the same token, we see a corresponding characteristic in his notion of state incompetence, that is, a sharp delineation between the religious realm and the temporal realm. Murray's separationism is so complete that he does not even take notice of so-called "mixed" questions that, as other authors acknowledge, legitimately concern both Church and state.[95] Instead, Murray assumes that every possible issue falls neatly on one side or the other of the Church-state divide. Similarly here, Murray's understanding of state incompetence has the same air of unreality about it. As already discussed, despite his claim that the incompetence argument is indispensable, he neglects almost entirely the need to delineate the precise areas in which the state is excluded from interfering. Thus, as discussed more fully below (in subsection 10.3.5.1), he entirely ignores the many practical and concrete contexts in which the temporal and religious realms inevitably must meet.

10.3.5. Can the Incompetence Argument (Possibly) Mean What It Says?

If the principle of the incompetence of the state in religious matters is to provide the foundation for the right to religious liberty, it is certain that this principle must be well-defined, and it is almost certain that this principle must be broad. It must be well-defined because otherwise it is not possible to verify that the state truly is excluded from the religious realm (or from a particular state action in regard to religion that arises as a concern). By the same token, it would seem to require breadth so that it would extend not simply to the relatively uncontroversial and narrow category of *ecclesiastical matters* but also to the broader category of *religious matters*.[96]

---

[93] On the more traditional understanding of the boundary between the two realms as something like a "semi-porous membrane" rather than a high and wide "wall of separation," see section 4.3. See also subsection 10.2.2, discussing Leo XIII and Pius XII on cooperation between the two realms.

[94] Cf. Pelotte, *Theologian in Conflict*, 124: For Murray, the character of the spiritual power is "absolutely spiritual." By the same token, an author cited by Murray, A. F. Carrillo de Albornoz, quite clearly assumes that one can classify any possible question as "purely religious" or "purely human" (cf. "Roman Catholicism and Religious Liberty," 33–34).

[95] Cf. Russell Hittinger, "How to Read *Dignitatis Humanae* on Establishment of Religion," *Catholic Dossier* 6, no. 2 (March–April 2000): 16; Biffi, "Chiesa, società civile e persona," 134, 137; Lorenzo Spinelli, *Il diritto pubblico ecclesiastico dopo il Concilio Vaticano II* (Milan: Dott. A. Giuffrè Editore, 1985), 93, 97.

[96] Exclusion of the state merely from *ecclesiastical matters* does not necessarily give rise to

However, the notion is by no means well-defined. Carrillo, although enthusiastic about the theory, concedes this.[97] Moreover, Grasso demonstrates this with special relevance in the case of Murray's own conception of state incompetence.[98] Despite promoting the incompetence argument as the only sufficient foundation for religious liberty, Murray makes little effort to define it. Other proponents make more of an effort to do so, but the results are limited and seem largely to reflect particular personal concerns. As for breadth, most proponents seem to envision a broad realm of state incompetence, but their listings of prohibited state action seem always to remain limited and incomplete.

Perhaps most importantly, the proponents fail to provide either definition or breadth to their notions of state incompetence because they ignore a number of practical matters. These matters include areas in which religion and the temporal authorities unavoidably come together.

10.3.5.1. Abstraction and Unreality (Inadequacy of the Incompetence Argument to Address Necessary Questions)

In a 1993 symposium on Pope Paul VI and *Dignitatis Humanae*, canonist Robert T. Kennedy delivered a paper on the contributions of DH to relations between Church and state in the United States.[99] He argues that DH is a corrective to much thinking on the relationship between the two realms. That is, while the declaration makes clear that the Church is autonomous and independent of the state, its notion of independence is nuanced. It is not the absolute claim of independence represented by canon 1254 of the 1917 code, which asserts the Church's claim to administer temporal goods independent of civil power.[100] Rather, it is "a qualified or responsible independence, a claim of freedom from all *arbitrary* interference by civil authority, but not freedom from all reasonable regulation by civil authority in the interests of justice, peace, and public morality."[101] Thus, the declaration

---

a right to religious liberty on the part of all persons (see subsections 10.3.1 and 10.3.2). Exclusion of the state from all *religious matters* would indeed seem to do so, although such a foundation for the right raises other difficulties (see generally sections 10.3 and 10.4).

[97] Carrillo de Albornoz, *The Basis of Religious Liberty*, 76 (difficulty of identifying exact boundaries on limitations of state incompetence).

[98] Cf. Grasso, "Murray, 'the Juridical State,' and Religious Freedom," 35–36.

[99] Kennedy, "Church-State Relations."

[100] Kennedy, "Church-State Relations," 94. Kennedy calls this "a remarkable claim" not because it includes the Church's contention that her property rights arise independently of civil power, but rather because it includes a claim to be able to *exercise* those property rights independently of civil power (Kennedy, 94).

[101] Kennedy, "Church-State Relations," 96.

recognizes the state's prerogative reasonably to regulate religious practice, that is, its right to limit religious activity that violates the just public order mentioned in article 7.[102] This serves as a corrective for absolute conceptions of the relationship between Church and state that have little connection to practical realities and lived experience.

> Whether put forward by church or state, a claim to independence or separation in any absolute sense is not realizable in the theoretical order. Churches, quite simply, cannot separate themselves from the civil order of law and government in regard to the acquisition, use, and disposition of temporal possessions; nor can civil government pretend to a neutrality born of a supposed separation of church and state when it comes to the property interests of organized religion.[103]

As an application of this principle, Kennedy identifies the issue of taxation. Should the civil authority tax religious communities, or should it grant an exemption? There is no "neutral" option. "[C]hurches either bear the burden of taxation or enjoy the boon of tax exemption. In either case, there is unavoidable involvement of civil government with churches. Complete separation of church and state in such a context is an illusion."[104]

Murray's conception of state incompetence takes no account of such practical realities. Its sole guidance is to tell us that the state's only role is to protect religious freedom. Is taxation, on the one hand, irrelevant to religious freedom because it steers clear of regulating religious acts directly, or, on the other hand, is it entirely relevant because it affects the availability of resources to carry out the community's religious mission? Among the proponents of state incompetence discussed above, none addresses this question or provides an application of the incompetence theory that would speak to it. Note that, in this matter of taxation, there is no option for state inaction or noninterference. The state has only two options, one of which is harmful to religion and one of which is helpful, but neither of which amounts to noninterference.

Note how inadequate the argument from state incompetence proves to be. Murray's formulation excludes the state from "religious matters" quite broadly. Thus, it might well lead to the conclusion that legislation specifically in favor of religious communities (including the grant of a religious

---

[102] Kennedy, "Church-State Relations," 95.
[103] Kennedy, "Church-State Relations," 97.
[104] Kennedy, "Church-State Relations," 97.

tax exemption) lies beyond the proper competence of the civil authority. Murray's lone exception is that the state may (and should) act to preserve and defend religious freedom. Is taxation a matter of religious freedom? In the strict sense, no. Despite being subject to taxation, a community and its members nonetheless could continue to worship freely and to engage in religious practice. However, the ability of the community to achieve its purposes depends on available funds, and taxation significantly reduces those funds. Could the civil authority then enact a religious exemption from taxation as an *indirect* way to promote religious freedom? Murray's notion of incompetence provides no clear answer. First, it does not distinguish between direct and indirect measures, and second, it provides no principle for resolving a dispute like this one, where a contemplated state measure arguably could be considered *either* an indirect promotion of religious liberty *or* an illegitimate action in the religious realm falling outside of the state's proper competence.

Lorenzo Spinelli makes a similar point in connection with the way that the Church holds property. He is particularly concerned with the organizational forms available to the Church, and he notes that this is a special challenge in common law countries. The difficulty is that the usual organizational forms in common law countries often are unsuited to the distinct origin and structure of ecclesiastical entities such as parishes and dioceses.[105] That is, the ecclesiastical entities do not fit well into the available organizational forms for corporations and private associations. Spinelli describes this situation not merely as an inconvenience but as a distinct problem for the freedom of the Church (*libertas Ecclesiae*) itself.[106]

Again, the leading formulations of state incompetence provide no assistance with resolving these problems. Indeed, they do not even take notice

---

[105] Spinelli does not specify the precise inadequacy in common law models, but one difficulty in the United States in the nineteenth century was that some of the individual states prohibited the Church from holding property. (Catholics did not come to the United States in large numbers until the mid nineteenth century, and some of the individual states had laws that were hostile to Catholicism.) As a result, individual pastors often would hold title to parish property, but this created a difficulty, namely, that the right of a parish to its own property was not secure. That is, the pastors sometimes failed to transfer the property to their successor pastors. In response to this problem, laymen sometimes were made trustees of Church property, but this development in turn gave rise to further problems in Church governance, especially the nineteenth-century American crisis of "lay trusteeism."

[106] Lorenzo Spinelli, *Libertas Ecclesiae. Lezioni di diritto canonico* (Milano: Dott. A. Giuffrè Editore, 1979), 211–12. Another problem for the *libertas Ecclesiae* identified by Spinelli is that the need for the Church to provide for her faithful in one part of the world may be hampered by laws limiting the movement of capital from one country to another. Cf. Spinelli, 212–13.

of them. Yet, these questions of organizational structure are connected with the identity of the ecclesiastical entity itself. The parish and the diocese may not be able to fulfill their purposes if the applicable civil law does not provide organizational forms that provide for their distinctive origin and structure.[107] Again, simply urging the state to remain neutral is no solution. The state either will provide new corporate forms that correspond more closely to the reality of these religious entities, or it will not. If it does not, the effect is to require the Church to use the existing corporate forms that developed for very different entities, especially commercial enterprises and private associations. It seems possible that Murray's understanding of state incompetence might even *prevent* a solution here. That is, if Murray is correct that the state is incompetent in religious matters (considered rather broadly), then the state's decision to accommodate religious organizations by providing special corporate structures to correspond to distinctly religious entities might well amount to its exceeding its competence by purporting to act in the religious realm.[108]

Perhaps the signal weakness of the theories of state incompetence is that they are, at the same time, both overbroad and insufficiently broad. By declaring the state incompetent in religious matters, Murray's theory very possibly would disable the state from solving the problem identified by Spinelli. However, because the incompetence argument seems quite clearly to depend on the breadth of its assertion of state noninterference, it seems

---

[107] Another difficulty in the U.S. has been that diocesan bishops often have held title (as *corporations sole*) to all of the Church property in their dioceses. Some states recognize the organizational form of the corporation sole and permit dioceses to use it, but others do not recognize it. This mode of ownership presents the difficulty of the parish lacking control of its own assets and of the pastor being unduly constrained in his ability to administer parish goods. This possibility continues to exist today, but in the wake of the sexual abuse crisis, many dioceses in recent years (even in states recognizing the corporation sole) have adopted models giving parishes primary control over their own property. The reason for the shift is the attempt to protect parish assets from being used to satisfy judgments for sexual abuse against dioceses.

[108] Consider how the notion of property ownership varies from common law countries to the canonical system. Common law includes various notions of ownership of real property, including *fee simple absolute* ownership. In this type, the owner is in near-total control of his property. Little interference is possible, provided that his use is lawful and does not harm the rights of others. By contrast, the canonical notion of ownership is less absolute. A parish is a public juridical person and is able to acquire real property, and, in the ordinary course of things, the pastor administers the parish's property with relative freedom. However, for transactions of a sufficiently high value, he will require the approval of the diocesan bishop (cf. *Codex Iuris Canonici* [1983], cann. 1291 and 1292, §1), and for some of an especially high value, he will require the approval of the Holy See (cf. can. 1292, §2).

difficult or impossible for any single theorist to anticipate and to specify all the various areas (or even categories of action) in which the state should be understood as incompetent. The daunting nature of this latter challenge may account for Murray's almost complete lack of an attempt to provide content for his understanding of state incompetence, and it also may account for the approach of most of the other proponents of the theory, who tend to describe it rather broadly but to explain it with reference to only a few examples or a couple of clear areas of necessary state noninterference.[109]

By contrast, if one understands state incompetence not as the *foundation* of the right to religious liberty but as a *consequence* of its grounding in human dignity, this problem resolves (or at least decreases to a manageable proportion). Once the right to religious liberty is defined with sufficient precision and once it is established as a human right, it necessarily follows that civil authority may not violate the right.[110] That is, the state is indeed incompetent, but its incompetence is sharply focused rather than unduly

---

[109] Note how Martín de Agar addresses state incompetence in a different context. He describes the state as incompetent in religious matters but as competent to regulate *manifestations* of religious belief or expression (cf. "Derecho y relaciones iglesia—sociedad civil," 52). Why did Murray not adopt a standard like this to help to distinguish legitimate state action from illegitimate enactments? Martín de Agar's principle is flexible and realistic. It does not directly resolve the question of taxation raised above in the main text, but it leaves sufficient room for the resolution of that issue (probably through the ordinary political process) without calling into question the foundation of religious liberty. However, Martín de Agar is writing in the tradition of Gelasian dualism, and, as a result, his conception of the two orders—religious and temporal—is distinct but not entirely separated (cf. "Derecho y relaciones iglesia—sociedad civil," 28, cited and quoted in section 4.3 above). Although Murray, too, adopts the language of Gelasian dualism, his notion of Church-state relations in fact is a different one, namely, one of strict, nearly absolute separationism (see section 4.3, discussing Murray's Jeffersonian-type separationism). My own sense is that Murray would not regard Martín de Agar's standard as limiting governmental action sufficiently. As discussed below, one of the drafts of the declaration for which Murray had primary responsibility contained language that alarmed many council fathers because it seemed to deny the state's authority to regulate external acts of religion at all (see section 11.5 discussing the *Textus Emendatus*). Thus, Murray's broad notion of state incompetence may provide a theoretical foundation for religious liberty, but his notion is so broad that it takes almost no account of the many areas in which religion and government inevitably meet.

[110] "[I]f civil authorities pass laws or command anything opposed to the moral order and consequently contrary to the will of God, neither the laws made nor the authorizations granted can be binding on the consciences of the citizens, since God has more right to be obeyed than men" (PT, §51). See also Javier Hervada, *Critical Introduction to Natural Law*, trans. Mindy Emmons (Montreal: Wilson & Lafleur, 2006), 153: "Law contrary to Natural Law lacks the force and nature of law."

10.3. The Practical Problems with the "Incompetence Argument"

broad. It is an incompetence to violate the natural right to religious liberty.[111] There no longer is any need to define state incompetence in such broad terms as Murray's. It is not necessary to prove state incompetence in all (or almost all) religious matters but only to insist on it when it comes to state action that would purport to violate the right of religious liberty by commanding or inhibiting religious acts.

(Basile Valuet argues in favor of state incompetence, but he avoids most of the pitfalls of the other proponents of the argument. The reason is that he acknowledges that the Council based the right to religious liberty on human dignity, and unlike Murray, he does not seek to supplant this foundation. What Valuet does, though, is to identify human dignity as the *internal* foundation of the right, and to assert that state incompetence is the *external* foundation.[112] Unfortunately, he does not say what he means by these terms. Where the terms come up in other contexts, though, they stand for the distinction between the personal aspect of the right and the social aspect.[113] As a result, I will assume tentatively that Valuet intends the same meaning by these terms, or at least a similar one. It is not certain that this is his understanding, but it seems at least likely. There is, however, no need for a separate *external* foundation for religious liberty. As already noted, once religious liberty is established as a natural right and a human right by virtue of its foundation in human dignity—particularly in the nature of the person as a seeker of truth—then the *external* or *social* consequence necessarily follows. That is, the state is indeed incompetent to violate this natural right or, indeed, any other. No so-called *external* foundation is necessary because

---

[111] This is exactly what the declaration said (DH, §3e). See also PT, §61: "[I]f any government does not acknowledge the rights of man or violates them, it not only fails in its duty, but its orders completely lack juridical force."

[112] See subsection 9.5.4, citing Valuet, LRTE, 554.

[113] See the final paragraphs of this chapter at the end of section 11.4: "That freedom which is internal and personal and that which is external and social are both equal in their origin" (Sept. 24, 1964, oral intervention of Bishop Ernest J. Primeau of Manchester, New Hampshire, possibly ghost-written by Murray [AS III/2, 495–97]); English translation in William K. Leahy and Anthony T. Massimini, eds., *Third Session Council Speeches of Vatican II* (Glen Rock, NJ: Paulist Press, 1966), 48–50. Note that the opponents of the Primeau/Murray proposal also use the words internal and external in the same way (see section 11.4, citations to interventions of Brizgys and Garcia de Sierra y Méndez). Regan, too, uses these terms in the same way. Cf. Regan, asserting that the Ancel/Colombo argument "involved a problem of linking the internal, personal order to the external, social order." Richard Regan, "John Courtney Murray, the American Bishops, and the *Declaration on Religious Liberty*," in John T. Ford, ed., *Religious Liberty: Paul VI and Dignitatis Humanae* (Brescia, Italy: Istituto Paolo VI, 1995), 57.

the *consequence* in the *external* realm, namely, state incompetence, follows as a function of the so-called *internal* foundation, that is, the basis of the right in human dignity. The *internal* foundation establishes religious liberty as a natural right, and as a result of this status itself, the state is incompetent to violate the right.[114] That is, state incompetence is a consequence of the right's foundation in human dignity. It is not itself a foundation for the right.)[115]

To return to the matters of taxation and property identified by Kennedy and Spinelli, these questions might seem to be somewhat distantly removed from considerations of conscience and religious freedom, but they are not. Indeed, the declaration itself refers to the need of religious communities to acquire funds and properties and to engage in many other practical activities that are necessary for the full exercise of religious rights (including communications, training clergy, and erecting buildings) (DH, §4c). In addition, inquiry into the law of taxation is warranted because of the clear breadth of Murray's notion of state incompetence and the apparent breadth of the corresponding notions of other proponents of the theory. Moreover, if we consider questions that lie even closer to the heart of concerns over conscience and religious freedom, we will see that the incompetence argument (especially in its broad, Murrayite formulation) remains problematic.

Murray asserts that "it is neither within the power nor within the competence of government to judge whether conscience be erroneous or not, in good faith or in bad faith."[116] Along similar lines, Pavan describes the state as incompetent to evaluate (*apprecier*) interior human acts or to have authority over them.[117] These are ringing principles, and most people of good will would have sympathy with them. However, they should not go unexamined.

There are situations in which civil authorities provide some benefit or accommodation to religion, and, to prevent the abuse of the measure in question, they may find it necessary to consider the sincerity of the person's religious beliefs. To return to the Kennedy example, consider the situation in which a state provides exemption from taxation for churches and religious communities. The benefit of tax exemption is so decisive that

---

[114] Cf. Hervada, *Critical Introduction*, 153.

[115] Even the explanation offered here in the main text may separate the internal and external aspects excessively. Man is indeed naturally a seeker of truth, but this fact is relevant not only internally but also externally or socially. That is, man is also a social being, and as a result, the way that he seeks the truth is in dialogue and communication with other men. See section 11.2 below.

[116] Murray, "Religious Freedom" (Georgetown speech), 137.

[117] Pavan, "Le droit à la liberté religieuse en ses éléments essentiels," 173 (from the author's discussion of the principle of interiority).

10.3. The Practical Problems with the "Incompetence Argument"

some persons and entities may seek to obtain it fraudulently. To prevent this abuse, the government may seek to verify that the directors truly are founding their organization with a religious purpose rather than seeking to shield their enterprise from tax liability for purely financial motives. The inquiry could be limited and respectful, but because the purpose is to verify that the founders have a truly religious motive in establishing their church or religious community, the inquiry would be at least a minimal investigation into the sincerity of their beliefs.[118]

Along similar lines, the civil authority might allow those with a conscientious objection to military service to avoid compulsory duty or to substitute a different type of service. However, it is possible that a person might seek to avoid military service by invoking this provision, even though his true motives were economic, political, or simply a general aversion to military service.[119] In this scenario, could the civil authority legitimately seek to verify that the person truly is motivated by reasons of conscience in seeking the status of a conscientious objector?

It does not seem that the formulations of either Murray or Pavan would permit these types of inquiries. They both refer to a "reserved zone" or a protected sphere of activity concerning religious freedom and conscience. (Minnerath does as well.) Both of the scenarios described involve some inquiry, at least minimally, into the sincerity of one's beliefs or perhaps even one's conscience or good faith. Thus, both involve intrusion not only into the general protected zone of religious matters but even into what is found at the core of that zone, namely, conscience and interior acts.

Yet, one also can appreciate a government's legitimate need to ensure that its benefits and accommodations to religion and conscience fall to persons and organizations entitled and qualified to receive them. (Note that it is precisely a government's disposition to protect and advance religious

---

[118] U.S. tax law allows for civil inquiries and examinations of churches, but it limits the government's authority to initiate such an inquiry. In particular, a high-level official of the U.S. Treasury must reasonably believe (based on facts recorded in writing) that the entity does not qualify for the tax exemption or is engaged in taxable activity (cf. Internal Revenue Code, §7611). See also "Special Rules Limiting IRS Authority to Audit a Church," IRS, accessed May 15, 2021, https://www.irs.gov/charities-non-profits/churches-religious-organizations/special-rules-limiting-irs-authority-to-audit-a-church; "Church Audit Process," IRS, accessed May 15, 2021, https://www.irs.gov/charities-non-profits/churches-religious-organizations/church-audit-process; Robert W. Wood, "IRS Can't Tax Churches, but Fake Ones Can Trigger Tax Evasion Charges," Forbes, Apr. 13, 2017, accessed May 17, 2021, https://www.forbes.com/sites/robertwood/2017/04/13/irs-cant-tax-churches-but-fake-churches-can-trigger-tax-evasion-charges/.

[119] See generally Gillette v. United States, 401 U.S. 437, 452–60 (1971).

rights that gives rise to the occasion for inquiring about one's sincerity, so as to verify eligibility for the religious benefit that the government seeks to provide.) Indeed, if the civil authorities are prevented from making this verification, they may decide to abandon altogether these efforts to accommodate religion and conscience. One can appreciate fears and concerns that the authorities might use their legitimate inquiry as a pretext for further, more intrusive, and unwarranted inquiries into conscience or interior acts. Several council fathers expressed this concern, and it is indeed a serious one. However, the incompetence argument, especially as proposed by Murray, has a certain air of unreality about it. That is, it seemingly would prohibit even the limited and seemingly legitimate inquiry and, as a consequence, might well result in a withdrawal altogether of the governmental accommodations to religion and conscience.

This idea of a protected or reserved zone for religious activity described by Pavan, Murray, and Minnerath is comforting and reassuring. However, the image that it suggests may not comport all that closely to juridic reality. It tends to suggest the idea of an impenetrable enclave into which the state is absolutely excluded from reaching. Murray's tendency to stark separation and absolute formulations seems particularly likely to suggest this image.[120] The idea of a reserved zone is not necessarily incorrect, but the image of an impenetrable enclave is misleading. The problem is that this is not how juridic guarantees work. They do indeed provide some assurance against governmental interference, but they do not necessarily exclude state action altogether. Rather, the protected zone often represents a *raising of the bar* against state action. Stated differently, because protected interests are at stake, the state will be required to demonstrate a sufficiently important governmental need if it seeks to interfere in the protected activity. Thus, there is a safeguard against abusive state action but not necessarily an exclusion of state action altogether.

The four issues raised here—taxation, corporate form, state recognition of religious communities, and conscientious objection—are important ones,

---

[120] Murray's writings themselves, of course, make clear that he is aware of the need for limitations on religious practice in some contexts. Indeed, Murray worked on this very issue at the Council, and one of the drafts under his care was the first one to propose "public order" as the correct standard for such interventions. The problem addressed in the main text, however, concerns not Murray's own understanding in this area but rather the images that his (and Pavan's and Minnerath's) writings suggest when they refer to a protected zone or sphere for religious activity. In the case of Murray, his neglect to elaborate on his idea of state incompetence would seem to increase the likelihood that readers will envision his idea of incompetence as an impenetrable sphere of freedom from state interference.

but none is new or particularly unusual. Yet, it does not seem that the incompetence argument is able to resolve them in concrete situations. None of the formulations considered above addresses (or even seems to contemplate) the practical realities of taxation and corporate form, despite nearly always conceiving of the ambit of state incompetence broadly. Many of them do discuss matters of conscience and interior human acts, but even these seem to lack a principle for resolution of the conscience questions discussed here. Worse yet, to the extent that one might attempt to apply the proponents' formulations to questions such as conscientious objection, the incompetence argument may well lead to the exclusion of the contemplated state action (that is, verifying an applicant's sincerity). In this event, the unintended but almost inevitable result likely would be the government's decision to cease recognizing conscientious objector status altogether.

10.3.5.2. A New Hypocrisy

The argument from state incompetence presents a logical problem as well. Murray's basic and oft-repeated formula is that the state is incompetent in religious matters (broadly considered), except for the protection of religious freedom. This is a familiar idea, especially in commentary on the declaration. However, it masks an incongruity or a logical difficulty.

If religion is an area in which the state lacks the competence to act, how can it be that, in this important—undoubtedly religious—question of personal and communal religious freedom, the state is indeed competent?

The obvious answer is that Murray simply has created an *exception* to his own rule. This is a convenient solution, but it is one that arguably calls the rule itself into question. In addition to the preceding observations on important areas of Church-state interaction that the incompetence argument ignores, this quality of relying on one (or more likely, many, exceptions) gives the argument its air of detachment from concrete realities.

This also accounts for the often-confused expression of the incompetence principle. Hamer and Riva assert that the state is incompetent in religious matters, but they immediately add that the state nonetheless may not be completely neglectful of religion.[121] This is incongruous. If the state truly is incompetent, then it would seem obligatory for it to neglect religion, at least in large part. Hamer and Riva are correct that, under DH's doctrine, the state is enjoined *not* to neglect religion and indeed is urged positively to promote the religious life of the citizenry. The difficulty is that these authors seek to join this principle with one that the declaration never voices, namely,

---

[121] Cf. Hamer/Riva, 187.

a somewhat broad notion of state incompetence in religious matters. DH never uses the language of incompetence, and even where it preserves this principle, it does so only after limiting it drastically (to apply only to actual state compulsion or inhibition of religious acts rather than to extend to all religious matters).

The Murrayite principle of state incompetence simply is a poor match for the declaration's insistence on state action to promote the religious life of citizens. Murray scholar (and admirer) Kenneth Grasso provides a valuable and exacting analysis of Murray's conception of state incompetence. He makes clear that the latter's understanding of "public order" is exceedingly "thin."[122] That is, Murray sees the civil authority as little more than a police officer or a "night-watchman." By contrast, the declaration envisions the public powers as positively promoting religion. Grasso demonstrates that Murray's notion of state incompetence leaves little or no room for the state to undertake the responsibilities that the declaration enjoins upon it.[123]

The preceding subsection discussed the failure of the proponents of state incompetence to address (or to provide a theory of incompetence capable of addressing) a number of practical issues. If one were to engage in dialogue with them, these learned commentators surely would be able to formulate answers to the questions raised above. However, these answers would be merely personal (that is, the considered opinions of thoughtful scholars, but detached from their incompetence theories) or else they would need to be incorporated by way of new exceptions to their formulations of state incompetence.[124] The assertion of state incompetence—if it is to serve as the foundation for religious liberty—must be broad, but a broad notion

---

[122] Cf. Grasso, "Murray, 'the Juridical State,' and Religious Freedom," 31: "At times, Murray's analysis seems to suggest that it [the concept of public order] possesses a rather thin content."

[123] Cf. Grasso, "Murray, 'the Juridical State,' and Religious Freedom," 31–32. Russell Hittinger raises the question of whether the argument from state incompetence even allows the state to recognize religion as good (cf. Hittinger, "*Dignitatis Humanae* on Establishment," 16).

[124] Murray's treatment of *special civil recognition* of religion is an example of his willingness to create a new exception to his incompetence argument when circumstances render it necessary or useful. See section 4.5 and subsection 9.3.4. His familiar formulation provides that the state's only competence in religion is to promote and protect religious freedom. As a result, his theory seems incompatible with state establishment of religion, even in the muted form in which the declaration acknowledges it. Yet, Murray does approve of this *special civil recognition* of religion, provided that the recognition is based on historical circumstances alone rather than truth claims. Note, however, that recognition even for historical reasons seems inconsistent with Murray's fundamental principle of state incompetence in religious matters. He is able to approve of *special civil recognition* of religion only by creating an exception to his theory of incompetence. See subsection 9.3.4 above.

10.3. The Practical Problems with the "Incompetence Argument"

(as we have seen) raises problems of definition and fails to take account of numerous significant areas in which religion and the state inevitably meet.

One can imagine a formulation of state incompetence containing multiple exceptions, but such a prospect raises the question of whether, in light of the need for so many exceptions, the state truly remains incompetent in religious matters in any meaningful sense. Murray's apparent solution to this problem is to limit himself to a single exception, namely, the state's duty to protect religious freedom, but the price of this solution is a formulation that is nearly empty of content, and that therefore provides no practical guidance on matters involving the unavoidable intersection of Church and state. As a result of these difficulties, Grasso suggests that state incompetence in religious matters simply may be an unworkable concept.[125]

Another danger is hypocrisy. If we seek actually to apply a broad principle of state incompetence in an attempt to resolve concrete problems and disputes, it seems almost certain that the solution to each concrete problem often will require a new exception to the incompetence formulation. That is, instead of having a vigorous principle to apply to concrete problems, we will be constantly adjusting the principle itself. The key danger, of course, is that of falling into the trap of repeatedly reworking the principle to fit a predetermined result.[126]

The Polish bishops at the Council objected to Murray's incompetence argument on different but not unrelated grounds. They voiced strong objection to a Murrayite passage that remained in the fifth draft of the declaration (the *Textus Recognitus*, dated October 28, 1965). That passage said, "The civil power, therefore, must be said to exceed its limits if it either

---

[125] "Seen in this context [confusion over whether the state may recognize religious truth], one might well wonder if the very language of the religious 'incompetence' of the state does not invite needless confusion" (Grasso, "Murray, 'the Juridical State,' and Religious Freedom," 40). Grasso's focus here is the specific problem of whether the state may recognize religious truth, but he is at least as concerned with Murray's "thin" conception of public order, and, as a result, I believe that his misgivings about the language of incompetence are equally justified on the latter grounds.

[126] Indeed, Murray seems to have fallen into this trap already. His familiar definition of state incompetence in religious matters already contains one exception, namely, for the protection of religious freedom. In addition, his treatment of *special civil recognition* of religion subtly incorporates a second exception, that is, one based on the *historical circumstances* of the people of a particular state. In addition, if one were to attempt to apply Murray's principle of state incompetence to the issues discussed in the preceding subsection (that is, the questions identified by Kennedy and Spinelli), this application likely would require additional exceptions (such as the distinction between *direct* and *indirect* state action impacting religion or religious communities).

impedes or directs those matters that by their nature transcend the earthly and temporal order of things."[127] Led by Stefan Cardinal Wyszyński, the Polish bishops expressed fear over the malleability of this incompetence principle. Their fear was that oppressive governments would use the stark delineation between the two spheres to maximize the temporal and to minimize the religious, so as to exclude any religious voice in public affairs.[128]

One of the circumstances that favored the adoption of a religious liberty declaration was the widespread impression that the pre-conciliar Catholic position on tolerance and liberty had been hypocritical. That is, the argument ran, Church leaders demand freedom for Catholics when they are the minority religion in a given place, but when they are in the majority and especially where Catholicism is the state religion, they recognize the religious rights only of Catholics, while for others they recognize only the possibility of tolerance.[129]

One of the Council's objectives and successes was to put this impression to rest through the adoption of a religious liberty declaration. However, the shadow of the incompetence argument raises anew the risk of hypocrisy, albeit of a different sort. The Polish bishops were alive to this threat at the Council. In addition, however, the possibility of the incompetence argument giving rise to a regime of convenient exceptions is by no means a problem only of our own day.

The incompetence argument in fact dates back to the early Church. An important argument against persecution or unwarranted state interference with the Church was the assertion that the state is incompetent in religious matters or in ecclesiastical matters. The problem is that the application of this principle was quite inconsistent. When the civil authority opposed the Church, the leaders of the Church objected on the ground of incompetence or inappropriate interference by the temporal power. However, when the temporal authorities interposed themselves in ways that aided the Church, her leaders very often turned a blind eye.[130]

---

[127] *Textus Recognitus*, §3 [AS IV/5, 81]; English translation in Schindler/Healy, 353.

[128] Cf. Silvia Scatena, *La fatica della libertà. L'elaborazione della dichiarazione* Dignitatis humanae *sulla libertà religiosa del Vaticano II*, Istituto per le scienze religiose—Bologna, Testi e ricerche di scienze religiose, nuova serie, 31 (Bologna, Italy: Il Mulino, 2003), 539–40.

[129] Cf. Jérôme Hamer, "Histoire du texte de la Déclaration," *Unam Sanctam* 60 (1967): 56: Dupanloup's nineteenth-century "thesis/hypothesis" formula exposes the Church to charges of opportunism; Carrillo de Albornoz, "Roman Catholicism and Religious Liberty," 405–21, reviewing authors who charge the Church with opportunism by insisting upon liberty when Catholics are in the minority but denying external liberty to non-Catholics in countries where Catholics form a large majority.

[130] Cf. Joseph Lecler, *Toleration and the Reformation*, vol. 1, trans. T. L. Westow (London/

The argument from state incompetence is a seemingly attractive theory. It is relatively straightforward and, at least in logical terms, it provides a basis for the right to religious liberty. Moreover, the argument has deep roots in Christian history, and it also resonates with contemporary sensibilities, especially in the liberal Western democracies. Nevertheless, a close inquiry into the argument reveals it as poorly-defined, ill-suited to addressing concrete problems, and vulnerable to erosion from a regime of convenient exceptions. Thus, this popular but very problematic notion threatens to supplant the arguable pre-conciliar hypocrisy with an entirely new hypocrisy.

10.4. Doctrinal Difficulties

In addition to the practical problems discussed at length in section 10.2, the incompetence argument presents doctrinal difficulties as well. These include the duty of the civic community to God and the compatibility of this argument with other provisions of DH and other Council documents.

10.4.1. The Duty of the Civic Community to God (Part 1)

The key doctrinal question about DH is whether it contradicts the teachings of the nineteenth-century and early twentieth-century popes. This entire work is an attempt to answer this question. A full response requires inquiry into several areas including the relationship between Church and state (see chapter 4), the issue of whether DH embraces indifferentism (see chapter 8), and the situations in which the civil power legitimately may limit religious activity (see chapter 12). A factor that is relevant to more than one of these areas is the teaching of the nineteenth-century and twentieth-century papal magisterium on the duty of the civic community to God.[131]

Papal teaching on this point is clear. Leo XIII taught that the civic community must not be godless (cf. ID, §6; LP, §21) and, indeed, that it is obliged to worship God (ID, §21). Pius XI taught that the rulers of a people

---

New York: Longmans/Association Press, 1960), 47–51. When the civil authority supports heresy or opposes the interests of the Church, "the bishops or Popes insist . . . on the distinction between the spiritual and the temporal" (Lecler, 47). However, when (especially in the fourth and fifth centuries) the imperial power supports her, "the Church is much less rigid in the practical application of its principles. It lets the emperors summon the councils, rejoices in their zeal for the observation of ecclesiastical discipline, and asks for their support against schism and heresy" (Lecler, 51).

[131] I am adopting Harrison's usage in this context of usually referring to the *civic community* rather than to the *state* (see section 4.5).

are obliged publicly to honor God.[132] The teaching of Pope Pius XII affirms the notion of "a legitimate and healthy secularity of the State" (*la legittima sana laicità dello Stato*),[133] but it also rejects the separation of civil authority from dependence upon God.[134]

(This section addresses the duty of the state or the civic community to God and to the Church in the context of the conciliar debate over state *establishment* of religion. The reason is that this is where the issue first arose. At the same time, it is important to recall Harrison's cogent observation that legal establishment of a state religion is only a single "historically-conditioned" form of the attempt to fulfill this duty.)[135]

The first appearance of the incompetence argument alarmed a number of council fathers because they saw it as excluding state establishment of religion (and apparently, by implication, preventing the state from fulfilling its duties to the Creator). The second draft of the declaration (the *Declaratio Prior*, dated April 27, 1964) was the first one to feature a version of the incompetence argument, and when the Council debated it in its third session (in September 1964), this passage proved to be controversial.[136] Responding to several fathers' concern that this principle would exclude legal establishment of religion, Archbishop John Heenan of Westminster and Bishop John Wright of Pittsburgh assured the assembly that religious freedom was compatible with state establishment.[137]

Note that the presence of the incompetence argument necessitated Heenan's and Wright's defense of the second draft, that is, their assertion that religious liberty is compatible with state establishment of religion. This presents a difficulty for Murray (and for the incompetence argument), however.[138] Murray's notion of state incompetence has two equally import-

---

[132] Pope Pius XI, Encyclical *Quas Primas* (Dec. 11, 1925), §32: "Not only private individuals but also rulers and princes are bound to give public honour and obedience to Christ ... for His kingly dignity demands that the State should take account of the commandments of God and of Christian principles."

[133] Pope Pius XII, Discorso *Ai marchigiani residenti in Roma* (Mar. 23, 1958) [AAS 50 (1958): 220].

[134] Pope Pius XII, *Summi Pontificatus* (Oct. 20, 1939) [AAS 31 (1939): 431]; cf. *Summi Pontificatus* [AAS 31 (1939): 424]. NB, Valuet notes that two pages of the text are missing from the AAS (cf. LRTC, vol. IIA, 1185n5312).

[135] See section 4.5 and subsection 9.3.4 above (citing and discussing Harrison).

[136] Regan, *Conflict and Consensus*, 90: "The paragraph denying the 'direct capacity and competence' of the state in religious matters was the most controversial of the additions to the second conciliar text on religious freedom."

[137] Regan, *Conflict and Consensus*, 90–91. For Heenan's and Wright's interventions, see AS III/2, 570 (Heenan), 575 (Wright).

[138] Note, however, that at this time Murray was a member of the drafting committee, but he

ant purposes, that is, to ground the right to religious liberty and to preclude state establishment of religion. (See section 4.3 above.) He did not believe that establishment was compatible with religious liberty. Moreover, nearly all proponents of the incompetence argument likewise reject state establishment of religion or assert that the state is incompetent to recognize religious truth.[139] (See section 10.3.3.)

Richard Regan was a protégé of Murray, and his book *Conflict and Consensus* provides a history of the elaboration of DH. Although he seems to appreciate the efforts of Heenan and Wright to defend the second draft, Regan concedes the critics' point. "On principle, however, legal establishment remains difficult to reconcile with an affirmation of the state's incompetence in religious matters."[140]

Heenan and Wright were correct that state establishment is not necessarily incompatible with religious liberty. The Council would make this clear in providing for the possibility of special civil recognition of a given religion.[141] However, the declaration's language on civil recognition took shape

---

was not chiefly responsible for the draft that contained the first mention of the incompetence argument (the second draft, or *Declaratio Prior*, dated April 27, 1964). He recently had published an article in the Jesuit periodical *America*, urging the Council to adopt the incompetence argument. Cf. "On Religious Liberty: Freedom is the most distinctively American issue before the Council," *America* 109 (Nov. 30, 1963): 704–6. However, he suffered a heart attack in January 1964, and, as a result, he was absent from the principal drafting session in February and early March of that year (cf. Scatena, *La fatica della libertà*, 131–32). However, Pietro Pavan played an important role in the drafting of the *Declaratio Prior* (Scatena, 131, 145). His positions were close to Murray's, and he promoted the inclusion of the incompetence argument (cf. Scatena, 140, 145–46).

[139] Valuet is a clear exception.

[140] Regan, *Conflict and Consensus*, 91.

[141] Cf. DH, §6c. Needless to say, *establishment* and *special civil recognition* are different terms, but it is not clear that there is a great deal of difference between them. As a result, I will treat them as at least roughly equivalent. Indeed, Murray, Regan, and Canavan all appear to equate the terms *establishment* and *special civil recognition*. Cf. John Courtney Murray, "Religious Freedom," in *The Documents of Vatican II*, ed. Walter M. Abbott (New York: Herder and Herder, 1966), 685n17: "[E]stablishment . . . is a matter of historical circumstance"; Murray, "The Issue of Church and State at Vatican Council II," *Theological Studies* 27, no. 4 (December 1966): 595 (similar); Regan, *Conflict and Consensus*, 175: DH "make[s] clear that . . . establishment is the product of historical circumstance"; Francis Canavan, "The Catholic Concept of Religious Freedom as a Human Right," in *Religious Liberty: An End and a Beginning*, ed. John Courtney Murray (New York: MacMillan, 1966), 77–78, discussing *special civil recognition* in terms of *establishment*.

For the purposes of comparison, Valuet's distinction of four different types of confessionality is helpful. Chapter 4 above contains a discussion of special civil recognition and concludes that DH at least permits (in Valuet's terminology) *formal confessionality of the historico-sociological type* (see section 4.2). In addition, Brian Harrison's scholarship on the

only in the fifth and sixth drafts of the document, and it is not coincidental that these same two drafts first scaled back the incompetence argument and then eliminated it almost entirely. (Note also that Heenan and Wright had asserted the compatibility between establishment and *religious liberty*, not necessarily between establishment and the *incompetence argument*.)

Before arriving at the fifth and sixth schemata, however, the drafting process passed through a stage where Murray had primary responsibility for the document. He was the main author of the third and fourth drafts, and in those versions the incompetence argument increased in prominence. (See subsections 9.3.1 and 9.3.2.) Indeed, in Murray's drafts, it became the primary foundation for the right to religious liberty. The third draft (the *Textus Emendatus*, dated November 17, 1964) said that the state's competence was "restricted to the earthly and temporal order," and the fourth (the *Textus Reemendatus*, dated May 28, 1965) contained similar language.[142] This was the highpoint of the incompetence argument, and from this juncture, it quickly and decisively declined in importance.

10.4.1.1. Amendments concerning State Establishment of Religion

The fathers debated the fourth draft in the fourth session of the Council (in September 1965). Again, a number of interventions criticized the incompetence language on several grounds. Pope Paul VI was moved by these criticisms, and after the debate, he met with the relator for the declaration, Bishop De Smedt. Paul provided instructions for the further redaction of the

---

last-minute addition of the phrase "and societies" to article 1 of DH (referring to duties, not only of individuals but also of societies toward the Church) suggests that *formal confessionality of the doctrinal type* (again, Valuet's terminology) is not necessarily inconsistent with DH, provided that the state ensures the religious liberty of all (see sections 4.5–4.7 above).

[142] The third schema or *Textus Emendatus* provided as follows: "In performing these [religious] acts, therefore, man is not subject to the civil power, whose competence, on account of its end, is restricted to the earthly and temporal order. . . . The public power completely exceeds its limits if it involves itself in any way in the governing of minds or the care of souls" (*Textus Emendatus*, §4e) [AS III/8, 432; English translation by Brannon and Camacho in Schindler/Healy, 293]. Note that the idea of the state being "restricted to the earthly and temporal order" is absolute for Murray, but not for Leo XIII or the other popes.

The fourth draft (the *Textus Reemendatus*) was similar: "[R]eligious acts, in which men and women privately and publicly order themselves toward God out of a sense of inner conviction, by their nature transcend the earthly and temporal order of things. The competence of the civil power, however, on account of its proper end—which today is more accurately perceived and described in terms of the demands of the dignity of the person and his rights—is restricted in its purpose to the earthly and temporal order. . . . The civil power must therefore be said to exceed its limits if it involves itself in those matters that concern the very ordination of man to God" (*Textus Reemendatus*, §3) [AS IV/1, 150; English translation by Brannon and Camacho in Schindler/Healy, 323].

document, and these included the charge to present the traditional teaching of the magisterium and to make clear to secular states that they continue to have obligations to the Church.[143]

Note here that the dynamism of the last few weeks of redaction, in large measure, is a sharp move away from the incompetence argument. The reason should be clear. A broad formulation of this argument, such as Murray's, is incompatible with state establishment of religion (even in the muted language that the Council would adopt, namely, "special civil recognition"). Murray says outright that the state's sole competence in the religious field is to promote religious liberty. (See subsection 10.3.4.2.) Although the declaration preserves the possibility of state establishment (without endorsing it), Murray's notion of state incompetence excludes it.[144]

If this had not been apparent already from Murray's argument itself, it became clearer after the Council in light of Murray's repeated misrepresentations of the final text of article 6 of the declaration. (See subsection 9.3.4 above.) The *fifth* conciliar schema (the *Textus Recognitus*) had provided for special civil recognition of religion, based on the "*historical* circumstances" of the people in question. In the *sixth* and final schema (the *Textus Denuo Recognitus*), though, the Secretariat revised (and apparently broadened) this standard to provide for such civil recognition on account of the people's "*peculiar* circumstances." The language of the fifth draft was satisfactory to Murray in some sense, but the language of the final text was not. Thus, despite this amendment, Murray—in his articles and speeches following the Council—almost invariably describes the relevant passage (article 6) as if it still contained the "historical circumstances" language that the Secretariat had discarded. (See subsection 9.3.4 above.)

The only apparent reason for Murray's inability to accept the final version of article 6 is its inconsistency with his incompetence argument. The

---

[143] See section 4.6 above, quoting De Smedt's note from his September 30, 1965, meeting with Pope Paul VI.

[144] Although the difficulty addressed here is the *breadth* of the incompetence argument (especially Murray's version of it), it does not seem that narrowing the concept would provide a remedy. The difficulty with a narrower version of state incompetence is that it would not sufficiently exclude the state from religious matters so as to provide the foundation for the right to religious liberty. For example, the narrower term, state incompetence in *ecclesiastical* matters (as opposed to all *religious* matters), is *sufficiently limited* to avoid the problem of excluding official establishment of religion, but it is *insufficiently broad* to provide the foundation for religious liberty. (See subsection 10.3.2.) As a result, it does not seem that any version of the incompetence argument could provide a proper foundation for this right.

passage on special civil recognition of religion does not present a difficulty in harmonizing with any other part of Murray's juridical approach.

Note, however, that even Murray's qualified acceptance of the "historical circumstances" language from the fifth schema appears to be inconsistent with his basic notion of state incompetence. That is, it amounts to state action in connection with religion, for a purpose other than what Murray says is the state's sole competence in this area, namely, protecting religious freedom. Stated differently, it seems that Murray is able to accept civil recognition of a particular religion (on the basis of historical circumstances) only by implicitly creating a *new exception* to his own incompetence theory. (See subsection 10.3.5.2.) Even this exception, however, reconciles the Murray theory only with the fifth conciliar text, not the final version of the declaration.

10.4.1.2. Amendments concerning the Incompetence Language Itself

The late changes to the document in the Council's fourth session concerned not only the parameters for special civil recognition of religion but also the incompetence language itself. As with the third draft (the *Textus Emendatus*, dated November 17, 1964), Murray was the chief author of the fourth draft as well, and it (the fourth, the *Textus Reemendatus*, dated May 28, 1965) contained a sentence limiting the state's competence "to the earthly and temporal order."[145] The fifth draft (the *Textus Recognitus*, dated October 22, 1965) *deleted* this sentence. Murray's fourth schema also excluded the civil authority's competence from "those matters that concern the very ordination of man to God." In the fifth schema, this language was revised and limited to read, "The civil power must therefore be said to exceed its limits if it either impedes or directs those matters that by their nature transcend the earthly and temporal order of things."[146] Despite this scaling back of Murray's argument, however, complaints about the incompetence language persisted.

The conservative International Group of Fathers (which included Archbishop Marcel Lefebvre) continued to object to the passage as insufficiently consistent with the teachings of previous popes on the duties of the state to religion. In addition, the Polish bishops objected on different grounds. They feared that certain regimes, such as those behind the Iron Curtain, would use this language to exclude the Church from public life.[147]

---

[145] Nicholas J. Healy, "The Drafting of *Dignitatis Humanae*," in Schindler/Healy, 229.

[146] Healy, "The Drafting of *Dignitatis Humanae*," in Schindler/Healy, 230, citing *Textus Recognitus*, §3 [AS IV/5, 81; English translation at Schindler/Healy, 353].

[147] Cf. Scatena, *La fatica della libertà*, 547 (complaints regarding fifth draft). See also Scatena,

10.4. Doctrinal Difficulties

The Polish bishops advocated the suppression of this entire passage,[148] and although they did not achieve this goal, the final version limited the reach of the incompetence argument still more. That is, the final text of the declaration would affirm that religious acts "transcend by their nature the order of terrestrial and temporal affairs." In addition, it stated that a government "would clearly transgress the limits set to its power, were it to presume to command or inhibit acts that are religious" (DH, §3e). Furthermore, although the final text would identify the temporal common good as government's distinctive purpose, it would avoid the Murrayite language restricting it solely to this purpose (cf. DH, §3e; see also subsection 9.5.1, citing Harrison).

This discussion (from subsection 10.4.1 to this one) has addressed state establishment of religion at some length, and therefore it has raised only *indirectly* the question of the civic community's duty to God and to the Church.[149] The reason for this focus is that much of the criticism of the incompetence argument in the actual Council debates was based on its incompatibility with state establishment of religion. The final declaration implicitly acknowledges the compatibility of legal establishment (or special civil recognition) with religious liberty. One of the factors that made this harmonization possible was the Secretariat's severe reduction of the incompetence argument.[150] If it had continued along Murray's path of founding religious liberty on the incompetence of the state in religious matters, this argument seemingly would have undermined the declaration's affirmation of the possibility of special civil recognition of a particular religion.[151]

539–40 (similar complaints regarding fourth draft).

[148] Scatena, *La fatica della libertà*, 547.

[149] The reason that the raising of the question is indirect is that, as Valuet explains, not all forms of legal establishment (or confessionality) make truth claims for the established religion (see section 4.2). In addition, as noted in subsection 3.2.4, section 4.5, and subsection 9.3.4, article 6 of the declaration refers to establishment—or rather, special civil recognition—of religion in general terms. That is, this single passage addresses the establishment question as it concerns both Catholicism and other religions.

[150] Another factor that made it possible was Bernard Cardinal Alfrink's influential suggestion to treat establishment or civil recognition in the conditional mood. Cf. Sept. 15, 1965, intervention of Alfrink (AS IV/1, 218). The Secretariat adopted this suggestion, and it remained in the final document. "If, in view of peculiar circumstances obtaining among peoples..." (DH, §6c). The result is a somewhat convoluted passage, but one that proved to be broadly acceptable, because it both acknowledges legal establishment and, at the same time, avoids endorsing it.

[151] This at least is the case with Murray's own notion of state incompetence in religious matters. Its inclusion in the third and fourth drafts drew many objections, and the stalemate regarding establishment or civil recognition resolved only with its omission. The final version

The following section will address more *directly* the state's duty to the Creator and to the Church. That is, it will consider not simply whether the incompetence argument is reconcilable with state establishment of religion but whether it is compatible with the community's duty toward the Creator and religion.

10.4.2. The Duty of the Civic Community to God (Part 2)

The final version of the declaration was strengthened (from the standpoint of the Council minority) in a significant way.[152] That is, the fifth draft (the *Textus Recognitus*, dated October 22, 1965) already had stated that the declaration "leaves intact the Catholic teaching on the one true religion, the one Church of Christ, and the moral duty individuals have toward the Church."[153] The final draft (the *Textus Denuo Recognitus*, dated November 19, 1965), however, was further revised to make clear that what was remaining intact was "the *traditional* Catholic teaching" and that this duty to the Church falls not only to individuals but also to "*societies*."[154]

Commentators continue to debate whether this reference to "societies" means that the state or the civic community itself has a duty to the Church. De Smedt's final *relatio* explains that the term "societies" is to be understood as including "the public authority."[155] As a result, he says, the Council does not neglect (although it does decline to emphasize) this part of the traditional teaching. Harrison significantly notes that because De Smedt was the relator for the declaration, this *relatio* is the sole official interpretation of article 1's reference to "societies."[156] This interpretation also is supported by an influential commentator on the declaration, Jérôme Hamer, who was

---

of the declaration never mentions the word incompetence, and the only faint remnants of this theme are in a more flexible and moderate vein than Murray's very separationist understanding of state incompetence (cf. DH, §3e).

[152] See section 4.6 above.

[153] AS IV/5, 78; English translation in Schindler/Healy, 351.

[154] Thus, the final version reads, "Religious freedom ... leaves untouched traditional Catholic doctrine on the moral duty of men and societies toward the true religion and toward the one Church of Christ" (DH, §1c). A new English translation published in Schindler/Healy reads: "[R]eligious freedom ... leaves intact the traditional Catholic teaching on the moral duty individuals and society have toward the true religion and the one Church of Christ" (Schindler/Healy, 385).

[155] See section 4.6, citing Brian W. Harrison, *Religious Liberty and Contraception: Did Vatican II Open the Way for a New Sexual Ethic?* (Melbourne: John XXIII Fellowship Co-op., Ltd., 1988), 75, quoting De Smedt's final oral *relatio* (AS IV/6, 719).

[156] Harrison's scholarship was made possible by the publication of the Acts of the Council—the *Acta Synodalia*—in 1979.

10.4. Doctrinal Difficulties

involved in all stages of the document's progress. Hamer said in his 1967 article on the history of the text that the duty mentioned in article 1 applies not only to individuals but also to social groups, from the most modest all the way up to nations and states, including all social bodies in-between.[157]

The incompetence argument, as propounded by Murray and other prominent commentators, seems to be incompatible with De Smedt's official interpretation of article 1. The reason is that Murray binds his notion of incompetence not only to religious liberty but to a very strict separationism as well. Murray asserts that the state is entirely incompetent in religious matters, except to protect religious freedom. He makes an apparent exception to allow for the state's special civil recognition of a particular religion, but only if the state bases that recognition on the historical circumstances of the people rather than the truth claims of religion. (See section 9.3.4 above.) It would seem then that the public authority as conceived by Murray lacks the competence to fulfill the moral duty to the Church that the declaration continues to recognize as binding. As discussed above, Murray goes into few specifics in his theory, but he does say that the state may not promote or protect religious truth. (See subsection 10.3.4.2.) Other proponents of the incompetence argument are more detailed, and their apparent rejection of this duty is explicit. That is, nearly all argue that the state may not even recognize religious truth. These include Biffi, Hamer and Riva,[158] Pavan, and D'Avack.[159] (By contrast, Ocáriz argues that the state may recognize the true religion, and Harrison and Valuet take similar or equivalent positions.)[160] As with the relatively late revisions to article 6, it is challenging indeed to get a firm grasp on these last-minute amendments to article 1.

---

[157] See section 4.6, quoting Hamer's history of the DH text.

[158] Hamer's position is surprising. He asserts that all societies have a duty to God (cf. "Histoire du texte de la Déclaration," 60), and that states have a moral duty to the Church (Hamer, 99–100), but he nonetheless says that the state is incompetent to judge a religion as true or false (Hamer, 88; Jérôme Hamer and Clemente Riva, *La libertà religiosa nel Vaticano II* [Torino, Italy: Elle di Ci, 1966], 179).

[159] Valuet, by contrast, is not a proponent of the incompetence argument in the usual way, and his notion does not preclude the state from recognizing religious truth. See subsection 10.3.5.1.

[160] Cf. Fernando Ocáriz, "Sulla libertà religiosa. Continuità del Vaticano II con il Magistero precedente," *Annales theologici* 3 (1989): 93; Harrison, RL&C, 77; Brian W. Harrison, "John Courtney Murray: A Reliable Interpreter of *Dignitatis Humanae*?" in *We Hold These Truths and More*, ed. Donald J. D'Elia and Stephen M. Krason (Steubenville, OH: Franciscan University Press, 1993), 160; Valuet, LRTE, 394. See also sections 4.2 and 4.5 above. Bradley is sympathetic to this position, but frames it in terms of DH's silence on the question. Gerard Bradley, "Pope John Paul II and Religious Liberty," *Ave Maria Law Review* 6, no. 1 (2007): 41.

What questions do these late amendments raise? *What precisely are societies* (including, as De Smedt says, civil rulers) *required to do in fulfillment of their duty to the true religion?* Article 1 refers to this duty as *moral*. *Is this reference to a* moral *duty to be understood in distinction from a* juridic duty? Is article 6's acknowledgement of the factual hypothesis of civil recognition of religion in tension with the article 1 duty of all men and societies to the true religion?

The text of the declaration—by design—provides little help in addressing these questions. The relator, Bishop De Smedt, says outright that the document does not directly address the juridical relations between Church and state.[161] By the same token, he says that it does not present a full description of all the Church's rights.[162]

In addition, the drafting history of the revisions sheds only limited light on these questions. The history of the late amendments to article 1 suggests that the impetus for the change came from Pope Paul VI and indirectly from persisting complaints that the document was not sufficiently consistent with the teachings of earlier popes. (See section 4.6 and subsection 10.4.1.1 above.) In addition, Bishop De Smedt provides an explanation of the passage in his final oral *relatio*:

> Some Fathers affirm that the Declaration does not sufficiently show how our doctrine is not opposed to ecclesiastical documents up till the time of the Supreme Pontiff Leo XIII. As we said in the last *relatio*, this is a matter for future theological and historical studies to bring to light more fully. As regards the substance of the problem, the point should be made that while the papal documents up to Leo XIII insisted more on the moral duty of public authorities toward the true religion, the recent Supreme Pontiffs, while retaining this doctrine, complement it by highlighting another duty of the same authorities, namely, that of observing the exigencies of the dignity

---

[161] Émile De Smedt, Oral *Relatio* on the *Textus Emendatus* (Nov. 19, 1964) [AS III/8, 452]. NB, see the discussion of this *relatio* in section 4.2 above for an explanation of why I rely on it there and here, despite my criticism of Thomas Pink's use of the same document (in subsection 9.5.1 above).

[162] Cf. Oral *Relatio* on the *Textus Recognitus* [AS IV/5, 102]. See also Mathijs Lamberigts, "Msgr. Emiel-Jozef De Smedt, Bishop of Bruges, and the Second Vatican Council," in *Experience, Organisations and Bodies at Vatican II: Proceedings of the Bologna Conference, December 1996*, ed. M. T. Fattori and A. Melloni (Leuven, Belgium: Bibliotheek van de Faculteit Godgeleerdheid, 1999), 463; Turner, "*Dignitatis Humanae* and the Development of Moral Doctrine," 307.

of the human person in religious matters, as a necessary element of the common good. The text presented to you today recalls more clearly (see nos. 1 and 3) the duties of the public authority towards the true religion (*officia potestatis publicae erga veram religionem*); from which it is manifest that this part of the doctrine has not been overlooked (*ex quo patet hanc doctrinae partem non praetermitti*). However, the special object of our Declaration is to clarify the second part of the doctrine of recent Supreme Pontiffs—that dealing with the rights and duties which emerge from a consideration of the dignity of the human person.[163]

De Smedt's *relatio* does not answer all the questions raised by these late amendments. Indeed, he disclaims an intention to do so. However, he does provide some clarification. He interprets the relevant pronouncements of the earlier popes as standing for the moral duty of public authorities toward the true religion. In this regard, Harrison's position is apt, namely, that the civic community has a duty to God and to religion, but that official recognition of Catholicism in a constitutional or statutory text is only one historically-conditioned expression of this duty, and not one that the Church ever has demanded.[164] In addition, De Smedt makes clear that although recent popes have shifted their focus to human rights and to the requirements of the dignity of the human person in religious matters, they have done so while retaining the previous doctrine. Indeed, he says, the recent teaching *complements* the older teaching.

Another interesting question left open is the precise relationship between state and society. The declaration does appear to adopt this distinction precisely by referring to "societies" in article 1. This is a signature theme of Murray's, though it is not unique to him, and indeed it is an appropriate and important distinction. That is, it is an implicit acknowledgement that government is limited, and that it may not occupy and dominate the entirety of the public space. It is a fundamentally anti-totalitarian principle.

However, although this reference to society addresses one difficulty, it perhaps gives rise to another. How does society as a whole fulfill its duty? Certainly one could point to customs, the activity of civic associations (or intermediary bodies), and the public exercise of religion. However, might society's commitment sometimes require legal enactments or other actions

---

[163] Émile De Smedt, Oral *Relatio* on the *Textus Denuo Recognitus* (Nov. 19, 1965) [AS IV/6, 719; English translation in Harrison, RL&C, 75].

[164] See section 4.5 above, quoting Harrison, RL&C, 70.

by the public authority? The declaration does not answer this question directly, but De Smedt's comment in the final oral *relatio* is intriguing. As already noted, when the declaration speaks of the moral duty of societies to the true religion, De Smedt says that the term *societies* specifically includes the public powers.

But what does it mean? What would it look like for society to fulfill this duty? Again, the declaration does not say.[165] De Smedt's statement does seem to suggest, however, that although it is indeed proper to distinguish between society and state, this distinction should be in the Gelasian mode, that is, indeed a *real distinction*, but not the seemingly *absolute separation* that Murray advocates.

The late amendments to article 1 (and the relatively late revisions to article 6 as well) are important in their own right, but Murray has raised the stakes by inextricably binding together the issues of (1) religious liberty, (2) state incompetence in religious matters, and (3) / (4) Church-state separation / official establishment of religion. The drafting commission as a whole did not consider religious liberty to be incompatible with official establishment of religion,[166] but Murray did, and Murray's opinion—although it did not prevail at the Council—has been influential in the aftermath and may even reflect the prevalent interpretation.[167] Moreover, for Murray, the incompetence of the state is what binds all of these issues together. That is, for him, state incompetence is the foundation of *both* religious liberty *and* separationism (and, it seems clear, of anti-establishmentism too). Note that I have grouped separationism and establishment above in such a way that one might consider them either as distinct issues or as two aspects of the same issue. The reason is that they often seem to be *two sides of the same coin*, such that adopting a position on separationism necessarily seems to imply a corresponding inverse position on establishment or confessionality.

Does the declaration have anything further to say about these two sides of the coin?

---

[165] Harrison, for his part, points to the presence of the president of the Philippines at a large open-air Mass of thanksgiving and prayer for the nation in 1986 following the restoration of democracy. The Mass was celebrated in the capital city by the cardinal of that see, and the president occupied a prominent place. There is no established religion in the Philippines, but Harrison points to this as an example of an action in fulfillment of the article 1 duty (cf. RL&C, 80). My own sense is that Harrison is correct. That is, this episode does indeed illustrate how a civil ruler might fulfill the duties mentioned in DH §1 while remaining within the framework of contemporary constitutional government.

[166] Cf. Turner, "*Dignitatis Humanae* and the Development of Moral Doctrine," 305, 307.

[167] Cf. Turner, "*Dignitatis Humanae* and the Development of Moral Doctrine," 304.

The *establishment or confessionality side of the coin* is quite indistinct and undefined, as if its image largely had been worn away. The Council intended to say little about Church-state relations, and it remained firm in this resolution. On the basis of the text and the *relationes*, one can make only a few observations. The chief one is simply that with appropriate safeguards, confessionality or establishment is not contrary to the teaching of the declaration (although the document itself avoids either encouraging or discouraging it). In addition, the previous papal teaching on the moral duty of men and societies to the true religion remains intact, and the term *societies* here specifically includes the *public powers*. If one confines oneself to the Council's text and the relator's *relationes*, there is little further that one can say with certainty.[168]

When one turns the coin over, however, one encounters a surprise. That is, the *separationist side of the coin* is not nearly as faint and obscure as the establishment side. The final document remains close to Murray's views on a number of important topics (see section 9.2 above), but it departs sharply from Murray's Jeffersonian embrace of a near-absolute separationism. That is, article 6 leaves room for official establishment of religion, and article 1— although its full implications remain undefined—recognizes (through De Smedt's official interpretation) a moral duty to the Church on the part of rulers that seems quite foreign to any regime of strict separationism. Thus, when Murray says after the Council that "the final text of the declaration is inadequate in its treatment of the limitations imposed on government by sound political doctrine,"[169] he seems almost certainly to have both articles 1 and 6 in mind. That is, he seems to refer to late or relatively late changes that he believes do not limit government sufficiently. It is virtually certain that he at least has article 6 in mind, given his record of attempting to reinterpret that passage after the Council (see subsections 9.3.4 and 10.4.1.1). In addition, as discussed below (see subsection 10.4.3), the final text recognizes a number of affirmative governmental duties in the religious realm that are inconsistent with Murray's strict separationism.

Thus, the final version of the declaration seems to be *more clearly*

---

[168] I do not mean to suggest that one necessarily must confine oneself to the document alone. For example, recourse to other conciliar documents—especially *Gaudium et Spes*—is entirely justified. See section 4.8 above (using passages from LG and GS to interpret DH). Article 76 of that constitution says that the Church does not place her hope in privileges from civil authority, but in the same context, it also refers to legitimately acquired rights and indicates that they might or might not be consistent with the Church's witness. As a result, I do not believe that GS §76 resolves the questions noted above.

[169] Murray, "Church and State at Vatican II," 587.

anti-separationist than pro-establishment. However, if a position on one of these issues usually implies an inverse position on the other, does this mean that the document's apparent anti-separationism implies an unstated position in favor of establishment?

No.

Rather, the Council as a whole is reaffirming the principle of Gelasian dualism (see section 4.3 above). That is, it is distinguishing the two orders (religious and temporal) clearly, but it is avoiding the error of insisting on a radical separation between them. Murray's approach binds together all four of the issues listed above, but the Council's does not. Although Murray's strict separationism necessarily implies a corresponding position against official establishment of religion, the Council's moderate and flexible Gelasian dualism does not necessarily imply any position on establishment, either for or against it. By the same token, Murray's separationism is wholly incompatible with the notion of civil rulers having a moral duty to the true religion.

Perhaps the crucial word is *untouched*. Reading DH §1 together with GS §76 suggests that there is indeed a way for the two orders to remain distinct, but in such a way that the Council can leave *untouched* the earlier teaching on this moral duty. The Council is able to do so because its teaching on the autonomy of the temporal realm is grounded in long experience, and because it is flexible enough to prevent the necessary *distinction* between the two orders from hardening into an impregnable *wall of separation* between them.

Although the Council is not emphasizing the traditional teaching, neither is it contradicting or repudiating that teaching. Could it have made this affirmation if it had chosen the religious incompetence of the state as the foundation of this right? I cannot see how. The reason is that the incompetence argument—especially as formulated by Murray, but also by others who would found religious liberty on it—by no means leaves the traditional teaching *untouched*.

10.4.3. The State's Duty to Promote Religious Life

The first difficulty in Murray's notion of state incompetence is its breadth. His exclusion of the state from taking action in regard to religion is so nearly complete as to leave little or no room for civil rulers to fulfill the moral duty that article 1 reaffirms. Indeed, in his extensive commentary on DH in the Walter Abbot edition of the Vatican II documents, Murray takes no notice of the crucial late addition of the phrase "and societies" to article 1.[170]

---

[170] Cf. Harrison, "Reliable Interpreter," 155.

By the same token, although DH remains open to state establishment of religion ("special civil recognition"), the logic of Murray's theory leaves no such space. Indeed, for Murray, the incompetence argument itself is the basis of both religious liberty and the prohibition on establishment. Even Murray's qualified attempt to remain theoretically open to civil recognition of religion ultimately demonstrates the incompatibility between his notion of state incompetence and the type of civil recognition acknowledged by the declaration.[171]

Most of the other notions of state incompetence described above (in subsection 10.3.3) are similarly broad.[172] They may be slightly narrower than Murray's, but to fulfill the purpose of providing a foundation for the right to religious liberty, their proponents nearly always find a broad formulation necessary.[173]

This breadth of scope is the first difficulty with Murray's notion of state incompetence, but there are others as well. As discussed in chapter 4 on Church-state relations, Murray's division between religious and secular matters is absolute and stark. He seems to take no account of "mixed questions" that are legitimate concerns of both the religious and the temporal realm, and he seems to view every issue as falling clearly into one category or the other.[174]

All of these characteristics of Murray's notion of state incompetence render it incompatible—not only with the provisions of DH already discussed but with additional ones as well. The declaration announces in article 1 its intention to develop the doctrine of recent popes on human rights and on the constitutional order of society. Somewhat surprisingly, the document makes few further references to constitutional government. The key passages

---

[171] Murray makes an apparent exception to his incompetence argument to provide for special civil recognition, but only on the basis of "historical circumstances." However, this concession has no relevance to the final version of the document, which allows for such recognition on the broader basis of the "peculiar circumstances" of a people. (See subsections 9.3.4 and 10.3.5.2.)

[172] Similar to Murray, Roland Minnerath recognizes the state's only competence with regard to religion as rendering effective the citizens' exercise of their rights. Cf. Roland Minnerath, "La concezione della chiesa sulla libertà religiosa," 56.

[173] As discussed above (in subsections 10.3.2 and 10.3.3), limiting state incompetence to "ecclesiastical matters," rather than extending it to all "religious matters," results in a more reasonable, manageable, and acceptable theory of state incompetence. However, it is not sufficient to provide a foundation for the right to religious liberty.

[174] See sections 4.3 and 4.4, citing Murray's articles "Problem of Religious Freedom" and "Church and State at Vatican II," and also Pelotte's biography of Murray, *Theologian in Conflict*.

are its approval of contemporary man's demand for constitutional limitations on the powers of government (DH, §1a) and its proviso that where a state grants civil recognition to a particular religion, it also must respect the right of all citizens to religious liberty (DH, §6c; cf. DH, §6d–e). In addition, the document concludes by approving constitutional recognition of religious freedom and by deploring the fact that, in some states, this guarantee is merely illusory (DH, §15b).

The declaration contains several other mentions of government in general and the duties incumbent on it. It does not specify constitutional government in particular, but rather it refers to government generally. The reason seems to be to make clear that whether they recognize them or not, all governments have these duties. In addition to the duties already discussed, these include noninterference with religious communities (in communications, training ministers, acquiring property, etc.) (DH, §4c) and with parents in choosing schools for their children (DH, §5).

The most interesting duties, however, are not mere obligations of noninterference but positive obligations to take account of the religious life of the citizens and to show it favor (article 3), to establish conditions favorable for the fostering of religious life (article 6), and to protect against abuses committed on the pretext of religious liberty (article 7). The declaration envisions cooperation between the two realms (as the popes also had promoted), but Murray does not share this vision (at least not to any appreciable degree). All of the key characteristics of Murray's incompetence theory come together to render it incompatible with the important role that the declaration envisions for civil government in favoring and promoting religious life.

Murray had difficulty even understanding these provisions of article 3 and article 6. The right to religious liberty is an immunity, and so, he wondered, how could one speak of promoting an immunity?[175] In addition, despite the Council's clarity in formulating these duties as affirmative ones, Murray considered them to be "primarily negative," that is, as "meant to exclude either a hostile or an indifferent attitude toward religion on the part of government."[176]

Kenneth Grasso embraces many of Murray's arguments (including ones related to state incompetence), but he nonetheless criticizes the

---

[175] John Courtney Murray, "The Declaration on Religious Freedom," in *Vatican II: An Interfaith Appraisal*, ed. John Miller (Notre Dame: Associated Press, 1966), 580, cited in Schindler/Healy, 57.

[176] Murray, "Church and State at Vatican II," 597. Murray does, however, acknowledge the positive content of the duty. Cf. Murray, 598: "The positive intention, however, is not in doubt."

10.4. Doctrinal Difficulties

incompetence argument insightfully.[177] The almost complete lack of content in Murray's notion of state incompetence (noted by Grasso) already has been discussed. In addition, Grasso criticizes Murray's excessively "thin" notion of public order. Sometimes, he says, Murray seems to see the state as little more than a night-watchman.[178] As a result, Grasso finds Murray's idea of state incompetence difficult or impossible to square with the state's duties to religion. The following is Grasso's *tour de force* summary of the problems presented by a number of Murray's formulations (contrasting quotations from DH with ones from Murray's 1966 article, "A Moment in Its [DH's] Legislative History"):

> How can the affirmative duties imposed by *DH* on the state in religious matters be reconciled with the claims that "the positive values inherent in religious belief, profession and practice" are "juridically irrelevant" [Murray, "A Moment in Its Legislative History," 28] and that "the higher ends of human existence" [Murray, 29] lie totally beyond the scope of the government's legitimate concerns? How can the state's obligation to "take account of the religious life of the people and show it favor" [DH, §3] be reconciled with the view that with regard to religion "the only matters that are juridically relevant are, first, the limits that may reasonably [be] set to the free exercise of religion and, second, the duty of government and of society not to transgress these limits" [Murray, 28–29]? How can a conception of public order rooted in "the objective moral order," [DH, §7] and hence in the truth about the nature of man and the human good, be embraced by a state committed to a posture of intellectual agnosticism? More broadly, inasmuch as a true understanding of the juridical order—involving as it does the proper ordering of intersubjective relations among men—can take shape only in light of the truth about the human person, how can a state arrive at such an understanding if "the higher ends of human existence" [Murray, 28–29] lie beyond its competence? It is hard to see, in short, how a conception of the state's competence in religious matters that involves a posture of intellectual agnosticism

---

[177] Grasso is a professor of government at Texas State University (San Marcos), and his main object is the formulation of a Catholic theory of the state. He believes that Murray made important advances toward this goal, but that he ultimately left the project unfinished.
[178] Grasso, "Murray, 'The Juridical State,' and Religious Freedom," 31.

can be reconciled with a theory of religious liberty predicated on a substantive vision of man and the human good.[179]

The effect of Murray's theory is to separate the religious and temporal realms almost completely and to preclude the state from taking almost any action concerning religion (except for protecting religious liberty). In this case, Murray's incompetence argument collides with the declaration's passages on the duties of the state. Quite simply, the positive duties that DH recognizes on the part of the state, namely, to promote and to foster religious practice, are ones that the state—as conceived by Murray—is incompetent to undertake.

10.4.4. A Brief Word on the General Sense of the Declaration and of the Council

The incompetence argument presents problems not only with other provisions of the declaration but with provisions contained in other Council documents as well. These problems may not rise to the level of actual doctrinal contradictions, but they do at least reveal a divergence in assumptions and approach between Murray and the overall sense of some of these passages.

10.4.4.1. The Decree on the Laity

The Decree on the Apostolate of the Laity calls upon the laity "to infuse a Christian spirit into the mentality, customs, laws, and structures of the community in which one lives."[180] This presents another difficulty for the incompetence theory, especially Murray's formulation of it. For Murray, the distinction between the temporal and religious realms is nearly absolute.[181] It is more the Jeffersonian wall of separation than the flexible Gelasian distinction (or the *semi-porous membrane* that I suggest as a metaphor in section 4.3 above).

The Decree on the Laity calls the faithful to infuse the spirit of the Gospel not only into the community's culture and social life but even into its laws and structures. Murray does not seem to have addressed this passage, perhaps because it arguably concerns religious competence or incompetence in temporal matters rather than state incompetence in religious matters.[182] Yet

---

[179] Grasso, "Murray, 'The Juridical State,' and Religious Freedom," 37–38.
[180] Second Vatican Council, Decree on the Apostolate of the Laity *Apostolicam Actuositatem* (Nov. 18, 1965), §13 [AAS 58 (1966): 849].
[181] See section 4.3 above, citing Pelotte, *Theologian in Conflict*, 124–35, and articles by Murray.
[182] He mentions the Decree on the Laity in a 1966 article, but only in passing and without analyzing any specific provisions. Cf. Murray, "Church and State at Vatican II," 601–2,

the incompetence argument seems necessarily to imply the corresponding religious incompetence in the temporal sphere. Murray's absolute sense of the separation between the two realms would seem to exclude the infusion of the Christian spirit into a society's laws. Even if this is not altogether certain, however, it at least seems clear that his notion of state incompetence fits uneasily with this passage on the lay apostolate.

10.4.4.2. An Embrace of Constitutionalism? (An Indian Summer of Catholicism)

The most prominent proponents of the incompetence argument—Murray and Pavan—assert that DH marks the Church's embrace of constitutional government. "The Council," Murray says, "makes a political commitment, however discreet, to constitutional government—or, if you will, to the juridical state."[183] By the same token, Pavan asserts that "the doctrine of the Declaration agrees with the basic tendency of the modern view of the State."[184] Grasso and other commentators agree.[185]

Francis J. Canavan takes a more guarded approach. The declaration, he says, does indeed "seem to consider constitutional government as normal."[186] However, rather than speaking of a commitment to, or an agreement with, constitutional government, Canavan describes the declaration's attitude in

---

mentioning the Decree's doctrine on the laity as the proper agent for the Church's mission in the temporal order, but noting that "a mere reference to this doctrine must here suffice."

[183] Murray, "Church and State at Vatican II," 599.

[184] Pietro Pavan, "Introduction and Commentary on the Declaration on Religious Freedom," in *Commentary on the Documents of Vatican II*, vol. 4, ed. Herbert Vorgrimler (New York/London: Herder and Herder/Burns & Oates Limited, 1969), 64, commentary on article 1 of DH.

[185] Kenneth L. Grasso and Robert P. Hunt, introduction to *Catholicism and Religious Freedom: Contemporary Reflections on Vatican II's Declaration on Religious Liberty* (Lanham, Maryland: Rowman & Littlefield Publishers, Inc., 2006), xx–xxi, cites the Murray quotation with approval. Elsewhere Grasso credits Murray with having demonstrated "how a principled commitment to the institutions and practices of constitutional democracy flow from the Catholic vision of man, society, and the human good" (Grasso, "Murray, 'The Juridical State,' and Religious Freedom," 48–49). John F. Crosby does not speak to this particular point, but he does describe DH as embracing related ideas connected with Murray's thought, such as the discontinuation of privileges for the Church and the conception of the civil law as merely "securing the space" in which religious activity takes place. Cf. John F. Crosby, "On Proposing the Truth and Not Imposing It: John Paul's Personalism and the Teaching of *Dignitatis Humanae*," in C&RF, 138, 153.

[186] Canavan, "Catholic Concept," 76.

subtler terms. "It cannot be said that the declaration advocates constitutional government in this passage, but it certainly shows a bias in that direction."[187]

At the outset, it is important to note that one could adopt the incompetence argument without claiming that the Council embraced constitutionalism or the juridical state. At the same time, though, it is not at all surprising to find the same persons adopting both ideas. The tenor of Murray's 1963 letter to Cardinal Spellman is that the Council should adopt the American system, and in some of his commentaries on the declaration, Murray claims that this is exactly what the Council did do.[188]

This, however, is an area in which one should tread carefully. One of the challenges in working with historical documents related to tolerance and liberty is that authors (even popes) naturally tend to take the political regimes existing in their own day—or in the recent past—as their point of reference. Difficulties thus arise in the future when it comes to disentangling the enduring teaching from the historically-contingent assertions.[189]

Murray was very much alive to this challenge as it related to the nineteenth-century Continental anti-clerical secular nation-state. Despite his admiration for Leo XIII, he contends that the Pope's vision was limited to that context and that it prevented him from really understanding the very different form that Liberalism took in America.[190] Regardless of whether his judgment about Leo is correct,[191] his commentary in this area is a reminder of the need to take an author's historical context into account, especially in an area such as this where historical shifts can be significant and dramatic.

It is not clear that Murray appreciated the application of this reality to his own work, however. He certainly was aware of historical contingencies, and although he sometimes used the language of natural law, he more often described state incompetence and religious liberty in terms of developments brought about by an increase of historical and political consciousness. Despite this emphasis, though, he does not seem to contemplate any further development or evolution of consciousness that might give rise to new

---

[187] Canavan, "Catholic Concept," 77.
[188] See section 4.1 and subsection 10.3.3.2 above.
[189] Cf. Congregation for the Doctrine of the Faith, Instruction on the Ecclesial Vocation of the Theologian *Donum Veritatis* (May 24, 1990), §24 [AAS 82 (1990): 1560–61].
[190] Murray seems to have felt that the council fathers themselves had trouble making the same distinction. Cf. Schindler, "Freedom, Truth, and Human Dignity," in Schindler/Healy, 57.
[191] Murray undoubtedly is correct that it is necessary to distinguish eighteenth-century and nineteenth-century Continental (especially French) Liberalism from American Liberalism, but his critique of Leo's appreciation of the situation is less convincing. See section 4.1 above.

10.4. Doctrinal Difficulties

forms of government.[192] Stated differently, although Murray is aware of the limitations that Leo XIII's historical context imposed on the Pope's thought and writing, he seems less aware that he is working within the same constraints. Indeed, although all authors must labor under this limitation, this fact—this influence of one's own time and circumstances on one's work—is as apparent in Murray as in any other author, and indeed perhaps even more apparent than in most.[193]

The conciliar pronouncement that most directly addresses this question is the pastoral constitution *Gaudium et Spes*. As discussed above in chapter 4, this document and the Declaration on Religious Liberty treat some of the same subjects, and each treats topics that are complementary to ones addressed in the other document. On the important question of political regimes, the Council says:

> Christ, to be sure, gave His Church no proper mission in the political, economic or social order. The purpose which He set before her is a religious one. . . . [I]n virtue of her mission and nature she is bound to no particular form of human culture, nor to any political, economic or social system. (GS, §42)[194]

The claim that the Council embraced constitutional government, at the least, is in tension with this principle. That is, at least generally, it seems to tend toward binding the Church—if not to a particular political system then to a particular *type* of political system.

As with the incompetence argument in general, so with the assertion

---

[192] Murray's concept of religious liberty is so tied to the Western liberal democracies (especially in his locating of the right's foundation in state incompetence in religious matters) that a widespread shift away from this form of government would endanger the right as understood by Murray. Pavan, especially in his later writings, is attuned to this danger, and as a result, he takes pains to assert that religious liberty is a permanent achievement. He calls it an irreversible doctrinal position that is not bound to historical contingency (cf. Pavan, *La dichiarazione conciliare*, 28). Pavan thus asserts more clearly than Murray ever did that religious liberty is a natural right, a fundamental human right that belongs to all, today and always (cf. Pavan, 38).

[193] An American author from the same period who did seem to appreciate the possibility of new types of regimes arising was the Notre Dame professor of government, E. A. Goerner. Cf. Goerner, *Peter and Caesar: Political Authority and the Catholic Church* (New York: Herder and Herder, 1965), 225–27.

[194] See also PT, §67: "It is impossible to determine, in all cases, what is the most suitable form of government, or how civil authorities can most effectively fulfill their respective functions, i.e., the legislative, judicial and executive functions of the State."

of a conciliar embrace of constitutionalism, there is some truth in this claim. The declaration certainly treats constitutional government with a certain *warmth of disposition*. The great virtue of this type of regime is its limitation on the powers of government.[195] At least with regard to this key feature of constitutionalism, one can indeed say that the Church fully embraces it. However, this is a principle that does not necessarily originate with the modern democracies, but that finds expression in different ways in the Church's own tradition, such as the principles of Gelasian dualism and subsidiarity.[196] Modern constitutionalism, however, is a new and effectual application of this principle.

What constitutional government adds is a structure that—at its best—is actually effective in constraining the government to respect those limitations.[197] At its best, one can say that constitutional government does two crucial things, one substantive and one procedural. That is, it recognizes human rights, and it establishes structures and procedures that provide effective protection for those rights. Moreover, with regard to the recognition of rights, the American form of Liberalism locates the origin of these rights in the Creator.

Another virtue of this form of government must have been prominent in the minds of the council fathers meeting scarcely a decade and a half following the end of the Second World War, namely, the Western democracies' defeat—both military and moral—of the totalitarian Nazi regime and their opposition to the totalitarian Soviet regime. One need only recall Pope Pius XI's ringing condemnations of the latter regimes[198] to note the difference in judgment on (or at least the Holy See's approach to) these two types of government.

At its best, Liberalism or Constitutionalism embodies some basic truths about the human person and about government, and (again, at its best) it

---

[195] See section 9.4 above (on the meaning of *limited government*).

[196] Properly conceived, subsidiarity is a co-principle with solidarity, and the two never must be separated. The reason is that subsidiarity without solidarity tends toward atomistic individualism, while solidarity without subsidiarity tends toward statist collectivism.

[197] As noted above in section 9.4, the language of Catholic social teaching likely would describe these realities differently. In particular, it probably would describe the optimal operation of governmental structures in more positive terms, such as the promotion of the common good in the sense of advancing the flourishing of persons both as individuals and as members of groups.

[198] Cf. Pius XI, Encyclical *Mit Brennender Sorge* (Mar. 14, 1937), §8: Whoever divinizes race or the state "distorts and perverts an order of the world planned and created by God" (AAS 29 [1937]: 149); Pius XI, Encyclical *Divini Redemptoris* (Mar. 19, 1937), §10: Communism strips man of his liberty (AAS 29 [1937]: 70).

10.4. DOCTRINAL DIFFICULTIES

also respects and provides substantial protection of the rights of the person. For these reasons, this form is preferable to many others, and its virtues are most readily apparent when one considers the counter-example of modern totalitarianism.

Given the virtues of constitutionalism and its historical record, why should one be at all reticent in claiming that the Council embraced this form of government?[199] One reason concerns the duties of government that the declaration insists upon. In large measure, constitutionalism measures up well, especially with regard to respecting the right to religious liberty, the freedom of associations, and the necessary freedom of religious communities to train clergy, acquire property, and communicate with their members. However, when it comes to the *positive* duties of government, the attitude of these governments might resemble Murray's own, that is, surprise at the declaration's assertion that governments have a duty positively to promote the religious life of the people.[200] The same is even more true with regard to the moral duty that societies (including the public authorities) have to the Church (DH, §1c).

Another difficulty concerns the decline of political regimes. Murray was writing in a time of unprecedented comity between the Church and the American regime. As already discussed, the U.S., above all, presented a stark contrast with the totalitarian regimes of mid-twentieth-century Europe. Its role in the war and the post-war European recovery still was fresh in the minds of the council fathers, and despite the presence of anti-Catholicism in periods of American history, the U.S. in its most recent election had elected a Catholic as president.

This comity, above all, characterized American society between the mid-1940s and the mid-1960s.

---

[199] My observations in this paragraph largely are limited to the American context, though I believe that some may apply as well to the Western democracies generally.

[200] This idea is by no means foreign to the American context. The Northwest Ordinance of 1787 (which, along with the Declaration of Independence, the Constitution, and the Bill of Rights, is one of the four organic documents of American government) called for the establishment of schools in the great undeveloped territory to the northwest of the original thirteen colonies, and it did so in ringing terms: "Religion, morality and virtue being necessary to good government and the happiness of mankind, schools and the means of education shall forever be encouraged." Thus, DH's very idea of promoting religious life resonates with deeply-rooted American traditions. These traditions remain alive, but in academia and the judiciary, the Jeffersonian idea of a "wall of separation" (which appears to have influenced Murray) often obscures them.

Murray came along at exactly the right moment in American Catholic history.... Those two decades following World War II represent a kind of peak in both the internal flourishing of the Church in the United States and, more to the point here, of a fairly general acceptance of Catholicism by America at large.[201]

In a marvelous turn of phrase, philosopher Frederick Wilhelmsen describes this period as an "Indian summer" of Catholicism in America.[202]

"Indian summer" is a phrase that Americans in some regions loosely apply to any period of warm weather during the season of autumn. However, it has a more precise climatological meaning. That is, it refers to a period in autumn following the first freeze, when the temperature rises back up to the levels of early autumn.[203] It is perhaps the most beautiful time of the year, but it is also the most evanescent, indeed perhaps so beautiful precisely because of its evanescence. As miraculously lovely as this brief season within the season is, it also is melancholy, because, having followed the first freeze, it comes with its own reminder that, inevitably, it soon will end, and with its end, winter will follow.

Why is Wilhelmsen's beautiful image so apt a description of Murray's period and work? In America, esteem for Catholicism was at its height, and among European Churchmen, regard for the Church in America was increasing. Indeed, Murray may have been only the second truly prominent Catholic intellectual that America had produced (after Orestes Brownson in the nineteenth century). In addition, Murray's 1967 death came even before the end of that "Indian summer" that Wilhelmsen evokes. The following years would be much more challenging ones for Catholicism in America. Writing in 1993, Wilhelmsen is clear that winter has set in and that, at least in some influential sectors, the American sensibility has shifted (or shifted back) to one of "massive hostility today to all things Catholic in the media."[204]

---

[201] Frederick D. Wilhelmsen, "John Courtney Murray: The Optimism of the 1950s," in *We Hold These Truths and More*, ed. Donald J. D'Elia and Stephen M. Krason (Steubenville, OH: Franciscan University Press, 1993), 24.

[202] "Murray wrote in that very favorable if somewhat odd Indian summer" (Wilhelmsen, "John Courtney Murray," 26).

[203] An even more precise definition appears on the website of the National Weather Service: "True Indian Summer is a period of abnormally warm weather following the killing freeze of autumn. A killing freeze occurs when the overnight temperature reaches 28 degrees [- 2 Celsius] or colder and may or may not occur with frost. Indian Summer typically occurs in mid to late autumn and can occur more than once." Weather Forecast Office, Quad Cities, Iowa/Illinois, National Weather Service, accessed May 16, 2021, www.weather.gov.

[204] Wilhelmsen, "John Courtney Murray," 25.

10.4. Doctrinal Difficulties

David L. Schindler has been famously critical of the American system, charging that Liberalism itself necessarily abstracts freedom from truth. As a result, he says, every liberal society ends in relativism.[205] One need not agree with Schindler's argument in its entirety to grasp his point. As I say above, at their best, liberal constitutional regimes respect human rights and provide effective structures for protecting them. However, constitutionalism remains vibrant and legitimate only so long as its recognition of rights is grounded in truth.[206] In recent decades, though, citizens in the Western democracies have seen their judicial systems extend protection to asserted rights that are not rights at all, especially, the so-called rights to abortion, same-sex marriage, and the choice of one's own gender identity.[207]

Schindler likely would say that this degeneration is inevitable, that is, that it was "baked in" to all forms of Liberalism from the beginning. Others would argue that these developments amount to a corruption of (or at least a strong force of corruption within) the American system. This is an important question, but it is beyond the scope of this work.

In any event, the experience of both the "Indian summer" and the succeeding winter reveal the wisdom of the Council's (and, of course, the Church's) declining to bind Catholicism to any particular type of political regime. Some key *elements* of Liberalism do indeed seem to represent a permanent achievement, namely, the need for limitations on government and the obligations of the government to honor human rights and to provide effective protection for them. This is as far as one prudently may go in characterizing the Council's warmth of disposition toward constitutionalism.[208]

---

[205] Cf. Schindler, "Freedom, Truth, and Human Dignity," in Schindler/Healy, 66. See also Schindler/Healy, 57–59, adopting a skeptical stance regarding Murray's attempt to distinguish American Liberalism from Continental Liberalism.

[206] Cf. Pope John Paul II, Encyclical *Evangelium Vitae* (Mar. 25, 1995), §70 [AAS 87 (1995): 481–83]. See also *Evangelium Vitae*, §4 [AAS 87 (1995): 404–5].

[207] Cf. *Roe v. Wade*, 410 U.S. 113 (1973) [abortion]; *Obergefell v. Hodges*, 576 U.S. 644 (2015) [same-sex marriage]; *Bostock v. Clayton County*, 140 S. Ct. 1731 (2020) [gender identity].

[208] Russell Hittinger argues forcefully that DH is compatible with a variety of political regimes. Cf. "Political Pluralism and Religious Liberty: The Teaching of *Dignitatis Humanae*," in *Universal Rights in a World of Diversity: The Case of Religious Freedom*, Proceedings of the 17th Plenary Session, Pontifical Academy of Social Sciences, Acta 17, ed. Mary Ann Glendon and Hans F. Zacher (Vatican City: Pontifical Academy of Social Sciences, 2012), 39: "*DH* can comport with many kinds of constitutional regimes"; "*DH* presupposes that there is more than one legitimate form of government" (46); "Peoples who have a serious commitment to religious liberty cannot be fit into a single model governing the relationship between state, religion, and society" (54–55). Elsewhere, however, Hittinger had described the "liberal conception of political and juridical institutions" as "at least germinally contained in *Dignitatis*." Russell Hittinger, "The Problem of the State in *Centesimus Annus*,"

The Council does indeed accord constitutionalism a type of *primacy*. However, the basis of this primacy is not necessarily a judgment that constitutionalism is (or will remain) the best form of government, but rather that today it is the most widespread and influential form of government. That is, the Council recognizes in constitutionalism a *primacy of prevalence* rather than a *primacy of perfection*.

10.5. A Response to the Question: "Might It Have Been Otherwise?"

This chapter began with the question *Might it have been otherwise?* That is, might the Council have chosen state incompetence as the foundation for the right to religious liberty? Despite the resilience of the argument and despite its strong intuitive appeal, the answer is no.

As mentioned at the outset, the idea of state incompetence contains some truth, especially if one restricts the idea to incompetence in ecclesiastical matters rather than to the broad category of all religious matters. In addition, a form of state incompetence has a place in the analysis and exposition of this right. However, its place is as a *consequence*—rather than the *foundation*—of the right. That is, once the right is established as a natural right, then it follows that the state is incompetent to violate it, either by compelling religious action or by hindering it without a sufficient reason.

However, the attempt to establish state incompetence as the foundation of the right to religious liberty entails several difficulties. The practical problems include the basic matter of even establishing the meaning of state incompetence. In addition, for this notion to serve as the foundation, its formulation apparently needs to be rather broad. The difficulty is that a broad notion of state incompetence yields an unrealistic standard that fails to take account of several concrete areas and situations in which the temporal power and the religious power inevitably must come into contact. Furthermore, this notion presents doctrinal difficulties, such as problems of consistency with other provisions of DH and with passages in other conciliar documents. In particular, contrary to the declaration, it seems to demand an end to legal establishment of religion. Moreover, it leaves little room for the civil government to fulfill the positive duties toward religion that the declaration enjoins on it.

Fordham International Law Journal 15 (1991–1992): 978. It seems clear from the context, though, that Hittinger had in mind the characteristic liberal feature of limiting state power, and of doing so on the basis of human rights (cf. Hittinger, 978–79).

10.5. A Response to the Question: "Might It Have Been Otherwise?"

This chapter has attempted to demonstrate that the foundation proposed by the declaration's most celebrated interpreter is unworkable. The question of whether any viable foundation remains is the subject of the next chapter.

CHAPTER 11

Starting with the Person, Not the State

> *I have seen men in real life who so long deceived others that at last their true nature could not reveal itself.... Or can you think of anything more frightful than that it might end with your nature being resolved into a multiplicity, that you really might become many, become, like those unhappy demoniacs, a legion, and you thus would have lost the inmost and holiest thing of all in a man, the unifying power of personality.*
>
> — SØREN KIERKEGAARD[1]

The sole remaining question for the analysis proper of the right to religious liberty (the focus of parts 3A and 3B of this study) concerns Murray's "sufficiency" argument. Murray argued after the Council that state incompetence had to be included in the foundation of the right to religious liberty because no other foundation was sufficient fully to justify or ground the right. (See section 9.6.) He did not object to other foundations being included, but he did not consider them necessary. Chapter 10 has attempted to exclude Murray's incompetence argument as the proper foundation for the right, but if Murray's argument against the other possible foundations is correct, then the right to religious liberty would be left without any sufficient foundation.

11.1. THE ONTOLOGICAL ARGUMENT

The argument that displaced Murray's incompetence argument was the "theological" or "ontological" argument of Bishops Ancel and Colombo. It

---

[1] Søren Kierkegaard, *Either/Or* (1843), 2 vols., trans. David F. Swenson et al. (Garden City, N.Y.: Doubleday & Co., 1959), 2:164.

starts with human dignity, and it proceeds to specify the key feature of this dignity as man's duty to seek the truth. Murray did not object to inclusion of the ontological argument, but he claimed that it was insufficient to ground the right to religious liberty. His reason was that the state's prevention of the public dissemination of religious error would not necessarily be inconsistent with man's duty to seek the truth (and might even appear as an aid in pursuit of the truth).

In a strictly logical sense, Murray might be correct. There is a certain logic to the assertion that the suppression of error is no hindrance to the search for truth (and may even be a help in focusing that search).

However, the Ancel argument also includes (though it does not much develop) the need for man to pursue truth in a way that is in keeping with his own nature. This requires psychological freedom and immunity from coercion. Strictly speaking, Murray may be correct that suppression of religious error does not prevent one's search for the truth. It still would permit that search, but only in private. It would cut this freedom off from the public realm. That is, it would hinder the social creature from pursuing truth in social contexts. As a result, even if suppression of all religious error might be consistent with man's search for the truth, it is at least inconsistent with his social nature.[2]

That said, notwithstanding Murray's intriguing argument, the suppression of all public dissemination of religious error (even dissemination within the bounds of the just public order) might well be contrary to man's search for the truth as well. That is, it arguably makes a sham of man's freedom. By eliminating or restricting the availability of information on other religions present in one's own society, Murray's hypothetical proposal comes close to foreordaining the result of one's "search" and perhaps even foreclosing the opportunity for authentic faith, which one is to embrace freely and fully. Depending on the thoroughness of the suppression, the person may be left with only a single choice. In that event, could one truly call one's embrace

---

[2] Correction of religious error is, of course, an obligation within the Church. In the wider society, however, the Council teaches that interference with religious practice is justified only when it violates the *just public order*. Cf. Second Vatican Council, Declaration on Religious Liberty *Dignitatis Humanae* (December 7, 1965), §7c. As discussed below in chapters 12 and 13, this is an innovation in the *public law* of the Church. In her *lived experience*, however, it arguably amounts to little or no innovation, given that the historical reason for the suppression of religious error has been its social harm rather than its falsity. Cf. A. Vermeersch, *Tolerance*, trans. W. Humphrey Page (New York: Benziger Brothers, 1912), 161: "[T]he heresies which were really hunted to death were those which, when spread abroad among the masses, sowed the seed of religious anarchy, and tended to the ruin and overthrow of the Church and society."

of the faith the result of a real "search" and a free embrace? Murray sees suppression as consistent with the ontological argument, but in truth this type of suppression would be consistent only with a narrow (and distorted) version of this argument.

11.2. The Social Argument (Part 1)

Murray also asserts that the argument from man's social nature is insufficient to ground the right to religious liberty. That is, he says, this argument does not necessarily amount to the preclusion of the state from hindering one's religious actions. In fact, Murray says, this argument "begs the question," or results in assuming what needs to be proven (namely, the state's inability to interfere).

Murray, however, may be ignoring (or missing) the full import of the social argument. This argument goes to man's nature, and Murray's idiosyncratic approach to natural law seems to prevent him from appreciating it fully. (See subsections 10.2.1 and 10.4.4.2.) The social argument concerns man's nature itself, and it potentially has an impact on how man must be permitted to search for the truth, so as to allow him to do so in accordance with his nature. If it is demonstrated that man has a certain right by nature, then it necessarily follows that the state may not act in violation of it.[3]

Murray never really puts this together. In fact, although he had written extensively about natural law in his earlier writings, he largely would set this interest aside. As a result, he justifies religious liberty on the basis of a development of historical consciousness much more than as a consequence of natural law. Indeed, during and after the Council, he seemed to have little interest in defending religious liberty as a natural right. Even where Murray does continue to speak of natural law and natural rights in his later writings (from 1964 until his death in 1967), his understanding is very different from traditional natural rights theory. In fact, he subordinates natural law to historical and political consciousness so thoroughly that, for him, natural law comes to mean the requirements of human nature "under today's conditions."[4] (See also section 10.1.)

---

[3] "Human laws in flagrant contradiction with the natural law are vitiated with a taint which no force, no power can mend." Pius XI, *Mit Brennender Sorge*, §30 (AAS 29 [1937]: 159). See also Javier Hervada, *Critical Introduction to Natural Law*, trans. Mindy Emmons (Montreal: Wilson & Lafleur, 2006), 153: "Law contrary to Natural Law lacks the force and nature of law."

[4] "It is not exact to say flatly that the state is incompetent in religious matters, as if this were some sort of transtemporal principle, derivative from some eternal law. The exact

If religious liberty is a natural right, then civil governments necessarily lack the authority to interfere with that right. Murray misses this point because by the time of his arguments in the mid-1960s, he largely has abandoned his interest in natural law and, to the extent that he has held on to the idea, it has been only in a very idiosyncratic and impoverished form.

11.3. The Social Argument (Part 2: An Excursus on Thomas Pink)

Thomas Pink offers a novel theory that intersects with Murray's thought in several places. (See subsection 9.5.1.) He argues that the state has no authority of its own to coerce in religious matters,[5] and as a result, whenever a Catholic ruler did so in the past, he acted as the Church's agent or instrument. Pink asserts that when Catholic rulers repressed non-Catholic worship, they did so largely for religious—rather than secular—ends.[6] Pink concludes that when Catholic princes engaged in religious coercion, they were exercising not their own power but a power delegated to them by the Church.[7] What DH represents in Pink's view is a *policy* shift on the

---

formula is that the State, under today's conditions of growth in the personal and political consciousness, is competent to do only one thing in respect of religion, that is, to recognize, guarantee, protect, and promote the religious freedom of the people. This is the full extent of the competence of the contemporary constitutional state." John Courtney Murray, "The Problem of Religious Freedom," *Theological Studies* 25, no. 4 (1964): 528. See also Murray, "Vers une intelligence du développement de la doctrine de l'Église sur la liberté religieuse," *Unam Sanctam* 60 (1967): 115: "Cette affirmation [de la liberté religieuse] n'est pas une 'vérité éternelle' de type platonicien. Elle est le produit d'une prise de conscience historique, d'une disposition nouvelle de l'Église enseignante qui la tourne y vers l'histoire pour y apprendre sur elle-même, aussi bien que sur l'homme."

[5] Cf. Thomas Pink, "Continuity after Leo XIII," in *Dignitatis Humanae Colloquium*, Dialogos Institute Proceedings, vol. I (Dialogos Institute, 2017), 114: State "has no coercive authority of its own in religious matters"; Pink, 145: State "is denied authority over religion ... because all authority over religion has been given to another *potestas*"; Thomas Pink, "Pink-Rhonheimer Debate on the Interpretation of Dignitatis Humanae—Opening Address" (University of Notre Dame, Nov. 20, 2015), §§1–2, Academia, Accessed July 11, 2022, https://www.academia.edu/19136187/Pink_Rhonheimer_debate_at_Notre_Dame_on_the_interpretation_of_Dignitatis_Humanae_opening_address.

[6] Cf. Pink, "Continuity after Leo XIII," 105–6: Popes "demand[ed] state legal protection of Catholicism not just to preserve just public order of a civil kind but for specifically religious ends"; Pink, 110: The state's privileging of Catholicism "was primarily to protect the spiritual goods of its citizens, and not simply to protect just public order under [different] civil and social conditions."

[7] Cf. Pink, "Continuity after Leo XIII," 113: "[W]hen the state was involved in coercion for religious ends, this was only under a borrowed authority"; Pink, 127: The state's "coercion

11.3. The Social Argument (Part 2: An Excursus on Thomas Pink)

part of the Church,[8] namely, the Church's withdrawal from the state of authorization to coerce in religious matters on her behalf.[9]

Pink's argument has a powerful allure. First, it is easy to understand in its broad outlines because it tracks the distinction between doctrine and discipline that should be so familiar to Catholics. Second, the Pink theory is especially attractive (or at least potentially attractive) to traditionalist critics of the declaration. The reason is that it interprets DH as a *policy* decision rather than as a *teaching* document. (Pink does sometimes refer to the *teaching* of DH, but when he does, he interprets it through the lens of policy. There is a right to religious liberty, he says, because in DH the Church now has withdrawn from the state its authorization to coerce in religious matters. That is, Pink understands the right as flowing from this policy change.)[10] As a result, this argument appears to hold out the promise of reconciling the SSPX and others in a similar position by providing a reading of the declaration as largely empty of doctrinal content, and therefore as posing no threat of contradicting the teachings of the nineteenth-century popes.

However, there are several difficulties with Pink's interpretation. It generally is far removed from the actual text of the declaration and sometimes even contradicts it. As discussed below in chapter 13, there is indeed a policy (or ecclesiastical law) component to DH, but the document cannot be reduced to a policy decision. On the contrary, the declaration announces early on that it is indeed a teaching document: "[T]he council intends to

---

for specifically religious ends ... involved a delegated exercise within the order of religion of the Church's own authority."

[8] "And she is now teaching, as she did not teach before, that people have a moral right not to be coerced religiously by the state. But all this arises from a reform at the level of policy and from accompanying change in religious and political circumstance, not from any reform of underlying doctrine." Thomas Pink, "The Interpretation of *Dignitatis Humanae*: A Reply to Martin Rhonheimer," *Nova et Vetera* (English ed.) 11, no. 1 (2013): 79. Cf. Pink, 110–11: "*Dignitatis Humanae* ... constitute[s] the Church's abandonment, *for our time at least*, of a *policy* reaching back to late antiquity—her use of the Christian state as her coercive agent"; Pink, "Conscience and Coercion: Vatican II's Teaching on Religious Freedom Changed Policy, Not Doctrine," *First Things* 225 (August 2012): 50: DH is "a great reform in the *policy* of the Catholic Church" (the emphases in the quotations in this note are my own).

[9] "Religious coercion by the state is now morally wrong, and a violation of people's rights, not because religious coercion by any authority is wrong, but because the Church no longer authorizes it." Pink, "Conscience and Coercion," 46.

[10] Cf. Pink, "Reply to Rhonheimer," 79: "[A]ll this arises from a reform at the level of policy." In a more recent essay, however, Pink quite surprisingly challenges another commentator's assertion that he (Pink) interprets DH merely as a matter of policy. Pink wrote this essay in response to Thomas Storck, and I discuss it in subsection 11.3.2.

343

develop the doctrine of recent popes on the inviolable rights of the human person and the constitutional order of society" (DH, §1c).[11]

A related difficulty with Pink's theory is that, unlike the Council, he seems not to conceive of religious liberty as a true natural right. Let us return to the discussion of natural law and natural rights from the previous subsection.

Like Murray, Pink sometimes uses the language of natural law, but his concept is narrower in scope than the declaration's understanding. Although Pink does connect religious liberty to natural law, he does so in only a limited way. He argues that, under natural law, the state has no authority of its own to coerce in religious matters.[12] Thus, when the state does coerce, it is acting as the Church's instrument or agent.[13] Now that the Church at Vatican II has withdrawn her authorization for the state to do so, Pink says, the state no longer has any authority to coerce in religious matters.[14]

---

[11] "While it is true that *DH* touches directly on policy matters concerning all mankind ... *DH* has an undoubted doctrinal character." Barrett Hamilton Turner, "*Dignitatis Humanae* and the Development of Moral Doctrine: Assessing Change in Catholic Social Teaching on Religious Liberty" (PhD diss., Catholic University of America, 2015), 252. See also Turner, 276–77.

[12] Cf. Pink, "Reply to Rhonheimer," 80, characterizing DH as teaching "that the state lacks an authority of its own to coerce religiously"; Pink, 108: "Since no one has any religious obligations to the state, so the state has no specifically religious authority, and so no authority of its own to coerce or direct anyone in any way in religious matters."

[13] Pink, "Conscience and Coercion," 46: "The state could act only as the Church's agent." Thomas Pink, "What is the Catholic Doctrine of Religious Liberty?" (expanded version June 15, 2012), §7n53, at 48: "The state's involvement [in religious coercion] ... could only be as the Church's agent" (Academia, accessed July 16, 2022, https://www.academia.edu/es/639061/What_is_the_Catholic_doctrine_of_religious_liberty). The idea that Catholic princes and states were acting in a purely *instrumental* capacity is a key premise of Pink's theory. Among those who dispute its accuracy, however, are Roger Nutt and Michael De Salvo. They agree with Pink that DH represents a policy shift (and that it essentially is a document about the state), but they believe that Pink's reliance on Charles Journet's famous treatise *L'Église du Verbe incarné* is selective and partial. That is, although Journet does indeed discuss a type of recourse to the secular arm that is "instrumental," he (unlike Pink) acknowledges another non-instrumental mode of the Church's use of the secular arm, in which the state remains an "autonomous cause." Cf. Roger W. Nutt and Michael R. De Salvo, "The Debate over Dignitatis Humanae at Vatican II: The Contribution of Charles Cardinal Journet," *The Thomist* 85 (2021): 193, 201, 205, 207.

[14] Cf. Pink, "Conscience and Coercion," 46: Coercion no longer is permitted "not because religious coercion by any authority is wrong, but because the Church no longer authorizes it." Nutt and De Salvo, however, note that Pink "does not consider whether the state might

A consequence of this argument is that Pink seems to understand religious liberty merely as a civil right rather than as a true natural right.[15] He describes the declaration as prohibiting religious coercion *only by the state*.[16] He does sometimes discuss this prohibition in terms of natural law,[17] but what he generally has in mind is a limitation on the state's authority or competence (somewhat akin to Murray's understanding)[18] rather than the existence of a right based in human dignity and owing to man as a result of the requirements of his very nature.[19] Pink also sometimes refers to human dignity or human nature, but even when he does so, it remains apparent that he conceives of the right as arising in the first instance from the state's lack of authority to coerce.[20] Indeed, to the extent that Pink refers to natural

---

accidentally have authority to coerce in materially spiritual or religious matters, if only within the context of a kind of Christendom not to be seen again" (Nutt and De Salvo, "Debate over Dignitatis Humanae," 206). See also Nutt and De Salvo, 207 (similar).

[15] See subsection 7.4.2 above (discussing Pink).

[16] Cf. "Conscience and Coercion," 46: "The declaration ... does not oppose religious coercion in general, but coercion *by the state*"; "Reply to Rhonheimer," 79: "[P]eople have a moral right not to be coerced religiously *by the state*"; "Continuity after Leo XIII," 105: Asserts that DH stands for freedom from religious coercion "*by the state*"; "Continuity after Leo XIII," 129: DH's strict teaching is on the "right to religious liberty *against the state*." The emphases in the quotations are my own. See also subsection 7.4.2; Pink, "What is the Catholic Doctrine of Religious Liberty?" §6, pp. 30–31, 36.

[17] Cf. Pink, "Reply to Rhonheimer," 108: "The declaration was intended to address only the coercive role of the state as fixed by natural law." Pink, 109: "Its [DH's] subject matter is state and civil coercion under natural law; and it teaches the moral wrongness of the state's involvement in religious coercion."

[18] Thus, like Murray, Pink adopts a strictly separationist view of the relationship between Church and state. This is not to say that Pink is a promotor of separationism, as Murray was. He is not. Rather, what he has in common with Murray is a sharp differentiation between the religious and temporal realms. Both seem to assume that nearly every question can be assigned to one of the two realms, and as a result, they take little account of "mixed questions" that pertain to both realms. See section 15.3 on the critique of Pink by Nutt and De Salvo.

[19] By the same token, although Pink occasionally refers to religious liberty as a moral right, he does not seem to think of it as something due to the human person as such. As a result, he limits this supposed moral right to freedom from religious coercion only when the state is the coercing party. Cf. Pink, "Reply to Rhonheimer," 79: The Church "is now teaching, as she did not teach before, that people have a moral right not to be coerced religiously by the state."

[20] "Once it is detached from the Church, the state entirely lacks competent authority to coerce us in matters of religion; and so our human dignity gives us a right not to be coerced religiously by the state" (Pink, "Continuity after Leo XIII," 119). Elsewhere, Pink says that "given rights against the state attaching to human nature, state coercion of religion cannot be justified" (Pink, "Conscience and Coercion," 50). This particular phrase tracks

law, he is more interested in the nature of the *state* than the nature of the *human person*.[21] Pink even suggests that one should not take at face value DH's assertion that the right to religious liberty is based on human dignity. Rather, he says, the right depends on other conditions as well, especially whether the person is subject to the Church's jurisdiction. If this is indeed the case (that is, if one is baptized), Pink says, then one is indeed subject to religious coercion by the Church.

> Whenever the right to liberty is grounded by the declaration on considerations X and Y, it must be left open that X or Y might not strictly be enough—that [what is] also necessary must be an absence of the kind of normative juridical relation that a baptized person has to the Church.[22]

This is an astonishing assertion. If Pink is correct, then none of the baptized has the right to immunity from coercion in civil society as practiced by the Church herself or by the state acting at the Church's direction!

Nothing in the declaration's text or drafting history supports the Pink theory, and the drafting history directly refutes it. The next subsection discusses Pink's assertion that the declaration does not prohibit coercion by the Church.

11.3.1. Various Species of Coercion

As discussed in the preceding subsection, although the plain language of DH prohibits religious coercion "on the part of individuals or of social groups

---

DH more closely, and it raises the possibility that perhaps Pink interprets the right as the Council does, that is, as arising from human nature. The article as a whole, however, makes clear that Pink continues to see the right as originating not from what is due to the human person as such but from the state's lack of competence to act. Cf. Pink, "Conscience and Coercion," 46: "The state is forbidden to coerce in matters of religion, not because such coercion is illicit for any authority whatsoever, but because such coercion lies beyond the state's particular competence"; Pink, 46: "Religious coercion by the state is now morally wrong... because the Church no longer authorizes it."

[21] Cf. Pink, "Conscience and Coercion," 50, criticizing "mainstream" view of religious liberty as "person-centered" and favoring instead "a quite different, jurisdiction-centered model" that Pink claims historically was the assumption behind Church teaching and canon law.

[22] Thomas Pink, "The Right to Religious Liberty and the Coercion of Belief," in *Reason, Morality, and Law: The Philosophy of John Finnis*, ed. John Keown and Robert P. George (Oxford: Oxford University Press, 2013), 439.

and of any human power" (DH, §2a),[23] Pink seems to ignore this language in his repeated insistance that the declaration prohibits coercion only "by the state." See subsection 7.4.2 and section 11.3. He does not ignore this language entirely, however. In fact, he puts forward his own interpretation of the article 2 term "any human power." Pink's interpretation, though, is incorrect.

The question that article 2 gives rise to is whether the Church herself is a "human power" who is prohibited from engaging in coercion in civil society.

Pink interprets "any human power" in article 2 in light of the similar term "no merely human power" in article 3 of the declaration.[24] Arnold Guminski calls this "a great error of omission on Pink's part,"[25] and he is indeed correct. That is, Guminski convincingly shows that the terms "human power" and "merely human power" are indeed distinct.

Where article 3 says that "no merely human power" may command or inhibit internal acts of religion, the Church *is not* included within this prohibition. That is, the Church is not a "merely human power." Indeed, the Council chose this phrasing specifically "so as not to prejudice the disputed question regarding the power of the Church to command internal acts."[26] However, where article 2 says that religious coercion in civil society is excluded by "any human power," here the Church *is* included as a "human power" that may not coerce.[27] That is, in article 2, a power is described as "human" not because its *origin* is human but because the subjects who exercise its power are human.[28]

---

[23] "This Vatican Council declares that the human person has a right to religious freedom. This freedom means that all men are to be immune from coercion on the part of individuals or of social groups and of any human power, in such wise that no one is to be forced to act in a manner contrary to his own beliefs, whether privately or publicly, whether alone or in association with others, within due limits" (DH, §2a).

[24] "[T]he exercise of religion, by its very nature, consists before all else in those internal, voluntary and free acts whereby man sets the course of his life directly toward God. No merely human power can either command or prohibit acts of this kind" (DH, §3c).

[25] Arnold T. Guminski, "An Examination of Thomas Pink's Theory of the Doctrine Concerning Religious Freedom in *Dignitatis Humanae*" (Dec. 6, 2015), Academia, §14, accessed July 16, 2022, https://www.academia.edu/19523482/An_Examination_of_Thomas_Pinks_Theory_of_the_Doctrine_concerning_Religious_Freedom_in_Dignitatis_Humanae.

[26] In his *relatio* of November 19, 1965, Bishop De Smedt, commenting on DH §3c, explained: "The words 'merely human' have been deliberately used so as not to prejudice the disputed question regarding the power of the Church to command internal acts" (AS IV/6, 730); English translation by Brian Harrison in Arnold T. Guminski and Brian W. Harrison, *Religious Freedom: Did Vatican II Contradict Traditional Catholic Doctrine? A Debate* (South Bend, IN: St. Augustine Press, 2013), 237n27.

[27] Guminski, "An Examination," §§9–18.

[28] Guminski, "An Examination," §26, citing Bernard Lucien, *Gregoire XVI, Pie IX et Vatican*

If the Church is excluded from religious coercion, then how can it be that she may direct acts of religion?

The official relator for the declaration addressed this very question in his written *relatio* on the final draft of the document. Barrett Turner demonstrates that the answer lies in the distinction between two different types of pressure. "The *relatio* draws some kind of a distinction between the state's use of force in protecting public order (*coactio*, from *cogere*) and the Church's use of canonical penalties (*potestas coercitiva*, from *coercitio/coercere*)."[29]

In view of the final draft's exclusion of "every manner of coercion on the part of men" in religious matters (cf. DH, §10),[30] a proposed amendment would have changed the text to exclude only *unjust* coercion. The apparent motivation was to safeguard the use of ecclesiastical sanctions. Turner explains the rejection of this proposal and its relevance to ecclesiastical sanctions:

> The amendment therefore implies that there is a just form of coercion in religious matters. The drafting commission rejected this suggested amendment because "coercion [*coactio*] towards adults in society and in the state, in religious matters, in the sense expressed in the first part of the Declaration, is itself unjust [*de se iniusta est*]." The response continues: "Ecclesiastical penalties that sanction delict acts are from the compelling power [*coercitiva potestate*] of the Church toward her members, but they are not coercion [*non sunt coactio*]."[31]

That is, the Church has coercive authority, but the sanctions that she imposes under her penal law do not amount to coercion in the sense meant

---

II. *Études sur la Liberté Religieuse dans la Doctrine Catholique* (Tours: Editions Forts dans la Foi, 1990), 256–57n39.

[29] Turner, "*Dignitatis Humanae* and the Development of Moral Doctrine," 318.

[30] Despite the seemingly absolute language in article 10, this provision should be read as taking for granted that coercion is legitimate to safeguard the just public order (cf. DH, §7c). "The limits are dealt with extensively in article 7, which obviously holds good for the entire schema, without it being necessary to keep summing them up at every point." De Smedt, responses to *modi* on the *Textus Denuo Recognitus* (Nov. 19, 1965) [AS IV/6, 742] (interpreting DH §3); English translation in Brian W. Harrison, *Religious Liberty and Contraception: Did Vatican II Open the Way for a New Sexual Ethic?* (Melbourne: John XXIII Fellowship Co-op., Ltd., 1988), 96.

[31] Turner, "*Dignitatis Humanae* and the Development of Moral Doctrine," 318, quoting AS IV/6, 761.

in article 2 of DH. (The distinction certainly is fine, and De Smedt's explanation is far from a model of clarity or thorough explanation.)[32]

Stated differently, one might think in terms of a *genus* of various types of *pressuring activity*. What article 2 rejects is *coercion proper*. Ecclesiastical sanctions, however, are a different *species* of pressuring activity. They do not amount to coercion proper, and DH does not address them. They are a part of the Church's *compelling power*. Penal sanctions are part of the internal life of the Church, and the relator made clear that religious liberty within the Church and other religious communities is not the subject of the declaration.[33] As he explained in an article shortly after the Council, one perceives the penal character of ecclesiastical sanctions only in the light of faith, and, by the same token, it is only in this light that one acknowledges the authority behind the sanctions.[34]

What is the difference between these two *species* of coercion? Turner, Guminski, and John Finnis offer various answers. Their answers are not identical, but they tend more to mutually reinforce each other than to oppose each other. Finnis (in a response to Pink) acknowledges that the Church has the authority to impose penalties on the faithful, but he describes these sanctions as "coercive only in a relatively weak, extended sense."[35] Turner makes a similar point. Unlike the coercion meant in article 2 (especially coercion by the civil authority), he says, ecclesiastical sanctions do not touch or force the body.[36] Guminski's understanding is close to Turner's. He says that the type of actions that article 2 forbids are *coercive practices typical only of the civil authority* (such as arrest and detention).[37] He and Turner agree (on the basis

---

[32] Cf. Guminski/Harrison, 232: The relator's response "vividly discloses that coercion is a very ambiguous term. And it can also be plausibly said, with all due respect, that the Secretariat engaged in a bit of confusing double-talk." See also John Finnis, "Reflections and Responses [26: Response to Thomas Pink]," in *Reason, Morality, and Law: The Philosophy of John Finnis*, ed. John Keown and Robert P. George (Oxford: Oxford University Press, 2013), 571.

[33] De Smedt, *Relatio oralis de textu recognito* (Oct. 25, 1965), AS IV/5, 99–104: "The Declaration does not concern relations ... between man and God (or relations between the faithful and authorities in the Church)."

[34] "Nous avons vu que même les peines spirituelles émanant des autorités ecclésiastiques ne sont pas opposées à la liberté religieuse, puisque leur caractère pénal ne peut être perçu qu'à la lumière de la foi, qui seule aussi permet de reconnaître comme valable l'autorité de celui quie les inflige." Émile-Joseph De Smedt, "Les conséquences pastorales de la Déclaration," *Unam Sanctam* 60 (1967): 226.

[35] John Finnis, "Response to Pink," 571.

[36] Turner, "*Dignitatis Humanae* and the Development of Moral Doctrine," 319.

[37] Cf. Guminski, "An Examination," §8n18.

of the *relatio*) that these are forbidden even to the Church under DH, §2a. Church sanctions are (1) spiritual penalties and (2) temporal penalties of a certain kind, namely, ones (a) that are not typical of civil authority, and (b) that are of a type that have their final end in the sanction of excommunication.[38] Guminski does not exclude some physical aspect, however, because he would include the Church's right physically to exclude someone from her property or ceremonies.[39]

The text of DH and the *relatio* show that Guminski and Turner are correct. That is, article 2's prohibition of coercion by "any human power" includes the Church. However, the declaration addresses religious liberty in civil society not within the Church or other religious communities. (This is clear from DH's subtitle.) Thus, the Church's application of penal sanctions is fully consistent with the declaration. However, the *relatio* insists, the Church's coercive power is of a different kind than that of the civil authority.[40]

Pink, however, does not make this distinction. On the contrary, he asserts that the Church's exercise of her coercive power is of the same nature as the civil authority's exercise of its own.[41] Crucial to this argument is Pink's assertion that the civil authority has no power of its own to coerce in matters of religion. Guminski and other commentators have challenged Pink on this point.[42] Even aside from the debates between Pink and his critics, the

---

[38] Cf. Guminski/Harrison, 229–30.

[39] Cf. Guminski/Harrison, 259. Although their criteria seem to diverge on this point, I doubt that Turner would disagree with Guminski here.

[40] Another *species* within the *genus* of *pressuring activity* would be *social pressure*. De Smedt addressed this topic in his capacity as relator, and he stated that mere social pressure does not amount to coercion within the meaning of the declaration. Cf. AS IV/6, 733 (cited in Guminski/Harrison, 222n193).

[41] "By attaching real costs to heresy, and describing those costs as punishment for what is presented as a crime, the Church is conveying the very same coercive message that states do when they attach similarly penal costs to actions classed by them as criminal—namely that what has been penalized really is wrong, and so is not to be done" (Pink, "Religious Liberty and the Coercion of Belief," 430). "[F]or the Church to threaten ... job loss ... is precisely to act like any authority seeking coercively to regulate and influence what people believe and do and to pressure them away from whatever is being classed as wrong" (Pink, "What is the Catholic Doctrine of Religious Liberty?" §5). Cf. Pink, §5: "[T]he Church is conveying the very same coercive message that states do."

[42] Cf. Arnold T. Guminski, "Further Reflections about Thomas Pink's Theory of the Meaning of *Dignitatis Humanae*" (Apr. 2, 2020), §§6–10, 12–15, 17, Academia, accessed July 16, 2022, https://www.academia.edu/42924123/Further_Reflections_About_Thomas_Pinks_Theory_of_the_Meaning_of_Dignitatis_Humanae; Nutt and De Salvo, "Debate over Dignitatis Humanae," 206: Pink "does not consider whether the state might accidentally have authority to coerce in materially spiritual or religious matters, if only within the

11.3. The Social Argument (Part 2: An Excursus on Thomas Pink)

drafting history of the declaration shows that the official relator, Bishop De Smedt, made a distinction that Pink refuses to make, namely, that between different *species* in the *genus* of coercion (or, as I would prefer to call it, the *genus* of *pressuring activity*). The key distinction is between, on the one hand, state coercion (or what I call *coercion proper*) and, on the other hand, ecclesiastical sanctions (an exercise of what De Smedt calls the Church's *compelling power*).[43]

Other episodes in the declaration's drafting history undermine Pink's claim even more clearly. That is, the interventions of the council fathers and the drafting commission's responses to them strongly indicate that the Church is indeed a human power within the meaning of DH §2.

Recall that Guminski faults Pink for interpreting article 2 ("human power") in light of article 3 ("merely human power"). That criticism is well placed, not only for the reasons already discussed above but also because the drafting history discloses that DH §2 formerly—in the third draft or

---

context of a kind of Christendom not to be seen again"; Nutt and De Salvo, 207 (similar). See also Turner, "*Dignitatis Humanae* and the Development of Moral Doctrine," 317. At the least, these critics demonstrate that Catholic tradition is far from clear and univocal in supporting this pillar of the Pink thesis.

[43] In one of his essays, Pink acknowledges (or at least seems to acknowledge) that DH prohibits coercion even by the Church (cf. "Continuity after Leo XIII," 124–26). Even in this essay, however, Pink continues to describe the prohibited coercion as action done by the state (cf. "Continuity after Leo XIII," 105–6, 129, 131, and 134). Indeed, both here and elsewhere, he argues that DH does not address the coercive authority of the Church. Cf. "Reply to Rhonheimer," 105: "We anyway know that the declaration was intended to bypass the coercive authority of the Church"; "Conscience and Coercion," 49: DH "was carefully drafted to bypass all questions of the coercive authority and jurisdiction of the Church herself." See also "Continuity after Leo XIII," 129 (similar). *How can Pink acknowledge that DH prohibits coercion even by the Church, while continuing to assert that the declaration addresses only state coercion?* If I understand him correctly, he does so with reference to the two orders (or the respective ends of the two orders). That is, he seems to acknowledge that the Church would be prohibited from coercion only if she were to engage in it *for civil or temporal ends*. "[I]n contexts where her revealed authority was not engaged, the Church would indeed have no more licence to coerce religiously than would the state or distinctively civil power" (Pink, "Continuity after Leo XIII," 125). However, while Pink almost always seems to have the two realms in mind, the declaration refers to them only rarely (primarily in a very brief reference at the end of article 3). On the contrary, De Smedt's distinctions primarily concern the *type* of coercive or pressuring action that is done. Ecclesiastical sanctions and social pressure simply are actions that do not amount to coercion within the meaning of article 2. Pink's references to the two orders are not irrelevant, but the accent in De Smedt's statements is on the character of the coercive or pressuring action itself. As a result, Finnis, Turner, and Guminski are correct in focusing here to distinguish *ecclesiastical sanctions* from *coercion proper*.

Textus Emendatus—did use the phrase "*merely* human power" to describe the entities that may not coerce in religious matters. However, several fathers issued written comments objecting to the word "merely" and asked for it to be deleted. The principal reason for the request was to make clear that the Church, too, was prohibited from coercing in religious matters within the meaning of article 2.[44] As a result, the word "merely" was suppressed in the following drafts and in the final version of the declaration.[45]

Guminski's arguments regarding the text and the drafting history of DH demonstrate that Pink is incorrect in arguing that the declaration does not address the Church's exercise of coercion and that the Church is not a "human power" within the meaning of article 2. Although these two arguments are sufficient in themselves, Guminski offers additional ones as well.

Guminski discusses the official pre-conciliar usage of the key terms. With regard to "human power," he shows that in one instance, the 1917 code of canon law excludes the Church, but in another, the code uses it as including the Church.[46] Guminski also shows that Pope Pius XI's use of equivalent terms in his 1930 encyclical *Casti Connubii* is remarkably similar to the Council's distinction between the terms "human power" and "merely human power."[47]

Guminski also addresses Pink's attempt to enlist the Catechism in support of his argument that DH prohibits religious coercion only as applied by the state (and, therefore, that the term "human power" in DH §2 does not include the Church). The Catechism does indeed contain language that seems consistent with Pink's argument. "The right to religious liberty is ... immunity, within just limits, from external constraint in religious matters *by political authorities*."[48]

An examination of the text of the declaration, however, leaves no doubt

---

[44] Cf. Guminski, "An Examination," §27, citing AS IV/1, 644 (intervention of Silvia-Henriquez), 677 (Buckley), 756 (Gufflet), and 866–68 (bishops of western France).

[45] Guminski discusses Basile Valuet's surprising and ambiguous position on this question. He notes that, although Valuet asserts that the Church is not included as a "human power" within the meaning of article 2, he nonetheless describes the contrary position, as argued by Bernard Lucien, as "enjoy[ing] a good probability." Cf. Guminski, "An Examination," §§29–31, citing Valuet, *La liberté religieuse et la tradition catholique. Un cas de développement doctrinal homogène dans le magistère authentique*, 3rd rev. ed. (Barroux: Éditions Sainte-Madeleine, 2011), vol. IB, 631–33, 633n2693; LRTC, 491–92.

[46] Cf. Guminski, "An Examination," §§20–21, agreeing with Pink that canon 2214, §1, of the 1917 code on the Church's coercive power excludes the Church from the term "any human authority," with Guminski, §23, noting that canon 1118 of the 1917 code on ratified and consummated marriages includes the Church when it says that such marriages cannot be dissolved "by any human power."

[47] Cf. Guminski, "An Examination," §23.

[48] CCC, §2108 (citing DH, §2) (emphasis added).

that the Catechism in this passage fails to transmit the full teaching of DH §2. Even aside from the question of whether the Church is included within the term "human power," article 2's reference to individuals and social groups makes it clear that religious liberty is not limited to immunity from coercion by the state only. In addition, Guminski notes that in their *Introduction to the Catechism of the Catholic Church*, then Cardinal Ratzinger and Christoph Cardinal Schönborn state that the original document itself is the controlling text: "The individual doctrines which the Catechism presents receive no other weight than that which they already possess."[49]

Finally, Guminski shares a passage from a personal message from Father Brian Harrison on this subject.[50] It is in the form of a *reductio ad absurdum* argument against the Pink theory. Harrison perceptively notes that if Pink were correct that religious liberty were a right only against the state, then the implication would be "that vigilante and terrorist groups, who enjoy no political authority, are not prohibited by DH #2 from using such coercion; but such an implied conclusion is preposterous."[51] Rather, Harrison suggests, one should read the relevant language of §2108 of the Catechism as "simply an inexact form of wording."

11.3.2. A Lack of Permanence

Pink's interpretation of the declaration reveals difficulties not only with his own theory but also with Murray's. Pink certainly does not follow Murray in all things connected with religious liberty, but he does share Murray's insistence that the state is incompetent in religious matters,[52] and that this incompetence is or should be the foundation of the right to religious liberty. Indeed, although Murray is the thinker most closely connected with the latter idea, Pink takes it further than Murray does. That is, while Murray seeks (in a sense) to "re-found" the right to religious liberty on the

---

[49] Joseph Ratzinger and Christoph Schönborn, *Introduction to the Catechism of the Catholic Church* (San Francisco: Ignatius Press, 1994), 26, cited by Guminski, "An Examination," §36.
[50] Guminski, "An Examination," §39, discussing and quoting the May 11, 2015, message from B. Harrison.
[51] Memorandum of B. Harrison attached to the May 11, 2015, email message to A. Guminski, quoted in Guminski, "An Examination," §39.
[52] For Pink, the declaration marks the Church's withdrawal of her authorization for the state to act as her agent to coerce in religious matters (cf. "Continuity after Leo XIII," 130, 145). Murray, by contrast, usually describes the incompetence of the state in terms connected with a modern increase in historical and political consciousness (see section 11.2 above). Despite this difference in reasoning, however, both Murray and Pink arrive at the conclusion of the state's incompetence.

incompetence of the state, Pink simply asserts outright that the Council founded the right on this basis.[53]

In fact, the Council did nothing of the sort.

Although the Murrayite texts (the third and fourth) in the middle of the drafting process had attempted to found the right to religious liberty on the state's incompetence in religious matters, the fifth and sixth (final) drafts eliminated the incompetence argument as a foundation and preserved it only minimally as a "further consideration" and without even a mention of the word "incompetence." See section 9.4 above on the Council's basing the right on the dignity of the person.[54]

The difficulty present in both the Pink and the Murray readings of the declaration is that if the right to religious liberty is (or as Murray says, should be) based on *state* incompetence in religious matters, then—just as Pink claims—the only prohibited coercion is coercion "by the state." One problem with the Pink and Murray readings noted above is simply that they depart from the text of the declaration (sometimes to the point of contradiction). In sharp contrast to Pink's repeated assertions that the document prohibits only coercion "by the state,"[55] the declaration itself makes clear that it does

---

[53] Cf. Pink, "Conscience and Coercion," 46: "The state is forbidden to coerce in matters of religion . . . because such coercion lies beyond the state's particular competence"; Pink, "Continuity after Leo XIII," 119: "[T]he state [detached from the Church] entirely lacks competent authority to coerce us in matters of religion"; Pink, "Continuity after Leo XIII," 131: "*Dignitatis humanae* bases the right to religious liberty on a claim that religion transcends the authority of the state." See also subsection 9.5.1 above.

[54] See also subsection 9.5.1, on the difficulties with Pink's reliance on the November 19, 1964, and September 15, 1965, *relationes*. Pink does accurately relate the content of these *relationes*, but he neglects to take account of the fact that they were describing the right as understood in the two Murrayite drafts, the *Textus Emendatus* and the *Textus Reemendatus*. Those texts did indeed base religious liberty on the incompetence of the state, or, as Pink says, the distinction between the temporal and religious orders. However, the editing process was by no means finished in November 1964 or even in September 1965, and the final document would base the right not on state incompetence but on human dignity.

[55] Pink occasionally will broaden his reading to include "civic institutions" as well as the state. Cf. Pink, "Reply to Rhonheimer," 80: "*Dignitatis Humanae* is a declaration, not on religious liberty and coercion in relation to any authority whatsoever, but rather on religious liberty and coercion in relation to the state and civic institutions." However, he does not define which "civic institutions" he means. What seems most likely is that he is referring to smaller governmental agencies that are subordinate to the state. In any event, however, even thus slightly broadened, Pink's terminology remains distant from that of the declaration, which excludes coercion, not only from human powers, but also from "individuals" and "social groups" (cf. DH, §2a). That is, it would be nonsensical to include "individuals" in Pink's category of "civic *institutions*," and it would be nearly as absurd to interpret this category as encompassing all "social groups."

not limit its reach to state action. On the contrary, it rejects coercion "on the part of individuals or of social groups and of any human power" (DH, §2a).[56] Murray does not emphasize the point as Pink does, but he too seems incorrectly to read the declaration as reaching only state action.[57]

If they understood religious liberty as something due to the human person *as such*, then, like the Council, they would have understood the immunity from coercion to apply even to *private* action. It is clear that the Council embraces this understanding by excluding coercion not only from state actors but also "on the part of individuals or of social groups and of any human power" (DH, §2a). *Murray and Pink err by conceiving of DH primarily as a pronouncement about the state rather than the human person.* Why do they insist on reading DH as a prohibition only on *state* coercion when the clear language of the declaration extends further? They do not acknowledge the full reach of DH because their theories cannot explain it. Stated differently, their theories do not permit them to recognize the full extent of the declaration's reach.

By reading DH fundamentally as a document about the *state*, Murray and Pink can explain only a *state* disability from engaging in religious coercion. Murray's emphasis on state incompetence and Pink's emphasis on the limitations of the temporal power shed no light whatsoever on whether individuals or social groups may coerce. To explain DH's prohibition on religious coercion by individuals, social groups, and every human power, one must read DH as it is written, that is, in the first instance as a pronouncement about the human person rather than the state.

By the same token, the right to religious liberty is not a permanent achievement for Pink, and it does not seem to be for Murray either. Pink says outright that the declaration effects a policy change merely "for our time."[58] As discussed in section 10.1, Murray probably did not anticipate a shift away from recognition of the right to religious liberty, but his theory

---

[56] Cf. Gerard Bradley, "Pope John Paul II and Religious Liberty," *Ave Maria Law Review* 6, no. 1 (2007): 40: DH concerns not only state action but individual action as well.

[57] Murray argues that the "passive subject" of the right to religious liberty is only the civil power and not the individual or a social group: "Le terme essentiel du rapport—son sujet passif, pourrait-on dire—est le pouvoir civil. Si une puissance humaine pouvait légitimement contester l'immunité en question, ce ne pourrait être que la plus haute autorité politique et juridique de la société, et certainement pas un individu ou un groupe social." Murray, "Vers une intelligence," 116.

[58] "[T]he Council intended . . . to abandon, *at least for our time*, the tradition of *using* the temporal power of the state in the service of the spiritual power." Pink, "Reply to Rhonheimer," 110 (emphasis added). See also Thomas Pink, "Jacques Maritain and the Problem of Church and State," *The Thomist* 79 (2015): 37: DH provides a framework

leaves the way open for such a change. His concept is beholden not so much to natural law as to developments in historical and political consciousness. As a result, future developments of consciousness, albeit in a different direction, conceivably could place the right in jeopardy.[59] Similarly, if Pink is correct that religious coercion is prohibited only as a function of current ecclesiastical policy, then the Church theoretically could revise her policy to make religious coercion permissible once again. Thus, although the Council describes the natural right to religious liberty as "inviolable" (cf. DH, §1c), the theories of Murray and Pink leave the right excessively vulnerable to violation and change. As a result, the right that they are describing is not truly a natural right.[60]

In a recent essay, Pink appears to anticipate this criticism. However, in that work, Pink surprisingly challenges Thomas Storck's assertion that he (Pink) interprets DH as a matter of policy. "[O]ne interpretation Storck gives of my position is not accurate. He claims that on my view *Dignitatis humanae* was simply a policy decision by the church."[61] This is an unexpected objection, because by now Pink has asserted many times that DH is a matter of policy, rather than doctrine. Indeed, this idea seems to be the very hallmark of his theory.[62]

The reason for Pink's surprising challenge to Storck's characterization of his theory seems to be a slight shift in Pink's own position. The implication of Pink's theory is that as a policy decision, DH is not necessarily permanent. Pink himself acknowledges this outright. "*Dignitatis humanae* ... constitute[s] the Church's abandonment, *for our time at least*, of a policy

---

"for the foreseeable future"; DH expresses "for our time" what Catholic tradition already implied about the state's ceasing to act as the Church's agent.

[59] See section 10.1 above.

[60] Cf. Martin Rhonheimer, "*Dignitatis Humanae*—Not a Mere Question of Church Policy: A Response to Thomas Pink," *Nova et Vetera* (English ed.) 12, no. 2 (2014): 462–63, contrasting Pink's understanding of DH as a policy change with DH's own understanding of the right as "something given with human existence itself" and as something by no means intended "for our time" only.

[61] Thomas Pink, "On *Dignitatis Humanae*—A Reply to Thomas Storck," *The Josias* (Oct. 28, 2021), §3, available from The Josias website, accessed July 16, 2022, https://thejosias.com/2021/10/28/on-dignitatis-humanae-a-reply-to-thomas-storck/.

[62] "Policy may have changed through the Vatican II declaration, but the underlying doctrine of coercive authority has not" (Pink, "Religious Liberty and the Coercion of Belief," 427). See also Pink, "Conscience and Coercion," 46, describing DH as a "policy change" and (Pink, 50) "a great reform in the policy of the Catholic Church"; "Reply to Rhonheimer," 79, teaching of DH "arises from a reform at the level of policy."

reaching back to late antiquity."[63] In his reply to Thomas Storck, however, Pink now asserts that as the result of the near disappearance of the Catholic state in recent times, "the church no longer had the capacity to employ these states as her religious agents even if she wanted to."[64] Thus, in response to Storck's critique that Pink sees DH "merely" as a matter of policy, Pink seems to be saying that this particular policy shift possesses a degree of stability that other ecclesiastical policies may lack. The reason is that as a result of the diminishing prevalence of Catholic states, the Church as a practical matter lacks the ability to reimplement the previous policy, even if she wished to do so.

This shift might indeed place a "policy change" on more solid ground, but it does not establish it as permanent. It does not amount to the recognition of religious liberty as something due to the human person as such. On the contrary, it secures religious liberty only for the foreseeable future, that is, only so long as current trends continue or remain stable.

11.4. The Argument about "Avoiding the Political"

Let us now return to Murray's critique of the ontological argument.

After purporting to dispatch the ontological argument and the social argument, Murray concludes that one simply cannot avoid the political. That is, one cannot avoid the notion of state incompetence.

This may be true, but one need not put the political in the first place, as Murray does. That is, one need not establish state incompetence as the foundation for the right to religious liberty. If a right truly is a requirement of man's nature, then one need not start with the political. Rather, the political consequence follows necessarily. This approach does not ignore the political, but neither does it make state incompetence the foundation of the right. Rather, it recognizes that if a certain right can be found to be a requirement of man's nature, then it necessarily follows that the state (and others) are disabled from violating that right.

Murray is wrong that this argument (expressed above as the social argument) necessarily begs the question. Rather, what Murray calls the assumption (that no power can coerce or hinder) is not an assumption at

---

[63] Pink, "Reply to Rhonheimer" (2013), 110–11 (emphasis added). See also subsection 9.5.1 and the several other essays and articles by Pink cited in this subsection and the preceding two.
[64] Pink, "Reply to Storck" (2021), §3.

all, but rather it is the consequence of a conclusion about the requirements of man's nature.

11.5. Human Integrity

Thus, Murray seems to have failed in his attempt to establish the incompetence argument as the only sufficient foundation for the right to religious liberty. His analysis of the ontological argument does not take adequate account of the social aspect of man's search for the truth. Moreover, in addressing the social argument itself, Murray's impoverished notion of natural law prevents him from recognizing some of the force of the social argument.

Yet, the social argument is not as complete as it could be. The ontological argument and the argument from man's social nature do indeed specify what it is about man's dignity that provides the foundation for the right to religious liberty. That is, they are sufficient. Even though sufficient, however, they may not be entirely complete. There is another aspect of human dignity that could add even more solidity and strength to the right's foundation. It is the principle of *human integrity*.

Chapter 7 above discussed the principle of human integrity as a key issue in interpreting the pronouncements of the nineteenth-century popes and in discerning the continuity between the Vatican II religious liberty teaching and those pronouncements. In the nineteenth-century papal teachings of Gregory XVI and Bl. Pius IX, one finds an implicit teaching on human integrity. That is why these popes, in warning against the nineteenth-century notion of liberty of conscience, always are concerned with both the individual moral realm and the social or juridical realm. Sometimes they speak of a single right (liberty of conscience or liberty of conscience and of worship) having ramifications in both realms, and sometimes they speak of two different rights, namely, liberty of conscience in the private realm and the unbridled liberty of speech, worship, and publication in the social realm. Even when they speak of two different rights, their concerns with both the individual realm and the social realm remain closely connected.

This teaching on human integrity is either implicit or in an early stage of development in the encyclicals of Gregory and Pius. The key figure in understanding these papal pronouncements is Lamennais. He advocated a radical split between the private and the public realm. That is, in the realm of personal individual morality, he rejected indifferentism, but in the social or public realm, he embraced indifferentism. (See section 7.3.2.) The popes, however, always insist on addressing both realms. Moreover, they also insist on a close connection between one's personal morality and his public actions.

Although this teaching on human integrity is largely implicit in Gregory XVI and Pius IX, Pope Leo XIII makes it explicit:

> [I]t is unlawful to follow one line of conduct in private life and another in public, respecting privately the authority of the Church, but publicly rejecting it; for this would amount to joining together good and evil, and to putting man in conflict with himself; whereas he ought always to be consistent, and never in the least point nor in any condition of life to swerve from Christian virtue. (ID, §47)

Vatican II likewise teaches the necessity of harmony or continuity between private belief and public behavior. This is the reason for its announcement of a right to religious liberty that applies both in private and in public.

Moreover, Vatican II extends the nineteenth-century papal teaching. Just as Leo had extended Thomas's teaching on toleration (Thomas applied it to Jews and Muslims, but Leo extended it to non-Catholic Christians), so does Vatican II extend this principle of integrity. As the above quotation from Leo shows, the nineteenth-century popes' concern was with the integrity of the *Catholic* person, and what the declaration does is to widen the umbrella of concern to encompass all people. One reason for this development is the brutal twentieth-century experience with totalitarian regimes and their attempt to swallow up the individual person and family into the collective. Thus, as early as 1930, Pope Pius XI was moved to deplore the violation of the religious rights of the Russian Orthodox within the Soviet regime.[65]

This experience (and others) shed new light on the Catholic state, if it ever should return to prominence. (See section 4.7.) If governmental authority forbids public non-Catholic worship and other religious expression (without regard to whether it violates the "just public order"), what then is the government really doing? It is sundering the two realms in the lives of the non-Catholic citizens and residents. The Jew may be a Jew in private, but the law effectively prevents him from living as a Jew in public. That is, it forces non-Catholics to live according to the Lamennaisian error—the error of radically separating private individual moral belief from public behavior. In a word, it attacks the integrity of the person. (See section 7.5 above.)

---

[65] Cf. Pius XI, Chirograph *Ci Commuovono* (Feb. 2, 1930) [AAS 22 (1930): 89].

One of the most moving interventions of the entire Council was on this theme. During the fourth session debate on the fourth draft of the religious liberty text (the *Textus Reemendatus*), Josef Cardinal Beran of Prague, who only recently had been released from imprisonment, rose to address the assembly:

> From the very moment in which freedom of conscience was radically restricted in my country, I witnessed the grave temptations which, under such conditions, confront so many. In my whole flock, even among the priests, I have observed not only grave temptations to faith, but also to lying, hypocrisy and other moral vices which easily corrupt people who lack true freedom of conscience.[66]

In substance, the presence of this principle of integrity is apparent in the final declaration. The very definition of the right to religious liberty says that the right applies in public and in private, regardless of whether one practices it alone or in association with others (cf. DH, §2a). In addition, the text draws out the implications of the Ancel argument. All persons not only have a duty to seek the truth but also a right to embrace the truth "and to order their whole lives in accord with the demands of truth" (DH, §2b). In addition, although the exercise of religion consists primarily in internal free acts, "the social nature of man . . . itself requires that he should give external expression to his internal acts of religion" (DH, §3c). The social nature of man is closely connected to the principle of integrity, and the declaration mentions it several times. By the same token, the document recognizes that religious communities themselves "are a requirement of the social nature both of man and of religion itself" (DH, §4a).

If the principle of integrity is present in substance, however, it is regrettable that the Council does not name or identify it outright. More explicit emphasis on the principle of human integrity could have illustrated the

---

[66] Sept. 20, 1965, intervention of Josef Cardinal Beran of Prague (AS IV/1, 393–94); English translation in Vincent A. Yzermans, ed., *American Participation in the Second Vatican Council* (New York: Sheed & Ward, 1967), 621–22. See also AS IV/1, 393–94: "Everywhere, and always, the violation of liberty of conscience gives birth to hypocrisy in many people. And, perhaps, one can say that hypocrisy in the profession of the faith is more harmful to the Church than the hypocrisy of hiding the faith, which, anyway, is more common in our times. So in my country the Catholic Church at this time seems to be suffering expiation for defects and sins committed in times gone by in her name against religious liberty, such as in the fifteenth century in the burning of the priest John Hus and during the seventeenth century the forced reconversion of a great part of the Czech people to the Catholic faith under the rule 'the people of a territory follow the religion of its ruler.'"

continuity between the nineteenth-century teaching and Vatican II, and it also would have bolstered the foundation of the right on human dignity.

An explicit mention of human integrity also would have provided a further response to Murray regarding the "sufficiency" of the foundation of the right to religious liberty on human dignity. That is, the principle of integrity shows more clearly than the ontological argument why the state generally is disabled from suppressing public religious error. In a narrow sense, Murray may be correct that technically and logically the suppression of religious error does not impede one's search for the truth (though, as discussed above, Murray's argument is problematic on other grounds). However, the suppression of all non-Catholic public religious expression— even though peaceful and within the bounds of the just public order—would inevitably be an attack on the integrity of the non-Catholic citizen. It would prevent their living as Methodists or Muslims in the public sphere. It would fragment their private and public lives, thus condemning them to live the Lamennaisian error.

This error, moreover, is a catastrophic one. "[W]herever constraint and violence appear over man to adhere to a religion or to renounce a religious position," Hamer and Riva say, "there takes place an affront and a mutilation of the human person."[67] The reason is that both man and religion are inherently social.

> [T]he conciliar Declaration wishes above all to emphasize the moral duty to search for the truth, in the first place religious truth, on the part of all intelligent beings, naturally within the limits and capacity of their own intelligence. This "moral obligation" is extended to the practice of the truth known and to "order their whole life according to its requirements." Religious truth requires a profound coherence in conduct and life, because the truth itself postulates it, also because the unity of the person requires a logical and coordinated order between its various aspects, especially between thought and action. The truth in thought has the function of guiding action; action becomes testimony and "profession" of the truth.[68]

Perhaps surprisingly, a review of the history of the elaboration of the declaration shows that there actually was a time when one of the drafts did indeed expressly base religious liberty on human integrity:

---

[67] Jérôme Hamer and Clemente Riva, *La libertà religiosa nel Vaticano II* (Torino, Italy: Elle di Ci, 1966), 159 (translation mine).

[68] Hamer/Riva, 177.

Man, as a person is by his very nature social. In all his actions, this social dimension of man is inseparably joined to his interior dimension. It is therefore an injustice for anyone to recognize man's personal freedom in religious matters and simultaneously deny him the free exercise of religion in society, since this would violate *the very integrity of the person*. The connection between interior freedom and its social manifestation is wholly indissoluble. Religious freedom is one, undivided and indivisible, and it inheres in one integral subject; at the same time, it refers to two different dimensions: namely, to interior freedom or freedom of conscience, on the one hand, and to the free exercise of religion, on the other.

What may be even more surprising is that this passage appeared in a draft that was under Murray's care, the third draft or the *Textus Emendatus*.[69] Moreover, this passage did not simply enter the draft under Murray's supervision, but it seems virtually certain that Murray himself wrote it. The reason is that it is similar to a passage from a famous article that Murray wrote around this same time:

> [A] true metaphysic of the human person affirms that human existence is essentially social-historic existence. It is not permitted *to introduce a dichotomy into man*, to separate his personal-interior existence and his social-historical existence. Hence it is not permitted to recognize freedom of conscience and to deny freedom of religious expression. Both freedoms are given in the same one instance; they are coequal and coordinate, inseparable, equally constitutive of *the dignity and integrity of man*.[70]

As mentioned above (see section 9.2), Murray made several enduring contributions to the declaration, and he deserves credit for them. As also noted, these contributions mostly are well known, except for one that has received little or no attention. That one is Murray's integrity argument in the *Textus Emendatus*.

Murray had an active and creative mind, and as a result he generated

---

[69] *Textus Emendatus*, §4a [AS III/8, 430]; English translation in *Freedom, Truth, and Human Dignity: The Second Vatican Council's Declaration on Religious Freedom—A New Translation, Redaction History, and Interpretation of* Dignitatis Humanae, ed. David L. Schindler and Nicholas J. Healy (Grand Rapids, MI / Cambridge, UK: William B. Eerdmans Publishing Company, 2015), 291 (emphasis added).

[70] Murray, "Problem of Religious Freedom," 526–27 (emphasis added).

a number of possible arguments or foundations for the right to religious liberty. In the quotation above from his 1964 *Theological Studies* article, note that he even intermingles the integrity argument with his historical consciousness argument. Although he could come up with multiple arguments, his evaluation of his own arguments was wanting. The arguments of his own that he preferred were the ones based on state incompetence and on historical consciousness, and, as already discussed at length in the preceding two chapters, these arguments have serious drawbacks.

This was not exactly the downfall of Murray's argument concerning human integrity, however. Despite his clarity and effectiveness in framing the argument, it does seem clear from the 1964 article that Murray's strong emphasis was on state incompetence. However, the integrity argument might have survived alongside the incompetence argument if it had not encountered serious opposition.

Note the language of Murray's integrity argument in the third draft. "The connection between interior freedom and its social manifestation is wholly indissoluble. Religious freedom is one, undivided and indivisible." Several council fathers were alarmed by this statement. One of the key questions throughout the religious liberty debate was the question of legitimate governmental limitation on religious expression. However, Murray's principle would seem to have allowed for no such limitation. The rule against coercing belief is an absolute one, and if the connection between man's interior life and his social action is "wholly indissoluble," then this argument would seem to allow for no limitation whatsoever on religious expression or action.[71]

This barrage of criticism points to a Murray characteristic that we have seen before, namely, his tendency to view issues as "black or white" and to formulate his ideas in absolute terms. Thus, his principle of state incompetence is nearly absolute, and his distinction between religious and secular issues is so "black and white" that he largely neglects "mixed questions" (that

---

[71] Valuet summarizes the interventions of the council fathers between the third draft (November 1964) and the fourth (May 1965). See Valuet, LRTC, vol. IIB, 1678–1710. See especially the interventions of Brizgys (AS IV/1, 676): If the "nexus" between internal and external liberty is true, then the right in question would be absolute and unlimited; García de Sierra y Méndez (AS IV/1, 752): The "nexus" is exaggerated; AS IV/1, 753: Passage contains an illegitimate transition from internal to external; Hervás y Benet (AS IV/1, 768): The idea of interior/exterior nexus is too absolute; Modrego y Casáus (AS IV/1, 808): The "nexus" is exaggerated; Moro-Briz (AS IV/1, 818): "[N]exus" is exaggerated; and Marcellino Olaechea Loizaga (AS IV/1, 822): The "nexus" is too absolute, and it destroys authority.

is, he fails to see the "grey" areas). Similarly here, the council fathers repeatedly singled out two words in criticizing this passage, "indissoluble nexus."

Murray's next draft would omit this argument,[72] but the omission was regrettable. This is especially true here, where the remedy for Murray's stark and absolute language was so obvious. A simple reformulation of the idea around an "intimate connection"—rather than an "indissoluble nexus"—between the private and the public would have been sufficient to address nearly all of the fathers' complaints about this passage.

The fourth draft contained new language on the social nature of the human person, and with these passages, some elements of Murray's "integrity" argument returned.[73] Moreover, man's social nature would remain a theme of the document throughout the drafting process. This is fortunate, and it is the reason that one can say that although the integrity argument may not enjoy the prominence that it deserves, it nonetheless is present in the declaration in substance.

Murray's fullest exposition of his integrity argument is found in an intervention that he seems to have prepared for Bishop Ernest Primeau of Manchester, New Hampshire. It is well known that Murray prepared a number of interventions for various American bishops,[74] and one of these almost certainly was Primeau's speech in the second session (in September 1964). This seems clear from the close similarity between one of the paragraphs in the intervention and the passage from Murray's 1964 article quoted above.[75] I will give the last word on the foundation of this right and on the importance of human integrity to Primeau/Murray:

> The right to the free exercise of religion must not be considered as being some logical conclusion deduced from the right to freedom of conscience. A deduction of this type would rest upon certain implied premises that are false. It would presuppose that rationalistic conception of man which was somewhat rife during the 19th

---

[72] Cf. Silvia Scatena, *La fatica della libertà. L'elaborazione della dichiarazione* Dignitatis humanae *sulla libertà religiosa del Vaticano II*, Istituto per le scienze religiose—Bologna, Testi e ricerche di scienze religiose, nuova serie, 31 (Bologna, Italy: Il Mulino, 2003), 373. Scatena is one of the few commentators who displays a great deal of interest in the "integrity" argument (which sometimes is called the "anthropological" argument).

[73] Scatena, *La fatica della libertà*, 375–76.

[74] Cf. Pelotte, *Theologian in Conflict*, 92.

[75] Cf. Richard J. Regan, *Conflict and Consensus: Religious Freedom and the Second Vatican Council* (New York/London: Macmillan/Collier-Macmillan Ltd., 1967), 79; Regan, 93n26: "The striking similarity of Primeau's intervention to Murray's thought is no accident. Murray was consulted by many American bishops."

century. According to this concept, man is first of all and primarily an individual and only secondarily is he a social being. This concept of man is false.

In accordance with the true metaphysics of the human person commonly held in Catholic philosophy, human existence is essentially social and historical. In one and the same instance the human person is an individual, or a certain 'I' (ego), and he is also a social being, or a certain 'I' (ego) with others and related to others in the world. On that account it is not permissible to introduce any dichotomy of the human person, i.e., between his personal interior existence and his social historical existence.

From this true metaphysics of the human person there follows a conclusion of the greatest importance to this question. It is certainly clear that it is not permissible to concede to man freedom of conscience and at the same time—in some way or other—to deny him the free exercise of religion. Both these liberties are given in the same instant so that the connection between them is absolutely indissoluble. That freedom which is internal and personal and that which is external and social are both equal in their origin; they are coequal and coordinate and, taken simultaneously, they pertain with equal claim to the dignity and integrity of the human person.

It should be added—if we are to teach clearly—that the free exercise of religion is not a mere logical inference based on the freedom of conscience. This will also be a clearer answer to the objection raised against this teaching of the Declaration. According to this objection, the teaching concerning the right to the free exercise of religion involves a transition or illicit inference from the subjective order of conscience to the objective order of rights. But, *de facto*, there is by no means any such inference made. On the contrary, we arrive at a true notion of religious liberty—one containing two inseparable elements, an internal and an external one. This is not arrived at by means of an inference from the rights of conscience to social religious rights, but rather by means of a simple analysis of the human person himself, who is a single subject having a single right. Indeed, this right applies simultaneously to two elements: to freedom of conscience and to the free exercise of religion.[76]

---

[76] Sept. 24, 1964, intervention of Bishop Ernest J. Primeau (AS III/2, 495–97); English translation in William K. Leahy and Anthony T. Massimini, eds., *Third Session Council Speeches of Vatican II* (Glen Rock, NJ: Paulist Press, 1966), 48–50.

PART 4

LIMITATIONS ON THE RIGHT TO RELIGIOUS LIBERTY

CHAPTER 12

The Challenge of *Quanta Cura*

> *The right to religious freedom is exercised in human society: hence its exercise is subject to certain regulatory norms.*
>
> — DIGNITATIS HUMANAE, §7a

The teachings of both the nineteenth-century popes and Vatican II agree that there are some circumstances in which the state legitimately may restrict religious practice, whether public or private. That is, a person may not perform absolutely any act that he chooses simply because he does so in the name of religion.

However, the question of *when* restriction on religious practice is justified is a crucial one. It is especially important for this discussion because some traditionalist Catholic commentators have charged Vatican II with contradicting previous teaching—namely that of Pope Bl. Pius IX—on this point.[1]

12.1. THE NEED FOR LIMITATIONS ON RELIGIOUS PRACTICE

To begin, history and experience make clear that one must acknowledge at least some right on the state's part to restrict religious practice. For example, although Charlemagne allowed most of his vanquished barbarian foes (such

---

[1] Cf. Marcel Lefebvre, *Religious Liberty Questioned*, trans. Jaime Pazat de Lys (Kansas City, MO: Angelus Press, 2002), 125–30; Marcel de Corte et al., *Lettre à Quelques Évêques* (Paris: Société Saint-Thomas-d'Aquin, 1983), 78–79; Bernard Lucien, "La Liberté Religieuse a Vatican II: Une Rémise en Question Fondamentale," in *Une Démarche Catholique* (Nice: Éditions Association Saint-Herménégilde, 1984), 44–48 (hereinafter, "Une Rémise").

as the Slavs and the Avars) to continue to practice their religion, he dealt much more severely with his most tenacious opponents, the Saxon tribes of northeastern Germany. Once he finally conquered them, Charlemagne converted the Saxons forcibly and entirely stamped out their pagan religion. The reason for this severity was that the Saxon religion was particularly hideous, incorporating as it did practices of human sacrifice and cannibalism.[2] Similarly, the sixteenth-century Portuguese explorers initially tolerated all religious practices in Goa, their outpost in India, except only for their prohibition of the Hindu practice of widow-burning (*suttee*).[3] By the same token, the explorers who voyaged to the New World and the governors who followed them forcibly prohibited Aztec human sacrifice rituals.

The fact of religious practices such as human sacrifice and widow-burning makes it clear that some repression of religious worship or practice must be considered licit. However, more controversy arises when one considers less dramatic practices, and when one inquires into the *standard* that should be used to judge whether a particular act of religious repression is justified.

Before proceeding to consider the proper *standard*, it is necessary to acknowledge that legitimate religious repression easily can give way to policies that exceed the bounds of justice (cf. DH, §12a). Thus, although Charlemagne's repression of Saxon religious atrocities is defensible, he also gave into vindictiveness in his treatment of the Saxons. He not only prohibited the repugnant Saxon rituals, but he also massacred a great number of Saxons, forcibly converted the others, and enacted harsh anti-Saxon laws. Charlemagne's laws were intended to combat the Saxon anti-Christian practices of destroying churches and assaulting the clergy. In addition, the Saxons were considered to pose a physical threat to both the Church and the civil order. However, it nonetheless seems clear that the measures that Charlemagne took against the Saxons went beyond the limits of justice.[4]

The fact that legitimate religious repression can give way to excessively harsh measures is a sober reminder of the need for caution in restricting religious activity, but it does not change the fact that such repression sometimes

---

[2] Cf. Warren H. Carroll, *A History of Christendom*, vol. 2, *The Building of Christendom* (Front Royal, Va.: Christendom College Press, 1987), 310–11.

[3] Cf. Warren H. Carroll, *A History of Christendom*, vol. 3, *The Glory of Christendom* (Front Royal, Va.: Christendom College Press, 1993), 700.

[4] Cf. Carroll, *Building of Christendom*, 315. It is also important to note that the Portuguese policy of general toleration in India lasted only a short time. It was abandoned after the Muslims rebelled against the Portuguese and reconquered Goa. When the Portuguese in turn took back Goa, they executed the Muslims and abandoned their previous policy of religious toleration (Carroll, *Glory of Christendom*, 701).

is just. Thus, the popes taught that it was legitimate for a Catholic state sometimes to restrict public religious worship by non-Catholics. However, the key question concerns the *standard* for determining when this type of repression is justified.

12.2. *Quanta Cura* (1864)

Archbishop Marcel Lefebvre and other leading traditionalist critics argue that *Dignitatis Humanae* contradicts the famous 1864 encyclical of Pope Bl. Pius IX, *Quanta Cura*.[5] In that encyclical, Pius condemned the idea that the best condition of society is that in which "offenders against the Catholic religion" (*violatores Catholicae religionis*) are not punished by the civil authority with "enacted penalties" unless they endanger the "public peace" (*pax publica*) (QC, §3).[6] The pontiff then would proceed to condemn this and other propositions in forceful terms:

> Therefore, by our Apostolic authority, we reprobate, proscribe, and condemn all the singular and evil opinions and doctrines severally mentioned in this letter, and will command that they be thoroughly held by all children of the Catholic Church as reprobated, proscribed and condemned. (QC, §6)[7]

---

[5] Cf. Lefebvre, *Religious Liberty Questioned*, 128; de Corte et al., *Lettre à Quelques Évêques*, 78–79, 81, 108–12; Lucien, "Une Rémise," 44–48.

[6] "Atque contra sacrarum Litterarum, Ecclesiae, sanctorumque Patrum doctrinam, asserere non dubitant, 'optimam esse conditionem societatis, in qua Imperio non agnoscitur officium coercendi sancitis poenis violatores catholicae religionis, nisi quatenus pax publica postulet.'" Pope Pius IX, Encyclical *Quanta Cura* (Dec. 8, 1864), §3. The English translation in the main text is from the EWTN, https://www.ewtn.com/catholicism/library/condemning-current-errors-3608.

[7] English translation from the EWTN. Several commentators assert that Pius IX's invocation of his Apostolic authority indicates an intention to make an infallible declaration. Valuet says that the document has exceptional authority and may amount to a confirmation of an infallible teaching of the ordinary magisterium. Cf. Basile Valuet, *Le droit à la liberté religieuse dans la Tradition de l'Eglise. Un cas de développement doctrinal homogène par le magistère authentique*, 2nd rev. ed. (Barroux: Éditions Sainte-Madeleine, 2011), 234n1231. Harrison considers QC §3 to belong to the secondary object of infallibility, while his interlocutor Guminski disagrees. Cf. Arnold T. Guminski and Brian W. Harrison, *Religious Freedom: Did Vatican II Contradict Traditional Catholic Doctrine? A Debate* (South Bend, IN: St. Augustine Press, 2013), 97–99 (Guminski's position), 155 (Harrison's position). Harrison repeats his opinion as to the document's infallibility in his review of Michael Davies's book on the declaration. Cf. Brian W. Harrison, "The Center is Holding," review of *The Second Vatican Council and Religious Liberty*, by Michael Davies, *Living Tradition*

However, the exact meaning of the condemned idea is not readily apparent. At the outset, one must take notice that two of the pontiff's terms—*violatores* or offenders against the Catholic religion, and *public peace*—contain a significant degree of ambiguity. One prominent traditionalist commentator critical of the declaration is Marcel de Corte. He is the primary author of *Lettre à Quelques Évêques*, a 1983 critique of DH signed by twenty-seven traditionalist leaders. In the *Lettre*, de Corte argues that to understand this passage from *Quanta Cura*, one need only read the words in their "ordinary" or "natural" sense. However, another prominent traditionalist critic, Bernard Lucien, acknowledges the ambiguity.[8]

Is Pius IX asserting that in the best possible society, the civil government should punish anyone who deviates from Catholic faith or worship? Lefebvre seems to answer *yes*.[9] He and other traditionalist critics—including Lucien—interpret Pius's reference to "offenders against the Catholic religion" to mean those who transgress Catholic laws. Lefebvre, in particular, specifies disciplinary and worship laws.[10]

However, such a broad reading of *Quanta Cura* is problematic. For one thing, it would be irreconcilable with numerous long-standing papal decrees requiring that Jewish rites remain undisturbed.[11] Second, such a reading would fail to distinguish between public and private action. The universal

---

44 (1993), Roman Theological Forum, accessed Oct. 29, 2000, http://www.rtforum.org/lt/lt44.html. See also Lefebvre, *Religious Liberty Questioned*, 29–30, arguing in favor of infallibility; Michael Davies, *The Second Vatican Council and Religious Liberty* (Long Prairie, MN: Neumann Press, 1992), 270: "*Quanta Cura* certainly fulfils all the requirements for an infallible pronouncement."

[8] Compare de Corte et al., *Lettre à Quelques Évêques*, 81, 111, and Bernard Lucien, *Gregoire XVI, Pie IX et Vatican II. Études sur la Liberté Religieuse dans la Doctrine Catholique* (Tours: Editions Forts dans la Foi, 1990), 130.

[9] Cf. Lefebvre, *Religious Liberty Questioned*, 128.

[10] Cf. Lefebvre, *Religious Liberty Questioned*, 128; Lucien, "Une Rémise," 44. Marcel de Corte takes a similar position. Cf. de Corte et al., *Lettre à Quelques Évêques*, 111: "Le mot 'violator' a donc ici son sens ordinaire: celui qui viole une règle, c'est celui qui fait ce que cette règle interdit. Celui qui viole la religion catholique, c'est celui qui pose des actes interdits par cette religion." Lucien later would modify his position to some degree. He would continue to favor the interpretation of *violatores* as those who transgress Catholic law, but would acknowledge that the term also may signify those who undermine the Church (cf. Lucien, *Gregoire XVI, Pie IX et Vatican II*, 129–30).

[11] See generally Valuet, LRTE, 224: The popes never have taught a duty in principle to repress Jewish worship. On the toleration of Jewish rites, see also LRTE, 137, discussing the twelfth-century pope Clement III; LTRE, 141, discussing the thirteenth-century popes Innocent III and Gregory IX; and LRTE, 153, discussing the obligatory tolerance of Jewish rites, according to St. Thomas Aquinas, citing *Summa Theologica* II-II, q. 10, a. 11.

or nearly universal policy of the popes who urged repression of non-Catholic religious practice was to do so on account of the *social* harm caused (or perceived to be caused) by such propaganda or worship.[12] A broad literal reading of this passage from *Quanta Cura*, however, would reach even *private* action that causes few, if any, social or public repercussions. Third, the term *violatores*, if taken literally to refer to all who violate Catholic teachings or laws, would apply to a great number of Catholics themselves! This would be an absurd result, as the context suggests that this was not the Pope's concern here. (No commentator—whether arguing for or against the continuity of *Dignitatis Humanae* with tradition—asserts that, in this passage of *Quanta Cura*, Pius is deploring the absence of civil penalties against Catholics.)

Marcel de Corte and his coauthors address this difficulty by reading into their interpretation the element of *public* action. That is, they assert that the encyclical's aim is to reach only *public* non-Catholic religious activity, apparently leaving private religious practice undisturbed.[13] This proviso renders the de Corte reading more reasonable, but it comes at the price of undermining de Corte's own claim that to understand *Quanta Cura*, it is sufficient simply to read the terms in their "ordinary" or "natural" sense. De Corte reads this crucial passage of *Quanta Cura* as referring to the transgression of Catholic "laws" and as being limited to "public" activity (and apparently as being limited to violations of Catholic law *by non-Catholics alone*, and not by Catholics themselves), though *none* of these three precisions is found in the text itself. Even more significantly, as the following observation of C. Goethals shows, although the qualification regarding public action does improve the de Corte interpretation, it ultimately fails to rescue it from overbreadth:

---

[12] Cf. A. Vermeersch, *Tolerance*, trans. W. Humphrey Page (New York: Benziger Brothers, 1912), 161: "[T]he heresies which were really hunted to death were those which, when spread abroad among the masses, sowed the seed of religious anarchy, and tended to the ruin and overthrow of the Church and society. In other words, the heresy persecuted was a revolutionary reformist movement." See also Vermeersch, 157, 158, 164, 174n2, 216. See also Brian W. Harrison, *Religious Liberty and Contraception: Did Vatican II Open the Way for a New Sexual Ethic?* (Melbourne: John XXIII Fellowship Co-op., Ltd., 1988), 93; Valuet, LRTE, 519: The type of harm to public order specified in DH §7.3 often was presupposed; Roland H. Bainton, *The Travail of Religious Liberty: Nine Biographical Sketches* (Philadelphia: Westminster Press, 1951), 17: "Neither Catholic nor Protestant persecuted mere error but only obstinate error. Both persecuted heresy as heresy, and both believed that heresy, if unchecked, would disintegrate society."

[13] Cf. de Corte et al., *Lettre à Quelques Évêques*, 76.

> This definition evidently is false. If it were true, the Pope would have every sinner punished by the public power, because every sinner "takes action forbidden by that (Catholic) religion." Even if we limit "violator" to public sinners, the definition still remains false. The baptized Catholic who does not assist at Sunday Mass, who does not perform his Easter duty, who does not have his children baptized, who states publicly that the Church's conjugal morality has nothing to do with him, takes actions forbidden by the Catholic religion. The public Power thus would be obliged to fix penalties for such offenders, and to have the police track them down. Come now!
>
> That is not all. All adherents of non-Catholic religions take actions forbidden by the Catholic religion. Thus, the "tolerance" of such religions always and everywhere would be a grave public sin, though it sometimes has been approved by the Holy Church.[14]

How then should one interpret this passage? It is clear from the same passage of the encyclical that Pius IX is concerned with the errors of naturalism and indifferentism, and more generally with the attempt to organize society without any reference to religion. Indeed, he identifies naturalism

---

[14] C. Goethals, *La liberté religieuse d'après "Dignitatis Humanae Personae" de Vatican II* (Dendermonde (B): Chez l'A., 1987), 12–13, quoted in Lucien, *Gregoire XVI, Pie IX et Vatican II*, 129–30n13. The English translation is mine. The original reads as follows: "Cette définition est évidemment fausse. Si elle était vraie, le Pape voudrait que tout pécheur fût puni par le pouvoir public, car tout pécheur 'pose des actes interdits par cette religion (catholique).' Si nous limitons 'violateur' aux pécheurs publics, la définition n' en reste pas moins fausse. Le baptisé catholique qui n' assiste pas à la Messe du dimanche, qui ne fait pas ses pâques, qui ne fait pas baptiser ses enfants, qui dit publiquement que la morale conjugale de l' Église ne l' intéresse pas, pose des actes interdits par la religion catholique. Le Pouvoir public serai donc obligé de fixer des peines pour ces violateurs, et de charger la police de les dépister. Allons donc!

"Ce n' est pas tout. Tous les adhérents des religions non-catholiques posent des actes interdits par la religion catholique. Par conséquent, la 'tolérance' de ces religions serait toujours et partout un péché grave public, approuvé parfois par la Sainte Église."

Lucien responds by criticizing Goethals's interpretation, but not by denying that Goethals correctly has captured the import of the traditionalist interpretation. Rather, Lucien responds that the situation described by Goethals would exist only in the best condition of society. In addition, he asserts that the relevant passage from *Quanta Cura* refers not to the government's obligation but to its function (cf. Lucien, *Gregoire XVI, Pie IX et Vatican II*, 130n13). The import of Lucien's response seems to be that all of the government interventions that Goethals lists would indeed be legitimate, but that they would not necessarily be obligatory.

as the source of the proposition quoted above concerning offenders against the Catholic religion. However, traditionalist critics are correct in pointing out that the pontiff does not simply *equate* this condemned proposition with indifferentism or naturalism.[15]

Pius IX, like his immediate predecessor Gregory XVI, seems to have been responding to the ideas of the French priest Félicité de Lamennais, one of the founders of the Catholic Liberalism movement.[16] Interestingly, serious critics on both sides of the larger debate agree on this point. Among those arguing for continuity between Vatican II and previous teaching, Brian Harrison takes this position. Among those arguing for discontinuity, Marcel de Corte and Bernard Lucien do so as well.[17] However, although all these commentators agree that Lamennais is a key to the interpretation of *Quanta Cura*, they disagree on the import of this observation.

The commentators arguing for discontinuity put forward the broad reading discussed above. That is, they argue that one may not limit the proposition on "offenders against the Catholic religion" to a rejection of indifferentism or naturalism because Lamennais's thought quite clearly was at issue, but Lamennais was not an indifferentist.[18] Disengaging Pius IX's condemnation from indifferentism paves the way for de Corte and his coauthors to argue for the broad reading of *violatores* that would encompass all who publicly transgress Catholic laws (or at least all *non-Catholics* who do so).

However, the question of Lamennais is more complex than these critics acknowledge. It is indeed true that on the *personal* level, Lamennais was not an indifferentist. On the contrary, he was a strong supporter of the papacy. By the same token, he acknowledged the uniqueness of Catholicism and did not consider all religions to be equally true. (See section 7.3.1.3 above.) If this is the case, then how can it be that Lamennais's name is so closely tied to the encyclicals of Gregory XVI and Pius IX deploring indifferentism and naturalism?

The reason is that there is a severe disjunction between Lamennais's personal or individual beliefs and his public or social program. Despite his

---

[15] Cf. de Corte et al., *Lettre à Quelques Évêques*, 85–86. As a result, it will not do to interpret the passage simply as a condemnation of indifferentism and naturalism.

[16] Cf. Brian W. Harrison, "Pius IX, Vatican II and Religious Liberty," *Living Tradition* 9 (1987), available on Roman Theological Forum, accessed Apr. 14, 2003, http://www.rtforum.org/lt/lt9.html. See also subsections 7.3.1.2 and 7.3.1.3 above.

[17] Cf. Harrison, RL&C, 34–37, 39–40, 51, and 109; de Corte et al., *Lettre à Quelques Évêques*, 88–95; Lucien, "Une Rémise," 49: "il est bien connu aussi selon les affirmations mêmes du Saint-Siège, que ces condamnations visaient Lamennais, et donc le 'libéralisme catholique.'"

[18] Cf. de Corte et al., *Lettre à Quelques Évêques*, 86, 90–91; Lucien, "Une Rémise," 49.

strong support of the papacy, Lamennais argued that the state should be completely secular.[19] As a result, in his view, the state could not recognize God or defend the rights or teaching of the Church. The only time that Lamennais considered it legitimate for the state to defend the Church was when it was necessary to preserve the *public peace*, namely, to prevent riots, sedition, or the violation of civil rights.[20] As Harrison says, although not personally an indifferentist himself, Lamennais did indeed essentially argue for an indifferentism on the part of the state.[21]

In *Quanta Cura*, Pius IX seems to have been reiterating Gregory XVI's condemnation of Lamennais's ideas in the landmark encyclical *Mirari Vos*.[22] Thus, the thrust of *Quanta Cura* in this context is that it is wrong to say the *only* time the state may act in aid of the Church is to preserve the *public peace*. Stated differently, one may not maltreat the Church or violate her rights or the rights of her members up to the point of—and only stopping short of—inciting a riot or making an actual physical attack.[23]

Valuet puts it succinctly: The standard for repression in *Quanta Cura* is something *more* than violation of the public peace and something *less* than any non-conformity to Catholicism.[24] Between these two poles, he says, the theory of Lamennais and Catholic Liberalism would *approve* all religious

---

[19] Cf. Lamennais, "What Catholicism Will Be in the New Society," *L'Avenir* (June 30, 1831); English translation in Peter N. Stearns, *Priest and Revolutionary: Lamennais and the Dilemma of French Catholicism* (New York: Harper & Row, 1967), 177: "The mixture of the spiritual and the temporal was always, ultimately, harmful to religion; it will be manifestly impossible in societies where the government will be only the administration of material things". See also Lamennais, "De la séparation de l'Église et de l'État," in *Articles de l'Avenir*, vol. 1, 23–30, calling for total Church-state separation, cited in Alec R. Vidler, *Prophecy and Papacy: A Study of Lamennais, the Church, and the Revolution* (London: SCM Press Ltd., 1954), 164.

[20] Cf. Lamennais, article, *L'Avenir* (Oct. 16, 1830), English translation in Stearns, *Priest and Revolutionary*, 172: "Let us rally frankly, completely, to any government that will maintain order and will legitimize itself by justice and respect for the rights of all. We ask no privileges of it; we ask liberty, offering it our strength in exchange." See also Harrison, RL&C, 36, quoting *L'Avenir*, cited in *Dictionnaire de Théologie Catholique*, vol. 9, part I (Paris: Librairie Letouzey et Ané, 1926), s.v. "Libéralisme Catholique," column 550: Government may only repress crimes and attacks on liberties; it may take action "only in the order of material interests"; Valuet, LRTE, 208, citing and quoting the *Acte d'union* proposed by *L'Avenir*.

[21] Harrison, RL&C, 36: "In effect, Lamennais was demanding a State which would be indifferent not only as regards Catholicism versus other religions, but between religion of any sort and irreligion." See also subsection 7.3.2 above.

[22] Cf. Harrison, "Pius IX, Vatican II and Religious Liberty."

[23] Cf. Valuet, LRTE, 222.

[24] Cf. Valuet, LRTE, 227.

expression or public propaganda. By contrast, the broad reading of de Corte and his coauthors would *disapprove* all such expression.

As discussed above, the de Corte reading is untenable. It is unable to follow through on its commitment to limit itself to the ordinary sense of the words found in the encyclical; its breadth leads to the anomalous, if not the absurd, result of empowering the government to police individual sins that have little or no impact on the common good; and it neglects to take account of the strain in Lamennais's thought that is indifferentist—not in the individual sense but in the public or political sense.

Valuet suggests that Pius understood *violatores* ("offenders against the Catholic religion") not to mean *all* transgressors of Catholic laws but rather those who attacked the Church or endangered the Catholic faithful in ways particularly damaging to the common good.[25] The import of this condemnation is that even if one does not take up arms against the Church or assault her faithful physically, one still can cause sufficient harm to the Church or her members, such that the public authority may take action to defend her. Thus, the *public peace* criterion is too narrow of a restriction on state action.

Concerning Valuet's interpretation of *violatore* as one who attacks the Church or who harms the faithful in a particularly damaging way, it would be difficult to prove conclusively that this was Pius's understanding. However, this reading seems eminently reasonable in light of the considerations discussed above and throughout this section. In addition, I would add in support of this reading that one should give due consideration to Pius IX's reference to "enacted penalties." A careful reading of this term can shed some light on the meaning of the larger passage in *Quanta Cura*.

Pius IX says that the civil authority should punish violators of the Catholic religion by "enacted penalties" (*sancitis poenis*). This reference to penalties suggests that the pontiff has criminal or penal sanctions in mind, and if so, it lends support to this reading of *violatores* as those who cause a particularly serious harm to the Church rather than those who simply profess a non-Catholic religion. Indeed, if Pius had in mind the application to non-Catholics of some kind of civil disability (as de Corte implies), one would not expect him to have used the word *penalties*. For example, when a nation disallows non-citizens from voting, one does not consider those non-citizens to be under criminal penalty, but rather one concludes simply that they fail to meet the legal requirements for voting. If de Corte is correct that "penalties" for "offenders against the Catholic religion" means the prohibition of public non-Catholic rites, then the choice of the phrase "enacted

---

[25] Cf. Valuet, LRTE, 224–25.

penalties" is curious. Such provisions would not amount to actual criminal *penalties* against the non-Catholics, but rather they would be considered protective measures in favor of the Catholic citizens. Indeed, even the traditionalist critics themselves do not seem to have any criminal penalties in mind—such as fines or imprisonment—but rather a prohibition on public non-Catholic worship. As a result, it seems incongruous that such measures would be termed *penalties*. By contrast, if Valuet is correct that a *violatore* is one who causes a particularly significant harm to the Church or the faithful, then the idea of criminal sanctions and the use of the term *enacted penalties* is readily understandable. (This observation still may not convince all readers that the Valuet interpretation of *violatores* is correct. After all, the term *penalties* sometimes is used in contexts besides criminal law. However, its most common and correct usage is indeed in the criminal or penal context, and as a result, it is another indication that the Valuet reading is correct and that the de Corte interpretation is overbroad.)

Pius IX does not provide examples of specific harms or violations that he has in mind when he refers to *offenders against the Catholic religion*. Thus, Harrison is careful to note that it may be impossible to determine for certain exactly what Pius meant.[26] Nevertheless, he says that we at least can identify with certainty some of the ideas that he condemned elsewhere in *Quanta Cura*, including a notion of "liberty of conscience and worship" that "involves an unlimited freedom of propaganda."[27] This too was one of the hallmarks of Lamennais's thought.[28] In this light, it is not difficult to imagine some examples of actions that could damage the Church or her faithful in the public realm, but that would not go so far as to violate the public peace by causing violence or bloodshed.[29] Harrison identifies abusive anti-Catholic religious proselytism as one example, and Valuet mentions the exhibition

---

[26] Cf. Harrison, RL&C, 103. Harrison here refers to ambiguity in the term *public peace* in particular, but this observation applies with at least as much force to the term *offenders against the Catholic religion*.

[27] Harrison, RL&C, 103–4.

[28] Cf. Vidler, *Prophecy and Papacy*, 165, citing several articles from *L'Avenir*. See also subsection 7.3.1.4 above.

[29] Somewhat paradoxically, Valuet notes that some violent attacks might not violate the public peace. He makes this point in response to Lucien's assertion that such attackers already are protected against by the public peace standard (cf. Lucien, *Gregoire XVI, Pie IX et Vatican II*, 129). Valuet's point is that in the case of state-sanctioned confiscation of Church property, the violent action against the Church would not necessarily violate the public peace because it would take place under the state's own auspices and in accordance with enacted laws (cf. Valuet, LRTE, 226).

of blasphemous films as another.[30] Both are persuasive in arguing that DH would allow repression in these cases.

As Harrison says, it likely is impossible to determine with certainty and precision what Pius IX meant by this passage. My own conclusion is that the observations of Harrison and Valuet are on target, but it seems that the most that one can do is to put forward the most plausible reading. If some readers remain uncomfortable that a higher degree of certainty seems elusive, then Harrison provides at least one way out of this difficulty. He invokes the maxim *odiosa sunt restringenda*, according to which favorable laws enjoy a broad interpretation and restrictive laws receive a narrow one. The import of the maxim in this context is that we may not interpret Pius IX to condemn a broader category of things than what he *certainly* condemned.[31] Thus, if significant doubt remains—for example, concerning whether a certain group of persons qualifies as *offenders against the Catholic religion*—then one must assume that such persons are *not* included within the condemnation.

Below I will return to this question and to a comparison of the standards contained in *Quanta Cura* and the declaration. I intend to show that the Vatican II standard is significantly broader than *public peace* and, therefore, that DH does not contradict *Quanta Cura*.

12.3. A Matter of Translation

A particular difficulty arose in the 1980s for those studying this issue in English. That is, an inaccurate translation of *Quanta Cura* caused confusion by using the phrase *public order* instead of *public peace*.[32] That is, the mistranslation claimed that *Quanta Cura* had criticized and rejected the standard of *public order* in discussing restrictions on religious activity. This created a difficulty because the Vatican II Declaration on Religious Liberty specifically had approved a certain understanding of *public order* as the correct standard for judging when repression of religious activity is just. "[T]he exercise of this right is not to be impeded, provided that just public order [*iustus ordo publicus*] be observed" (DH, §2b).[33] Thus, juxtaposing the Vatican

---

[30] Guminski/Harrison, 217–18, Harrison's final reply to Guminski; Valuet, LRTE, 227.
[31] Harrison, RL&C, 102–3, 106.
[32] Cf. Harrison, "Pius IX, Vatican II and Religious Liberty," n2.
[33] The Council used the term *public order* because it was one that was familiar in secular law and, therefore, one that governmental authorities readily would understand. Cf. De Smedt, Oral *Relatio* on the *Textus Denuo Recognitus* (Nov. 19, 1965) [AS IV/6, 722]. In addition, however, as discussed below, the fathers put forward their own definition specifying what the content of the term *public order* should be. Cf. *Textus Denuo Recognitus* [AS IV/6,

II endorsement of a *public order* standard with the mistranslation of *Quanta Cura* made it appear that Vatican II had adopted the precise standard that Pope Pius IX specifically had condemned.

This mistranslation of *Quanta Cura* is found in three articles by Father William G. Most from the early- and mid-1980s. However, it is not clear which translation of *Quanta Cura* Father Most is citing or quoting. One of his articles contains a footnote to this passage, but the actual text of that footnote itself says only "Missing."[34] Appparently a footnote was placed in the draft, but no source was added. The passage containing the mistranslation says the following:

> [*Quanta Cura*] . . . says it is wrong to hold that the *best* condition of society is one in which there is no recognition of the duty of the government to repress *violatores* of the Catholic religion, except to the extent that public order demands.[35]

An earlier article in the same journal and by the same author had contained the same mistranslation of "public peace" in *Quanta Cura* §3 as "public order," but it had contained no citation or footnote at all.[36] Harrison points out that Most "has quoted from an inaccurate translation of *Quanta Cura*, which wrongly attributes the expression 'public order' to Pius IX in this passage."[37] Given the lack of citations, however, it also appears possible that the faulty translation may be Most's own.

In any event, Harrison's identification of the mistranslation in Most's articles sheds the necessary light on this issue. If the Vatican II adoption of the *public order* standard had amounted to an embrace of a standard that Pius IX specifically had rejected, then *Dignitatis Humanae* indeed might be impossible to reconcile with the teachings of the nineteenth-century popes. Actually, however, there is no contradiction because Pius IX had rejected

---

722]; Second Vatican Council, Declaration on Religious Liberty *Dignitatis Humanae* (December 7, 1965), §7c.

[34] Cf. William G. Most, "Religious Liberty: What the Texts Demand," *Faith & Reason* 9, no. 3 (Fall 1983): 208n10 ("Missing").

[35] Most, "Religious Liberty," 201.

[36] Cf. William G. Most, "Vatican II vs. Pius IX? A Study in Lefebvrism," *Faith & Reason* 6, no. 3 (Fall 1980): 223.

[37] Harrison, "Pius IX, Vatican II and Religious Liberty," n2. See also RL&C, 50–51n46. Harrison also cites an article that Most published in the *Wanderer* on October 23, 1986, "Vatican II on Religion and the State." This article, too, apparently contains the same mistranslation, but I have been unable to locate a copy of it.

only *public peace* as the correct standard, not *public order*.[38] The following section discusses the *substantive* difference between these terms as used in *Quanta Cura* and the declaration.

12.4. A Limitless Freedom?

Needless to say, it is not sufficient simply to point out that *Quanta Cura* and the declaration refer to different terms—*public peace* (with disapproval) and *just public order* (with approval), respectively—in specifying the standard for legitimate restriction of religious activity. Rather, it is necessary also to show that the *substance* of what is signified by these terms truly is different, and thus that DH did not adopt a standard that *Quanta Cura* had condemned.

Lefebvre acknowledges that the two documents refer to different standards, that is, that DH does not actually say that *public peace* is the sole limitation on religious activity.[39] However, he implies that Vatican II's adoption of a different standard is, in fact, illusory. Mocking the Vatican II standard, he says, "'Within the limits of a just public order'—which limits nothing!" and "Always 'within due limits'—which are nothing of the kind!"[40] Lucien makes a similar argument. He asserts that according to the traditional doctrine (especially as embodied in *Mirari Vos* and *Quanta Cura*), *per se* religious liberty is not a right, and *per accidens*, toleration is permissible in certain historical circumstances. The declaration, Lucien continues, turns the traditional teaching on its head by recognizing religious liberty *per se* as a right, while recognizing limitations on this right only *per accidens*, or according to circumstances.[41] (Like Lucien, de Corte and his coauthors also see the limitations contained in DH as accidental.)[42]

Harrison rightly points out that these critiques reduce the conciliar and pre-conciliar teachings to *philosophical propositions* and then compare whether the propositions themselves are contradictory. However, this method *truly* demonstrates a contradiction between the underlying papal and conciliar pronouncements *only* if the philosophical propositions accurately capture the substance of the magisterial documents. The difficulty in this particular case is that these critics interpret DH as *more expansive*

---

[38] Harrison, "Pius IX, Vatican II and Religious Liberty" n2.
[39] Cf. Lefebvre, *Religious Liberty Questioned*, 127–28.
[40] Marcel Lefebvre, Letter to Cardinal Seper (Feb. 26, 1978), in Michael Davies, *Apologia Pro Marcel Lefebvre*, vol. 2, *1977–1979* (Dickinson, TX: Angelus Press, 1983), 153.
[41] Cf. Lucien, "Une Rémise," 47. For Harrison's English translation of the relevant passage, see RL&C, 45.
[42] Cf. de Corte et al., *Lettre à Quelques Évêques*, 108–9.

than it really is (and, as discussed above, *Quanta Cura* as *more restrictive* than it really is).[43]

Lefebvre and Lucien underestimate the limitations that DH places on the exercise of the right of religious liberty. Notwithstanding Lucien's characterization, Vatican II never defines the limitations on the exercise of religious liberty *as merely accidental*.[44] On the contrary, these limitations are included in the very definition of the right to religious liberty itself. The key provision of DH is section 2, which contains the definition of religious liberty. This passage includes the limitations on the exercise of that right, not as an *afterthought* or as something *accidental* but rather as an inherent qualification on the right:

> This Vatican Council declares that the human person has a right to religious freedom. Such freedom consists in this, that all men and women should be immune from coercion on the part of individuals, social groups or any human power, so that no one is to be forced to act against his conscience in religious matters, or prevented from acting according to his conscience, in private or in public, whether alone or in association with others, within due limits. (DH, §2a)[45]

Note that (as discussed in chapter 9, especially in section 9.2) there are two parts to the right. The first is the right *not to be coerced* into acting against one's conscience in religious matters, and the second is the right *not to be prevented* from acting according to one's conscience. The next section of DH—section 3—reiterates the second part of the right. That is, just as one may not be *forced* into making a religious profession, neither may one be prohibited or *impeded* from doing the religious acts that he chooses to do. "Nor, on the other hand, is he to be restrained from acting in accordance with his conscience, especially in religious matters" (DH, §3c).[46] During the

---

[43] Cf. Harrison, RL&C, 45–48, 107.

[44] Cf. Harrison, RL&C, 46.

[45] Translation from David L. Schindler and Nicholas J. Healy, eds., *Freedom, Truth, and Human Dignity: The Second Vatican Council's Declaration on Religious Freedom—A New Translation, Redaction History, and Interpretation of* Dignitatis Humanae (Grand Rapids, MI / Cambridge, UK: William B. Eerdmans Publishing Company, 2015), 387. Note that a problem is present in some prominent English translations of DH §2, including the one on the Vatican website. The problem is that they translate DH §2 as providing a right to freedom from coercion, but do not include the right not to be prevented from acting in accordance with one's conscience. See also the NCWC translation published by St. Paul Books & Media (Boston) (same problem).

[46] DH, §3 [AAS 58 (1966): 932].

Council, some bishops pointed out that this passage on non-restraint (DH, §3c), unlike the preceding one (DH, §2a), does not repeat the qualification that the right must be exercised "within due limits."[47] As a critique of the drafting and style of the declaration, this is a fair point. It does indeed seem that a brief reiteration of this qualification would have enhanced the document's clarity. However, as an indictment that DH contradicts *Quanta Cura*, it misses the mark.

That is, even if DH §3 neglects to refer to due limits expressly, both logic and the context of the declaration indicate that such limitations apply even here. Section 2 asserts that both parts of the right apply "within due limits." Note that the first part of the right (non-coercion) contained in DH §2 is a broader version of the perennial Catholic teaching on the freedom of the act of faith. It is not identical to the ancient teaching, but it can be understood as flowing from it.[48] By contrast, the second part of the right (contained in both articles 2 and 3) presents the greater challenge because it goes further in asserting that this immunity applies as well to one's *affirmative religious actions*. This is the more expansive right (and the truly challenging doctrinal development). As a result, logic itself dictates that *if* the far less debatable right of freedom from coercion exists only "within due limits," *then* certainly the more extensive (and more controversial) immunity for one's religious acts must be similarly limited.[49]

In addition, another provision in the text itself supports this conclusion.

---

[47] Cf. Harrison, RL&C, 96.

[48] See section 9.6 above, citing John Courtney Murray, "The Declaration on Religious Liberty: A Moment in Its Legislative History," in *Religious Liberty: An End and a Beginning*, ed. John Courtney Murray (New York: MacMillan, 1966), 30. This part of the right also could be based on the duty to follow one's conscience.

[49] John Courtney Murray believed that the right of non-coercion was absolute. That is, he believed that it never is licit to coerce someone to act against his beliefs. Cf. Richard Regan, "John Courtney Murray, the American Bishops, and the *Declaration on Religious Liberty*," in John T. Ford, ed., *Religious Liberty: Paul VI and Dignitatis Humanae* (Brescia, Italy: Istituto Paolo VI, 1995), 55, noting that the *Textus Emendatus*, for which Murray had primary responsibility, takes this position. Luigi Mistò takes the same position. Cf. "Discussion Summary," in John T. Ford, ed., *Religious Liberty: Paul VI and Dignitatis Humanae* (Brescia, Italy: Istituto Paulo VI, 1995), 43 (comment by Mistò at symposium on DH). However, Regan and Valuet call into question the absolute character of this right. Cf. Richard J. Regan, *Conflict and Consensus: Religious Freedom and the Second Vatican Council* (New York/London: Macmillan/Collier-Macmillan Ltd., 1967), 123–24; Valuet, LRTE, 424n2336). Indeed, a famous U.S. civil case addressed one of these contexts, namely, the licitness of ordering life-saving medical care that violates the religious convictions of a patient. Cf. *Application of the President and Directors of Georgetown College*, 331 F., 2nd 1000 (DC Cir. 1964), permitting hospital's administration of blood transfusions to

The declaration contains another section (article 7) devoted entirely to the subject of limitations on the right to religious liberty, and its qualifications are by no means limited to the first part of the right (the immunity from coercion). The official relator for the declaration, Bishop Émile De Smedt of Bruges, Belgium, addressed this precise issue: "The limits are dealt with extensively in article 7, which obviously holds good for the entire schema, without it being necessary to keep summing them up at every point."[50] In fact, the text makes clear that these limitations come into play much more often in connection with the second part of the right to religious freedom, namely, the immunity from restraint in acting according to one's conscience in religious matters. "The right to religious freedom is exercised in human society: hence its exercise is subject to certain regulatory norms. . . . Furthermore, society has the right to defend itself against possible abuses committed on the pretext of religion. It is the special duty of government to provide this protection" (DH, §7c).

Another provision of the declaration—section 4—provides a concrete example of such an abuse, namely, coercive or misleading proselytism (DH, §4d). Such activity does not rise to the level of a breach of the public peace since it does not involve violence (at least not usually), but the declaration makes clear that such activity amounts to an abuse of the right to religious liberty, not a legitimate exercise of the right. That is, the declaration, like Pius IX, recognizes a scope of legitimate restriction of religious activity that extends beyond breaches of the public peace.

Lefebvre and Lucien charge that DH—like Lamennais—promotes a freedom that is limitless or that is bound only by illusory limitations. However, this simply is not the case. Article 2 defines the right as one that must be exercised "within due limits," and several provisions of the declaration specify *public order* or the *just public order* as the limiting principle or governing standard (cf. DH, §§2b, 3d, 4b, 7c). That is, one must exercise one's right to religious freedom within the limitations of the (just) public order. Indeed, the Council provides a definition of the term *public order*, and this definition makes clear that this standard is broader than the term *public peace*. (Note the three components indicated by added brackets in the following quotation.)

---

incompetent Jehovah's Witness patient over the objections of her husband; *cert. denied*, 84 S. Ct. 1883 (1964).

[50] AS IV/6, 742; English translation by Harrison in RL&C, 96.

[G]overnment is not to act in an arbitrary fashion or in an unfair spirit of partisanship. Its action is to be controlled by juridical norms which are in conformity with the objective moral order. These norms arise out of [1] the need for the effective safeguard of the rights of all citizens and for the peaceful settlement of conflicts of rights, also out of [2] the need for an adequate care of genuine public peace, which comes about when men live together in good order and in true justice, and finally out of [3] the need for a proper guardianship of public morality. These matters constitute the basic component of the common welfare: they are what is meant by public order. (DH, §7c)

Note several things about this definition. First, as mentioned, it contains three distinct components. Second, these components *include*—but are *not limited to*—public peace. It is indeed true that the civil authority may restrict religious activity that violates the public peace, and thus, the passage refers to "the need for an adequate care of genuine public peace." However, Vatican II—like Pope Pius IX—recognizes that there are additional circumstances in which the civil authority may restrict religious activity. These additional justifications for restrictions are, first, to protect the rights of other citizens and, second, to safeguard public morality.

Thus, Lefebvre and Lucien have interpreted DH as *more expansive* than it really is. That is, the limitations on the exercise of the right to religious liberty are by no means accidental, but rather they are real and they are integral to the Vatican II understanding of the right. By the same token, Lefebvre and de Corte also interpret *Quanta Cura* as *more restrictive* than it really is.[51] They assert that the encyclical stands for the idea that the civil authority may repress non-Catholic religious activity, not only on account of the harm that it causes but simply because it is false.[52] Some manuals took this position,[53] and Harrison acknowledges that perhaps Pius IX and other

---

[51] Cf. Harrison, RL&C, 107: "[O]ur authors' case that 'public peace' in *Quanta Cura* means the same as 'just public order' in *Dignitatis Humanae* does not rest only upon a more conservative interpretation of the former document than the evidence *requires*; it rests also upon a more liberal interpretation of the latter than the evidence *permits*." See also RL&C, 42.

[52] Lefebvre, *Religious Liberty Questioned*, 128. De Corte seems to take the same position, namely, that violating the Catholic religion always amounts to a disturbance of the public peace. Cf. de Corte et al., *Lettre à Quelques Évêques*, 112.

[53] Cf. Valuet, LRTE, 359.

popes personally believed this.[54] However, none actually taught it as Catholic doctrine. That is, Catholic doctrine never has required the state as such to persecute error as such.[55]

There are three possible positions that one might take with regard to peaceful non-Catholic religious activity, that is, religious activity that does not breach the public peace:[56]

(a) *All* of it is entitled to immunity;
(b) *Some* of it is entitled to immunity; or
(c) *None* of it is entitled to immunity.

Quanta Cura rejects position (a). This is the specific error mentioned in QC §3, namely, that the civil authority may not intervene except when there is a riot, a physical attack, or some other breach of the public peace. Lefebvre accuses DH of taking this position, but it does not. On the contrary, DH recognizes that the civil authority sometimes may restrict religious activity, even if it is peaceful.

Lefebvre contends that *Quanta Cura* embraces position (c). If this were true, there would be a difficulty in reconciling the declaration with the encyclical. However, the Church never has required the repression of

---

[54] Harrison, RL&C, 44.
[55] Cf. Valuet, LRTE, 179: Catholic doctrine never required suppression of error as such. Note, however, that Harrison reads *Mirari Vos* (the 1832 encyclical of Gregory XVI) as calling for repression of non-Catholic worship *as such* (cf. Guminski/Harrison, 83, 177n77). Even in *Mirari Vos*, though, one can see that the call for repression is based not only on account of the falsity of the underlying worship or propaganda but also on an intention to protect the Catholic faithful. Thus, the encyclical says that where restraints are lifted, men are propelled to ruin. By the same token, Gregory says, the state is endangered as well. "Thence [from liberty of conscience] comes transformation of minds, corruption of youths, contempt of sacred things and holy laws—in other words, a pestilence more deadly to the state than any other." Pope Gregory XVI, Encyclical *Mirari Vos* (Aug. 15, 1832), §14. Moreover, even if some papal documents neglected to identify such harms or potential harms, Valuet notes, they at least presupposed dangers to the Church, the faithful, or society as a whole (cf. LRTE, 519). Harrison bases his reading of *Mirari Vos* in part on Gregory's reference to Augustine, and it is indeed true that some passages in Augustine do call for repression on account of the falsity of the non-Catholic doctrine. However, as discussed more fully in chapter 15, Augustine nearly always emphasizes the violence and criminal behavior of those whose repression he is urging. In light of the fact that the actual members of these sects nearly always were violent, Valuet concludes that the issue of the sincere and peaceable non-Catholic religious practitioner simply was not practically posed in ancient or medieval times (cf. LRTE, 181).
[56] Cf. Harrison, RL&C, 44.

all public non-Catholic religious activity, and never has required repression for the sole reason that the worship or teaching is false. As discussed in the next chapter, the justification for such repression (usually stated, but at least implied) was the social harm that it caused or was believed to cause to the Church, the Catholic faithful, or society as a whole. As a result, *Quanta Cura* leaves the way open for the assertion of position (b), namely, that some peaceful non-Catholic religious activity is entitled to immunity, and some is not. This is precisely the position that DH takes.[57] If a particular religious action respects the just public order, then it is entitled to immunity; if it violates that order, then it is not.

12.5. The Public Order and the Common Good

Despite the difference between the declaration's *public order* standard and the *public peace* standard rejected by Pius IX, some traditionalists still contend that Vatican II contradicts *Quanta Cura*. Marcel de Corte and his coauthors attempt to equate the two standards by asserting that both include considerations of public morality. Discussing the "just limits" of DH §7, de Corte says, "They concern requirements of peace and public morality, which correspond well to the 'public tranquility' which *Quanta Cura* mentioned."[58] This is mere assertion. De Corte provides no support for inclusion of public morality within the *public peace* standard. Contrary to his implication that the two standards "correspond," *Quanta Cura*—unlike DH—never mentions public morality as a component of the relevant standard for repression of religious activity.

De Corte makes another attempt to equate the two standards by recalling that the error in question (insufficient public intervention against offenders of the Catholic religion) finds its origin in naturalism. However, naturalism, he says, does not exclude all morality but only *supernatural* morality.[59] Thus, perhaps the *public peace* standard embraces considerations at least of *natural* morality. If so, the argument runs, then the *public order* standard (embraced by Vatican II) and the *public peace* standard (rejected

---

[57] Harrison, RL&C, 44. See also RL&C, 51: *Mirari Vos* and *Quanta Cura* condemn only the proposition that *all* peaceful non-Catholic propaganda has a right to immunity from civil coercion.

[58] de Corte et al., *Lettre à Quelques Évêques*, 79. The English translation is mine. The original French reads: "Il s'agit des exigences de la paix et de la moralité publique, ce qui correspond bien à la 'tranquilité publique' dont fait mention *Quanta Cura*."

[59] Cf. de Corte et al., *Lettre à Quelques Évêques*, 111.

by Pius IX) would appear to be quite similar, and the assertion that DH embraced a standard that *Quanta Cura* had rejected would gain strength.

This argument may seem plausible at first blush, but there are several difficulties with it. First, it conflates the error in question with naturalism itself (its cause), a mistake that de Corte himself specifically had warned against in connection with indifferentism.[60] Naturalism indeed may purport to accept natural morality, but Pius says that what it *gives rise to* is an error that recognizes no limit but public peace. Second, the fact is that Pius IX does not mention public morality, and he certainly never suggests that the public peace standard includes it. Third, the whole context of *Quanta Cura* makes clear that Pius does not view the public peace standard as protecting even *natural* morality. On the contrary, only a few lines after his reference to *violatores* against the Catholic religion, Pius describes the practical disappearance of morality in the absence of religion:

> [W]here religion has been removed from civil society, and the doctrine and authority of divine revelation repudiated, the genuine notion itself of justice and human right is darkened and lost, and the place of true justice and legitimate right is supplied by material force.... But who, does not see and clearly perceive that human society, when set loose from the bonds of religion and true justice, can have, in truth, no other end than the purpose of obtaining and amassing wealth, and that society (under such circumstances) follows no other law in its actions, except the unchastened desire of ministering to its own pleasures and interests? (QC, §4)

Thus, it seems that Pius IX would be the last person to agree with de Corte in crediting the *public peace* standard (originating in naturalism) with preserving *any* authentic sense of morality, whether supernatural or natural. Fourth, de Corte forgets one of his own interpretive keys, namely, that Pius is concerned especially with the errors of Lamennais. Again, although Lamennais did not exclude religious truth or morality from *private* life, he did indeed exclude them from the proper concerns of the civil authority in *public* life. That is, Lamennais's concept of the state was entirely secular, and his understanding of its duties was simply material. Thus, de Corte's attempt to enlarge the ambit of the *public peace* standard to include public morality ultimately fails, and with it so does his attempt to charge DH with embracing a standard that Pius IX had condemned.

---

[60] Cf. de Corte et al., *Lettre à Quelques Évêques*, 85–86.

12.5. The Public Order and the Common Good

Some critics also complain about the Council's preference for the term *just public order* over the *common good*. Archbishop Lefebvre, Bishop Carli, and other council fathers had proposed replacing the term *public order* with the term *common good*.[61] The standard of the *common good* had been used in previous papal teaching, notably that of Popes Leo XIII and Pius XII. This standard, too, would have made it clear that the state may defend the Church to a greater extent than simply to prevent bloodshed. That is, the effect of these proposed amendments would have been to allow repression of religious activity to the extent permitted by the *common good*. These proposed amendments, however, were rejected. One reason for this decision was that the standard of the common good likely would provide too broad of an allowance for the civil authority to repress religion.[62]

Archbishop Karol Wojtyła of Krakow proposed a different amendment to clarify the meaning of *public order*. This amendment specified that although the Council was adopting a term—public order—that was familiar in secular law, the meaning that the Church was giving to that term was broader than the secular understanding of it. This amendment contained the three components of the just public order discussed above (public morality, the rights of others, and the public peace). In addition, it mentioned both

---

[61] In his final *relatio*, the official relator for the declaration, Émile De Smedt, refers to these proposals generally (cf. AS IV/6, 722; English translation in Harrison, RL&C, 90). See also AS II/5, 797–98 (Lefebvre), discussed in Silvia Scatena, *La fatica della libertà. L'elaborazione della dichiarazione* Dignitatis humanae *sulla libertà religiosa del Vaticano II*, Istituto per le scienze religiose—Bologna, Testi e ricerche di scienze religiose, nuova serie, 31 (Bologna, Italy: Il Mulino, 2003), 138n123; AS IV/2, 99 (Carli), quoted in part and summarized in Basile Valuet, *La liberté religieuse et la tradition catholique. Un cas de développement doctrinal homogène dans le magistère authentique*, 3rd rev. ed. (Barroux: Éditions Sainte-Madeleine, 2011), vol. IIB, 1491.

[62] In his debate with Harrison, Guminski quotes a 1964 De Smedt *relatio* explaining why the term *common good*, although contained in the first draft of the declaration, was omitted in the second and succeeding drafts: "In the draft of the Declaration that we proposed last year [the first draft], we affirmed that the exercise of religious liberty was limited by the common good. But very numerous Fathers have remarked with just reason that this rule is too broad and opens the way to multiple abuses." De Smedt, Oral *Relatio* on the *Textus Emendatus* [AS III/8, 454; translation by Michael Woodward, quoted in Guminski/Harrison, 143]. In his *relatio* on the final version of the declaration, De Smedt discusses proposals to replace the term *just public order* with the term *common good*. He gives an explanation consistent with what he had said in the earlier *relatio*, but he is more circumspect, referring to the Council's duties toward those fathers "who are living in dangerous circumstances." De Smedt, Oral *Relatio* on the *Textus Denuo Recognitus* [AS IV/6, 722; English translation in Harrison, RL&C, 90]. A number of council fathers were particularly concerned about possible abuses and distortions of the common good standard in Communist nations. Cf. Scatena, *La fatica della libertà*, 138–39.

objective morality and the *common good* as well. This amendment was included in *Dignitatis Humanae* in the following language (this quotation is somewhat duplicative of one contained in the previous section, but this version provides additional context both before and after the specification of the components included in the public order):

> Furthermore, society has the right to defend itself against possible abuses committed on the pretext of freedom of religion. It is the special duty of government to provide this protection. However, government is not to act in an arbitrary fashion or in an unfair spirit of partisanship. Its action is to be controlled by juridical norms which are in conformity with *the objective moral order*. These norms arise out of the need for the effective safeguard of the rights of all citizens and for the peaceful settlement of conflicts of rights, also out of the need for an adequate care of genuine public peace, which comes about when men live together in good order and in true justice, and finally out of the need for a proper guardianship of public morality. These matters constitute the basic component of the *common welfare*: they are what is meant by public order. (DH, §7c [emphasis added])

The significance of this passage is that despite using the phrase *public order*, which is derived from secular law, the Council makes clear that it understands this term to include reference to the *objective moral order* and to the basic component of the *common welfare* or the *common good*. As a result, the text of *Dignitatis Humanae* proves that the meaning of *public order* embraced by the Council is by no means *equivalent* to the meaning of *public peace* that was condemned by Pius IX, even though the Vatican II definition does *encompass* the concept of public peace. By the same token, by requiring that such restrictions conform to the objective moral order, the declaration is addressing the problem with articles 10 and 11 of the DDHC, namely, that the only limits on religious activity that they recognized were those set by the positive civil law.

In fact, the Council's broad interpretation of *public order* actually is a reaffirmation of *Quanta Cura*. That is, it makes clear that the state has a greater interest in religion and morality than in simply preventing bloodshed or protecting property rights. However, the standard of *public order* or the *just public order* is narrower than the *common good* standard. Note that the Wojtyła amendment does not identify the *public order* standard with the *common good* in its totality but rather with the *basic component of the common good*. The relator, Bishop De Smedt, explains the difference:

> The common good is taken in its full extent (*sumitur in sua amplitudine*) as a norm when it is a question of guarding or promoting the right to religious liberty. When it comes to imposing limits, however, the more basic component (*parte fundamentali*) of the common good is taken to be the norm.[63]

Harrison explains that the basic component of the common good concerns those interests that the civil authority may protect with coercion, that is, interests closely tied to the *survival* of society itself. As DH §7 says, these essential societal interests comprising the public order are the preservation of public peace, the protection of rights, and the promotion of public morality. However, the common good considered in its totality includes not only those interests that are strictly necessary for society's *survival* but also additional ones that are valuable but not essential, namely, those interests that are oriented to society's *perfection*.[64]

As discussed in the next chapter, the question of how much to repress problematic religious practice is one of prudence rather than doctrine. Harrison will frame it as a matter of public ecclesiastical law. As Bishop De Smedt notes, this judgment necessarily is one that varies across different historical periods and, as a result, the concrete requirements of the common good (or, one might add, even the requirements of the *basic component* of the common good) always are relative.[65]

In addition, even this distinction between *public order* and the *common good* may be less significant than it appears. By definition, *public order* is a narrower standard because it encompasses only the *core content* of the

---

[63] De Smedt, Oral *Relatio* on the *Textus Denuo Recognitus* [AS IV/6, 722]; English translation in Harrison, RL&C, 90.

[64] Cf. Guminski/Harrison, 57. Murray's understanding of the basic component of the public order is similar to Harrison's. Cf. Murray, "A Moment in Its Legislative History," 41–42: Government may coerce only "in the case of a violation of public order; a contravention of the necessary conditions of social coexistence; a public offense that imperils the pillars of society, which are an order of equal justice for all citizens; the public peace which is the work of justice; and that minimum of realizable public morality whose maintenance is the just requirement of the citizenry."

[65] Cf. De Smedt, Oral *Relatio* on the *Textus Denuo Recognitus* [AS IV/6, 723]: "The common good, as everyone knows, is something relative: it is linked to the cultural evolution of peoples and has to be judged according to that development" (English translation in Harrison, RL&C, 89).

common good. In actuality, however, even when previous popes referred to the standard of the *common good*, what they apparently had in mind were measures necessary for the survival of society, that is, measures that would fall within the *basic component* of the common good.⁶⁶ Moreover, in explaining the reasons for the choice of the phrase *public order* over the *common good*, De Smedt emphasizes above all else the fact that the former term is one that is familiar to civil authorities.⁶⁷ Thus, the Wojtyła amendment remains important as a marker for the proper standard to guide civil authorities. However, when it comes to the Church's lived experience since the eighteenth or nineteenth centuries—specifically the question of allowable religious repression—the difference between the *common good* and the *public order* as guidelines often seems to be more theoretical than practical.⁶⁸

12.6. Contemporary Applications

A relevant contemporary application of these principles concerns not the repression of non-Catholic religious activity but the enactment of laws in accord with Catholic moral teaching. The *public order* standard has a very practical significance. If it were true that Vatican II had adopted the standard

---

⁶⁶ Guminski/Harrison, 58: Despite reference to the common good, the repression in question often qualified as necessary for society's survival; Guminski/Harrison, 220: Commentators and Church authorities, though referring to the common good, "nevertheless saw these restrictions . . . as protecting pretty much the same VSCs [valued social conditions] that come under the *extension* of the term 'public order' as this is explained in *DH*, #7.3." NB, the citations here to Guminski/Harrison are to positions taken by Harrison rather than Guminski. Valuet takes a similar position, noting that in Church enactments concerning religious repression, the types of harms specified in DH §7c often were presupposed (cf. LRTE, 519).

⁶⁷ "This basic component of the common good is referred to today in modern civil law and in many state Constitutions as the 'public order.' In order for our document to be readily intelligible in the modern world, it should use this technical term according to accepted modern usage. In what way would it serve our purpose to speak of the 'common good,' if that term is not used in this sense in modern civil law? A great deal of confusion would arise." De Smedt, Oral *Relatio* on the *Textus Denuo Recognitus* [AS IV/6, 722]; English translation in Harrison, RL&C, 90.

⁶⁸ Harrison notes that with the publication of the Catechism of the Catholic Church, the term *common good* has been revived as a standard for judging when restriction of religious activity is legitimate. Indeed, the Catechism uses both terms—the *just public order* and the *common good*—in discussing legitimate restriction of religious activity. Cf. Brian W. Harrison, "Roma Locuta Est—Causa Finita Est," citing CCC, §§1738, 2109, available from Roman Theological Forum, accessed Oct. 29, 2000, http://www.rtforum.org/lt/lt57.html. This circumstance bolsters his argument regarding the relatively small difference between the two terms.

12.6. Contemporary Applications

of public peace that Pius IX had rejected, then a possible implication might be that Vatican II had taken the position that the state may not enact laws in support of Catholic principles or Catholic morality. The reason is that the *public peace* standard endorses laws in aid of the Church only to avoid bloodshed or perhaps to protect property rights. However, the Council's definition of public order as encompassing the *objective moral order* and the basic component of the *common good* means that it is indeed legitimate for secular laws to follow the principles of Catholic morality. Thus, laws against divorce and abortion are just as consistent with *Dignitatis Humanae* as they are with *Quanta Cura*.[69]

Michael Davies, another leading traditionalist critic of the declaration, accepts that this is indeed the effect of the Wojtyła amendment, namely, that such laws informed by Catholic teaching are consistent with *Dignitatis Humanae*. Accordingly, Davies welcomes this amendment, but at the same time he asserts that the *practical* effect of the declaration as a whole is to render such laws less likely rather than more likely.[70] The reason that such laws have become less likely, Davies asserts, is because DH has abandoned the idea of the Catholic state. As a result, he finds the Wojtyła amendment to be "of no practical value."[71]

Davies's critique is significant for several reasons. His reference to the amendment as lacking *practical* value, taken together with his acknowledgement that—at least on the level of principle—the amendment legitimates laws against divorce, etcetera, suggests that he accepts the conclusion that there is no *doctrinal* dispute between the declaration and *Quanta Cura* on this question. By the same token, Davies acknowledges that the *just*

---

[69] Guminski argues that DH §7's reference to the *objective moral order* is limited to the *natural* moral order (cf. Guminski/Harrison, 132). However, the text contains no such limitation, and other esteemed commentators have the better of the argument in asserting that the objective moral order must include moral principles known from revelation. Cf. Valuet, LRTE, 506–8; Fernando Ocáriz, "Sulla libertà religiosa. Continuità del Vaticano II con il Magistero precedente," *Annales theologici* 3 (1989): 80–81; Davies, SVC&RL, 193: "It is evident that 'the objective moral order' referred to in Archbishop Wojtyła's amendment can only be the moral order taught by the Magisterium of the Catholic Church." For his part, Guminski's interlocutor, Harrison, forcefully disagrees with Guminski on this point as well (cf. Guminski/Harrison, 209).

[70] Cf. Davies, SVC&RL, 193–94.

[71] Davies, SVC&RL, 194. As to Davies's assertion that DH has abandoned the notion of the Catholic state, see chapter 4 above. That chapter argues that DH did not necessarily close the door on the Catholic state. At the same time, however, it acknowledges that the declaration did indeed effect a decisive shift of emphasis toward the prevalent regime in our own day, namely, constitutional democracy.

public order standard of DH is considerably broader than the *public peace* standard of *Quanta Cura*. At the same time, however, he argues that the Council's choice of terminology has caused significant confusion.[72] Thus, room remains for a robust traditionalist critique of the declaration, but the Davies critique gives several indications that it is on the level of prudence rather than doctrine.

---

[72] Cf. Davies, SVC&RL, 196–97. Like other commentators, Davies notes that the French Revolution's *Declaration of the Rights of Man and the Citizen* also refers to the *public order*. He recognizes that the term has a different meaning in the context of DH, but he nonetheless regrets its use there (cf. Davies, 196).

CHAPTER 13

Public Law and Policy

[P]rinciples ... remain fixed. However, becoming incarnated in facts, they are clothed with a contingent character, determined by the center in which their application is produced.

— POPE LEO XIII[1]

And indeed, we do find some statements whose "form" makes them appear like exercises of the teaching office, but whose "matter" sounds more like something pertaining to the governing office.

— BRIAN HARRISON[2]

The previous chapter discussed the standard for permissible governmental restriction of religious activity, and it noted a commonality between *Dignitatis Humanae* and previous teaching and practice. That is, past repression of non-Catholic religious practice took place not (or not primarily) on the basis of the falsity of the religion in question but rather on the basis of actual or perceived social harm caused by that religious activity. (See section 12.4 above and chapter 15 below.) By the same token, the declaration affirms the necessity of governmental intervention against abusive religious practices, but the predicate for such an intervention is not the *falsity* of the religious expression but rather its causing of a breach of the *just public order*.

---

[1] Pope Leo XIII, Apostolic Letter *Au Milieu des Sollicitudes* (Feb. 16, 1892), §15 [ASS 24 (1891–1892): 523].

[2] Brian W. Harrison, *Religious Liberty and Contraception: Did Vatican II Open the Way for a New Sexual Ethic?* (Melbourne: John XXIII Fellowship Co-op., Ltd., 1988), 26.

However, the shift from a context favoring repression to one favoring freedom remains a dramatic one. How then is one to understand such a transition? Brian Harrison considers this shift in light of previous papal statements urging repression of non-Catholic religious worship or expression.[3]

13.1. Teaching and Policy

Harrison makes an important observation about categorizing the content of those statements. He argues that not every assertion is to be taken as Church *teaching*. The reason is that some of the matters that the popes address pertain to administration or *policy*. This is the case even though these statements sometimes read as if they were doctrinal. "And indeed, we do find some statements whose 'form' makes them appear like exercises of the teaching office, but whose 'matter' sounds more like something pertaining to the governing office."[4] This distinction is crucial because it is only Church teachings and not the administrative and prudential decisions of individual popes that enjoy protection from error. This is a specific application of the familiar distinction between doctrine and discipline.[5]

---

[3] For John T. Noonan, the question of previous pronouncements urging repression is the primary difficulty that *Dignitatis Humanae* leaves unresolved. John T. Noonan Jr., "Development in Moral Doctrine," *Theological Studies* 54, no. 4 (1993): 677; John T. Noonan Jr., *The Lustre of Our Country: The American Experience of Religious Freedom* (Berkeley: University of California Press, 1998), 351–52.

[4] Harrison, RL&C, 26.

[5] However, some theologians argue that disciplinary decisions partake of "a negative and indirect, rather than a positive and direct infallibility." That is, they contend that the Church cannot adopt a discipline that is contrary to natural or divine law. *The Catholic Encyclopedia* (New York: Encyclopedia Press, 1913), s.v. "Discipline, Ecclesiastical." See also *The New Catholic Encyclopedia* (New York: McGraw-Hill Book Co., 1967), s.v. "Discipline, Ecclesiastical" (similar). Harrison, too, entertains this idea. In particular, he considers whether disciplinary infallibility (also called practical infallibility) might be relevant to the Church's concordat practice, given that these agreements frequently provided for the prohibition of public non-Catholic worship in Catholic countries. His position is not completely clear. On the one hand, he does not believe that such a long-standing policy could be violative of the natural law. Cf. Brian W. Harrison, "The Center is Holding," review of *The Second Vatican Council and Religious Liberty*, by Michael Davies, *Living Tradition* 44 (1993), available from Roman Theological Forum, accessed Oct. 29, 2000, http://www.rtforum.org/lt/lt9.html. On the other hand, though, he seems finally (in his most recent work on the subject) to conclude that concordats are not a proper subject of disciplinary infallibility because they are by their nature particular to certain countries rather than universal. In addition, he says, the usual examples cited in support of disciplinary infallibility are not from this realm but rather nearly always concern the liturgy and the sacraments. Cf. Arnold T. Guminski and Brian W. Harrison, *Religious Freedom: Did Vatican II Contradict*

13.1. Teaching and Policy

One example of such a statement appears in an encyclical that figures into the wider discussion of religious liberty, namely, *Libertas* (1888) by Pope Leo XIII:

> Men have a right freely and prudently to propagate throughout the State what things so-ever are true and honorable, so that as many as possible may possess them; but lying opinions, than which no mental plague is greater, and vices which corrupt the heart and moral life should be diligently repressed by public authority, lest they insidiously work the ruin of the State. (LP, §23)

This particular passage does not refer to non-Catholic religious worship specifically, but it encompasses the propagation of any ideas whatsoever that vary from Catholic teaching.

Harrison argues that such statements urging repression are a matter not of doctrine but of *public ecclesiastical law*.[6] They do not necessarily pertain to doctrine because they concern, rather, the *means* for implementing Church teaching. They pertain to the Church's *public law*, which traditionally has been understood as the body of law that concerns the Church's external relationships, such as its relationship to the state and its relationship to other

---

Traditional Catholic Doctrine? A Debate (South Bend, IN: St. Augustine Press, 2013), 85–86. Harrison appears to resolve the larger question—not with reference to practical infallibility but rather with reference to the flexibility of the norm established by DH §7. That is, Harrison interprets DH §7 as not necessarily repudiating the previous concordat practice. Harrison believes that in overwhelmingly Catholic countries, during times when the government took a paternalistic approach to the citizens (who usually were poorly educated), a prohibition on public non-Catholic worship could have been consistent with the Vatican II understanding of *public order* (cf. Guminski/Harrison, 85–86, 222). On the question of formulating judgments about the justice of past instances of religious restriction, see section 13.2 below.

In addition, on the question of concordat practice, an observation by Valuet also is relevant, namely, that such documents do not always represent the actual preferred position of the Holy See but sometimes signify only a situation or circumstance that it is willing to tolerate. Cf. Basile Valuet, *Le droit à la liberté religieuse dans la Tradition de l'Eglise. Un cas de développement doctrinal homogène par le magistère authentique*, 2nd rev. ed. (Barroux: Éditions Sainte-Madeleine, 2011), 343.

On the general question of disciplinary (or practical) infallibility, Dulles finds this notion difficult to square with the teachings on infallibility found in both Vatican Councils. Cf. Avery Dulles, *Magisterium: Teacher and Guardian of the Faith* (Naples, FL: Sapientia Press, 2007), 78.

[6] On Harrison's choice to frame the issue in terms of public ecclesiastical law, see subsection 13.3.2 below.

religious bodies. The Church's public law, in itself—Harrison says—is not divine law and, as a result, is mutable.[7] (See subsection 13.3.2 below on the place of public ecclesiastical law in the life of the Church in the nineteenth century and the first half of the twentieth century.)

This is not to say that such pronouncements contain no doctrinal content. In a broad sense, all such statements pertain to the Catholic teaching that there is a social duty to Christ.[8] More specifically, however, Harrison attempts to set forth a principle that unifies the nineteenth-century teaching and Vatican II. He notes that the Church never has taught that non-Catholic religious teaching and worship could be repressed simply because it was non-Catholic. Rather, the justification for such repression was to protect the Catholic populace from the danger posed, or from the danger that authorities believed was posed, by public non-Catholic worship or expression.[9] The presumptive policy of previous popes was that non-Catholic worship generally constituted a danger to the Catholic populace and, therefore, generally should be repressed. (In his more recent writings, Harrison identifies specific circumstances that he believes rendered this policy suitable in previous contexts, including the low level of education among the populace, and the government's paternalistic attitude toward the citizens.[10])

13.2. The Vatican II Change in Policy or Public Law

However, this policy or this point of public ecclesiastical law changed with Vatican II. The presumptive position now is that non-Catholic worship usually does not constitute a danger to Catholics and, therefore, usually should not be repressed. "[T]he freedom of man is to be respected as far as possible and is not to be curtailed except when and insofar as necessary" (DH, §7c). By imposing the standard of public order on religious worship,

---

[7] Cf. Harrison, RL&C, 57–58, citing F. M. Cappello, *Summa iuris publici ecclesiastici*, 4th ed. (Rome: Pontifical Gregorian University Press, 1936), 334–40, 369–70. For additional passages in which Harrison advances this argument on the basis of public law, see RL&C, 57–60, 141–43; "Pius IX, Vatican II and Religious Liberty," available from Roman Theological Forum, accessed Oct. 29, 2000, http://www.rtforum.org/lt/lt9.html; "Review of SVC&RL"; "Towards Clarifying the Religious Liberty Quandary," *New Oxford Review* (November 1999): 11–12.

[8] Cf. Harrison, RL&C, 57. On the duty of the civic community to Christ, see generally Pope Pius XI, Encyclical *Quas Primas* (Dec. 11, 1925).

[9] Cf. Harrison, "Review of SVC&RL."

[10] Cf. Guminski/Harrison, 84. The following section addresses the evaluation of historical instances of religious restriction or repression.

however, Vatican II agrees with the previous pronouncements that *some* religious activity may be repressed. The question of how much repression is appropriate, Harrison says, is one of policy or public ecclesiastical law.

In his first writings in this area, Harrison attempted to craft a single formulation to reconcile the situations before and after Vatican II: non-Catholic worship should be repressed as far as the *common good* requires it. This formulation pertained to both periods, but it was sufficiently flexible to encompass both the nineteenth-century presumption of repression and the Vatican II presumption of freedom. However, this formulation was based on a position that Harrison held at the time, namely, that DH preserved the recourse to the *common good* contained in the pronouncements of Leo XIII and other popes.[11] As discussed in the previous chapter, however, the declaration's standard of the *just public order* is not in fact coextensive with the *common good*, but rather it refers to the *basic component* of the common good. That is, it refers to those conditions that are essential to society's *survival* rather than to the entire range of conditions that may lead to societal *flourishing*. Harrison acknowledges this in his most recent writings.[12]

As discussed in the previous chapter, however, the practical difference between the standards of the *common good* and the *public order* may be modest. As a result, it still may be possible to craft a single formulation to apply to the periods both before and after Vatican II.[13] However, although convenient, such a formulation is not strictly necessary. The reason is that the contours of Harrison's public ecclesiastical law argument already have explained the Vatican II shift. That is, he has described the narrowing of the circumstances in which non-Catholic religious expression may be repressed. A necessary adjustment to Harrison's original framework is to specify that the shift in *public ecclesiastical law* occurs not (as he originally had proposed) entirely within the realm of the *common good as a whole* but rather in a refinement from the broad range of justifications coextensive with the common good in its fullness (the Leo XIII position) to a narrower range of

---

[11] Cf. Harrison, RL&C, 94–95, 141.
[12] Cf. Guminski/Harrison, 57.
[13] The Catechism of the Catholic Church arguably offers such a formulation in asserting that "[t]he 'due limits' which are inherent in it [the right to religious liberty] must be determined for each social situation by political prudence, according to the requirements of the common good, and ratified by the civil authority in accordance with 'legal principles which are in conformity with the objective moral order.'" CCC, §2109, citing Second Vatican Council, Declaration on Religious Liberty *Dignitatis Humanae* (December 7, 1965), §7c.

acceptable justifications belonging to the *core content* of the common good (my term), that is, the just public order (the position of DH §7).

To return to Harrison's observation at the end of the previous section (that previous papal policy restricting public non-Catholic worship may have satisfied the standard of DH §7), my own sense is that the declaration primarily is forward-looking. However, I agree with Harrison that it provides resources for analyzing past practices as well (though DH itself is quite reticent about making such judgments). In the Catholic context, the key question for determining whether a particular restriction on religious activity was just *in an objective sense* is whether that activity posed (or reasonably was believed to pose) a danger to the just public order (that is, a threat to the rights of others, the public peace, or public morality). The difficulty, however, is that the public order standard becomes known only with Vatican II. As a result, it does not seem fair to judge civil authorities in previous times by a standard that had not yet been articulated and pronounced. (This is especially the case because the Church's recognition of religious liberty as a natural right also comes only with Vatican II, or perhaps slightly earlier in *Pacem in Terris*.) Thus, in times when the applicable standard was the common good, one might judge a civil authority's culpability (or lack of it) by applying that standard. That is, the question would be whether the particular restriction was justified by a danger to the common good. As discussed above in section 12.5, although these are different standards, there may be little difference between their application in actual practice.[14]

---

[14] What if a past act of repression were to satisfy the *common good* standard but to fall short of the more exacting Vatican II standard of the *just public order*? In that case, it would seem that the civil authority's action would be blameless. To hold otherwise would be to charge authorities with anticipating future revisions to policy or public law. However, could one say that while the authority was *subjectively* blameless, his action nevertheless was *objectively* unjust? Such a possibility has a certain appeal, but it is not without its own difficulty. The appeal of such a judgment is that it recognizes both the concrete circumstances of the civil authority and also the reality that it is a natural right that is at stake. The difficulty is that it still seems to involve the retroactive application of a revision in policy or public law. Resolution of this question is beyond the scope of this work, but chapter 16 might shed some light on it. That chapter concludes this study by considering the factors that delayed the Church's recognition of a natural right to religious liberty. As Valuet notes, one of the key developments that made this recognition possible is the widespread acceptance of the principle of *reciprocity*. Cf. Basile Valuet, *La liberté religieuse et la tradition catholique. Un cas de développement doctrinal homogène dans le magistère authentique*, 3rd rev. ed. (Barroux: Éditions Sainte-Madeleine, 2011), vol. IA, 273–74 [= LRTE, 183]; see also LRTC, 341–42, a short passage on reciprocity not contained in LRTE. One consideration in judging past repressive measures of civil authorities might be whether, in a given time,

For times before either standard was in effect, the appropriate question in connection with the authority's culpability would seem to be whether the measure was reasonable. This would mean inquiring whether the restriction on religious activity was proportionate to the danger posed (or reasonably believed to be posed).

Although public law or policy is the focus of this part of the analysis, one should not confuse this argument with that of Thomas Pink. Harrison recognizes the Council's teaching that religious liberty is a natural right. In this particular matter, he is discussing a teaching that *Quanta Cura* and *Dignitatis Humanae* have in common, namely, that the restriction of *some* non-Catholic religious activity is legitimate. (This framing is closer to the *Quanta Cura* formulation. *Dignitatis Humanae* frames the matter in terms of civil authorities generally, but if one considers the Catholic context in particular, the statement accurately reflects DH as well.[15]) The only point that belongs to policy or public law is the judgment on *how much* religious activity to restrict. By contrast, Pink considers the recognition of the *right itself* to be a matter of mere policy. That is, while Harrison makes an important policy argument, he also recognizes the doctrinal content of DH. Pink, however, apparently sees the entirety of DH's distinctive content as pertaining to policy rather than doctrine. (See generally section 11.3 above.)

13.3. Analysis of Harrison's Public Law Argument

13.3.1. The Rationale for Repression

It now remains to analyze Harrison's *public ecclesiastical law* argument. At the outset, it is clear that Harrison is on firm ground in his claim that the Church urged repression of religious worship in the past, not merely because such worship was non-Catholic but rather because the Church authorities

---

enough of the necessary developments were in place to render the particular repressive measure unnecessary or unreasonable.

[15] The declaration itself, of course, considers other contexts too. That is, although the focus here is on restriction of non-Catholic worship in a Catholic state, or a state where Catholicism receives special civil recognition, DH speaks about such recognition *generally* (cf. DH, §6c). That is, it encompasses contexts in which another religion is established or receives civil recognition. This work, however, focuses largely on the Catholic context because it is the scenario that gives rise to most of the doctrinal controversy.

believed that such worship posed a danger to Catholics.[16] This is discussed in the previous chapter and also in chapter 15.[17]

The same principle can be gleaned in the historical policies of some of the popes and the Christian monarchs. For example, although the Jews have suffered much persecution at the hands of Christians, it also is the case that many popes granted protection to the Jews. Pope Gregory I was the first to do so in 598, and a number of his successors followed this policy.[18] Notably, his namesake, Gregory X, issued a decree in 1272 granting general protection to the Jews and forbidding Christians to disturb their festivals. An example that confirms Harrison's assertion more directly is that of Pope Clement VI. Clement issued a number of papal bulls in 1348 and 1349 for the protection of the Jews, including penalizing with excommunication anyone who blamed the Jews for the Black Death.[19] However, he permitted the persecution of Muslims. There may have been theological reasons for this difference in treatment,[20] but Clement certainly was motivated as well by the practical consideration that the Muslims, unlike the Jews, possessed formidable military power and therefore posed a physical threat to Christians.[21] As discussed in the previous chapter, the policy that Charlemagne followed was roughly similar to that attributed by Harrison to the popes generally. That is, Charlemagne allowed most of the barbarians to continue to practice

---

[16] "[E]ven in the days of the most severe repression of heretics, the principal reason given by theologians for punitive action (which of course may not always have been the uppermost motive in the minds of the secular authorities who inflicted it) was that heretics endangered the eternal life of their Catholic neighbours" (Harrison, RL&C, 93). The Lutheran historian Roland Bainton makes a similar point when he says, "Neither Catholic nor Protestant ever persecuted mere error but only obstinate error. Both persecuted heresy as heresy, and both believed that heresy, if unchecked, would disintegrate society." Roland H. Bainton, *The Travail of Religious Liberty: Nine Biographical Sketches* (Philadelphia: Westminster Press, 1951), 17.

[17] One also can find support for this point in St. Thomas's writings. Thomas taught that it sometimes was proper to make war against non-Christians, but that such measures are undertaken not to compel the unbelievers to believe but rather "to prevent them from hindering the faith of Christ." St. Thomas Aquinas, *Summa Theologica*, Christian Classics ed. (Benziger Brothers, 1947), II-II, q. 10, a. 8.

[18] Cf. Diana Wood, "Infidels and Jews: Clement VI's Attitude to Persecution and Toleration," in *Persecution and Toleration*, ed. W. J. Sheils (Oxford: Basil Blackwell, 1984), 119–23.

[19] Warren H. Carroll, *A History of Christendom*, vol. 3, *The Glory of Christendom* (Front Royal, Va.: Christendom College Press, 1993), 392–93; cf. Wood, "Persecution and Toleration," 120.

[20] Cf. Valuet, LRTE, 153: Jewish rites were tolerated generally because they prefigured the truth of the faith and bore testimony to the Christian faith.

[21] Cf. Wood, "Persecution and Toleration," 124.

their pagan rites, but he actively persecuted those tribes whose religious practices posed a danger to the Church and the civil order. (See section 12.1 above. In addition, on the social harm caused, or believed to be caused, by non-Catholic public worship, see chapter 15 below.)

13.3.2. A Note on Harrison's Recourse to Public Ecclesiastical Law

The statements by the popes themselves urging repression, Harrison says, were matters of policy or public ecclesiastical law rather than Catholic doctrine. This choice to focus on public ecclesiastical law is unusual, perhaps even anachronistic. The reason is that although public ecclesiastical law was a prominent part of the study of canon law in the nineteenth century and into the twentieth century, it now has lost its former prominence. It no longer is a standard subject in the canon law curriculum, and the most recent textbooks on the subject date from around the time of World War II. The focus of public ecclesiastical law was the relationship between Church and state and the relationship between the Church and other religious communities. Its hallmark was the concept of the Church as a perfect society (*societas perfectas*), on a par with the state. In this sense, it had something of an apologetic purpose. That is, the nineteenth century was marked by encroachments on the Church's rights (especially in Europe), and a notable characteristic of public ecclesiastical law was to react with a reassertion of the Church's prerogatives.[22]

The subject matter of public ecclesiastical law remains relevant, and it continues to be studied today in canonical programs. However, the subject itself usually is described as *Church-state relations* or *the relations between the Church and civil society*. It no longer is understood to have an apologetic purpose, and the concern of the previous subject to compare the Church to the state has diminished or disappeared.

Thus, Harrison's appeal to public ecclesiastical law may seem dated or anachronistic. However, it does not hinder his argument. *First*, Harrison is not a canonist, and, as a result, it seems clear that his focus is on the subject matter—especially Church-state relations—rather than the distinct role that this field of study played in Church life in the nineteenth century and early twentieth century. *Second*, the point of his argument is clear, namely, that there is a distinction between doctrine and discipline, or between the Church's teaching office (*munus docendi*) and her governing office (*munus regendi*). That is, although others might have framed the discussion in

---

[22] See generally José Tomás Martín de Agar, "Derecho y relaciones iglesia—sociedad civil," *Ius Ecclesiae* 32, no. 1 (2020): 17–19, 65.

terms of policy or administrative decisions, Harrison's reference to public law similarly leaves no doubt that he is referring to exercises of the governing office rather than the teaching office. *Third*, the debate over religious liberty provides a specific reason for referring to public law. The reason is that Marcel Lefebvre, in rejecting the declaration, charged that it amounts to a repudiation of both Church doctrine and public ecclesiastical law. (See subsection 13.3.3 below.)

Thus, it remains to evaluate Harrison's public law argument. His argument can be divided into two parts: (1) his assertion that the papal statements urging repression belong to the field of public ecclesiastical law, and (2) his assertion that public ecclesiastical law is mutable. I will begin with the latter point.

13.3.3. The Mutability of Public Ecclesiastical Law

With regard to the second part of Harrison's argument, there is some disagreement as to whether the Church's public law is mutable. Archbishop Lefebvre's reason for opposing *Dignitatis Humanae* was his belief that it contradicted the Church's immutable public law. "[H]er public law is as unchangeable as her faith, because it is founded on it."[23] Indeed, there is some basis for this argument because the Church's public law, like its canon law, contains *elements* of immutable natural and divine law. In fact, this is truer of public law than of canon law generally. The reason is that public law is largely concerned with the Church's constitution, which is predominantly a matter of divine positive law (cf. Matt 16:18, 28:19; John 20:21–23). That is, the founding of the Church by Jesus Christ and the commission to teach all nations belong both to the Church's doctrine and to its public law. By the same token, Harrison states that the duty of the civic community to Christ is a matter not only of public law but also of doctrine and of divine law.

However, Harrison is correct that not all points of the Church's public law coincide with unchangeable divine law.[24] A canonical example illustrates this distinction. With regard to marriage, the right of persons to marry (can. 1058) belongs to *natural law*; the absolute indissolubility of consummated Christian marriage (can. 1141) belongs to *divine positive law* (Mark 10:9, 11–12; Luke 16:18; cf. Matt 5:31, 19:9); but the requirement that Catholics marry according to canonical form (can. 1108, §1) is a matter

---

[23] Marcel Lefebvre, Letter to Cardinal Seper (Feb. 26, 1978), in Michael Davies, *Apologia Pro Marcel Lefebvre*, vol. 2, *1977–1979* (Dickinson, TX: Angelus Press, 1983), 127.

[24] Cf. Ludovicus Bender, *Ius Publicum Ecclesiasticum* (Paulus Brand, 1948), 17.

only of *discipline*.[25] In a similar way, the Church's public law incorporates both mutable and immutable elements. Among the mutable elements are the various concordats and other international agreements between the Holy See and various states.[26] These agreements are influenced by the concrete circumstances present in the world and, as a result, are subject to change. Thus, although the Church historically preferred to receive special recognition from the state, it sometimes has been willing to solemnize concordats that accorded it a position of mere civil equality with other religious bodies or, in at least one instance, a position of legal inferiority.[27] The example of concordat practice and the analogy of canon law demonstrates the mutability of public ecclesiastical law, at least in some of its elements. However, it is now necessary to inquire whether papal statements urging religious repression belong to public law and, if so, whether they belong to that part of public law that is mutable.

Harrison's argument is based on F. M. Capello's 1936 treatise on public law.[28] Harrison contrasts Capello's passages on the duty of the civic community to Christ with his passages on toleration. In describing the state's social duty to Christ, Capello cites Scripture, the writings of the church fathers, the popes, and the councils. As a result, Harrison argues, the social duty of the community to Christ is a matter of immutable divine law. However, Capello's treatment of toleration is different. He treats it as an application of the foregoing principles (the social duty to Christ), and in supporting it, Capello cites not the councils or Scripture but only the writings of other authors. As a result, Harrison argues, the Church's previous posture on the extent of toleration and liberty of worship was a matter of public ecclesiastical law but not of unchanging divine law or Church doctrine.[29] Harrison

---

[25] The point of discipline contained in canon 1108, §1, was established by the Council of Trent to address the problem of secret marriages.

[26] Cf. Bender, *Ius Publicum Ecclesiasticum*, 18.

[27] Cf. William Nessel, *First Amendment Freedoms, Papal Pronouncements and Concordat Practice: A Comparative Study in American Law and Public Ecclesiastical Law* (Washington, DC: Catholic University of America Press, 1961), 207–8. The example of the Church accepting an inferior position in law was its concordat with Rumania in 1929. Nessel argues that it was remarkable that the Holy See would use the solemn instrument of a concordat to accept an inferior position in law. However, the Rumanian constitution recognized the Orthodox Church officially, and a concordat between the Holy See and Rumania was necessary to mitigate the effects of a constitutional provision that would have prohibited contact between the local Catholic Church and Rome.

[28] Cf. F. M. Cappello, *Summa iuris publici ecclesiastici*, 4th ed. (Rome: Pontifical Gregorian University Press, 1936).

[29] Cf. Harrison, RL&C, 57–58, citing Cappello, *Summa iuris*, 334–40, 369–70.

appears to be on solid ground in making this assertion. A later text on public ecclesiastical law by Emmanuel González Ruiz follows the same paradigm. That is, it too cites authoritative magisterial documents on some points but not on the parameters of toleration.[30] More importantly, however, this text contains an appendix listing those elements of public ecclesiastical law that are rooted in Catholic dogma, but this particular listing does not include directives regarding toleration and repression.[31] Thus, the González Ruiz text, too, indicates that toleration and repression belong to public ecclesiastical law but not to that portion that is immutable.

13.4. Papal Administrative Practice

As a result, the principles of public ecclesiastical law seem to provide some support for Harrison's position. At the same time, however, one would do well to seek additional support. The reason is that this public law argument is based largely on implication. It attributes significance to the types of sources cited and not cited rather than relying on direct statements by the author. However, papal statements lend additional support to the Harrison interpretation. At bottom, Harrison's argument is that papal encouragement for religious repression was not an *invocation* of divine law but merely an *application* of divine law (the duty of the community to Christ) to specific circumstances. That is, these statements represented judgments as to the *means* by which a community might fulfill its social duty to God.[32] Leo XIII himself, in his encyclical on the political situation in France, states that when broad theological principles are applied to facts, the resulting judgment is not absolute:

> In descending from the domain of abstractions to that of facts, we must beware of denying the principles just established: they remain fixed. However, becoming incarnated in facts, they are clothed with a contingent character, determined by the center in which their application is produced.[33]

Joseph Cardinal Ratzinger, as prefect of the Congregation for the Doctrine of the Faith, also acknowledged that some aspects of the nineteenth-century

---

[30] Cf. Emmanuel González Ruiz, *Lectiones iuris publici ecclesiastici* (Malacae: Seminarium Conciliare Malacitanum, 1947), 116–17.
[31] Cf. González Ruiz, *Lectiones*, 243–44.
[32] Cf. Harrison, RL&C, 54.
[33] Leo XIII, *Au Milieu des Sollicitudes*, §15 [ASS 24 (1891–1892): 523].

papal teaching on religious liberty are "contingent" and therefore may require "rectification" in certain details.[34] Similarly, one can find in Leo's works a distinction between papal teaching and papal administrative policy. Thus, he commands Catholics to "stand by the judgment" of his teaching on modern liberties (ID, §42), but, with regard to matters of policy, he employs the language of exhortation rather than command, urging that "the faithful *should follow* the practical political wisdom of the ecclesiastical authority."[35]

Most importantly, however, no magisterial document appears to contradict Harrison on this point. Harrison asserts that Catholic doctrine never went so far as to require repression of non-Catholic religious activity that posed no danger to the Church, the civil order, or the faith of Catholics.[36] Harrison is indeed correct. His argument on public law is that pronouncements along these lines may have the "form" of doctrinal statements, but they actually have the "matter" of administrative decisions or points of public law. His argument on public law lends some support to this theory, and Leo's treatment of these issues bolsters this argument.

In addition, however, it is important to note that even the papal pronouncements that urged repression most vigorously did so not simply to oppose non-Catholic religion in itself but rather to address other perceived dangers. Thus, Leo urged repression of "lying opinions . . . lest they insidiously work the ruin of the State" (LP, §23). Similarly, Pius IX stated that offenders against the Catholic religion should be punished to prevent the spread of other harmful opinions and to preserve justice in civil society (QC, §§3–4).

---

[34] In a press conference on the occasion of the publication of the Instruction on the Ecclesial Vocation of the Theologian, *Donum veritatis*, Cardinal Ratzinger said, "It states—perhaps for the first time with such clarity—that there are magisterial decisions which cannot and are not intended to be the last word on the matter as such, but are a substantial anchorage in the problem and are first and foremost an expression of pastoral prudence, a sort of provisional disposition. Their core remains valid, but the individual details influenced by the circumstances at the time may need further rectification. In this regard one can refer to the statements of the Popes during the last century on religious freedom." "Cardinal Ratzinger Speaks to the Press on New Instruction: Theology is not Private Idea of Theologian," *L'Osservatore Romano* (July 2, 1990), weekly English ed., 5.

[35] Leo XIII, *Sapientiae Christianae*, §37 (emphasis added) [ASS 22 (1889–1890): 400].

[36] Cf. Harrison, "Review of SVC&RL," available from Roman Theological Forum, accessed Oct. 29, 2000, http://www.rtforum.org/lt/lt44.html. See also Harrison, RL&C, 141–42; Valuet, LRTE, 179: "La doctrine catholique n'exigeait pas de *l'État comme tel* de poursuivre l'erreur en tant que telle."

13.5. Doctrine and Policy

Harrison acknowledges that the Vatican II formulation is new. The content of this new development is that all persons have a natural right to immunity in the private and public exercise of their religion provided that there is no harm to the just public order. Michael Davies sees in this a corruption of doctrine. Before Vatican II, a Catholic state could *permit* non-Catholic worship only for some good reason; after Vatican II, the state can *repress* non-Catholic worship only for some good reason.[37] However, Harrison argues that there is in fact no contradiction because the prerogative of the civil authority to repress *some* religious activity remains a constant, while the question of *how much* to repress is a matter of prudential judgement rather than doctrine. Moreover, the common good itself, as De Smedt made clear, is relative to time and circumstance, and accordingly, although the shift from a presumption of repression to a presumption of freedom is indeed a change, it is one that takes place not in the field of doctrine but in the realm of mutable policy or public law.[38]

Harrison's public law argument correctly concludes that no doctrinal contradiction exists between Vatican II and previous teaching. Vatican II effected a decided shift of emphasis, but this was simply a new *policy* application of a constant *doctrinal* principle.[39] The change in the Church's public law created no doctrinal crisis.

> Thus, the old and the new teachings on "tolerance" and "rights," though heading, so to speak, in different directions (one towards less liberty in society, the other towards more), do not collide head-on: like two well-driven vehicles approaching each other on the highway, they skim safely past one another.[40]

---

[37] Michael Davies, *The Second Vatican Council and Religious Liberty* (Long Prairie, MN: Neumann Press, 1992), 225.

[38] Cf. Émile De Smedt, Oral *Relatio* on the *Textus Denuo Recognitus* (Nov. 19, 1965) [AS IV/6, 723]: "[T]he norm for the care of religion is the common good. The common good, as everyone knows, is something relative: it is linked to the cultural evolution of peoples and has to be judged according to that development" (English translation in Harrison, RL&C, 89).

[39] The constant doctrinal principle is that restriction of some non-Catholic religious activity is legitimate. The Council's recognition of religious liberty as a natural right is a different matter. It is a development of doctrine but a noncontradictory one.

[40] Harrison, RL&C, 118.

CHAPTER 14

The Burning of Heretics

Yes, theology, like philosophy and jurisprudence, has great niceties of distinction, because, evidently, in questions of doctrine, as in questions of law, nice distinctions must be drawn, to avoid dangerous misapprehensions.

— FÉLIX DUPANLOUP[1]

The previous chapter discussed papal statements urging religious repression and argued that such pronouncements often fall within the realm of policy or public law rather than doctrine. The reason is that while the civil authority's general duty and right to restrict some religious expression is a matter of doctrine, the concrete judgment as to how much to repress in a given situation is largely a question of prudence. The authority must act according to the objective moral order, and it must recognize the religious liberty of all, unless the exercise of that right violates public order. Within these parameters, the civil authority may decide whether to restrict religious expression. Indeed, it even may allow some abuses to go unpunished if their correction would cause greater harm.

That being said, one particular papal statement on the specific question of religious repression deserves its own separate treatment. The reason is that its text and context indicate that the statement is more a matter of doctrine than mere discipline. In addition, it is a document of particular historical significance. Indeed, it may be the earliest papal pronouncement concerning the civil authority's repression of non-Catholic religious activity.[2]

---

[1] Félix Dupanloup, *Remarks on the Encyclical of the 8th of December 1864*, trans. W. J. M. Hutchinson (London: George Cheek, 1865), 21.
[2] Cf. Brian W. Harrison, *Religious Liberty and Contraception: Did Vatican II Open the Way*

It is the famous sixteenth-century papal bull directed at the positions of Martin Luther.

14.1. Leo X's Bull against Luther

In 1520 Pope Leo X issued the bull *Exsurge Domine* condemning forty-one of Luther's positions, including, "That heretics be burned is against the will of the Spirit."[3] However, Leo makes clear that although some of Luther's positions may be heretical, others are condemned for less serious reasons, such as that they are "offensive to pious ears or seductive of simple minds."[4]

> No one of sound mind is ignorant of how destructive, pernicious, scandalous, and seductive to pious and simple minds these various errors are, how opposed they are to all charity and reverence for the holy Roman Church who is the mother of all the faithful and teacher of the faith; how destructive they are of the vigor of ecclesiastical discipline, namely obedience.[5]

Leo requires the faithful to reject all forty-one positions, but he does not specify which ones are heretical and which ones are rejected for lesser reasons, such as their propensity to mislead the faithful. Stated differently, he does not specify whether his rejection of the proposition on the burning of heretics—or any of the rejected propositions—is a matter of doctrine or simply a matter of discipline or prudence. As a result, Leo's rejection of this particular proposition is troubling for a modern reader, but the bull does not establish this particular proposition of Luther's as heretical or as contrary to defined Catholic dogma.[6]

Brian Harrison draws a useful distinction between what the Pope himself may have believed personally and what he actually proposed as Catholic doctrine. Thus, Leo X likely was firm in the conviction that the burning of heretics was legitimate, but his bull *Exsurge Domine* does not establish this conviction as a point of Catholic doctrine. Harrison provides a reason that Luther's thesis concerning the burning of heretics might have been

---

for a New Sexual Ethic? (Melbourne: John XXIII Fellowship Co-op., Ltd., 1988), 32.

[3] Pope Leo X, Bull *Exsurge Domine* (June 15, 1520) [Latin original in *CIC Fontes* 1, 129–34]; English translation available at EWTN, https://www.ewtn.com/catholicism/library/condemning-the-errors-of-luther-8927.

[4] Leo X, *Exsurge Domine*.

[5] Leo X, *Exsurge Domine*.

[6] Cf. Harrison, RL&C, 32.

considered a dangerous position, even if it was not contrary to Catholic doctrine. That is, because the populace in the sixteenth century was accustomed to the practice of burning heretics, Harrison suggests, promotion of Luther's thesis might have been taken to imply that heresy was not a serious matter.[7] Valuet suggests another possible reason for Leo deeming this proposition dangerous or offensive to the faithful, namely, because there was a current of thought at the time urging total non-resistance to the Turks, even in the face of invasion.[8]

The strictly juridical portion of the bull contains the following declaration:

> [B]y the authority of almighty God, the blessed Apostles Peter and Paul, and our own authority, we condemn, reprobate, and reject completely each of these theses or errors as either heretical, scandalous, false, offensive to pious ears or seductive of simple minds, and against Catholic truth.

One must read this sentence carefully. In the first part of it, Leo declares that each of the rejected propositions, including the one on burning heretics, is "*either* heretical, scandalous, . . . *or* seductive of simple minds." From this use of the disjunctive, it is clear that Leo avoids categorizing any specific proposition as definitely heretical. Rather, the terms that Leo uses in the first part of this sentence are technical terms known as *theological censures*, and he lists them in descending order of seriousness.[9] Thus, the import of

---

[7] Harrison, RL&C, 32.

[8] Cf. Basile Valuet, *La liberté religieuse et la tradition catholique. Un cas de développement doctrinal homogène dans le magistère authentique*, 3rd rev. ed. (Barroux: Éditions Sainte-Madeleine, 2011), vol. IA, 246–47, quoting Pierre-Marie-Henri Dubarle, "Faut-il brûler les hérétiques?" *La Vie intellectuelle* (Jan. 1952): 5–34, at 12; Basile Valuet, *Le droit à la liberté religieuse dans la Tradition de l'Eglise. Un cas de développement doctrinal homogène par le magistère authentique*, 2nd rev. ed. (Barroux: Éditions Sainte-Madeleine, 2011), 166 (same). Valuet also emphasizes that the bull is not necessarily vindicating the coercive power of the Church but rather that of the secular power to employ coercion when heretics threaten the tranquility of society (LRTC, vol. IA, 246 [= LRTE, 166]). Vermeersch reads the bull as meaning simply that in certain circumstances, it is legitimate to execute heretics. Cf. A. Vermeersch, *Tolerance*, trans. W. Humphrey Page (New York: Benziger Brothers, 1912), 178n1.

[9] Cf. *The Catholic Encyclopedia* (New York: Encyclopedia Press, 1913), s.v. "Censures, Theological"; John A. Hardon, *Modern Catholic Dictionary* (Garden City, NY: Doubleday, 1966), s.v. "Theological Censures." One of the most comprehensive lists of theological censures is found in the following document: Pope Clement XI, Dogmatic Constitution *Unigenitus* (Sept. 8, 1713), listing errors of Paschasius Quesnel.

the first part of this sentence is that although all forty-one of Luther's propositions pose some danger (or posed some danger in the sixteenth century), no particular proposition is identified as heretical. (The context suggests that at least *some* of the errors do indeed amount to heresy, but there is no indication of how many or which ones.[10])

However, the second part of this declaration describes *each* of the rejected propositions not only as subject to one of the theological censures but also as "against Catholic truth" (*et veritate Catholicae obviantes*). What is the meaning of this phrase? At first blush, this term might seem to have the same meaning as heresy. Indeed, St. Albert the Great and St. Thomas Aquinas had used a similar term—*contra Catholicam veritatem*—as a synonym for heresy.[11]

However, this interpretation would result in an anomalous reading of *Exsurge Domine*. First, if "against Catholic truth" has the same meaning as heresy, then one would have expected Leo to have condemned all forty-one propositions simply as heretical. It would have made no sense to list the different degrees of theological censures if in fact all the propositions were subject to the same ultimate censure of heresy.

In addition, if all of the propositions were indeed heretical, it would have been irresponsible for Leo to suggest that some of them were subject only to one of the less severe censures, such as "offensive to pious ears" or "seductive of simple minds." Second, if the term "against Catholic truth" in fact had the same meaning as heresy, then it would have been redundant for the pontiff to describe the same statements as *both* heretical *and* against Catholic truth. It is significant that, unlike the terms used in the first part of the sentence, "against Catholic truth" was not among the technical terms recognized as theological censures.

Therefore, the true meaning of "against Catholic truth" in this context seems to be something other than heresy. The internal logic of *Exsurge Domine* would seem to foreclose one from interpreting "against Catholic

---

[10] However, even this is not certain, for if only one proposition had been condemned as "either heretical, scandalous . . . or seductive of simple minds," the declaration would appear to mean that the proposition is possibly, but not definitely, heretical and, in any event, dangerous. Thus, the context suggests that at least some of the propositions are heretical, but the text does not absolutely demand this conclusion.

[11] St. Albert the Great, *De Eucharistia*, dist. vi, tract 2, c. 1, in *On the Body of the Lord*, trans. Sr. Albert Marie Surmanski (Washington, DC: Catholic University of America, 2017), 327, refers to denial of transubstantiation; Thomas Aquinas, *Contra impugnantes Dei cultum*, pt. 2, c. 5, in *An Apology for the Religious Orders*, ed. John Procter (London/St. Louis: Sands & Co./B. Herder, 1902), 175, refers to the proposition that it is not lawful to leave all to follow Christ in poverty.

truth" as equivalent to heresy. Leo X seems to have used the phrase simply as a generic category or summary of all rejected propositions, regardless of whether the rejection was for dogmatic or other reasons (such as being scandalous, offensive, or likely to mislead the faithful).[12] Leo's phrase (*veritate Catholicae obviantes*) is not identical with the formula of Albert and Thomas (*contra Catholicam veritatem*), although both are translated into English as "against Catholic truth." In any event, however, even the latter phrase appears to have a more elastic meaning that is not necessarily equivalent to heresy.[13]

---

[12] Vermeersch notes that a proposition might be described as dangerous *either* because of its falsity *or* because of consequences to which it might lead (Vermeersch, *Tolerance*, 173–74n2).

[13] This phrase—"against Catholic truth"—was not a term that theologians or the magisterium were accustomed to using very often. Leo X appears to be the first pope to use the phrase, and later popes seem to use it (or, rather, roughly equivalent terms) only occasionally. Cf. Gregory XVI, Encyclical *Commissum Divinitus* (May 17, 1835), §9, referring to mixed marriages as "*assolutamente contrarie alla verità cattolica*"; Pius X, Encyclical *Pascendi Dominici Gregis* (Sept. 8, 1907), §15, describing Modernist emphasis on religious experience as "*quod catholicae veritati est omnino infestum*" (ASS 40 [1907]: 605); Pius X, Letter to the French Archbishops and Bishops *Our Apostolic Mandate* (Aug. 15, 1910), describing doctrine of the Sillon as "*contraire à la verité catholique*" (AAS 2 [1910]: 615). The popes also sometimes have used the phrase "Catholic truth" standing alone (cf. Vatican I; Leo XIII, *Sapientiae Christianae*; Leo XIII, *Providentissimus Deus*; Pius XI, *Quas Primas*; Pius XII, *Ad Apostolorum Principis*). It does not appear that any writer used precisely the same term as Leo—*veritate Catholicae obviantes*.

The phrase—or, rather, its more common equivalents—seems to be an elastic and somewhat general term that can mean heresy, but that also can mean something less, such as that a proposition is scandalous or poses a certain danger. The first to use the term may have been Lanfranc, the eleventh-century archbishop of Canterbury. He uses it in charging Berengarius with denying Catholic doctrine on the Eucharist, and, as a result, Lanfranc's usage initially seems similar to Albert's, that is, a synonym for heresy.

However, unlike Albert and Aquinas, Lanfranc applies the term not to a specific proposition but to an entire work. Lanfranc, *De corpore et sanguine Domini*, c. 1, in Gregory F. LaNave et al., eds., *The Fathers of the Church: Mediaeval Continuation*, vol. 10, *Lanfranc of Canterbury On the Body and Blood of the Lord* (Washington, DC: The Catholic University of America Press, 2009): "You . . . composed a document against the aforementioned synod [the Council of Rome in 1059], against Catholic truth, and against the opinion of the entire Church."

Moreover, Lanfranc acknowledges that not all of Berengarius's work is objectionable. The book contains "roses among the thorns," he says (Lanfranc, cap. 1, in *Body and Blood*, 31). Note also that in the same work, Lanfranc represents Berengarius himself as claiming to have been writing in opposition to a work of Humbert of Burgundy that "was written against Catholic truth" (Lanfranc, cap. 2, in *Body and Blood*, 31). As a result, although "against Catholic truth" (in Lanfranc's usage) can mean that a work contains heresy, the phrase seems not to be precisely or necessarily equivalent to heresy.

The theologian who seems to use this type of phrase most often is William of Ockham,

14.2. The Drafting of *Exsurge Domine*

The history of the drafting of *Exsurge Domine* demonstrates that Leo's usage is indeed along the lines of the more elastic meaning of this term. That is, the phrase is consistent with the presence of heresy, but does not necessarily demand it. It also may signify errors that do not rise to the level of heresy, such as rash pronouncements that are dangerous or scandalous. In fact, Leo's usage signifies that a number of problematic propositions are at issue, some of which are heretical and others of which are objectionable for lesser reasons, such as their offensiveness or their propensity to mislead.

The cardinals collaborated with Leo in the drafting of *Exsurge Domine* in 1520, and one of them—Cajetan—advocated specifying a precise censure for each of the forty-one condemned propositions.[14] In the end, however, the bull rejected Luther's propositions only "indiscriminately and without specification."[15] The reason was to prevent delay in the publication of the bull. As a result of rumors of an increasing number of German princes taking Luther's side, "prompt action" was essential.[16]

> It was obvious that under these circumstances it was out of the question to apportion the degree of censure to each proposition. The one thing to be done was to judge them as a whole, with a general reference to individual points.[17]

---

and his usage suggests that it has a range of possible meanings. In some contexts, the phrase is an apparent equivalent for heresy: "[E]very Christian . . . who errs pertinaciously against Catholic truth (*errans pertinaciter contra Catholicam veritatem*) is said to be a heretic." William of Ockham, *Dialogus*, pt. 1, bk. 3, ch. 2; Latin text and English translation available online at John Kilcullen and John Scott, "William of Ockham, *Dialogus*, Part 1, Book 3, Chapters 1–5," trans. John Kilcullen, *British Academy* (1999), accessed May 3, 2017, http://www.britac.ac.uk/pubs/dialogus/t1d3at.html. Elsewhere, however, it is clear that Ockham uses the term to denote an offense less serious than heresy. Thus, Ockham says that, although Catholic truth (cf. *Dialogus*, pt. 1, bk. 2, ch. 1, [http://www.britac.ac.uk/pubs/dialogus/t1d2a.html]) includes chronicles and histories that are worthy of belief (*Dialogus*, pt. 1, bk. 2, ch. 5 [http://www.britac.ac.uk/pubs/dialogus/t1d2a.html]), the denial of the accounts found in these chronicles or histories is condemned "not as heretical but as dangerous and pertinacious to the church" (*Dialogus*, pt. 1, bk. 2, ch. 33 [http://www.britac.ac.uk/pubs/dialogus/t1d2b.html]).

[14] Ludwig Freiherr von Pastor, *The History of the Popes: From the Close of the Middle Ages*, vol. 7, 2nd ed., ed. Ralph Francis Kerr (St. Louis, MO: B. Herder Book Co., 1923), 397. See also Pastor, 387–88, for a similar attempt earlier in the drafting process to specify more precisely the degree of objection in Luther's propositions.

[15] Pastor, *History of the Popes*, 397.

[16] Pastor, *History of the Popes*, 398.

[17] Pastor, *History of the Popes*, 399.

As a result of the need for near-immediate action, the bull *Exsurge Domine* sacrificed precision for speed. "These [forty-one articles] were condemned wholesale without sufficient regard to the distinction of their individual degree of offensiveness."[18] Thus, it is clear that "against Catholic truth," like the bull itself, was a general indication of some danger or error in each proposition. While heresy was included within this phrase, the phrase itself does not necessarily imply heresy, to the exclusion of lesser censures (like "offensive to pious ears"). Thus, with regard to the rejection of Luther's thesis against the burning of heretics, *Exsurge Domine* does not condemn it as heretical but only applies an indeterminate censure to it.

---

[18] Pastor, *History of the Popes*, 394.

CHAPTER 15

The Appeal to "Changed Circumstances," Part 2
Social Harm, Both Real and Perceived

> [H]eresy was perceived as the primal threat to social order, both by ecclesiastics and by secular rulers.
>
> — MICHAEL NOVAK[1]

This chapter revisits a theme discussed in chapter 5, the relevance of "changed circumstances." Such arguments standing alone seem insufficient to resolve the doctrinal issue, but they do illuminate various points in the discussion. That chapter discussed, in particular, the near disappearance of the Catholic state. This chapter and the following one concern some additional changed circumstances and their relevance to a possible harmonization of *Dignitatis Humanae* with the nineteenth-century papal teaching. This chapter considers especially the observations of Patrick O'Neil on historical changes in the assessment of dangers to civil society posed by non-Catholic religious expression, and the next chapter discusses the insights of Walter Kasper and Basile Valuet on changes in currents of thought that made possible the Church's Declaration on Religious Liberty.

---

[1] Michael Novak, "Aquinas and the Heretics," *First Things* 58 (1995): 37.

15.1. Noonan and O'Neil

Patrick O'Neil attempts to explain the doctrinal development of DH in both theological and historical terms.[2] O'Neil is responding to an earlier article by the distinguished Catholic jurist, John T. Noonan.[3] Noonan's article, which was published in *Theological Studies*, was called "Development in Moral Doctrine."[4] Noonan begins his article, "That the moral teachings of the Catholic Church have changed over time will, I suppose, be denied by almost no one today."[5] He proceeds to discuss four areas in which he asserts that the Church has changed its moral teachings—usury, marriage, slavery, and religious liberty. Noonan's conclusion is that change in moral doctrine is acceptable, provided that it is based on a fresh appeal to Christ. "[T]he principle of change," he concludes, "is the person of Christ."[6] In the specific area of religious liberty, Noonan argues that *Dignitatis Humanae* contradicts the Church's historical acquiescence in the *persecution of heretics*. He also identifies the historical practice of toleration and distinguishes it from religious liberty.[7]

O'Neil takes issue with Noonan's opening assertion that Church teaching has changed or reversed itself. In all four areas identified by Noonan, O'Neil offers explanations of the underlying consistency in Church teaching. O'Neil's method is to seek to determine the meaning of the Church's teaching and to show how the *application* of that teaching might take different forms in different historical circumstances. He discusses religious liberty last and begins by describing it as an "extremely troublesome issue."

O'Neil points out that for most of the Church's life, the predominant

---

[2] Cf. Patrick M. O'Neil, "A Response to John T. Noonan, Jr. Concerning the Development of Catholic Moral Doctrine," *Faith & Reason* (Spring/Summer 1996), EWTN, accessed Dec. 19, 2020, https://www.ewtn.com/catholicism/library/response-to-john-t-noonan-jr-concerning-the-development-of-catholic-moral-doctrine-10041.

[3] Noonan was a Judge of the U.S. Court of Appeals for the Ninth Circuit from 1985 until his death in 2017. He also served on the commission that studied the question of birth control before Pope Paul VI's issuance of *Humanae Vitae* in 1968. In addition, he is the author of books on usury, marriage, and religious freedom in the U.S.

[4] John T. Noonan Jr., "Development in Moral Doctrine," *Theological Studies* 54, no. 4 (1993): 662–77.

[5] Noonan, "Development in Moral Doctrine," 662.

[6] Noonan, "Development in Moral Doctrine," 677. Noonan's theory carries with it the same difficulties as the "historical circumstances" argument addressed in chapter 5. That is, it simply proves too much. A fresh appeal to Christ should indeed be a part of any Christian theory. However, such a standard provides no way of judging whether such a theory or teaching represents an *authentic development* of doctrine or a *corruption* of it. Indeed, it seems likely that such a theory would devolve into mere subjectivity.

[7] Cf. Noonan, "Development in Moral Doctrine," 667–68.

assumption was that heresy and heretics posed a serious danger both to the Church and to civil society. Primacy of conscience, he says, was a principle of Catholic teaching. However, it did not take precedence over the social good. As a result, as long as non-Catholic religions were considered a threat to the Church and the state, the general principle of religious liberty could not come into play. O'Neil formulates these assumptions into a single practical principle: "If and only if persecution were necessary to protect Church and state, then it would be morally justified—but prudential judgments may also justify as permissible a policy of religious toleration."

15.1.1. O'Neil's Focus on Factual Predicates

A key to O'Neil's argument is his observation that it is possible for the *factual predicate* of a particular teaching to be mistaken. For example, O'Neil argues, Pope Leo XIII's declaration on the invalidity of Anglican orders was based on "certain irregularities of form and defects of intention, but the existence of the facts backing the existence of such irregularities and defects depended on the assumption of the correctness of certain historical accounts by ecclesiastical historians." Thus, O'Neil says, the doctrinal content of Leo's declaration should be framed "as a hypothetical, 'If these events (S, T, U) occurred, then Anglican orders are invalid, because the validity of priestly orders depends upon conditions X, Y, Z.'" This statement is unquestionably true, he says, but Leo XIII's *Apostolicae Curae* also contains "a second premise, 'Events S, T, U did occur,' the truth of which is not a matter of faith and morals, but of historical fact." The protection from error that the Church enjoys, O'Neil says, is in the issuance of the strictly *doctrinal* statement, not in the correct recounting or evaluation of *historical* facts.[8]

O'Neil's theory largely is sound, though his choice to illustrate it by Pope Leo XIII's pronouncement on Anglican orders is an unfortunate one. In 1998 Pope John Paul II issued the apostolic letter *Ad Tuendam Fidem*,[9]

---

[8] As another example, recall John Paul's revision of the Catechism of the Catholic Church concerning capital punishment (cf. CCC, §2267). That revision similarly is based on a factual assertion: as a result of the ability of penal systems to render offenders harmless, John Paul asserts, the circumstances in which recourse to capital punishment is justified are practically non-existent. The factual predicate for this assertion may be accurate in some places and times but not in others. Pope Francis's further 2018 revision of the Catechism includes the same factual predicate but adds to it two additional rationales: one based on the dignity of the person, and one based on a new understanding of the significance of penal sanctions.

[9] John Paul II, Apostolic Letter Motu Proprio *Ad Tuendam Fidem* (May 18, 1998) [AAS 90 (1998): 457–61].

and in a doctrinal commentary accompanying it, the Congregation for the Doctrine of the Faith explained that Leo XIII's pronouncement on the invalidity of Anglican orders, *Apostolicae Curae*, is an example of a definitive teaching that, although not contained in revelation itself, is "connected to revelation by historical necessity"[10] or "necessarily connected with revelation by virtue of an historical relationship."[11]

Thus, it seems problematic for O'Neil to suggest that the factual predicate for this teaching may remain in doubt. In *Apostolicae Curae*, Leo XIII makes clear that he intends to resolve the question of the validity of Anglican orders,[12] and he bases his decision not primarily on the judgments of historians but on an analysis of the Anglican ordination formula itself.[13] To his credit, O'Neil identifies *Apostolicae Curae* as partaking of papal infallibility, but he seems to underestimate the significance of its connection to revelation by virtue of a historical relationship. That is, the relevance of history to Leo's pronouncement is not so much that it finds some basis in the judgments of historians, but rather that it is based on the Church's historical practice of three centuries, that is, the Church's unbroken practice of treating Anglican orders as invalid.[14] (In justice to O'Neil, one must acknowledge that the precise classification of this teaching became clear only in 1998, with the publication of the Congregation's doctrinal commentary. As recounted above, O'Neil was writing two years earlier.)

However, if O'Neil's example of Anglican orders does not survive *Ad Tuendam Fidem*,[15] his larger point does. That is, at least for authentic teaching of the magisterium, O'Neil's theory remains intact. Such teachings may be based on historical facts and assumptions that, in time, prove to have been incomplete, incorrect, or correct in only some circumstances. He succeeds in giving other examples along these lines.

For O'Neil, the important change in circumstances concerning religious liberty is the gradual realization that persecution is not necessary to protect the Church and civil society. Once this circumstance becomes known, the

---

[10] Congregation for the Doctrine of the Faith, Doctrinal Commentary on the Concluding Formula of the *Professio Fidei*, §11 (June 29, 1998) [AAS 90 (1998): 549].

[11] *Professio Fidei*, §7 [AAS 90 (1998): 547].

[12] Cf. Pope Leo XIII, Apostolic Letter *Apostolicae Curae* (Sept. 13, 1896), §§35–37, 40 [ASS 29 (1896–1897): 202–3].

[13] Cf. Leo XIII, *Apostolicae Curae*, §§29–30 [AAS 29 (1896–1897): 200–201].

[14] Cf. Leo XIII, *Apostolicae Curae*, §15 [AAS 29 (1896–1897): 197].

[15] Dulles, however, notes that debates continue regarding the validity of Anglican orders. Cf. Avery Dulles, *Magisterium: Teacher and Guardian of the Faith* (Naples, FL: Sapientia Press, 2007), 91.

moral justification for persecution falls away. As a result, the way is cleared for the general principles of conscience and religious liberty to come into prominence. As O'Neil says, "[R]eligious liberty becomes the operative principle in default of any alternative position."[16] Thus, as O'Neil interprets the Church's doctrine, it is not the teaching that has changed, but it is rather "judgments of circumstances in the world" that have changed.[17]

15.1.2. Observations on the O'Neil Approach

Before proceeding to evaluate O'Neil's argument, some observations are appropriate. There is some ambiguity in his account of the realization that persecution is not necessary to protect the Church or civil society. It is not clear whether he is saying that the popes were *mistaken* in believing that repression was necessary in previous periods, or that the actual historical-political situation changed over time so that public non-Catholic religious expression *no longer* poses a threat. The discussion below—concerning St. Augustine in particular—shows that the threat posed by heretics could be quite real.

By the same token, it is uncertain whether O'Neil is saying that we have arrived at a historical point where persecution—or limitation on religious expression—*never* is necessary, or *only rarely* is necessary. O'Neil seems to assume that such limitations never are necessary, but the text of DH itself makes clear that religious freedom is a right "within due limits," and that restriction remains a live possibility when religious activity breaches

---

[16] As discussed above, O'Neil's theory does not fully account for the second part of the right to religious liberty. Cf. Second Vatican Council, Declaration on Religious Liberty *Dignitatis Humanae* (December 7, 1965), §3c. However, our concern is with his treatment of changed historical circumstances, which provides at least a partial account of the delay in recognition of the right to religious liberty.

[17] Note that O'Neil's discussion sometimes emphasizes the *first* part of the right to religious liberty in particular, namely, freedom from coercion or freedom from being forced to worship in a way that does not correspond to one's own beliefs (cf. DH, §2a). He is indeed correct that the freedom of the act of faith always has been a principle of Catholic teaching. As discussed above in section 9.6, the first part of the right that the declaration recognizes can be understood as a broader version of the freedom of the act of faith, or as flowing from it in principle. However, O'Neil does not always focus equally on the *second* part of the right, namely, the immunity from being impeded in the religious acts that one chooses to perform according to his conscience (cf. DH, §3c). As discussed in chapter 9, the second part of the right presents the challenge in doctrinal development. As a result, the range of circumstances necessary for the right to become operative likely are broader than O'Neil acknowledges. These circumstances include the principle of reciprocity, and they are discussed below in chapter 16.

the public order (cf. DH, §2a). Indeed, another possibility is that the key change in circumstance is not the realization that non-Catholic religious expression poses no threat, but rather the realization that, despite any such threats, limitation on non-Catholic worship would result in consequences more harmful than those posed by exposure of the Catholic populace to non-Catholic religious worship. Even with these points of uncertainty, however, O'Neil's article remains useful and thought provoking.

Another crucial question is what concrete events or circumstances led to the realization that repression no longer was necessary (or the realization that repression might cause more harm than good). O'Neil's article is brief, and this issue likely was beyond its scope. However, this question is one that is illuminated by two authors discussed in the next chapter, Walter Kasper and Basile Valuet.

O'Neil's argument deserves serious consideration. At the outset, it is important to note that whether or not his historical argument is decisive, it is useful in providing perspective on previous periods in the Church's history. In addition, O'Neil does not use this argument as an attempt to avoid the theological issues, as some of the council fathers sometimes appeared to do with regard to the circumstance of the near disappearance of the Catholic state (and other differences between the political situations of the nineteenth and twentieth centuries). To begin the analysis of O'Neil's argument, one should acknowledge that O'Neil undoubtedly is correct that heresy formerly was considered a great danger to both Church and state. A review of the teachings of Saints Augustine and Thomas Aquinas illustrates this point.

15.2. St. Augustine

St. Augustine believed that the act of faith must be free. Pope Leo XIII would quote Augustine to this effect: "Man cannot believe otherwise than of his own will."[18] Indeed, the Catholic tradition appears to be unanimous on this point.[19] As a result, Augustine directly rejected the use of force against

---

[18] St. Augustine, *In Iohannis evangelium tractatus* [Tractates on the Gospel of John], 26, 2 [AD 416–417] (PL 35:1607); English translation, W. A. Jurgens, *The Faith of the Early Fathers*, vol. 3 (Collegeville, MN: Liturgical Press, 1979), 118. The Jurgens translation reads as follows: "A man is able to come into the Church unwillingly, he is able to approach the altar unwillingly, he is able to receive the Sacrament unwillingly; but he is not able to believe except willingly." The translation in the main text is from the quotation of Augustine in the English translation of *Immortale Dei*. Cf. Pope Leo XIII, Encyclical *Immortale Dei* (Nov. 1, 1885), §36.

[19] Cf. DH, §10. See also Basile Valuet, *Le droit à la liberté religieuse dans la Tradition de*

the Manichaean heretics. He also *initially* rejected the use of force against the Donatists.

Later, however, Augustine reversed his position regarding the coercion of heretics.[20] That is, despite insisting that the act of faith must be free, Augustine came to believe that a different principle applies to baptized Christians who later embraced heretical opinions or adhered to schismatic movements. Thus, Augustine came to advocate some measure of coercion in returning the Donatist heretics to the Church. The Donatists were moral rigorists who asserted that sacraments administered by priests and bishops who had apostatized during the Roman persecutions were invalid.

Basile Valuet identifies five distinct "anti-Donatist periods" in Augustine's thought.[21] In the first period (391–400), Augustine would rely only on persuasion to return the Donatists to the fold:

> [M]y desire is, not that anyone should against his will be coerced into the Catholic communion, but that to all who are in error the truth may be openly declared, and being by God's help clearly exhibited through my ministry, may so commend itself as to make them embrace and follow it.[22]

In the second period (400–405), however, Augustine took account of Donatist violence and began to see a role for the civil authority in creating a climate of liberty. The third period (405–408) marks the imperial edicts against the Donatists and Augustine's hesitant acceptance of those laws. In the fourth period (408–411), Augustine confirmed his acceptance of the civil authority's role, largely as a result of the efficacy of the imperial laws. By the same token, Augustine also opposed the law of liberty of conscience enacted in the year 410. Finally, in the fifth period (411–430), Augustine definitively set forth his theory and his acceptance of coercion.[23]

In support of forcibly bringing the Donatists back to Catholic orthodoxy,

---

l'Eglise. Un cas de développement doctrinal homogène par le magistère authentique, 2nd rev. ed. (Barroux: Éditions Sainte-Madeleine, 2011), 185.

[20] Cf. St. Augustine, *Retractationes* II, 5 [PL 32:632].

[21] Cf. Valuet, LRTE, 106. Most of Valuet's chapter on Augustine consists of a detailed examination of each of these five periods (cf. LRTE, 106–21).

[22] St. Augustine, Letter 34 (To Eusebius) [AD 396], §1 (PL 33:132); English translation from New Advent, accessed Sept. 29, 2015, https://www.newadvent.org/fathers/1102034.htm. This passage is cited in DH, §10.

[23] Cf. Valuet, LRTE, 105, 119–21.

Augustine (in the year 408) cited the parable of the great banquet.[24] In that parable, when the invited guests refuse to attend, the host orders his slave to go into the streets and to invite the poor and the lame. When there still is room at the banquet, the master orders the slave to go to the people in the roads and lanes. He says, "*Compel* people to come in, so that my house may be filled" (Luke 14:23 [emphasis added]; cf. Matt 22:9). Augustine drew the lesson from this parable that compulsion was permissible in some circumstances, namely in situations involving heretics and schismatics.[25] (Note, however, that when Augustine speaks of *coercion*, he is referring not to torture and the threat of death but to means such as exile, fines, and the confiscation of property.[26]) In addition, Augustine cites another passage in support of his position in favor of coercion. He remembered Paul's conversion on the road to Damascus (Acts 9:1–9) and argued that Paul "was compelled, by the great violence with which Christ coerced him, to know and to embrace the truth."[27]

Augustine's scriptural arguments are by no means decisive. Other interpreters would find support at least as strong in Scripture for toleration or liberty as Augustine finds for coercion. Joseph Lecler notes, "[T]he *compelle intrare* of the parable of the supper (Luke 14:23) has nothing to do with the use of compulsion either to bring pagans to the faith or to bring schismatics and heretics back into the Church."[28] Moreover, as early as the tenth century, Bishop Wazo of Liège had cited the parable of the wheat and the tares (Matt

---

[24] Cf. St. Augustine, Letter 93 (To Vincentius) [AD 408], §5 [PL 33:323; CSEL 34:449–50] (hereinafter, Letter 93); English translation in NPNF 1st Series, vol. 1, 382–401. See also St. Augustine, Letter 173 (To Donatus) [AD 416], §10 [PL 33:757]; English trans. NPNF 1st Series, vol. 1, 544–47; St. Augustine, Letter 208 (To the Lady Felicia) [AD 423], §7; English trans. NPNF 1st Series, vol. 1, 558–60; St. Augustine, "A Treatise Concerning the Correction of the Donatists," (= Letter 185) [ca. AD 417], §24 [PL 33:803–4] (hereinafter, "Donatists"); English trans. NPNF 1st Series, vol. 4, 633–51.

[25] Cf. "Donatists" (= Letter 185), §24 [PL 33:803–4].

[26] Cf. Letter 93, §14 (confiscation) [PL 33:328]; Letter 93, §10 (fines and exile) [PL 33:325–26]; "Donatists," §§25, 26 (fines and exile) [PL 33:804–5]; "Donatists," §14 (against capital punishment) [PL 33:799]; "Donatists," §26 (against capital punishment) [PL 33:805].

[27] Letter 93, §5 [PL 33:323; English trans. NPNF 1st Series, vol. 1, 383]. See also Letter 173, §3 [PL 33:754–55]; "Donatists," §22; [PL 33:802–3].

[28] Joseph Lecler, *Toleration and the Reformation*, vol. 1, trans. T. L. Westow (London/New York: Longmans/Association Press, 1960), 24. Lecler identifies Sebastian Castellio as the first critic seriously to question the use of these texts to justify persecution (cf. Lecler, 346). Castellio, and Andrew Modrzewski after him, argued in favor of returning heretics to the fold but only by spiritual means such as persuasion (cf. Lecler, 346, 396).

13:29–30) against the persecution of heretics.[29] The Second Vatican Council would follow suit, analogizing religious liberty to the same parable, in which the tares are left to grow alongside the wheat until the harvest.

In his Scriptural arguments, Augustine's strongest point is the one concerning St. Paul's conversion. However, despite the force that the Lord uses against Paul, it is not completely clear that He overbears Paul's will. Paul's later career gives the impression of a man whose passion was undiminished and whose will was redirected rather than broken. Ultimately, Paul's conversion remains mysterious. However, one can say for certain that this episode is an exception. In calling the other disciples, it is clear that the Lord extends an *invitation*. The account of the rich young man makes clear that the disciples are free either to accept or reject the call (cf. Matt 19:16–22; Mark 10:17–22; Luke 18:18–23). This aspect of the call is reinforced by the promises that Jesus makes to some of the Twelve—"I will make you fishers of men" (Matt 4:19; Mark 1:17) and "You shall see greater things than these" (John 1:50)—which almost give the impression that he is *bargaining* with them. Similarly, when some disciples find the teaching on the Eucharist to be a "hard saying," the Lord does not hinder them from departing (cf. John 6:60–66). Thus, to the extent that Scripture answers the question of coercion versus toleration or liberty, the predominant sense of the gospels is that coercion is not a valid way either to win persons to the faith or to maintain them in it.

However, despite Augustine's questionable (and indeed unconvincing) use of Scripture, one cannot simply dismiss his teachings. Rather, one must keep Augustine's historical context in mind. In particular, one should remember that the theological disputations with the Donatists were not simply intellectual affairs. The Donatists occupied Christian churches, refused to relinquish control of them, and resorted to cruel violence against Orthodox Christians who attempted to persuade them to return to the fold. This violence sometimes included cutting out the tongues of Christian missionaries or blinding them.[30] In addition, the Donatists threatened not only the Church but the civil order as well. They were associated with the Circumcellions, a group of rebels against the Roman landlords.[31] Thus, it is

---

[29] Cf. Lecler, 82, citing *Vita Vasonis*, c. 25 [PL 142:751–53].

[30] Cf. Warren H. Carroll, *A History of Christendom*, vol. 2, *The Building of Christendom* (Front Royal, Va.: Christendom College Press, 1987), 85. Augustine makes frequent reference to the violence of the Donatists. E.g., Letter 88, 6 and 8, recounting beatings, detentions, blindings, the burning of houses, and the ambush of bishops [PL 33:305, 307].

[31] Cf. *The Encyclopedic Dictionary of Religion* (Washington, DC: Corpus Publications, 1979), s.v. "Circumcellions."

not the case that our early Christian forbears were *deluded* into thinking that heretics posed a danger to the civil order. In the concrete situation of the Donatist controversy, they did indeed pose such a danger. The reason for the laws against heretics, Augustine said, was "the fury of their violence."[32] Such laws, he said, were necessary to protect the freedom of the weak,[33] and were a matter of self-defense rather than persecution:[34] "You trouble the repose and the peace, I do not say of the Church alone, but of the whole society."[35] Moreover, the situation in which Christian heretics were regarded as an equal threat to both the spiritual order and the temporal order was by no means limited to the Donatist controversy. For example, the Cathars or Albigensians posed a similarly serious threat in southern France and northern Italy from the eleventh century to the thirteenth century. Given the danger that they posed to civil society—particularly the antisocial character of the heresy and its adherents' refusal to follow the rules of the civil state—one author astutely notes that if a similar movement were to arise in modern times, states once again would find it necessary to protect themselves against it.[36]

Vatican II frankly and rightly acknowledges that the coercive methods in religious matters used in the past were not always in keeping with the Gospel (DH, §12a). However, one should resist the temptation to judge too harshly those who went before us. In considering the Donatist crisis and the many crises that followed it, one should not simply condemn the authorities outright as if they had punished persons simply for their sincerely held beliefs. Rather, in many or even most circumstances, one will find that such persons posed a physical threat to the Church, to her members, and often to the civil order as well.[37] A modern reader might tend to think of

---

[32] St. Augustine, Sermon 62, 18 (AD 399–400) [PL 38:423]; English trans. NPNF 1st Series, vol. 6, 303–4, identified here as Sermon 12.

[33] Cf. St. Augustine, *Epistula ad Catholicos de secta Donatistarum* (= *De Unitate Ecclesiae*), cap. XX, n55 [PL 43:434].

[34] Cf. St. Augustine, Letter 87, 7 [PL 33:299].

[35] St. Augustine, *Contra Cresconium grammaticum et Donatistam*, libri IV, III, xlii, 46 (AD 405) [PL 43:520]. The translation is my own.

[36] Cf. Édouard Jordan, "La Responsabilité de l' Église dans la répression de l'hérésie au moyen âge," *Annales de Philosophie chrétienne*, series IV, vol. VIII/6 (September 1909): 577–78, cited in Valuet, LRTE, 177.

[37] Cf. *The Catholic Encyclopedia* (New York: Encyclopedia Press, 1913), s.v. "Toleration, History." On the threat posed to civil society by the Donatists in particular, see Basile Valuet, *La liberté religieuse et la tradition catholique. Un cas de développement doctrinal homogène dans le magistère authentique*, 3rd rev. ed. (Barroux: Éditions Sainte-Madeleine, 2011), vol. IA, 166–69.

an Arian, a Donatist, or an Albigensian as something like a "conscientious objector," because such a person is remembered chiefly for his role in what is now recalled as an intellectual dispute. However, one must keep in mind the danger to civil society that such persons posed, or at least sincerely were believed to pose. Thus, if one wishes to understand a Donatist in the way that his orthodox Christian contemporaries understood him, then one's modern analogy for the Donatist will be more like an armed revolutionary than a conscientious objector.[38]

This need to protect both the Church and civil society is present throughout history, and, as a result, it is a crucial unifying theme in every stage of the life of the Church. Indeed, *Dignitatis Humanae* continues to affirm this principle in its insistence that religious activity and expression must be exercised *within due limits*, and that these limits are specified by the requirements of the *just public order* (DH, §§2a, 2b). Thus, in a very real sense, this principle has remained consistent throughout history. Nonetheless, it may be difficult to see the thread of consistency. Religious repression was so much more common in the past than today that it may seem strange to assert that a single principle applies to all times, whether they were periods of repression, toleration, or liberty. As discussed above in chapters 12 and 13, the key is to recognize that in the past, repression nearly always took place and was justified—not on the basis of the *falsity* of the religion that was repressed but rather because of the *danger* posed (or believed to be posed) to the Church, to the faithful, and to civil society.[39] Thus, in the Council's language, the justification for repression of public non-Catholic worship was not the *error* of the doctrine but rather the *threat* that it posed to the *just public order*. Moreover, in Harrison's language, the shift from a presumption in favor of repression toward a presumption in

---

[38] Cf. A. Vermeersch, *Tolerance*, trans. W. Humphrey Page (New York: Benziger Brothers, 1912), 161: "[T]he heresies which were really hunted to death were those which, when spread abroad among the masses, sowed the seed of religious anarchy, and tended to the ruin and overthrow of the Church and society. In other words, the heresy persecuted was a revolutionary reformist movement." Cf. Novak, "Aquinas and the Heretics," 37.

[39] Cf. Arnold T. Guminski and Brian W. Harrison, *Religious Freedom: Did Vatican II Contradict Traditional Catholic Doctrine? A Debate* (South Bend, IN: St. Augustine Press, 2013), 63 (position of Harrison): "Catholic doctrine never taught that religious repression was for the purpose of 'imposing' truth on unbelievers or dissidents themselves, but rather for preventing them from doing spiritual, moral or material harm to others." Even where repression was justified in the past, the repressive measures sometimes have been excessive (cf. DH, §12a). In addition, as O'Neil appears to suggest, it seems certain that there have been times when authorities have reached mistaken judgments as to whether non-Catholic public religious practice truly posed a threat and required repression.

favor of freedom takes place within the field of *policy* or *public ecclesiastical law* rather than *doctrine*. It remains a constant that suppression of abusive religious activity is legitimate, but the concrete determination of exactly how much repression is necessary in a given context is a question of policy.[40]

St. Augustine refers constantly to the atrocities committed by the Donatists. These assaults on orthodox Catholics were so numerous and frequent that they leave no doubt that the Donatists posed a serious threat to individual believers, the Church itself, and even civil society. Again, in the language of Vatican II, one can say that the harm threatened and caused to the public order justified repression of the Donatists.[41]

It is clear that this motive for religious repression—protection of the *just public order*—is a legitimate one in any historical period. However, is it clear that St. Augustine confined himself to this motive?

Valuet studies Augustine in depth and outlines the various justifications that he cites throughout his successive anti-Donatist periods.[42] He identifies Augustine's arguments based on public order as his most frequent and decisive ones.[43] However, they were not his only arguments. In addition to his public order arguments, Augustine made two kinds of *a priori* arguments, those based on Scripture (which are discussed above) and those based on theological reason (such as arguments from the nature of schism and the finality of coercion). He also made *a posteriori* arguments, that is, arguments based on the actual effectiveness of coercion in practice in returning Donatists to the fold. In addition, Augustine came to believe that virtue could be forced or compelled.[44]

---

[40] This is not to say that public ecclesiastical law is a blank slate. Now that the right to religious liberty has been recognized, public law must take account of the circumstance that restrictions may threaten the exercise of a natural right. The declaration does so by presuming freedom and by placing the burden on the authority that would restrict it. "[T]he freedom of man is to be respected as far as possible and is not to be curtailed except when and insofar as necessary" (DH, §7c). Likewise, the narrowing of the range of justifications for religious repression also should be understood as a consequence of the circumstance that a natural right is at issue (cf. DH, §7c).

[41] At the same time, given the close connection between ecclesiastical and civil society, it is difficult today to determine precisely how much of the threat was religious and how much was social or political. "The strands were so interwoven and confused that to this day it is hard to tell whether the difference in dogma was the occasion, the driving power, or merely the accompaniment of the political and social convulsions." Hermann Dörries, *Constantine and Religious Liberty*, trans. R. H. Bainton (London: Oxford University Press, 1961), 84–85, quoted in Valuet, LRTC, vol. IA, 169n656.

[42] Cf. Valuet, LRTE, 122; LRTC, vol. IA, 166–71.

[43] Cf. Valuet, LRTE, 122.

[44] Cf. Letter 93, §5 (PL 33:323); Letter 173, §2 (PL 33:754).

For all of Augustine's greatness, Valuet correctly notes that, as with any other private author, his is not the last word on Catholic tradition.[45] What this means for our question is that to the extent that Augustine's arguments are based on the requirements of the just public order—and recall that, to a large extent, they were indeed based on this rationale—they go forward and are entirely consistent with DH. His other arguments fare less well and do not go forward in the same way. That is, these latter arguments do not speak with the same relevance to the modern period and do not provide enduring principles of judgment and action.

15.3. St. Thomas Aquinas

St. Thomas Aquinas follows Augustine closely in this area. Like Augustine, Thomas distinguishes sharply between non-Christians and Christians who had lapsed into heresy. Non-Christians such as Jews and Muslims "are by no means to be compelled to the faith" because the act of faith depends on the will.[46] Thus, Thomas teaches that it is wrong to baptize Jewish children against the wishes of their parents.[47] Thomas also teaches that the rites of unbelievers such as Jews and Muslims may be tolerated to achieve some good or to avoid some evil.[48]

However, Thomas taught that Christian heretics were another matter entirely. Because they already had accepted the faith, Thomas taught, it was permissible to hold them to their promises and to compel them to return to the faith.[49] Thomas cited the same Scriptural passages that Augustine had cited on this point regarding the conversion of St. Paul and the parable of the great banquet. In fact, Thomas went further than Augustine by teaching that heretics may be turned over to the civil authorities for punishment by

---

[45] Cf. Valuet, LRTC, 171.

[46] St. Thomas Aquinas, *Summa Theologica*, Christian Classics ed. (Benziger Brothers, 1947), II-II, q. 10, a. 8. Thomas was not necessarily opposed to persecuting non-Christians, but he made clear that such measures legitimately are undertaken not to compel the unbelievers to believe but rather "to prevent them from hindering the faith of Christ" (ST II-II, q. 10, a. 8).

[47] Cf. ST II-II, q. 10, a. 12. The reason was that such a practice would be an offense against natural justice as a usurpation of parental authority.

[48] Cf. ST II-II, q. 10, a. 11. Thomas reasoned that human government should imitate divine government, which permits evils that it might otherwise prevent, so that unbelievers might gradually be won to the faith. This teaching would become very influential, especially in the nineteenth century during the reign of Pope Leo XIII, himself a Thomistic scholar.

[49] Cf. ST II-II, q. 10, a. 8.

death.[50] He also taught that if one relapsed into his heresy after having once been received back into the Church, then he should not be received again. He should be permitted to receive the sacrament of penance, but he should not be spared from death.[51]

How could Thomas take such a tolerant position with regard to Jews and Muslims but such a harsh stance against Christian heretics? Michael Novak provides perhaps the best answer possible. His article, "Aquinas and the Heretics," is a masterful attempt to recreate all the pressing circumstances of the thirteenth century to gain an understanding as to why Thomas's position would have been so convincing in his own time.[52] Novak explains Thomas but does not make excuses for him. He rejects Thomas's teaching on the heretics, but he also offers a sympathetic reading of that text. Novak's reading is based on three main explanatory observations.

First, Novak describes the sufferings that Thomas's own family endured at the hands of Emperor Frederick II, regarded by many as "the Great Heretic of the epoch."[53] Recalling that Frederick had two of Thomas's own brothers tortured and killed for rebellion, Novak reminds us, "When the term 'heretic' was used, it was not for Thomas Aquinas or his contemporaries an abstraction."[54]

Second, Novak explains in detail *why* heresy posed such a threat to the entire social order, both spiritual and temporal. The authority of the rulers themselves depended in large measure on universal acceptance of the Christian faith. As a result, *any* heresy tended to undercut kingly authority. As for the common people, they were especially vulnerable to anarchy because they were geographically isolated and subject to the shifting allegiances and feuds of their lords. The sole bond among the people (and, one might say, between the classes as well) was the Christian faith. Thus, heresy was not merely one of many dangers. "[H]eresy was perceived as *the primal threat* to social order, both by ecclesiastics and by secular rulers."[55]

---

[50] Cf. ST II-II, q. 10, a. 8, reply obj. 1.
[51] Cf. ST II-II, q. 11, a. 3–4.
[52] See generally Novak, "Aquinas and the Heretics."
[53] Novak, "Aquinas and the Heretics," 36.
[54] Novak, "Aquinas and the Heretics," 34.
[55] Novak, "Aquinas and the Heretics," 37 (emphasis added). Thomas Pink, in his scholarship on the declaration, largely neglects to take into account this intertwining of religious and temporal purposes. That is, he gives the impression that when Catholic rulers repressed or restricted non-Catholic worship, they did so almost entirely for religious—rather than secular—ends. Cf. Thomas Pink, "Continuity after Leo XIII," in *Dignitatis Humanae Colloquium*, Dialogos Institute Proceedings, vol. I (Dialogos Institute, 2017), 105–6, 110. As Novak notes here (and as Valuet notes shortly below in connection with the Inquisition),

15.3. St. Thomas Aquinas

Before proceeding to Novak's third observation, let us pause on this second one. The idea of the danger that heresy posed is critical, and, as discussed above in several different places, it was not only a religious threat but a civil and political danger as well. In the crises of Arianism, Donatism, and Albigensianism, it is clear that the civil order was threatened.

However, what about Donatists and Albigensians who might have been content to practice their religion peaceably without disturbing the public order? In one sense, Augustine had addressed this question, but in another sense, strange as it strikes a modern observer, Valuet shows that this circumstance was not *practically* posed in either the Patristic or the medieval eras.[56] Augustine's answer seems to be that it is irrelevant whether or not heretics are peaceable.[57] Toleration is permissible, he says, only when Catholics cannot hinder the heretics. That is, when there is no danger to the good wheat, the tares must be uprooted.[58] Thus, Augustine supported the imperial laws of 405 and 408 that not only repressed the Donatists but that outlawed Donatism

---

in fact, temporal and religious motivations were so closely intertwined in these periods that it often is difficult or impossible to distinguish them. Nutt and De Salvo make the same point in addressing Pink's work directly. "The medieval Church had greater recourse to a secular arm because, within medieval Christendom, the temporal and spiritual orders were commingled. Because citizenship was restricted within medieval consecrational Christendom to juridical Church members alone, threats to the good of the Church that otherwise would not have been more than an indirect threat to the state posed a direct threat to the temporal common good." Roger W. Nutt and Michael R. De Salvo, "The Debate over Dignitatis Humanae at Vatican II: The Contribution of Charles Cardinal Journet," *The Thomist* 85 (2021): 192. See also Nutt and De Salvo, 202 (similar). Pink does make reference to the presence or possible presence of both motives (cf. "Continuity after Leo XIII," 105–6, 110), but his emphasis is almost entirely on the religious ends. A key point for him is his assertion that the state lacks its own authority to coerce for religious purposes, and that when it did so, it was by virtue of authority delegated from the Church. (See subsection 9.5.1 and section 11.3 above for fuller descriptions of Pink's theory.) Nutt and De Salvo, however, assert that Pink neglects to consider other possible theories that might support the state's own authority to coerce in religious matters. Cf. Nutt and De Salvo, "Debate over Dignitatis Humanae," 206: Pink "does not consider whether the state might accidentally have authority to coerce in materially spiritual or religious matters, if only within the context of a kind of Christendom not to be seen again"; Nutt and De Salvo, 207 (similar). See also Arnold T. Guminski, "Further Reflections about Thomas Pink's Theory of the Meaning of *Dignitatis Humanae*" (Apr. 2, 2020), §§6–17, Academia, accessed July 16, 2022, https://www.academia.edu/42924123/Further_Reflections_About_Thomas_Pinks_Theory_of_the_Meaning_of_Dignitatis_Humanae.

[56] Cf. Valuet, LRTE, 181 [= LRTC, vol. IA, 268–69].

[57] Cf. St. Augustine, Letter 89 (To Festus) [AD 406], §2 [PL 33:309–10].

[58] St. Augustine, *Contra epistolam Parmeniani*, libri III, (ii), §13 [PL 43:92].

itself.[59] Valuet wrestles with this measure and concludes that although it was not justified as a legal matter, it may have been justified as a practical matter. The reason was that the Donatists appeared utterly incapable of practicing their religion without relying on violence and terror.[60] That is, a "peaceful Donatist" was practically a contradiction in terms. This is Valuet's reason for asserting that the question of the conscientious and peaceable heretic was not *practically* posed in Augustine's time (or in Thomas's). That is, it did not present a *live* option. In actual practice, the Donatists of Augustine's day (like the Albigensians of Thomas's) were not peaceable.[61] Thus, Augustine's occasional references to the possibility of peaceful heretics essentially were hypotheticals.

Valuet wrestles as well with the motivations behind the Inquisition. He doubts that the threat to the public order was the sole reason for the condemnation of heretics.[62] At the same time, he makes clear that Catholic doctrine itself did not oblige the civil authorities to pursue error *as such*.[63] Valuet asks whether the Inquisition pursued heresy because of its falsity or because of the social danger that it posed, and for an answer, he relies on historian Joseph Lecler. The inquisitors did indeed pursue the dogmatic error of the Cathars, but these errors were considered dangerous to the whole social order itself... because the whole social order rested on the Christian faith.[64] That is, even from the *civil* point of view, medieval society was founded on adherence to the Catholic faith.[65] Thus, as Novak says, both ecclesiastical and civil authorities considered heresy to be "the primal threat."[66] In such circumstances, even if heretics were to practice their religion peaceably, they still could pose (or reasonably could have been believed to pose) a threat to

---

[59] Cf. Valuet, LRTC, vol. IA, 169.
[60] Cf. Valuet, LRTC, vol. IA, 168–69.
[61] Cf. Valuet, LRTC, vol. IA, 168–69 (Donatists), 273n1190 (Cathars).
[62] Cf. Valuet, LRTE, 178. Valuet notes that scholars disagree on the question of whether the secular arm pursued heretics for reasons of public order (cf. LRTE, 179; see also LRTC, vol. IA, 271n1179). However, even if reasons of public order were not the *exclusive* motivation, Valuet says, they were the *principal* reason for the state's intervention (cf. LRTE, 179). He also asserts that heretics often violated temporal rights (LRTE, 179), and that the Inquisition pursued people not so much for error as for their bad faith (cf. LRTC, vol. IA, 276n1200).
[63] Cf. Valuet, LRTE, 179.
[64] Cf. Valuet, LRTC, vol. IA, 271n1179, citing Joseph Lecler, "Inquisition," *Catholicisme* 5 (1962): col. 1682–93, at col. 1685–86.
[65] Cf. Valuet, LRTE, 182.
[66] Cf. Novak, "Aquinas and the Heretics," 37.

the public order.[67] Valuet notes that the threat of their possible expansion would have constituted a danger to the religious liberty of Catholics,[68] and Thomas famously quotes St. Jerome on the dangers of moving too slowly against heresy: "Arius was but one spark in Alexandria, but as that spark was not at once put out, the whole earth was laid waste by its flame."[69]

Third among Novak's explanatory observations for Thomas's teaching on the heretics is that, for Thomas, heresy was not a mistaken intellectual idea but rather a willful choice to contradict the faith and to sever one's communion with the Church. That is, both Augustine and Aquinas saw heretics as acting in bad faith.[70] Vermeersch explains why the treatment of Christian heretics was harsher than the treatment of Jews and Muslims:

> [B]aptism makes a man the subject of the Church, and . . . heresy constitutes desertion and rebellion, which is a grievous sin in the sight of God, as the result of a *voluntary* abuse of grace.[71]

Again, the question of a heretic acting sincerely according to his conscience simply was not an option that presented itself concretely.[72] Valuet's historical and theological survey is exhaustive, and he identifies only one or two authors in these periods who grasped the possibility of a heretic embracing his belief in good faith.[73]

Perhaps there is a mistake of fact in Thomas's teaching. Both Novak and Brian Harrison observe that the teaching on heretics seems inconsistent with Thomas's own teaching that a person always is obliged to follow his own conscience, even if mistaken.[74] Although Thomas seems not to admit the

---

[67] Cf. Valuet, LRTE, 183.
[68] Cf. Valuet, LRTE, 183.
[69] ST II-II, q. 11, a. 3.
[70] Cf. Valuet, LRTC, vol. IA, 269n1169, citing Louis Janssens, Liberté de conscience et liberté religieuse (Paris: Desclée de Brouwer, 1964), 178n2; cf. Roger Aubert, "Le problème de la liberté religieuse à travers l'histoire du christianisme," *Scripta Theologica* 1 (1969): 377–401, at 385; cf. LRTE, 154, 181.
[71] Vermeersch, *Tolerance*, 55.
[72] Cf. Valuet, LRTC, vol. IA, 268–69.
[73] Salvian, a priest of Marseille in the mid fifth century, is one of the few who glimpsed the possibility of good faith on the part of heretics, namely, the Arian Goths. Cf. Valuet, LRTE, 123. See also Lecler, *Toleration and the Reformation*, 1:52: "It is true that they are heretics, but they are so unwittingly. From our point of view they are heretics, from theirs they are not" (quoting Salvian, *De gubernatione Dei*, V, 2 [PL 53:95–96]).
[74] Cf. Novak, "Aquinas and the Heretics," 36; Brian W. Harrison, *Religious Liberty and Contraception: Did Vatican II Open the Way for a New Sexual Ethic?* (Melbourne: John

possibility that a Christian heretic could be sincere in his beliefs,[75] Harrison notes that as a result of historical experience and the insights of modern psychology, we now know that the reasons for the continuing disunity among Christians are more complex than once were supposed.[76]

One can add that Harrison's and Novak's arguments are buttressed by the fact that Thomas compares a heretic's unbelief to the breaking of a vow.[77] This comparison makes clear that, for Thomas, heresy is a matter not of sincere belief but of certain knowledge of an obligation freely incurred, coupled with a willful refusal to fulfill that obligation. For Thomas, then, conscience provides no more justification for embracing a heresy than it does for breaking a wedding vow or a religious vow. John Finnis, however, notes that Thomas's premise is "unsound." That is, the rationale for coercing a heretic is that he has broken his promise, but this justification rests on a promise that not all heretics actually have made.[78]

In addition, Valuet notes that an important development occurred in the late seventeenth century. Indeed, he describes it as a rupture with the medieval position. In a 1690 decree condemning Jansenist propositions, the Holy

---

XXIII Fellowship Co-op., Ltd., 1988), 130. Similarly, Valuet identifies several components in Thomas's teaching that, taken together, generate a conclusion roughly equivalent to that of DH, namely, that the state is obliged to ensure the conditions necessary to allow man to act according to a correct or invincibly ignorant conscience and to be protected from having to act against his conscience (cf. LRTE, 160). Thomas, however, did not connect these strands in his own thought and thus did not arrive at such a teaching, except in a couple of distinct areas, such as the right of parents to educate their children.

In addition, in reviewing Thomas's treatment of how the civil authority treats individual vice (cf. ST I-II, q. 96, a. 2), namely, by reprobating it only if it disturbs the peace of the city, Valuet asserts that one logically should conclude from this that if religious propaganda (even when false) poses no harm to the peace of the city, then the civic authorities should not impede it (cf. LRTE, 151). Thomas, however, did not draw this conclusion.

[75] Walter Kasper makes a similar point with regard to atheism. He notes that both Scripture and the writings of the church fathers always view godlessness as a willful decision to refuse to acknowledge the God that one knows. Kasper, *The God of Jesus Christ* (New York: Crossroad, 1996), 48. "[A] complete ignorance of God that is also inculpable seems to them an impossibility" (Kasper, 49).

[76] Cf. Harrison, RL&C, 130. See also *Catholic Encyclopedia*, s.v. "Toleration, History."

[77] ST II-II, q. 10, a. 8, reply obj. 3.

[78] "In Aquinas's more famous, later discussion, in the *Summa Theologiae*, all the weight falls on that last idea: heretics have broken their promise, and like other promise-breakers are punishable by reason of that fault. This last argument is unsound in its reliance on a promise not all heretics had even actually made, but again there is no trace of a *punitive purpose of inducing belief*." John Finnis, "Reflections and Responses [26: Response to Thomas Pink]," in *Reason, Morality, and Law: The Philosophy of John Finnis*, ed. John Keown and Robert P. George (Oxford: Oxford University Press, 2013), 569.

Office addressed the principle of *invincible ignorance*. That is, it condemned the proposition that invincible ignorance of the natural law does *not* excuse one of formal sin.[79] Thus, Valuet asserts, it follows that invincible ignorance of revelation also can excuse a person of any formal sin of infidelity.

15.4. Coercion of the Baptized

Thomas Pink argues that the baptized remain subject to coercion by the Church, and potentially by states acting on behalf of the Church.[80] As a consequence, Pink says, the right of the baptized to religious liberty is qualified or conditioned by their baptism.[81] However, this seems to be a diplomatic way of saying that, once baptized, a person does not have the right to religious liberty. Stated differently, one is free to decide whether to enter the Church but not whether to remain in the Church or to depart. (Of course, Pink's theory would protect the person from coercion by the state as such but not by the Church or by the state acting at the Church's behest. See section 11.3 and subsection 11.3.2.) Moreover, for Pink, such coercion means actual coercion of belief:

> Part of the authority she [the Church] has from God to bind and loose is the authority coercively to hold the Christian faithful true to baptismal obligations—obligations to belief and practice that they can have incurred at baptism without their personal

---

[79] Cf. Valuet, LRTE, 173, citing Holy Office, Decree Condemning Jansenist Propositions (Dec. 7, 1690), *DzSch*, 2302.

[80] "The unbaptized had no obligation of fidelity to the Church, and so could never rightly be coerced into Catholic belief or practice. But the baptized did have such obligations; and so, once properly instructed, they could be threatened with punishments to coerce them into the faith, should their unbelief ever be expressed." Thomas Pink, "The Right to Religious Liberty and the Coercion of Belief," in *Reason, Morality, and Law: The Philosophy of John Finnis*, ed. John Keown and Robert P. George (Oxford: Oxford University Press, 2013), 428. Cf. Pink, 433: "[I]f the state is Christian, its rulers as baptized can in particular be under an obligation to assist the Church in coercion for religious ends, should such assistance be requested"; Pink, 435: The assertion in DH §12 that "it has always remained the teaching of the Church that no one's faith is to be coerced" applies only to the unbaptized; Pink, 439: "That the coercion would be equally wrong when the person is baptized and the authority behind the coercion is the Church cannot be assumed to follow," from DH §2.

[81] Cf. Pink, "Religious Liberty and the Coercion of Belief," 439: "Whenever the right to liberty is grounded by the declaration on considerations X and Y, it must be left open that X or Y might not strictly be enough—that also necessary must be an absence of the kind of normative juridical relation that a baptized person has to the Church."

consent, and that continue to bind them once baptized irrespective of whether they still consent.[82]

Dignitatis humanae in no way denies the doctrine of the right and authority to pressure religious belief and practice on which the Church's past policies, once very coercive indeed, were historically based. Policy may have changed through the Vatican II declaration, but the underlying doctrine of coercive authority has not.[83]

The second quotation immediately above is from an essay by Pink that was included in a *Festschrift* in honor of the noted philosopher John Finnis. In turn, Finnis responded to the various essays and, in his response to Pink, he challenged the notion that the object or purpose of ecclesiastical penalties—especially as understood by St. Thomas—is to coerce belief. "Such a project, precisely one of inflicting punishment in order to bring about Christian belief (albeit via 'impelled' attention to evidence), was always vigorously rejected by Aquinas."[84] Thomas's justification for proceeding against heretics, rather, was to prevent them from corrupting others.[85]

There can be no denying that the coercion of heretics has at times been a part of the life of the Church. This includes ecclesiastical policy and the common opinion of theologians and canonists in the medieval period and into the twentieth century. Guminski and Harrison frame the issue precisely. Church policy and common theological opinion asserted or assumed that the Church had the authority to coerce heretics even by temporal penalties typical of civil authorities (and to do so either by her own action or through the state).[86] At the same time, however, they note that "another legitimate well-founded probable theological opinion" to the contrary existed, namely, denying that the Church has the authority to inflict temporal penalties typical of the civil authority.[87]

---

[82] "What is the Catholic Doctrine of Religious Liberty?" (expanded version June 15, 2012), §7 [p. 44], Academia, accessed July 16, 2022, https://www.academia.edu/es/639061/What_is_the_Catholic_doctrine_of_religious_liberty.

[83] Pink, "Religious Liberty and the Coercion of Belief," 427.

[84] Finnis, "Response to Pink," 568.

[85] Cf. Finnis, "Response to Pink," 568. See also Finnis, 569, 577.

[86] Cf. Guminski/Harrison, 228–29, 256–57. Note that the work cited here is comprised primarily of a debate between the two authors on whether DH contradicts previous Church teaching. (Guminski believes that it does, and Harrison believes that it does not.) However, both authors collaborated on a substantial appendix entitled, "The Scope and Limits of the Church's Inherent Coercive Power" (cf. Guminski/Harrison, Appendix A, 225–62).

[87] Cf. Guminski/Harrison, 256–57. The proponents include respected figures such as

15.4. Coercion of the Baptized

If ecclesiastical policy and the common opinion of theologians provided abundant support for this type of coercion, however, Church doctrine did not. Guminski and Harrison acknowledge that several doctrinal pronouncements may be read as attributing this authority to the Church, but they note that these documents also are open to the interpretation that she does not have the authority to impose temporal penalties typical of the civil authority.[88]

For his part, Pink relies heavily on canon 14 of the seventh session of the Council of Trent. That canon concerned a proposal by Erasmus to the effect that persons baptized as children, upon reaching adulthood, should be asked whether they wish to continue to fulfill their baptismal obligations. If they do not wish to do so, then Erasmus proposed that, aside from being prohibited from receiving the sacraments, they should be left to themselves and should not be "coerced by any penalty into the Christian life." Canon 14 rejected this proposition and attached an anathema to it.[89]

Pink cites this canon as a pronouncement justifying the Church's coercive power over the baptized, even to the extent of coercing actual belief. The text of the canon does not speak of coercion of belief, though it does refer to coercion into the Christian life. All that it seems to stand for, however, is the idea that when faced with a person who refuses to fulfill his baptismal obligations, the Church is not limited solely to prohibiting

---

Arthur Vermeersch and Thomas-Marie-Joseph Cardinal Gousset (cf. Guminski/Harrison, 257–61). Guminski and Harrison are clear in acknowledging, however, that common theological opinion supported coercion of the sort typical of civil authorities (cf. Guminski/Harrison, 228–29).

[88] Cf. Guminski/Harrison, 229, 256–57. For their review of the specific pronouncements, see Guminski/Harrison, 251–56. The one discussed below is the one that Thomas Pink especially relies on.

[89] Pink asserts that this is a dogmatic canon, and he says that it long was understood as *de fide*. "Subsequent theologians viewed this decree as de fide, and as defining the legitimacy of the use of coercion to enforce baptismal obligations on heretics and apostates, including the central baptismal obligation to faith." Thomas Pink, "The Interpretation of *Dignitatis Humanae*: A Reply to Martin Rhonheimer," *Nova et Vetera* (English ed.) 11, no. 1 (2013): 98. Cf. Pink, "Religious Liberty and the Coercion of Belief," 429: "Trent's teaching is a dogmatic canon." Finnis, however, cites the noted authority on the Council of Trent, Hubert Jedin, as cautioning against too readily making such an assumption. "The modern theological historian of the Council [of Trent] reminds us that 'the canons, with their appended anathemas, are not to be regarded, without more ado, as so many definitions *de fide*'" (Finnis, "Response to Pink," 574n89, citing Jedin, *A History of the Council of Trent*, vol. 1, *The Struggle for the Council*, trans. Ernest Graf (London: Thomas Nelson, 1957), 381). For my own part, I have difficulty interpreting the canon as dogmatic, given that it concerns how a particular offense is to be punished.

the sacraments to this person. This is unremarkable, however. It merely means that the Church would have additional measures at her disposal, presumably including some temporal penalties. For example, if the person enjoyed an ecclesiastical office, he might be deprived of it. Guminski and Harrison note that canon 14 essentially describes the difference between the penalties of minor excommunication and major excommunication.[90] Minor excommunication referred to deprivation of the sacraments, and major excommunication added additional penalties as well. This canon from the Council of Trent presents no difficulty, however, because even the temporal penalties incident to excommunication are not of the same type as those typical of civil authorities.[91]

In one sense, Pink's claim is correct. That is, the baptized who commit ecclesiastical offenses are indeed subject to a certain type of *pressuring activity*. As in the past, even in some contexts today, this application of ecclesiastical penalties may be called the Church's *coercive authority*. However, discussion of the matter is complicated by Pink's refusal to distinguish between state coercion and Church penalties. (See subsection 11.3.1.) He insists that they are of the same nature. Pink's position, however, is inconsistent with the explanations of the official relator for the declaration. Bishop De Smedt made clear both that the Church herself is precluded from engaging in religious coercion in civil society and that her application of penal sanctions (though a part of her *compelling power*) does not amount to *coercion*. See section 11.3 and subsection 11.3.1.

The citations that appear in the final version of the declaration are limited to the names of the cited works themselves and the specific page or section of the work supporting the point at issue. No quotations are included. In the previous drafts, however, the cited passages actually were quoted for the benefit of the council fathers deliberating over them. Guminski and Harrison draw attention to two documents from Pope Pius XII (quoted in the earlier drafts of the declaration) strongly supporting the idea that

---

[90] In the Roman Catholic Church today, the penalty of excommunication remains, but it no longer is qualified as minor or major (cf. can. 1331). Rather, all excommunications essentially are major excommunications. However, in the Eastern Catholic Churches, the earlier terminology survives. Thus, the penalty that the Roman Church describes as interdict is called minor excommunication in the Eastern Churches (cf. *Codex Canonum Ecclesiarum Orientalium* [CCEO] [Vatican City: Typis Poliglottis Vaticanis, 1990], can. 1431, §1), and excommunication is called major excommunication (cf. CCEO, can. 1434).

[91] "[E]ven these more burdensome ecclesiastical penalties are still milder than the kinds of coercion typically used only by civil authorities" (Guminski/Harrison, 251).

15.4. Coercion of the Baptized

it is not only the unbaptized who enjoy freedom from coercion but the already-baptized as well.[92]

Leo XIII had stated in *Immortale Dei* that no one is to be forced to embrace the Catholic faith against his will (cf. ID, §36). It is not clear from the encyclical itself, however, whether Leo meant to refer only to the unbaptized or to the baptized as well. In *Mystici Corporis*, however, Pius XII cites this passage and seems to interpret it as applying even to the baptized. "Though We desire this unceasing prayer to rise to God from the whole Mystical Body in common that all the straying sheep may hasten to enter the one fold of Jesus Christ, yet We recognize that this must be done of their own free will; for no one believes unless he wills to believe."[93] Moreover, in an allocution to the Roman Rota three years later, Pius quoted Lactantius:

> There is no need of violence or injustice. Religion cannot be imposed by force. To obtain what we desire, words, not blows should be used. That is why we keep no one who does not wish to stay with us.... The man without loyalty and faith is useless before God.... There is nothing so voluntary as religion.[94]

Then the pontiff explains the passage's significance:

> According to the principles of Catholic teaching, conversion should be the result not of coercion from without but of sincere interior assent to the truths taught by the Catholic Church. That is why the Catholic Church grants admission to those adults desired to be received *or to return to her* only on condition that they are fully conscious of the meaning and effect of the action they propose to take.[95]

---

[92] Cf. Guminski/Harrison, 242–50. Guminski addresses this matter again in his essay, "An Examination of Thomas Pink's Theory of the Doctrine Concerning Religious Freedom in *Dignitatis Humanae*," (Dec. 6, 2015), Academia, §62, and Addendum II on "The Content of Notes 12 and 13 in the *Textus Denuo Recognitus*," accessed July 16, 2022, https://www.academia.edu/19523482/An_Examination_of_Thomas_Pinks_Theory_of_the_Doctrine_concerning_Religious_Freedom_in_Dignitatis_Humanae.

[93] Pius XII, Encyclical *Mystici Corporis* (1943), §104. Pius does not cite *Immortale Dei* for this particular sentence, but he cites it shortly afterwards in the same passage. Note that Guminski interprets the term "straying sheep" to refer to baptized Catholics who have fallen away, but Harrison disagrees. Nonetheless, both authors agree that Pius would think that if lapsed Catholics are to return, they must do so freely (cf. Guminski/Harrison, 244n37).

[94] Pius XII, Allocution to the Roman Rota (Oct. 6, 1946) [AAS 38 (1946): 391–97], quoting Lactantius, *Divinae institutiones*, t. 5, c. 19.

[95] Pius XII, Allocution to the Roman Rota, (emphasis added).

Note the full import of these passages, as discussed by Guminski and Harrison. First, these passages are fully consistent with the text of the declaration and with the relator's explanation that no adult is to be subject to religious coercion.[96] As a result, they necessarily support the teaching of DH. In addition, these very documents and these very passages in them were cited in the final version of the declaration. Finally, during the drafting process and the debates, the council fathers actually had these quotations before them because they were included in earlier drafts of the declaration.[97]

Thus, it seems apparent that the right to immunity from coercion applies not only to the unbaptized but to the baptized as well. In addition, despite the presence of coercion in the Church's history and policy, the Church's actual doctrine is consistent with the teaching of the declaration.

15.5. Insights and Limitations of the O'Neil Approach

O'Neil does not explain entirely the development of the Church's teaching on religious liberty, but he contributes to a more profound understanding of the question. He is correct that a significant shift takes place with the realization that nonacceptance of Catholic dogma does not necessarily pose a danger to the Church and civil society, and this insight partially explains the reason for the delay in the emergence of a teaching on religious liberty. To O'Neil's point, one may add that the impetus for the shift need not necessarily have been a conclusion that non-Catholic propaganda was harmless but rather a realization that repression often might do more harm than good.

O'Neil's theory also might point to a principle of consistency running throughout Catholic teaching and life in this area. This is the idea that religious liberty is not absolute, and that the requirements of the "public order" provide the standard for determining whether repression of religious expression is just (cf. DH, §§4b, 7c). This standard provides a way of interpreting past history in light of Vatican II, and explaining previous policies of persecution in terms of what was necessary for the protection of the public order. Of course, the benefit of hindsight might lead one to conclude that the perceived danger sometimes was more apparent than real.

---

[96] "[C]oercion [*coactio*] towards adults in society and in the state, in religious matters, in the sense expressed in the first part of the Declaration, is itself unjust [*de se iniusta est*]." AS IV/6, 761, quoted in Barrett Hamilton Turner, "*Dignitatis Humanae* and the Development of Moral Doctrine: Assessing Change in Catholic Social Teaching on Religious Liberty" (PhD diss., Catholic University of America, 2015), 318.

[97] Cf. Guminski, "An Examination," Addendum II.

15.5. Insights and Limitations of the O'Neil Approach

In this circumstance, the belief in the necessity of repression nonetheless may have been sincere and reasonable. However, as the Council recognizes, the desire to protect the public order or the common good sometimes resulted in measures that were excessive, disproportional, or unjust (cf. DH, §12a).

O'Neil's observations are indeed helpful. By focusing on judgments about the necessity (or perceived necessity) of religious repression, he provides another perspective for consideration of the Council's limitations on religious activity, according to the requirements of the *just public order*. His reflections on changes in both circumstances and thinking help to illuminate how the principle and standard of public order can remain more or less constant, even through many different historical periods. As discussed in chapter 12, Harrison develops this idea in a different way, particularly in his examination of how Church doctrine can remain consistent even amid significant modifications to the Church's public ecclesiastical law. Although O'Neil's article is premised on the eventual realization that religious repression no longer (or only rarely) is necessary to protect the just public order, he does not explain how or when this realization took hold. To shed light on this question, I turn to Basile Valuet and Walter Kasper in the next chapter and to the crucial issue of reciprocity.

CONCLUSION

CHAPTER 16

The Appeal to "Changed Circumstances," Part 3

The Delay in Recognizing the Right to Religious Liberty

[I]n centuries to come, there may be found out some way of uniting what is free in the new structure of society with what is authoritative in the old, without any base compromise with "Progress" and "Liberalism."

— ST. JOHN HENRY NEWMAN[1]

16.1. Murray after the Council

If anyone was an indispensable person on the journey toward the Church's recognition of the right to religious liberty, it may have been John Courtney Murray. It would be difficult to identify another person who made as many significant contributions to the declaration. (See section 9.2 above.) The only contenders that come to mind as contributors possibly even more significant than Murray are Pope St. Paul VI and the official relator of DH, Bishop Émile De Smedt, and, indeed, one could argue that either or both of them may have been even more important than Murray. However, their importance was especially in judging among the proposals of the various council fathers and in crafting a broadly acceptable declaration. Murray's contributions, on the other hand, largely were based on his own ideas. As a result, he justly occupies a unique place in the document's history, and

---

[1] John Henry Newman, Letter to the Duke of Norfolk (Dec. 27, 1874), reprinted in *Newman and Gladstone: The Vatican Decrees*, with an introduction by Alvan S. Ryan (Notre Dame, IN: University of Notre Dame Press, 1962), 144.

to a large degree, it is fitting that his name is identified so closely with the declaration.

Yet, as noted repeatedly in this work, Murray by no means prevailed in every dispute concerning DH. Indeed, in the crucial struggle over the foundation of the right, he won an important victory in moving the Secretariat away from the argument from conscience, but he failed in his attempt to base the right on the state's incompetence in religious matters. It is understandable that the final version of the declaration would be the source of mixed feelings for Murray, but what is startling is the degree to which some of his statements shortly after the Council minimize the document's importance and actually seem almost to border on disdain for the final version.

> It can hardly be maintained that the Declaration is a milestone in human history—moral, political, or intellectual. The principle of religious freedom has long been recognized in constitutional law, to the point where even Marxist-Leninist political ideology is obliged to pay lip-service to it. In all honesty it must be admitted that the Church is late in acknowledging the validity of the principle.[2]

By the same token, Murray's protégé Richard Regan, in his history of the drafting of the declaration, takes a very similar position, thus downplaying its importance, denying its originality, and lamenting its late arrival:

> The Declaration was hardly an earth-shaking intellectual, political, or theological event; it only recognized the consensus of modern thought, national constitutions, and professional theologians on principles of religious freedom. Indeed, nineteen hundred and sixty-five, two-thirds of the way to the twenty-first century, seemed rather late to lay a nineteenth-century problem to rest.[3]

---

[2] John Courtney Murray, "Religious Freedom," in *The Documents of Vatican II*, ed. Walter M. Abbott (New York: Herder and Herder, 1966), 673. See also Murray, "Vers une intelligence du développement de la doctrine de l'Église sur la liberté religieuse," *Unam Sanctam* 60 (1967): 111: "L'objet réel de la Déclaration était simplement de mettre l'Église de plain-pied avec la conscience commune de l'humanité civilisée, qui a déjà accepté le principe et l'institution légale de la liberté religieuse."

[3] Richard J. Regan, *Conflict and Consensus: Religious Freedom and the Second Vatican Council* (New York/London: Macmillan/Collier-Macmillan Ltd., 1967), 167. Regan goes on to say, "It is also true that the final text was neither the perfect nor the best of the series of conciliar texts, especially in the construction of the argument for the principle of religious freedom" (Regan, 167). This likely indicates his disappointment that the fifth and sixth

Journalist Henri Fesquet, who covered the Council, also lamented the perceived lateness of its taking up of the subject of religious liberty:

> Considerably later than the secular forces for liberty, Vatican II has come to the defense of the cause of man, irrespective of belief, in the wake of a unique encyclical, *Pacem in terris*. In a century of political totalitarianisms, it is high time the Church, which claims to be the authentic heir of the evangelical patrimony, solemnly proclaimed her belief in liberty.[4]

This distinct lack of enthusiasm on the part of Murray and others is surprising, but perhaps it is understandable. Given the long-standing recognition of the right to religious liberty, how does one account for the extensive delay in the Church's recognition of that right? Can a Catholic reflect on the declaration only with, at best, relief—that is, relief at the Church's finally *catching up* to the consensus of modern constitutional thought—or, at worst, with embarrassment at such a long delay?

16.2. An Assumption

The frustration of Murray, Regan, and Fesquet seems to be rooted in this apparent assumption that what the declaration stands for is indeed the Church's *catching up* to the modern consensus on religious liberty. Murray certainly was aware that DH was far from a simple adoption of secular rights theory, and Regan no doubt was as well. However, these particular observations noted above emphasize the commonalities, and this is the source of their disenchantment with the document.[5]

Other commentators, too, frame the issue along these lines. Thus, historian Thomas Bokenkotter views Vatican II as an acceptance of the Enlightenment and of Catholic Liberalism. Lamennais's Catholic Liberalism was an attempt to come to terms with the French Revolution, he says, and Vatican II marks the acceptance of liberal theory.[6]

---

drafts, the *Textus Recognitus* and the *Textus Denuo Recognitus*, moved away from Murray's position on the foundation of the right.

[4] Henri Fesquet, *The Drama of Vatican II* (New York: Random House, 1967), 335, commenting on the opening of the debate on religious liberty in the third session in September 1964.

[5] In other works, their emphasis falls elsewhere, and this somewhat startling expression of underappreciation of the declaration is absent or moderated.

[6] "[A] small number of Catholics . . . began a movement to reconcile the Church with the

The burden of this work has been to demonstrate that Vatican II, in fact, represents something very different. Murray and Regan are correct that there are commonalities among the Council and the modern consensus on human rights. However, Bokenkotter is quite mistaken to interpret the Vatican II achievement as the mere *taking over* of Lamennais's position or as nothing more than a simple *catching up* to the modern consensus.

Rather, Vatican II and the recent popes *join* the nineteenth-century popes in diagnosing the problems with the Enlightenment conception of rights, and then the Council (like the mid- and late-twentieth-century popes, and the popes up to today) *build* on the work of the nineteenth-century popes by *salvaging* the genuine insights of the Enlightenment and by placing them on an entirely new foundation. Parts 3A and 3B of this study examined the differences in these understandings of rights. They demonstrated, in particular, that the right that DH affirms differs in object, scope, and foundation from the right that the nineteenth-century popes had rejected.

What made the Vatican II affirmation possible? What enabled the Church to sift out the genuine insights and to locate a new foundation for them? Walter Kasper offers an insightful reflection on this question.

16.3. Kasper's Contribution

Walter Kasper has written about religious liberty in terms somewhat similar to those of Patrick O'Neil. (See chapter 15.) Kasper does not purport to explain the doctrinal development between the nineteenth century and Vatican II, but he does provide an explanation of the philosophical context of both *Dignitatis Humanae* and previous papal teaching. He does this in connection with providing the theological underpinnings for the Catholic acceptance of the idea of human rights.[7]

Most importantly, Kasper distinguishes between the philosophical ideas that the popes rejected in the nineteenth century and the ones that Vatican II embraces in the Declaration on Religious Liberty. As suggested in chapter 1, there is a danger that the Church's acceptance of religious liberty will be interpreted as a cynical capitulation to the same Enlightenment ideas that

---

Revolution—liberal Catholicism. It was to fail for many reasons, and not until Vatican II (1962–1965) would the Church finally lay to rest its antiliberal position and officially endorse the liberal doctrines on such issues as separation of church and state, freedom of conscience, freedom of speech, and freedom of the press." Thomas Bokenkotter, *Church and Revolution: Catholics in the Struggle for Democracy and Social Justice* (New York: Image Books, 1998), 39–40.

[7] See generally Walter Kasper, "The Theological Foundations of Human Rights," *The Jurist* 50 (1990): 148–66.

the popes formerly rejected. Kasper explains why such an accusation would be unfounded.

The popes did indeed reject the theories of rights that arose from the Enlightenment and nineteenth-century Catholic Liberalism. The reason was that the bases that were put forward for these rights were incompatible with Church teaching. Kasper does not expand on this conflict, but he seems to be referring to the way in which many Enlightenment thinkers valorized man's rational faculty and his ability to seek and obtain the truth. These thinkers often denigrated man's spiritual faculty and regarded revelation as an illegitimate, or at least inferior, source of knowledge.[8] Many Enlightenment thinkers were skeptical about the human capacity to know the truth in religious matters. The only possible exception concerned moral truths. John Locke believed that it was possible to deduce moral principles in a way similar to mathematical proofs. As a result, Enlightenment thinkers sought to simplify the doctrinal aspects of religion and to place a stronger emphasis on morality. In the words of Voltaire,

> There is no morality in superstition, it is not in ceremonies, it has nothing in common with dogmas. It cannot be too often repeated that all dogmas are different, and that morality is the same among all men who use their reason. Therefore morality comes from god like light. Our superstitions are nothing but darkness.[9]

The result was that the religion that a person chose was largely a matter of indifference by Enlightenment standards, so long as morality was maintained.[10]

---

[8] In the nineteenth century, proponents of a different intellectual trend, positivism, would identify sensory experience rather than reason as the sole source of knowledge. Needless to say, this theory was as incompatible with Catholicism as rationalism was. In addition, the proponents would establish a Positivist Church. Similar in structure to the Catholic Church but wholly secular, it was described as "Catholicism without Christianity." *The New Catholic Encyclopedia* (New York: McGraw-Hill Book Co., 1967), s.v. "Positivism."

[9] Voltaire, *Philosophical Dictionary*, ed. and trans. Theodore Besterman (Harmondsworth, England: Penguin Books, 1972), s.v. "Morality," 322. Cf. Voltaire, s.v. "Dogmas," 179–81. Voltaire's confidence in the unity of men in a common morality is emblematic of Enlightenment thought. He almost certainly overstates the actual consensus existing in the eighteenth century, but there is no doubt some truth to this observation. However, his apparent expectation that the consensus would endure was entirely mistaken. It was at least crumbling by the late nineteenth century, and it already had eroded significantly by the early twentieth century.

[10] However, because he considered Catholicism to be a danger to the state, Locke taught that it should not be tolerated. "That Church can have no right to be tolerated by the

At the time of the nineteenth-century papal pronouncements, Kasper argues, it was impossible to separate the rights that were advocated from the philosophical assumptions that supported them. That is, because rationalism, skepticism, and indifferentism were so utterly incompatible with Catholic teaching, there was no way for the popes to accept the assertion of the various liberties that sprang from these ideas. This was true not only for philosophical reasons but also because the governments that championed these rights attacked the Church so unmercifully throughout most of the nineteenth century and denied to her the rights that were claimed for others.

Kasper's insight is that despite the Church's eventual acceptance of religious liberty, this acceptance came without any acquiescence in the thought systems of the Enlightenment and Catholic Liberalism. Kasper recounts the history of *Dignitatis Humanae* to show how the Church was able both to embrace a modern theory of human rights and still respect the concerns of the nineteenth-century popes:

> [T]he council adopted a positive attitude toward the modern conception of human rights and human dignity; but it did not simply take it over.... It tried to judge the modern conception of human rights in the light of its own tradition. In so doing, it was able to recognize the positive aspects of human rights and to differentiate them from historically conditioned polemical, anti-clerical strictures.... Of the substantial concerns of the 19th century popes nothing was thereby relinquished. Rather, the council provided an original, specifically theological foundation in continuity with the tradition.[11]

Kasper argues that the Council based its idea of religious liberty not on the Enlightenment ideas of rationalism, skepticism, and indifferentism but on the original and distinctively Christian basis of the dignity of the human person. Human dignity itself has two theological bases: (1) the equal creation of all men and women in God's image, and (2) Christ's eradication of differences among persons. "There is neither Jew nor Greek, there is neither slave nor free, there is neither male nor female; for you are all one in Christ Jesus" (Gal 3:28). The transformation of the world by Christ

---

magistrate which is constituted upon such a bottom that all those who enter into it do thereby *ipso facto* deliver themselves up to the protection and service of another prince." John Locke, "A Letter Concerning Toleration," in *John Locke on Politics and Education*, with an introduction by Howard R. Penniman (Roslyn, NY: Walter J. Black, Inc., 1947), 57–58.

[11] Kasper, "Theological Foundations," 156.

affects not Christians alone, but, in a mysterious way, all persons.[12] "For, by his incarnation, he, the son of God, has in a certain way united himself with each man" (GS, §22b).

Although the Enlightenment reflected a general pessimism concerning the ability of the human person to arrive at religious truth, *Dignitatis Humanae* bases religious liberty on a concept of human dignity that specifically includes an ability to know and to seek the truth in religious matters. Kasper's insight is twofold. First, he shows that the liberty proclaimed in *Dignitatis Humanae* enjoys a different intellectual basis than the similar-sounding Enlightenment and Liberal ideas. Second, Kasper is astute in recognizing the novelty of the Church's approach. It is not the case, as it is often charged, that the Church simply is a latecomer to the cause for human rights. Nor is it the case that the Church has jumped onto the bandwagon of the Western democracies or the modern constitutional consensus. Rather, the Church is a true pioneer in this area, for in *Dignitatis Humanae* she has provided a distinctively Christian justification for religious liberty. In addition, the Church's approach holds out the possibility of avoiding or correcting the adverse consequences to which Enlightenment theories of rights lead.

Several circumstances show that Kasper's interpretation is indeed sound. The declaration's very title *Dignitatis Humanae* proclaims the centrality of human dignity to the question of religious liberty. Moreover, the text asserts directly that this right "has its foundation in the dignity of the person, whose exigencies have come to be . . . fully known to human reason through centuries of experience" (DH, §9). In this sense, *Dignitatis Humanae* represents the fulfillment of a dream to which St. John Henry Newman had given voice: "And thus, in centuries to come, there may be found out some way of uniting what is free in the new structure of society with what is authoritative in the old, without any base compromise with 'Progress' and 'Liberalism.'"[13]

Thus, Kasper, like O'Neil, provides a Catholic framework that comfortably accommodates the idea of religious liberty. Kasper does not purport to explain the doctrinal development itself, but he provides the philosophical counterpart to O'Neil's discussion of changed historical circumstances.

---

[12] Kasper's insights on human dignity all are valid. However, as discussed in chapter 9, one could draw out other aspects of human dignity as well. For example, Bishop Ancel emphasizes especially the human orientation toward the truth and his need for freedom in pursuing it. See subsection 9.3.3 and section 9.4 above. By the same token, one also could point to man's social nature. See section 11.2 above.

[13] Newman, Letter to the Duke of Norfolk, 144.

16.4. The Final Piece

As Kasper makes clear, the disengagement of the right to religious liberty from its initial foundation in rationalism, indifferentism, and skepticism required both time and reflection. More than that, a reformulation of the right itself was necessary to revise its object and scope. (See generally part 3A above.) The time required for this work accounts in large measure for the seeming delay in the Church's recognition of the right.

However, these were not the only factors delaying this recognition. Basile Valuet shows that another factor was crucial to clearing the way for this achievement. Moreover, this factor affected not only the Church but other entities as well.

The problem that Valuet identifies is the question of *reciprocity*. That is, as a result of the circumstances prevailing throughout much of history, the extension of liberty or even tolerance to members of minority religions could be dangerous. The difficulty was that no entity or religious community recognized a right to liberty on the part of the members of any other community.[14] As a result, the constant threat was that a minority religion or sect might seek tolerance when it was weak, bide its time to gain strength and to become a majority, and then attempt to supplant or marginalize the religion that formerly had enjoyed the majority.[15] Most religious minorities aspired to become the majority religion and, as a result, any significant growth of a minority tended to threaten the majority religion.[16]

The case of the American colony of Maryland is instructive. Led by Lord Baltimore, Catholic settlers in Maryland enacted the landmark Act of Toleration in 1649. As a result of the new law, Puritans facing persecution from Anglicans in Virginia began to move to Maryland. In fact, so many entered that they eventually came to outnumber the original Catholic settlers. Once they did, they enacted harsh anti-Catholic legislative measures.[17] As a result, the experiment in toleration abruptly came to an end.

The lack of reciprocity, Valuet says, was the chief factor that not only prevented the discernment of the principle of religious liberty but that also revealed why the principle was inapplicable before modern times.[18] Javier

---

[14] Cf. Basile Valuet, *Le droit à la liberté religieuse dans la Tradition de l'Eglise. Un cas de développement doctrinal homogène par le magistère authentique*, 2nd rev. ed. (Barroux: Éditions Sainte-Madeleine, 2011), 515.

[15] Cf. Valuet, LRTE, 172.

[16] Cf. Valuet, LRTE, 236.

[17] Cf. Steven Waldman, *Founding Faith: Providence, Politics, and the Birth of Religious Freedom in America* (New York: Random House, 2008), 16. See also Valuet, LRTE, 183.

[18] Cf. Valuet, LRTE, 183 = Basile Valuet, *La liberté religieuse et la tradition catholique. Un cas*

Hervada explains the impact of historical developments on the efficacy of natural rights. A natural right must be known to be incorporated into the juridical system. However, even natural rights that are rooted in human nature itself sometimes come to be known only *progressively*. This is particularly the case with human rights. Hervada calls this process of knowledge *positivation*, and it is necessary for the right to acquire historical validity. Before positivation occurs, the right already exists but not in its full development. A further step, *formalization*, is necessary to guarantee the efficacy of the right and to incorporate it fully into the juridical system.[19]

The solution to the problem of reciprocity comes with the advent of international and inter-religious agreements that recognize religious rights on the part of all persons and communities. The two key documents in this regard are the United Nations' Universal Declaration of Human Rights (1948) and the Declaration of the Ecumenical Council of Churches (1961). The inclusion of reciprocity in these pronouncements, Valuet says, made it not only possible but urgent for the Catholic Church to address the question of religious liberty.[20] The advent of reciprocity provides the indispensable condition for the recognition of a right to religious liberty, and indeed it results in a crucial development in the law of nations (*ius gentium*).[21]

16.5. Conclusion

Most fundamentally, this work has addressed the question, *What is the place of this Declaration in the life of the Church?* (See chapter 1.) There are two primary aspects of this question: *Does* Dignitatis Humanae *contradict the teachings of the nineteenth-century and twentieth-century popes?* and *What are the particular problems to which DH provides the solution?*

My answer to the first question is provided primarily in parts 3A and 3B (especially chapters 7 through 11), but also in part 4 (especially chapters 12 and 13). Chapters 7 through 11 concern the scope, object, and foundation of the right to religious liberty that Vatican II recognizes, and this

---

de développement doctrinal homogène dans le magistère authentique, 3rd rev. ed. (Barroux: Éditions Sainte-Madeleine, 2011), vol. IA, 273–74.

[19] Cf. Javier Hervada, *Critical Introduction to Natural Law*, trans. Mindy Emmons (Montreal: Wilson & Lafleur, 2006), 161–64.

[20] Cf. Valuet, LRTE, 515.

[21] Cf. Valuet, LRTE, 515. This development is a key theme in a recent dissertation. Cf. Barrett Hamilton Turner, dissertation "*Dignitatis Humanae* and the Development of Moral Doctrine: Assessing Change in Catholic Social Teaching on Religious Liberty" (Catholic University of America, 2015), 373–79.

investigation and analysis show that this right is not the same right that the nineteenth-century popes condemned. The Vatican II right does indeed share commonalities with the right discussed in the nineteenth-century pronouncements, namely, the subject matter of religious belief and practice. However, the Vatican II right differs in important respects. First, it is a right in civil society and not primarily a right situated in the moral realm (and not a right before God). Second, the content of the right is not a positive authorization to believe whatever one wishes, but rather it is an immunity from coercion and from interference. This difference, in particular, makes it possible for the Council to affirm a right to religious liberty without indifferently affirming the specific content of all religions. Finally, the right is founded on the dignity of the human person rather than on indifferentism or skepticism. In addition, chapters 12 and 13 make clear that the Vatican II right, unlike the right condemned by the nineteenth-century popes, is by no means unlimited. As a result, there is no contradiction between *Dignitatis Humanae* and the teachings of the nineteenth-century and twentieth-century popes.

With regard to the second question, *Dignitatis Humanae* makes clear that religious liberty is a natural right of the human person. That is, its foundation is not merely in positive law, political theory, or historical experience but, on the contrary, it is in the very nature of the person. Moreover, the specific aspects of the person that demand the acknowledgement of this right are above all his nature as a seeker of truth and his nature as a social being.

The declaration makes explicit what often was implicit in the earlier teaching, namely, the crucial importance of the integrity of the human person. That is, one's external life is to reflect one's internal convictions and, unless social harm results, the belief that one professes in private is to be lived out in public. Thus, the declaration not only avoids the modern errors that have led to the fragmentation and compartmentalization of the human person but, indeed, it provides a positive corrective to them.

Bibliography

Sources (Councils—U.S. Civil Decisions—Papal Documents—Roman Curia—U.S. Conference of Catholic Bishops [and subdivisions])

Acta Synodalia Sacrosancti Concilii Oecumenici Vaticani II. 32 vols. Vatican City: Typis Polyglottis Vaticanis, 1970–1999.

Application of the President and Directors of Georgetown College, 331 F., 2nd 1000 (DC Cir. 1964), *cert. denied*, 84 S. Ct. 1883 (1964).

Bertone, Tarcisio. "Magisterial Documents and Public Dissent." *L'Osservatore Romano*. January 29, 1997.

Bostock v. Clayton County, 140 S. Ct. 1731 (2020).

Catechism of the Catholic Church, 2nd ed. Vatican City: Libreria Editrice Vaticana, 1997.

Congregation for Divine Worship. Circular Letter *Quattuor Abhinc Annos*. October 3, 1984. AAS 76 (1984): 1088–89.

———. *Responsa ad Dubia*. On Certain Provisions of the Apostolic Letter *Traditionis Custodes*. December 4, 2021.

Congregation for the Doctrine of the Faith. Declaration on the Unicity and Salvific Universality of Jesus Christ and the Church *Dominus Iesus*. August 6, 2000. AAS 92 (2000): 742–65.

———. Doctrinal Commentary on the Concluding Formula of the *Professio Fidei*. June 29, 1998. AAS 90 (1998): 542–51.

———. Instruction on the Ecclesial Vocation of the Theologian *Donum Veritatis*. May 24, 1990. AAS 82 (1990): 1550–70.

———. Norms on Theological Dissent. June 29, 1997. AAS 89 (1997): 830–35.

Bibliography

———. "Note on Some Questions Concerning the Participation of Catholics in Political Life." November 24, 2002. AAS 96 (2004): 359–70.

———. "Observations on Father Charles Curran's Positions." *Origins* 15, no. 41 (1986): 170.

De Smedt, Émile. Oral *Relatio* on Chapter V of *De Oecumenismo*. November 19, 1963. AS II/5, 485–95.

———. Oral *Relatio* on the *Declaratio Prior*. September 23, 1964. AS III/2, 348–53.

———. Oral *Relatio* on the *Textus Denuo Recognitus*. November 19, 1965. AS IV/6, 719–23.

———. Oral *Relatio* on the *Textus Emendatus*. November 19, 1964. AS III/8, 449–56.

———. Oral *Relatio* on the *Textus Recognitus*. October 25, 1965. AS IV/5, 99–104.

Dichiarazione della Pontificia Commissione "Ecclesia Dei." October 27, 2012. Accessed December 19, 2020. https://web.archive.org/web/20121101161603/http://press.catholica.va/news_services/bulletin/news/29911.php?index=29911&lang=it#TESTO.

Everson v. Board of Education, 330 U.S. 1 (1947).

First Vatican Council. Dogmatic Constitution concerning the Catholic Faith *Dei Filius*. April 24, 1870. ASS 5 (1869–1870): 481–90.

———. Dogmatic Constitution on the Church of Christ *Pastor Aeternus*. July 18, 1870. ASS 6 (1870–1871): 40–47.

Gillette v. United States, 401 U.S. 437 (1971).

Holy Office. Decree *Lamentabili Sane*. July 3, 1907. ASS 40 (1907): 470–78.

Human Life in Our Day: A Collective Pastoral Letter of the American Hierarchy. November 15, 1968.

International Theological Commission. *Religious Freedom for the Good of All*. April 26, 2019.

Obergefell v. Hodges, 576 U.S. 644 (2015).

Pope Benedict XVI. Address to the Roman Curia. December 22, 2005. AAS 98 (2006): 40–53.

———. Wednesday Catechesis. "St. Irenaeus of Lyons." March 28, 2007.

———. Homily for Ash Wednesday. February 13, 2013. AAS 105 (2013): 269–72.

Pope Francis. Apostolic Letter *Misericordia et Misera*. November 20, 2016. AAS 108 (2016): 1311–27.

———. Apostolic Letter *Traditionis Custodes*. June 16, 2021.

Pope Gregory XVI. Encyclical *Commissum Divinitus*. On Church and State. Addressed to the Clergy of Switzerland. May 17, 1835. English translation from EWTN online library. https://www.ewtn.com/catholicism/library/on-church-and-state-3368.

———. Encyclical *Mirari Vos*. August 15, 1832. ASS 4 (1868): 336–45.

———. Encyclical *Singulari Nos*. June 25, 1834. *Acta Gregorii XVI*, vol. 1 (Rome 1901): 433–34.

Pope John XXIII. Encyclical *Pacem in Terris*. April 11, 1963. AAS 55 (1963): 257–304.

Pope John Paul II. Address to the Diplomatic Corps Accredited to the Holy See. January 13, 1990. AAS 82 (1990): 860–70.

———. Address to the Members of the Paasikivi Society. Helsinki. June 5, 1989. *L'Osservatore Romano*. English edition. June 19, 1989.

———. Apostolic Letter Motu Proprio *Ad Tuendam Fidem*. May 18, 1998. AAS 90 (1998): 457–61.

———. Apostlolic Letter Motu Proprio *Ecclesia Dei Adflicta*. July 2, 1988. AAS 80 (1988): 1495–98.

———. Apostolic Letter *Orientale Lumen*. May 2, 1995. AAS 87 (1995): 745–74.

———. Apostolic Letter *Tertio Millenio Adveniente*. November 10, 1994. AAS 87 (1995): 5–41.

———. Encyclical *Evangelium Vitae*. March 25, 1995. AAS 87 (1995): 401–522.

———. Encyclical *Veritatis Splendor*. August 6, 1993. AAS 85 (1993): 1132–1228.

———. Message to Congress on Secularism and Religious Liberty. December 7, 1995. In *L'Osservatore Romano*. English ed. December 10–27, 1995.

Pope Leo X. Bull *Exsurge Domine*. June 15, 1520. *CIC Fontes* 1, 129–34.

Pope Leo XII. Encyclical *Ubi Primum*. May 5, 1824. Bull. Rom. IV (Continuatio) (Prato), VIII (1854), 53–57.

Pope Leo XIII. Apostolic Letter *Apostolicae Curae*. September 13, 1896. ASS 29 (1896–1897): 193–203.

———. Apostolic Letter *Au Milieu des Sollicitudes*. February 16, 1892. ASS 24 (1891–1892): 519–59.

———. Encyclical *Diuturnum Illud*. June 29, 1881. ASS 14 (1881): 3–14.

———. Encyclical *Immortale Dei*. November 1, 1885. ASS 18 (1885–1886): 161–80.

———. Encyclical *Libertas*. June 20, 1888. ASS 20 (1887–1888): 593–613.

———. Encyclical *Longinqua Oceani*. January 6, 1895. *Acta Leonis XIII*, vol. 15 (1895) 3–21 = ASS 27 (1894–1895): 387–99.

———. Encyclical *Rerum Novarum*. May 15, 1891. ASS 23 (1890–1891): 641–670.

———. Encyclical *Sapientiae Christianae*. January 10, 1890. ASS 22 (1889–1890): 385–404.

———. Encyclical *Satis Cognitum*. June 29, 1896. ASS 28 (1895–1896): 708–39.

———. Encyclical *Testem Benevolentiae Nostrae*. January 22, 1899. AAS 32 (1898–1899): 470–79.

Pope Paul VI. Address from Bethlehem. January 6, 1964. AAS 56 (1964): 173–82.

———. Address to Rulers at the Close of the Second Vatican Council *Aux Gouvernants*. December 8, 1965. AAS 58 (1966): 10–11.

———. Christmas Radio Message December 23, 1965. AAS 58 (1966): 90–95.

———. Discours *Aux membres des missions extraordinaires*. December 7, 1965. AAS 58 (1966): 71–75.

———. Encyclical *Humanae Vitae*. July 25, 1968. AAS 60 (1968): 481–503.

———. Homily on the Occasion of the Closing of the Third Session of the Second Vatican Council. November 21, 1964. AAS 56 (1964): 1007–18.[1]

Pope Pius VI. *Quod Aliquantum*. March 10, 1791.

Pope Pius IX. Allocution *Acerbissimum*. September 27, 1852. *Acta Pii IX* 1:383–95.

———. Allocution *Maxima Quidem*. June 9, 1862. *Acta Pii IX* 3:451–61.

———. Allocution *Nemo Vestrum*. July 26, 1855. *Acta Pii IX* 2:441–46.

———. Apostolic Constitution *Ineffabilis Deus*. December 8, 1854. *Acta Pii IX*, pars 1, vol. 1.

———. Damnatio *Multiplices Inter*. June 10, 1851. *Acta Pii IX* 1:280–84.

———. Encyclical *Quanta Cura*. December 8, 1864. ASS 3 (1867): 160–67.

———. *Syllabus Errorum*. December 8, 1864. ASS 3 (1867): 170–76.

Pope Pius X. Encyclical *Pascendi Dominici Gregis*. September 8, 1907. ASS 40 (1907): 593–50.

———. Encyclical *Vehementer Nos*. February 11, 1906. ASS 39 (1906): 3–16.

---

[1] Valuet notes that there is some doubt as to whether this homily was delivered at St. Peter's or at St. Mary Major in Rome. Cf. Basile Valuet, *La liberté religieuse et la tradition catholique. Un cas de développement doctrinal homogène dans le magistère authentique*, 3rd rev. ed. (Barroux: Éditions Sainte-Madeleine, 2011), vol. IIA, 1271.

———. Letter to the French Archbishops and Bishops *Our Apostolic Mandate*. August 25, 1910. AAS 2 (1910): 607–33.

Pope Pius XI. Chirograph *Ci Commuovono*. February 2, 1930. AAS 22 (1930): 89–93.

———. Chirograph *Ci Si è Domandato*. May 30, 1929. AAS 21 (1929): 297–306.

———. Encyclical *Divini Illius Magistri*. December 31, 1929. AAS 22 (1930): 49–86.

———. Encyclical *Divini Redemptoris*. March 19, 1937. AAS 29 (1937): 65–106.

———. Encyclical *Mit Brennender Sorge*. March 14, 1937. AAS 29 (1937): 145–67.

———. Encyclical *Non Abbiamo Bisogno*. June 29, 1931. AAS 23 (1931): 285–312.

———. Encyclical *Quadragesimo Anno*. May 15, 1931. AAS 23 (1931): 177–228.

———. Encyclical *Quas Primas*. December 11, 1925. AAS 17 (1925): 593–610.

Pope Pius XII. Allocution "This Audience" to American Journalists. January 23, 1950. *L'Osservatore Romano* (Jan. 23–24, 1950) [not in AAS].

———. Allocution to the Roman Rota. October 6, 1946. AAS 38 (1946): 391–97.

———. Apostolic Constitution *Munificentissimus Deus*. November 1, 1950. AAS 42 (1950): 753–73.

———. Chirograph "We Have Just." In response to President Harry Truman. August 26, 1947. AAS 39 (1947): 380–82.

———. Christmas Radio Message. December 24, 1942. AAS 35 (1943): 9–24.

———. Christmas Radio Message. December 24, 1944. AAS 37 (1945): 10–23.

———. Discorso *Ai marchigiani residenti in Roma*. March 23, 1958. AAS 50 (1958): 216–20.

———. Discourse to Italian Jurists *Ci Riesce*. December 6, 1953. AAS 45 (1953): 794–802.

———. Discourse *Vous avez voulu* to the Tenth International Conference of Historical Sciences. September 7, 1955. AAS 47 (1955): 672–82.

———. Discourse "With the Special Affection" to Irish Prime Minister Eamon de Valera. October 4, 1957. AAS 49 (1957): 953–54.

———. Encyclical *Humani Generis*. August 12, 1950. AAS 42 (1950): 561–78.

———. Encyclical *Mystici Corporis*. June 29, 1943.

———. Encyclical *Summi Pontificatus*. October 20, 1939. AAS 31 (1939): 413–53. English translation, AAS 31 (1939): 538–64.

———. Radio Message "La Famiglia." March 23, 1952. AAS 44 (1952): 270–78.

———. Radio Message to the Whole World "La Solennità della Pentecoste." June 1, 1941. AAS 33 (1941): 195–205.

Ratzinger, Joseph, and Christoph Schönborn. *Introduction to the Catechism of the Catholic Church*. San Francisco: Ignatius Press, 1994.

———. Decree on the Apostolate of the Laity *Apostolicam Actuositatem*. November 18, 1965. AAS 58 (1966): 837–64.

———. Decree on Ecumenism *Unitatis Redintegratio*. November 21, 1964. AAS 57 (1965): 90–112.

———. Decree concerning the Pastoral Office of Bishops in the Church *Christus Dominus*. October 28, 1965. AAS 58 (1966): 673–96.

———. Dogmatic Constitution on the Church *Lumen Gentium*. November 21, 1964. AAS 57 (1965): 5–75.

———. Dogmatic Constitution on Divine Revelation *Dei Verbum*. November 18, 1965. AAS 58 (1966): 817–36.

———. Pastoral Constitution on the Church in the Modern World *Gaudium et Spes*. December 7, 1965. AAS 58 (1966): 1025–1115.

Roe v. Wade, 410 U.S. 113 (1973).

Second Vatican Council. Declaration on Religious Liberty *Dignitatis Humanae*. December 7, 1965. AAS 58 (1966): 929–46.

U.S. Conference of Catholic Bishops Office of Religious Liberty. "Discrimination Against Catholic Adoption Services." USCCB. 2018. Accessed September 3, 2018. http://usccb.org/issues-and-action/religious-liberty/discrimination-against-catholic-adoption-services.cfm.

Studies (Books, Online Articles, Articles, Reference Works)

Abbott, Walter M., ed. *The Documents of Vatican II*. New York: Herder and Herder, 1966.

St. Albert the Great. *De Eucharistia*. In *On the Body of the Lord*. Translated by Sr. Albert Marie Surmanski. Washington, DC: Catholic University of America, 2017.

Allen, Elise Ann. "Suspension of Ordinations in France an Unprecedented Surprise." *Crux*. June 8, 2022. Accessed June 18, 2022. https://cruxnow.com/church-in-europe/2022/06/suspension-of-ordinations-in-france-an-unprecedented-surprise.

Angerer, Carlo, and Ian Johnston. "Pope's Brother: Pontiff was Troubled by Butler's Revelations." February 12, 2013. Accessed June 15, 2013.

http://worldnews.nbcnews.com/_news/2013/02/12/16936793-popes-brother-pontiff-was-troubled-by-butlers-revelations?lite.

Associated Press. "Mormon President Denounces Polygamy." *Richmond Times-Dispatch*. October 11, 1998.

Aubert, Roger. "Le problème de la liberté religieuse à travers l'histoire du christianisme." *Scripta Theologica* 1 (1969): 377–401.

St. Augustine. *Contra Cresconium grammaticum et Donatistam*. AD 405. PL 43.

———. *Contra epistolam Parmeniani*. PL 43.

———. *Epistula ad Catholicos de secta Donatistarum* (= *De Unitate Ecclesiae*). PL 43.

———. *In Iohannis evangelium tractatus* [Tractates on the Gospel of John]. AD 406–430. PL 35:132–1976. CCL 36.

———. *Letters*. AD 386–429. PL 33:61–1162. CSEL 34, 44, 57, 58.

———. *Retractationes*. PL 32:583–656. CSEL 36. CCL 57.

———. *Sermon 62*. AD 399–400. PL 38.

Bainton, Roland H. *The Travail of Religious Liberty: Nine Biographical Sketches*. Philadelphia, PA: Westminster Press, 1951.

Barberini, Giovanni. "Riflessioni in tema di libertà religiosa, di libertà di coscienza e di relazioni fra stato e chiese." In *Raccolta di scritti in onore di Pio Fedele*, ed. Giovanni Barberini [Pubbl. della Fac. di Giurispr., 34], vol. 2, 793–814. Perugia: Univ., 1984.

Bender, Ludovicus. *Ius Publicum Ecclesiasticum*. Paulus Brand, 1948.

"Benedict XVI—SSPX: Quarter to midnight." *Rorate Caeli*. February 20, 2013. Accessed May 8, 2021. https://rorate-caeli.blogspot.com/2013/02/benedict-xvi-sspx-quarter-to-midnight.html.

Bennett, Isaiah. "Mormon Changes in Practice." *This Rock* (May 1999): 26–29.

Benoit, Pierre. "La droit à la liberté religieuse à la lumière de la Révélation." *Unam Sanctam* 60 (1967): 205–13.

Bentham, Jeremy. "An Introduction to the Principles of Morals and Legislation." In *A Bentham Reader*, ed. Mary Peter Mack. New York: Pegasus, 1969.

Biffi, Franco. "Chiesa, società civile e persona di fronte al problema della libertà religiosa. Dalla revoca dell'Editto di Nantes al Concilio Vaticano II." In *Teologia e diritto canonico*, 131–51. Città del Vaticano: Libreria Editrice Vaticana, 1987.

———. "Le droit à la liberté religieuse et le rôle des pouvoirs politics selon le Concilie Vatican II." In *I diritti fondamentali della persona umana e la libertà religiosa: Atti del V Colloquio Giuridico, 8–10 marzo 1984*, ed. Franco Biffi, 733–44. Città del Vaticano: Libreria Editrice Vaticana, 1985.

Bibliography

Blanshard, Paul. *Paul Blanshard on Vatican II*. Boston: Beacon Press, 1966.

Bokenkotter, Thomas. *A Concise History of the Catholic Church*. Garden City, NY: Image Books, 1979.

———. *Church and Revolution: Catholics in the Struggle for Democracy and Social Justice*. New York: Image Books, 1998.

Bork, Robert H. *Slouching Towards Gomorrah: Modern Liberalism and American Decline*. New York: ReganBooks/HarperCollins, 1996.

Bradley, Gerard V. "John Courtney Murray and the Privatization of American Religion." In *We Hold These Truths and More*, ed. Donald J. D'Elia and Stephen M. Krason, 120–33. Steubenville, OH: Franciscan University Press, 1993.

———. "Pope John Paul II and Religious Liberty." *Ave Maria Law Review* 6, no. 1 (2007): 33–59.

Canavan, Francis. "The Catholic Concept of Religious Freedom as a Human Right." In *Religious Liberty: An End and a Beginning*, ed. John Courtney Murray, 65–80. New York: MacMillan, 1966.

———. "Religious Freedom: John Courtney Murray, S.J., and Vatican II." *Faith & Reason* 13 (Summer 1987): 323–38. Reprinted in *John Courtney Murray and the American Civil Conversation*, ed. Robert P. Hunt and Kenneth L. Grasso, 167–80. Grand Rapids, MI: William B. Eerdmans Publishing Co., 1992.

Cappello, F. M. *Summa iuris publici ecclesiastici*. 4th edition. Rome: Pontifical Gregorian University Press, 1936.

Cardia, Carlo. "Società moderna e diritti di libertà." In *Teoria e prassi delle libertà di religione*, ed. P. Bellini et al., 23–102. Bologna, Italy: Società Editrice Il Mulino, 1975.

Carrillo de Albornoz, A. F. *The Basis of Religious Liberty*. Guildford and London: World Council of Churches, 1963.

———. "Roman Catholicism and Religious Liberty." *Ecumenical Review* 11, no. 4 (1959): 405–21.

Carroll, Warren H. *A History of Christendom*. Vol. 2, *The Building of Christendom*. Front Royal, VA: Christendom College Press, 1987.

———. *A History of Christendom*. Vol. 3, *The Glory of Christendom*. Front Royal, VA: Christendom College Press, 1993.

Carter, Stephen L. *The Culture of Disbelief: How American Law and Politics Trivialize Religious Devotion*. New York: Basic Books, 1993.

Chadwick, Owen. *From Bossuet to Newman: The Idea of Doctrinal Development*. Cambridge: Cambridge University Press, 1957.

Chesterton, G. K. *The Catholic Church and Conversion*. New York: MacMillan Company, 1926.

———. *Orthodoxy*. London: The Bodley Head, 1908.

———. "Why I am a Catholic." In *Twelve Modern Apostles and Their Creeds*. New York: Duffield & Co., 1926.

Côme de Prévigny. "Setting Things Straight about the SSPX-Vatican Talks: What Exactly Happened in April–June 2012?" *Rorate Caeli*. July 7, 2013. Accessed December 19, 2020. https://rorate-caeli.blogspot.com/search?updated-max= 2013-07-19T23:30:00Z&max-results=40.

Congar, Yves M.-J. "Que faut-il entendre par 'Déclaration'?" *Unam Sanctam* 60 (1967): 47–52.

Coppa, Frank J. *Pope Pius IX: Crusader in a Secular Age*. Boston: Twayne Publishers, 1979.

Craycraft, Kenneth R., Jr. *The American Myth of Religious Freedom*. Dallas: Spence Publishing Co., 1999.

Crosby, John F. "On Proposing the Truth and Not Imposing It: John Paul's Personalism and the Teaching of *Dignitatis Humanae*." In *Catholicism and Religious Freedom: Contemporary Reflections on Vatican II's Declaration on Religious Liberty*, ed. Kenneth L. Grasso and Robert P. Hunt, 135–159. Lanham, MD: Rowman & Littlefield Publishers, Inc., 2006.

Cuneo, Michael W. *The Smoke of Satan: Conservative and Traditionalist Dissent in Contemporary American Catholicism*. New York: Oxford University Press, 1997.

Curran, Charles. *Faithful Dissent*. Kansas City, MO: Sheed & Ward, 1986.

———. "Public Dissent in the Church." *Origins* 16, no. 9 (1986): 180.

———. "Response to Doctrinal Congregation's Decision." *Origins* 16, no. 11 (1986): 206.

Dalla Torre, Giuseppe. "Annotazioni minime sull'ascesa e declina dello stato laico." In *I Diritti fondamentali della persona umana e la libertà religiosa. Atti del V Colloquio Giuridico, 8–10 marzo 1984*, ed. Franco Biffi, 525–31. Rome: L.E.V. / Libreria Editrice Lateranense, 1985.

———. *Il primato della coscienza. Laicità e libertà nell'esperienza giuridica contemporanea*. Rome: Studium, 1992.

———. "Orientamenti e problemi sui rapporti tra Chiesa e Stato dopo il Vaticano II." In *Problemi e prospettive del diritto canonico*, ed. Ernesto Cappellini, 333–60. Brescia, Italy: Queriniana, 1977.

D'Avack, Pietro Agostino. "La Chiesa e lo Stato nella nuova impostazione conciliare." In *Il diritto ecclesiastico e rassegna di diritto matrimoniale*, 21–50. Milano, Italy: Giuffrè, 1971.

———. "La libertad religiosa en el magisterio actual de la Iglesia Católica." *Ius Canonicum* 5, no. 2 (1965): 365–84.

Davies, Michael. *Apologia Pro Marcel Lefebvre.* Vol. 2, *1977–1979.* Dickinson, TX: Angelus Press, 1983.

———. *Archbishop Lefebvre and Religious Liberty.* Rockford, IL: TAN Books and Publishers, 1980.

———. "Pope Leo XIII on True Liberty." *Latin Mass* (Summer 1998): 62–66.

———. *The Second Vatican Council and Religious Liberty.* Long Prairie, MN: Neumann Press, 1992.

de Corte, Marcel, et al. *Lettre à Quelques Évêques.* Paris: Société Saint-Thomas-d'Aquin, 1983.

D'Elia, Donald J., and Stephen M. Krason, eds. *We Hold These Truths and More: Further Catholic Reflections on the American Proposition.* Steubenville, OH: Franciscan University Press, 1993.

del Portillo, Álvaro. *Laici e fedeli nella Chiesa.* Milano, Italy: Giuffrè, 1999.

De Smedt, Émile-Joseph. "Les conséquences pastorales de la Déclaration." *Unam Sanctam* 60 (1967): 215–35.

Desmond, Joan Frawley. "Bishop Paprocki Discusses 'Traditionis Custodes': Liturgical Unity Doesn't Mean Liturgical Uniformity." *National Catholic Register.* August 4, 2021. Accessed June 18, 2022. https://www.ncregister.com/interview/bishop-paprocki-discusses-traditionis-custodes-liturgical-unity-doesn-t-mean-liturgical-uniformity.

Dörries, Hermann. *Constantine and Religious Liberty.* Translated by R. H. Bainton. London: Oxford University Press, 1961.

Doyle, Arthur Conan. "Silver Blaze." In *The Memoirs of Sherlock Holmes,* 11–35. Pleasantville, NY: The Reader's Digest Association, Inc., 1988.

Doyle, Dennis M. *The Church Emerging from Vatican II: A Popular Approach to Contemporary Catholicism.* Mystic, CT: Twenty-Third Publications, 1992.

Doyle, Peter. "Pope Pius IX and Religious Freedom." In *Persecution and Toleration: Papers Read at the Twenty-second Summer Meeting and the Twenty-third Winter Meeting of the Ecclesiastical History Society,* ed. W. J. Sheils, 329–41. Padstow, UK: Ecclesiastical History Society, 1984.

Dulles, Avery. "Dignitatis Humanae and the Development of Catholic Doctrine." In *Catholicism and Religious Freedom: Contemporary Reflections on Vatican II's Declaration on Religious Liberty,* ed. Kenneth L. Grasso and Robert P. Hunt, 43–67. Lanham, MD: Rowman & Littlefield Publishers, Inc., 2006.

———. *Magisterium: Teacher and Guardian of the Faith.* Naples, FL: Sapientia Press, 2007.

Dunnigan, R. Michael. "*Traditionis Custodes* and the Raw Data on the Latin Mass." *Catholic World Report.* July 19, 2021. Accessed June 18, 2022. https://

www.catholicworldreport.com/2021/07/19/traditionis-custodes-and-the-raw-data-of-the-latin-mass/.

Dupanloup, Félix. *La convention du 15 septembre et l'encyclique du 8 décembre*. Paris, 1865.

———. *Remarks on the Encyclical of the 8th of December 1864*. Translated by W. J. M. Hutchinson. London: George Cheek, 1865.

Eagan, Joseph F. *Restoration and Renewal: The Church in the Third Millennium*. Kansas City, MO: Sheed & Ward, 1995.

Ellis, John Tracy. "Religious Freedom: An American Reaction." In *Vatican II Revisited By Those Who Were There*, ed. Alberic Stacpoole, 291–97. Minneapolis, MN: Winston Press, 1986.

"Father Charles Curran Asked to Retract Positions." *Origins* 15, no. 41 (1986): 673.

Feliciani, Giorgio. "La libertà religiosa nel magistero di Giovanni Paolo II." In *Escritos en honor de Javier Hervada*, 921–29. Pamplona: Instituto Martín de Azpilcueta, 1999.

Fellay, Bernard. Letter 77. "To Friends and Benefactors." Reprinted in part on *Rorate Caeli*. December 6, 2010. Accessed December 19, 2020. https://rorate-caeli.blogspot.com/2010/12/fellay-it-is-still-quite-difficult-to.html.

"Fellay: 'I Thought That, with His Resignation, He Would Perhaps Make a Final Gesture in Our Favor as Pope' (Updated)." *Rorate Caeli*. February 15, 2013. Accessed December 19, 2020. https://rorate-caeli.blogspot.com/2013/02/fellay-i-thought-that-with-his.html.

"Fellay: 'To Defend the Faith, to Keep the Faith, to Die in the Faith, This is the Essential Thing!'" *Rorate Caeli*. February 2, 2013. Accessed December 19, 2020. https://rorate-caeli.blogspot.com/2013/02/fellay-to-defend-faith-to-keep-faith-to.html.

Fesquet, Henri. *The Drama of Vatican II*. New York: Random House, 1967.

Filibeck, Giorgio. *Human Rights in the Teaching of the Church: From John XXIII to John Paul II*. Vatican City: Libreria Editrice Vaticana, 1994.

———. *I diritti dell'uomo nell'insegnamento della Chiesa. Da Giovanni XXIII a Giovanni Paolo II*. Vatican City: Libreria Editrice Vaticana, 2001.

Finnis, John. "Reflections and Responses [26: Reply to Thomas Pink]." In *Reason, Morality, and Law: The Philosophy of John Finnis*, ed. John Keown and Robert P. George, 566–77. Oxford: Oxford University Press, 2013.

Finocchiaro, Francesco. "Libertà: VI. Libertà religiosa—Dir. Can." In *Enciclopedia giuridica*. Roma: Istituto della Enciclopedia Italiana fondata da Giovanni Treccani, 1990.

Flannery, Austin, ed. *Vatican Council II: The Conciliar and Post Conciliar Documents*. New rev. ed. Northport, NY: Costello Publishing Co., 1996.

Flannery, Kevin. "*Dignitatis Humanae* and the Development of Doctrine." *Catholic Dossier* 6, no. 2 (March–April 2000): 31–35.

Ford, John T., ed. *Religious Liberty: Paul VI and Dignitatis Humanae*. Brescia, Italy: Istituto Paolo VI, 1995.

"For the Record: Declaration of Bishops of Society of St. Pius X on the Occasion of the 25th Anniversary of the Episcopal Ordinations." *Rorate Caeli*. June 27, 2013. Accessed May 5, 2021. https://rorate-caeli.blogspot.com/2013/06/for-record-declaration-of-sspx-bishops.html.

"Full Text of Advent Letter of Archbishop J. Augustine Di Noia Vice-President of the Ecclesia Dei Commission to the Fraternity of St. Pius X." *Il Sismografo*. January 19, 2013. Accessed December 19, 2020. http://ilsismografo.blogspot.com/2013/01/vaticano-full-text-of-advent-letter.html.

Gabriel, Karl, Christian Spiess, and Katja Winkler. *Catholicism and Religious Freedom: Renewing the Church in the Second Vatican Council*. Boston, MA: Brill USA, Inc., 2019.

Garnsey, Peter. "Religious Toleration in Classical Antiquity." In *Persecution and Toleration*, ed. W. J. Sheils, 1–27. Studies in Church History 21. Oxford: Basil Blackwell, 1984.

González Ruiz, Emmanuel. *Lectiones iuris publici ecclesiastici*. Malacae: Seminarium Conciliare Malacitanum, 1947.

Grasso, Kenneth L. "John Courtney Murray, 'The Juridical State,' and the Catholic Theory of Religious Freedom." *The Political Science Reviewer* 33 (2004): 1–61.

———. "An Unfinished Argument: *Dignitatis Humanae*, John Courtney Murray, and the Catholic Theory of the State." In *Catholicism and Religious Freedom: Contemporary Reflections on Vatican II's Declaration on Religious Liberty*, ed. Kenneth L. Grasso and Robert P. Hunt, 161–93. Lanham, MD: Rowman & Littlefield Publishers, Inc., 2006. (This essay is a later version of the author's 2004 article in *The Political Science Reviewer*.)

Grasso, Kenneth L., and Robert P. Hunt, eds. *Catholicism and Religious Freedom. Contemporary Reflections on Vatican II's Declaration on Religious Liberty*. Lanham, MD: Rowman & Littlefield Publishers, Inc., 2006.

Grisez, Germain. *The Way of the Lord Jesus*. Vol. 1, *Christian Moral Principles*. Chicago: Franciscan Herald Press, 1983.

Guarino, Thomas G. *The Disputed Teachings of Vatican II: Continuity and Reversal in Catholic Doctrine*. Grand Rapids, MI: William B. Eerdmans Publishing Company, 2018.

Guminski, Arnold T., and Brian W. Harrison. *Religious Freedom: Did Vatican*

II Contradict Traditional Catholic Doctrine? A Debate. South Bend, IN: St. Augustine's Press, 2013.

Guminski, Arnold T. "An Examination of Thomas Pink's Theory of the Doctrine Concerning Religious Freedom in *Dignitatis Humanae*." December 6, 2015. Academia. Accessed July 16, 2022. https://www.academia.edu/19523482/An_Examination_of_Thomas_Pinks_Theory_of_the_Doctrine_concerning_Religious_Freedom_in_Dignitatis_Humanae.

———. "Further Reflections About Thomas Pink's Theory of the Meaning of *Dignitatis Humanae*." April 2, 2020. Academia. Accessed July 16, 2022. https://www.academia.edu/42924123/Further_Reflections_About_Thomas_Pinks_Theory_of_the_Meaning_of_Dignitatis_Humanae.

Hales, E. E. Y. *Pio Nono: A Study in European Politics and Religion in the Nineteenth Century*. London: Eyre & Spottiswoode, 1954.

Hamer, Jérôme. "Histoire du texte de la Déclaration." *Unam Sanctam* 60 (1967): 53–110.

———. *La libertà religiosa nel Vaticano II*. 2nd ed. Torino, Italy: Elle Di Ci, 1967.

Hamer, Jérôme and Clemente Riva. *La libertà religiosa nel Vaticano II*. Torino, Italy: Elle Di Ci, 1966.

Harrison, Brian W. "The Center is Holding." Review of *The Second Vatican Council and Religious Liberty*, by Michael Davies. Roman Theological Forum. Accessed October 29, 2000. http://www.rtforum.org/lt/lt44.html.

———. "John Courtney Murray: A Reliable Interpreter of *Dignitatis Humanae*?" In *We Hold These Truths and More*, ed. Donald J. D'Elia and Stephen M. Krason, 134–65. Steubenville, OH: Franciscan University Press, 1993.

———. "Pius IX, Vatican II and Religious Liberty." *Living Tradition* 9 (Jan. 1987). Roman Theological Forum. Accessed April 14, 2003. http://www.rtforum.org/lt/lt9.html.

———. *Religious Liberty and Contraception: Did Vatican II Open the Way for a New Sexual Ethic?* Melbourne: John XXIII Fellowship Co-op., 1988.

———. "Religious Liberty: 'Rights' versus 'Tolerance.'" *Living Tradition* 16 (March 1988). Roman Theological Forum. Accessed April 23, 2003. http://www.rtforum.org/lt/lt16.html#II.

———. "Roma Locuta Est—Causa Finita Est." *Living Tradition* 57 (March 1995). Roman Theological Forum. Accessed December 19, 2020. http://www.rtforum.org/lt/lt57.html.

———. "Towards Clarifying the Religious Liberty Quandary." *New Oxford Review* (November 1999): 11–12.

———. "Vatican II and Religious Liberty: Contradiction or Continuity?" *Catholic Dossier* 6 (March–April 2000): 21–30.

Healy, Nicholas J. "The Drafting of *Dignitatis Humanae*." In *Freedom, Truth, and Human Dignity: The Second Vatican Council's Declaration on Religious Freedom—A New Translation, Redaction History, and Interpretation of Dignitatis Humanae*, ed. David L. Schindler and Nicholas J. Healy, 211–42. Grand Rapids, MI / Cambridge, UK: William B. Eerdmans Publishing Company, 2015.

Hehir, J. Bryan. "*Dignitatis Humanae* in the Pontificate of John Paul II." In *Religious Liberty: Paul VI and Dignitatis Humanae*, ed. John T. Ford, 169–83. Brescia, Italy: Istituto Paulo VI, 1995.

Hervada, Javier. *Critical Introduction to Natural Law*. Translated by Mindy Emmons. Montreal: Wilson & Lafleur, 2006.

Hill, Brennan R., Paul Knitter, and William Madges. *Faith, Religion, & Theology: A Contemporary Introduction*, rev. ed. Mystic, CT: Twenty-Third Publications, 1997.

Himmelfarb, Gertrude. *On Looking Into the Abyss: Untimely Thoughts on Culture and Society*. New York: Alfred A. Knopf, 1994.

Hittinger, Russell. "The Declaration on Religious Liberty, *Dignitatis Humanae*." In *Vatican II: Renewal within Tradition*, ed. Matthew L. Lamb and Matthew Levering, 359–82. New York: Oxford University Press, 2008.

———. "How to Read *Dignitatis Humanae* on Establishment of Religion." *Catholic Dossier* 6, no. 2 (March–April 2000): 14–20.

———. "Political Pluralism and Religious Liberty: The Teaching of *Dignitatis Humanae*." In *Universal Rights in a World of Diversity: The Case of Religious Freedom*, Proceedings of the 17th Plenary Session, Pontifical Academy of Social Sciences, Acta 17, ed. Mary Ann Glendon and Hans F. Zacher, 39–55, 677–80. Vatican City: Pontifical Academy of Social Sciences, 2012.

———. "The Problem of the State in *Centesimus Annus*." *Fordham International Law Journal* 15 (1991–1992): 952–96.

———. "Religion, Human Law, and the Virtue of Religion: The Case of *Dignitatis Humanae*." *Nova et Vetera* (English ed.) 14, no. 1 (2016): 151–76.

Hollenbach, David, et al. "Theology and Philosophy in Public: A Symposium on John Courtney Murray's Unfinished Agenda." *Theological Studies* 40, no. 4 (1979): 700–715.

Hughes, Philip. *A Popular History of the Catholic Church*. Macmillan, 1947. Image Books Edition, 1954.

Janssens, Louis. *Liberté de conscience et liberté religieuse*. Paris: Desclée de Brouwer, 1964.

Jefferson, Thomas. Letter to the Danbury Baptist Association. January 1, 1802. In *The Portable Thomas Jefferson*, ed. Merrill D. Peterson. New York: Penguin Books, 1977.

Johnson, Paul. *A History of Christianity*. New York: Atheneum, 1985.

Jordan, Édouard. "La Responsabilité de l' Église dans la répression de l'hérésie au moyen âge." *Annales de Philosophie chrétienne*, series IV, vol. VIII/6 (September 1909): 561–80.

Kasper, Walter. "The Theological Foundations of Human Rights." *The Jurist* 50 (1990): 148–66.

———. *The God of Jesus Christ*. New York: Crossroad, 1996.

Kennedy, Robert T. "Contributions of *Dignitatis Humanae* to Church-State Relations in the United States." In *Religious Liberty: Paul VI and* Dignitatis Humanae, ed. John T. Ford, 93–113. Brescia, Italy: Istituto Paulo VI, 1995.

Ker, Ian. *Newman on Vatican II*. Oxford: Oxford University Press, 2014.

Kollmorgen, Gregor. "Interview with Ecclesia Dei Secretary—Full Text." New Liturgical Movement. December 3, 2010. Accessed December 19, 2020. http://www.newliturgicalmovement.org/2010/12/interview-with-ecclesia-dei-secretary_03.html#.Ub0Nwtgn_XQ.

König, Franz. "The Right to Religious Freedom: The Significance of *Dignitatis Humanae*." In *Vatican II Revisited By Those Who Were There*, ed. Alberic Stacpoole, 283–90. Minneapolis, MN: Winston Press, 1986.

Küng, Hans, Yves Congar, and Daniel O'Hanlon, eds. *Council Speeches of Vatican II*. Glen Rock, NJ: Paulist Press, 1964.

Lamberigts, Mathijs. "Msgr. Emiel-Jozef De Smedt, Bishop of Bruges, and the Second Vatican Council." In *Experience, Organisations and Bodies at Vatican II: Proceedings of the Bologna Conference, December 1996*, ed. M. T. Fattori and A. Melloni, 431–69. Leuven, Belgium: Bibliotheek van de Faculteit Godgeleerdheid, 1999.

Lanfranc. *De corpore et sanguine Domini*. In *The Fathers of the Church: Mediaeval Continuation*, Gregory F. LaNave et al., eds. Vol. 10, *Lanfranc of Canterbury On the Body and Blood of the Lord*. Washington, DC: The Catholic University of America Press, 2009.

Langan, Jeffrey. *The French Revolution Confronts Pius VI*. South Bend, IN: St. Augustine's Press, 2016.

"A Last Chance for the SSPX?" *Rorate Caeli*. February 13, 2013. Accessed December 19, 2020. https://rorate-caeli.blogspot.com/2013/02/a-last-chance-for-sspx-plus-sspx-in.html.

Leahy, William K., and Anthony T. Massimini, eds. *Third Session Council Speeches of Vatican II*. Glen Rock, NJ: Paulist Press, 1966.

Lecler, Joseph. *Toleration and the Reformation*. Vol. 1. Translated by T. L. Westow. London/New York: Longmans/Association Press, 1960.

Lefebvre, Marcel. *Religious Liberty Questioned*. Translated by Jaime Pazat de Lys. Kansas City, MO: Angelus Press, 2002. Original title *Mes doutes sur la liberté religieuse*. Clovis, 2000.

Littell, Franklin H. "A Response." In *The Documents of Vatican II*, ed. Walter M. Abbott, 697–700. New York: Herder and Herder, 1966.

Locke, John. "A Letter Concerning Toleration." In *John Locke on Politics and Education*. Roslyn, NY: Walter J. Black, Inc., 1947.

Lonergan, Bernard J. F. *Method in Theology*. London: Darton, Longman, & Todd Ltd., 1972. Reprint, Toronto: University of Toronto Press, 1996.

Lucien, Bernard. *Gregoire XVI, Pie IX et Vatican II. Études sur la Liberté Religieuse dans la Doctrine Catholique*. Tours: Éditions Forts dans la Foi, 1990.

———. "La Liberté Religieuse a Vatican II: Une Rémise en Question Fondamentale." In *Une Démarche Catholique*, 33–61. Nice: Éditions Association Saint-Herménégilde, 1984.

MacCaffrey, James. *History of the Catholic Church in the Nineteenth Century (1789–1908)*, 2nd rev. ed. 2 vols. Dublin/St. Louis: M.H. Gill and Son, Ltd./B. Herder, 1910.

Magister, Sandro. "Tra confidenze ed esorcismi, un Francesco tutto da decifrare." L'Espresso. May 25, 2013. Accessed June 15, 2013. http://magister.blogautore.espresso.repubblica.it/2013/05/25/tra-confidenze-ed-esorcismi-un-papa-tutto-da-decifrare/.

Marshner, William H. "*Dignitatis Humanae* and Traditional Teaching on Church and State." *Faith & Reason* 9, no. 3 (1983): 222–48.

Martín de Agar, José T. "Ecclesia y polis." *Ius Canonicum* (2008): 399–413.

———. "Derecho y relaciones iglesia—sociedad civil." *Ius Ecclesiae* 32, no. 1 (2020): 17–68.

———. "Problemas jurídicos de la objeción de conciencia." *Scripta Theologica* 27, no. 2 (1995): 519–43.

Martos, Joseph. *Doors to the Sacred*. Liguori, MO: Triumph Books, 1991.

McBrien, Richard P. *Catholicism*. New York: Harper & Row, 1981.

McElrath, Damian. *The Syllabus of Pius IX: Some Reactions in England*. Louvain, Belgium: Publications Universitaires de Louvain, 1964.

McEntee, Peg. "Why Do People Practice Polygamy?; Utah & the United States;

Nationally, Polygamists Cite Theological Roots." *Salt Lake Tribune.* September 20, 1998. Accessed December 2, 1999. https://archive.sltrib.com/article.php?itype=storyID&id=100F3CF37932951B.

Mead, Frank S., and Samuel S. Hill. *Handbook of Denominations in the United States.* Nashville, TN: Abingdon Press, 1995.

Melchin, Kenneth R. "Revisionists, Deontologists, and the Structure of Moral Understanding." *Theological Studies* 51, no. 3 (1990): 389–416.

Meyers, Marvin, ed. *The Mind of the Founder: Sources of the Political Thought of James Madison*, rev. ed. Hanover: University Press of New England, 1981.

Minnerath, Roland. "La concezione della Chiesa sulla libertà religiosa." In *La libertad religiosa: Memoria del IX Congreso Internacional de Derecho Canónico*, 43–59. Universidad Nacional Autónoma de México, 1996.

———. "How Should State and Church Interact?" *Jurist* 70, no. 2 (2010): 473–86.

Mistò, Luigi. "Paul VI and *Dignitatis Humanae*: Theory and Practice." In *Religious Liberty: Paul VI and Dignitatis Humanae*, ed. John T. Ford, 12–38. Brescia, Italy: Istituto Paulo VI, 1995.

Most, William G. "Religious Liberty: What the Texts Demand." *Faith & Reason* 9, no. 3 (Fall 1983): 196–209.

———. "Vatican II vs. Pius IX? A Study in Lefebvrism." *Faith & Reason* 6, no. 3 (Fall 1980): 220–29.

Murray, Charles. *Coming Apart: The State of White America, 1960–2010.* New York: Crown Forum, 2012.

Murray, John Courtney. "Arguments for the Human Right to Religious Freedom." Article based on a September 19, 1966, speech. In *Religious Liberty: Catholic Struggles with Pluralism*, ed. J. Leon Hooper, 229–44. Louisville, KY: Westminster/John Knox Press, 1993.

———. "Commentary." In *American Participation in the Second Vatican Council*, ed. Vincent A. Yzermans, 668–76. New York: Sheed & Ward, 1967.

———. "A Common Enemy, A Common Cause." *First Things*, no. 26 (October 1992): 29–37.

———. "Contemporary Orientations of Catholic Thought on Church and State in the Light of History." *Theological Studies* 10, no. 2 (1949): 177–234.

———. "Current Theology on Religious Freedom." *Theological Studies* 10, no. 3 (1949): 409–32.

———. "The Declaration on Religious Freedom." *Concilium* 5, no. 2 (May 1966): 3–10.

———. "The Declaration on Religious Freedom: Its Deeper Significance." *America* 114 (Apr. 23, 1966): 592–93.

———. "The Declaration on Religious Liberty: A Moment in Its Legislative History." In *Religious Liberty: An End and a Beginning*, ed. John Courtney Murray, 15–42. New York: MacMillan, 1966.

———. "The Issue of Church and State at Vatican Council II." *Theological Studies* 27, no. 4 (1966): 580–606.

———. "Leo XIII on Church and State: The General Structure of the Controversy." *Theological Studies* 14, no. 1 (1953): 1–30.

———. "Leo XIII: Separation of Church and State." *Theological Studies* 14, no. 2 (1953): 145–214.

———. "Leo XIII: Two Concepts of Government." *Theological Studies* 14, no. 4 (1953): 551–67.

———. "Leo XIII: Two Concepts of Government (II): Government and the Order of Culture." *Theological Studies* 15, no. 1 (1954): 1–33.

———. "The Problem of Religious Freedom." *Theological Studies* 25, no. 4 (1964): 503–75.

———. "Religious Freedom." In *The Documents of Vatican II*, ed. Walter M. Abbott, 672–96. New York: Herder and Herder, 1966.

———. "Religious Freedom." Speech at Georgetown University (Summer 1964). In *Freedom and Man*, 131–40. New York: P. J. Kenedy & Sons, 1965.

———. *Religious Liberty: Catholic Struggles with Pluralism*. Louisville, KY: Westminster/John Knox Press, 1993.

———. *Religious Liberty: An End and a Beginning*. New York: MacMillan, 1966.

———. "Vers une intelligence du développement de la doctrine de l'Église sur la liberté religieuse." *Unam Sanctam* 60 (1967): 111–47.

———. *We Hold These Truths: Catholic Reflections on the American Proposition*. Kansas City, MO: Sheed & Ward, 1960.

"Naming the 'False Brethren,' the 'Mute Dogs' and the 'Untrustworthy Leaders.'" *The Pastor's Corner*. U.S. District of the SSPX (website). Reprinted on *Rorate Caeli*. February 14, 2011. Accessed December 19, 2020. https://rorate-caeli.blogspot.com/2011/02/naming-false-brethren-mute-dogs-and.html.

Nessel, William. *First Amendment Freedoms, Papal Pronouncements and Concordat Practice: A Comparative Study in American Law and Public Ecclesiastical Law*. Washington, DC: Catholic University of America Press, 1961.

Neuhaus, Richard John. *The Naked Public Square: Religion and Democracy in America*. 2nd ed. Grand Rapids, MI: William B. Eerdmans Publishing Co., 1986.

Newman, John Henry. *An Essay on the Development of Christian Doctrine*. B. M.

Pickering, 1878. Reprint, Notre Dame, IN: University of Notre Dame Press, 1989.

———, and William E. Gladstone. *Newman and Gladstone: The Vatican Decrees*. Introduction by Alvan S. Ryan. Notre Dame, IN: University of Notre Dame Press, 1962.

Nichols, Aidan. *From Newman to Congar: The Idea of Doctrinal Development from the Victorians to the Second Vatican Council*. Edinburgh: T&T Clark, 1990.

Noonan, John T., Jr. "Development in Moral Doctrine." *Theological Studies* 54, no. 4 (1993): 662–77.

———. *The Lustre of Our Country: The American Experience of Religious Freedom*. Berkeley: University of California Press, 1998.

Novak, Michael. "Aquinas and the Heretics." *First Things* 58 (1995): 33–38.

Nutt, Roger W., and Michael R. De Salvo. "The Debate over Dignitatis Humanae at Vatican II: The Contribution of Charles Cardinal Journet." *The Thomist* 85 (2021): 175–226.

Ocáriz, Fernando. "On Adhesion to the Second Vatican Council," *L'Osservatore Romano*. December 2, 2011.

———. "Sulla libertà religiosa. Continuità del Vaticano II con il Magistero precedente." *Annales theologici* 3 (1989): 71–97.

O'Connor, Flannery. "The Fiction Writer and His Country." In Mystery and Manners: Occasional Prose, edited by Sally Fitzgerald and Robert Fitzgerald, 25–35. New York: Farrar, Straus & Giroux, 1969.

O'Connor, James T. *The Gift of Infallibility*. Boston: St. Paul Editions, 1986.

O'Neil, Patrick M. "A Response to John T. Noonan, Jr. Concerning the Development of Catholic Moral Doctrine." *Faith & Reason* (Spring/Summer 1996). EWTN. Accessed June 15, 2013. https://www.ewtn.com/catholicism/library/response-to-john-t-noonan-jr-concerning-the-development-of-catholic-moral-doctrine-10041.

Paprocki, Thomas J. *Vindication and Defense of the Rights of the Christian Faithful Through Administrative Recourse in the Local Church*. Ann Arbor, MI: UMI, 1995.

Pavan, Pietro. *La dichiarazione conciliare* Dignitatis humanae *a 20 anni dalla pubblicazione*. Casale Monferrato, Italy: Edizioni Piemme di Pietro Marietti, 1986.

———. "Le droit à la liberté religieuse en ses éléments essentiels." *Unam Sanctam* 60 (1967): 149–203.

———. "Introduction and Commentary on the Declaration on Religious Freedom." In *Commentary on the Documents of Vatican II*, vol. 4, ed. Herbert

Bibliography

Vorgrimler, 49–86. New York/London: Herder and Herder/Burns & Oates Limited, 1969.

Pelotte, Donald E. *John Courtney Murray: Theologian in Conflict*. New York: Paulist Press, 1975.

Pentin, Edward. "Pope Francis' Approval of SSPX Marriages Offers Hopeful Step to Unity." *National Catholic Register*. April 7, 2017. Accessed June 18, 2022. https://www.ncregister.com/news/pope-francis-approval-of-sspx-marriages-offers-hopeful-step-to-unity.

Peterson, Paul H. "The Manifesto of 1890." Light Planet (Mormons website). Accessed February 28, 2023. https://www.lightplanet.com/mormons/daily/history/plural_marriage/manifesto_eom.htm.

Pew Research Center. "Many Countries Favor Specific Religions, Officially or Unofficially." Pew Research Center. October 3, 2017. Accessed April 5, 2021. https://www.pewforum.org/2017/10/03/many-countries-favor-specific-religions-officially-or-unofficially/.

Pink, Thomas. "Conscience and Coercion: Vatican II's Teaching on Religious Freedom Changed Policy, Not Doctrine." *First Things* 225 (August 2012): 45–51.

———. "*Dignitatis Humanae*: Continuity after Leo XIII." In *Dignitatis Humanae Colloquium*, Dialogos Institute Proceedings, vol. 1, 105–45. Dialogos Institute, 2017.

———. "The Interpretation of *Dignitatis Humanae*: A Reply to Martin Rhonheimer." *Nova et Vetera* (English ed.) 11, no. 1 (2013): 77–121.

———. "Jacques Maritain and the Problem of Church and State." *The Thomist* 79 (2015): 1–42.

———. "John Finnis's Alternative History of Trent." November 27, 2018. Academia. Accessed July 16, 2022. https://www.academia.edu/37861294/John_Finniss_Alternative_History_of_Trent.

———. "On Dignitatis Humanae—A Reply to Thomas Storck." *The Josias*. October 28, 2021. Accessed July 16, 2022. https://thejosias.com/2021/10/28/on-dignitatis-humanae-a-reply-to-thomas-storck/.

———. "Suarez and Bellarmine on the Church as Coercive Lawgiver." Undated but apparently from a December 2013 lecture.[2] Academia. Accessed July

---

[2] Per Arnold T. Guminski. Cf. "An Examination of Thomas Pink's Theory of the Doctrine Concerning Religious Freedom in *Dignitatis Humanae*" (Dec. 6, 2015), Academia, §2n7, accessed July 16, 2022, https://www.academia.edu/19523482/An_Examination_of_Thomas_Pinks_Theory_of_the_Doctrine_concerning_Religious_Freedom_in_Dignitatis_Humanae.

16, 2022. https://www.academia.edu/8577465/Suarez_and_Bellarmine_on_the_Church_as_Coercive_Lawgiver?sm=b.

———. "The Right to Religious Liberty and the Coercion of Belief." In *Reason, Morality, and Law: The Philosophy of John Finnis*, ed. John Keown and Robert P. George, 427–42. Oxford: Oxford University Press, 2013.

———. "What is the Catholic Doctrine of Religious Liberty?" Expanded version. June 15, 2012. Academia. Accessed July 16, 2022. https://www.academia.edu/es/639061/What_is_the_Catholic_doctrine_of_religious_liberty.

"Pope to Latin American Religious: Full Text." *Rorate Caeli*. June 11, 2013. Accessed June 15, 2013. http://rorate-caeli.blogspot.com/2013/06/pope-to-latin-american-religious-full.html.

Poulet, Charles, and Sidney A. Raemers. *A History of the Catholic Church*. 2 vols. St. Louis, MO: B. Herder Book Co., 1934.

"The Priests of the Fraternity of St. Pius X Rally behind Bishop Fellay." *Rorate Caeli*. February 18, 2013. Accessed December 19, 2020. https://rorate-caeli.blogspot.com/2013/02/the-priests-of-fraternity-of-st-pius-x.html.

Prieto, Vicente. *Diritto dei rapporti tra Chiesa e società civile*. Rome: Edizioni Università della Santa Croce, 2003.

Rahner, Hugo. *Church and State in Early Christianity*. Translated by Leo Donald Davis. San Francisco: Ignatius Press, 1992.

Ratzinger, Joseph. *Church, Ecumenism and Politics: New Essays in Ecclesiology*. New York: Crossroad, 1988.

———. *God and the World*. San Francisco: Ignatius Press, 2002.

———. *Salt of the Earth*. San Francisco: Ignatius Press, 1997.

Regan, Richard J. *The American Constitution and Religion*. Washington, DC: Catholic University of America Press, 2013.

———. *Conflict and Consensus: Religious Freedom and the Second Vatican Council*. New York/London: Macmillan/Collier-Macmillan Ltd., 1967.

———. "John Courtney Murray, the American Bishops, and the *Declaration on Religious Liberty*." In *Religious Liberty: Paul VI and Dignitatis Humanae*, ed. John T. Ford, 51–66. Brescia, Italy: Istituto Paolo VI, 1995.

Rhonheimer, Martin. "Benedict XVI's 'Hermeneutic of Reform' and Religious Freedom." *Nova et Vetera* (English ed.) 9, no. 4 (2011): 1029–54.

———. "*Dignitatis Humanae*—Not a Mere Question of Church Policy: A Response to Thomas Pink." *Nova et Vetera* (English ed.) 12, no. 2 (2014): 445–70.

Rodríguez, Victorino. "Estudio histórico-doctrinal de la declaración sobre la libertad religiosa del Concilio Vaticano II." *Ciencia Tomista* 93 (1966): 193–339.

———. "Sobre la libertad religiosa." *Ciencia Tomista* 91 (1964): 311–429.

Rooney, David. "Murray: Beacon of Light?" Review of *We Hold These Truths and More*, ed. Donald J. D'Elia and Stephen M. Krason. *Lay Witness Newsletter*, May 1994, 7–10.

Rousselle, Christine. "Traditionis Custodes: Arkansas Bishop Limits Traditional Latin Mass across State to Two Parishes Administered by FSSP." *National Catholic Register*. July 19, 2021. Accessed June 18, 2022. https://www.ncregister.com/news/traditionis-custodes-arkansas-bishop-limits-traditional-latin-mass-across-state-to-two-parishes-administered-by-fssp.

Rynne, Xavier. *Vatican II: An Authoritative One-Volume Version of the Four Historic Books*. New York: Farrar, Straus, and Giroux, 1968.

Scatena, Silvia. *La fatica della libertà. L'elaborazione della dichiarazione* Dignitatis humanae *sulla libertà religiosa del Vaticano II*. Istituto per le scienze religiose—Bologna, Testi e ricerche di scienze religiose, nuova serie, 31. Bologna, Italy: Il Mulino, 2003.

Schaff, Philip, ed. *A Select Library of the Nicene and Post-Nicene Fathers of the Christian Church*, First Series. 14 vols. Edinburgh: T&T Clark, 1886–1900. Reprint, Grand Rapids, MI: William B. Eerdmans Publishing Co., 1989.

Schindler, David L. "Freedom, Truth, and Human Dignity: An Interpretation of *Dignitatis Humanae* on the Right to Religious Freedom." In *Freedom, Truth, and Human Dignity: The Second Vatican Council's Declaration on Religious Freedom—A New Translation, Redaction History, and Interpretation of* Dignitatis Humanae, ed. David L. Schindler and Nicholas J. Healy Jr., 39–209. Grand Rapids, MI / Cambridge, UK: William B. Eerdmans Publishing Company, 2015.

———. "Religious Freedom, Truth, and American Liberalism: Another Look at John Courtney Murray." *Communio* 21 (Winter 1994): 696–741.

———, and Nicholas J. Healy Jr., eds. *Freedom, Truth, and Human Dignity: The Second Vatican Council's Declaration on Religious Freedom—A New Translation, Redaction History, and Interpretation of* Dignitatis Humanae. Grand Rapids, MI / Cambridge, UK: William B. Eerdmans Publishing Company, 2015.

Sheils, W. J., ed. *Persecution and Toleration*. Oxford: Basil Blackwell, 1984.

Sockey, E. William, III. "Religious Freedom and Human Rights." *Faith & Reason* 9, no. 3 (1983): 210–21.

Spinelli, Lorenzo. *Il diritto pubblico ecclesiastico dopo il Concilio Vaticano II*. Milan: Dott. A. Giuffrè Editore, 1985.

———. *Libertas Ecclesiae. Lezioni di diritto canonico*. Milan: Dott. A. Giuffrè Editore, 1979.

———. *Lo Stato e la Chiesa. Venti secoli di relazioni*. Turin, Italy: UTET, 1988.

Stacpoole, Alberic, ed. *Vatican II Revisited By Those Who Were There*. Minneapolis, MN: Winston Press, 1986.

Stearns, Peter N. *Priest and Revolutionary: Lamennais and the Dilemma of French Catholicism*. New York: Harper & Row, 1967.

Storck, Thomas. "Recent Discussions of Religious Liberty." *The Josias*. June 3, 2021. Accessed July 16, 2022. https://thejosias.com/2021/06/03/recent-discussions-of-religious-liberty/.

St. Thomas Aquinas. *Contra impugnantes Dei cultum*. In *An Apology for the Religious Orders*, ed. John Procter. London/St. Louis: Sands & Co./B. Herder, 1902.

———. *Summa Theologica*. Christian Classics ed. Benziger Bros., 1947.

Tierney, Brian. *The Idea of Natural Rights: Studies on Natural Rights, Natural Law, and Church Law (1150–1625)*. Atlanta, GA: Emory University, 1997.

Turner, Barrett Hamilton. "*Dignitatis Humanae* and the Development of Moral Doctrine: Assessing Change in Catholic Social Teaching on Religious Liberty." PhD diss., Catholic University of America, 2015.

———. Review, *Freedom, Truth, and Human Dignity: The Second Vatican Council's Declaration on Religious Freedom—A New Translation, Redaction History, and Interpretation of* Dignitatis Humanae. *The Thomist* 80, no. 2 (April 2016): 309–14.

———. "Is Conscience the Ultimate Ground of Religious Liberty?" *Political Theology*. June 10, 2016. Political Theology Network. Accessed May 15, 2021. https://politicaltheology.com/is-conscience-the-ultimate-ground-of-religious-liberty-barrett-turner/.

Valuet, Basile. *La liberté religieuse et la tradition catholique. Un cas de développement doctrinal homogène dans le magistère authentique*. 3rd rev. ed. 6 vols. Barroux: Éditions Sainte-Madeleine, 2011.

———. *Le droit à la liberté religieuse dans la Tradition de l'Eglise. Un cas de développement doctrinal homogène par le magistère authentique*, 2nd rev. ed. Barroux: Éditions Sainte-Madeleine, 2011.

"Vatican Says Father Curran Can't Teach Theology." *Origins* 16, no. 11 (1986): 203.

Vermeersch, A. *Tolerance*. Translated by W. Humphrey Page. New York: Benziger Brothers, 1912.

Vidler, Alec R. *Prophecy and Papacy: A Study of Lamennais, the Church, and the Revolution*. London: SCM Press Ltd., 1954.

Voltaire. *Philosophical Dictionary*. Edited and translated by Theodore Besterman. Harmondsworth, England: Penguin Books, 1972.

von Pastor, Ludwig Freiherr. *The History of the Popes: From the Close of the Middle Ages.* Vol. 7. 2nd ed. St. Louis, MO: B. Herder Book Co., 1923.

Waldman, Steven. *Founding Faith: Providence, Politics, and the Birth of Religious Freedom in America.* New York: Random House, 2008.

Walsh, W. John. "Why Did the Church Abandon Polygamy?" Light Planet (Mormons website). Accessed February 28, 2023. https://www.lightplanet.com/mormons/response/qa/plural_revelation.htm.

———, and Jeff Lindsay. "Have Your Doctrines Changed?" Light Planet (Mormons website). Accessed February 28, 2023. http://www.lightplanet.com/mormons/response/qa/doctrines_changed.htm.

Weigel, George. "Liberal Authoritarianism and the Traditional Latin Mass." *First Things.* July 21, 2021. Accessed July 16, 2022. https://www.firstthings.com/web-exclusives/2021/07/liberal-authoritarianism-and-the-traditional-latin-mass.

Whitehead, Kenneth D. "Summarizing the Controversy." *Catholic Dossier* 6, no. 2 (March–April 2000): 6–13.

Whitmore, Todd David. "Immunity or Empowerment? John Courtney Murray and the Question of Religious Liberty." In *John Courtney Murray and the Growth of Tradition*, ed. J. Leon Hooper and Todd David Whitmore, 149–74. Kansas City, MO: Sheed & Ward, 1996.

Wilhelmsen, Frederick D. "John Courtney Murray: The Optimism of the 1950s." In *We Hold These Truths and More*, ed. Donald J. D'Elia and Stephen M. Krason, 20–32. Steubenville, OH: Franciscan University Press, 1993.

Willebrands, Jean. "La liberté religieuse et l'œcuménisme." *Unam Sanctam* 60 (1967): 237–51.

William of Ockham. *Dialogus.* Latin text and English translation available at *British Academy* (website). Accessed May 3, 2017. https://publications.thebritishacademy.ac.uk/pubs/dialogus/wtc.html#part1.

Wiltgen, Ralph M. *The Rhine Flows into the Tiber: A History of Vatican II.* Rockford, IL: TAN Books, 1985.

Wolfe, Christopher. "The Church's Teaching on Religious Liberty." *Faith & Reason* 9, no. 3 (Fall 1983): 182–95.

Wood, Diana. "Infidels and Jews: Clement VI's Attitude to Persecution and Toleration." In *Persecution and Toleration*, ed. W. J. Sheils, 115–24. Oxford: Basil Blackwell, 1984.

Yzermans, Vincent A., ed. *American Participation in the Second Vatican Council.* New York: Sheed & Ward, 1967.

Index

A

Ad Tuendam Fidem, 419, 420
Albert the Great, 412, 413
Albigensians, 426–27, 431–32
Alfrink, Bernard, 89, 317
Ancel, Alfred, 211, 221, 232–35, 237, 242, 247, 249, 254, 257, 265, 303, 339–40, 360, 451
Antonelli, Giacomo, 137, 138–39
Apostolicae Curae, 419–20
Apostolicam *Actuositatem*, 103, 155, 328–29
Aquinas, Thomas, 148, 179, 193, 199–200, 203, 205, 230, 359, 372, 402, 412, 413, 417, 422, 427, 429–36
Arianism, 426–27, 431, 433
Aristotle, 170
Arius, 433
atheism, 117–18, 157, 178, 199, 230, 255, 434
Augustine, 386, 421–29, 431–33
Aux gouvernants, 55, 56, 101–13

B

Balthasar, Hans Urs von, 78
Bea, Augustin, 251
Benedict XVI, 6–7, 12, 15–18, 20, 22, 32, 42, 51, 65, 97–98, 275. See also Ratzinger, Joseph
Beran, Josef, 179, 360
Biffi, Franco, 178–79, 227, 228, 237, 281, 288, 289, 292, 297, 319
Bradley, Gerard V., 80, 87, 96, 226, 253–54, 319, 355
Brownson, Orestes, 334

C

Cajetan, 414
canon law (ecclesiastical law), 11, 13, 15–16, 19, 33, 137, 236–37, 252, 298, 301, 343, 346, 348–50, 352, 373, 403–5, 438
Carrillo de Albornoz, A. F., 123, 279, 280, 285–86, 297, 298, 310
Castellio, Sébastien, 178, 424
Cathars, 426, 432
Chalcedon, Council of, 36–37, 43
Charlemagne, 369–70, 402–3
Chesterton, G. K., 9, 147, 185–86
China, 1, 32
Christus Dominus, 111, 112
Church. See also doctrine, development of
    coercive power of, 241, 342–53, 411, 431, 435–40
    diplomacy, 3, 33–34, 53, 106–7
    freedom of (*libertas Ecclesiae*), 101–2, 112, 120, 186, 283–84, 293, 300
    and the state, 48, 55, 61–62, 72–73, 105, 122, 144–45, 227, 273, 302, 307, 323, 325, 403
Ci riesce, 189, 200, 201–2, 211
Civil Constitution of the Clergy, 129, 156

Cold War, 117, 221
collectivism, 7, 332
Colombia, 67, 91, 122, 142
Colombo, Carlo, 221, 232–35, 247, 257, 303, 339
common good, 79, 86, 145, 148, 149, 155–56, 192–93, 215, 230, 244, 258, 259, 265, 278, 293, 317, 320–21, 332, 377, 387–93, 399–400, 408, 431, 441
communism, 84–85, 267, 332, 389
confessional state, 2, 3, 4, 47, 55, 57, 62–63, 64, 66–70, 81, 82, 85, 86–91, 92, 94–99, 100, 101, 105, 107, 112, 115–16, 121, 122, 123, 142, 144–45, 173–74, 178–79, 182, 190–92, 196, 216, 226, 236–37, 284, 313–14, 317, 322–23, 357, 359, 371, 393, 401, 408, 417, 422
Congar, Yves, 78, 250
Congregation for the Doctrine of the Faith (Holy Office), 12–13, 15–16, 19, 22–27, 30, 38, 39, 42, 43, 44–45, 51, 52, 95, 120, 194, 230, 282, 330, 406–7, 420, 435
conscience, 32, 107–8, 152–54, 157, 159–60, 162, 175, 195, 203, 210–14, 217, 218, 229–30, 234, 235, 239, 242, 249, 254–57, 265, 283, 288, 294, 302, 304–7, 342, 382, 383, 384, 419, 421, 433, 434, 446. *See also* liberty of conscience (and of cults)

consciousness (historical consciousness, political consciousness), 153, 215, 216, 231, 233, 264, 270, 272, 279, 289, 295–96, 330–31, 341–42, 353, 356, 363
Constantinople, First Council of, 36–37
constitutionalism, 57, 67, 69, 87, 88, 91, 98, 118–19, 122, 177, 212, 221–22, 230–31, 245, 270–71, 272, 275, 276–77, 289, 292, 294, 322, 325–26, 329–36, 341–42, 343–44, 392, 393, 405, 446, 447, 451
Crosby, John F., 246, 329
Curran, Charles, 9, 21–27, 28–31, 52–53
Cushing, Richard, 116–17

D

D'Avack, Pietro A., 69–70, 87, 88, 236–37, 281, 284, 288–89, 292, 319
Davies, Michael, 10, 11–12, 27, 66, 91, 99–101, 137, 143–44, 190, 198–202, 210, 371–72, 381, 393–94, 396, 404, 408
Declaration of the Rights of Man and the Citizen (DDHC), 129–31, 154, 156, 204, 205, 390, 394
de Corte, Marcel, 133–34, 151, 369, 371, 372–73, 375, 377–78, 381, 385, 387–88
De Lubac, Henri, 78
de Maistre, Joseph, 164

Dei Filius, 39, 41, 42.
Dei Verbum, 39, 40, 41, 42, 109, 183, 185
De Smedt, Émile, 66, 80, 82, 92–94, 96, 100, 105, 113, 117–18, 154, 162, 174, 176–77, 206, 219, 223, 238, 240, 241, 248, 250–51, 314–15, 318–23, 347, 348, 349, 350–51, 379, 384, 389, 391–92, 408, 438, 445
Dignitatis Humanae. *See also* religious freedom, doctrine
    Council debates, 1, 31–32, 78, 115, 116, 121, 176–77, 179, 180–81, 186, 199, 218, 232–34, 238, 247–49, 312–15, 317, 344–45, 360, 363, 404, 431, 440, 447
    drafts
        chapter V (*De libertate religiosa*) of *De Oecumenismo* (Nov. 18, 1963), 66, 82, 118, 154, 162, 177, 211, 213, 231
        Declaratio prior (Apr. 27, 1964), 82, 211, 213, 220, 231, 232, 233, 312–13
        Textus Emendatus (Nov. 17, 1964), 66, 73–74, 77, 80, 83, 85, 214, 217–19, 220, 221, 231, 234, 239, 240, 302, 314, 316, 320, 351–52, 354, 362, 383, 389
        Textus Reemendatus (May 28, 1965), 74, 83–84, 85, 219–20, 221, 231, 234, 239, 240, 241, 314, 316, 354, 360
        Textus Recognitus (Oct. 25, 1965), 84, 85, 86, 88, 89, 92, 105, 113, 150, 174, 220, 221–22, 224, 231, 241–42, 309, 310, 313–14, 315, 316, 318, 320, 354, 447
        Textus Denuo Recognitus (Nov. 19, 1965), 84, 92, 93, 94, 206, 220, 221–22, 223, 313–14, 315, 318, 321, 348, 354, 379–80, 389, 391, 392, 408, 439, 447
    redaction (drafting) history in general, 1, 32, 66, 73–74, 76–77, 81–86, 88–89, 92–95, 96, 99, 102, 120, 177, 204, 211–22, 224–26, 228, 231–35, 237, 239–43, 245–46, 251, 257, 263, 265, 267–68, 280, 296, 302, 306, 309–10, 312–17, 318, 320, 346, 348–52, 354, 360–64, 383, 389, 438–40, 446–47
    relator, 66, 80, 117, 174, 206, 222, 238, 240, 318, 320, 323, 348–49, 350, 351, 384, 391, 438, 440, 445
    repetition of its teaching by postconciliar popes, 53–54
dignity. *See* person, dignity of

Di Noia, Augustine, 14–15
Divini Redemptoris, 267, 276, 332
doctrine. *See also Dignitatis Humanae*
   authentic, 25, 44, 51–52, 53, 134, 139, 420
   development of, 3, 26, 28, 35–42, 43, 44–47, 49–51, 56, 57, 67, 68, 118, 119, 120, 122, 177, 182–85, 200, 206, 230, 325, 335, 343–44, 383, 418, 421, 434, 440, 448, 451
   infallible, 25–26, 46, 51, 53, 54, 134, 136–37, 142, 151–52, 154, 371–72, 396–97, 420
   levels of authority, 26–27, 51–54, 137
   possible deficiencies in some statements, 43–44, 51–52
   reversal or corruption of (actual or alleged), 1–4, 9, 16, 20, 24, 26, 27, 35–37, 48–49, 54–56, 61, 67, 95, 99, 116–17, 120, 127, 134, 144, 146, 151, 162, 183–84, 189, 229, 311, 324, 343, 369, 371, 379–81, 383, 387, 404, 408, 418, 436, 453–54
Donatism, 423–28, 431–32
Doyle, Arthur Conan, 261, 295
Duke of Norfolk, 139, 151–52
Dulles, Avery, 40, 397, 420
Dupanloup, Félix, 49–50, 132, 140–41, 310, 409

E

Eagan, Joseph, 27–29, 30, 35–36, 43–44, 52, 57
Ecclesia Dei adflicta, 11, 12

ecumenism, 5, 18–19, 31, 82, 194
Enlightenment, the, 5–7, 34, 48, 132, 163, 164, 165, 170, 180, 181, 185, 447–51
Ephesus, Council of, 37, 41
Erasmus, Desiderius, 249–50, 437
Exsurge Domine, 56, 127, 410–15

F

fascism, 266, 267
Fellay, Bernard, 14–16, 18, 19
Fesquet, Henri, 1, 5, 27, 66, 80, 100, 193, 200, 274, 447
Finocchiaro, Francesco, 252
Finnis, John, 238, 349, 351, 434, 436, 437
France, 10, 21, 49, 117, 131, 140, 142, 164, 180, 194, 232, 352, 406, 426
Francis, 17–21, 32, 419
French Revolution, 65, 73, 117, 127, 129–31, 132, 150, 154, 156, 164–65, 187, 394, 447

G

Gallicanism, 132–33, 164–65, 166
Garrone, Gabriel-Marie, 117, 162, 181
Gaudium et Spes, 10, 70, 71, 72–73, 74, 75, 79, 80–81, 97, 103–4, 107–9, 111–13, 173, 220, 227, 323–24, 331, 450–51
Gelasian dualism, 47, 70–81, 85–86, 113, 184, 220, 227–28, 268, 273, 278, 296–97, 302, 322, 324, 328, 332
Gelasius I, 70, 71, 73, 77, 98, 228

Gladstone, William, 49, 139, 151–54, 159–60, 163, 445
Goerner, E. A., 331
Grasso, Kenneth L., 76, 213–14, 244, 246, 254, 259, 261, 292–96, 298, 308–9, 326–28, 329
Gregory XVI, 2, 48, 54–55, 127, 128–29, 131, 132–34, 135, 137, 150–51, 152, 156, 158, 159, 160, 162, 163, 166–69, 171, 174, 268, 281, 282, 358–59, 375, 376, 386, 413
Grisez, Germain, 29, 50, 152–53
Guminski, Arnold T., 80, 133–34, 137, 226, 238, 239, 240, 241, 253, 347–53, 371, 379, 386, 389, 391, 392, 393, 396, 397, 398, 399, 427, 431, 436–40

H

Hamer, Jérôme, 89, 94, 150, 177, 223, 230, 243, 248, 280, 281, 286, 288, 291, 292, 307–8, 310, 318–19, 361
Harrison, Brian W., 4, 30, 55–56, 61, 66, 67, 69–70, 75, 82, 87, 88, 89–94, 99–100, 104–7, 112–13, 124, 128, 129, 130, 134, 136–37, 142, 156, 159, 160–63, 166, 167–70, 176–77, 193, 196, 197–202, 204, 205, 206, 223, 224–26, 240, 241, 251, 253–54, 311, 312, 313, 317, 318, 319, 321, 322, 324, 347, 348, 349, 350, 353, 371, 373, 375–76, 378–82, 383, 384, 385–86, 387, 389, 391, 392, 393, 395, 396–408, 409, 410–11, 427–28, 433–34, 436–38, 439, 440, 441
Healy, Nicholas, J., 83, 84, 85, 213, 225, 232, 235, 242, 265, 316, 318
Heenan, John, 98, 199, 234, 312, 314
heresy, 4, 37, 56, 179, 311, 350, 373, 402, 410–15, 417, 418–19, 422–26, 429–34, 436, 437
hermeneutic
  of discontinuity and rupture, 12, 18, 51, 209–10, 375
  of human integrity, 170–74, 180–84, 186, 358
  jurisprudential, 49–51, 54–57
  of reform in continuity, 6–7, 17, 18, 51, 52, 97

Hervada, Javier, 149, 191, 302, 304, 341, 452–53
Hittinger, F. Russell, 55, 65, 66, 80–81, 82, 102, 103–4, 107, 112, 219, 297, 308, 335–36
Hooper, Leon, 27, 214, 254, 257, 264, 273–74
human being. *See* person
Humanae Vitae, 21–22, 418
humility, 65–67, 71
Hus, John, 360
hypostasis, 37

I

Immaculate Conception, 26, 42, 46

Immortale Dei, 48, 68, 70, 73, 74, 75, 77, 139, 143–46, 157, 169, 171–72, 178, 181, 191, 193, 194, 229, 239, 268, 311, 359, 407, 422, 439
India, 370
Indian summer, 329, 334–35
indifferentism, 18, 96, 128, 133, 144–45, 149, 156–58, 160–63, 165, 166–67, 168–69, 173, 184, 186, 191, 194, 204–5, 206, 234, 311, 326, 358–59, 374–77, 388, 449–50, 452, 454
individualism, 6–7, 17, 94, 179, 223, 332
Inquisition, 430–31, 432
International Group of Fathers, 84, 316
Ireland, 154, 234, 272
Islam, 32, 68, 123–24, 179, 193, 359, 361, 370, 402, 429–30, 433
Italy, 17, 117, 137, 138, 200, 266, 267, 426

J

Jansenism, 434–35
Jefferson, Thomas, 74, 77, 78, 86, 278, 302, 323, 328, 333
Jerome, 433
John XXIII, 78–79, 83, 172, 200, 206, 210, 211, 266, 275–78
John Paul II, 10–12, 20, 25, 29, 30, 31–32, 42, 50, 104, 246, 329, 335, 419–20
Judaism, 178, 179, 193, 199–200, 359, 372, 400, 429–30, 433
juridical approach to religious freedom. *See* religious freedom, juridical approach
just public order. *See* public order

K

Kasper, Walter, 34, 417, 422, 434, 441, 448–52
Kennedy, John F., 118
Kennedy, Robert T., 289, 298–99, 304, 309
Kierkegaard, Søren, 339
Komonchak, Joseph, 246
König, Franz, 118
Küng, Hans, 27

L

Lactantius, 439
Lamennais, Félicité de, 128–29, 131, 132–33, 135, 138, 155, 163–71, 174, 178, 180, 187, 358–59, 361, 375–78, 384, 388, 447–48
La Mennais, Jean-Marie Robert de, 164
Lanfranc of Canterbury, 413
Lateran Agreements (1929), 117
Lecler, Joseph, 274, 310–311, 424, 425, 432, 433
Lefebvre, Marcel, 3, 9, 10–13, 18, 31, 84, 136–137, 143, 210, 316, 369, 371–72, 381–82, 384–87, 389, 404
Leo X, 4, 127, 410–13
Leo XII, 133, 140, 160, 166
Leo XIII, 2, 3, 34, 41, 48, 54–55, 63–64, 65, 67, 68, 70–71, 73, 74, 78–79, 81, 83, 99, 101, 106, 115–16, 117–18, 120–21, 127, 139, 142–46, 150, 151, 153,

154, 157–58, 160, 168, 169, 171–73, 178–79, 190, 191–94, 195, 196, 199–200, 201, 203, 206, 220, 228–29, 239, 251, 268, 297, 311–12, 314, 320, 330–31, 359, 389, 395, 397, 399, 406, 407, 413, 419–20, 422, 429, 439

liberalism
- American versus Continental, 117, 330, 332–33
- Catholic, 132, 138, 165–66, 168, 169, 375, 376–77, 447–48, 449–50
- generally, 64, 157–58, 162, 171, 335, 445, 451

Libertas, 2, 48, 64, 73, 78, 143–46, 151, 153, 157–58, 168, 171, 172, 178, 191–94, 196, 220, 239, 311, 397, 407

liberty of conscience (and of cults), 1–2, 48, 92, 128–29, 131–35, 141, 149–69, 174, 179, 212, 213, 214, 230, 358, 360, 362, 364–65, 378, 386, 423, 448

Locke, John, 449–50
Lonergan, Bernard, 35, 153, 170
Longinqua Oceani, 64, 79, 106, 118, 194, 220
Lucien, Bernard, 347–48, 352, 369, 371, 372–73, 374, 375, 378, 381–82, 384–85
Lumen Gentium, 25, 52–53, 70, 74, 81, 109, 134, 142, 172, 184, 194, 227, 323
Luther, Martin, 127, 410–12, 414–15

M

Madison, James, 280.
magisterium, 1, 13–14, 22–26, 28–30, 35–36, 39–41, 43–44, 46, 51, 52–53, 54, 92–93, 127–28 135, 137, 170–71, 183, 190, 269, 311, 314–15, 371, 381, 406, 407, 413, 420
Manicheans, 422–23
Martín de Agar, José Tomás, 71, 72–73, 74, 86, 91, 95–96, 145, 146, 184, 201, 212, 217, 228, 263, 274, 277, 279, 302, 403
Marshner, William, 203–4, 212
Marxism, 5, 31, 117–18, 182, 446
materialism, 117–18
McBrien, Richard, 27
Melchin, Kenneth, 29, 119
Meyer, Albert, 118
Minnerath, Roland, 67–68, 80, 87, 124, 286–88, 289, 292, 305, 306, 325
Mirari vos, 2, 48, 53, 128–29, 131, 132–35, 137, 138, 144, 150–52, 156, 159–61, 163, 166–69, 171, 376, 381, 386, 387
Mit brennender Sorge, 210, 267, 276, 332, 341
Montalembert, Charles, 138
moral teaching, 1, 3, 9, 21–22, 25–32, 43–46, 50, 66, 89, 92–94, 100, 108, 119–20, 127, 128, 148–51, 152–53, 155–59, 160–63, 168–75, 177, 179, 180, 187, 189, 191, 195, 199, 200, 202, 203, 204, 206, 222–23,

485

256, 273, 287, 302, 318, 319–24, 327, 333, 343, 358–61, 385, 392–93, 397, 399, 409, 418, 419, 420–21, 427, 446, 449
morality (public morality), 3, 6, 29–30, 31, 42, 50, 128, 148, 149, 155, 157–58, 160–61, 171, 174–75, 179–80, 183, 215, 249, 282–83, 298, 332, 358–59, 374, 387–91, 393, 400
Mormons (Church of Jesus Christ of Latter Day Saints), 37–38
Most, William, 380–381
Müller, Gerhard, 15
Murray, Charles, 6
Murray, John Courtney, 3, 4, 5, 27, 32, 54, 55, 56, 61, 63–65, 66, 69, 70, 72–78, 79–80, 81–83, 85–86, 87–88, 89, 91, 95–99, 100–101, 103, 105, 106–7, 110–13, 116–17, 120–21, 146, 175, 194–95, 206, 210, 212–15, 216–28, 230, 232–46, 247–51, 253–59, 261, 262, 263, 264–69, 272, 273, 275–78, 279–80, 284, 285–86, 287, 292–309, 312–17, 318, 319, 321–31, 333–34, 335, 339–42, 344–45, 354–56, 357–58, 361–64, 383, 391, 445–48

N

Napoleon, 131–32, 164
Napoleon III, 137–38

National Socialism (Nazism), 210, 267, 332
natural law, 65, 152, 177, 210, 270–72, 276, 302, 330, 341–46, 356, 358, 396, 404, 435
naturalism, 134, 157–58, 168, 374–75, 387–88
Nestorianism, 37, 57
Nestorius, 37
Newman, John Henry, 35–37, 40, 42–43, 44–47, 49–51, 139, 151–54, 158–63, 167, 175, 182–84, 445, 451
Nicaea, First Council of, 36–37, 41, 43, 274
Noonan, John T., 192, 396, 418–19
Non Abbiamo Bisogno, 154, 266, 267–68, 276
Nostra Aetate, 110–11
Novak, Michael, 417, 427, 430–34

O

Obama, Barack, 32
Ocáriz, Fernando, 2, 4, 46, 65, 69–70, 87, 145, 150, 155, 175, 176, 189, 198, 201, 227, 229, 230, 237, 319, 393
Ockham, William of, 413–14
O'Connor, Flannery, 143
O'Neil, Patrick, 2, 45, 57, 127, 145, 417–22, 427, 440–41, 448, 451
Orthodox Churches, 26, 67–68, 194, 210, 359, 405

P

Pacem in Terris, 78–79, 172, 200,

INDEX

211, 274, 276–78, 302, 303, 331, 400, 447
Pacca, Bartolomeo, 129, 133, 167–68
Paprocki, Thomas J., 20, 200
Pastor Aeternus, 38, 39, 40, 41, 142
Paul, 16, 39, 249, 425, 429
Paul VI, 10, 20, 22, 42, 55, 56, 83–84, 92–93, 100, 101–3, 105–9, 110–12, 183, 198, 206, 232, 237, 252, 280, 298, 314, 315, 320, 418, 445
Pavan, Pietro, 56, 76–77, 176, 189, 196, 202, 218, 229–30, 231, 242, 245–46, 250, 262, 264, 286, 288–92, 304–6, 313, 319, 329, 331
Pelotte, Donald, 73, 76, 77, 83, 87, 100, 223, 293, 296, 297, 325, 328, 364
person, human
  compartmentalization, 6, 163, 454
  dignity of, 7, 83–84, 85, 91, 94, 153, 155, 182, 199, 209, 213, 218, 228–35, 245, 247, 248–49, 252, 257, 261, 262–63, 266, 270, 278–79, 280, 282, 285, 287, 289, 291, 296, 302, 303, 304, 312, 314, 320–21, 339–40, 345–46, 354, 358, 360–61, 362, 365, 419, 450–51, 454
  fragmentation of, 163, 170, 178, 361, 362, 454
  integrity of, 7, 56, 158, 169, 170–74, 178–84, 186, 216, 218, 358–59, 360–65, 454

  nature of, 180–81, 215, 229, 230, 231, 257, 258, 263, 277–78, 341, 345–46, 364, 453
  as seeker of truth, 92, 141, 150, 155, 162, 174–75, 179, 187, 190, 199, 218, 221, 232–35, 245, 247, 257, 258–59, 262, 287, 303, 304, 340–41, 360, 449, 451, 454
  social nature of, 82, 7, 158, 170–74, 180–82, 183, 257–59, 260, 340, 341, 358, 360, 361, 364, 451
Philippines, the, 67, 91, 322
Pink, Thomas, 66, 176, 177, 237–42, 320, 342–57, 401, 430–31, 434, 435–39
Pius VI, 127, 130–31, 135, 142, 155–56, 158, 162
Pius VII, 127, 131–32, 142
Pius IX, 2, 4, 26, 40, 41, 42, 48–49, 54–55, 63, 67, 68, 121, 127, 128, 129, 134–41, 142, 143, 150–51, 152, 156–57, 158, 159, 160, 161–62, 167, 168, 169, 171, 283, 358, 359, 371–81, 384–85, 387–88, 390, 392–93, 398, 407
Pius X, 39, 41, 42, 64, 67, 139, 172, 413
Pius XI, 68, 91, 98, 146, 154, 173, 193, 210, 266–70, 276, 311, 332, 341, 352, 359, 398, 413
Pius XII, 26, 31, 40–41, 42, 74, 77, 78, 79, 83, 189, 195, 200, 206, 210–11, 266, 268,

487

270–75, 277, 297, 312, 389, 413, 438–39
Plato, 170, 342
Poland, 84–85, 232–33, 249–50, 309–10, 316–17
policy (discipline), 21, 102, 105–7, 111, 112–13, 145, 178–79, 193, 237, 343–44, 355–57, 370, 372–73, 396, 398–99, 400–404, 407–8, 409, 419, 427–28, 436–37, 440
political science (political theory), 85, 269–70, 272, 454
polygamy, 37–38
Pontifical Commission *Ecclesia Dei*, 13–14, 19
Primeau, Ernest, 181, 204–5, 303, 364–65
proportionalism, 29–30
proselytism, 378–79, 384
Protestant Reformation, 127
Protestants, 5, 67, 74, 123, 140, 154, 178, 194, 294, 361, 373, 402, 419–20, 452
public ecclesiastical law, 4, 33, 343, 391, 397–406, 408, 427–28, 441
public order, 54, 71, 98, 108, 129, 180, 187, 197–98, 202, 203, 214, 215, 222, 241, 243, 244, 255–56, 265, 293, 299, 306, 308, 309, 327, 340, 342, 348, 359, 361, 373, 379–81, 384–85, 387–94, 395, 397, 398–400, 408–9, 422, 427–29, 431–32, 440–41
public peace, 136, 284, 371–72, 376–81, 384–94, 400

Q

Quadragesimo Anno, 98
Quanta Cura, 2, 4, 48–49, 53, 55, 68, 134–37, 138, 150–52, 156, 159–61, 163, 167, 168, 169, 171, 369, 371–88, 390, 393–94, 401, 407
Quas Primas, 91, 146, 173, 193, 312, 398, 413
Quod Aliquantum, 130–31, 135, 156, 162

R

Rahner, Hugo, 71
Rahner, Karl, 78
rationalism, 34, 449, 450, 452
Ratzinger, Joseph, 12, 22–23, 25, 26, 29–30, 53, 77, 78, 275, 353, 406, 407. *See also* Benedict XVI.
Regan, Richard, 69, 79, 85, 87, 89, 203, 210–12, 213, 214, 218, 219, 220–22, 225, 232, 233, 234, 243–44, 250–51, 280, 294, 303, 312, 313, 364, 383, 446–48
religious freedom (religious liberty)
  as a civil right, 97, 122, 156–57, 160, 161–62, 174, 176–77, 199, 345
  and duties to God and to the Church, 47, 62, 67, 68, 70, 87, 89, 90–95, 100, 105, 173, 178, 180, 187, 197, 199, 222, 223, 243, 285, 312, 313–14, 317, 318–24, 390, 404, 406
  as a right in civil society, 116, 150, 155, 162, 175, 187,

INDEX

199, 204, 242, 347, 350, 438, 454
foundation of, 3–4, 7, 55–56, 82–83, 85, 86, 113, 123, 147, 148, 150, 151, 155, 175, 177, 186, 190, 209–10, 212–14, 216–18, 219–20, 222, 228–35, 240, 242–59, 261–66, 270, 278–79, 280, 282, 284–91, 293, 296, 297–98, 302, 303–4, 308–9, 314, 315, 322, 324, 325, 331, 336–37, 339, 353–54, 357, 358, 360–61, 362–63, 364, 447, 448, 450, 451, 452
as immunity from coercion, 136, 150, 175–76, 177, 179, 182, 187, 189–90, 196–200, 202, 204, 205, 213, 215, 222, 232, 234, 245, 247, 249, 254–58, 265–66, 293, 326, 340, 346–47, 352–53, 355, 383–84, 387, 408, 421, 440, 454
juridical approach to, 215, 216–22, 226, 228, 232–35, 242, 244–45, 249, 251, 254, 257, 265–66, 270, 276, 315–16
and the juridical realm, 147–49, 150, 151, 155–59, 161, 163, 174, 175, 176, 179, 186, 187, 189, 202, 358
limitations of, 4, 135, 136, 143–44, 147–48, 149–50, 187, 190, 195, 203, 217, 255, 256, 265, 342, 347, 348, 352, 363, 369–70, 381–84,

387, 391, 393, 399, 421, 427, 441
as a natural right, 54, 122, 176–77, 199, 210, 217, 243, 262, 264, 265, 291, 303, 304, 331, 341–42, 344, 345, 354, 356, 357–58, 400, 401, 408, 428, 454
object, 55–56, 123, 147, 148, 186, 190, 196
ontological approach to, 171, 211, 221, 229–30, 232–33, 235, 242, 245, 249, 251, 254, 257–58, 265–66, 339–41, 357–58, 361
in private and in public, 2, 83, 145, 147, 149, 155–56, 178–80, 182, 195, 197, 210, 211, 255–56, 314, 340, 347, 354, 359, 360, 369, 382, 408, 454
scope, 3, 4, 47, 55–56, 123, 147–50, 155, 174–77, 186–87, 190, 202, 246, 278, 448, 452, 453
Render to Caesar (Matt 22:21), 71, 72, 246, 273–75, 280
Rerum Novarum, 99, 199
Rhonheimer, Martin, 52, 97–98, 156–57, 161–62, 238, 241, 275, 342, 343, 344, 345, 351, 354, 355–56, 357, 437
rights
civil, 97, 122, 156–57, 160, 161–62, 174, 176–77, 199, 345
as immunities from coercion, 136, 150, 175–76, 177, 179, 182, 189, 196–201, 202, 204–5, 215, 222, 234,

INDEX

245, 249, 254–58, 265, 266, 326, 355, 383–84, 387, 454
as natural, 199–200, 203, 263–64, 267, 268, 270, 277–78, 291, 336, 341, 344, 453
negative versus positive, 175–76, 195–97, 200, 202–6, 263, 265
origin, 199–200
reciprocity, 123, 400, 421, 441, 452–53
versus tolerance (toleration), 2, 48, 66, 115, 120–21, 127–28, 132, 143–46, 171–73, 177, 179, 190, 192–200, 201–2, 310, 330, 359, 372, 374, 381, 402, 405–6, 408, 418–19, 424–25, 427, 429–31, 449–50, 452
Ritter, Joseph, 121, 247–48
Riva, Clemente, 177, 230, 243, 280, 281, 286, 288, 291–92, 307, 319, 361
Roosevelt, Franklin, D., 269

S

Salvian, 433
Scatena, Silvia, 82, 84, 85, 89, 93, 100, 171, 214, 223, 237, 240, 251, 310, 313, 316–17, 364, 389
Schindler, David L., 78, 80, 93, 97–98, 170–71, 175–76, 214, 215, 225, 232, 235, 242, 249, 251, 253–54, 265, 273–74, 275, 318, 330, 335
Secretariat for Promoting Christian Unity, 66, 214, 217, 234, 243, 315, 317, 349, 446
secular (secularism), 234, 375–76
Shehan, Lawrence, 120, 199
skepticism, 6, 34, 124, 450, 452, 454
Smith, Joseph, 37–38
Society of St. Pius V, 11, 31
Society of St. Pius X, 10–16, 18–19, 20–21, 22–23, 31, 343
Spain, 107, 141–42
Spellman, Francis, 293–94, 296, 330
Spinelli, Lorenzo, 74, 297, 300–301, 304, 309
state
and care for religion, 62, 63–64, 220, 293, 294–95, 296
and the Church, 48, 55, 61–67, 70, 72–73, 81, 83, 105, 122, 144–45, 227, 273, 302, 307, 323, 325, 403
competence in religious matters, 55, 56, 82–86, 216, 218, 221–23, 226, 228, 233–34, 235–37, 240–41, 243, 244, 246–47, 261–319, 322, 324–32, 336, 339, 341–42, 345, 346, 353–55, 357, 358, 363, 446
duties to religion, 84, 91, 92, 121, 136, 144, 172, 174, 186, 187, 193, 222, 223, 244, 271–72, 277–78, 285, 309, 311, 312, 316, 317–22, 323, 324–28, 333, 336, 384, 390

490

as limited in its powers, 98, 118,
   184, 198, 219–21, 223,
   230, 231, 240–41, 243,
   245, 247, 259, 262–63,
   266, 267, 270, 271, 275,
   293, 294–95, 309–10, 314,
   316, 317, 321, 323, 325–
   26, 332, 335, 345, 355
and religious establishment,
   32–33, 62–63, 69, 72, 73,
   74, 79–80, 83, 85, 88–89,
   91, 95–96, 97, 123–24,
   138, 141–42, 154, 216,
   224, 225, 226, 233–34,
   236, 275, 278, 280, 289,
   308, 312–18, 322–25, 336
separation from the Church,
   63–65, 66–67, 71, 73,
   79–80, 81, 85, 86, 113,
   216, 297, 318, 322, 328,
   345, 376
and society, 76, 87, 89, 93, 321
special civil recognition of religion, 67, 68, 69–70, 86–92,
   98, 223–27, 243, 253, 285,
   308, 309, 313–14, 315–17,
   319, 325, 405
Storck, Thomas, 343, 356–57
Summorum Pontificum, 12, 17
Syllabus Errorum, 48, 49–50, 63,
   121–22, 128, 137–43,
   151–52, 159–60, 282–83

T

Tertullian, 164
Thomism, 78, 204, 429
totalitarianism, 117–18, 179, 181,
   182, 221, 230, 265–68,
   270, 276, 321, 332–33,
   359, 447

Traditionis custodes, 19–21
Trent, Council of, 26, 405, 437–38
Truman, Harry S, 273
Turner, Barrett H., 80, 88–89, 96,
   105, 206, 212, 226, 237,
   250, 265–66, 320, 322,
   344, 348–51, 440, 453

U

Ultramontanism, 164, 166, 169
Unitatis Redintegratio, 194
United Nations, 453
United States of America, 10,
   32–33, 61, 62, 64–65, 73,
   74, 76, 106, 118–19, 120–
   21, 196, 215, 218, 242, 245,
   289, 293, 300, 301, 305,
   313, 330, 332–35, 364,
   383–84, 452
Universal Declaration of Human
   Rights, 453
U.S. Constitution, 64–65, 73, 74,
   79, 106, 118, 196, 263–64,
   269, 280, 293–94

V

Valuet, Basile, 53, 55–56, 68–70,
   79, 82, 85, 90, 91, 92, 94,
   95–96, 99, 104, 106–7,
   120, 127, 129, 130, 131,
   132, 133–34, 135, 137,
   139, 150, 155, 156, 162,
   175–76, 190, 195, 196,
   197, 199–200, 201–5,
   210, 215, 225, 226, 250,
   252–53, 273, 280, 281,
   285, 303, 312, 313–14,
   317, 319, 352, 363,
   371–72, 373, 376–79, 383,
   385, 386, 389, 392, 393,

397, 400–401, 402, 407,
411, 417, 422, 423, 426,
428–29, 430–431–435,
441, 452–53, 458
Vatican Council, First, 39, 41,
134, 152. *See also Pastor
Aeternus*
Vatican Council, Second. *See
Apostolicam Actuositatem,
Christus Dominus, Dei
Verbum, Dignitatis
Humanae, Gaudium et
Spes, Lumen Gentium,
Nostra Aetate, Unitatis
Redintegratio*, religious
freedom
Vigil, Francisco de Paola, 141
Vincent of Lérins, 40
voluntarism, 50

W

Wazo of Liège, 424–25
Whitehead, Kenneth D., 85
Wilhelmsen, Frederick, 334
Williams, Roger, 178
Wojtyła, Karol, 232, 237, 247,
389–90, 392, 393. *See also*
John Paul II
Wolfe, Christopher, 116, 121–23
World War II, 32–33, 118, 221,
270, 332, 334, 403
Wright, John, 98, 115, 121, 234,
312–14
Wyszyński, Stefan, 310